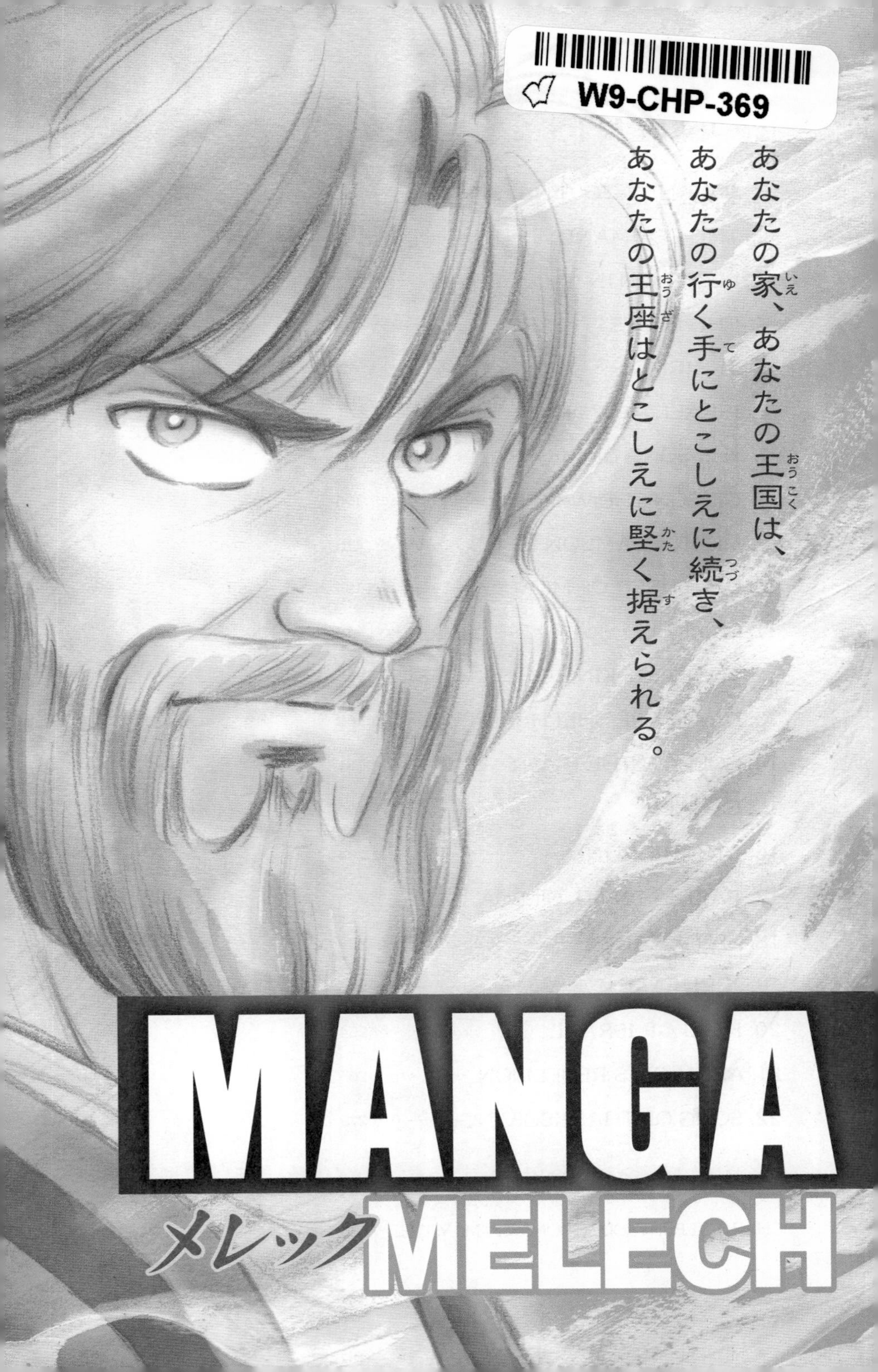
あなたの家、あなたの王国は、
あなたの行く手にとこしえに続き、
あなたの王座はとこしえに堅く据えられる。
MANGA
メレック
MELECH

CONTENTS

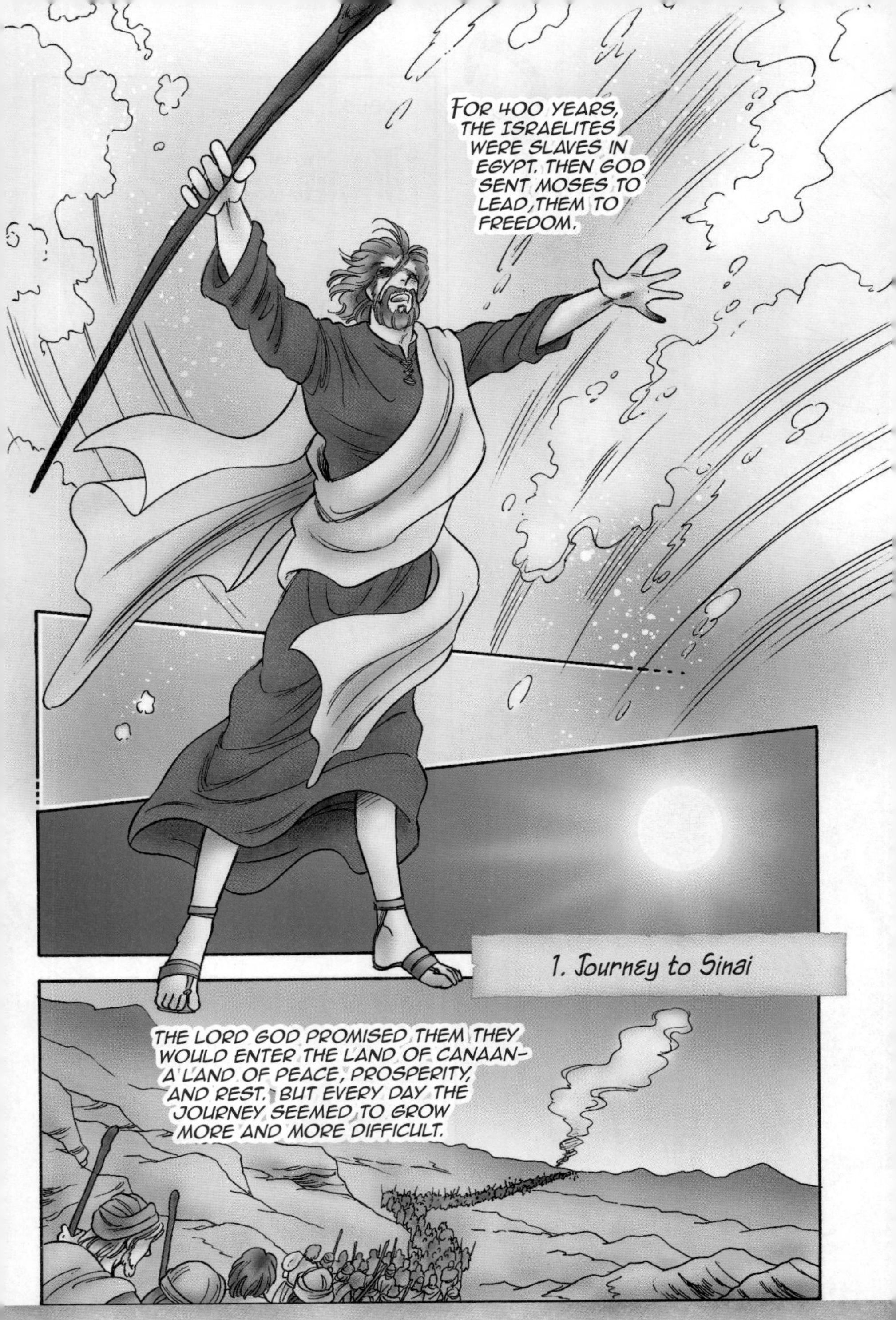
FOR 400 YEARS, THE ISRAELITES WERE SLAVES IN EGYPT. THEN GOD SENT MOSES TO LEAD THEM TO FREEDOM.
1. Journey to Sinai
THE LORD GOD PROMISED THEM THEY WOULD ENTER THE LAND OF CANAAN— A LAND OF PEACE, PROSPERITY, AND REST. BUT EVERY DAY THE JOURNEY SEEMED TO GROW MORE AND MORE DIFFICULT.

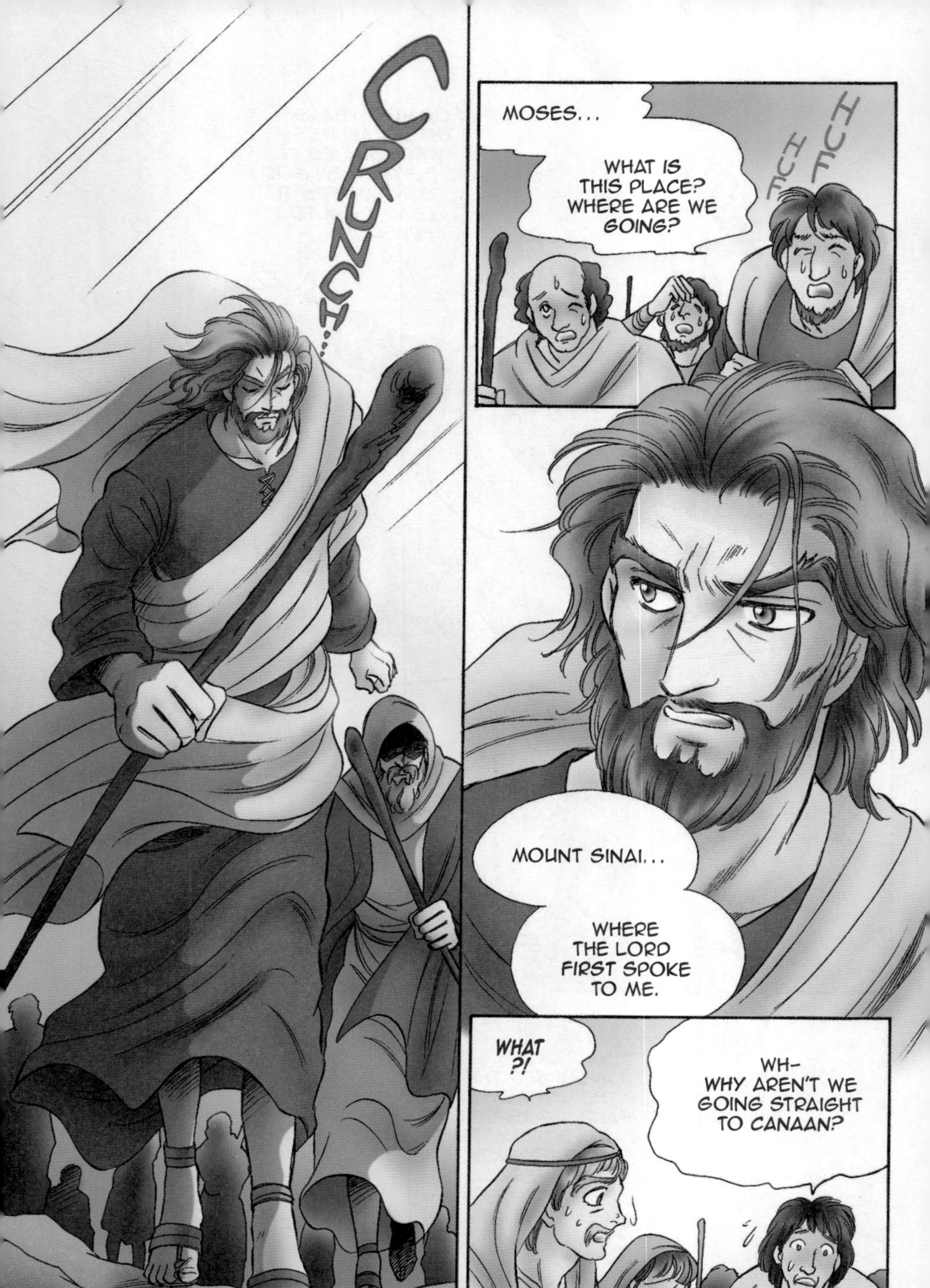
CRUNCH...
MOSES...
WHAT IS THIS PLACE? WHERE ARE WE GOING?
HUF HUF
MOUNT SINAI...
WHERE THE LORD FIRST SPOKE TO ME.
WHAT ?!
WH- WHY AREN'T WE GOING STRAIGHT TO CANAAN?

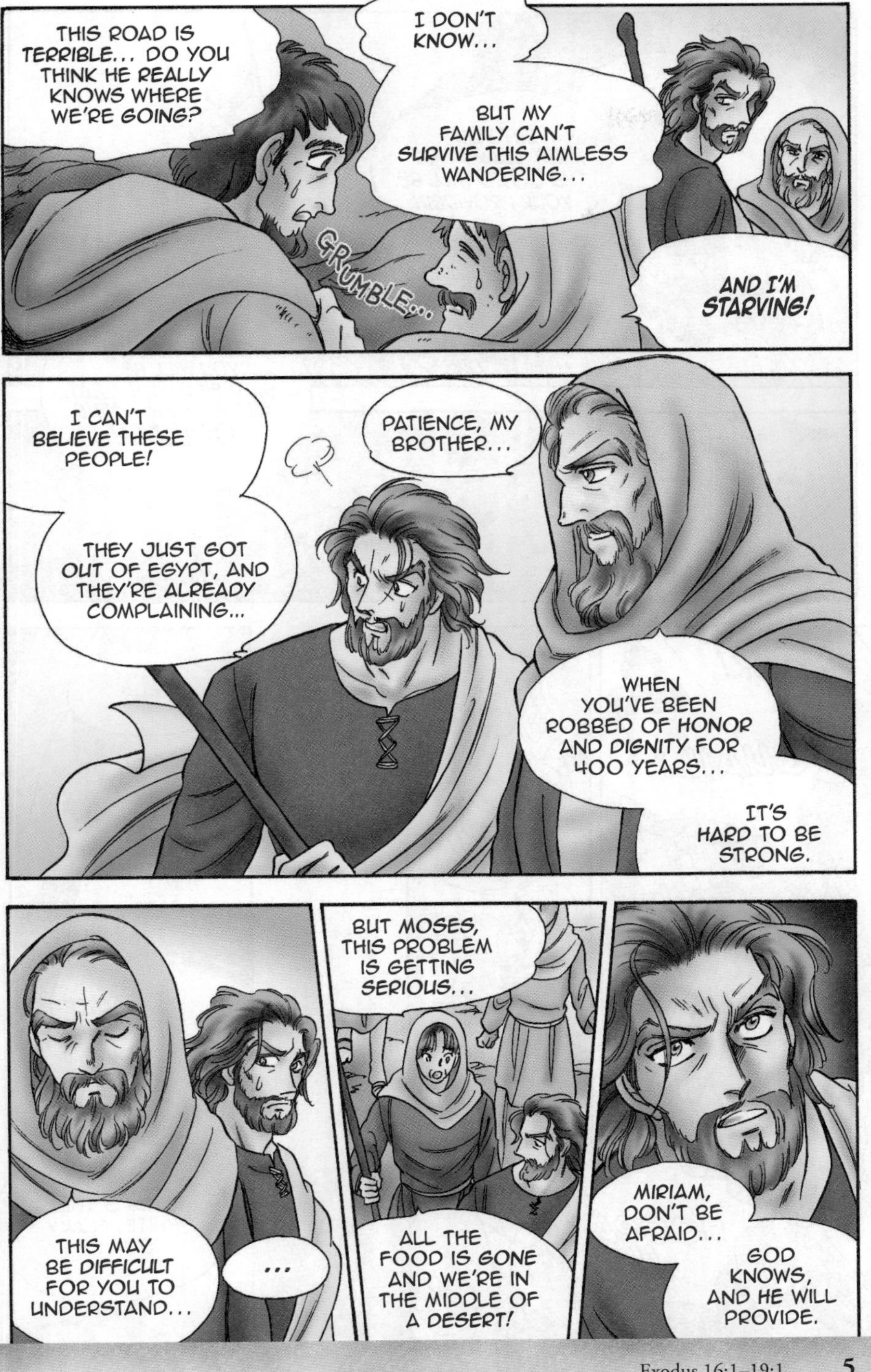
THIS ROAD IS TERRIBLE... DO YOU THINK HE REALLY KNOWS WHERE WE'RE GOING?
I DON'T KNOW...
BUT MY FAMILY CAN'T SURVIVE THIS AIMLESS WANDERING...
GRUMBLE...
AND I'M STARVING!
I CAN'T BELIEVE THESE PEOPLE!
THEY JUST GOT OUT OF EGYPT, AND THEY'RE ALREADY COMPLAINING...
PATIENCE, MY BROTHER...
WHEN YOU'VE BEEN ROBBED OF HONOR AND DIGNITY FOR 400 YEARS...
IT'S HARD TO BE STRONG.
THIS MAY BE DIFFICULT FOR YOU TO UNDERSTAND...
...
BUT MOSES, THIS PROBLEM IS GETTING SERIOUS...
ALL THE FOOD IS GONE AND WE'RE IN THE MIDDLE OF A DESERT!
MIRIAM, DON'T BE AFRAID...
GOD KNOWS, AND HE WILL PROVIDE.

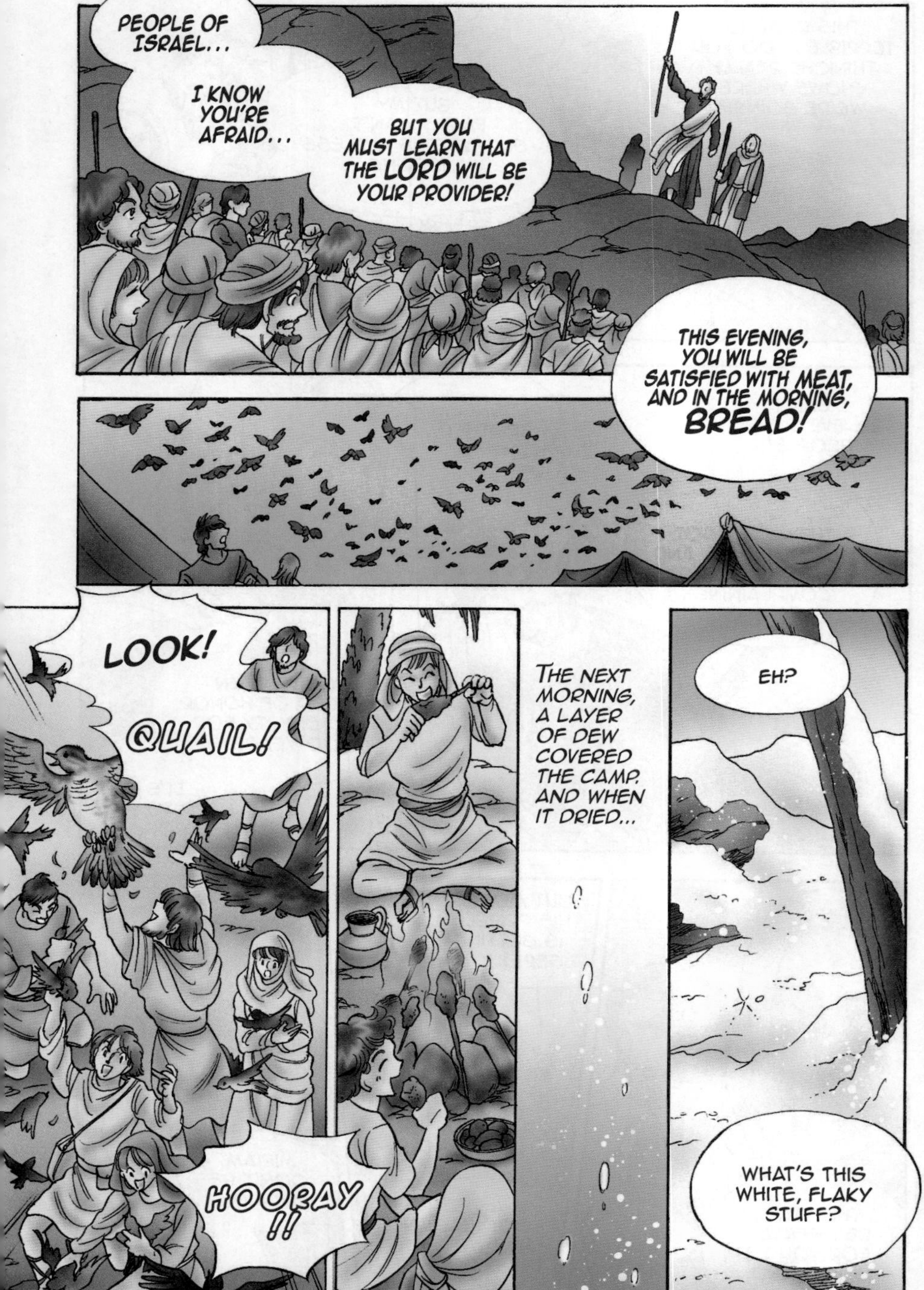
PEOPLE OF ISRAEL...
I KNOW YOU'RE AFRAID...
BUT YOU MUST LEARN THAT THE LORD WILL BE YOUR PROVIDER!
THIS EVENING, YOU WILL BE SATISFIED WITH MEAT, AND IN THE MORNING, BREAD!
LOOK!
QUAIL!
HOORAY !!
THE NEXT MORNING, A LAYER OF DEW COVERED THE CAMP. AND WHEN IT DRIED...
EH?
WHAT'S THIS WHITE, FLAKY STUFF?

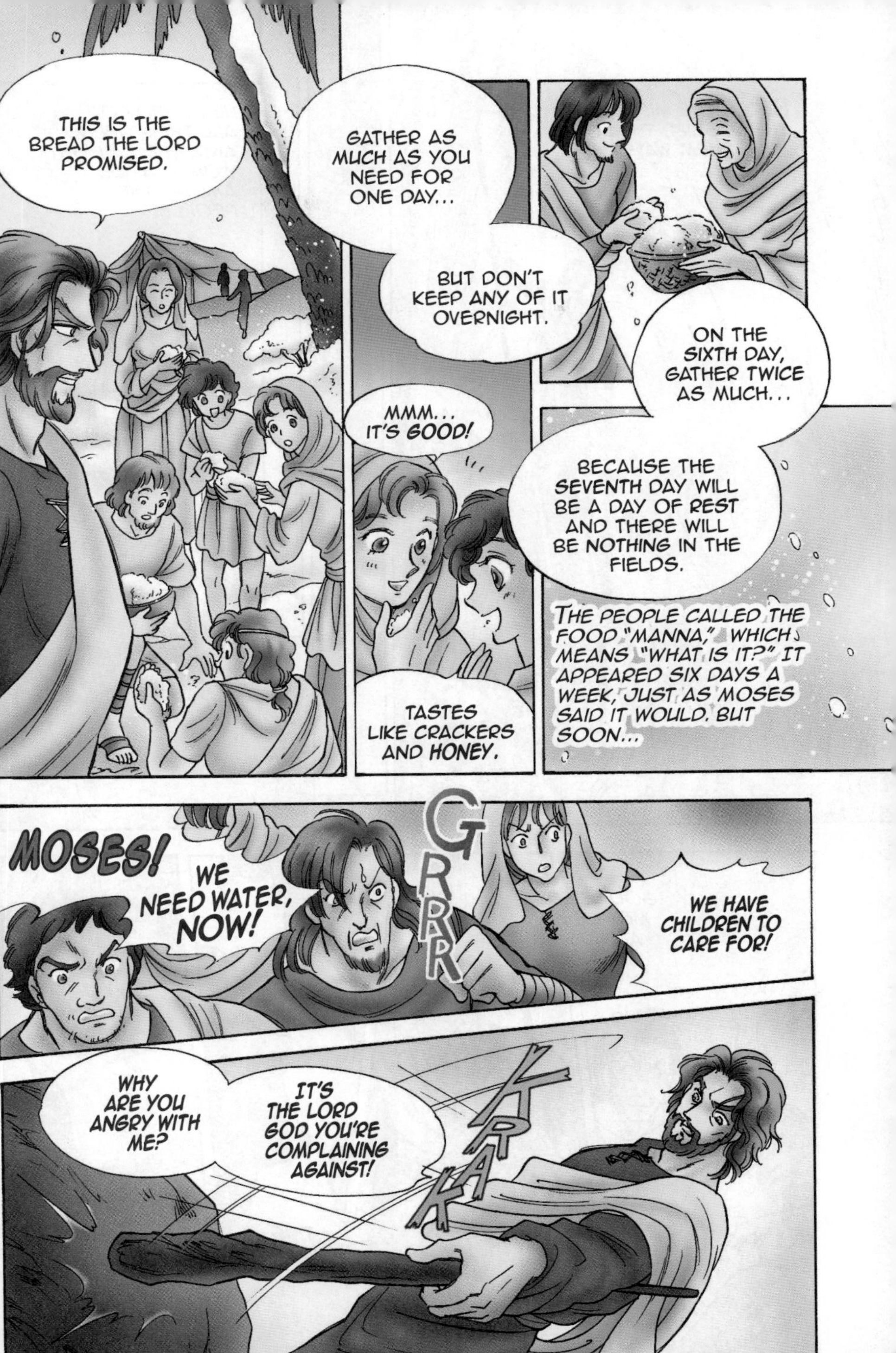
THIS IS THE BREAD THE LORD PROMISED.
GATHER AS MUCH AS YOU NEED FOR ONE DAY...
BUT DON'T KEEP ANY OF IT OVERNIGHT.
ON THE SIXTH DAY, GATHER TWICE AS MUCH...
MMM... IT'S GOOD!
TASTES LIKE CRACKERS AND HONEY.
BECAUSE THE SEVENTH DAY WILL BE A DAY OF REST AND THERE WILL BE NOTHING IN THE FIELDS.
THE PEOPLE CALLED THE FOOD "MANNA," WHICH MEANS "WHAT IS IT?" IT APPEARED SIX DAYS A WEEK, JUST AS MOSES SAID IT WOULD. BUT SOON...
MOSES!
WE NEED WATER, NOW!
GRRR
WE HAVE CHILDREN TO CARE FOR!
WHY ARE YOU ANGRY WITH ME?
IT'S THE LORD GOD YOU'RE COMPLAINING AGAINST!
KRAK

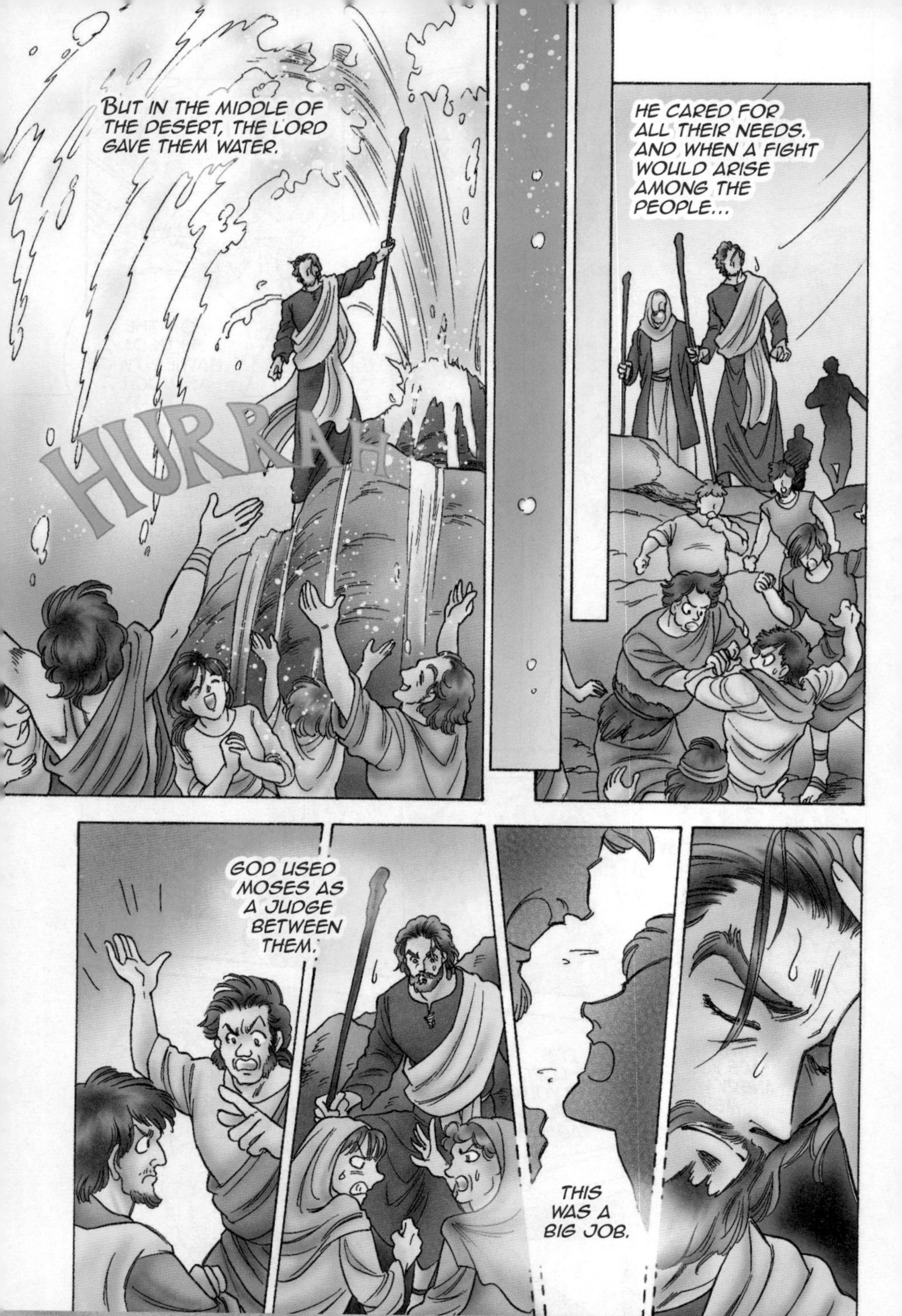

BUT IN THE MIDDLE OF THE DESERT, THE LORD GAVE THEM WATER.
HURRAH
HE CARED FOR ALL THEIR NEEDS. AND WHEN A FIGHT WOULD ARISE AMONG THE PEOPLE...
GOD USED MOSES AS A JUDGE BETWEEN THEM.
THIS WAS A BIG JOB.

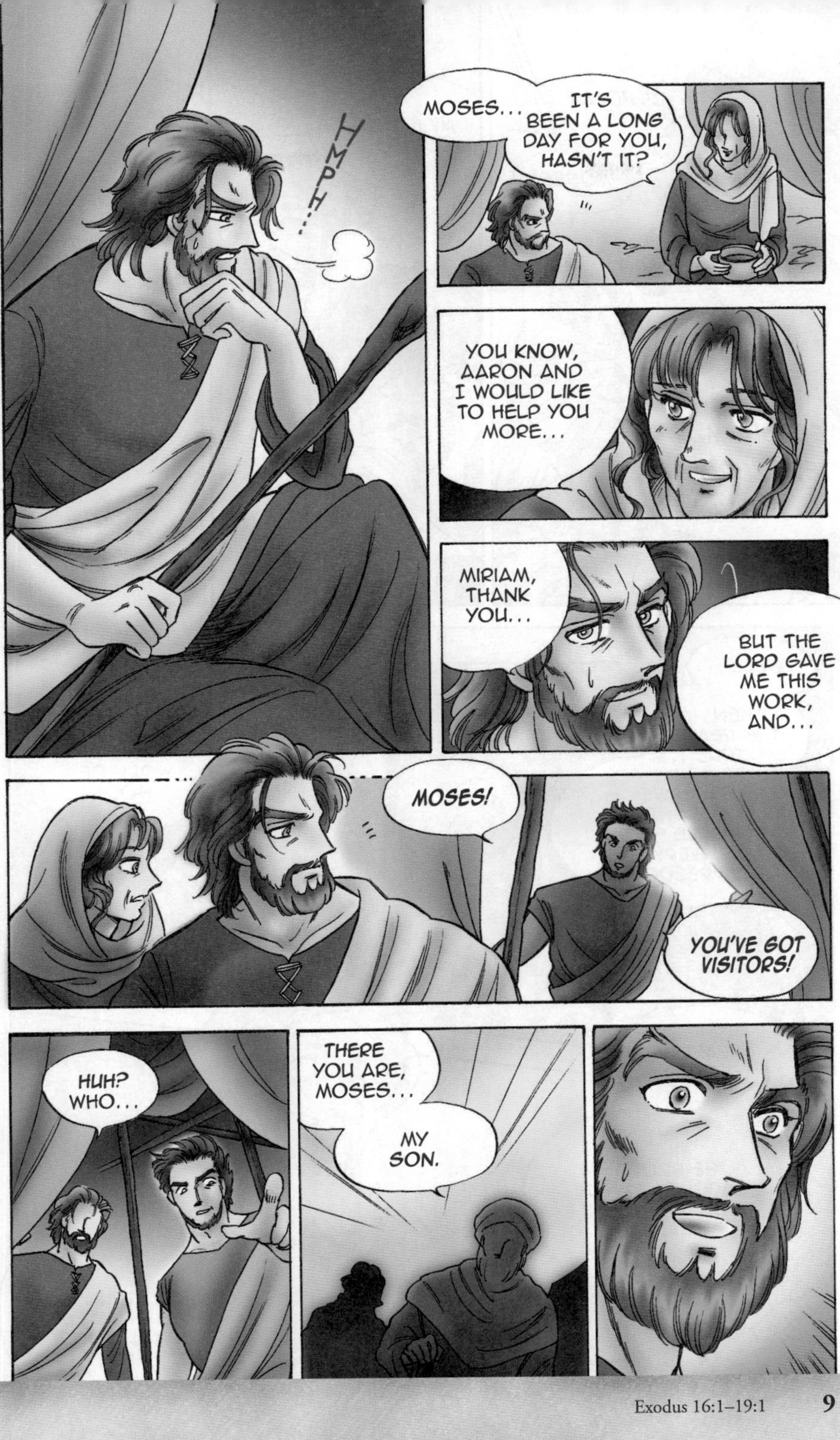
HMPH!...
MOSES...
IT'S BEEN A LONG DAY FOR YOU, HASN'T IT?
YOU KNOW, AARON AND I WOULD LIKE TO HELP YOU MORE...
MIRIAM, THANK YOU...
BUT THE LORD GAVE ME THIS WORK, AND...
MOSES!
YOU'VE GOT VISITORS!
HUH? WHO...
THERE YOU ARE, MOSES...
MY SON.

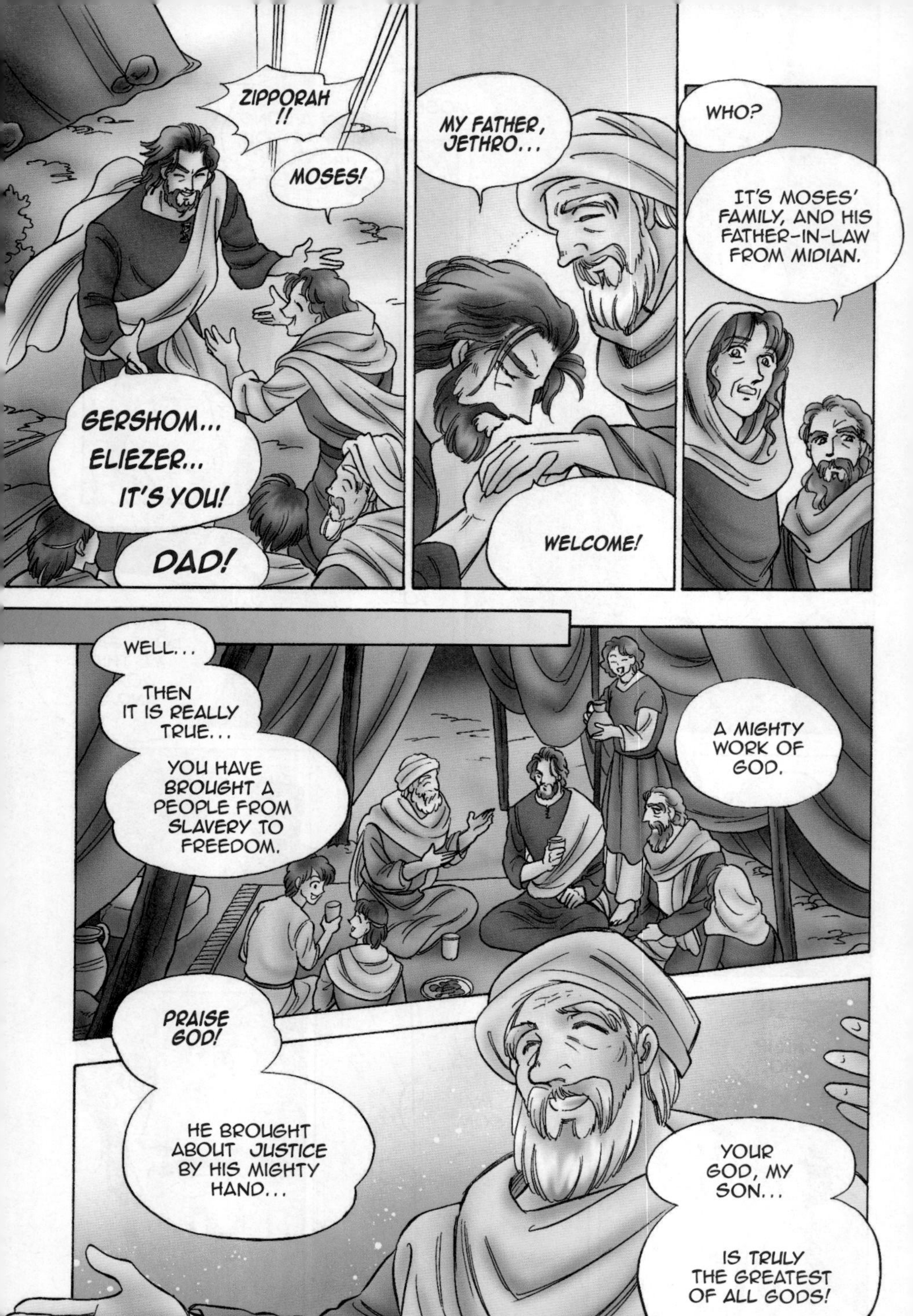
ZIPPORAH !!
MOSES!
GERSHOM... ELIEZER... IT'S YOU!
DAD!
MY FATHER, JETHRO...
WELCOME!
WHO?
IT'S MOSES' FAMILY, AND HIS FATHER-IN-LAW FROM MIDIAN.
WELL...
THEN IT IS REALLY TRUE...
YOU HAVE BROUGHT A PEOPLE FROM SLAVERY TO FREEDOM.
A MIGHTY WORK OF GOD.
PRAISE GOD!
HE BROUGHT ABOUT JUSTICE BY HIS MIGHTY HAND...
YOUR GOD, MY SON...
IS TRULY THE GREATEST OF ALL GODS!

MOSES, I AM ASTOUNDED BY THE SIZE OF YOUR CAMP...

HOW MANY PEOPLE DID THE LORD RESCUE FROM EGYPT?

THE MEN ALONE NUMBER ABOUT 600,000...

WHA—MORE THAN A *MILLION* PEOPLE?!

YES. AND ALL OF THEM ARE CHILDREN OF OUR ANCESTOR ABRAHAM.

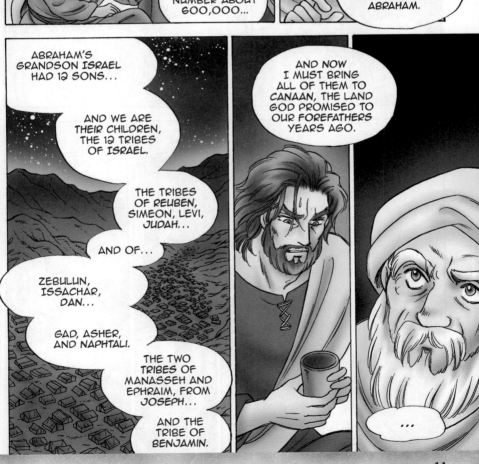

ABRAHAM'S GRANDSON ISRAEL HAD 12 SONS...

AND WE ARE THEIR CHILDREN, THE 12 TRIBES OF ISRAEL.

THE TRIBES OF REUBEN, SIMEON, LEVI, JUDAH...

AND OF...

ZEBULUN, ISSACHAR, DAN...

GAD, ASHER, AND NAPHTALI.

THE TWO TRIBES OF MANASSEH AND EPHRAIM, FROM JOSEPH...

AND THE TRIBE OF BENJAMIN.

AND NOW I MUST BRING ALL OF THEM TO CANAAN, THE LAND GOD PROMISED TO OUR FOREFATHERS YEARS AGO.

...

Exodus 16:1–19:1   **11**

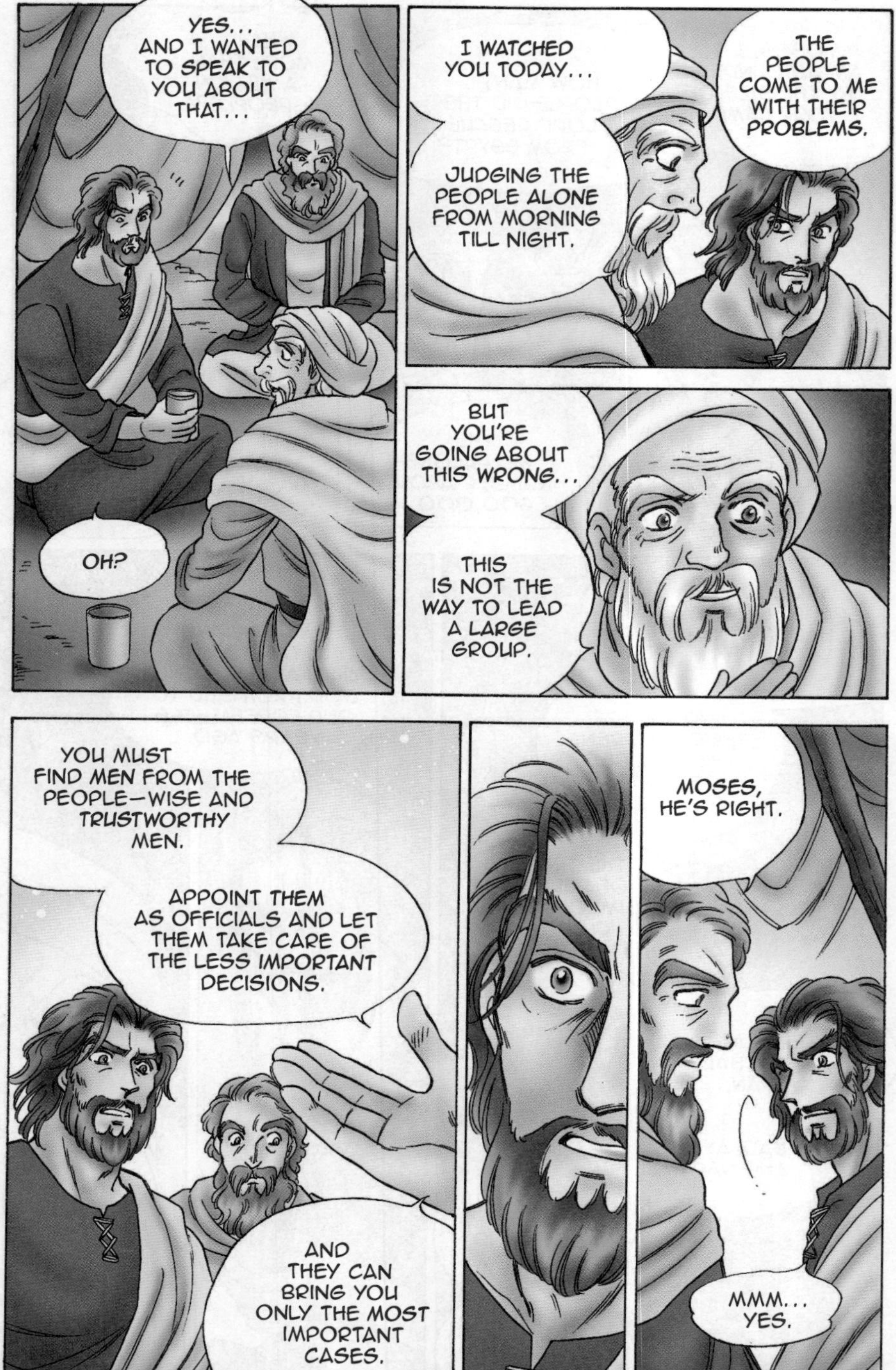
YES... AND I WANTED TO SPEAK TO YOU ABOUT THAT...
OH?
I WATCHED YOU TODAY...
JUDGING THE PEOPLE ALONE FROM MORNING TILL NIGHT.
THE PEOPLE COME TO ME WITH THEIR PROBLEMS.
BUT YOU'RE GOING ABOUT THIS WRONG...
THIS IS NOT THE WAY TO LEAD A LARGE GROUP.
YOU MUST FIND MEN FROM THE PEOPLE—WISE AND TRUSTWORTHY MEN.
APPOINT THEM AS OFFICIALS AND LET THEM TAKE CARE OF THE LESS IMPORTANT DECISIONS.
AND THEY CAN BRING YOU ONLY THE MOST IMPORTANT CASES.
MOSES, HE'S RIGHT.
MMM... YES.

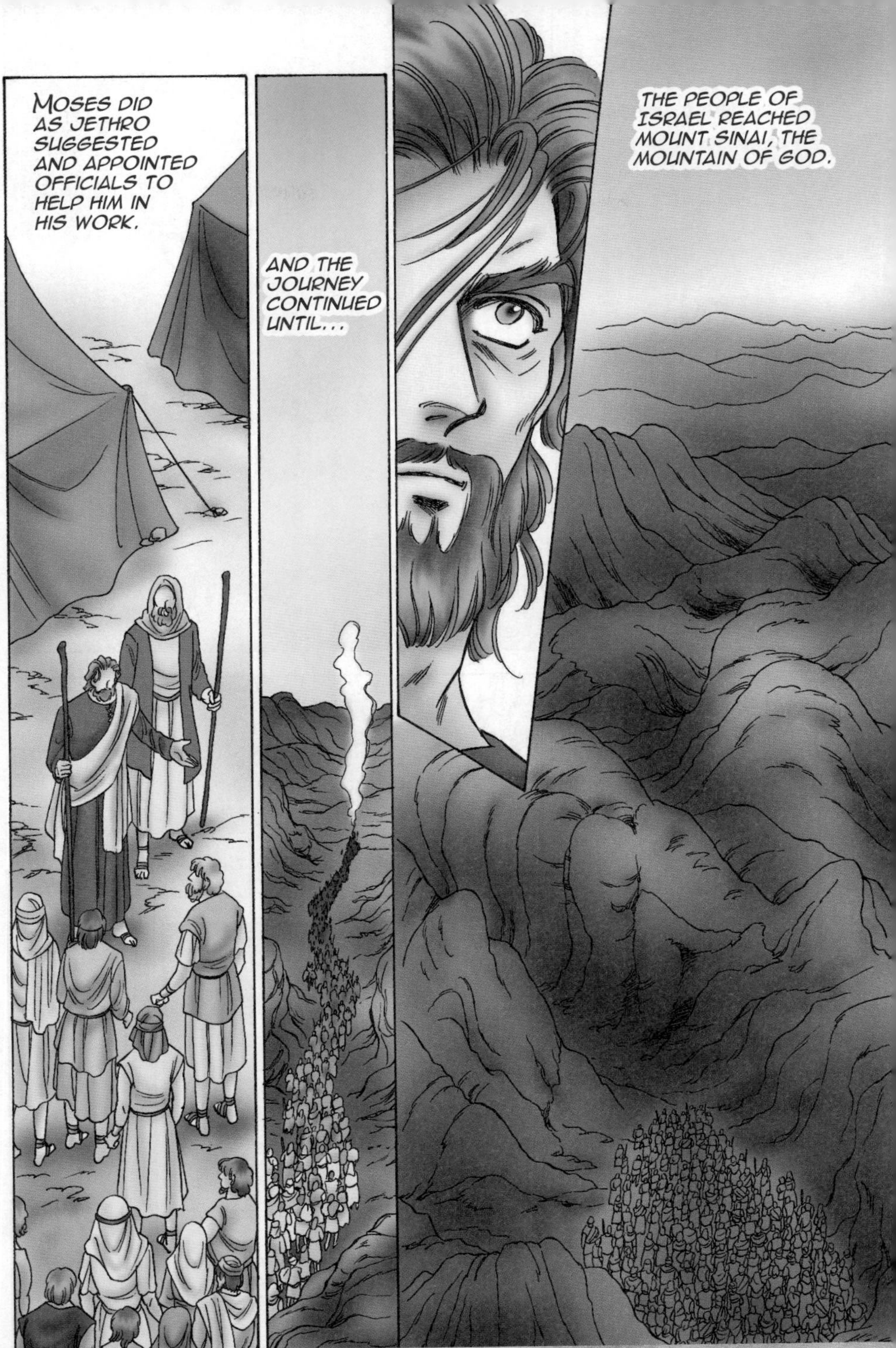
MOSES DID AS JETHRO SUGGESTED AND APPOINTED OFFICIALS TO HELP HIM IN HIS WORK.
AND THE JOURNEY CONTINUED UNTIL...
THE PEOPLE OF ISRAEL REACHED MOUNT SINAI, THE MOUNTAIN OF GOD.

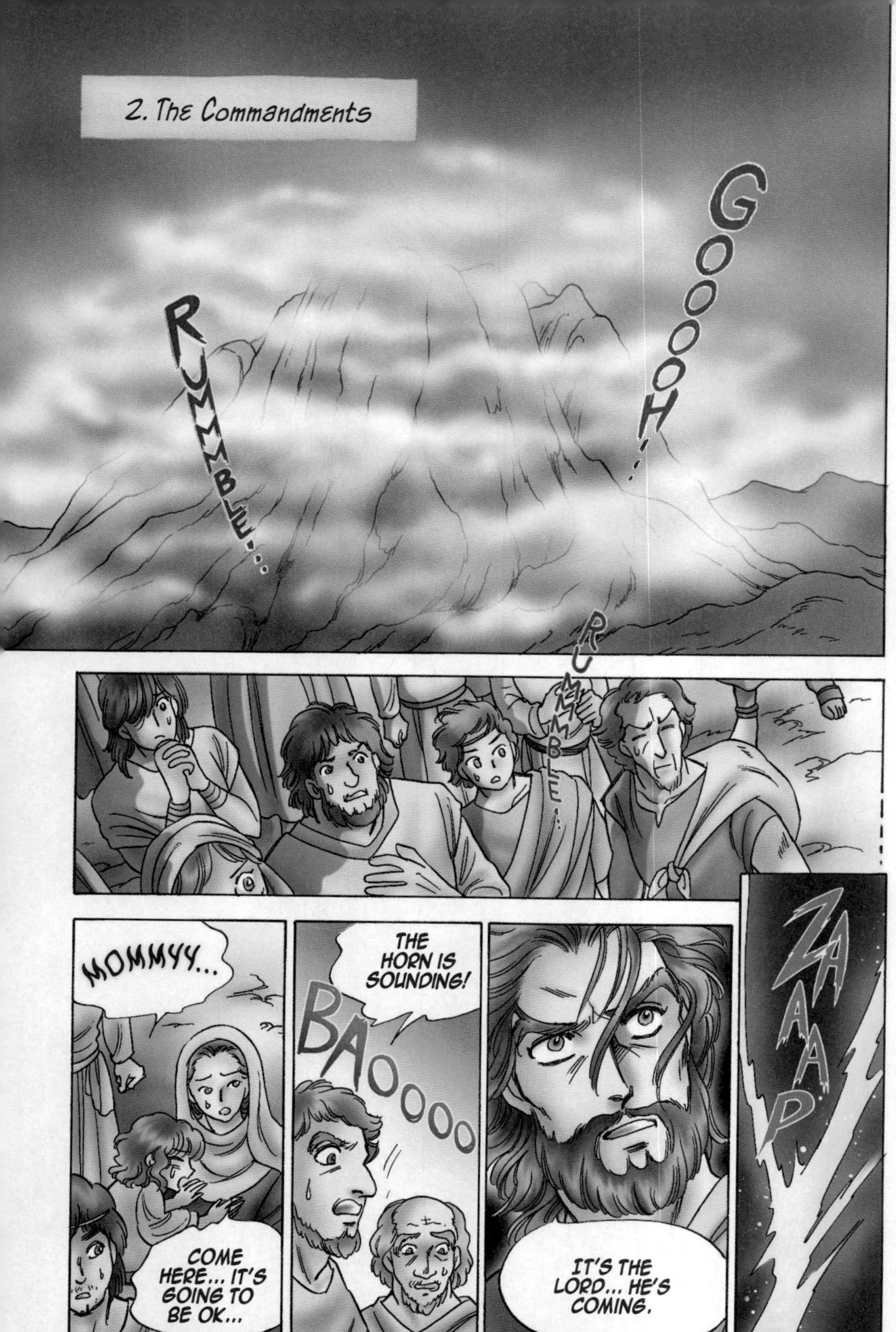
2. The Commandments
RUMMBLE...
GOOOOOH...
RUMMBLE...
MOMMYY...
COME HERE... IT'S GOING TO BE OK...
THE HORN IS SOUNDING!
BAOOOOO
IT'S THE LORD... HE'S COMING.
ZAAAAP

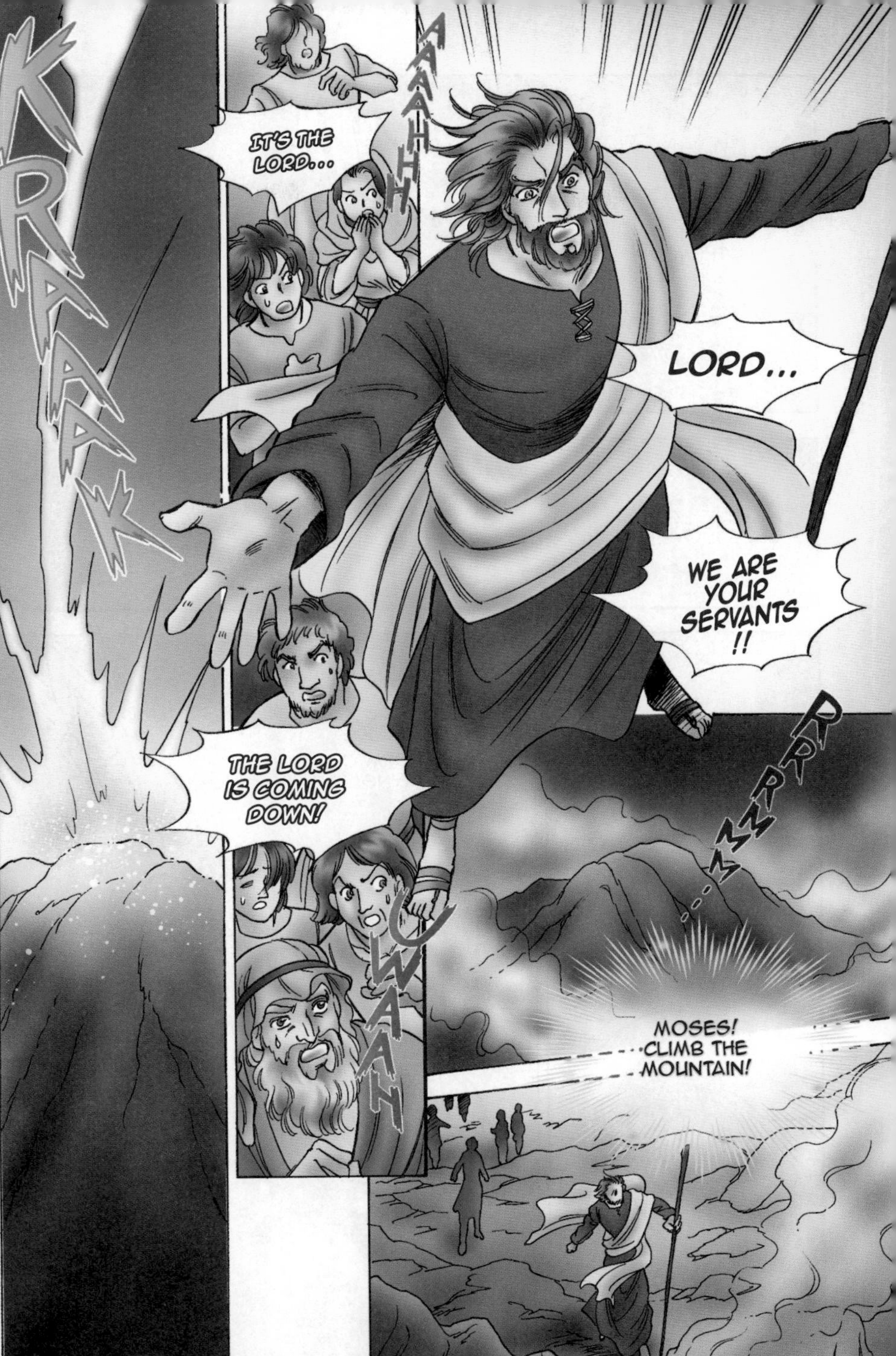
KRRAAAK
AAAAHHH
IT'S THE LORD...
LORD...
WE ARE YOUR SERVANTS !!
THE LORD IS COMING DOWN!
UWAAAH
RRRMMM...
MOSES! CLIMB THE MOUNTAIN!

SPEAK TO THE PEOPLE OF ISRAEL, TELLING THEM...

THAT I AM THE LORD...

THE LORD YOUR GOD!

I BROUGHT YOU OUT OF EGYPT, OUT OF THE LAND OF SLAVERY!

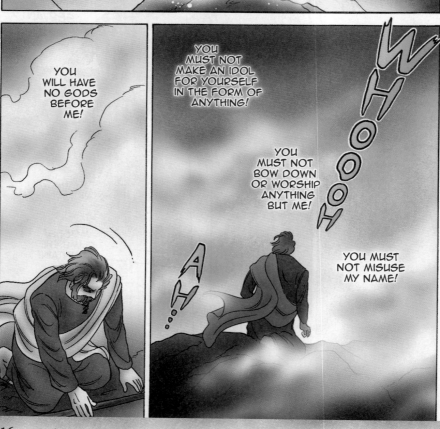

YOU WILL HAVE NO GODS BEFORE ME!

YOU MUST NOT MAKE AN IDOL FOR YOURSELF IN THE FORM OF ANYTHING!

YOU MUST NOT BOW DOWN OR WORSHIP ANYTHING BUT ME!

YOU MUST NOT MISUSE MY NAME!

WHOOOOH

AH...!

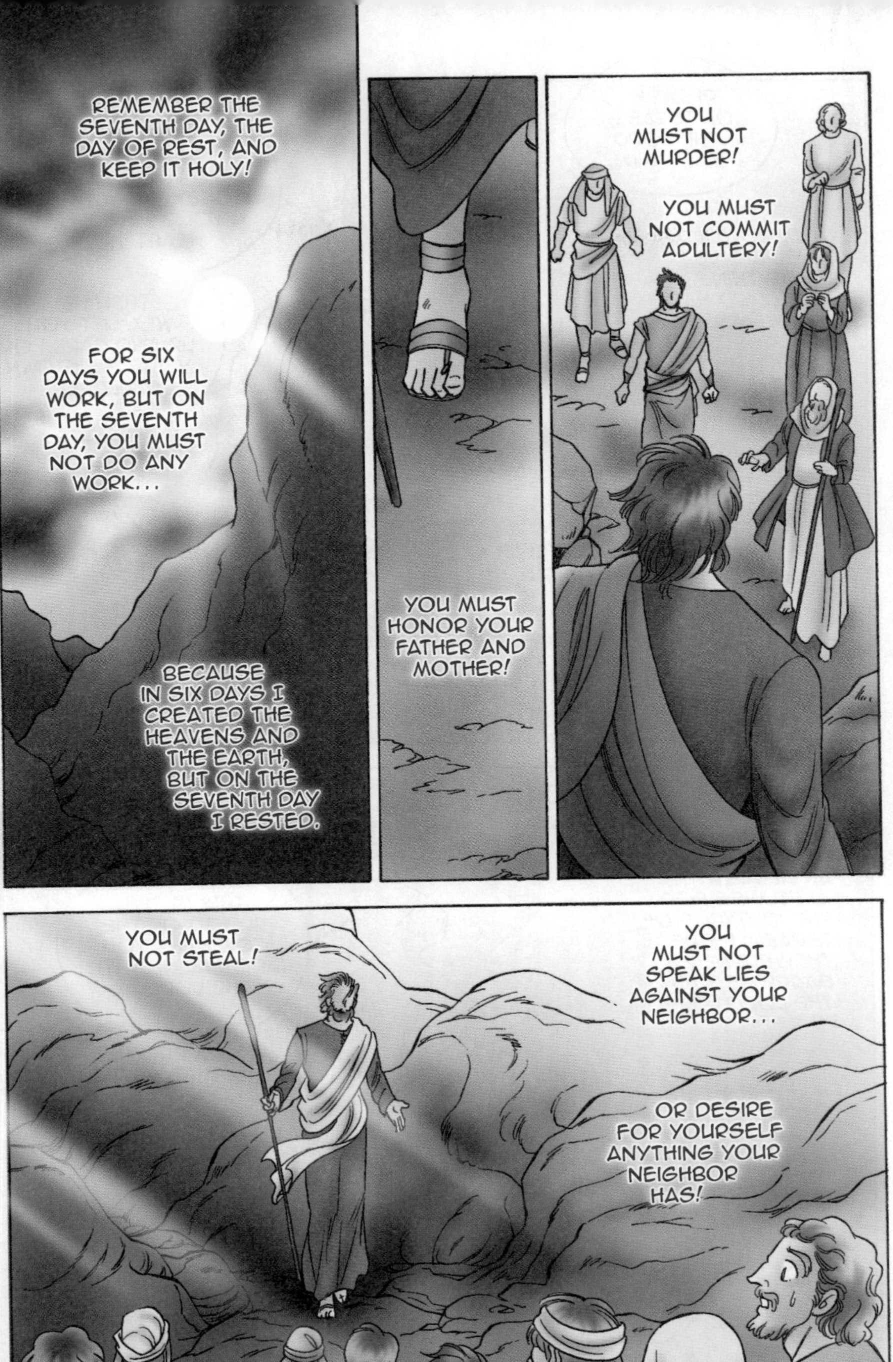
REMEMBER THE SEVENTH DAY, THE DAY OF REST, AND KEEP IT HOLY!
FOR SIX DAYS YOU WILL WORK, BUT ON THE SEVENTH DAY, YOU MUST NOT DO ANY WORK...
BECAUSE IN SIX DAYS I CREATED THE HEAVENS AND THE EARTH, BUT ON THE SEVENTH DAY I RESTED.
YOU MUST HONOR YOUR FATHER AND MOTHER!
YOU MUST NOT MURDER!
YOU MUST NOT COMMIT ADULTERY!
YOU MUST NOT STEAL!
YOU MUST NOT SPEAK LIES AGAINST YOUR NEIGHBOR...
OR DESIRE FOR YOURSELF ANYTHING YOUR NEIGHBOR HAS!

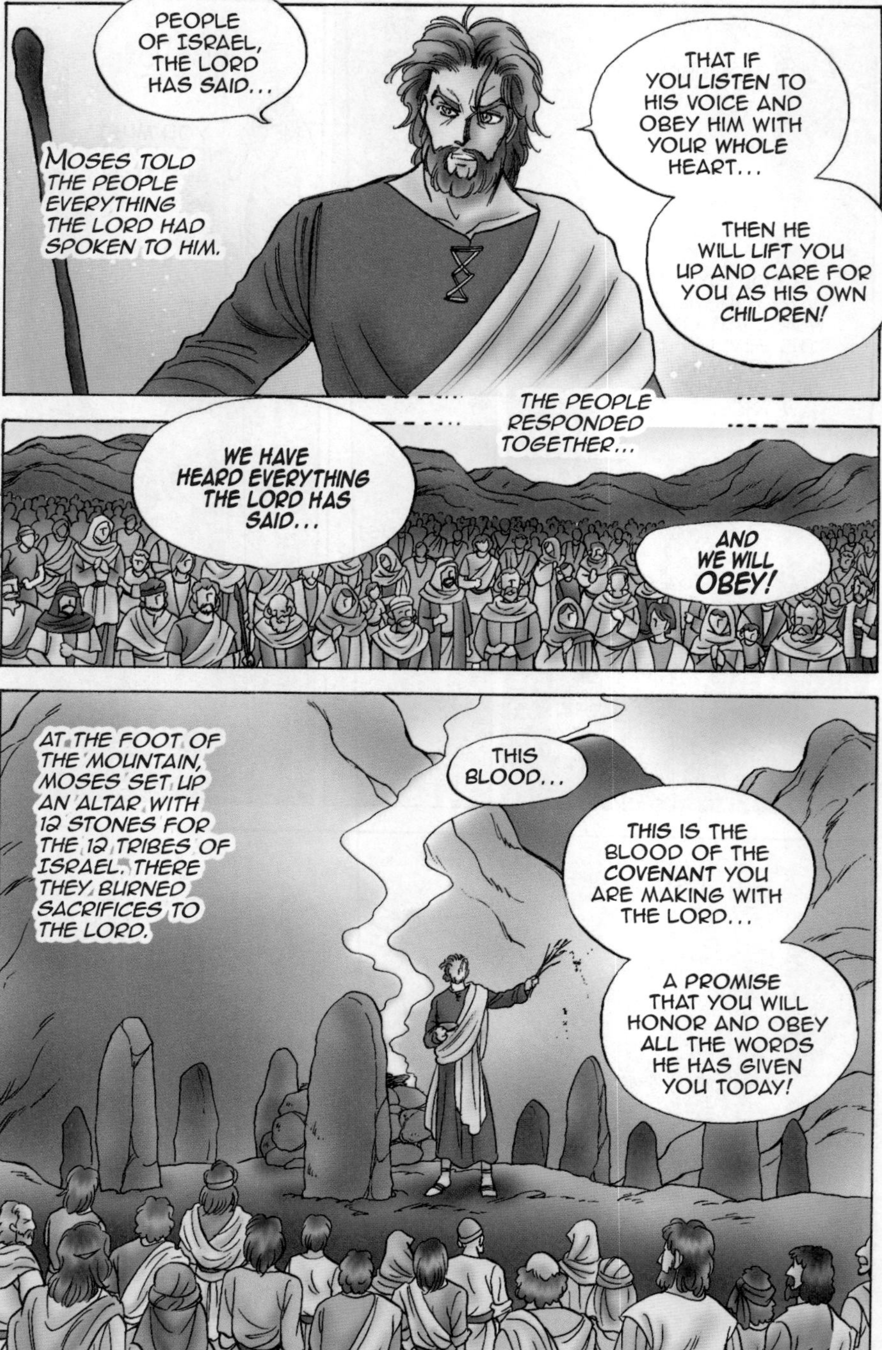

PEOPLE OF ISRAEL, THE LORD HAS SAID...
MOSES TOLD THE PEOPLE EVERYTHING THE LORD HAD SPOKEN TO HIM.
THAT IF YOU LISTEN TO HIS VOICE AND OBEY HIM WITH YOUR WHOLE HEART...
THEN HE WILL LIFT YOU UP AND CARE FOR YOU AS HIS OWN CHILDREN!
THE PEOPLE RESPONDED TOGETHER...
WE HAVE HEARD EVERYTHING THE LORD HAS SAID...
AND WE WILL OBEY!
AT THE FOOT OF THE MOUNTAIN, MOSES SET UP AN ALTAR WITH 12 STONES FOR THE 12 TRIBES OF ISRAEL. THERE THEY BURNED SACRIFICES TO THE LORD.
THIS BLOOD...
THIS IS THE BLOOD OF THE COVENANT YOU ARE MAKING WITH THE LORD...
A PROMISE THAT YOU WILL HONOR AND OBEY ALL THE WORDS HE HAS GIVEN YOU TODAY!

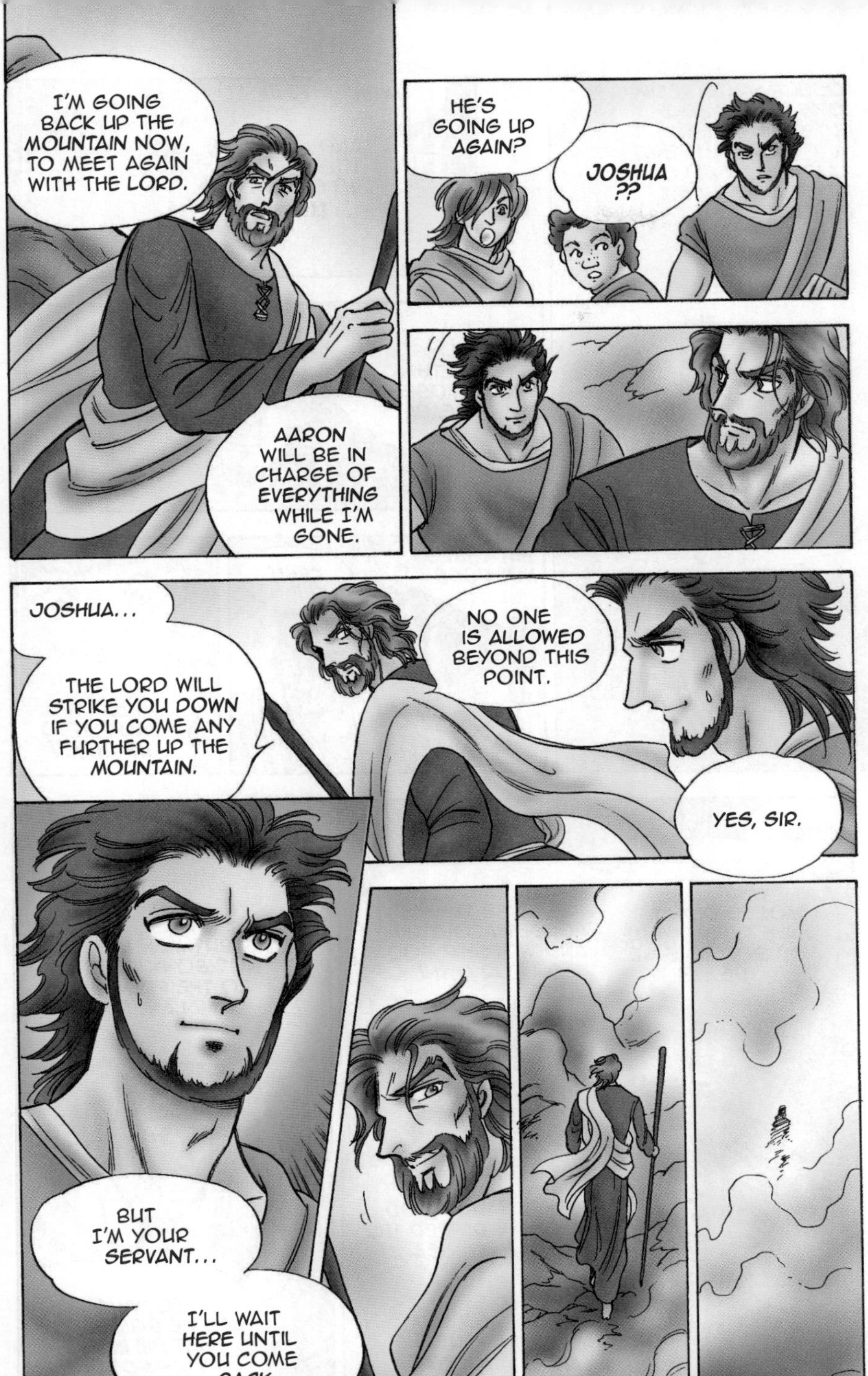
I'M GOING BACK UP THE MOUNTAIN NOW, TO MEET AGAIN WITH THE LORD.
HE'S GOING UP AGAIN?
JOSHUA ??
AARON WILL BE IN CHARGE OF EVERYTHING WHILE I'M GONE.
JOSHUA...
THE LORD WILL STRIKE YOU DOWN IF YOU COME ANY FURTHER UP THE MOUNTAIN.
NO ONE IS ALLOWED BEYOND THIS POINT.
YES, SIR.
BUT I'M YOUR SERVANT...
I'LL WAIT HERE UNTIL YOU COME BACK.

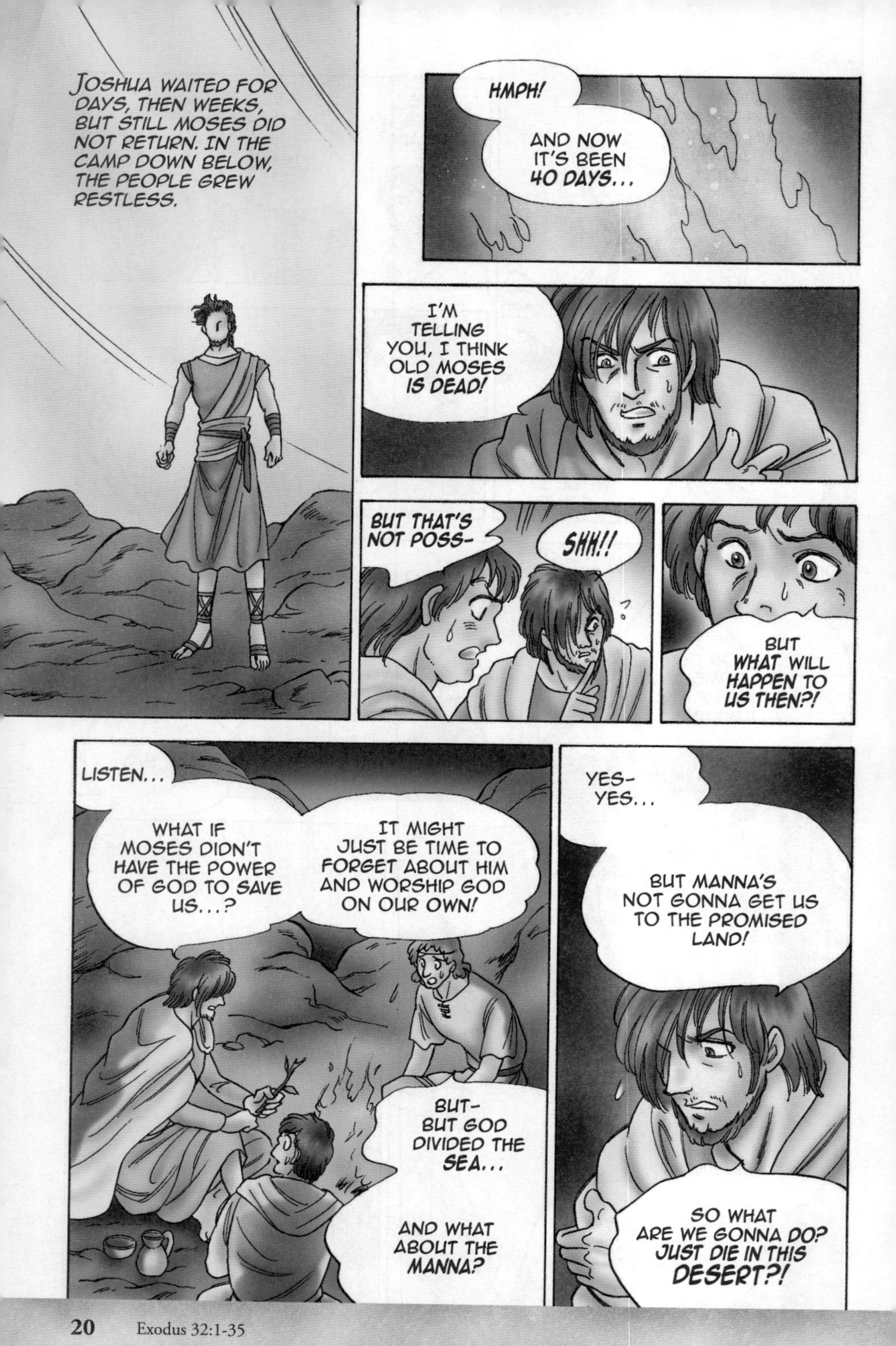

JOSHUA WAITED FOR DAYS, THEN WEEKS, BUT STILL MOSES DID NOT RETURN. IN THE CAMP DOWN BELOW, THE PEOPLE GREW RESTLESS.
HMPH!
AND NOW IT'S BEEN 40 DAYS...
I'M TELLING YOU, I THINK OLD MOSES IS DEAD!
BUT THAT'S NOT POSS-
SHH!!
BUT WHAT WILL HAPPEN TO US THEN?!
LISTEN...
WHAT IF MOSES DIDN'T HAVE THE POWER OF GOD TO SAVE US...?
IT MIGHT JUST BE TIME TO FORGET ABOUT HIM AND WORSHIP GOD ON OUR OWN!
BUT- BUT GOD DIVIDED THE SEA...
AND WHAT ABOUT THE MANNA?
YES- YES...
BUT MANNA'S NOT GONNA GET US TO THE PROMISED LAND!
SO WHAT ARE WE GONNA DO? JUST DIE IN THIS DESERT?!

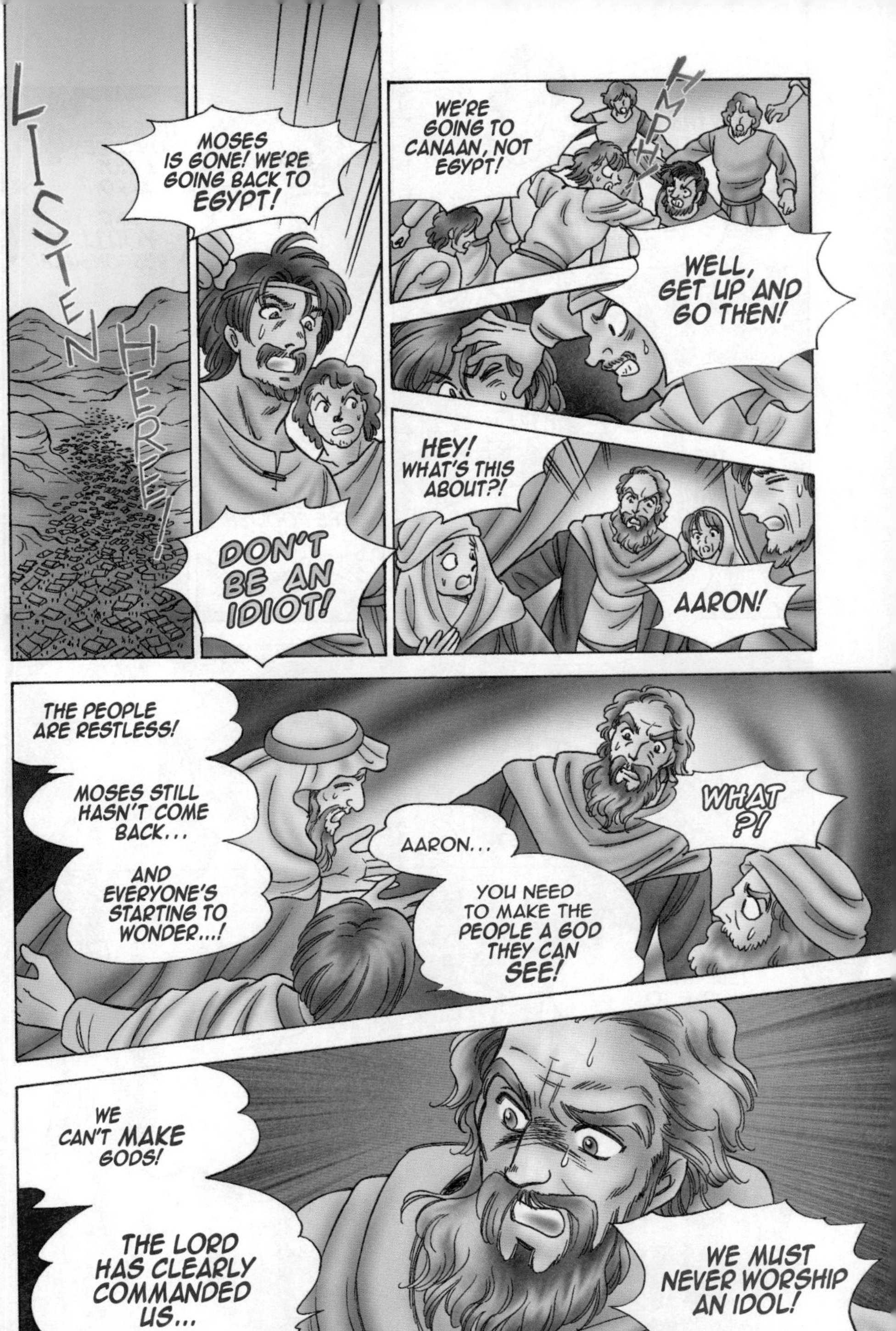
LISTEN HERE!
MOSES IS GONE! WE'RE GOING BACK TO EGYPT!
DON'T BE AN IDIOT!
WE'RE GOING TO CANAAN, NOT EGYPT!
HMPH!
WELL, GET UP AND GO THEN!
HEY! WHAT'S THIS ABOUT?!
AARON!
THE PEOPLE ARE RESTLESS!
MOSES STILL HASN'T COME BACK...
AND EVERYONE'S STARTING TO WONDER...!
AARON...
YOU NEED TO MAKE THE PEOPLE A GOD THEY CAN SEE!
WHAT?!
WE CAN'T MAKE GODS!
THE LORD HAS CLEARLY COMMANDED US...
WE MUST NEVER WORSHIP AN IDOL!

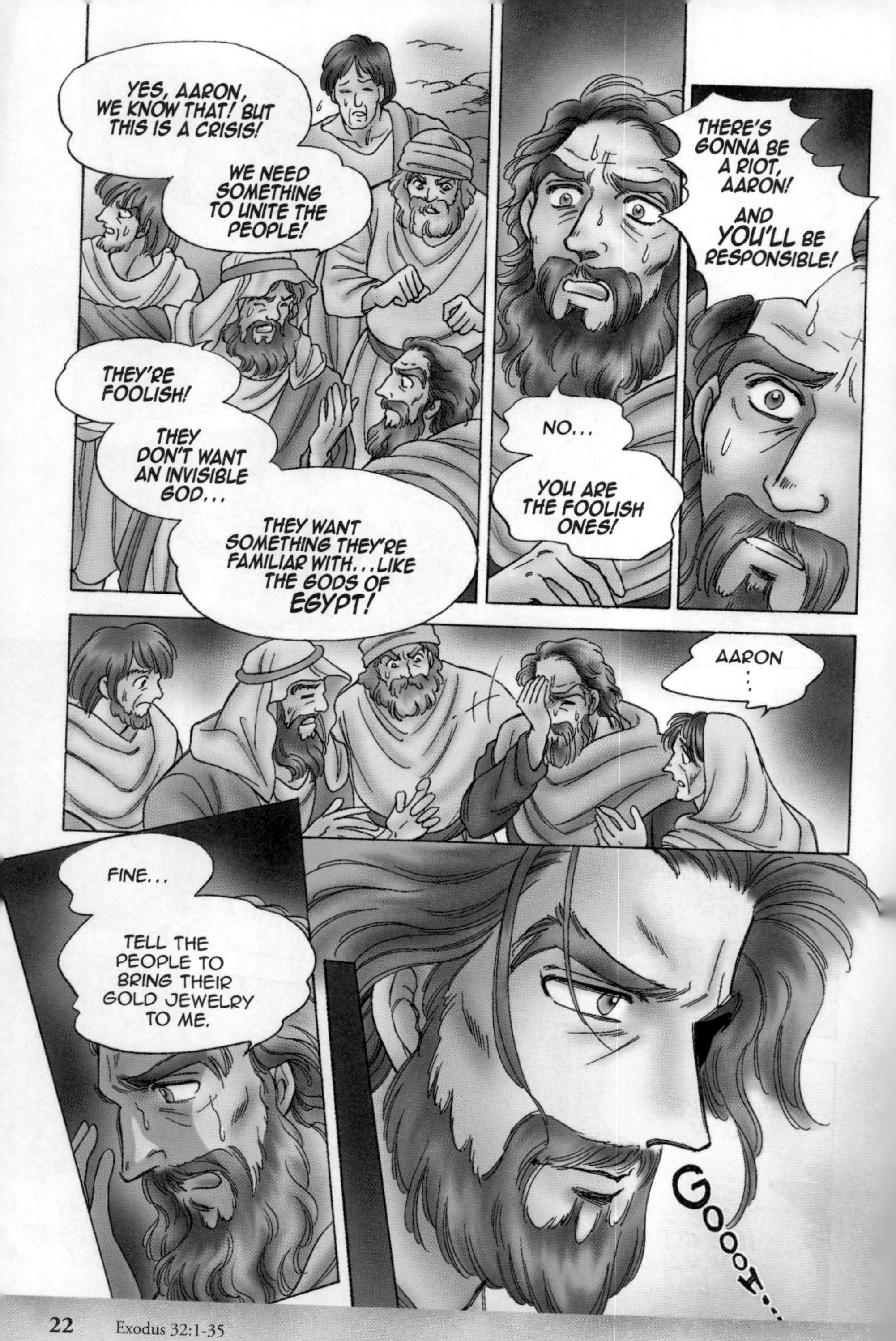
YES, AARON, WE KNOW THAT! BUT THIS IS A CRISIS!
WE NEED SOMETHING TO UNITE THE PEOPLE!
THEY'RE FOOLISH!
THEY DON'T WANT AN INVISIBLE GOD...
THEY WANT SOMETHING THEY'RE FAMILIAR WITH...LIKE THE GODS OF EGYPT!
NO...
YOU ARE THE FOOLISH ONES!
THERE'S GONNA BE A RIOT, AARON!
AND YOU'LL BE RESPONSIBLE!
AARON
...
FINE...
TELL THE PEOPLE TO BRING THEIR GOLD JEWELRY TO ME.
GOOOT...

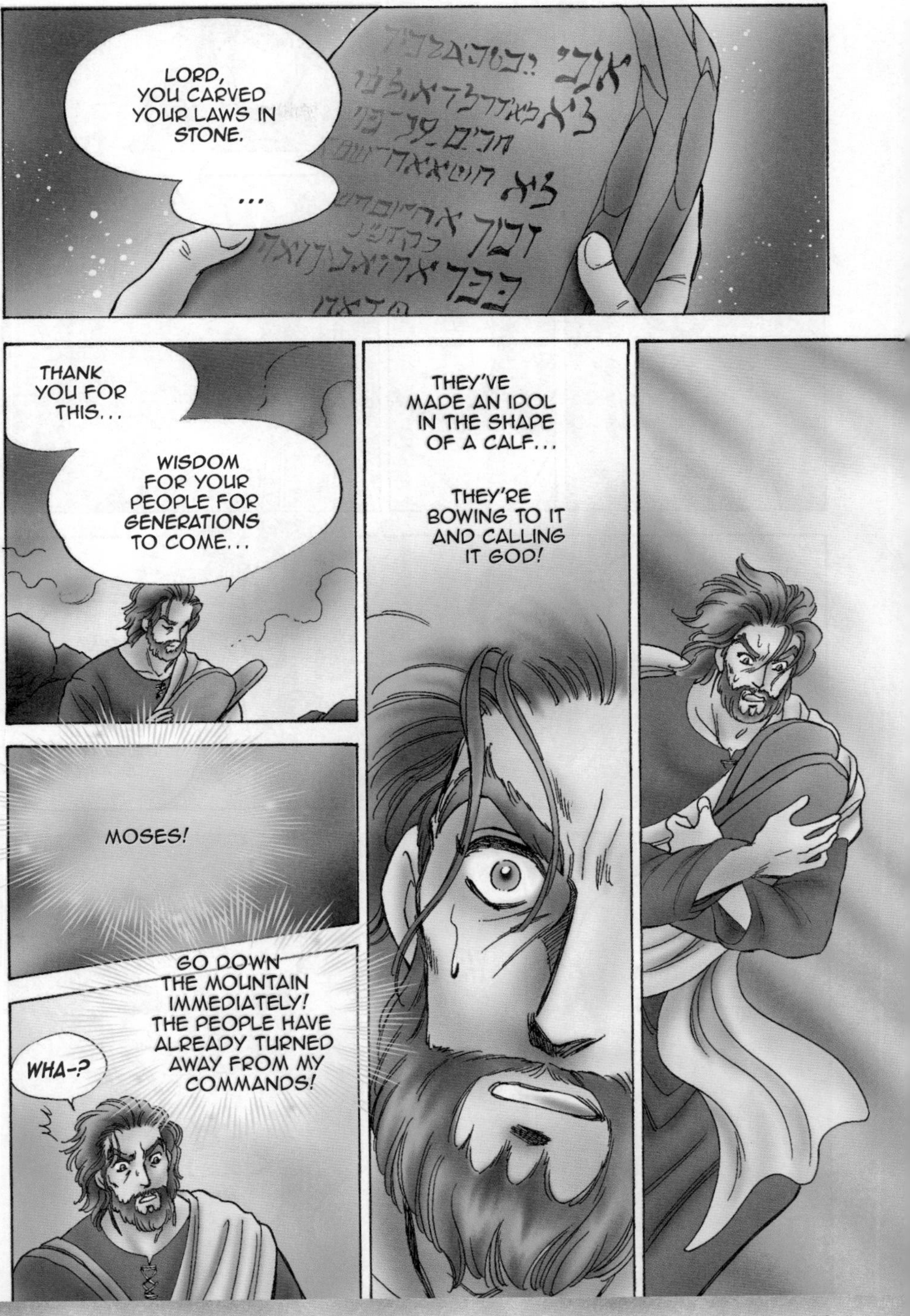
LORD, YOU CARVED YOUR LAWS IN STONE.
...
THANK YOU FOR THIS...
WISDOM FOR YOUR PEOPLE FOR GENERATIONS TO COME...
MOSES!
GO DOWN THE MOUNTAIN IMMEDIATELY! THE PEOPLE HAVE ALREADY TURNED AWAY FROM MY COMMANDS!
WHA-?
THEY'VE MADE AN IDOL IN THE SHAPE OF A CALF...
THEY'RE BOWING TO IT AND CALLING IT GOD!

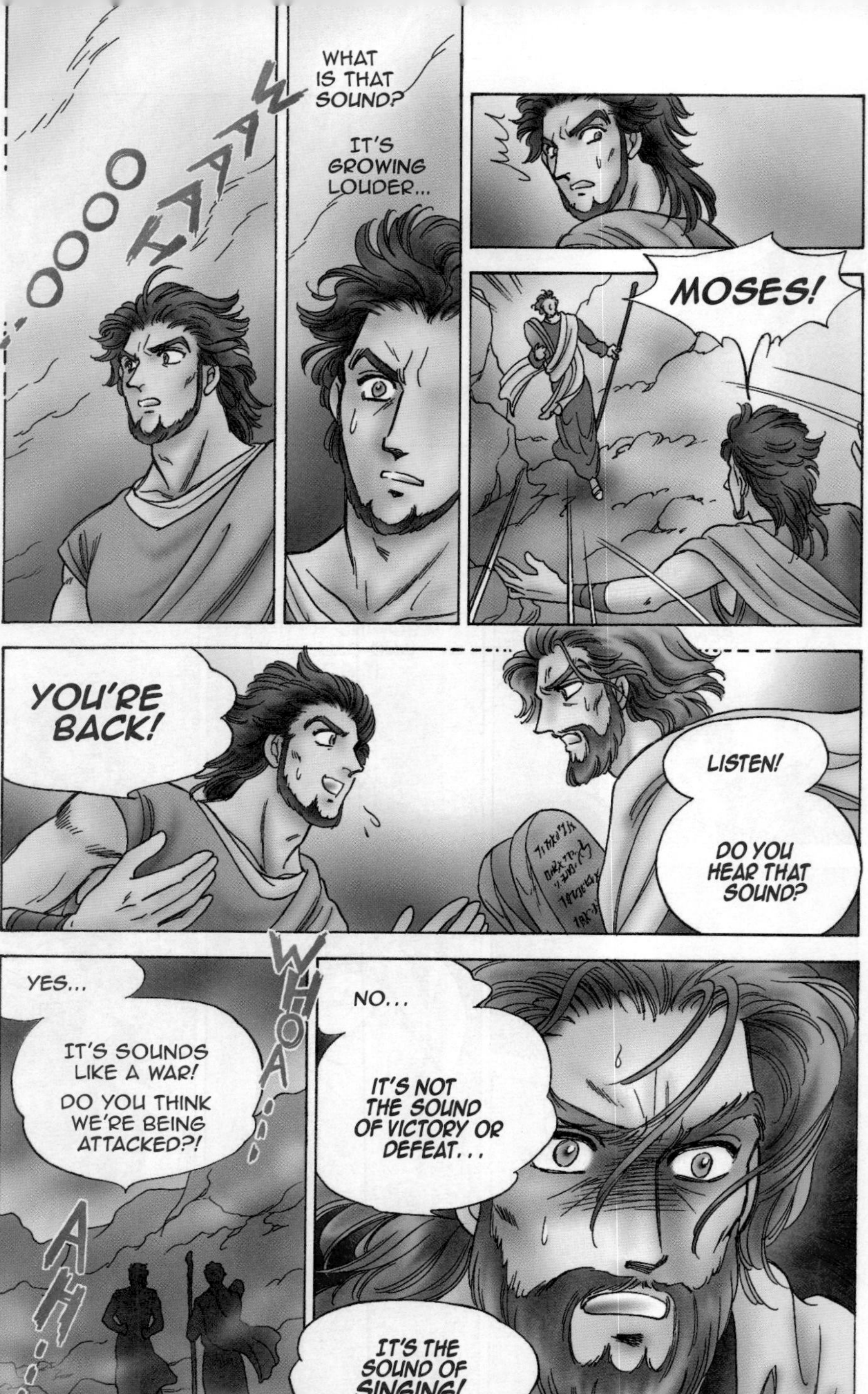
OOOOOHAAAAW
WHAT IS THAT SOUND?
IT'S GROWING LOUDER...
MOSES!
YOU'RE BACK!
LISTEN!
DO YOU HEAR THAT SOUND?
YES...
IT'S SOUNDS LIKE A WAR!
DO YOU THINK WE'RE BEING ATTACKED?!
WHOA...
AAH...
NO...
IT'S NOT THE SOUND OF VICTORY OR DEFEAT...
IT'S THE SOUND OF SINGING!

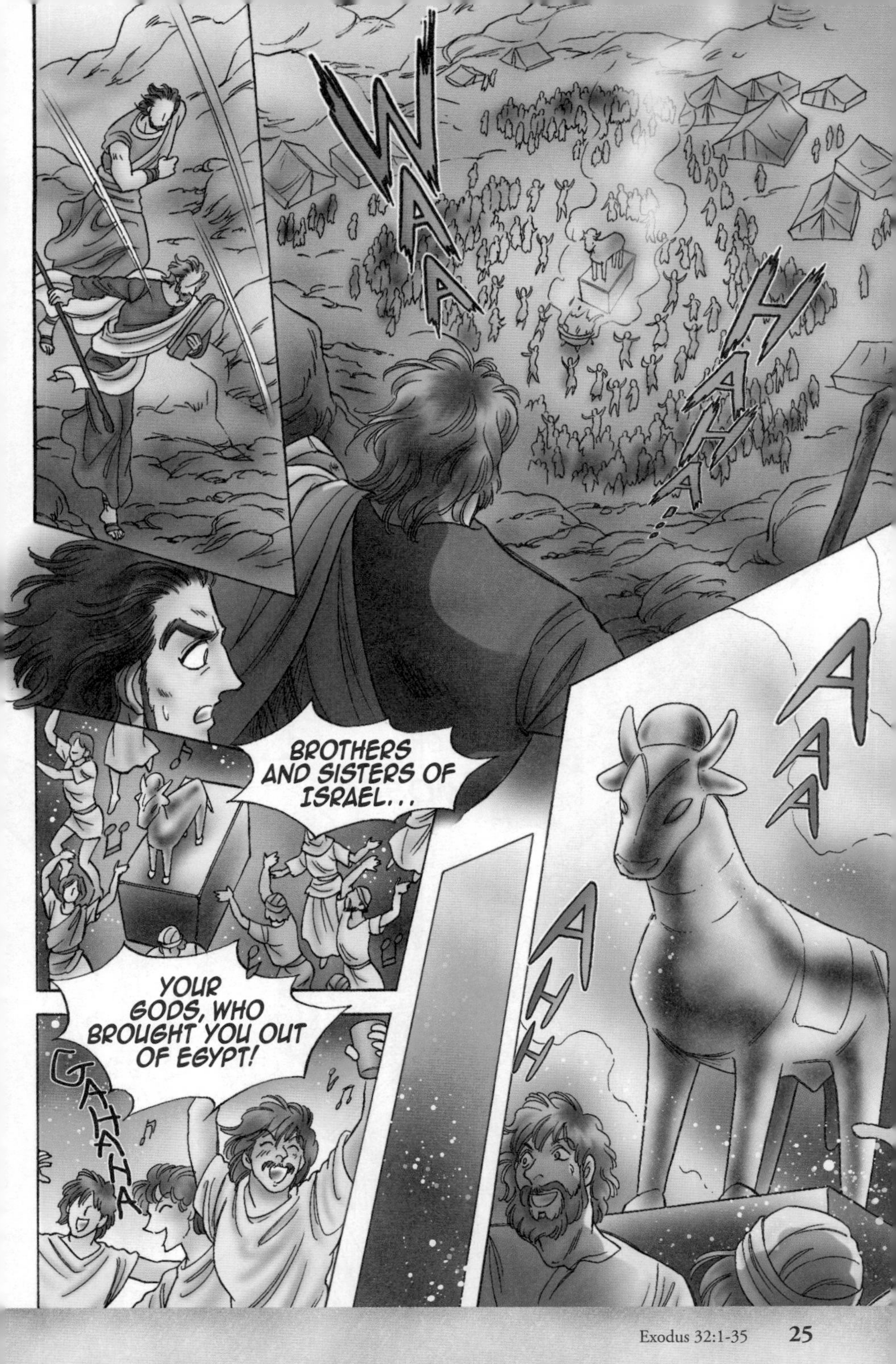
WAA
HAHAA
BROTHERS AND SISTERS OF ISRAEL...
YOUR GODS, WHO BROUGHT YOU OUT OF EGYPT!
GAHAHA
AAAA
AHHH

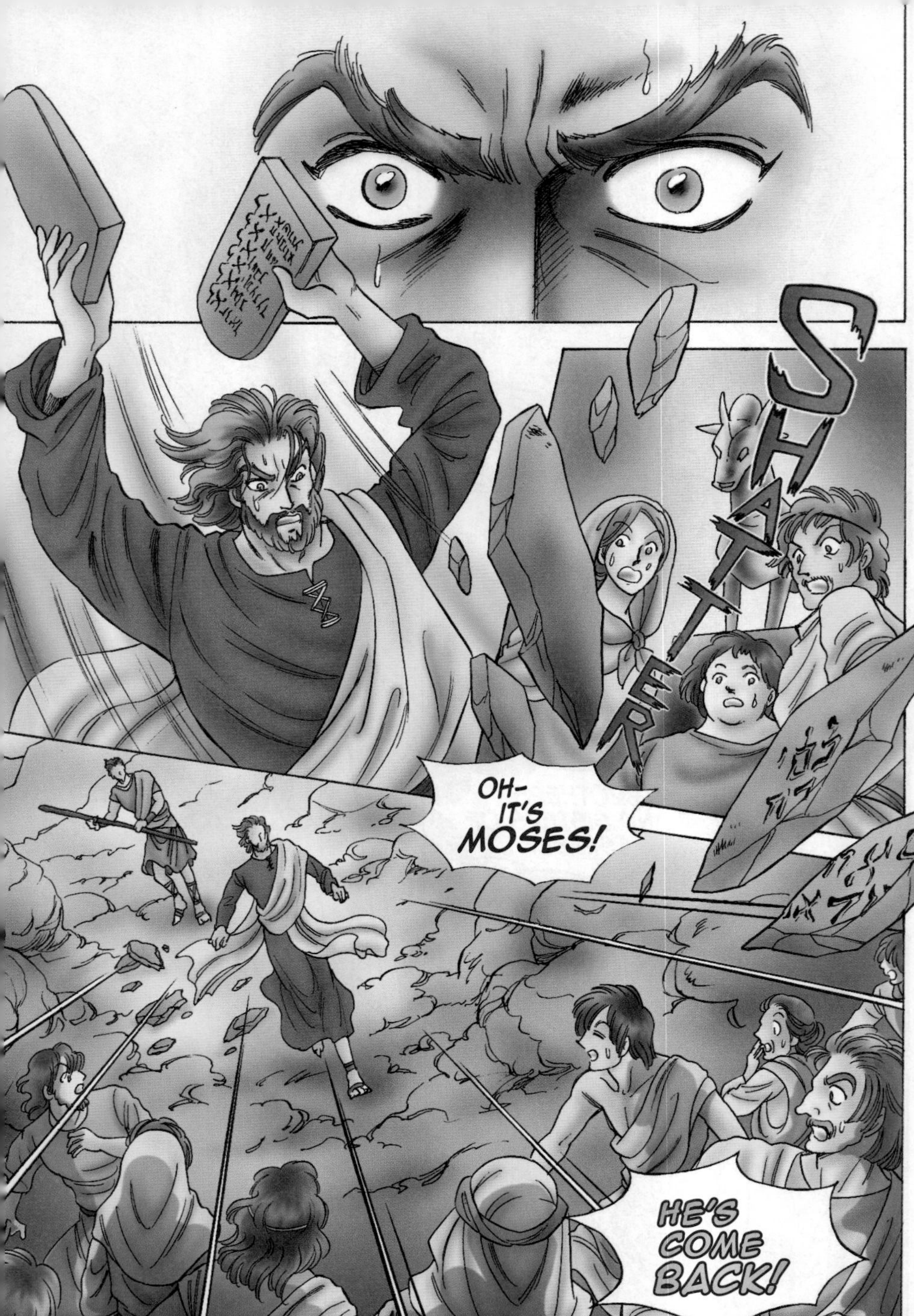
SHATTER
OH- IT'S MOSES!
HE'S COME BACK!

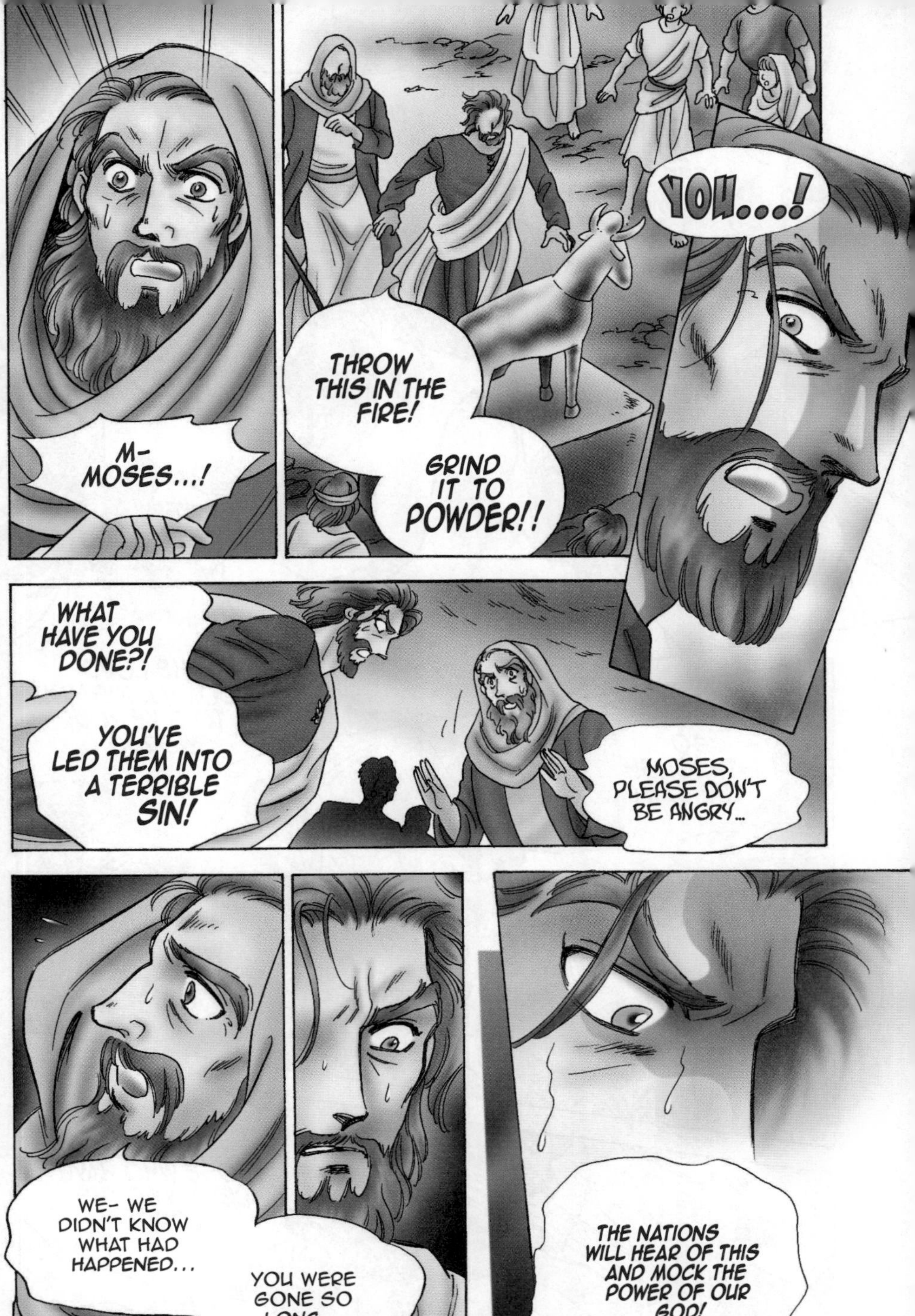
M- MOSES...!
THROW THIS IN THE FIRE!
GRIND IT TO POWDER!!
YOU...!
WHAT HAVE YOU DONE?!
YOU'VE LED THEM INTO A TERRIBLE SIN!
MOSES, PLEASE DON'T BE ANGRY...
WE- WE DIDN'T KNOW WHAT HAD HAPPENED...
YOU WERE GONE SO LONG...
THE NATIONS WILL HEAR OF THIS AND MOCK THE POWER OF OUR GOD!

Exodus 32:1-35

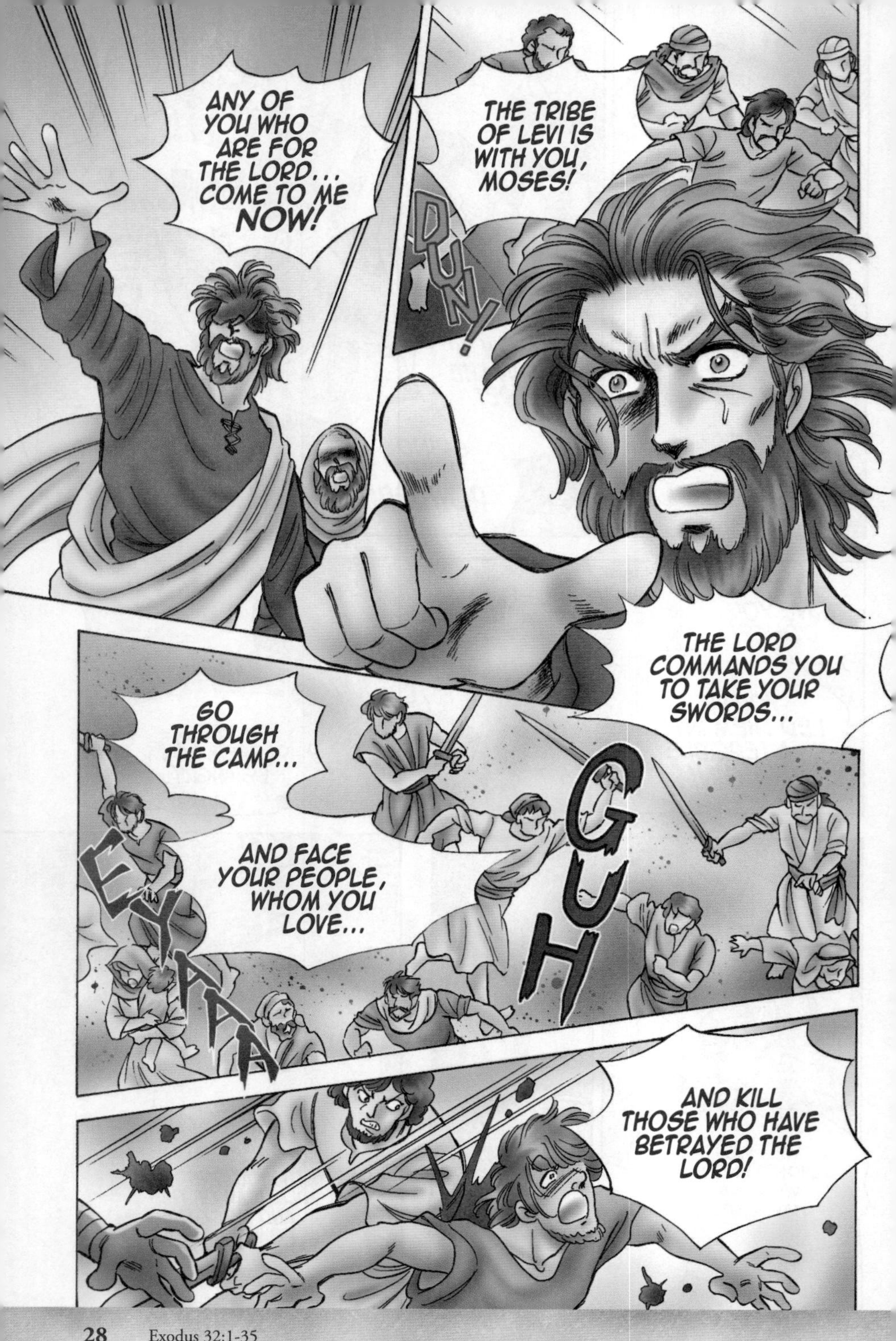
ANY OF YOU WHO ARE FOR THE LORD... COME TO ME NOW!
THE TRIBE OF LEVI IS WITH YOU, MOSES!
DUN!
THE LORD COMMANDS YOU TO TAKE YOUR SWORDS...
GO THROUGH THE CAMP...
AND FACE YOUR PEOPLE, WHOM YOU LOVE...
GUH
EYAAA
AND KILL THOSE WHO HAVE BETRAYED THE LORD!

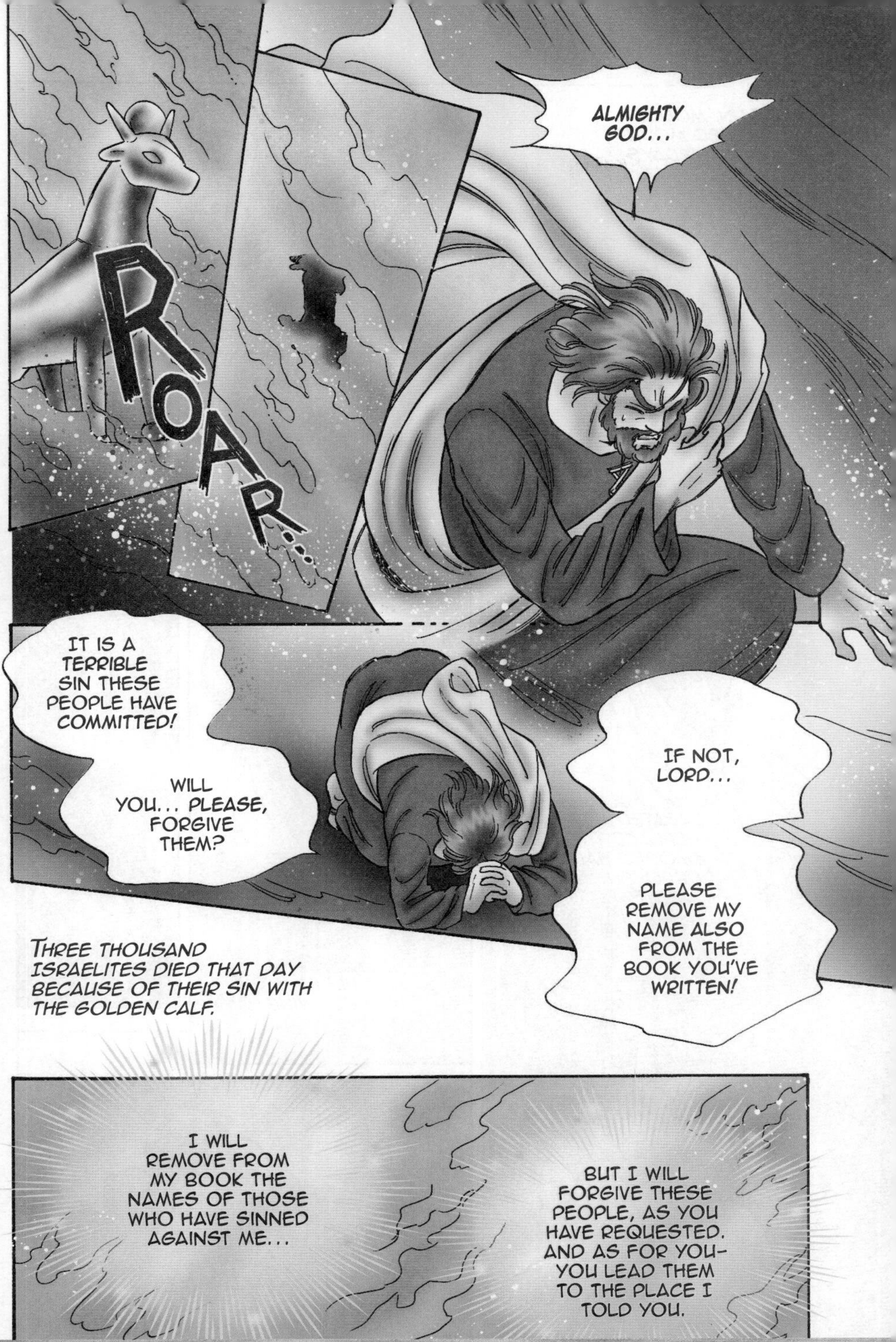
ROAR...
ALMIGHTY GOD...
IT IS A TERRIBLE SIN THESE PEOPLE HAVE COMMITTED!
WILL YOU... PLEASE, FORGIVE THEM?
IF NOT, LORD...
PLEASE REMOVE MY NAME ALSO FROM THE BOOK YOU'VE WRITTEN!
THREE THOUSAND ISRAELITES DIED THAT DAY BECAUSE OF THEIR SIN WITH THE GOLDEN CALF.
I WILL REMOVE FROM MY BOOK THE NAMES OF THOSE WHO HAVE SINNED AGAINST ME...
BUT I WILL FORGIVE THESE PEOPLE, AS YOU HAVE REQUESTED. AND AS FOR YOU- YOU LEAD THEM TO THE PLACE I TOLD YOU.

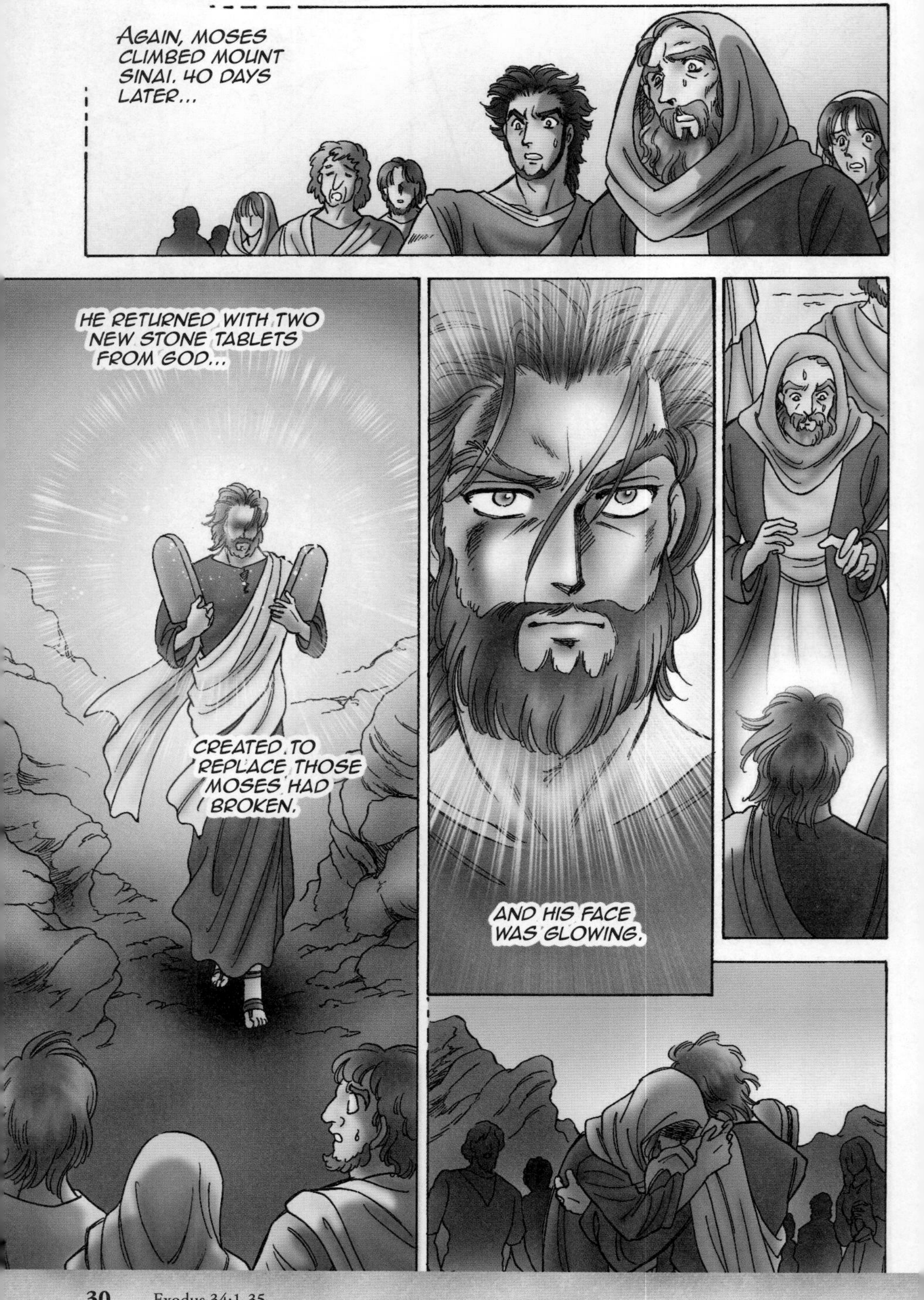
AGAIN, MOSES CLIMBED MOUNT SINAI. 40 DAYS LATER...
HE RETURNED WITH TWO NEW STONE TABLETS FROM GOD...
CREATED TO REPLACE THOSE MOSES HAD BROKEN.
AND HIS FACE WAS GLOWING.

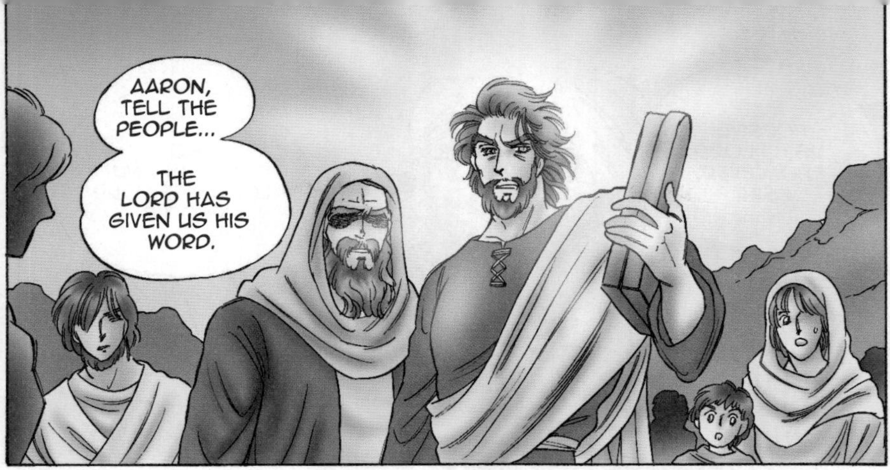
AARON, TELL THE PEOPLE...
THE LORD HAS GIVEN US HIS WORD.

3. Rebellion in the Desert

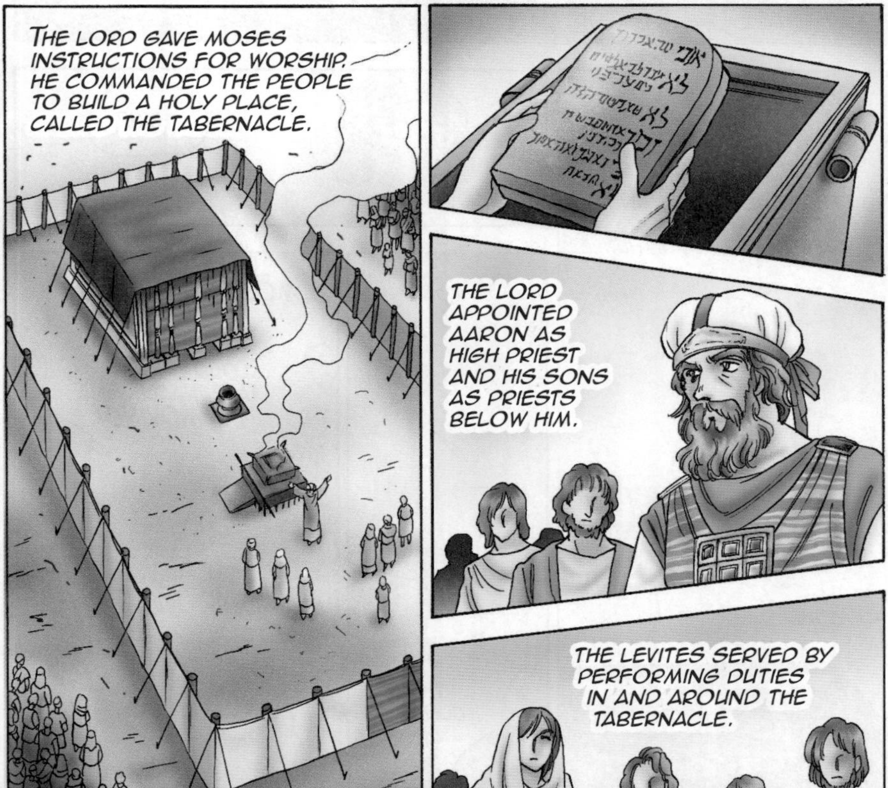
THE LORD GAVE MOSES INSTRUCTIONS FOR WORSHIP. HE COMMANDED THE PEOPLE TO BUILD A HOLY PLACE, CALLED THE TABERNACLE.
THE LORD APPOINTED AARON AS HIGH PRIEST AND HIS SONS AS PRIESTS BELOW HIM.
THE LEVITES SERVED BY PERFORMING DUTIES IN AND AROUND THE TABERNACLE.

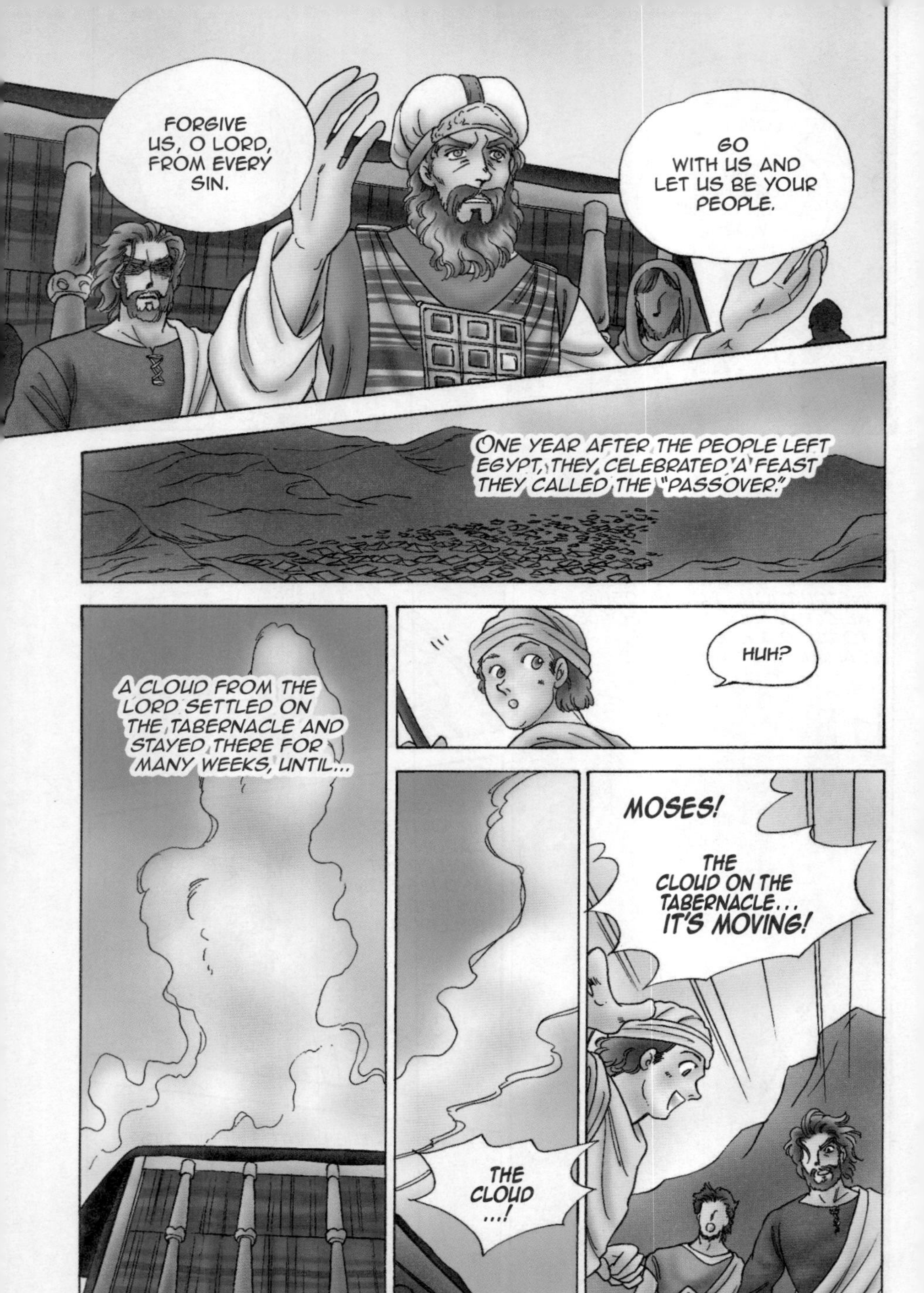
FORGIVE US, O LORD, FROM EVERY SIN.
GO WITH US AND LET US BE YOUR PEOPLE.
ONE YEAR AFTER THE PEOPLE LEFT EGYPT, THEY CELEBRATED A FEAST THEY CALLED THE "PASSOVER."
A CLOUD FROM THE LORD SETTLED ON THE TABERNACLE AND STAYED THERE FOR MANY WEEKS, UNTIL...
HUH?
THE CLOUD ...!
MOSES!
THE CLOUD ON THE TABERNACLE... IT'S MOVING!

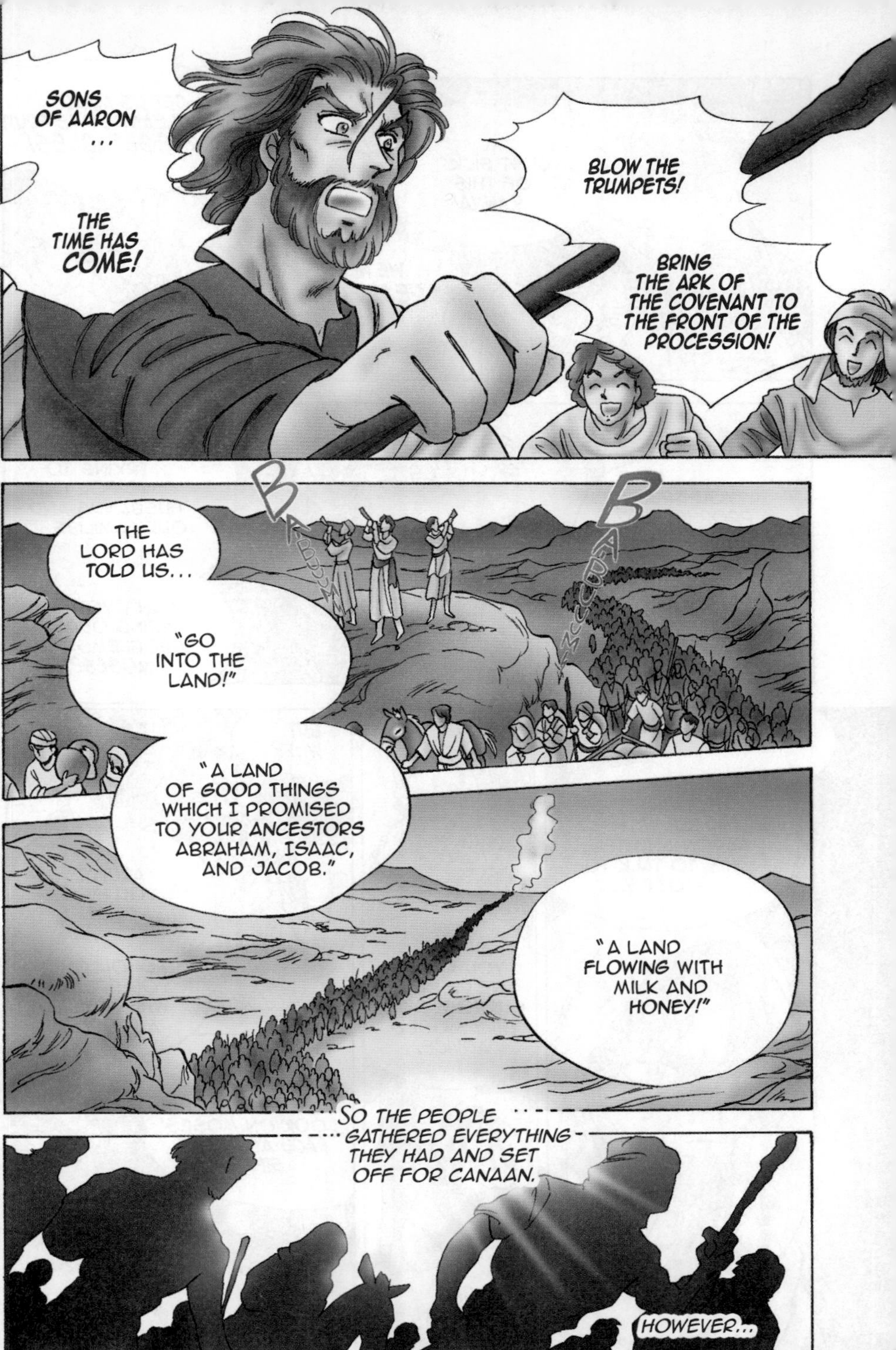
SONS OF AARON . . .
THE TIME HAS COME!
BLOW THE TRUMPETS!
BRING THE ARK OF THE COVENANT TO THE FRONT OF THE PROCESSION!
BABUUUM
BABUUUM
THE LORD HAS TOLD US...
"GO INTO THE LAND!"
"A LAND OF GOOD THINGS WHICH I PROMISED TO YOUR ANCESTORS ABRAHAM, ISAAC, AND JACOB."
"A LAND FLOWING WITH MILK AND HONEY!"
SO THE PEOPLE GATHERED EVERYTHING THEY HAD AND SET OFF FOR CANAAN.
HOWEVER...

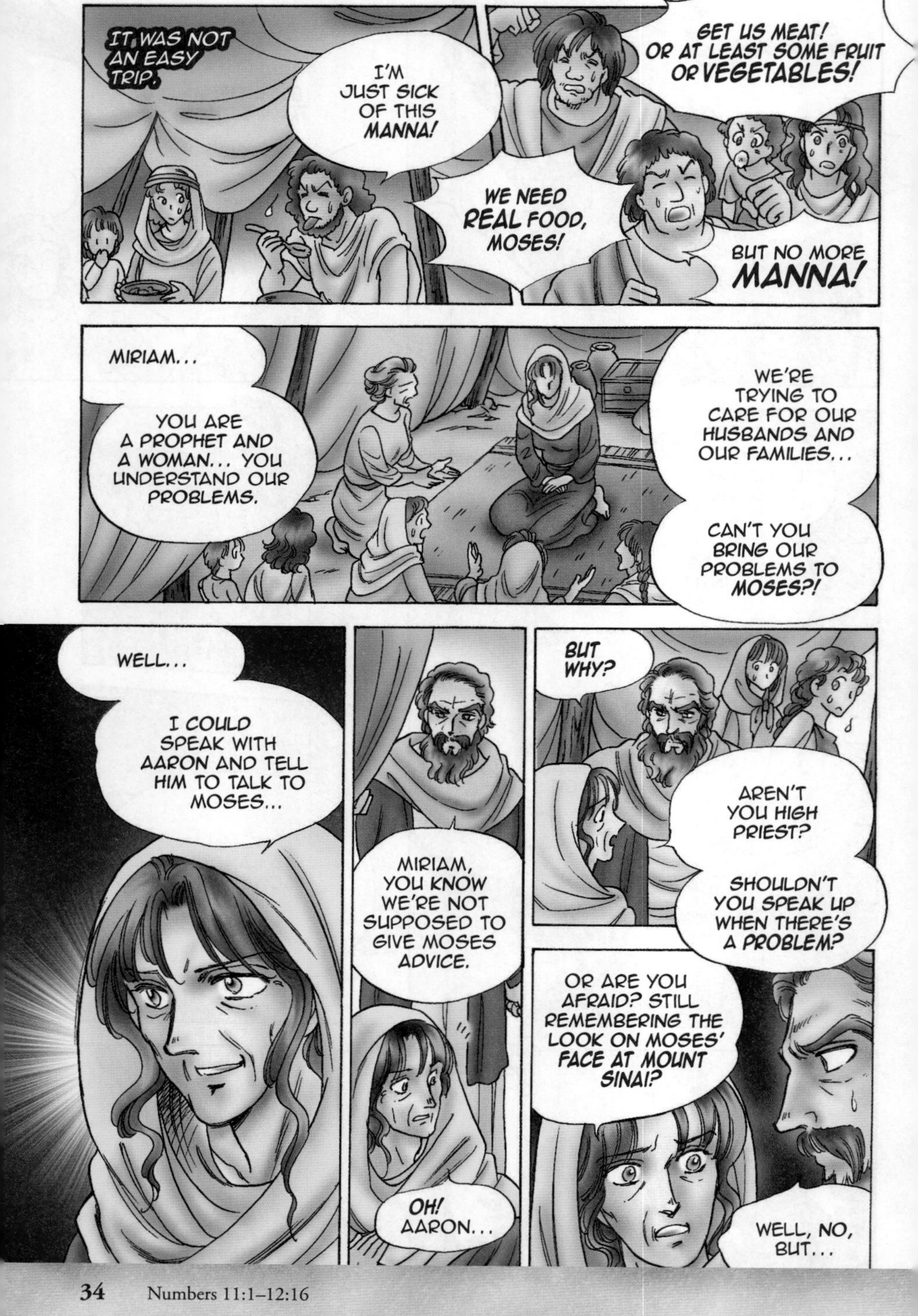
IT WAS NOT AN EASY TRIP.
I'M JUST SICK OF THIS MANNA!
GET US MEAT! OR AT LEAST SOME FRUIT OR VEGETABLES!
WE NEED REAL FOOD, MOSES!
BUT NO MORE MANNA!
MIRIAM...
YOU ARE A PROPHET AND A WOMAN... YOU UNDERSTAND OUR PROBLEMS.
WE'RE TRYING TO CARE FOR OUR HUSBANDS AND OUR FAMILIES...
CAN'T YOU BRING OUR PROBLEMS TO MOSES?!
WELL...
I COULD SPEAK WITH AARON AND TELL HIM TO TALK TO MOSES...
MIRIAM, YOU KNOW WE'RE NOT SUPPOSED TO GIVE MOSES ADVICE.
OH! AARON...
BUT WHY?
AREN'T YOU HIGH PRIEST?
SHOULDN'T YOU SPEAK UP WHEN THERE'S A PROBLEM?
OR ARE YOU AFRAID? STILL REMEMBERING THE LOOK ON MOSES' FACE AT MOUNT SINAI?
WELL, NO, BUT...

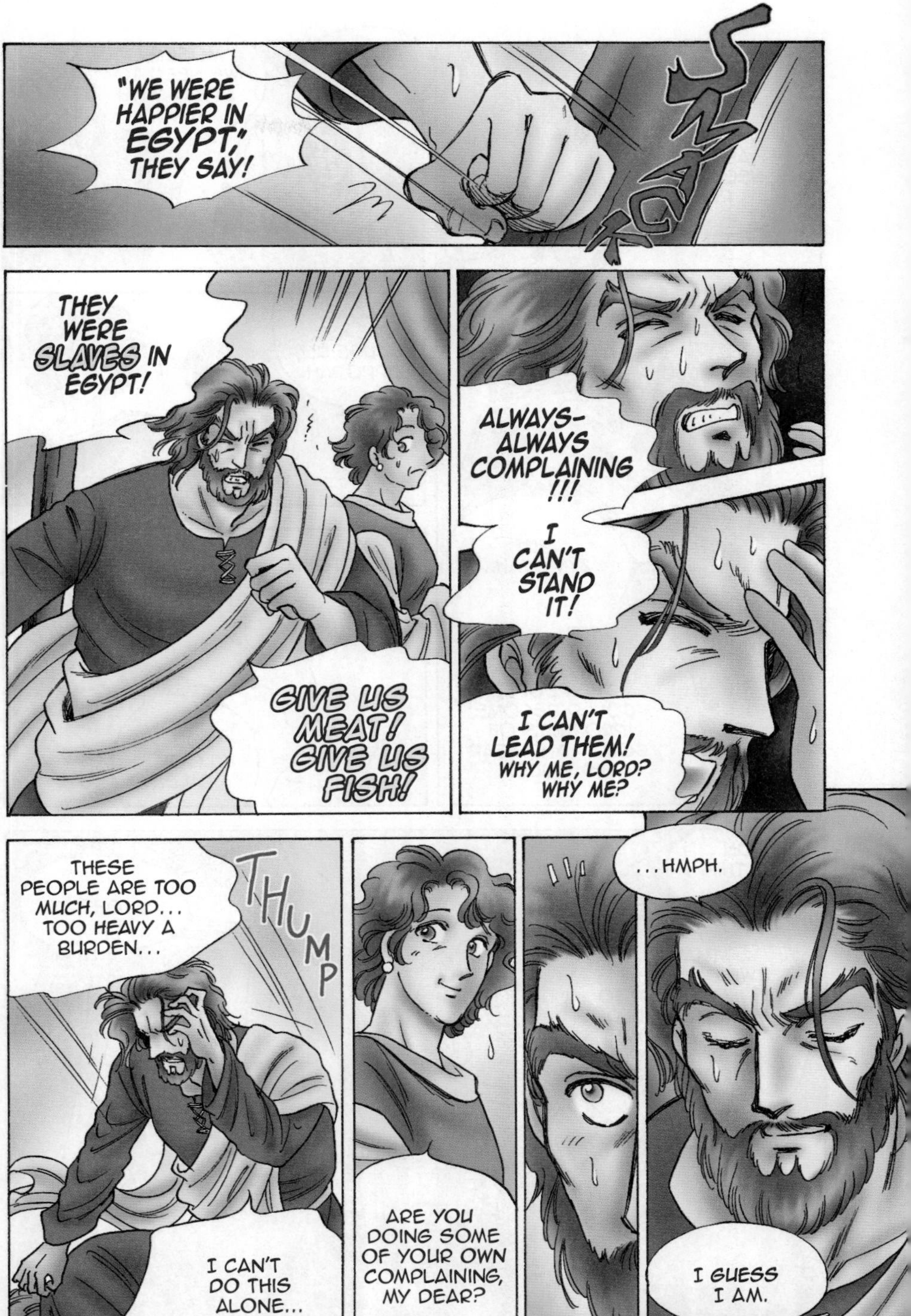
"WE WERE HAPPIER IN EGYPT," THEY SAY!
SMACK
THEY WERE SLAVES IN EGYPT!
GIVE US MEAT! GIVE US FISH!
ALWAYS-ALWAYS COMPLAINING !!!
I CAN'T STAND IT!
I CAN'T LEAD THEM! WHY ME, LORD? WHY ME?
THESE PEOPLE ARE TOO MUCH, LORD... TOO HEAVY A BURDEN...
THUMP
I CAN'T DO THIS ALONE...
ARE YOU DOING SOME OF YOUR OWN COMPLAINING, MY DEAR?
...HMPH.
I GUESS I AM.

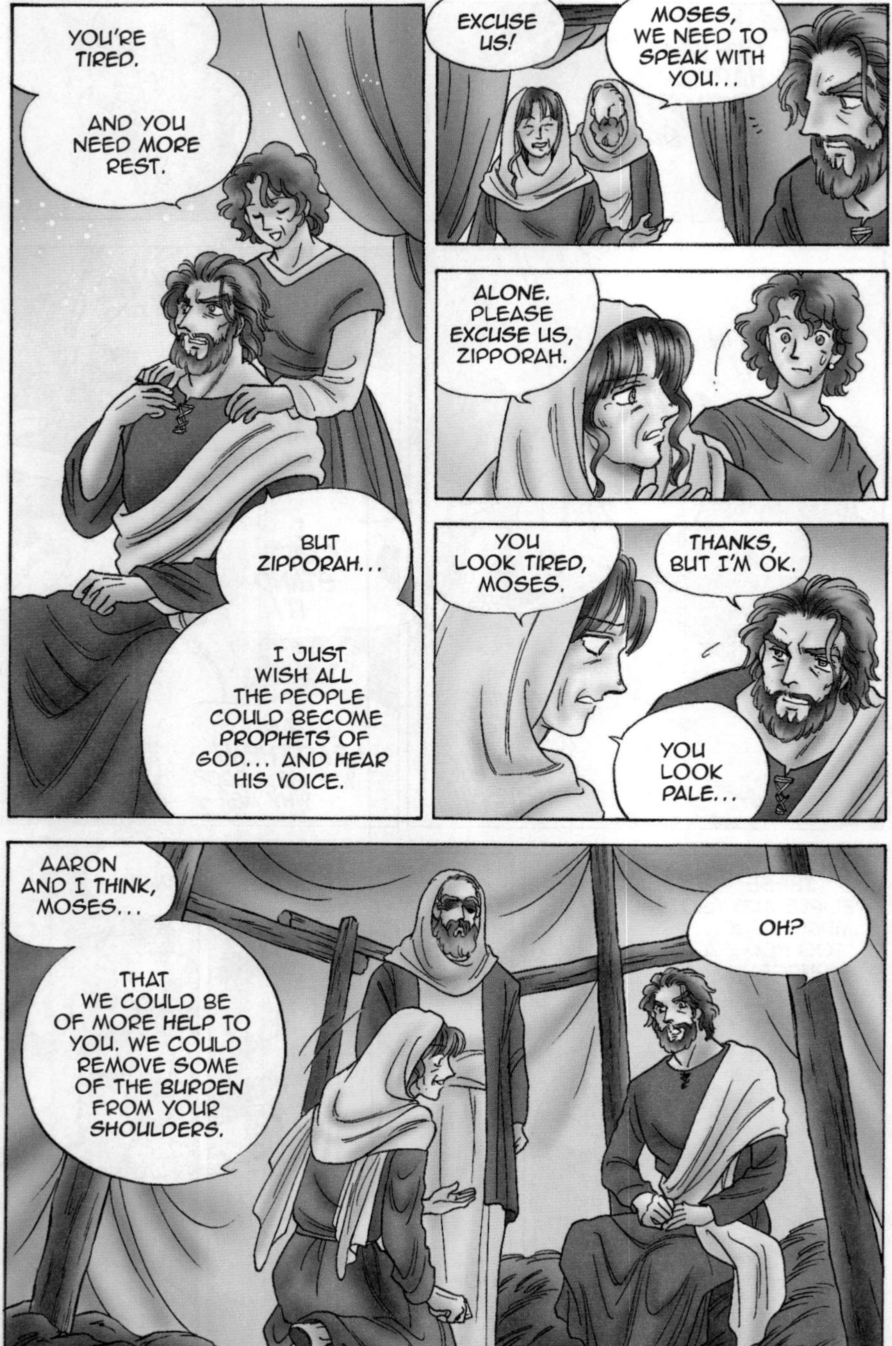
YOU'RE TIRED.
AND YOU NEED MORE REST.
BUT ZIPPORAH...
I JUST WISH ALL THE PEOPLE COULD BECOME PROPHETS OF GOD... AND HEAR HIS VOICE.
EXCUSE US!
MOSES, WE NEED TO SPEAK WITH YOU...
ALONE. PLEASE EXCUSE US, ZIPPORAH.
YOU LOOK TIRED, MOSES.
THANKS, BUT I'M OK.
YOU LOOK PALE...
AARON AND I THINK, MOSES...
THAT WE COULD BE OF MORE HELP TO YOU. WE COULD REMOVE SOME OF THE BURDEN FROM YOUR SHOULDERS.
OH?

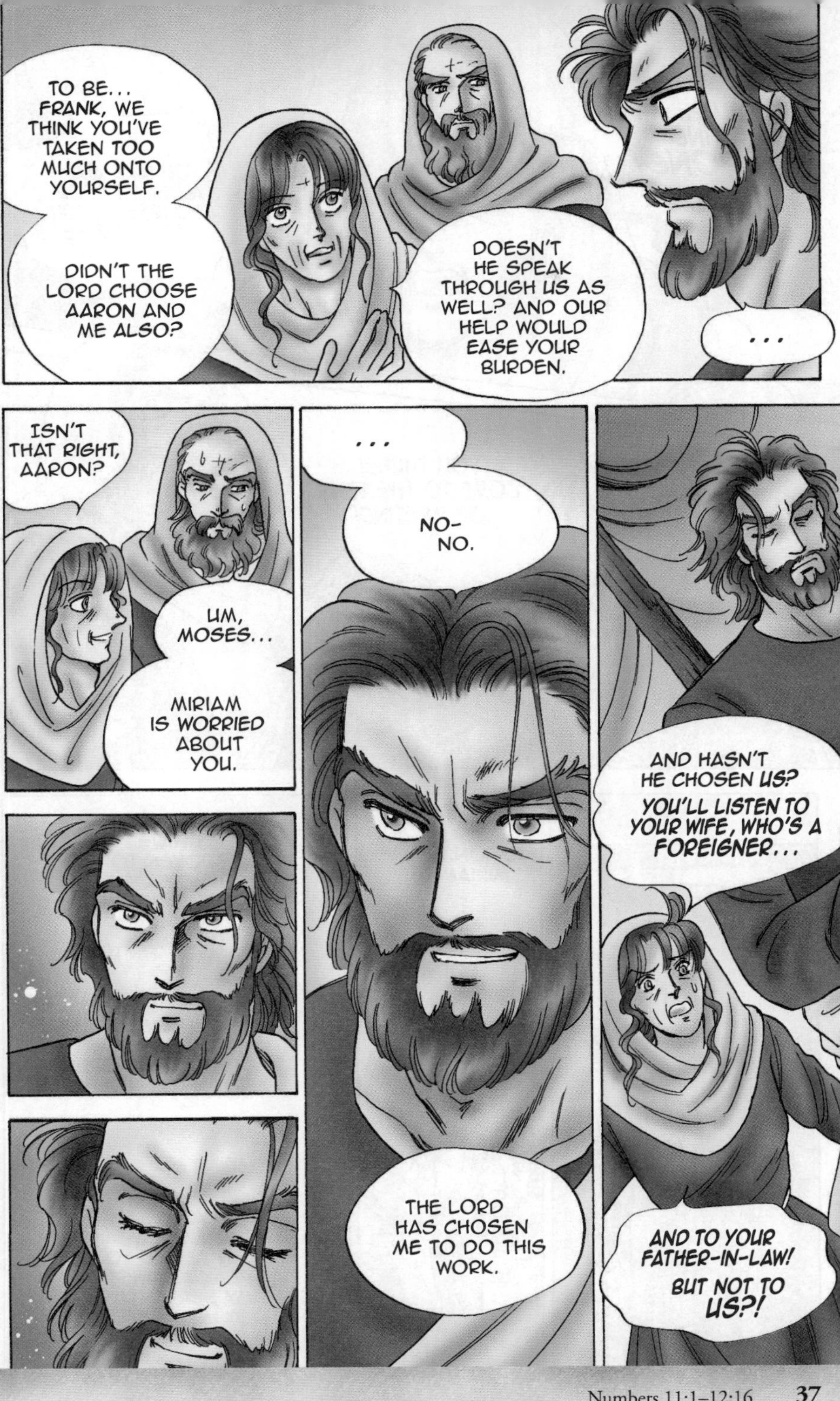
TO BE... FRANK, WE THINK YOU'VE TAKEN TOO MUCH ONTO YOURSELF.
DIDN'T THE LORD CHOOSE AARON AND ME ALSO?
DOESN'T HE SPEAK THROUGH US AS WELL? AND OUR HELP WOULD EASE YOUR BURDEN.
...
ISN'T THAT RIGHT, AARON?
UM, MOSES...
MIRIAM IS WORRIED ABOUT YOU.
...
NO- NO.
THE LORD HAS CHOSEN ME TO DO THIS WORK.
AND HASN'T HE CHOSEN US?
YOU'LL LISTEN TO YOUR WIFE, WHO'S A FOREIGNER...
AND TO YOUR FATHER-IN-LAW!
BUT NOT TO US?!

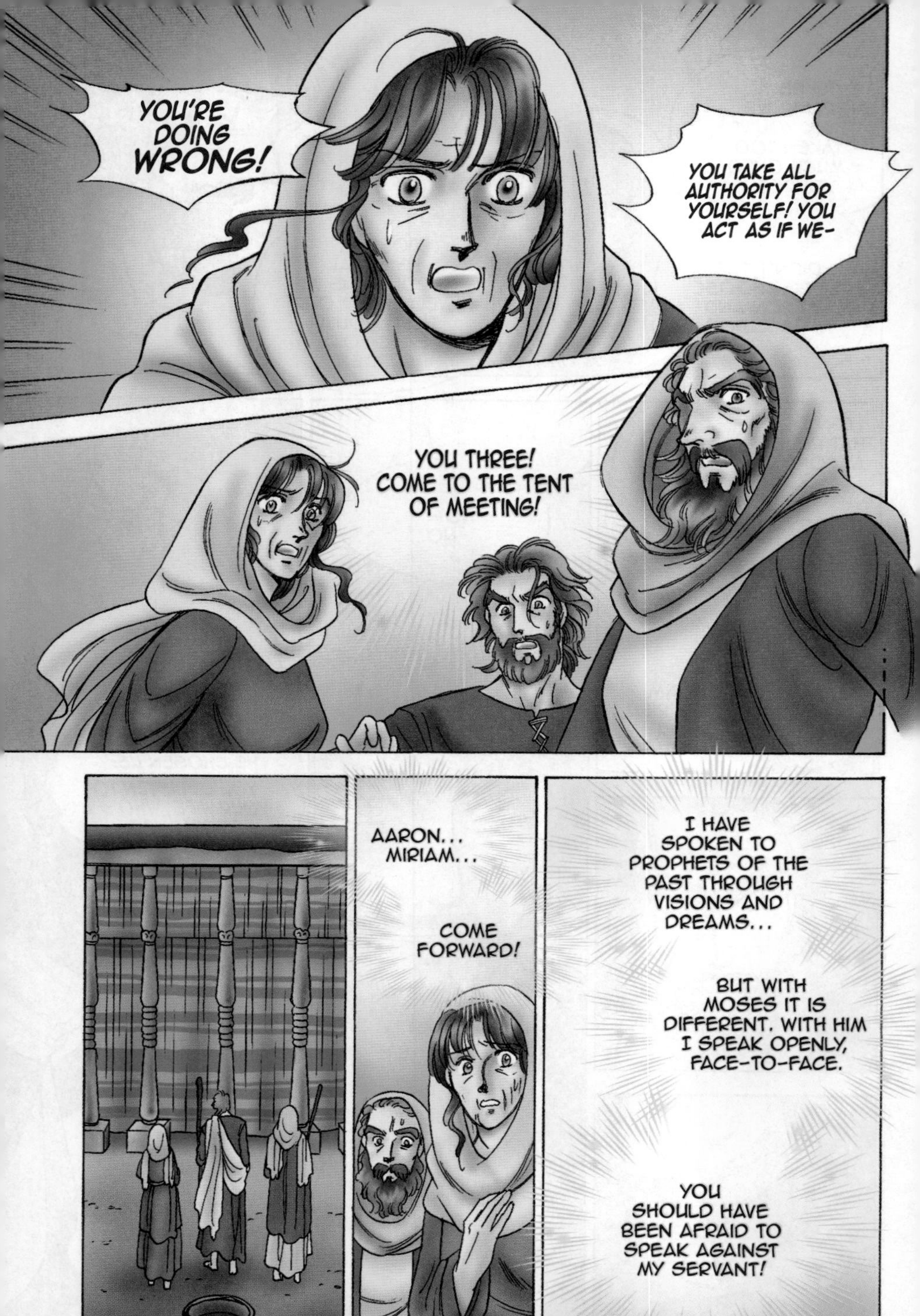
YOU'RE DOING WRONG!
YOU TAKE ALL AUTHORITY FOR YOURSELF! YOU ACT AS IF WE-
YOU THREE! COME TO THE TENT OF MEETING!
AARON... MIRIAM...
COME FORWARD!
I HAVE SPOKEN TO PROPHETS OF THE PAST THROUGH VISIONS AND DREAMS...
BUT WITH MOSES IT IS DIFFERENT. WITH HIM I SPEAK OPENLY, FACE-TO-FACE.
YOU SHOULD HAVE BEEN AFRAID TO SPEAK AGAINST MY SERVANT!

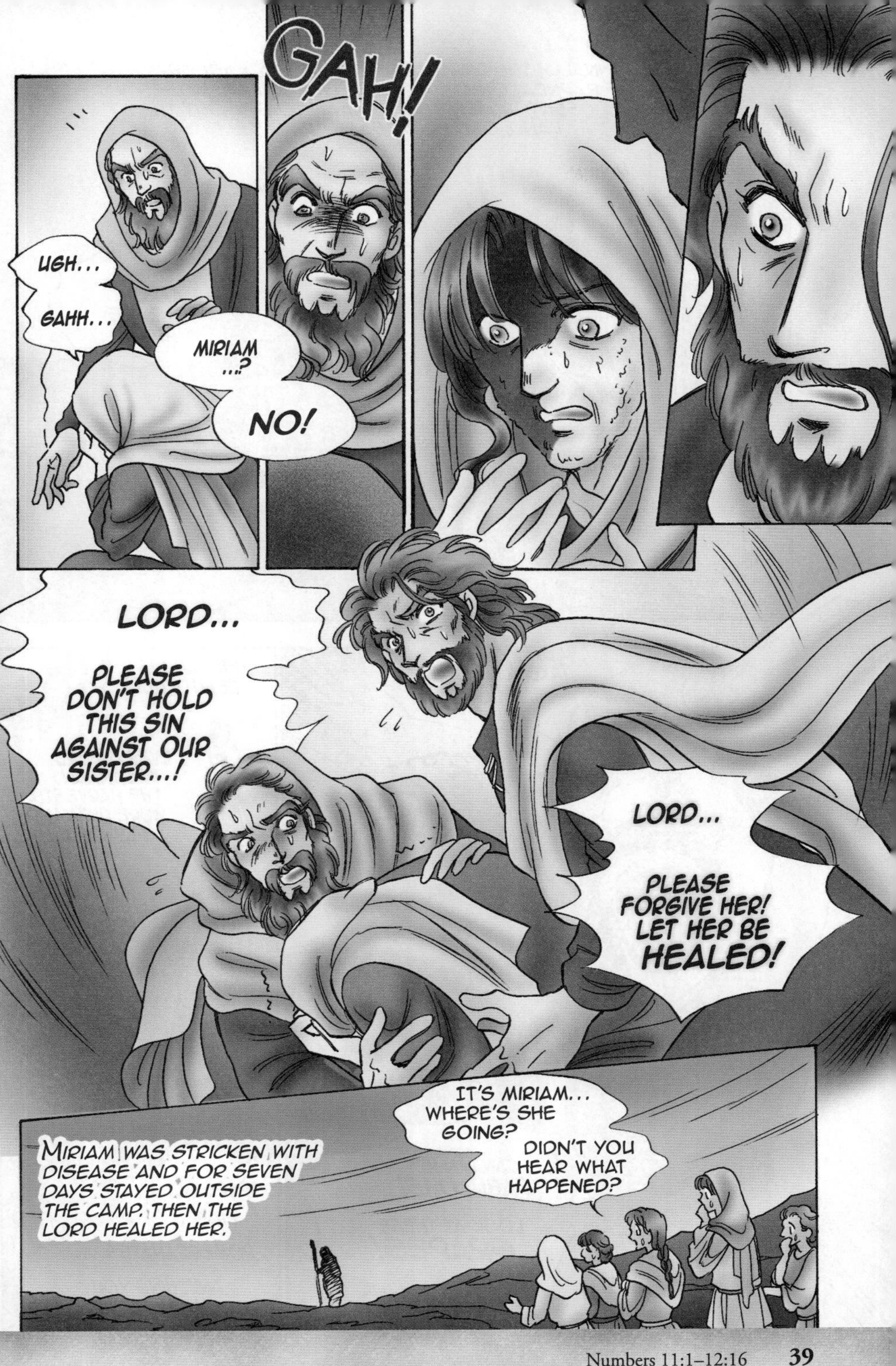
GAH!
UGH...
GAHH...
MIRIAM ...?
NO!
LORD...
PLEASE DON'T HOLD THIS SIN AGAINST OUR SISTER...!
LORD...
PLEASE FORGIVE HER! LET HER BE HEALED!
MIRIAM WAS STRICKEN WITH DISEASE AND FOR SEVEN DAYS STAYED OUTSIDE THE CAMP. THEN THE LORD HEALED HER.
IT'S MIRIAM... WHERE'S SHE GOING?
DIDN'T YOU HEAR WHAT HAPPENED?

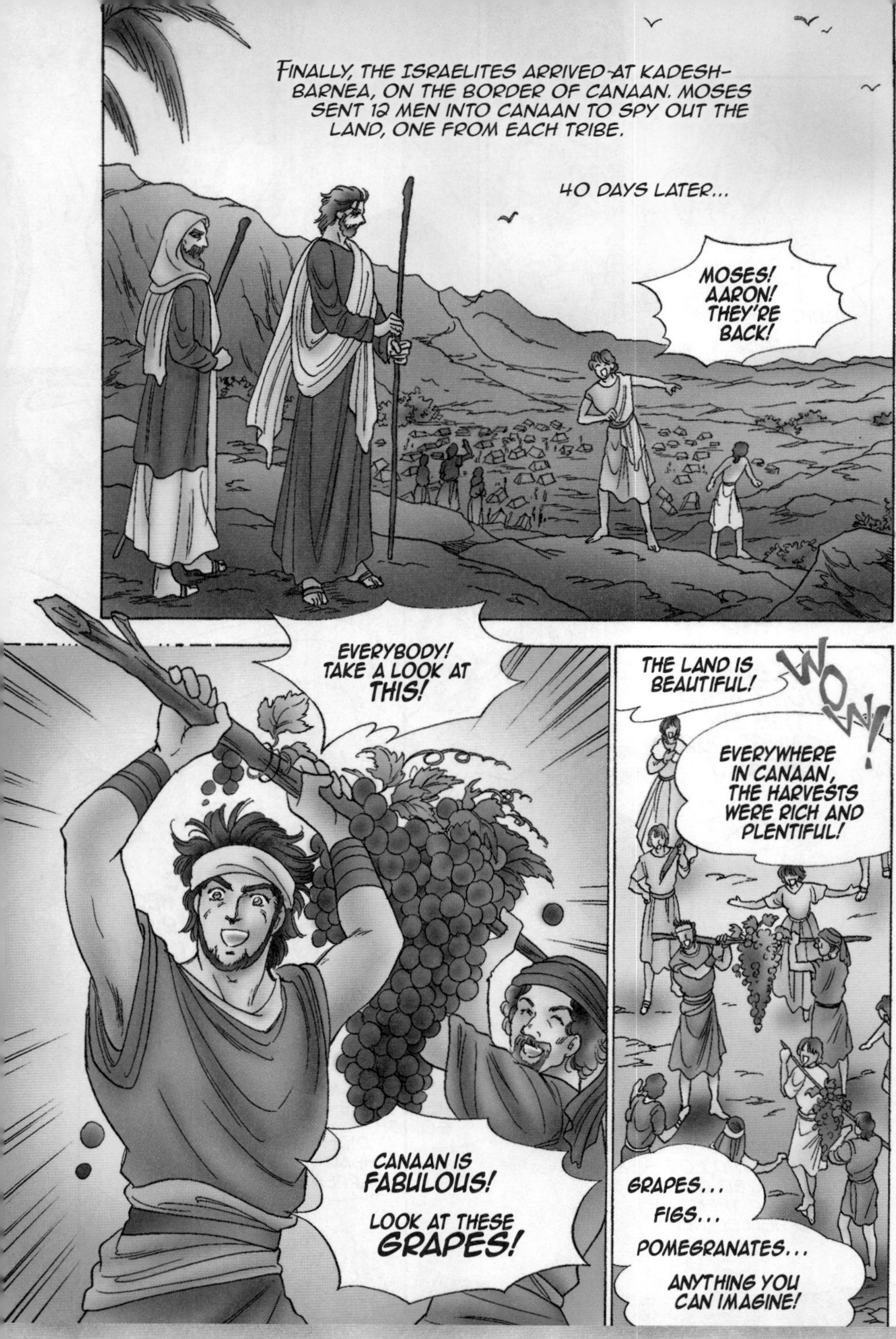

FINALLY, THE ISRAELITES ARRIVED AT KADESH-BARNEA, ON THE BORDER OF CANAAN. MOSES SENT 12 MEN INTO CANAAN TO SPY OUT THE LAND, ONE FROM EACH TRIBE.
40 DAYS LATER...
MOSES! AARON! THEY'RE BACK!
EVERYBODY! TAKE A LOOK AT THIS!
CANAAN IS FABULOUS!
LOOK AT THESE GRAPES!
THE LAND IS BEAUTIFUL!
WOW!
EVERYWHERE IN CANAAN, THE HARVESTS WERE RICH AND PLENTIFUL!
GRAPES...
FIGS...
POMEGRANATES...
ANYTHING YOU CAN IMAGINE!

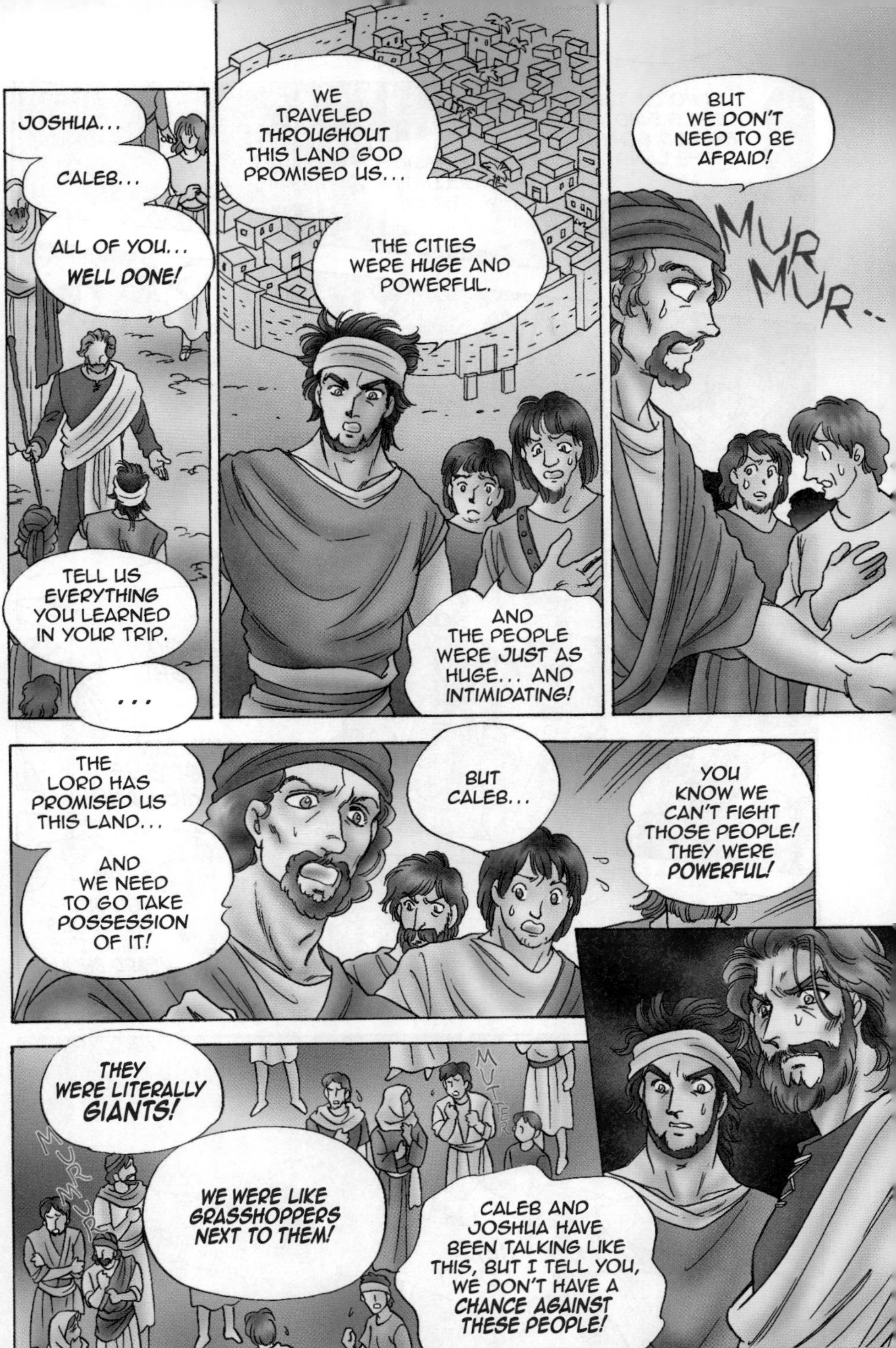
JOSHUA...
CALEB...
ALL OF YOU... WELL DONE!
TELL US EVERYTHING YOU LEARNED IN YOUR TRIP.
...
WE TRAVELED THROUGHOUT THIS LAND GOD PROMISED US...
THE CITIES WERE HUGE AND POWERFUL.
AND THE PEOPLE WERE JUST AS HUGE... AND INTIMIDATING!
BUT WE DON'T NEED TO BE AFRAID!
MUR MUR...
THE LORD HAS PROMISED US THIS LAND...
AND WE NEED TO GO TAKE POSSESSION OF IT!
BUT CALEB...
YOU KNOW WE CAN'T FIGHT THOSE PEOPLE! THEY WERE POWERFUL!
THEY WERE LITERALLY GIANTS!
MURMUR
MUTTER
WE WERE LIKE GRASSHOPPERS NEXT TO THEM!
CALEB AND JOSHUA HAVE BEEN TALKING LIKE THIS, BUT I TELL YOU, WE DON'T HAVE A CHANCE AGAINST THESE PEOPLE!

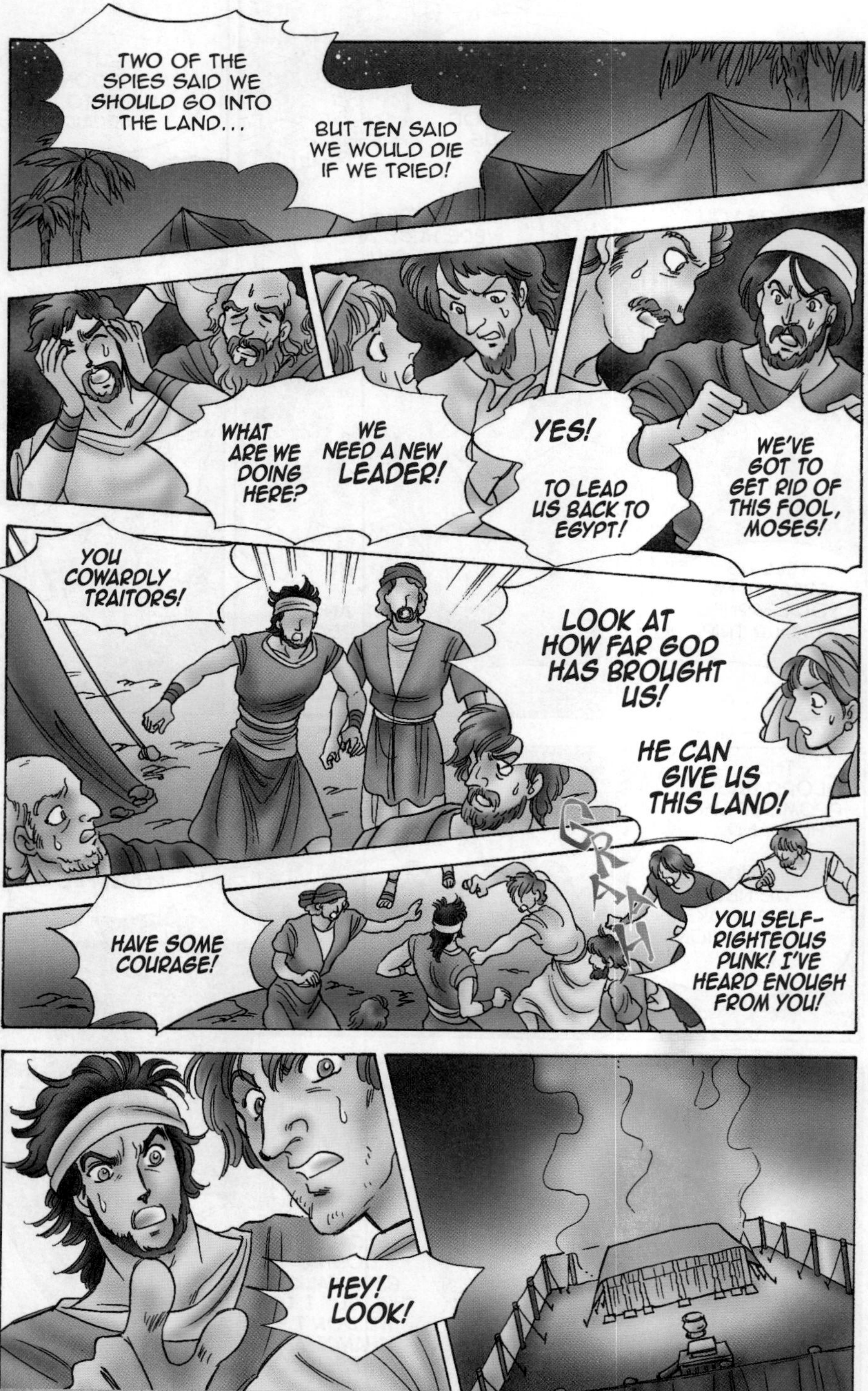
TWO OF THE SPIES SAID WE SHOULD GO INTO THE LAND...
BUT TEN SAID WE WOULD DIE IF WE TRIED!
WHAT ARE WE DOING HERE?
WE NEED A NEW LEADER!
YES!
TO LEAD US BACK TO EGYPT!
WE'VE GOT TO GET RID OF THIS FOOL, MOSES!
YOU COWARDLY TRAITORS!
LOOK AT HOW FAR GOD HAS BROUGHT US!
HE CAN GIVE US THIS LAND!
GRAAH
HAVE SOME COURAGE!
YOU SELF-RIGHTEOUS PUNK! I'VE HEARD ENOUGH FROM YOU!
HEY! LOOK!

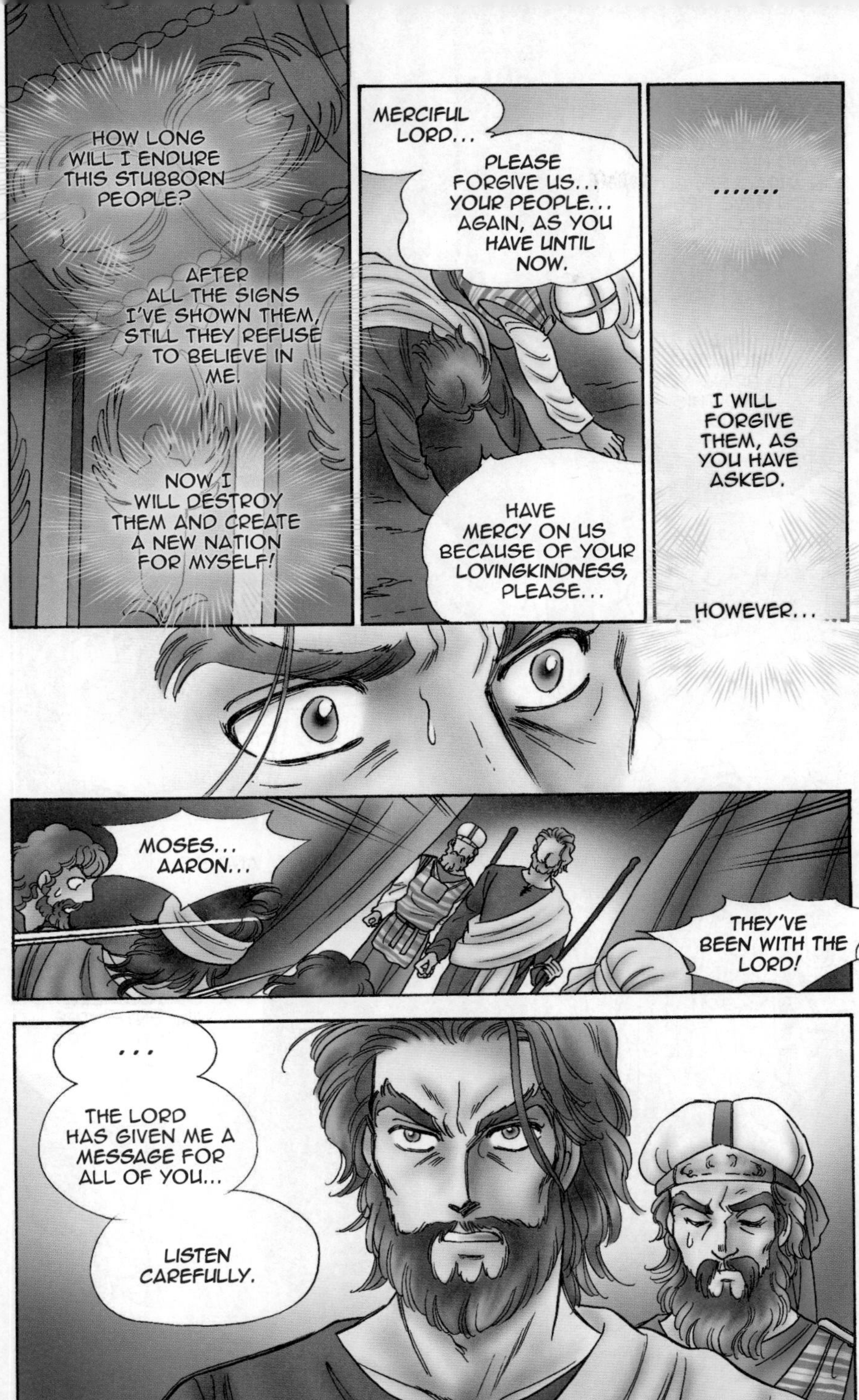
HOW LONG WILL I ENDURE THIS STUBBORN PEOPLE?
AFTER ALL THE SIGNS I'VE SHOWN THEM, STILL THEY REFUSE TO BELIEVE IN ME.
NOW I WILL DESTROY THEM AND CREATE A NEW NATION FOR MYSELF!
MERCIFUL LORD...
PLEASE FORGIVE US... YOUR PEOPLE... AGAIN, AS YOU HAVE UNTIL NOW.
HAVE MERCY ON US BECAUSE OF YOUR LOVINGKINDNESS, PLEASE...
....
I WILL FORGIVE THEM, AS YOU HAVE ASKED.
HOWEVER...
MOSES... AARON...
THEY'VE BEEN WITH THE LORD!
...
THE LORD HAS GIVEN ME A MESSAGE FOR ALL OF YOU...
LISTEN CAREFULLY.

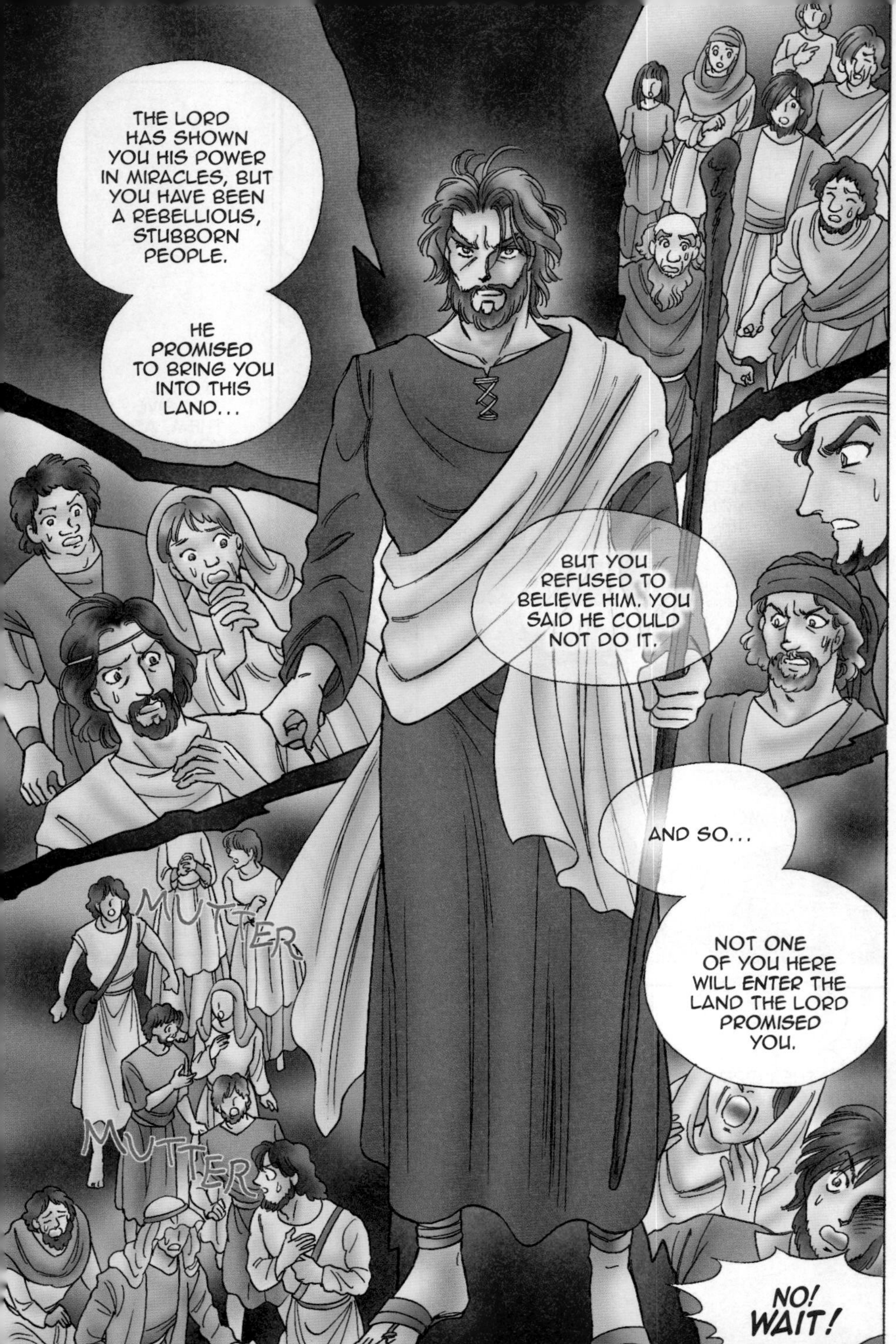
THE LORD HAS SHOWN YOU HIS POWER IN MIRACLES, BUT YOU HAVE BEEN A REBELLIOUS, STUBBORN PEOPLE.
HE PROMISED TO BRING YOU INTO THIS LAND...
BUT YOU REFUSED TO BELIEVE HIM. YOU SAID HE COULD NOT DO IT.
AND SO...
NOT ONE OF YOU HERE WILL ENTER THE LAND THE LORD PROMISED YOU.
MUTTER
MUTTER
NO! WAIT!

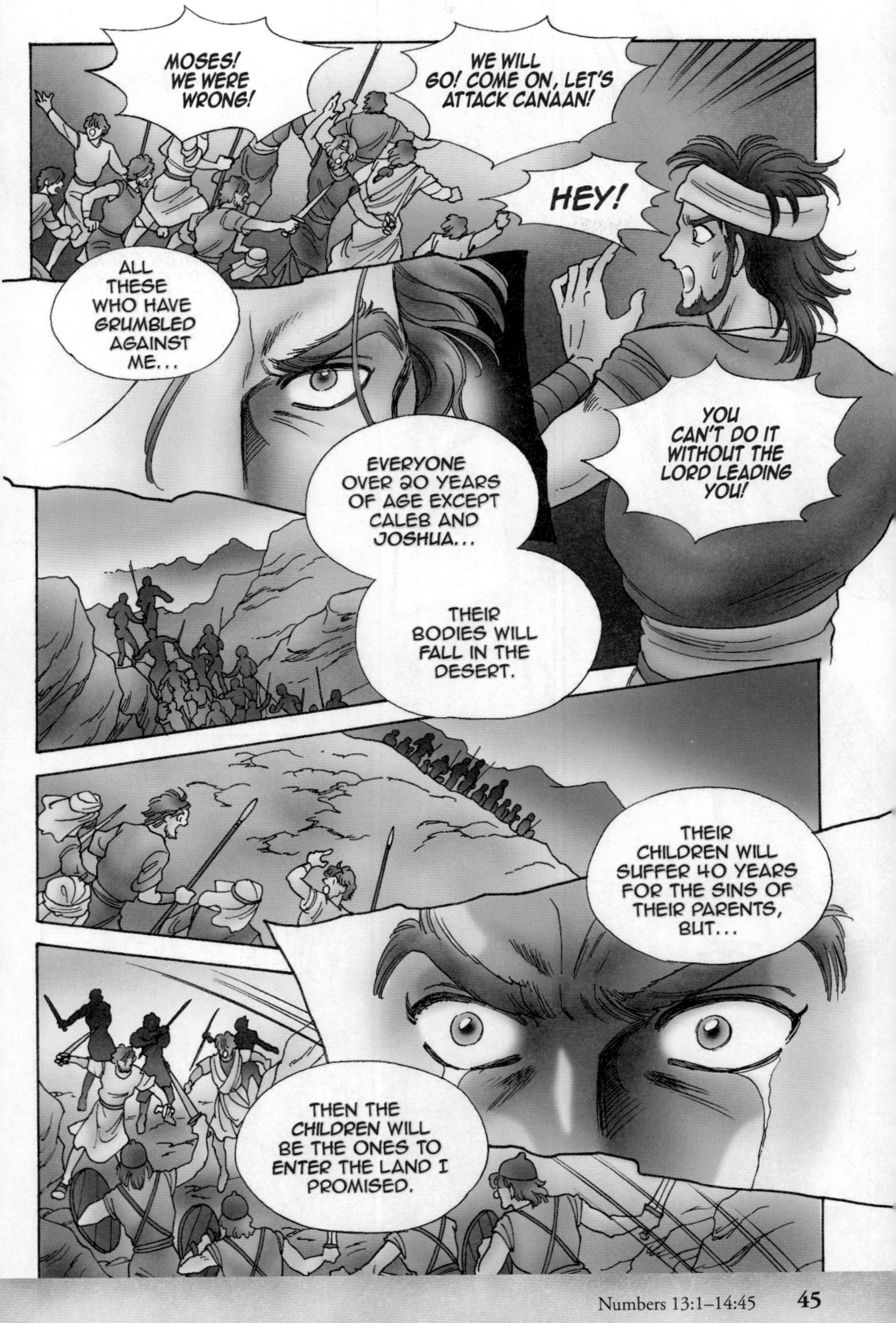
MOSES! WE WERE WRONG!
WE WILL GO! COME ON, LET'S ATTACK CANAAN!
HEY!
ALL THESE WHO HAVE GRUMBLED AGAINST ME...
YOU CAN'T DO IT WITHOUT THE LORD LEADING YOU!
EVERYONE OVER 20 YEARS OF AGE EXCEPT CALEB AND JOSHUA...
THEIR BODIES WILL FALL IN THE DESERT.
THEIR CHILDREN WILL SUFFER 40 YEARS FOR THE SINS OF THEIR PARENTS, BUT...
THEN THE CHILDREN WILL BE THE ONES TO ENTER THE LAND I PROMISED.

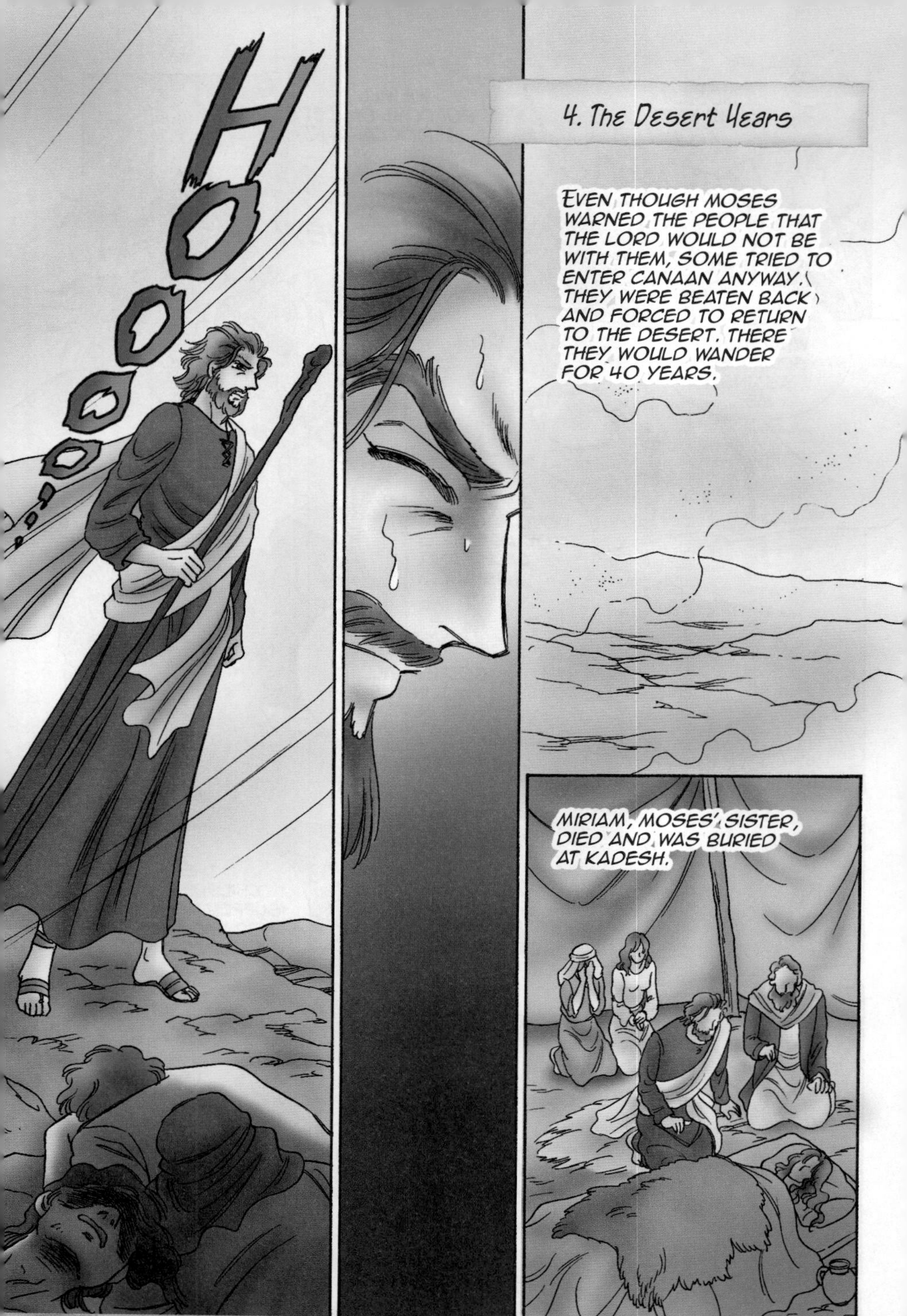

HOOOOO
4. The Desert Years
EVEN THOUGH MOSES WARNED THE PEOPLE THAT THE LORD WOULD NOT BE WITH THEM, SOME TRIED TO ENTER CANAAN ANYWAY. THEY WERE BEATEN BACK AND FORCED TO RETURN TO THE DESERT. THERE THEY WOULD WANDER FOR 40 YEARS.
MIRIAM, MOSES' SISTER, DIED AND WAS BURIED AT KADESH.

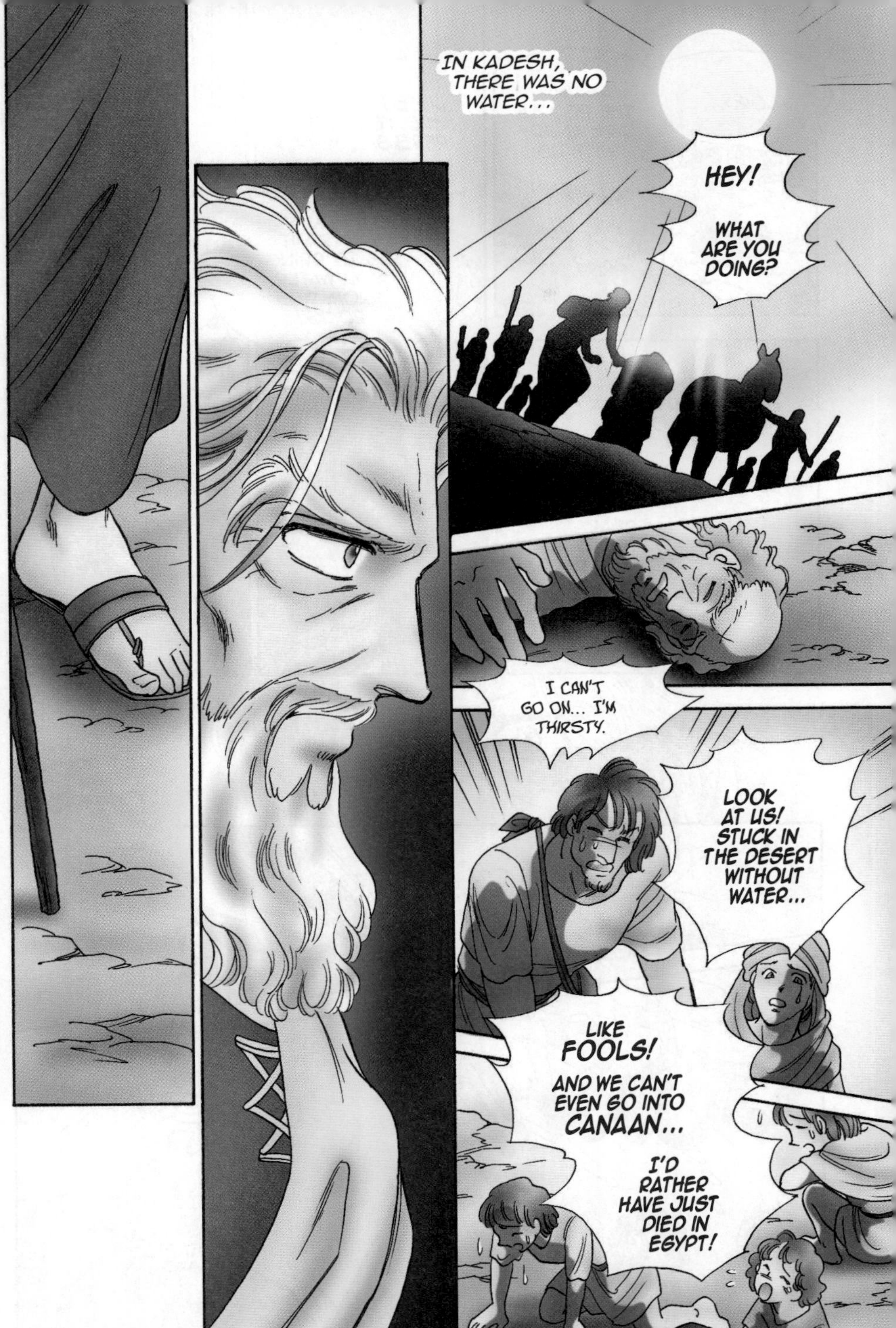
IN KADESH, THERE WAS NO WATER...
HEY!
WHAT ARE YOU DOING?
I CAN'T GO ON... I'M THIRSTY.
LOOK AT US! STUCK IN THE DESERT WITHOUT WATER...
LIKE FOOLS!
AND WE CAN'T EVEN GO INTO CANAAN...
I'D RATHER HAVE JUST DIED IN EGYPT!

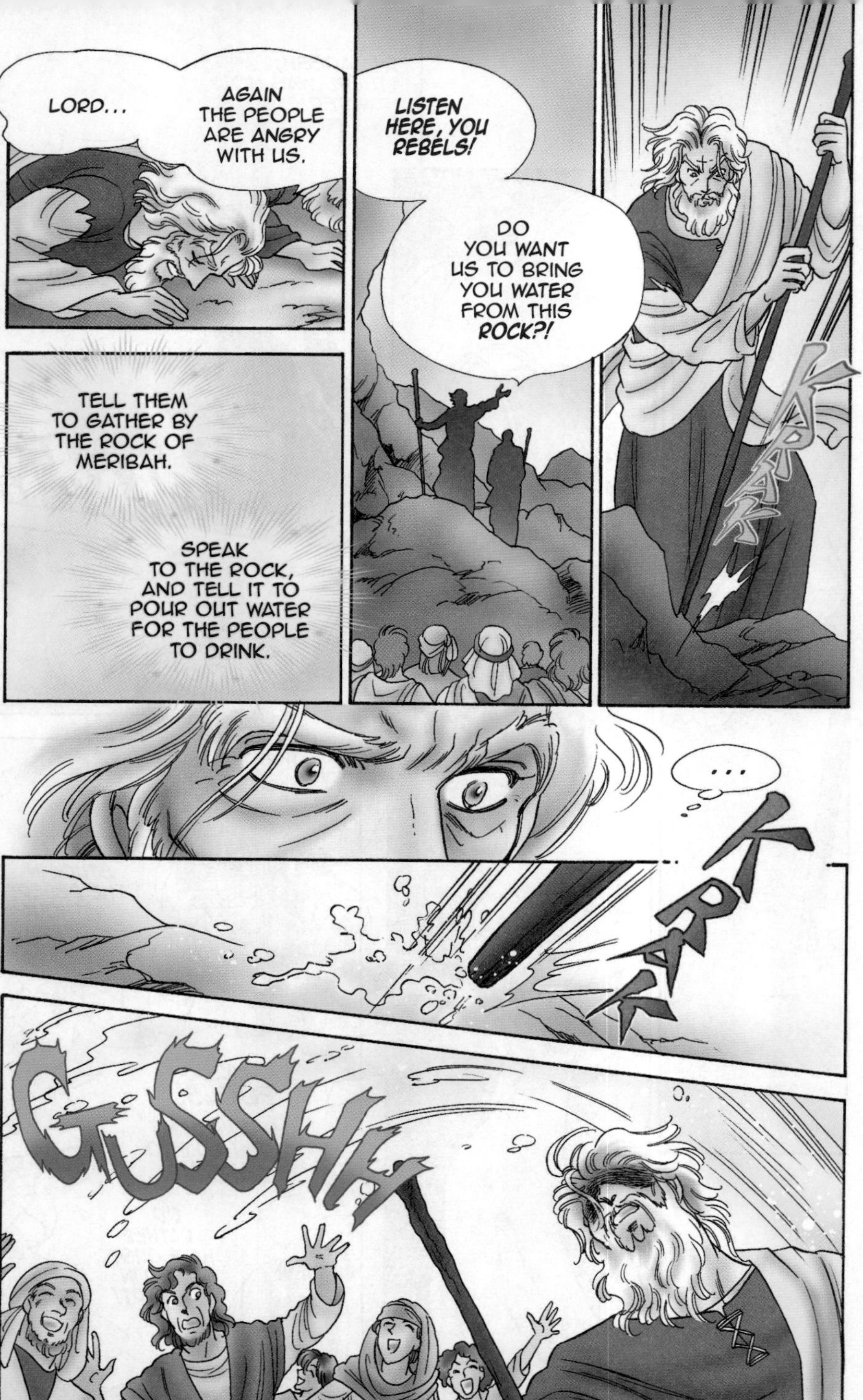

LORD...
AGAIN THE PEOPLE ARE ANGRY WITH US.
TELL THEM TO GATHER BY THE ROCK OF MERIBAH.
SPEAK TO THE ROCK, AND TELL IT TO POUR OUT WATER FOR THE PEOPLE TO DRINK.
LISTEN HERE, YOU REBELS!
DO YOU WANT US TO BRING YOU WATER FROM THIS ROCK?!
KRAK
...
KRAK
GUSSH

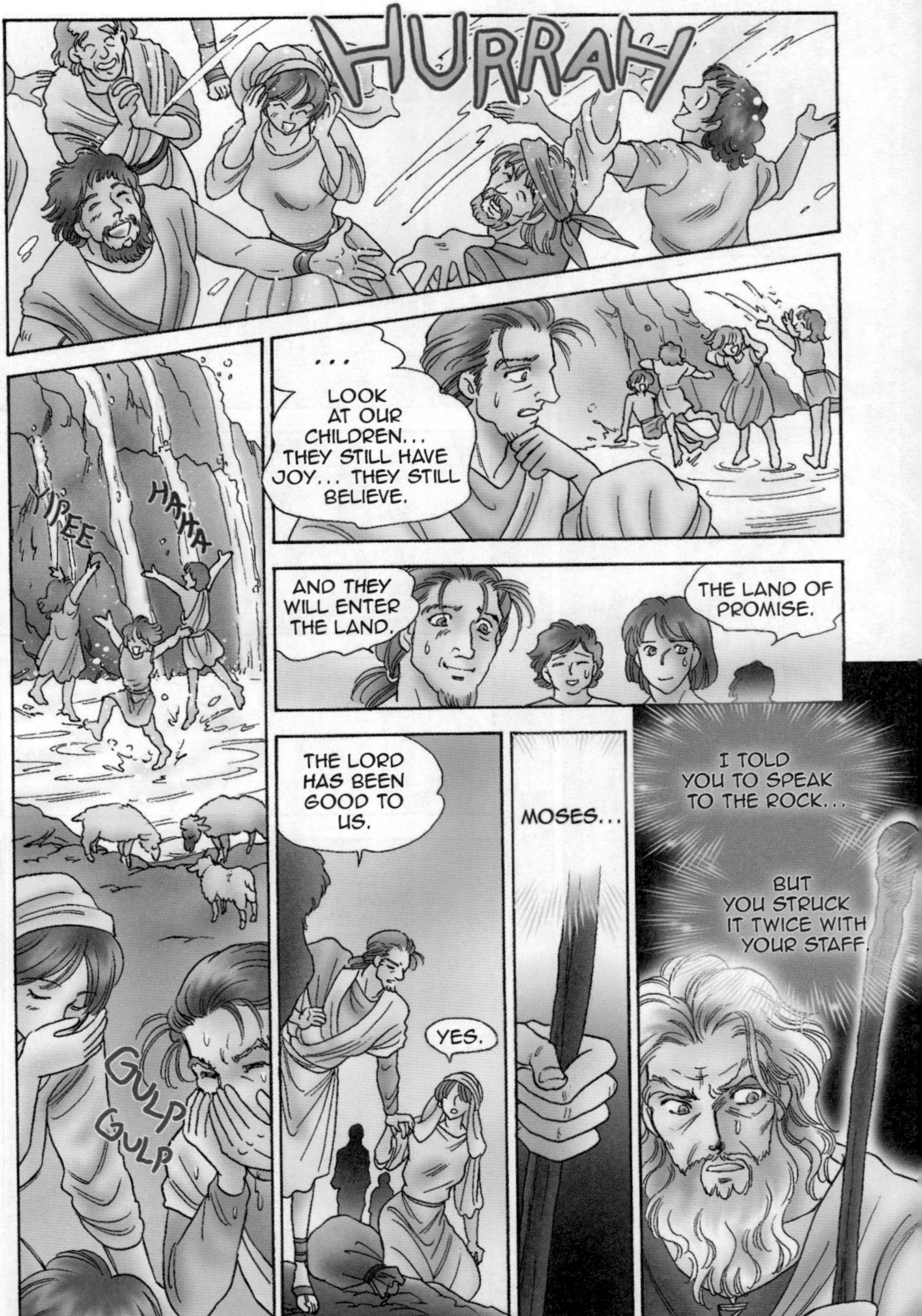
HURRAH
...
LOOK AT OUR CHILDREN... THEY STILL HAVE JOY... THEY STILL BELIEVE.
YIPEE
HAHA
AND THEY WILL ENTER THE LAND.
THE LAND OF PROMISE.
GULP
GULP
THE LORD HAS BEEN GOOD TO US.
YES.
MOSES...
I TOLD YOU TO SPEAK TO THE ROCK...
BUT YOU STRUCK IT TWICE WITH YOUR STAFF.

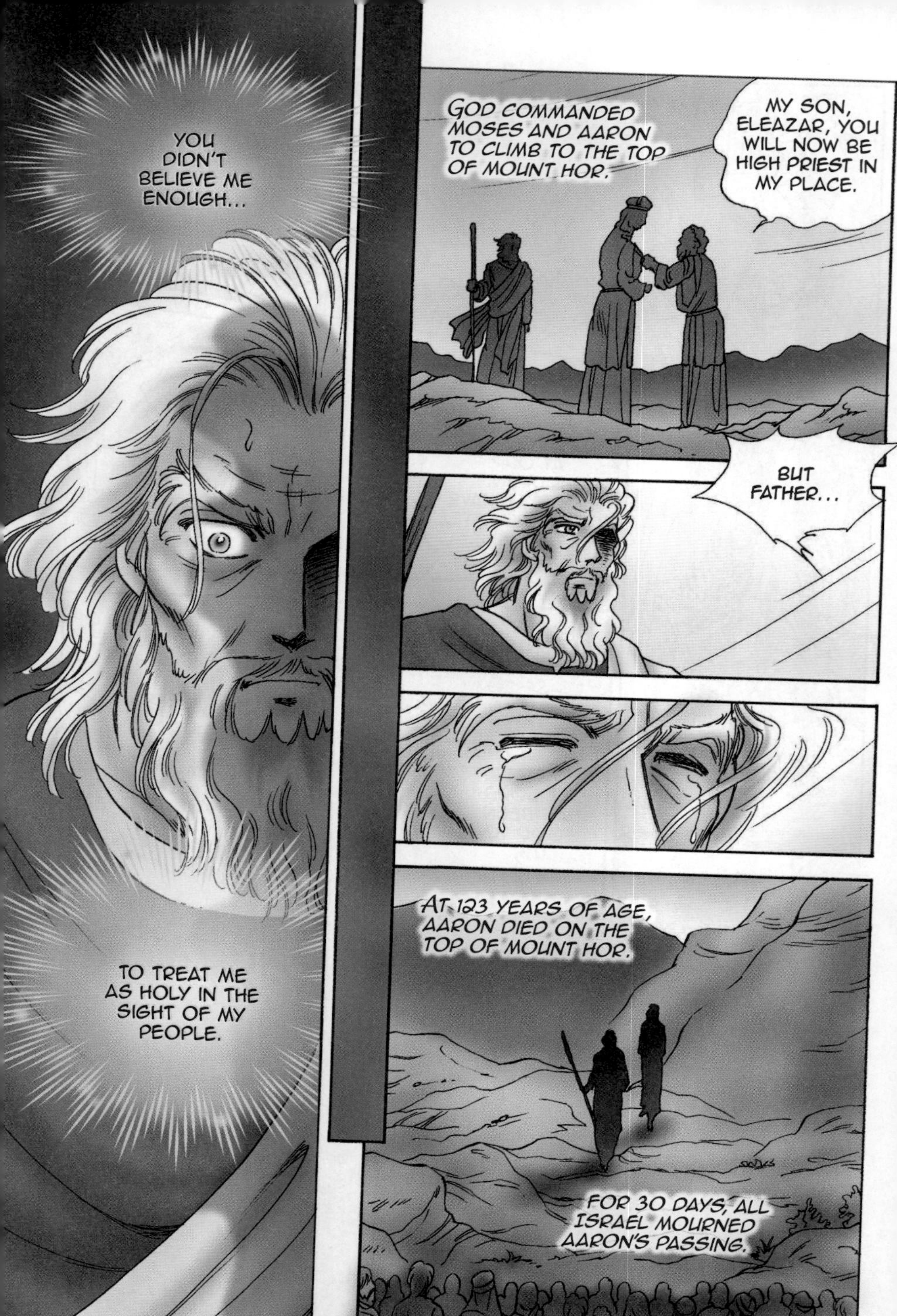
YOU DIDN'T BELIEVE ME ENOUGH...
TO TREAT ME AS HOLY IN THE SIGHT OF MY PEOPLE.
GOD COMMANDED MOSES AND AARON TO CLIMB TO THE TOP OF MOUNT HOR.
MY SON, ELEAZAR, YOU WILL NOW BE HIGH PRIEST IN MY PLACE.
BUT FATHER...
AT 123 YEARS OF AGE, AARON DIED ON THE TOP OF MOUNT HOR.
FOR 30 DAYS, ALL ISRAEL MOURNED AARON'S PASSING.

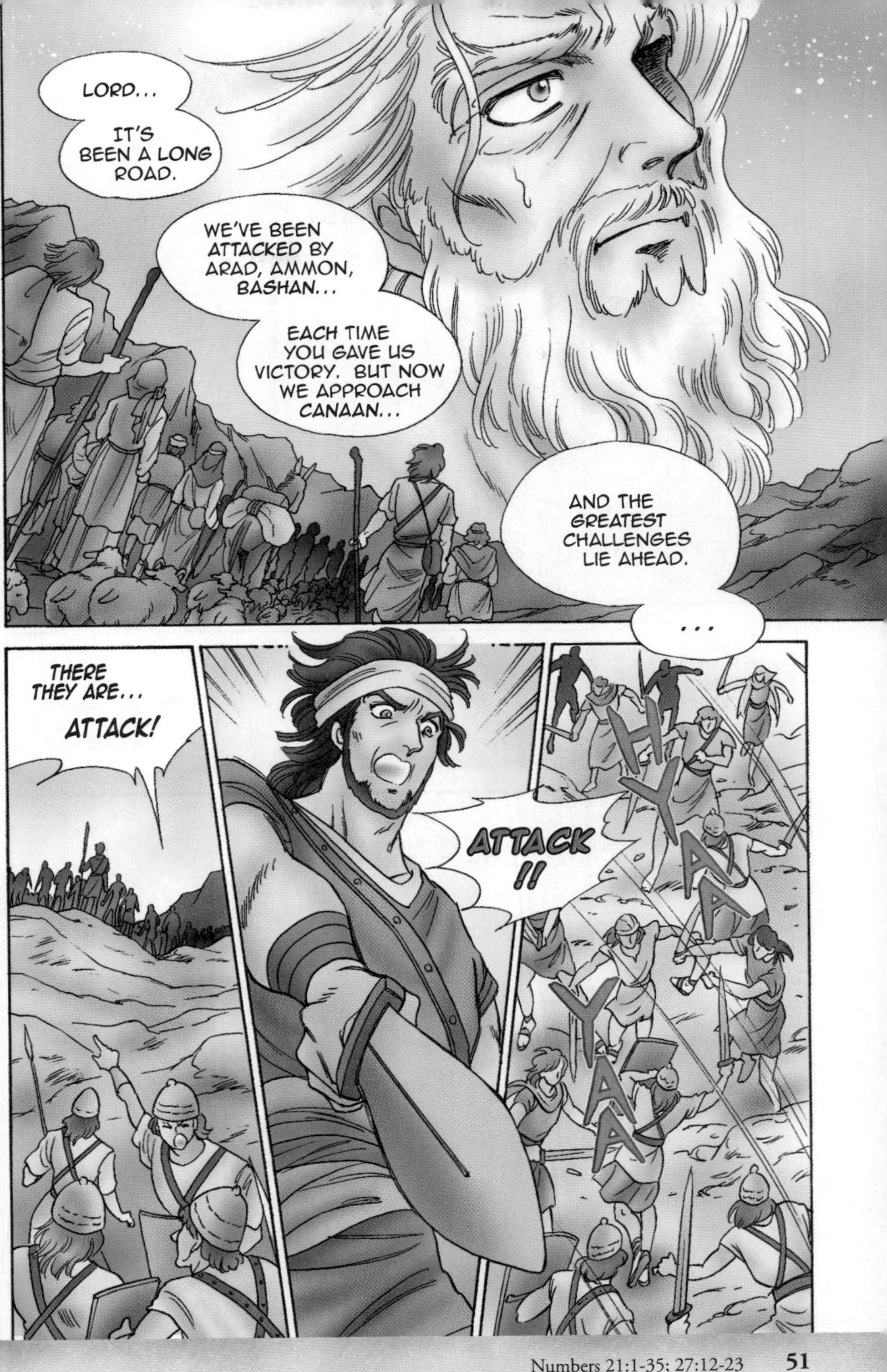
LORD...
IT'S BEEN A LONG ROAD.
WE'VE BEEN ATTACKED BY ARAD, AMMON, BASHAN...
EACH TIME YOU GAVE US VICTORY. BUT NOW WE APPROACH CANAAN...
AND THE GREATEST CHALLENGES LIE AHEAD.
...
THERE THEY ARE...
ATTACK!
ATTACK !!
HYAA
YAA

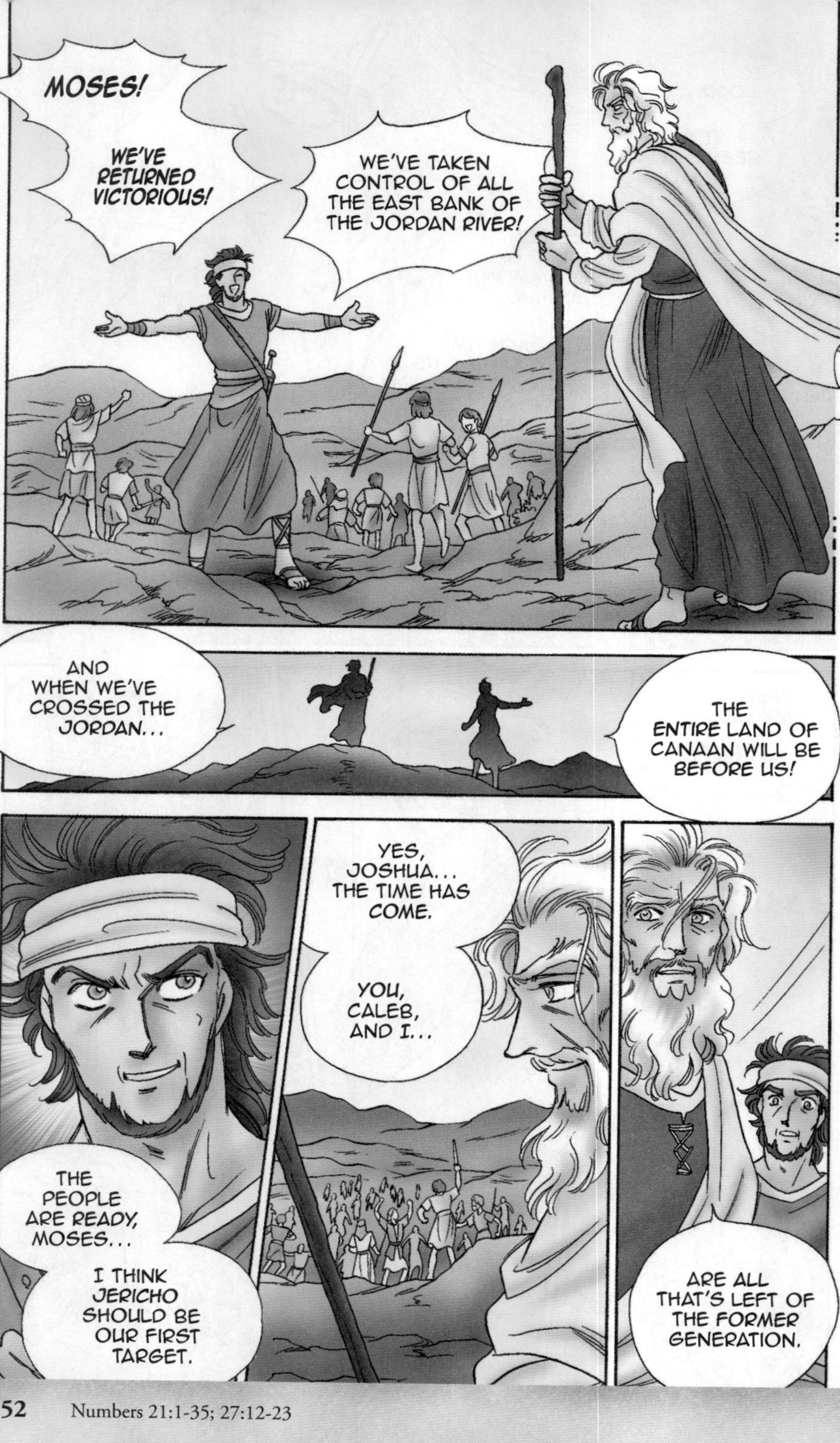
MOSES!
WE'VE RETURNED VICTORIOUS!
WE'VE TAKEN CONTROL OF ALL THE EAST BANK OF THE JORDAN RIVER!
AND WHEN WE'VE CROSSED THE JORDAN...
THE ENTIRE LAND OF CANAAN WILL BE BEFORE US!
THE PEOPLE ARE READY, MOSES...
I THINK JERICHO SHOULD BE OUR FIRST TARGET.
YES, JOSHUA... THE TIME HAS COME.
YOU, CALEB, AND I...
ARE ALL THAT'S LEFT OF THE FORMER GENERATION.

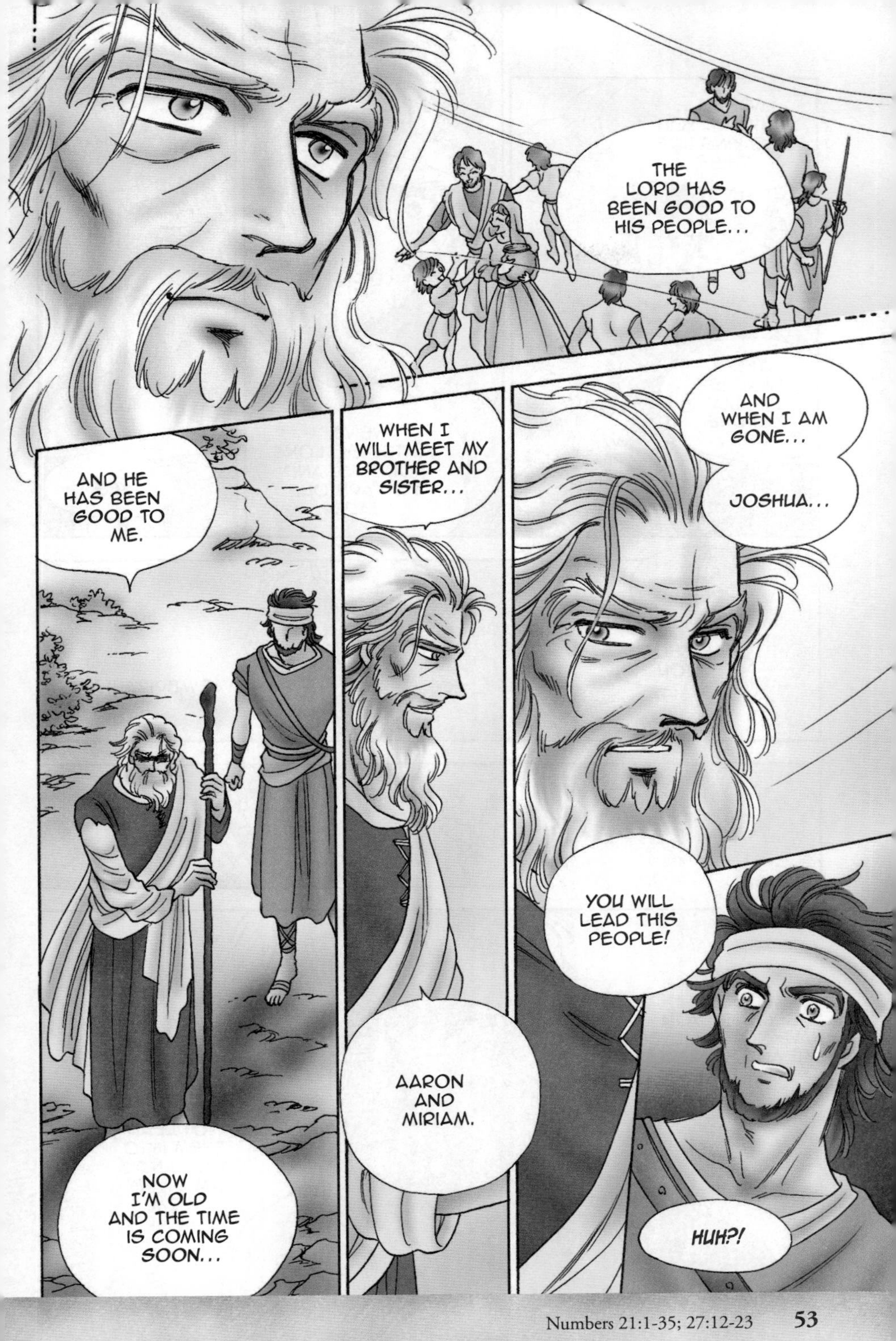
THE LORD HAS BEEN GOOD TO HIS PEOPLE...
AND HE HAS BEEN GOOD TO ME.
NOW I'M OLD AND THE TIME IS COMING SOON...
WHEN I WILL MEET MY BROTHER AND SISTER...
AARON AND MIRIAM.
AND WHEN I AM GONE...
JOSHUA...
YOU WILL LEAD THIS PEOPLE!
HUH?!

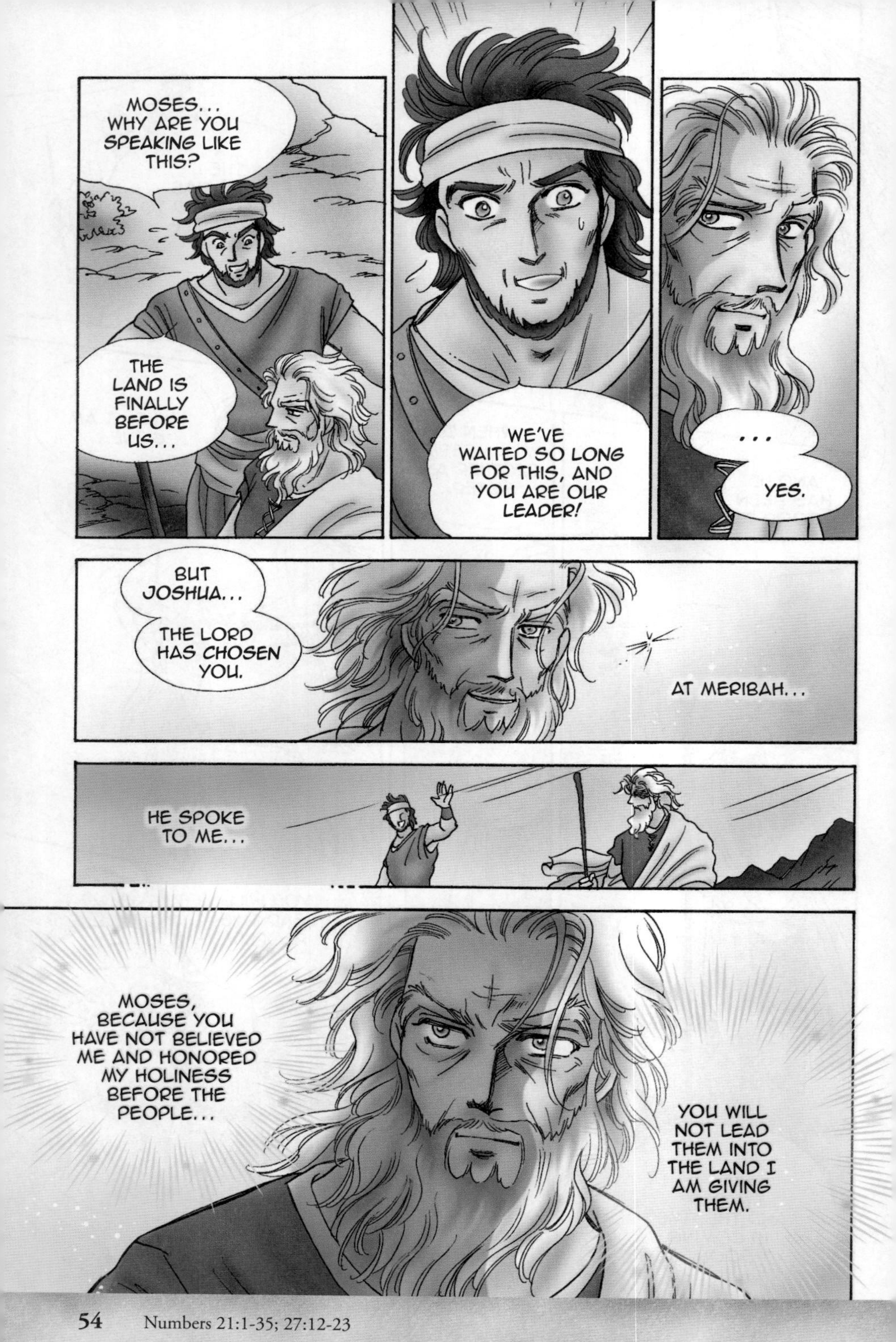
MOSES... WHY ARE YOU SPEAKING LIKE THIS?
THE LAND IS FINALLY BEFORE US...
WE'VE WAITED SO LONG FOR THIS, AND YOU ARE OUR LEADER!
...
YES.
BUT JOSHUA...
THE LORD HAS CHOSEN YOU.
AT MERIBAH...
HE SPOKE TO ME...
MOSES, BECAUSE YOU HAVE NOT BELIEVED ME AND HONORED MY HOLINESS BEFORE THE PEOPLE...
YOU WILL NOT LEAD THEM INTO THE LAND I AM GIVING THEM.

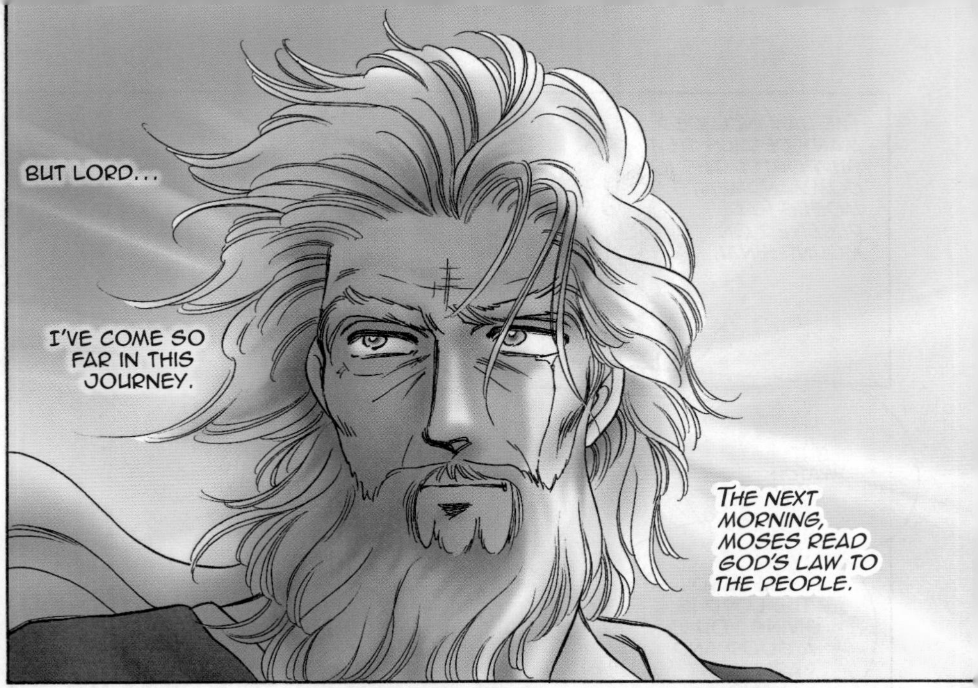
BUT LORD...
I'VE COME SO FAR IN THIS JOURNEY.
THE NEXT MORNING, MOSES READ GOD'S LAW TO THE PEOPLE.

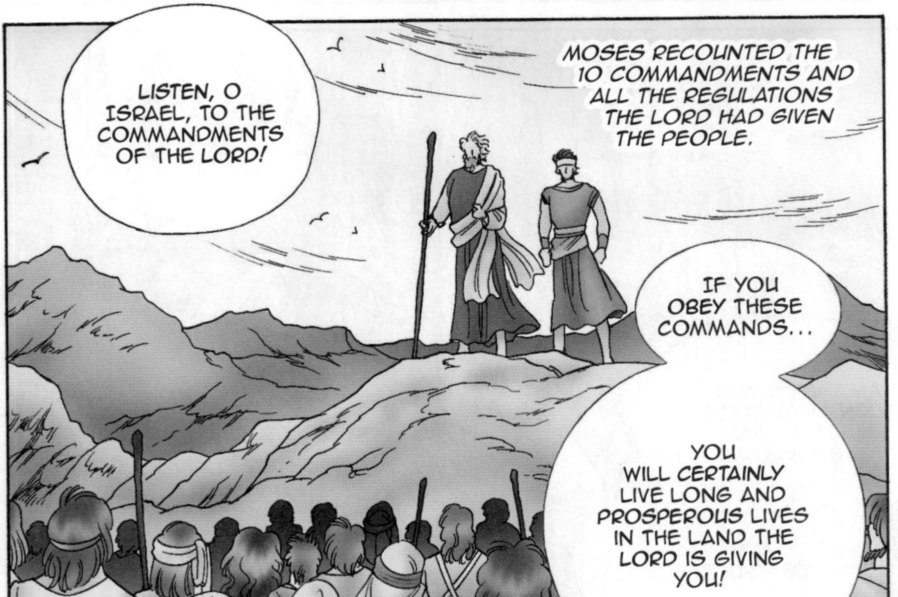
LISTEN, O ISRAEL, TO THE COMMANDMENTS OF THE LORD!
MOSES RECOUNTED THE 10 COMMANDMENTS AND ALL THE REGULATIONS THE LORD HAD GIVEN THE PEOPLE.
IF YOU OBEY THESE COMMANDS...
YOU WILL CERTAINLY LIVE LONG AND PROSPEROUS LIVES IN THE LAND THE LORD IS GIVING YOU!

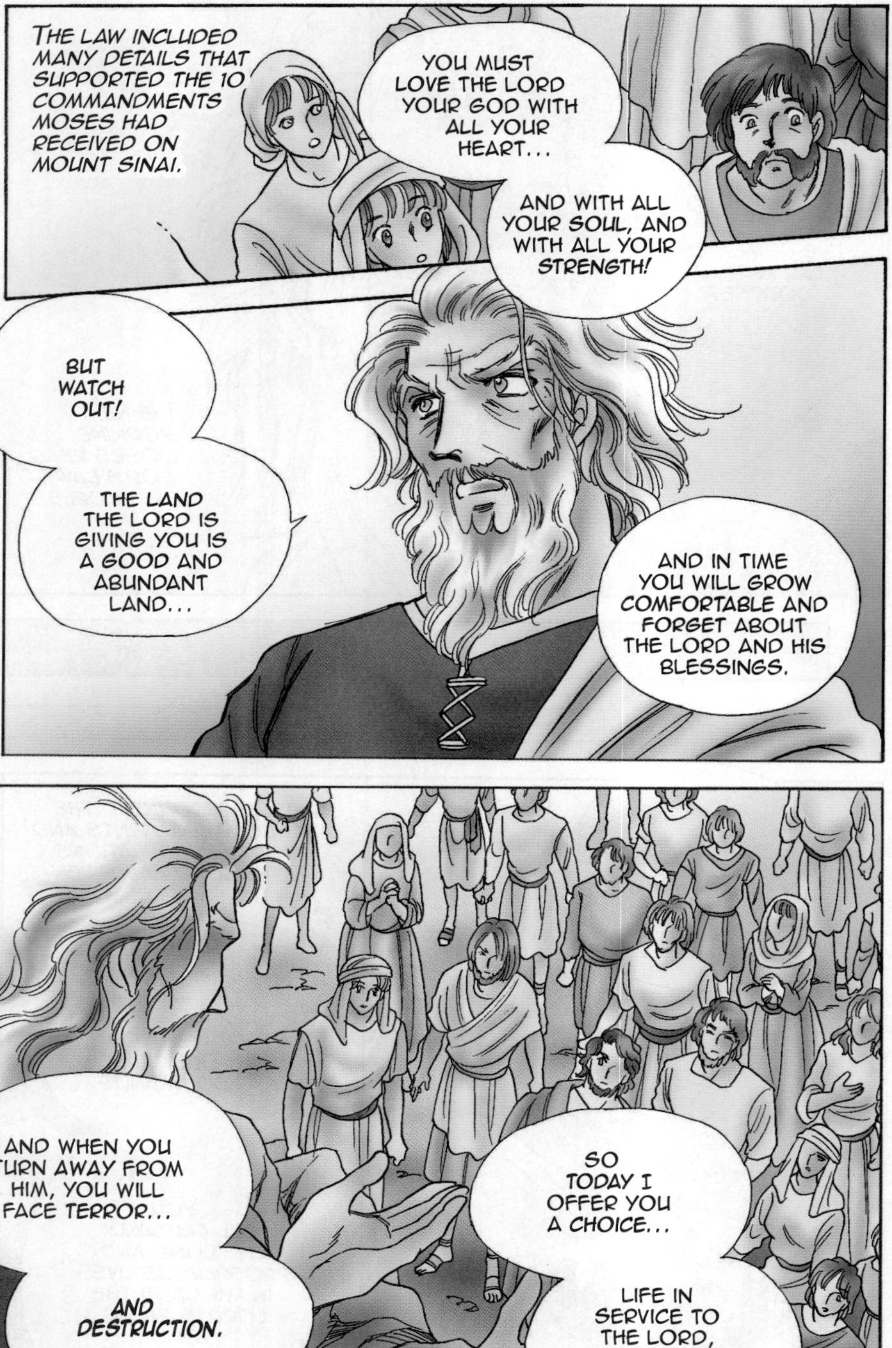
THE LAW INCLUDED MANY DETAILS THAT SUPPORTED THE 10 COMMANDMENTS MOSES HAD RECEIVED ON MOUNT SINAI.
YOU MUST LOVE THE LORD YOUR GOD WITH ALL YOUR HEART...
AND WITH ALL YOUR SOUL, AND WITH ALL YOUR STRENGTH!
BUT WATCH OUT!
THE LAND THE LORD IS GIVING YOU IS A GOOD AND ABUNDANT LAND...
AND IN TIME YOU WILL GROW COMFORTABLE AND FORGET ABOUT THE LORD AND HIS BLESSINGS.
AND WHEN YOU TURN AWAY FROM HIM, YOU WILL FACE TERROR...
AND DESTRUCTION.
SO TODAY I OFFER YOU A CHOICE...
LIFE IN SERVICE TO THE LORD, OR DEATH!

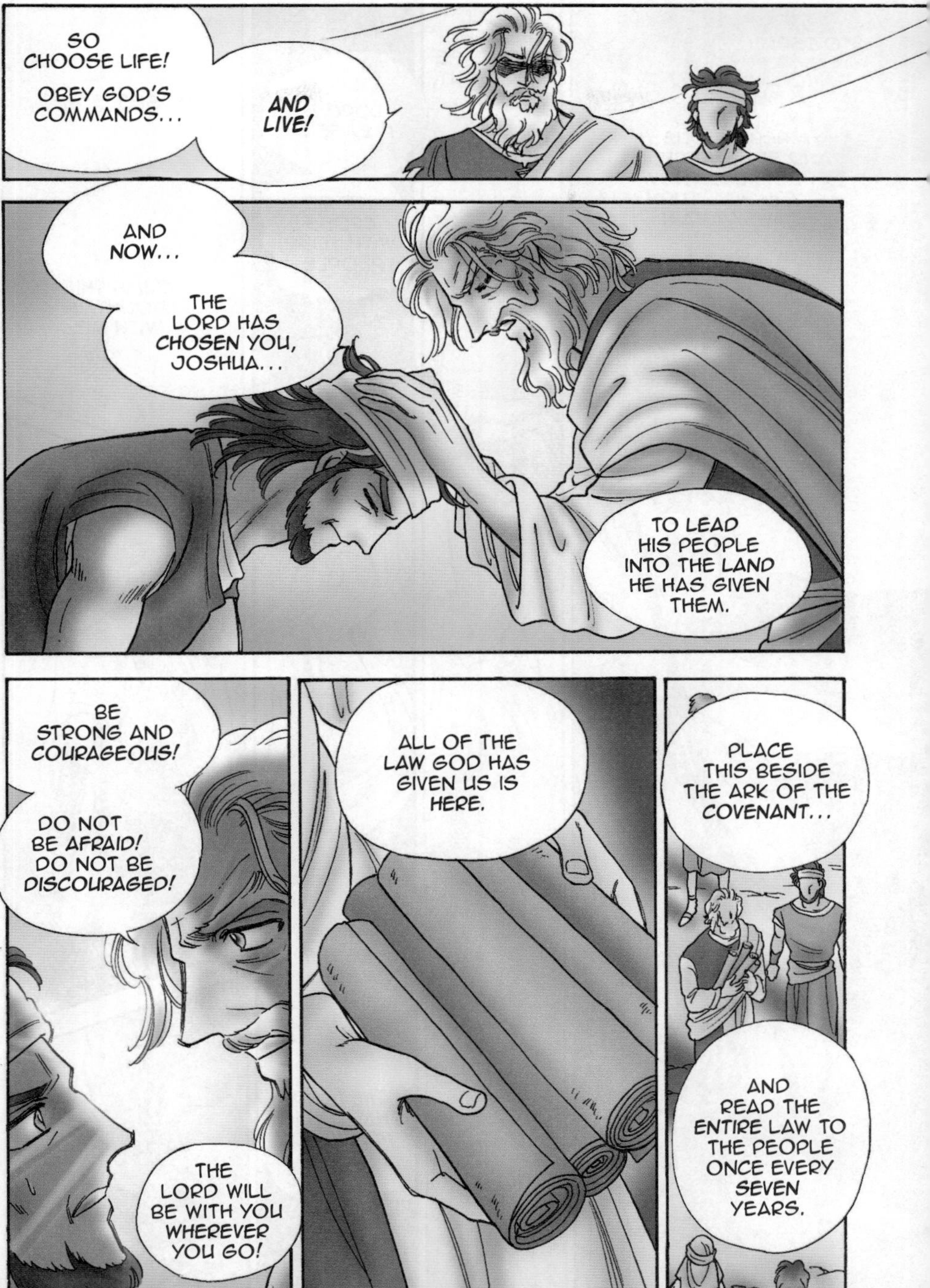
SO CHOOSE LIFE!
OBEY GOD'S COMMANDS...
AND LIVE!
AND NOW...
THE LORD HAS CHOSEN YOU, JOSHUA...
TO LEAD HIS PEOPLE INTO THE LAND HE HAS GIVEN THEM.
BE STRONG AND COURAGEOUS!
DO NOT BE AFRAID! DO NOT BE DISCOURAGED!
THE LORD WILL BE WITH YOU WHEREVER YOU GO!
ALL OF THE LAW GOD HAS GIVEN US IS HERE.
PLACE THIS BESIDE THE ARK OF THE COVENANT...
AND READ THE ENTIRE LAW TO THE PEOPLE ONCE EVERY SEVEN YEARS.

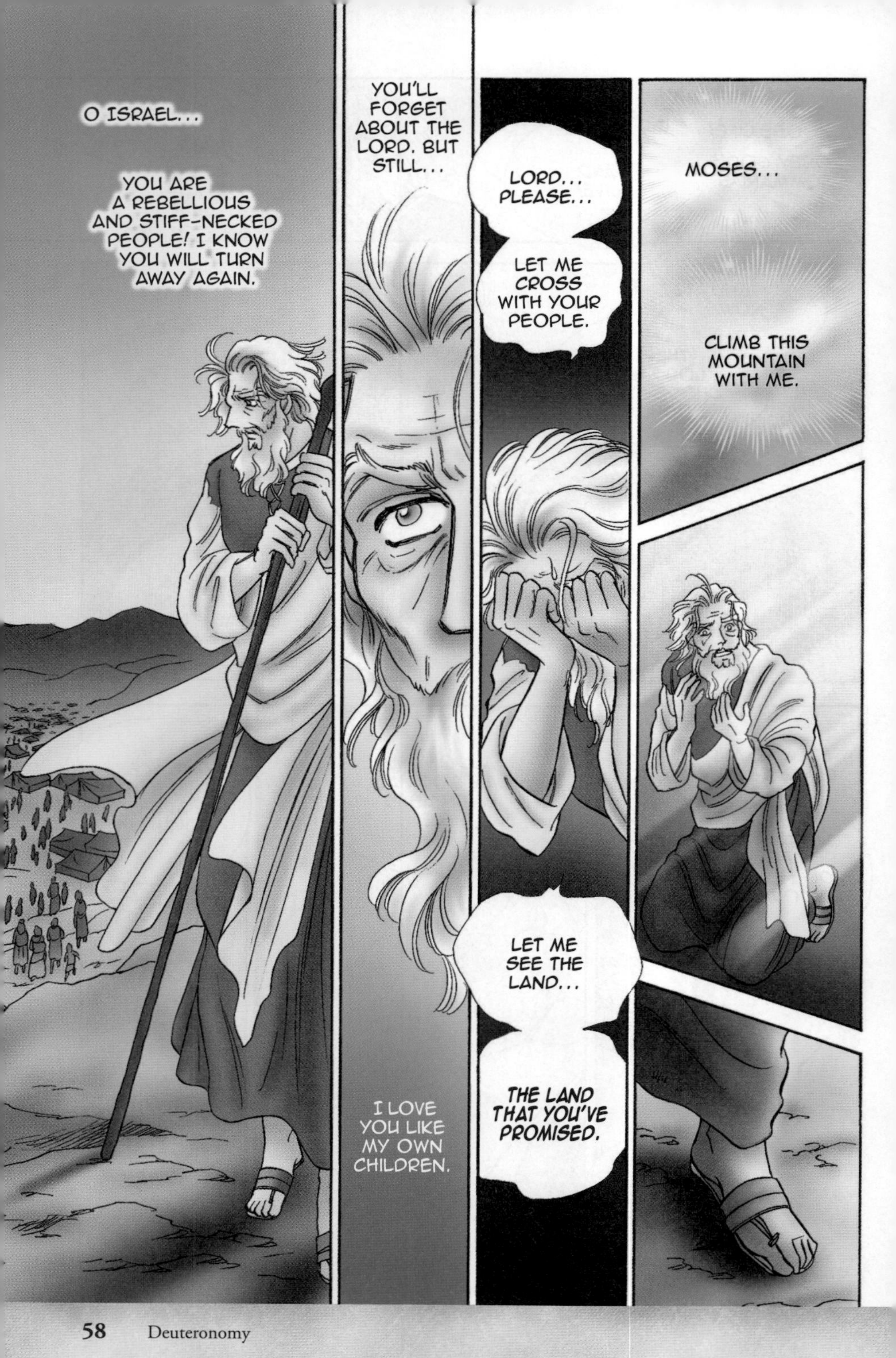
O ISRAEL...
YOU ARE A REBELLIOUS AND STIFF-NECKED PEOPLE! I KNOW YOU WILL TURN AWAY AGAIN.
YOU'LL FORGET ABOUT THE LORD. BUT STILL...
I LOVE YOU LIKE MY OWN CHILDREN.
LORD... PLEASE...
LET ME CROSS WITH YOUR PEOPLE.
LET ME SEE THE LAND...
THE LAND THAT YOU'VE PROMISED.
MOSES...
CLIMB THIS MOUNTAIN WITH ME.

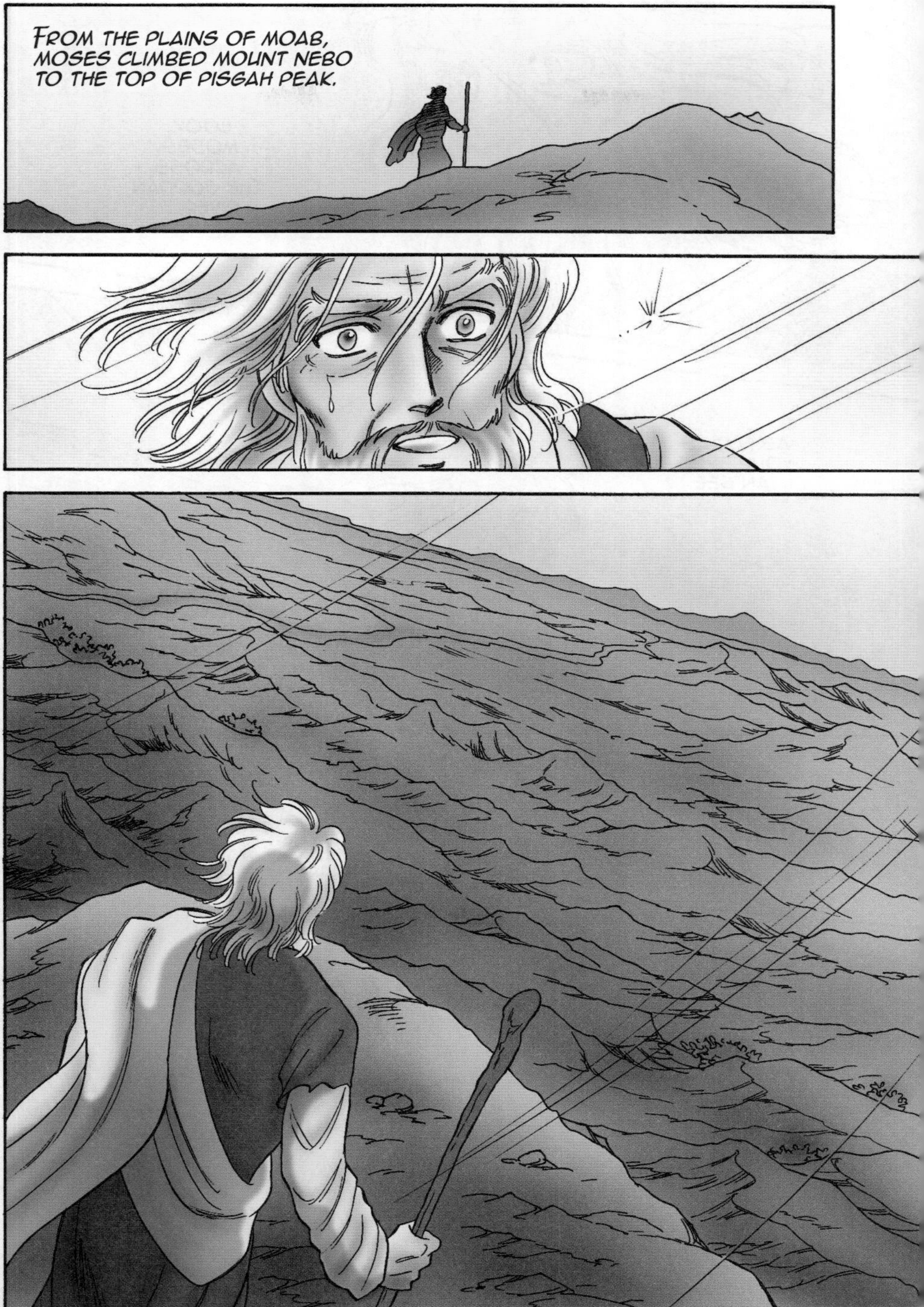
FROM THE PLAINS OF MOAB, MOSES CLIMBED MOUNT NEBO TO THE TOP OF PISGAH PEAK.

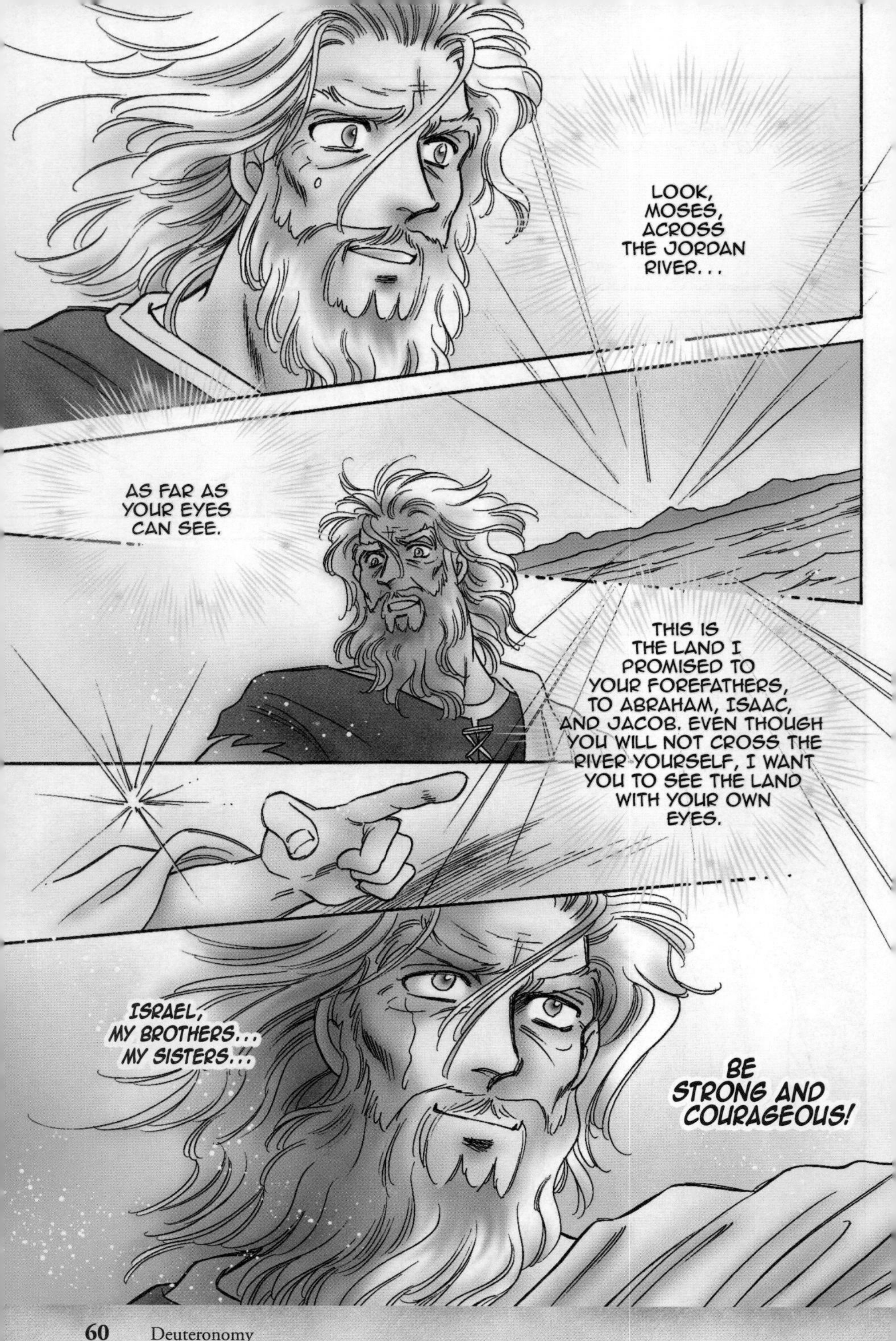
LOOK, MOSES, ACROSS THE JORDAN RIVER. . .
AS FAR AS YOUR EYES CAN SEE.
THIS IS THE LAND I PROMISED TO YOUR FOREFATHERS, TO ABRAHAM, ISAAC, AND JACOB. EVEN THOUGH YOU WILL NOT CROSS THE RIVER YOURSELF, I WANT YOU TO SEE THE LAND WITH YOUR OWN EYES.
ISRAEL, MY BROTHERS... MY SISTERS...
BE STRONG AND COURAGEOUS!

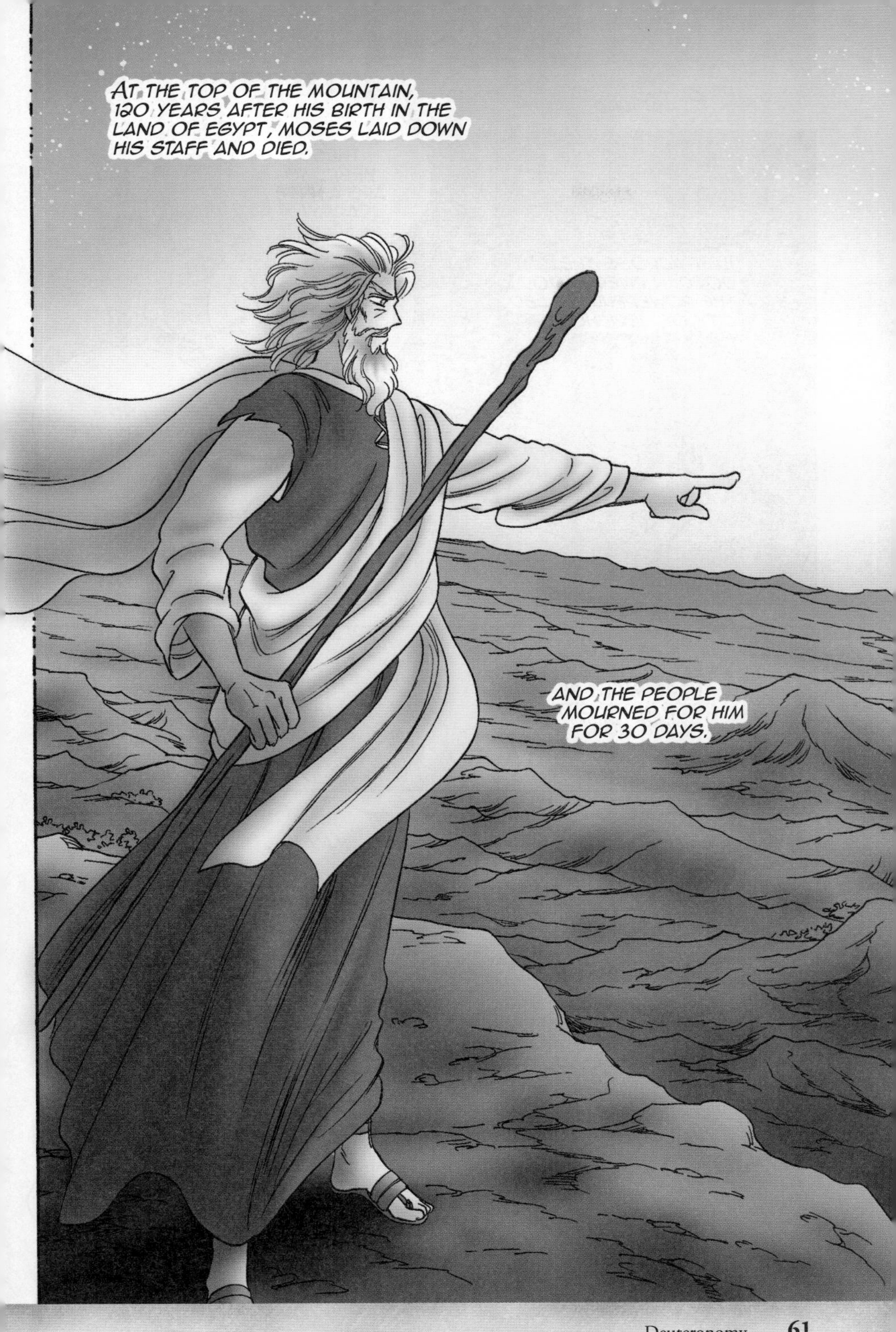
AT THE TOP OF THE MOUNTAIN, 120 YEARS AFTER HIS BIRTH IN THE LAND OF EGYPT, MOSES LAID DOWN HIS STAFF AND DIED.
AND THE PEOPLE MOURNED FOR HIM FOR 30 DAYS.

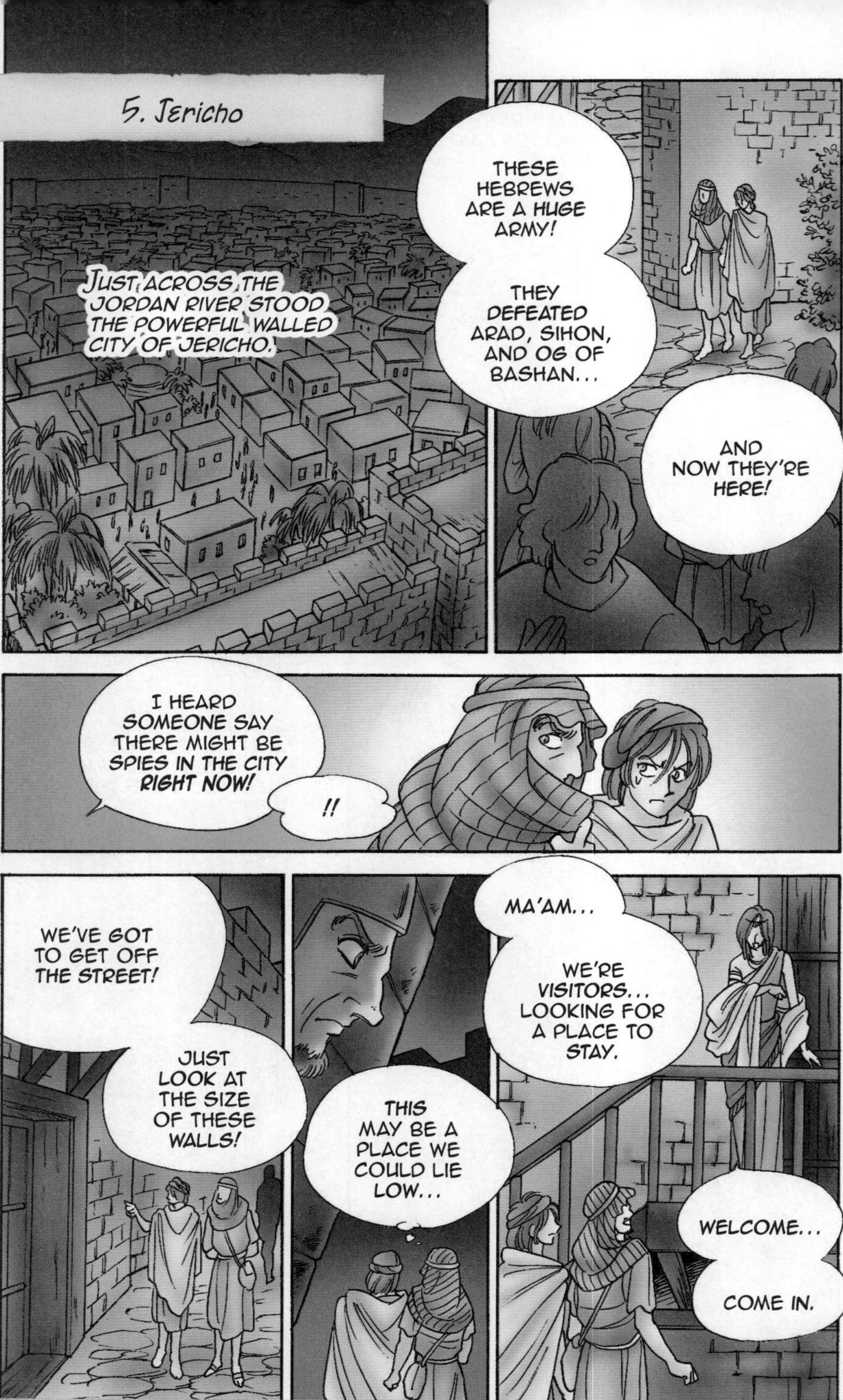
5. Jericho
JUST ACROSS THE JORDAN RIVER STOOD THE POWERFUL WALLED CITY OF JERICHO.
THESE HEBREWS ARE A HUGE ARMY!
THEY DEFEATED ARAD, SIHON, AND OG OF BASHAN...
AND NOW THEY'RE HERE!
I HEARD SOMEONE SAY THERE MIGHT BE SPIES IN THE CITY RIGHT NOW!
!!
WE'VE GOT TO GET OFF THE STREET!
JUST LOOK AT THE SIZE OF THESE WALLS!
THIS MAY BE A PLACE WE COULD LIE LOW...
MA'AM...
WE'RE VISITORS... LOOKING FOR A PLACE TO STAY.
WELCOME...
COME IN.

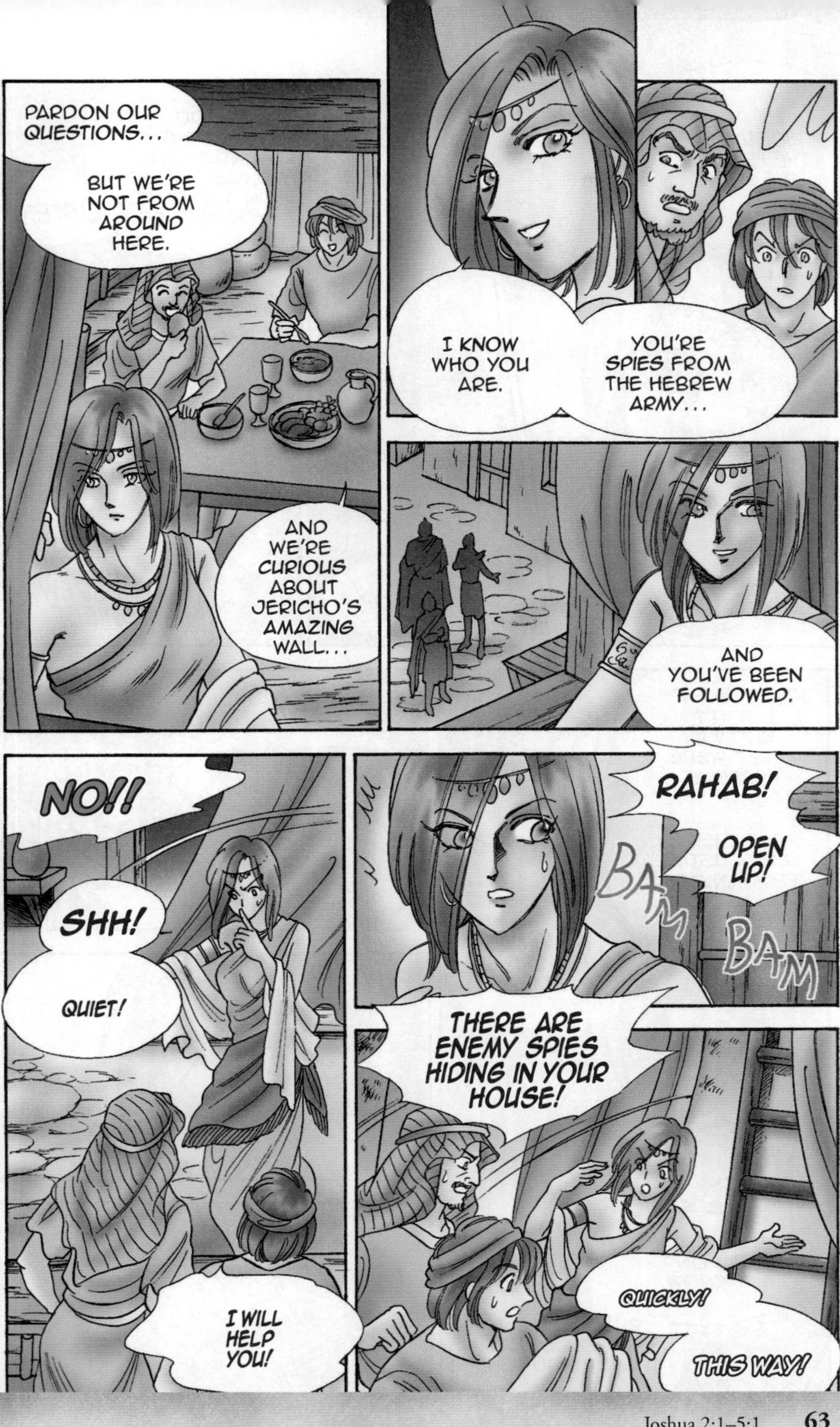
PARDON OUR QUESTIONS...
BUT WE'RE NOT FROM AROUND HERE.
AND WE'RE CURIOUS ABOUT JERICHO'S AMAZING WALL...
I KNOW WHO YOU ARE.
YOU'RE SPIES FROM THE HEBREW ARMY...
AND YOU'VE BEEN FOLLOWED.
RAHAB!
OPEN UP!
BAM
BAM
NO!!
SHH!
QUIET!
THERE ARE ENEMY SPIES HIDING IN YOUR HOUSE!
I WILL HELP YOU!
QUICKLY!
THIS WAY!

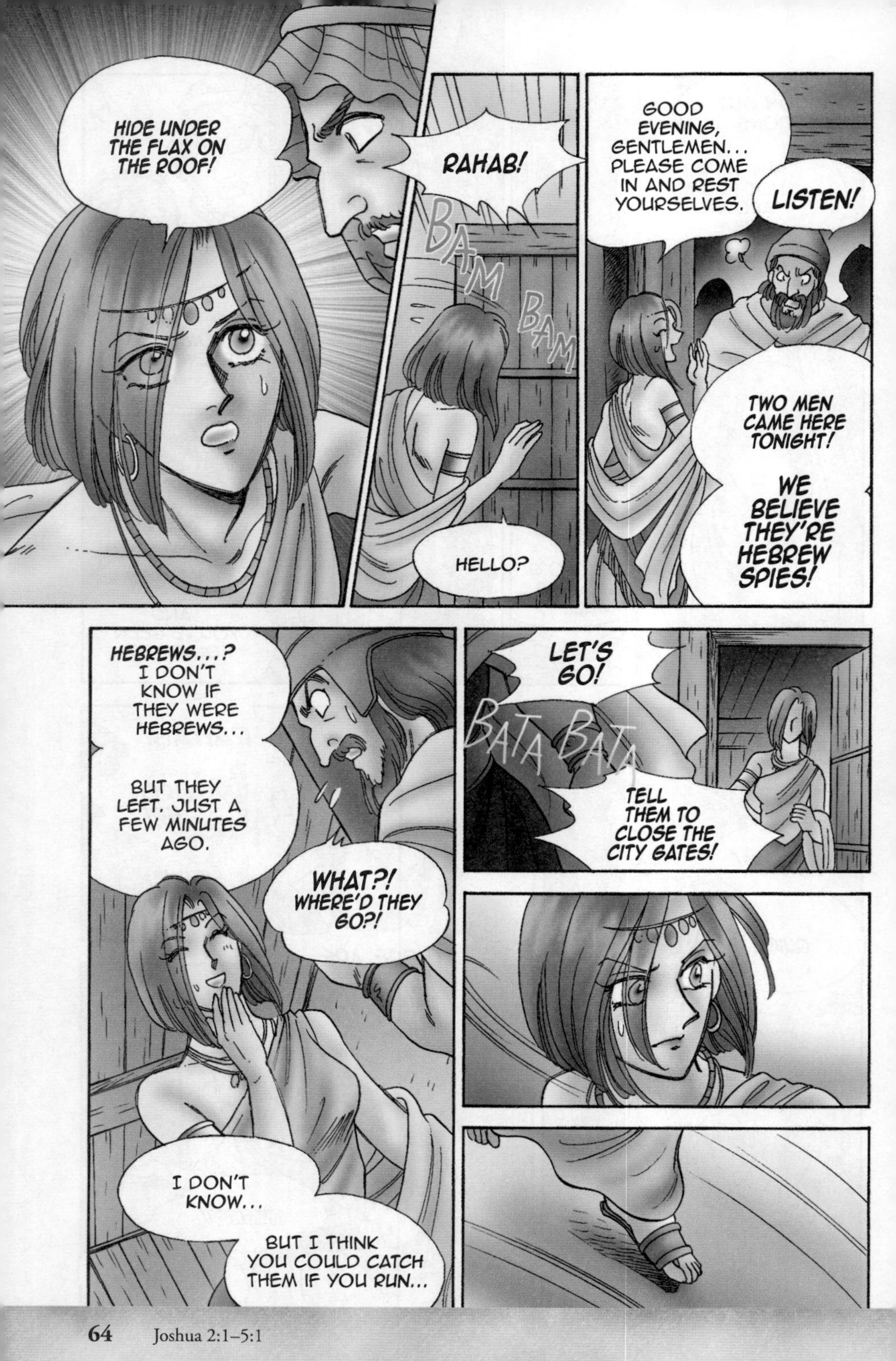
HIDE UNDER THE FLAX ON THE ROOF!
RAHAB!
BAM BAM
HELLO?
GOOD EVENING, GENTLEMEN... PLEASE COME IN AND REST YOURSELVES.
LISTEN!
TWO MEN CAME HERE TONIGHT!
WE BELIEVE THEY'RE HEBREW SPIES!
HEBREWS...? I DON'T KNOW IF THEY WERE HEBREWS...
BUT THEY LEFT. JUST A FEW MINUTES AGO.
WHAT?! WHERE'D THEY GO?!
I DON'T KNOW...
BUT I THINK YOU COULD CATCH THEM IF YOU RUN...
LET'S GO!
BATA BATA
TELL THEM TO CLOSE THE CITY GATES!

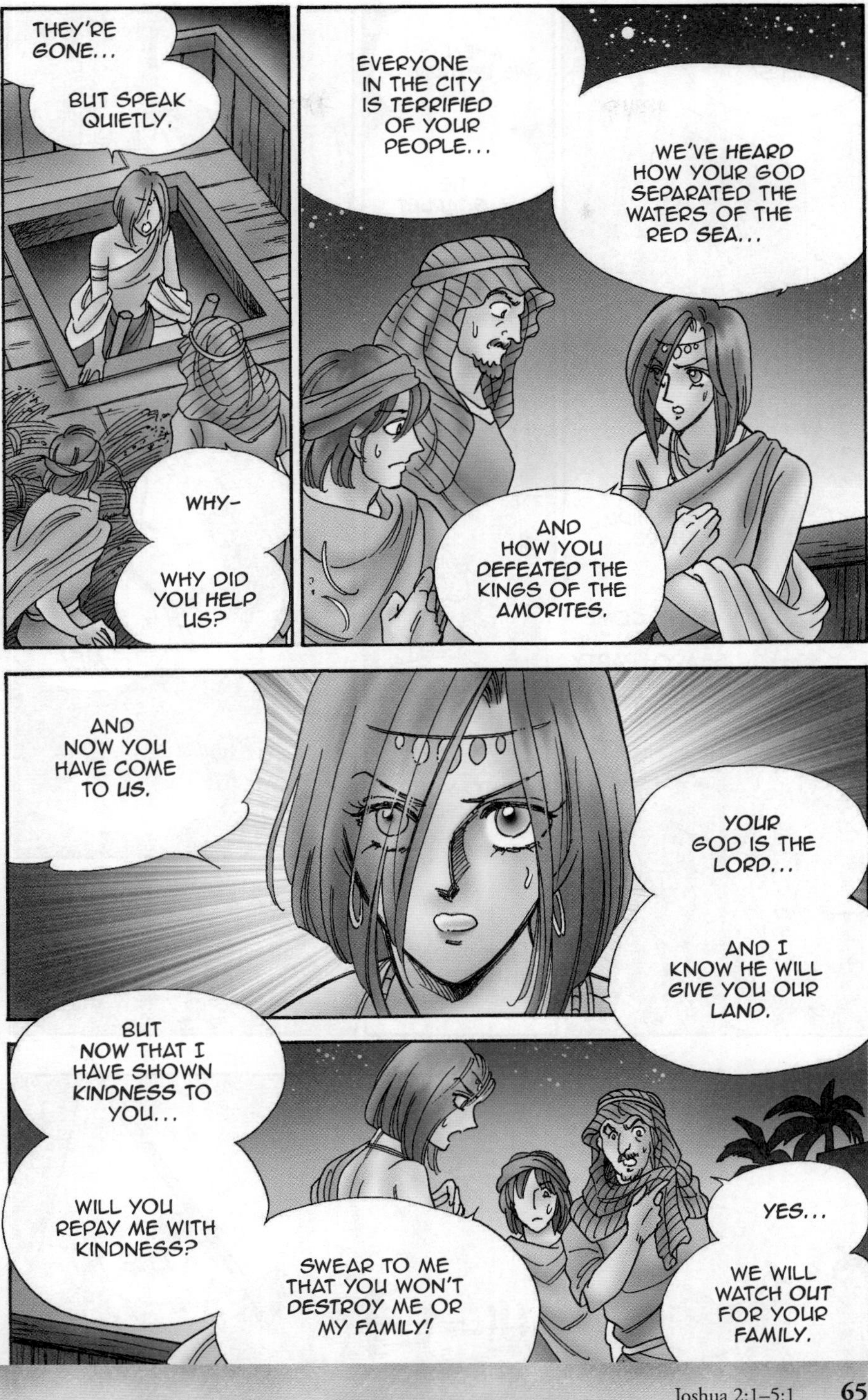
THEY'RE GONE...
BUT SPEAK QUIETLY.
WHY-
WHY DID YOU HELP US?
EVERYONE IN THE CITY IS TERRIFIED OF YOUR PEOPLE...
WE'VE HEARD HOW YOUR GOD SEPARATED THE WATERS OF THE RED SEA...
AND HOW YOU DEFEATED THE KINGS OF THE AMORITES.
AND NOW YOU HAVE COME TO US.
YOUR GOD IS THE LORD...
AND I KNOW HE WILL GIVE YOU OUR LAND.
BUT NOW THAT I HAVE SHOWN KINDNESS TO YOU...
WILL YOU REPAY ME WITH KINDNESS?
SWEAR TO ME THAT YOU WON'T DESTROY ME OR MY FAMILY!
YES...
WE WILL WATCH OUT FOR YOUR FAMILY.

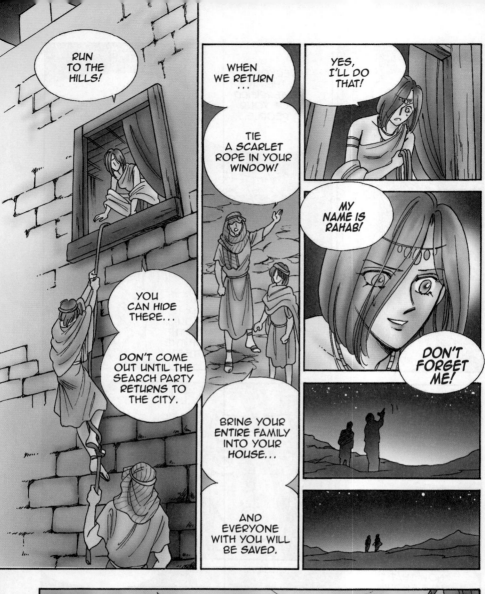

RUN TO THE HILLS!

WHEN WE RETURN...

TIE A SCARLET ROPE IN YOUR WINDOW!

YES, I'LL DO THAT!

YOU CAN HIDE THERE...

DON'T COME OUT UNTIL THE SEARCH PARTY RETURNS TO THE CITY.

MY NAME IS RAHAB!

DON'T FORGET ME!

BRING YOUR ENTIRE FAMILY INTO YOUR HOUSE...

AND EVERYONE WITH YOU WILL BE SAVED.

THE SPIES ARE BACK!

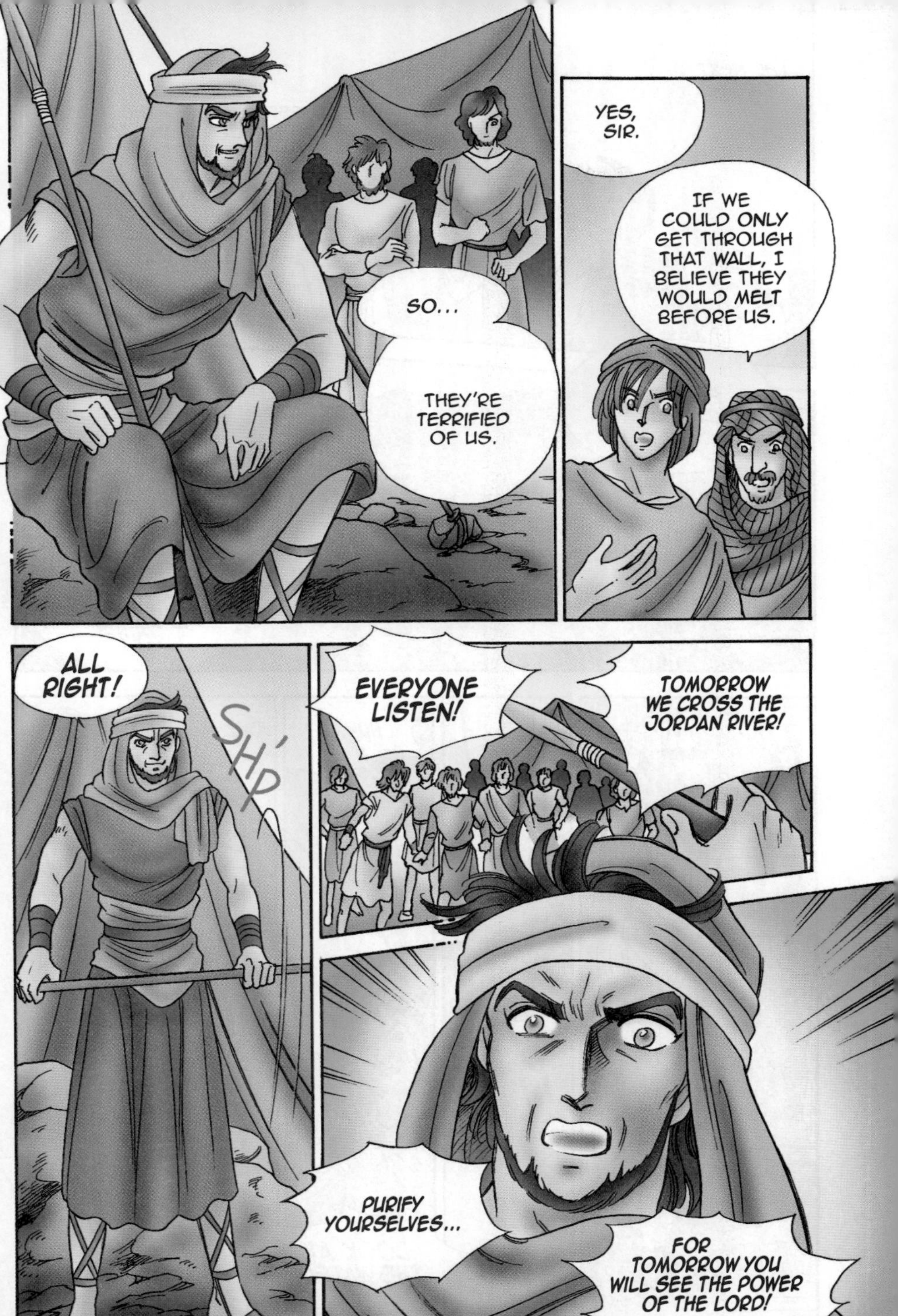
SO...
THEY'RE TERRIFIED OF US.
YES, SIR.
IF WE COULD ONLY GET THROUGH THAT WALL, I BELIEVE THEY WOULD MELT BEFORE US.
ALL RIGHT!
SH'P
EVERYONE LISTEN!
TOMORROW WE CROSS THE JORDAN RIVER!
PURIFY YOURSELVES...
FOR TOMORROW YOU WILL SEE THE POWER OF THE LORD!

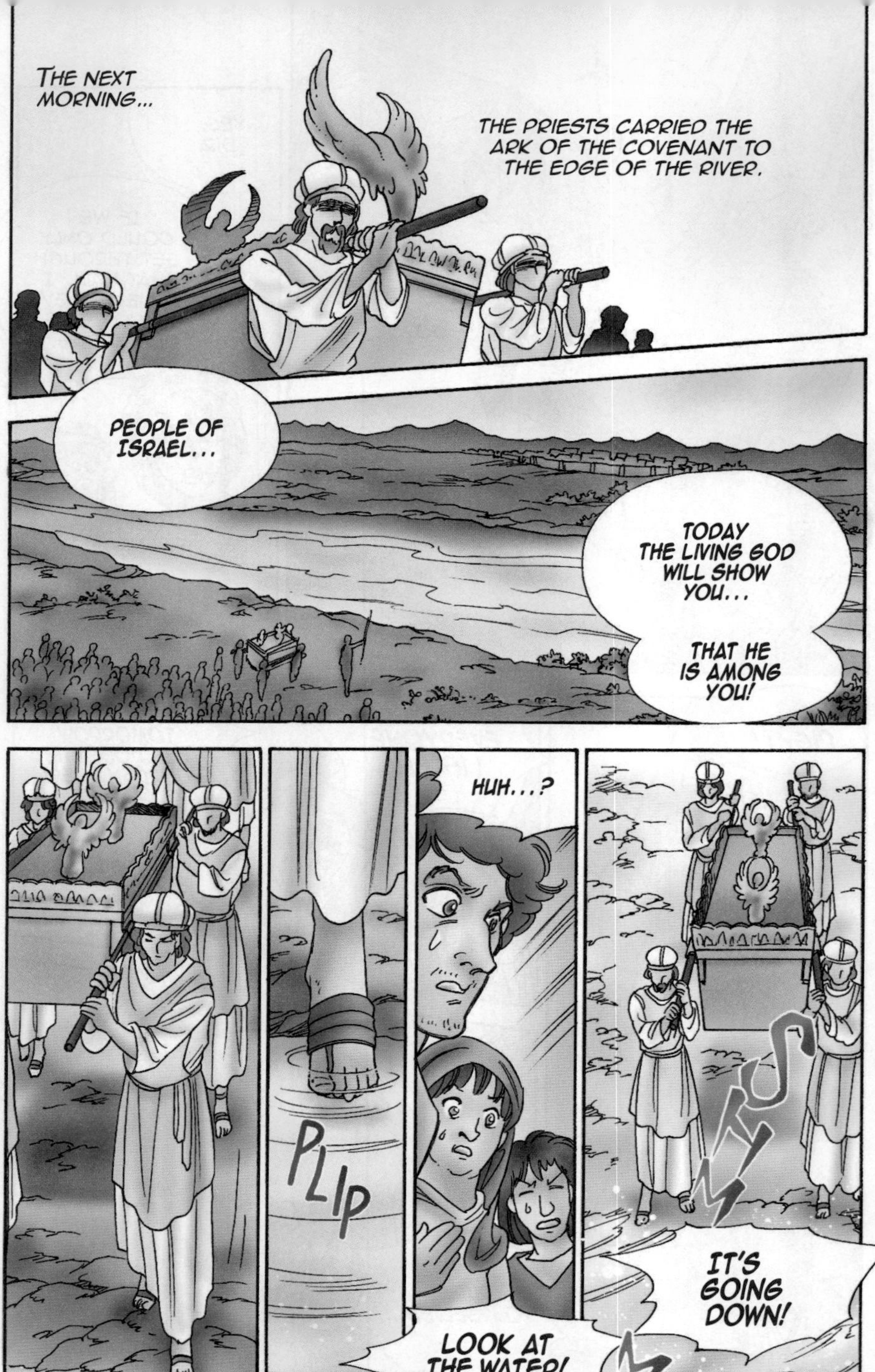
THE NEXT MORNING...
THE PRIESTS CARRIED THE ARK OF THE COVENANT TO THE EDGE OF THE RIVER.
PEOPLE OF ISRAEL...
TODAY THE LIVING GOD WILL SHOW YOU...
THAT HE IS AMONG YOU!
PLIP
HUH...?
LOOK AT THE WATER!
IT'S GOING DOWN!

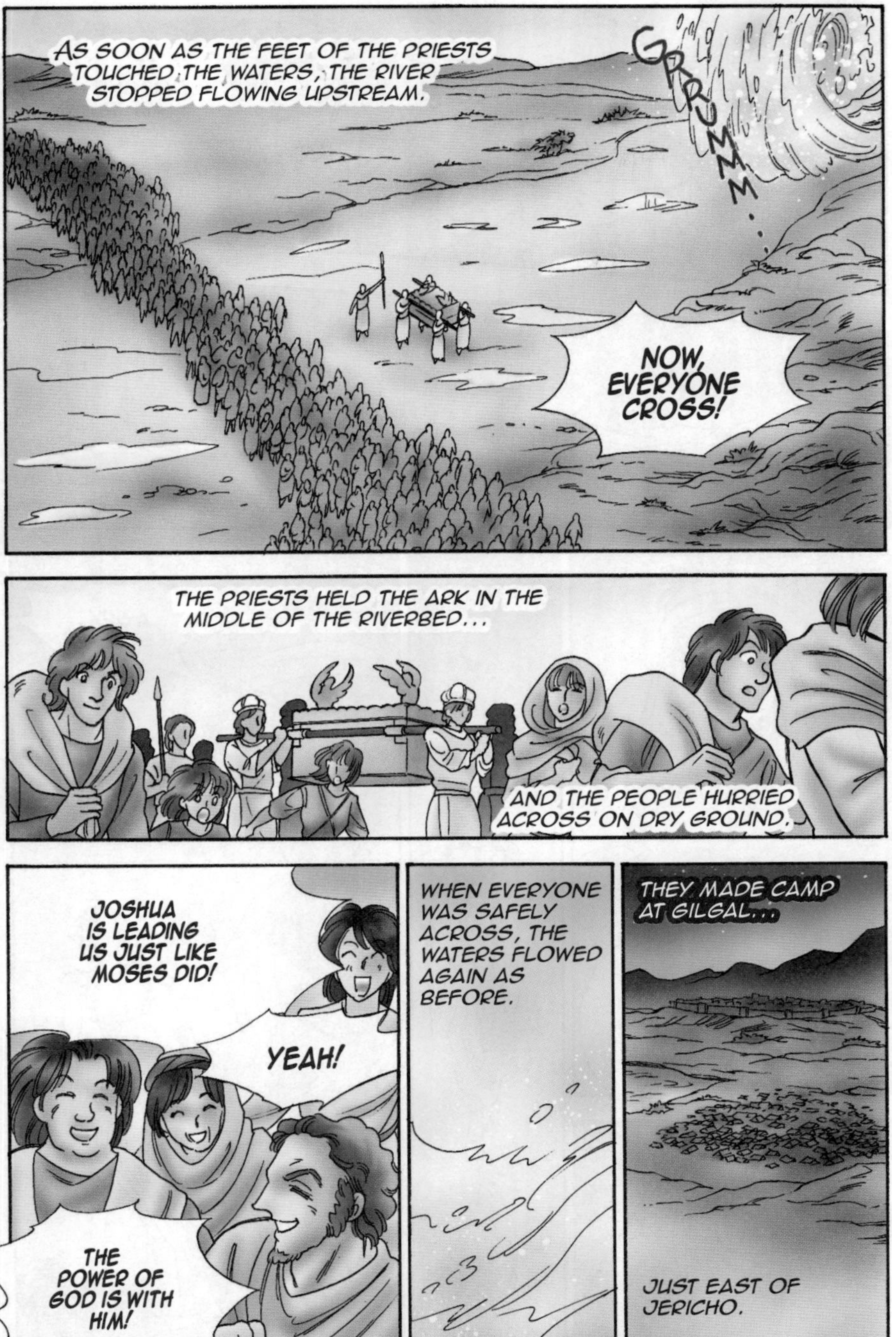
AS SOON AS THE FEET OF THE PRIESTS TOUCHED THE WATERS, THE RIVER STOPPED FLOWING UPSTREAM.
GRRUMMM...
NOW, EVERYONE CROSS!
THE PRIESTS HELD THE ARK IN THE MIDDLE OF THE RIVERBED...
AND THE PEOPLE HURRIED ACROSS ON DRY GROUND.
JOSHUA IS LEADING US JUST LIKE MOSES DID!
YEAH!
THE POWER OF GOD IS WITH HIM!
WHEN EVERYONE WAS SAFELY ACROSS, THE WATERS FLOWED AGAIN AS BEFORE.
THEY MADE CAMP AT GILGAL...
JUST EAST OF JERICHO.

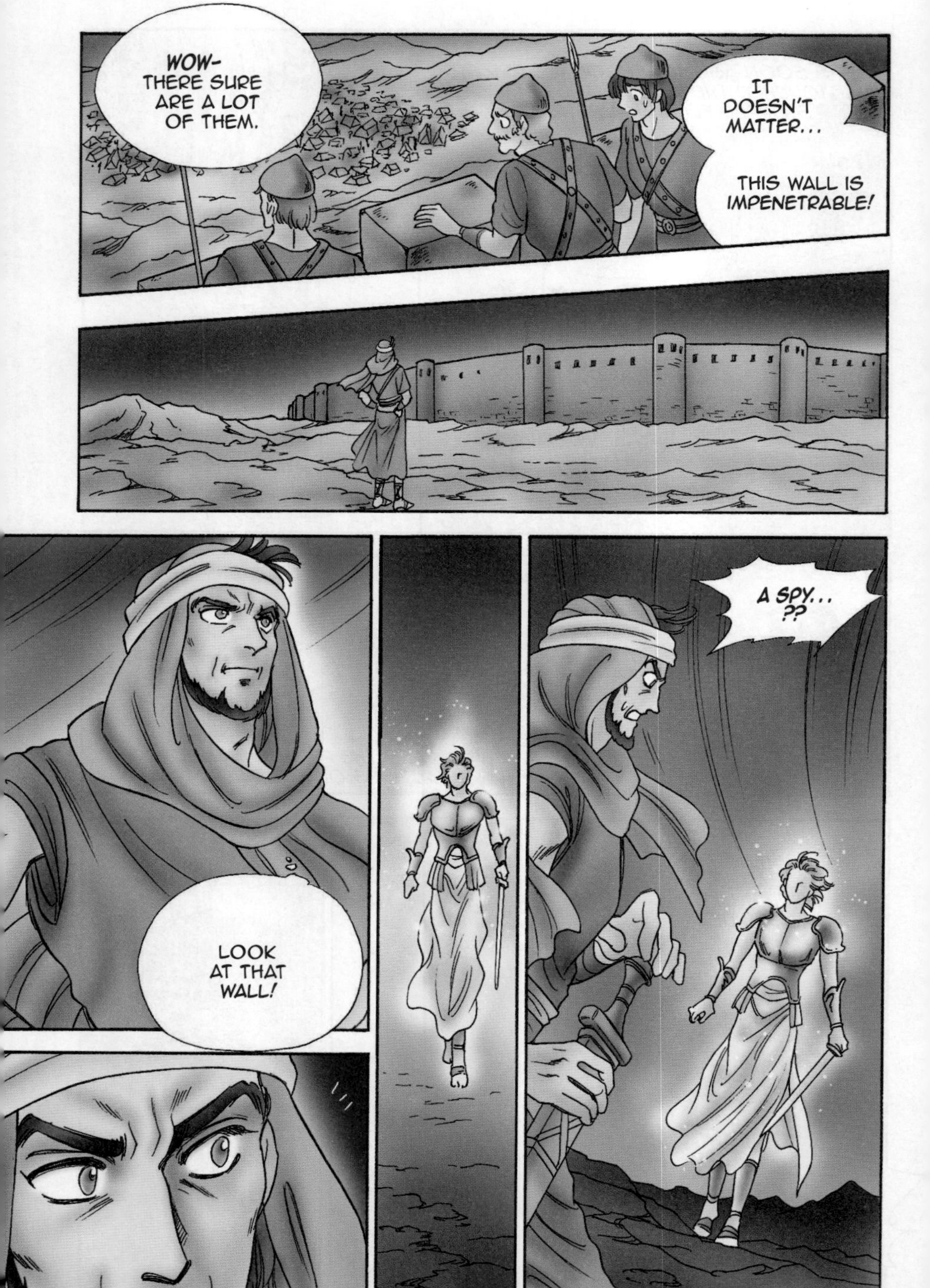
WOW-
THERE SURE
ARE A LOT
OF THEM.
IT
DOESN'T
MATTER...
THIS WALL IS
IMPENETRABLE!
LOOK
AT THAT
WALL!
A SPY...
??

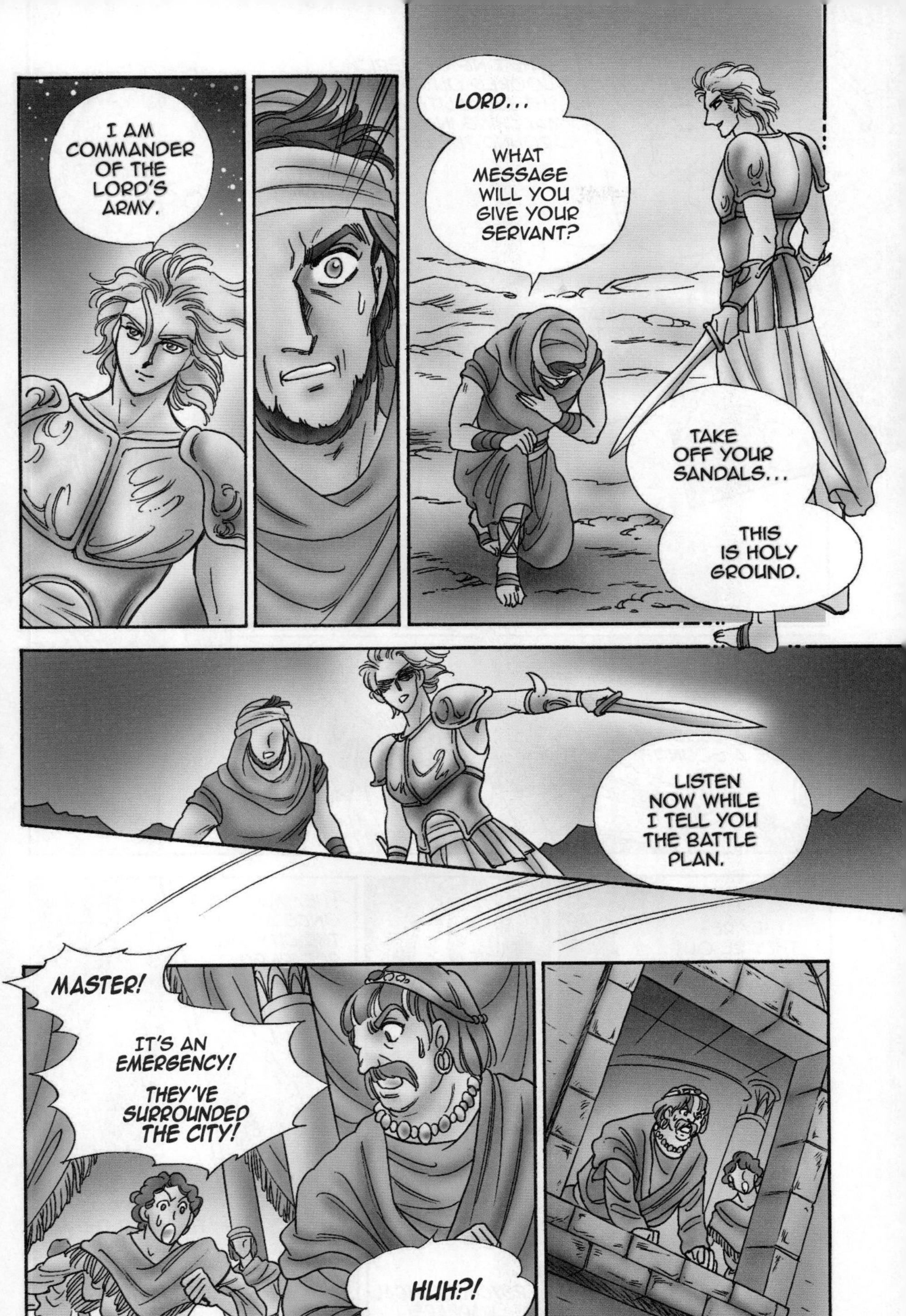
I AM COMMANDER OF THE LORD'S ARMY.
LORD...
WHAT MESSAGE WILL YOU GIVE YOUR SERVANT?
TAKE OFF YOUR SANDALS...
THIS IS HOLY GROUND.
LISTEN NOW WHILE I TELL YOU THE BATTLE PLAN.
MASTER!
IT'S AN EMERGENCY!
THEY'VE SURROUNDED THE CITY!
HUH?!

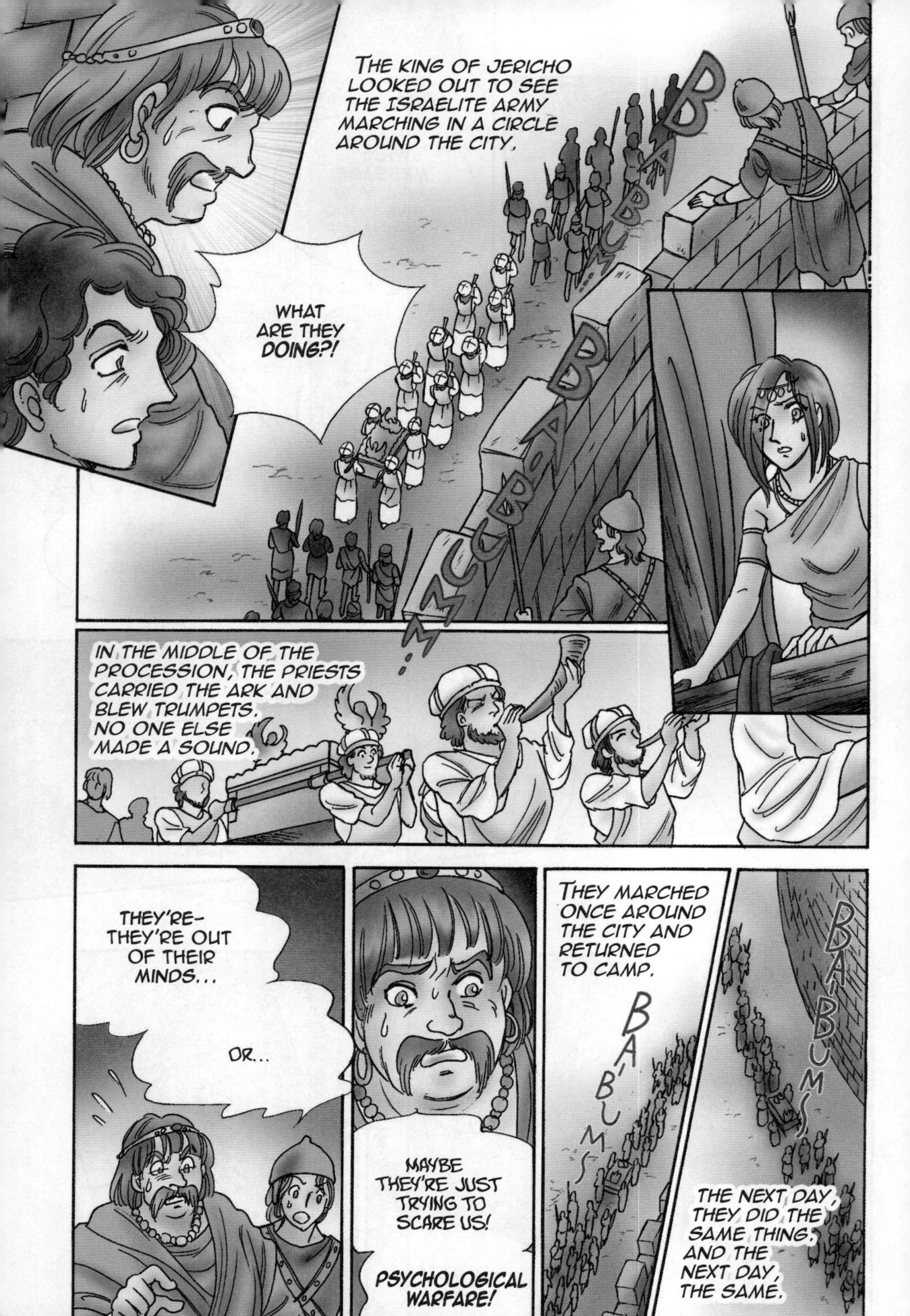
THE KING OF JERICHO LOOKED OUT TO SEE THE ISRAELITE ARMY MARCHING IN A CIRCLE AROUND THE CITY.
WHAT ARE THEY DOING?!
BABUMS...
BABUMS...
BA-BUMS...
IN THE MIDDLE OF THE PROCESSION, THE PRIESTS CARRIED THE ARK AND BLEW TRUMPETS. NO ONE ELSE MADE A SOUND.
THEY'RE- THEY'RE OUT OF THEIR MINDS...
OR...
MAYBE THEY'RE JUST TRYING TO SCARE US!
PSYCHOLOGICAL WARFARE!
THEY MARCHED ONCE AROUND THE CITY AND RETURNED TO CAMP.
BA-BUMS
BA-BUMS
THE NEXT DAY, THEY DID THE SAME THING. AND THE NEXT DAY, THE SAME.

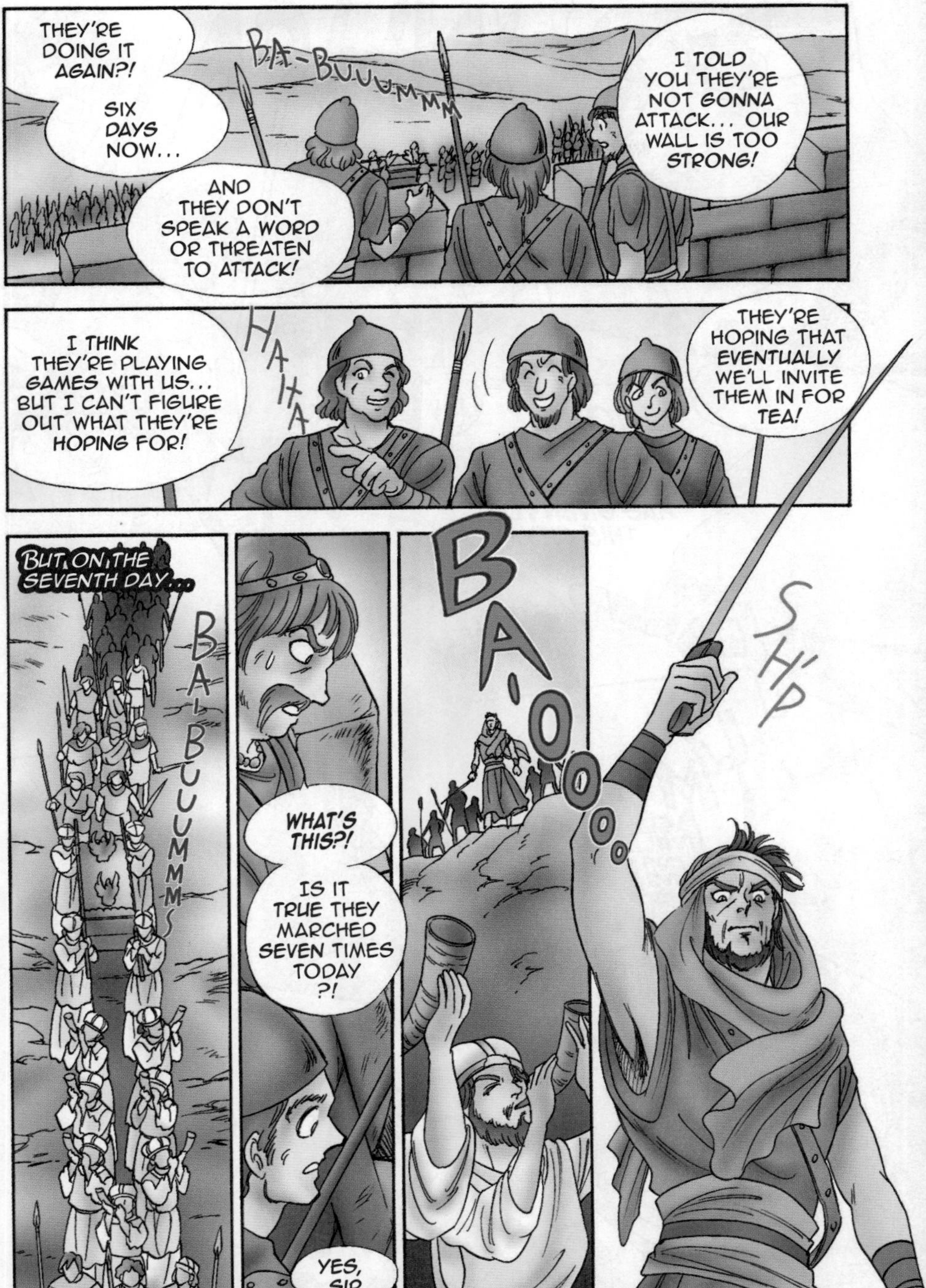
THEY'RE DOING IT AGAIN?!
SIX DAYS NOW...
BA-BUUUMMM
AND THEY DON'T SPEAK A WORD OR THREATEN TO ATTACK!
I TOLD YOU THEY'RE NOT GONNA ATTACK... OUR WALL IS TOO STRONG!
I THINK THEY'RE PLAYING GAMES WITH US... BUT I CAN'T FIGURE OUT WHAT THEY'RE HOPING FOR!
HAHA
THEY'RE HOPING THAT EVENTUALLY WE'LL INVITE THEM IN FOR TEA!
BUT, ON THE SEVENTH DAY...
BA-BUUUMMMS
WHAT'S THIS?!
IS IT TRUE THEY MARCHED SEVEN TIMES TODAY ?!
YES, SIR.
BAOOOOO
SH'P

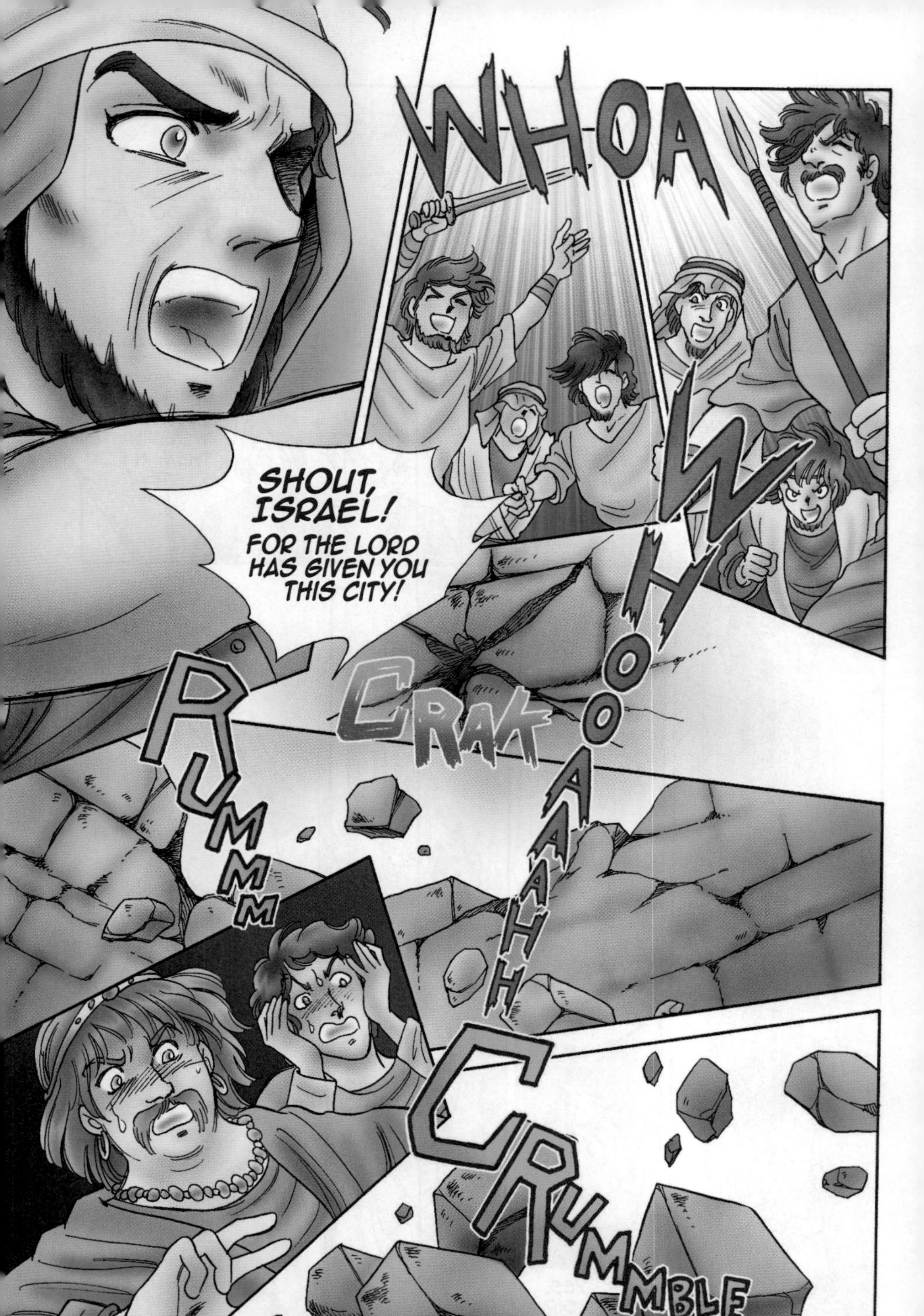
WHOA
SHOUT, ISRAEL!
FOR THE LORD HAS GIVEN YOU THIS CITY!
WHOOOAAAHHH
CRAK
RUMMM
CRUMMBLE

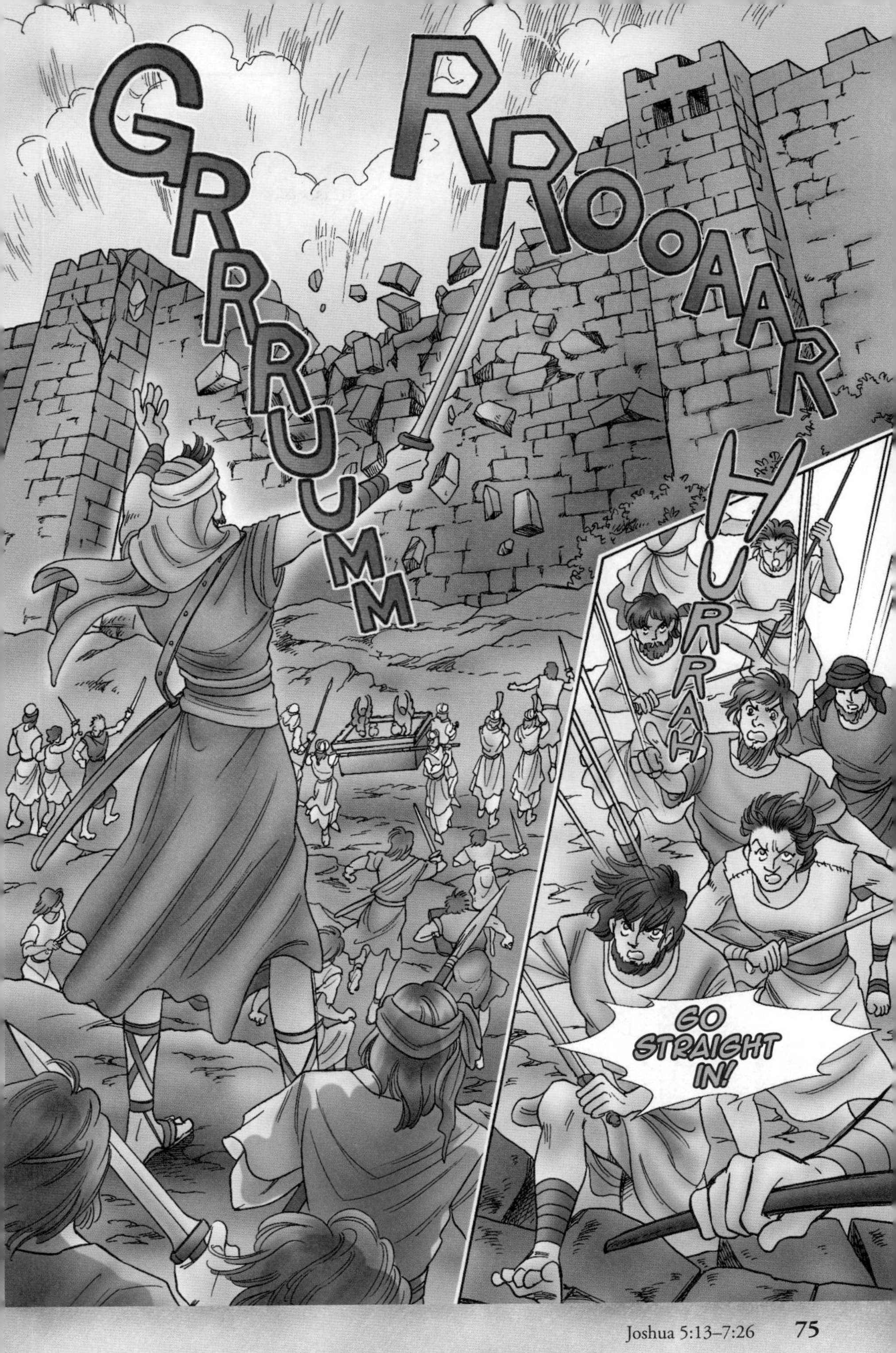
GRRRRUUMM
RROOAAR
HURRAH
GO STRAIGHT IN!

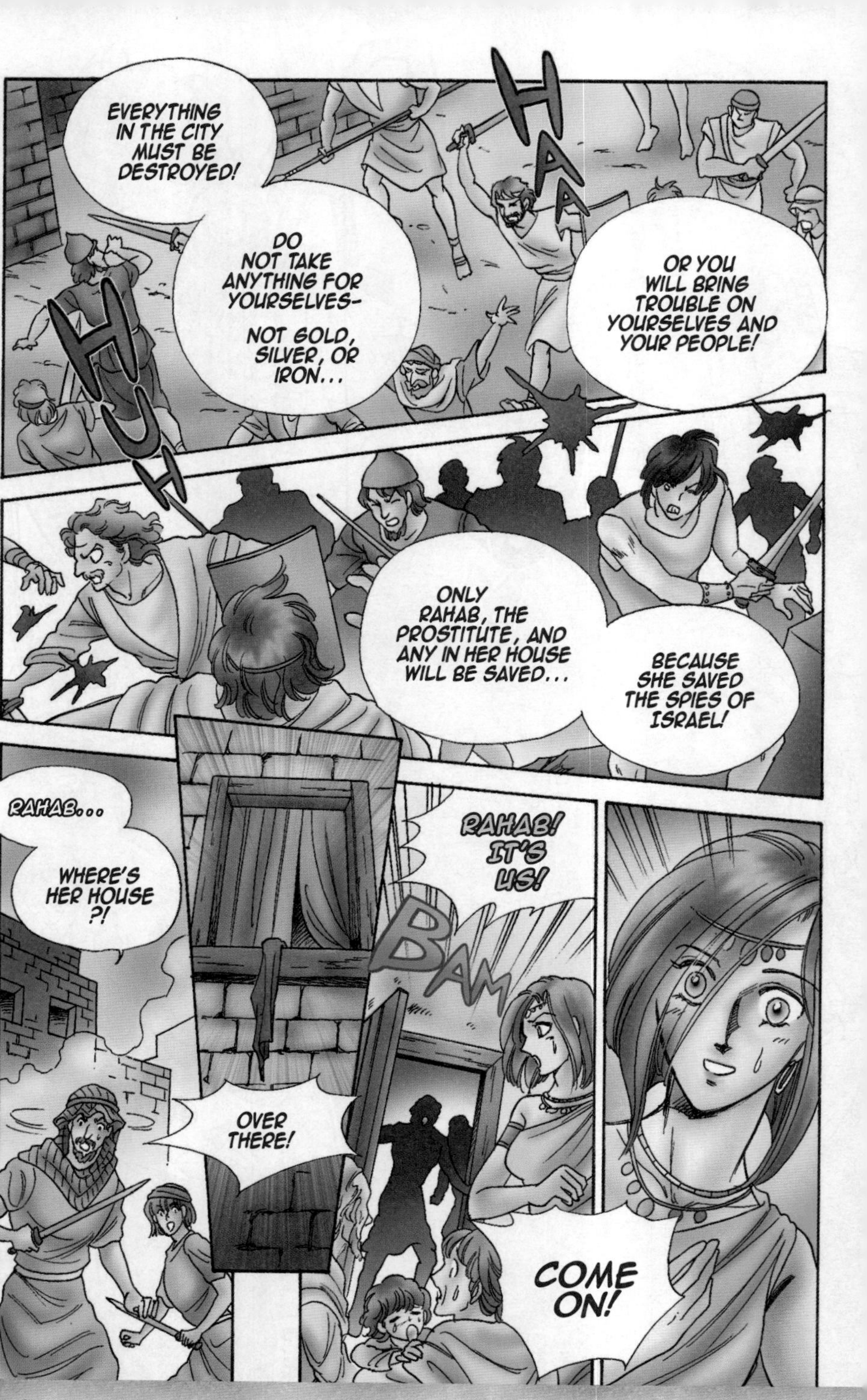
EVERYTHING IN THE CITY MUST BE DESTROYED!
DO NOT TAKE ANYTHING FOR YOURSELVES-
NOT GOLD, SILVER, OR IRON...
HAA
OR YOU WILL BRING TROUBLE ON YOURSELVES AND YOUR PEOPLE!
HUH
ONLY RAHAB, THE PROSTITUTE, AND ANY IN HER HOUSE WILL BE SAVED...
BECAUSE SHE SAVED THE SPIES OF ISRAEL!
RAHAB...
WHERE'S HER HOUSE ?!
OVER THERE!
RAHAB! IT'S US!
BAM
COME ON!

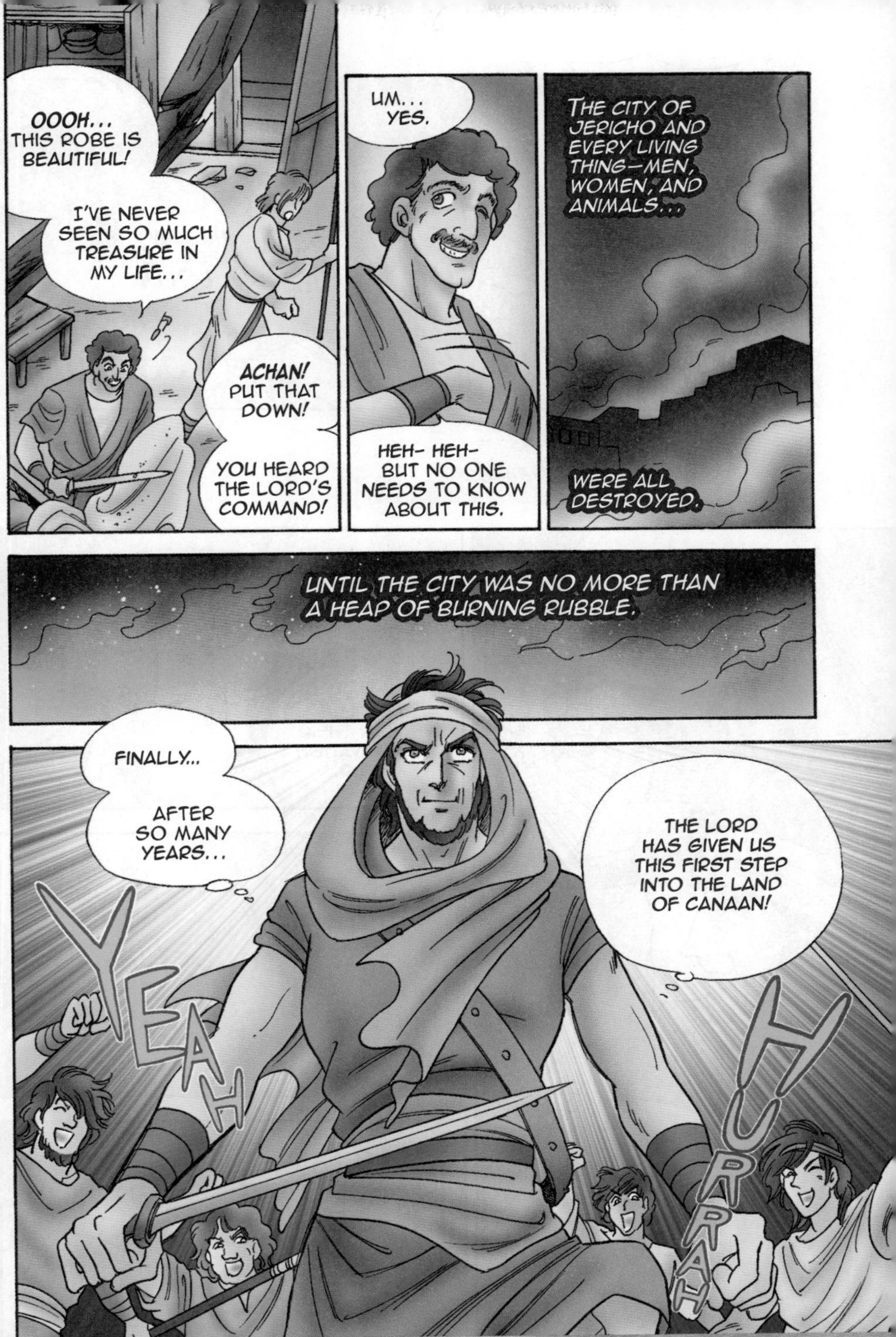
OOOH... THIS ROBE IS BEAUTIFUL!
I'VE NEVER SEEN SO MUCH TREASURE IN MY LIFE...
ACHAN! PUT THAT DOWN!
YOU HEARD THE LORD'S COMMAND!
UM... YES.
HEH- HEH- BUT NO ONE NEEDS TO KNOW ABOUT THIS.
THE CITY OF JERICHO AND EVERY LIVING THING—MEN, WOMEN, AND ANIMALS...
WERE ALL DESTROYED.
UNTIL THE CITY WAS NO MORE THAN A HEAP OF BURNING RUBBLE.
FINALLY...
AFTER SO MANY YEARS...
THE LORD HAS GIVEN US THIS FIRST STEP INTO THE LAND OF CANAAN!
YEAH
HURRAH

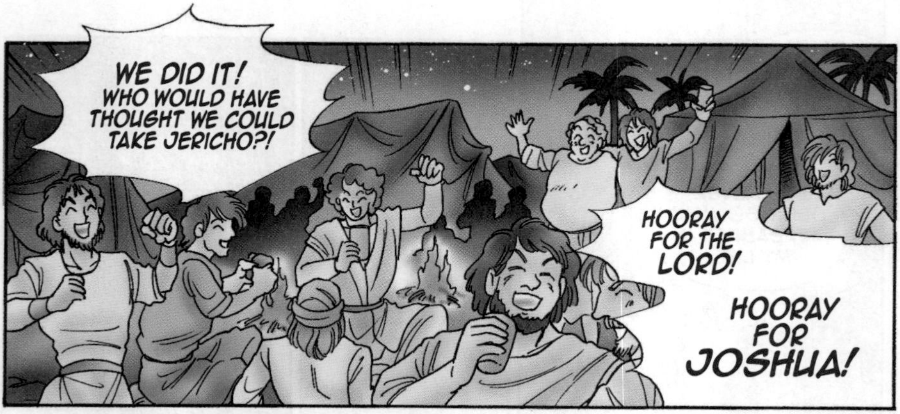
WE DID IT! WHO WOULD HAVE THOUGHT WE COULD TAKE JERICHO?!
HOORAY FOR THE LORD!
HOORAY FOR JOSHUA!

6. Israel Advances

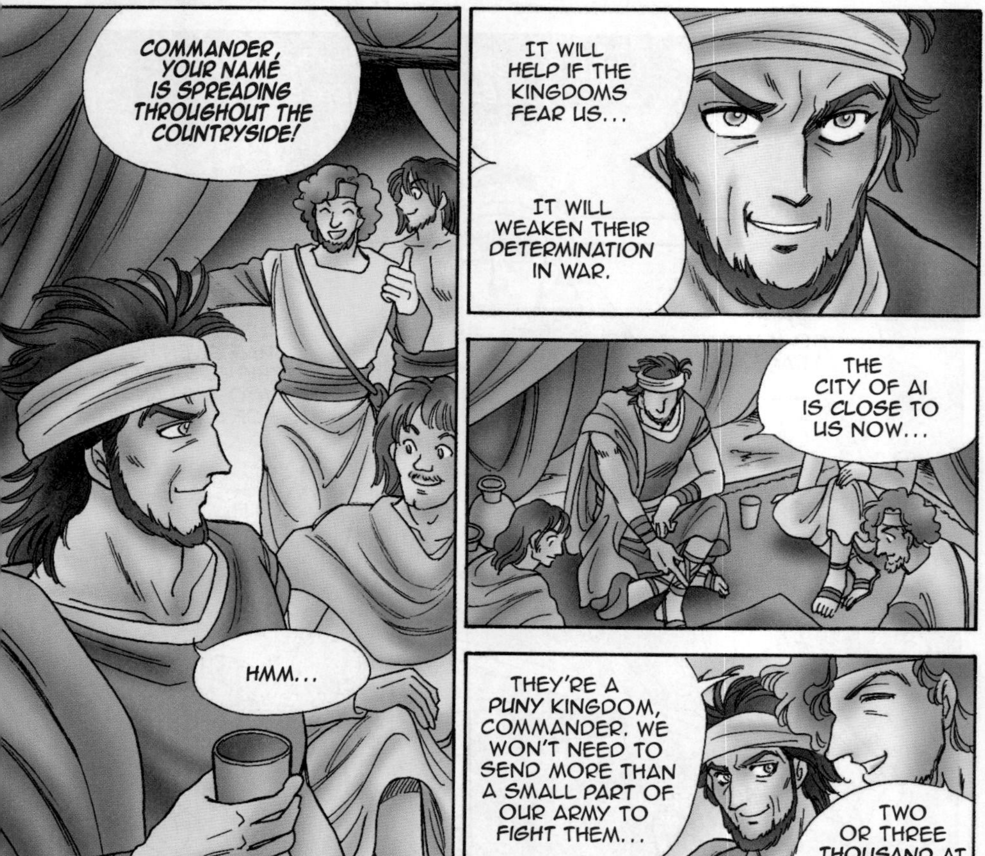
COMMANDER, YOUR NAME IS SPREADING THROUGHOUT THE COUNTRYSIDE!
HMM...
IT WILL HELP IF THE KINGDOMS FEAR US...
IT WILL WEAKEN THEIR DETERMINATION IN WAR.
THE CITY OF AI IS CLOSE TO US NOW...
THEY'RE A PUNY KINGDOM, COMMANDER. WE WON'T NEED TO SEND MORE THAN A SMALL PART OF OUR ARMY TO FIGHT THEM...
TWO OR THREE THOUSAND AT THE MOST.

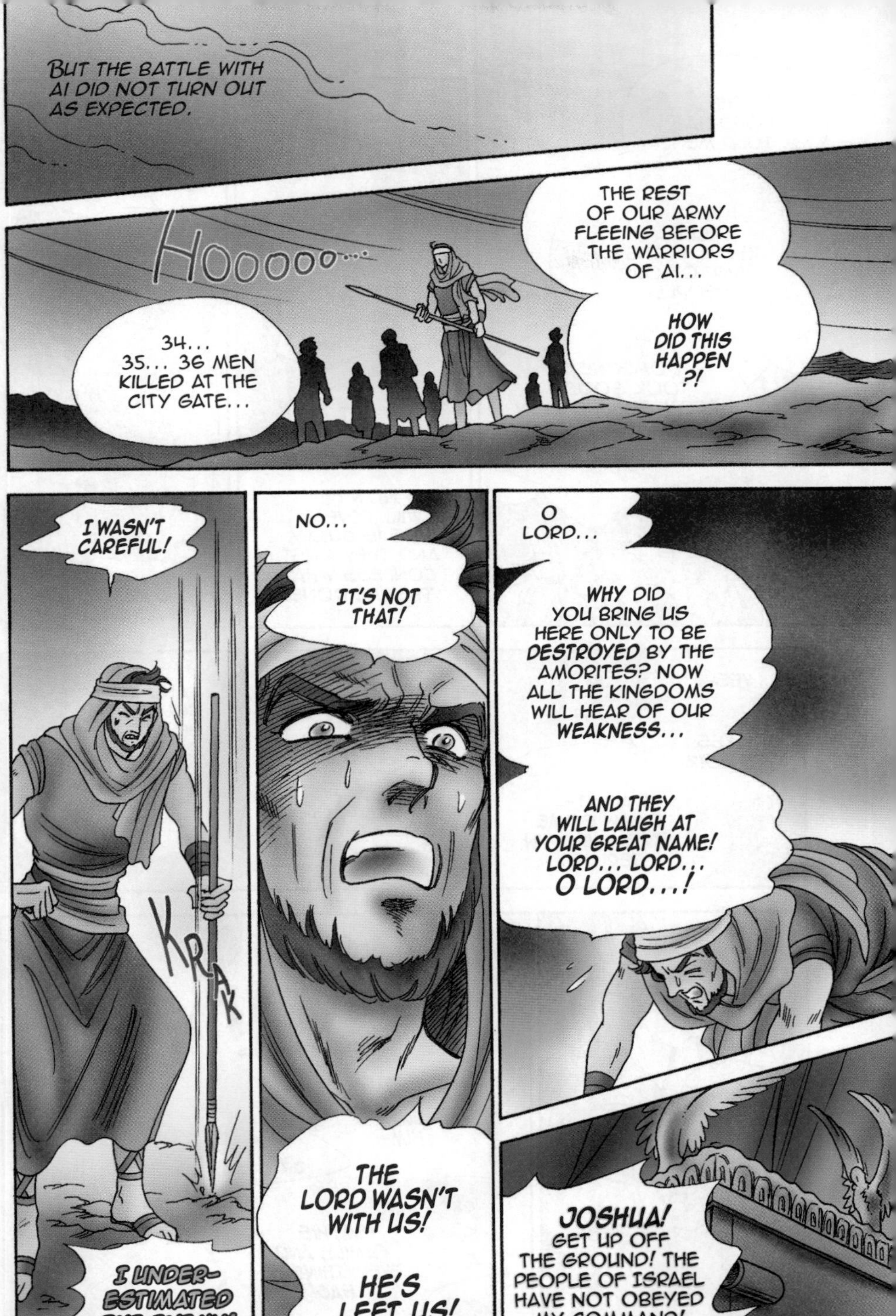
BUT THE BATTLE WITH AI DID NOT TURN OUT AS EXPECTED.
HOOOOO...
THE REST OF OUR ARMY FLEEING BEFORE THE WARRIORS OF AI...
34... 35... 36 MEN KILLED AT THE CITY GATE...
HOW DID THIS HAPPEN ?!
I WASN'T CAREFUL!
KRAK
I UNDER-ESTIMATED THE ENEMY!
NO...
IT'S NOT THAT!
THE LORD WASN'T WITH US!
HE'S LEFT US!
O LORD...
WHY DID YOU BRING US HERE ONLY TO BE DESTROYED BY THE AMORITES? NOW ALL THE KINGDOMS WILL HEAR OF OUR WEAKNESS...
AND THEY WILL LAUGH AT YOUR GREAT NAME! LORD... LORD... O LORD...!
JOSHUA! GET UP OFF THE GROUND! THE PEOPLE OF ISRAEL HAVE NOT OBEYED MY COMMAND!

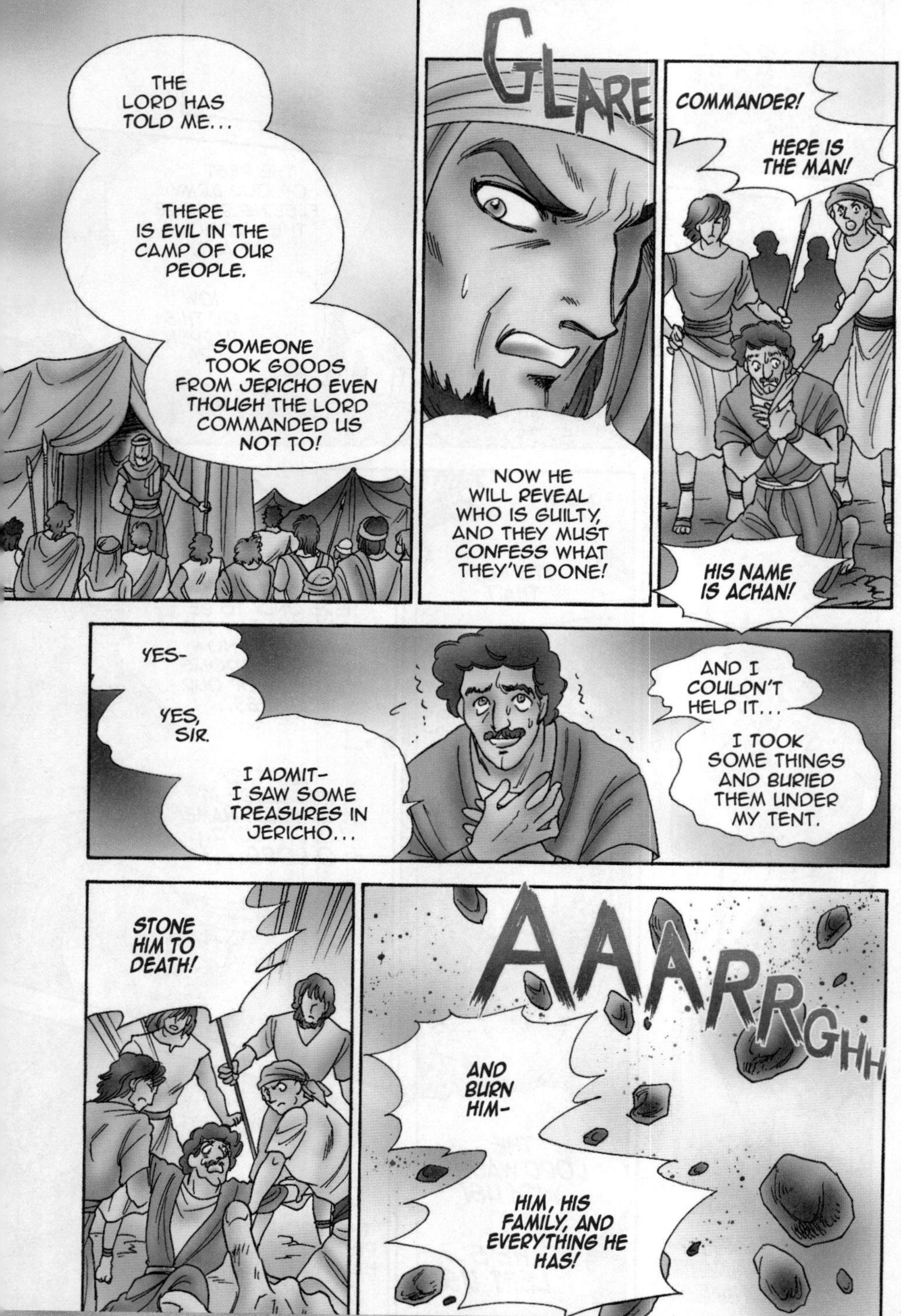
THE LORD HAS TOLD ME...
THERE IS EVIL IN THE CAMP OF OUR PEOPLE.
SOMEONE TOOK GOODS FROM JERICHO EVEN THOUGH THE LORD COMMANDED US NOT TO!
GLARE
NOW HE WILL REVEAL WHO IS GUILTY, AND THEY MUST CONFESS WHAT THEY'VE DONE!
COMMANDER!
HERE IS THE MAN!
HIS NAME IS ACHAN!
YES-
YES, SIR.
I ADMIT- I SAW SOME TREASURES IN JERICHO...
AND I COULDN'T HELP IT...
I TOOK SOME THINGS AND BURIED THEM UNDER MY TENT.
STONE HIM TO DEATH!
AND BURN HIM-
HIM, HIS FAMILY, AND EVERYTHING HE HAS!
AAARRGHH

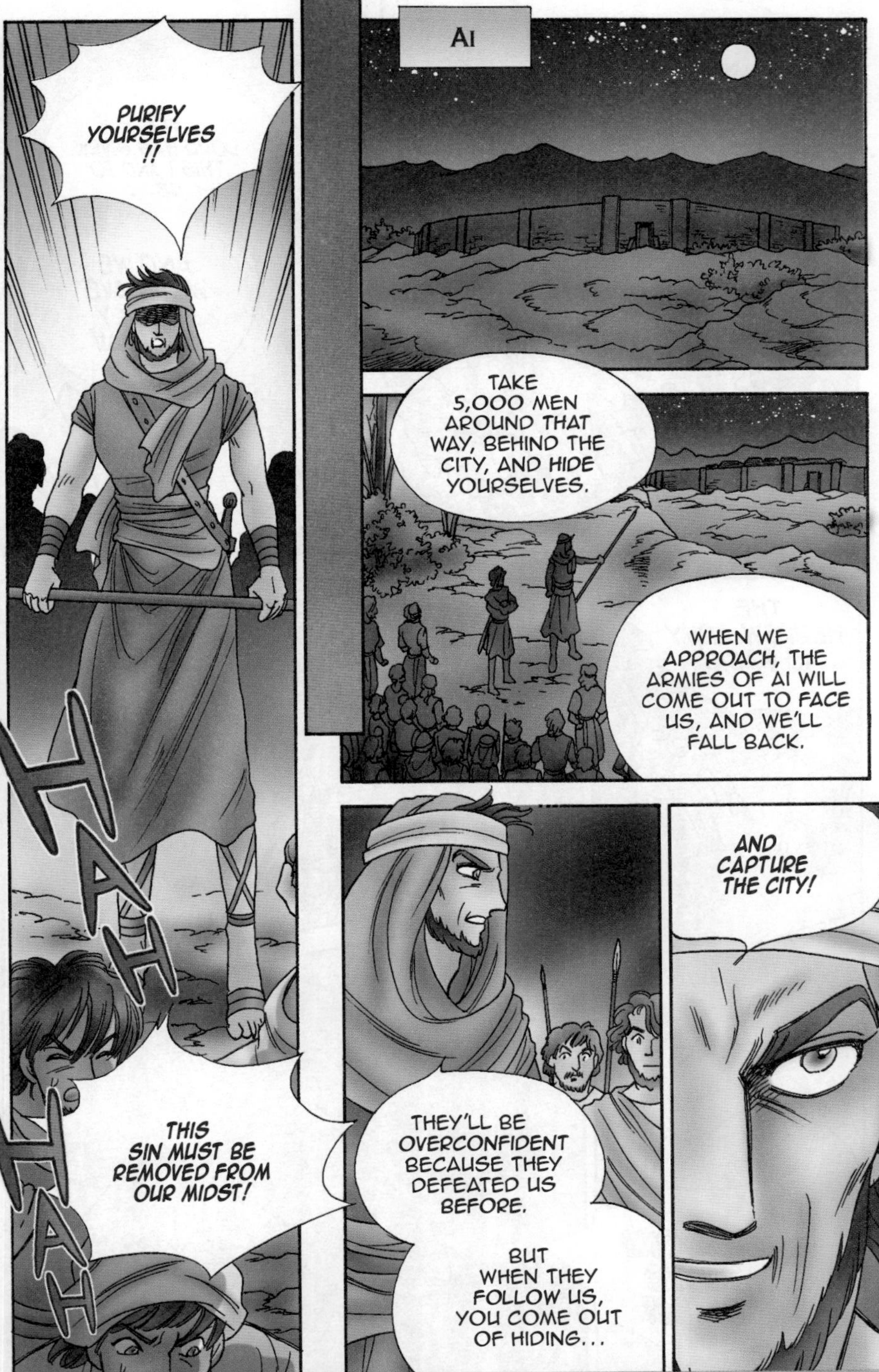
PURIFY YOURSELVES !!
HAH
HAH
THIS SIN MUST BE REMOVED FROM OUR MIDST!
AI
TAKE 5,000 MEN AROUND THAT WAY, BEHIND THE CITY, AND HIDE YOURSELVES.
WHEN WE APPROACH, THE ARMIES OF AI WILL COME OUT TO FACE US, AND WE'LL FALL BACK.
THEY'LL BE OVERCONFIDENT BECAUSE THEY DEFEATED US BEFORE.
BUT WHEN THEY FOLLOW US, YOU COME OUT OF HIDING...
AND CAPTURE THE CITY!

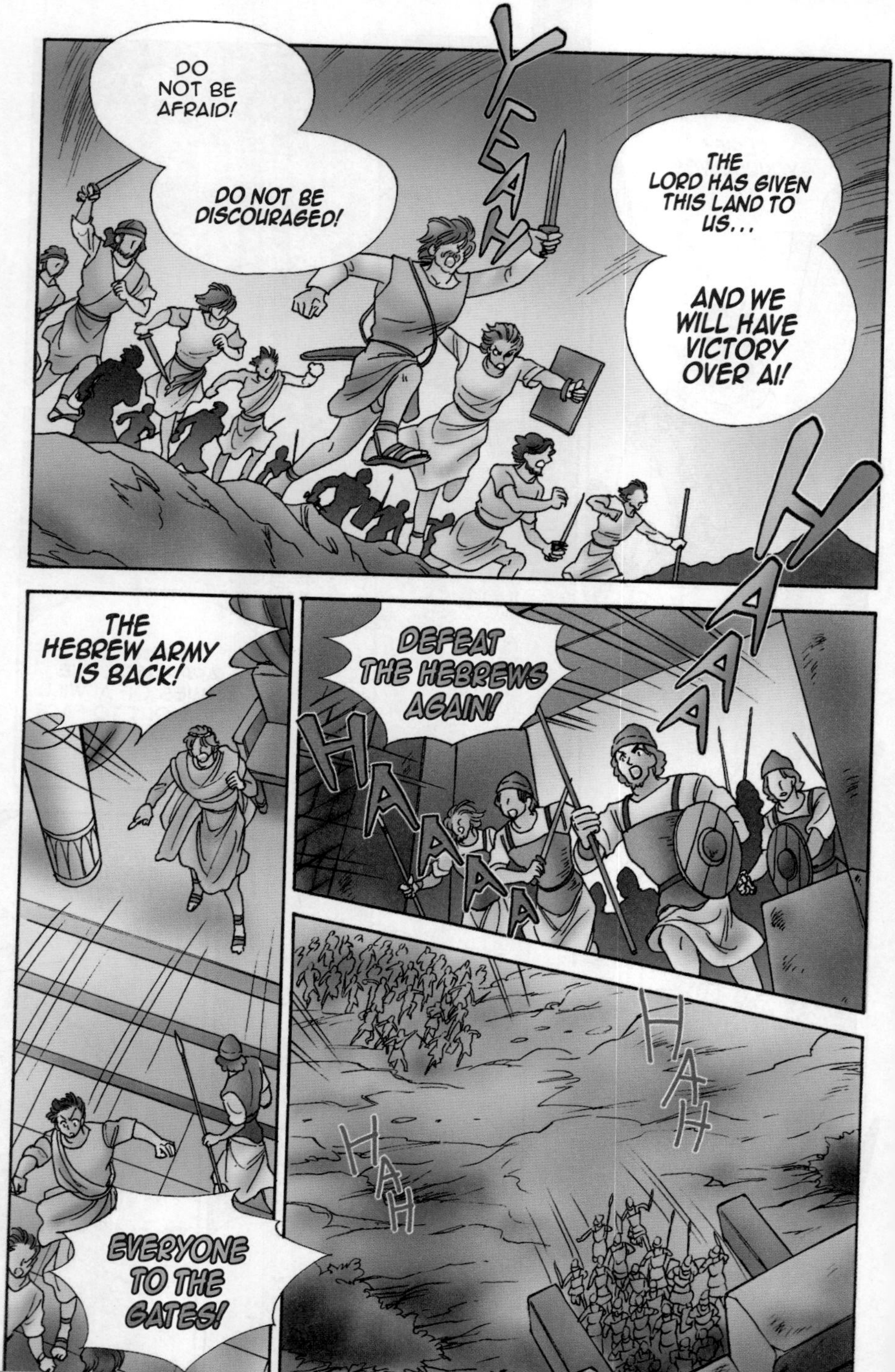
DO NOT BE AFRAID!
DO NOT BE DISCOURAGED!
YEAH
THE LORD HAS GIVEN THIS LAND TO US...
AND WE WILL HAVE VICTORY OVER AI!
HAAAA
THE HEBREW ARMY IS BACK!
DEFEAT THE HEBREWS AGAIN!
HAAAAA
EVERYONE TO THE GATES!
HAH
HAH

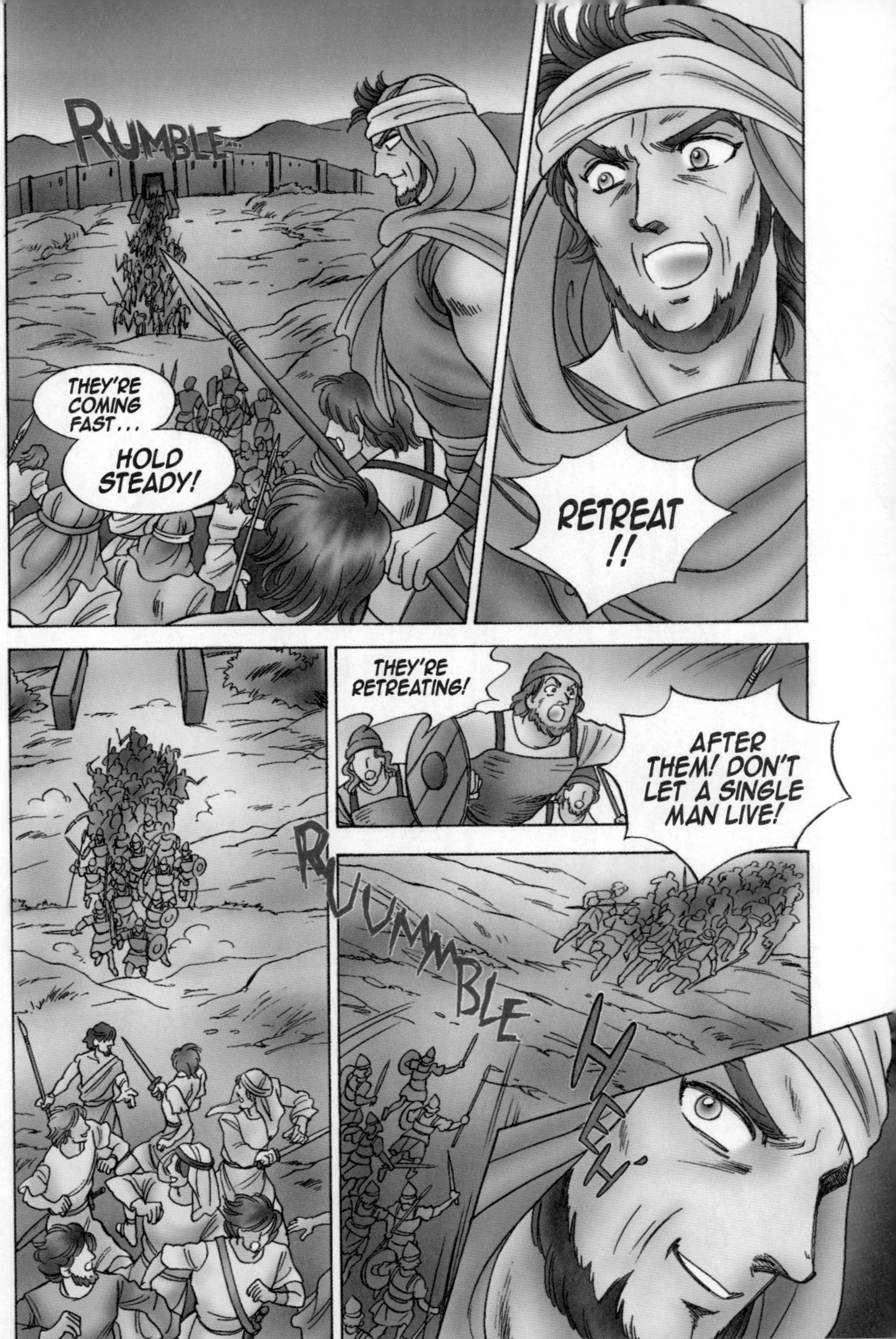
RUMBLE...
THEY'RE COMING FAST...
HOLD STEADY!
RETREAT !!
THEY'RE RETREATING!
AFTER THEM! DON'T LET A SINGLE MAN LIVE!
RUUMMBLE
HEH

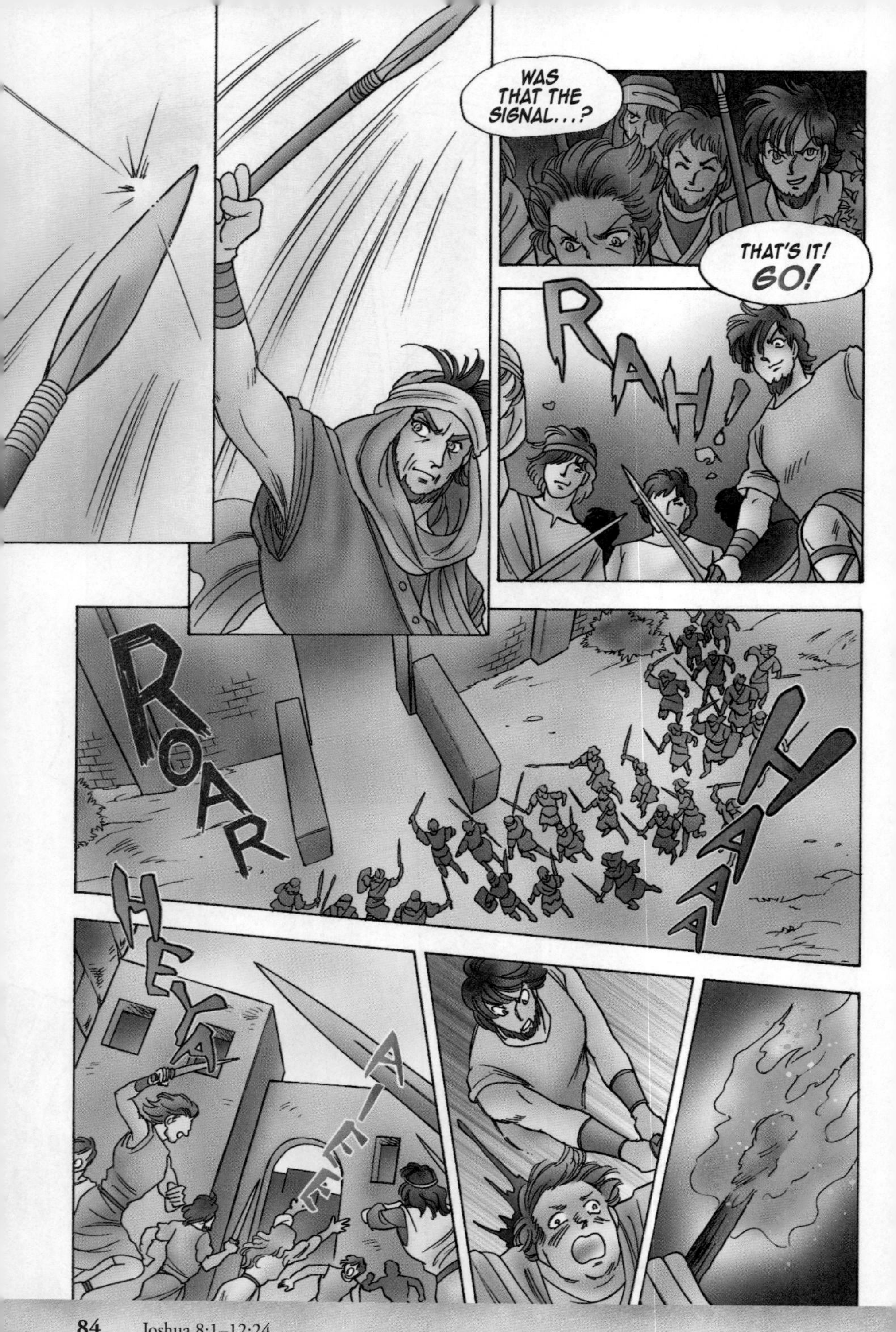
WAS THAT THE SIGNAL...?
THAT'S IT! GO!
RAH!
ROAR
HAAA
HEYA
AIEEE

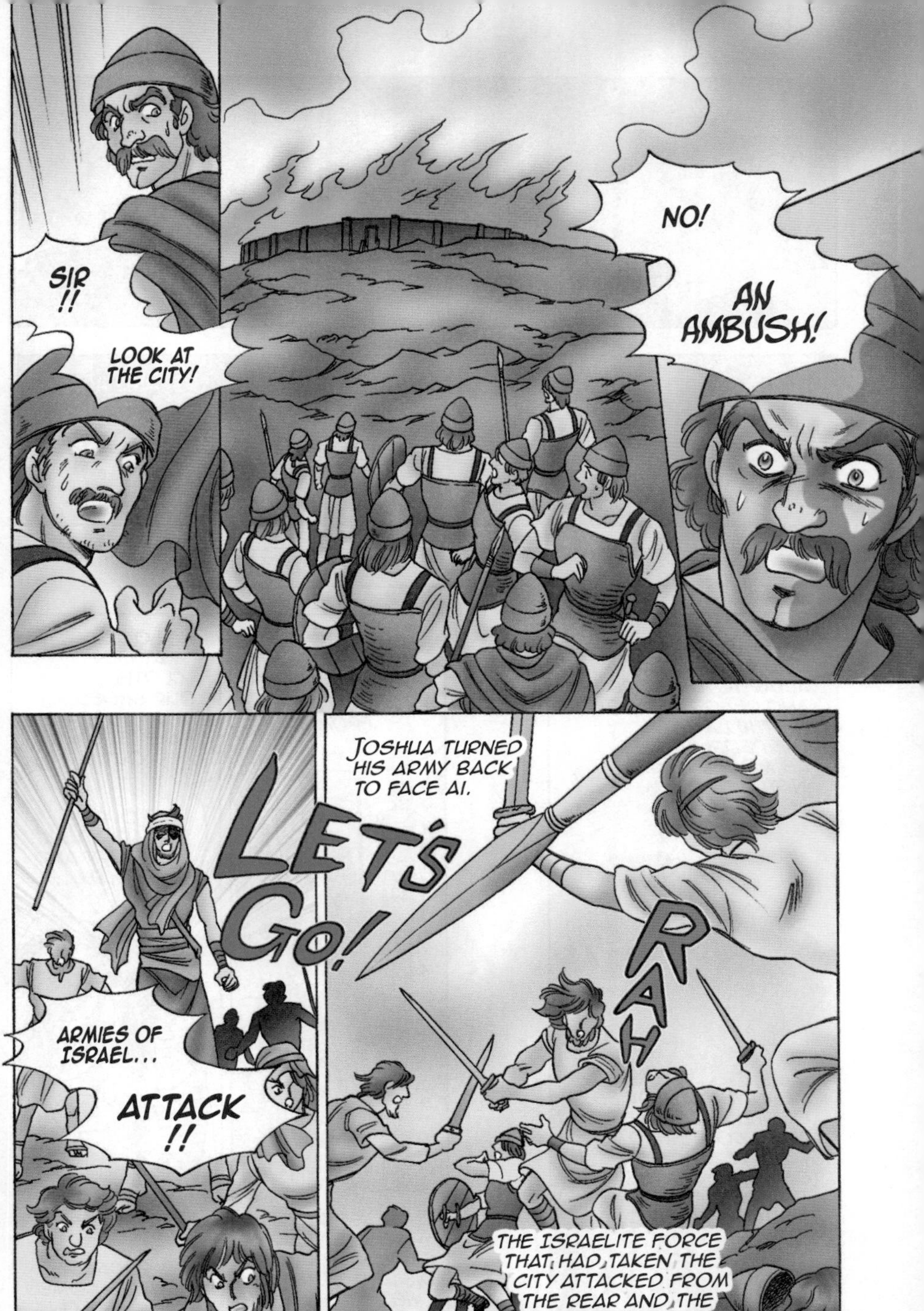
SIR !!
LOOK AT THE CITY!
NO!
AN AMBUSH!
ARMIES OF ISRAEL...
ATTACK !!
LET'S GO!
JOSHUA TURNED HIS ARMY BACK TO FACE AI.
RAH
THE ISRAELITE FORCE THAT HAD TAKEN THE CITY ATTACKED FROM THE REAR AND THE ARMY OF AI WAS SURROUNDED.

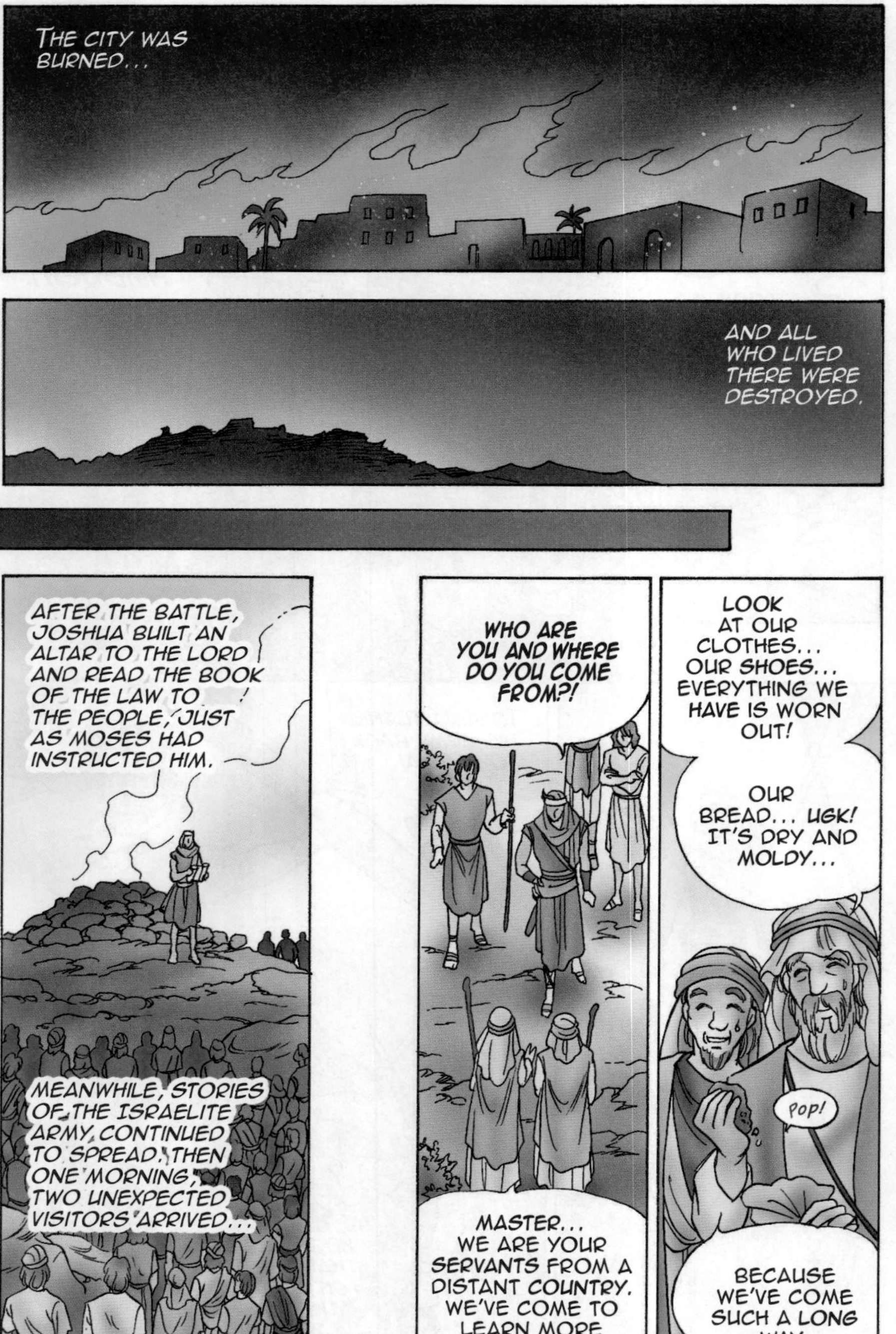
THE CITY WAS BURNED...
AND ALL WHO LIVED THERE WERE DESTROYED.
AFTER THE BATTLE, JOSHUA BUILT AN ALTAR TO THE LORD AND READ THE BOOK OF THE LAW TO THE PEOPLE, JUST AS MOSES HAD INSTRUCTED HIM.
MEANWHILE, STORIES OF THE ISRAELITE ARMY CONTINUED TO SPREAD. THEN ONE MORNING, TWO UNEXPECTED VISITORS ARRIVED...
WHO ARE YOU AND WHERE DO YOU COME FROM?!
MASTER... WE ARE YOUR SERVANTS FROM A DISTANT COUNTRY. WE'VE COME TO LEARN MORE ABOUT YOUR GOD.
LOOK AT OUR CLOTHES... OUR SHOES... EVERYTHING WE HAVE IS WORN OUT!
OUR BREAD... UGK! IT'S DRY AND MOLDY...
POP!
BECAUSE WE'VE COME SUCH A LONG WAY.

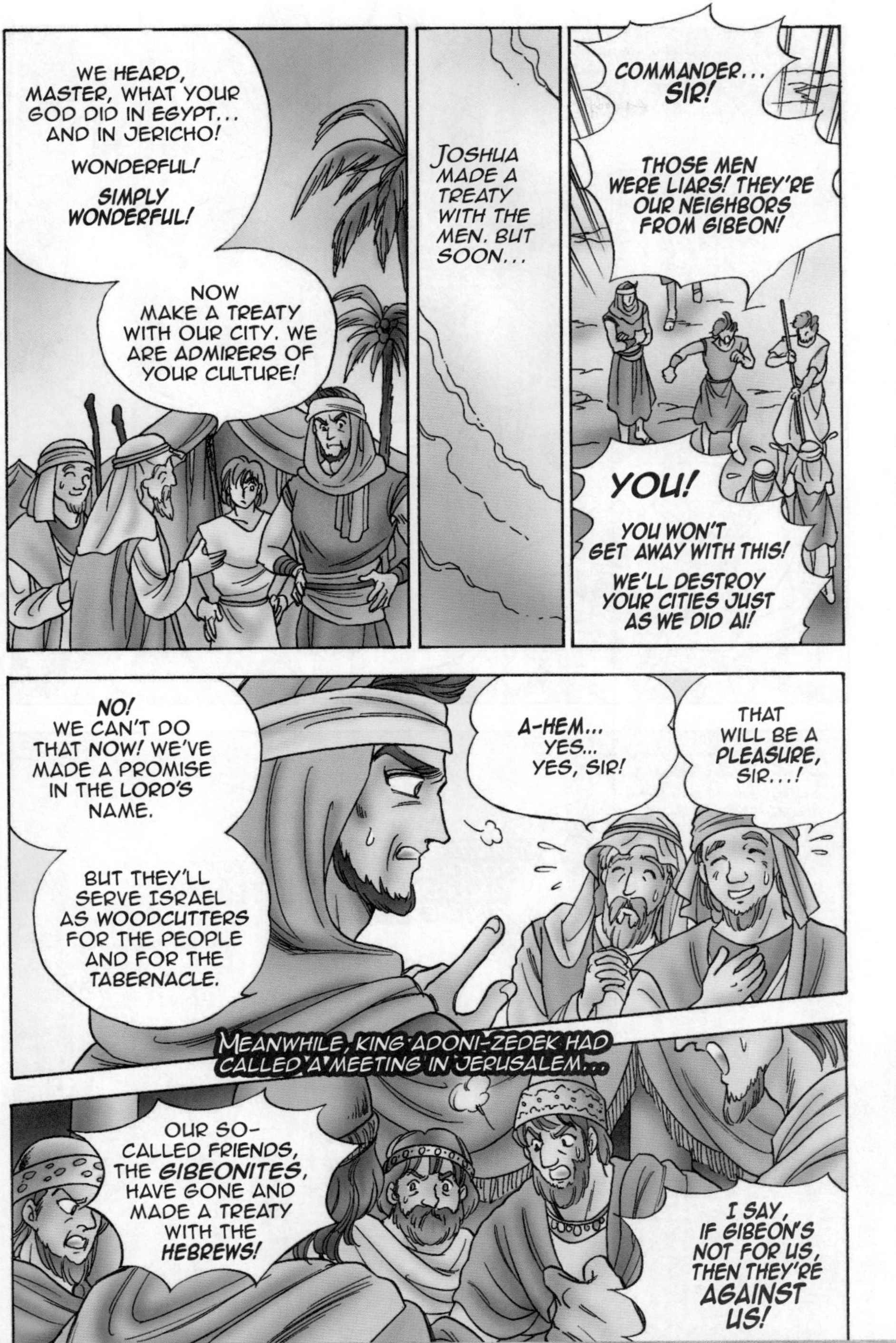

WE HEARD, MASTER, WHAT YOUR GOD DID IN EGYPT... AND IN JERICHO!
WONDERFUL!
SIMPLY WONDERFUL!
NOW MAKE A TREATY WITH OUR CITY. WE ARE ADMIRERS OF YOUR CULTURE!
JOSHUA MADE A TREATY WITH THE MEN. BUT SOON...
COMMANDER... SIR!
THOSE MEN WERE LIARS! THEY'RE OUR NEIGHBORS FROM GIBEON!
YOU!
YOU WON'T GET AWAY WITH THIS!
WE'LL DESTROY YOUR CITIES JUST AS WE DID AI!
NO! WE CAN'T DO THAT NOW! WE'VE MADE A PROMISE IN THE LORD'S NAME.
BUT THEY'LL SERVE ISRAEL AS WOODCUTTERS FOR THE PEOPLE AND FOR THE TABERNACLE.
A-HEM... YES... YES, SIR!
THAT WILL BE A PLEASURE, SIR...!
MEANWHILE, KING ADONI-ZEDEK HAD CALLED A MEETING IN JERUSALEM...
OUR SO-CALLED FRIENDS, THE GIBEONITES, HAVE GONE AND MADE A TREATY WITH THE HEBREWS!
I SAY, IF GIBEON'S NOT FOR US, THEN THEY'RE AGAINST US!

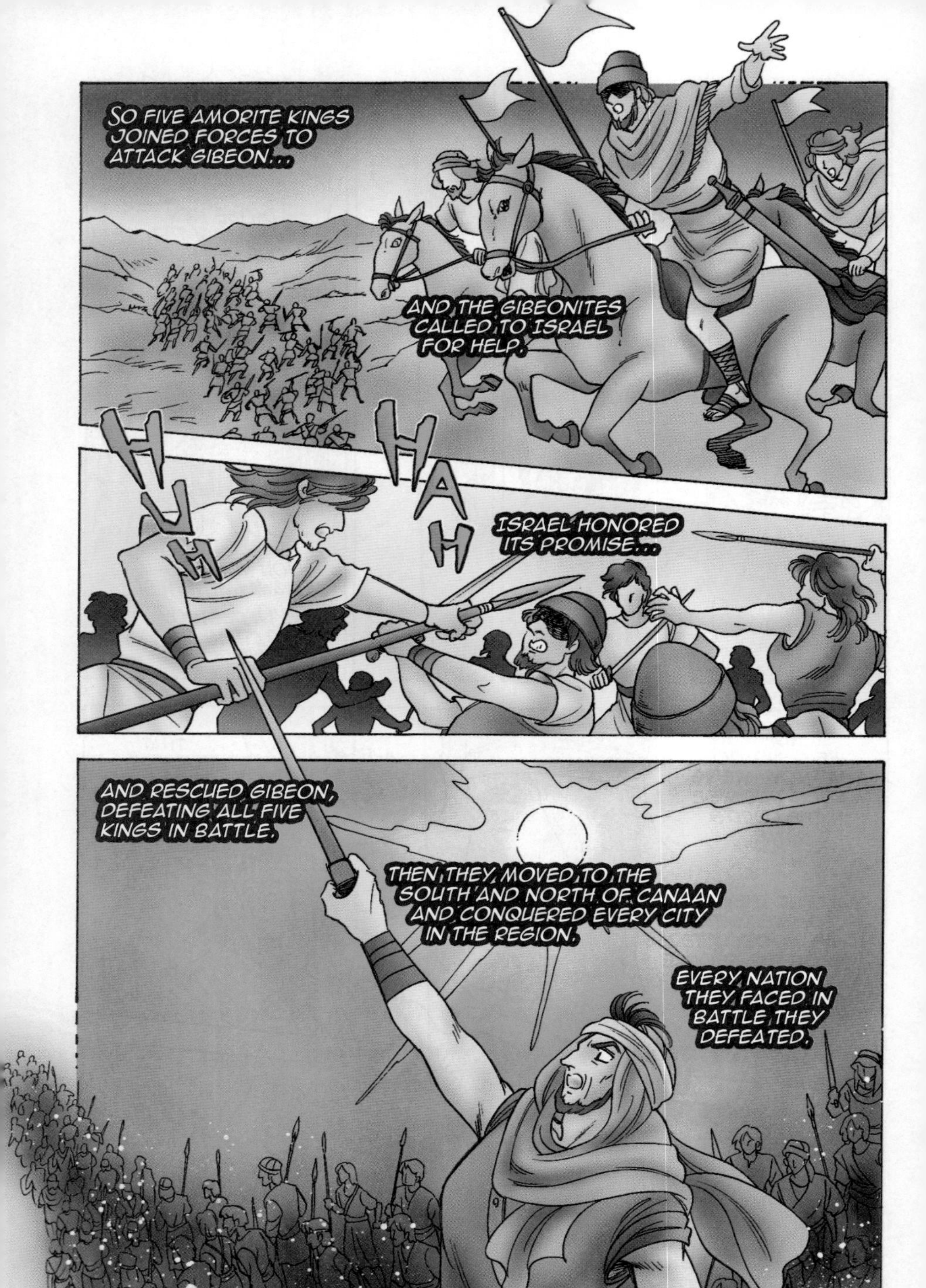
SO FIVE AMORITE KINGS JOINED FORCES TO ATTACK GIBEON...
AND THE GIBEONITES CALLED TO ISRAEL FOR HELP.
HUH
HAH
ISRAEL HONORED ITS PROMISE...
AND RESCUED GIBEON, DEFEATING ALL FIVE KINGS IN BATTLE.
THEN THEY MOVED TO THE SOUTH AND NORTH OF CANAAN AND CONQUERED EVERY CITY IN THE REGION.
EVERY NATION THEY FACED IN BATTLE THEY DEFEATED.

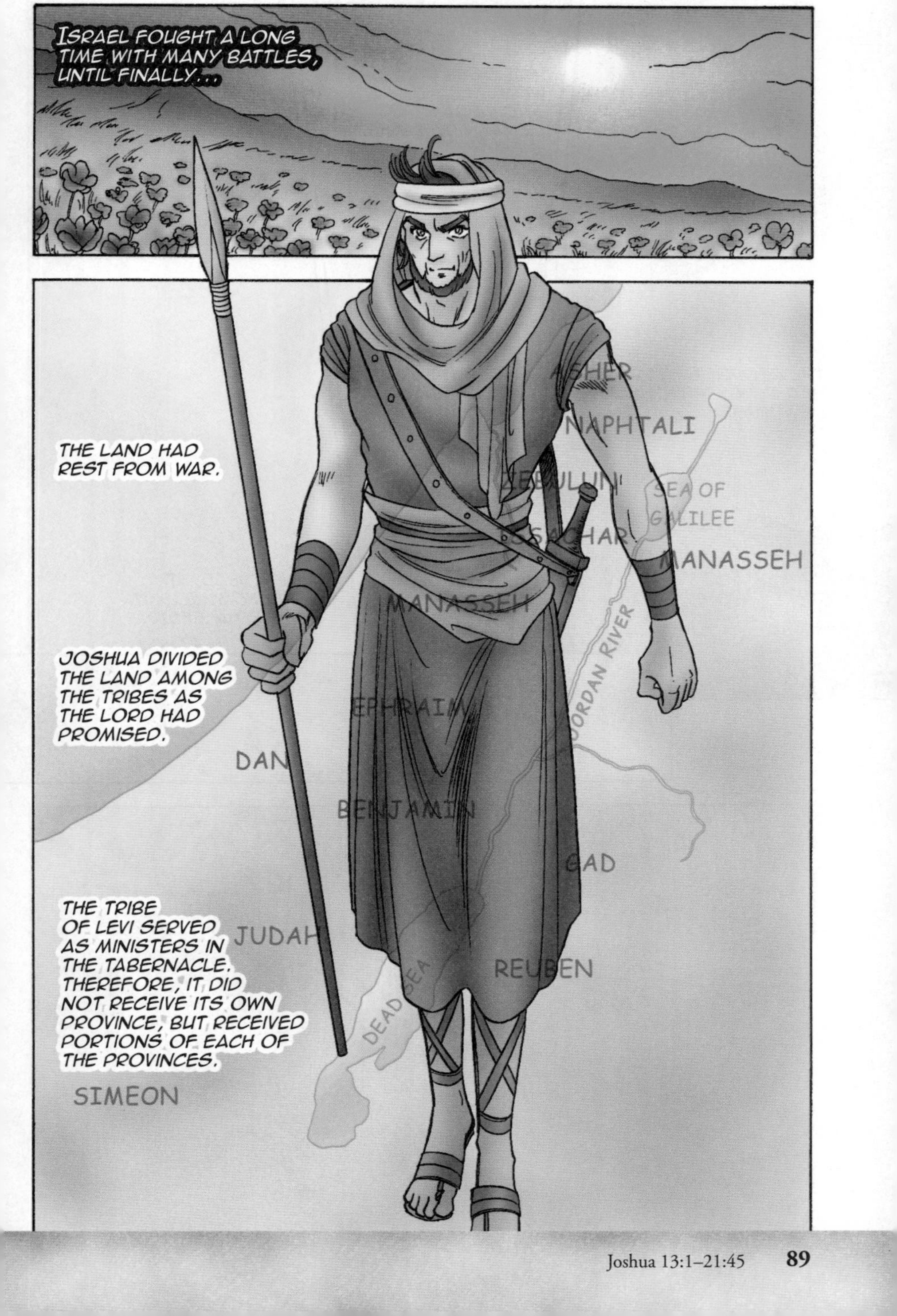
ISRAEL FOUGHT A LONG TIME WITH MANY BATTLES, UNTIL FINALLY...
THE LAND HAD REST FROM WAR.
JOSHUA DIVIDED THE LAND AMONG THE TRIBES AS THE LORD HAD PROMISED.
THE TRIBE OF LEVI SERVED AS MINISTERS IN THE TABERNACLE. THEREFORE, IT DID NOT RECEIVE ITS OWN PROVINCE, BUT RECEIVED PORTIONS OF EACH OF THE PROVINCES.
NAPHTALI
SEA OF GALILEE
MANASSEH
MANASSEH
DAN
GAD
JUDAH
REUBEN
SIMEON

AFTER NEARLY 50 YEARS OF TRAVELING, GATHERING FOOD, FINDING WATER, AND LIVING IN TENTS...

ALMOST 500 YEARS EARLIER, JACOB'S SON JOSEPH HAD PREDICTED THAT SOMEDAY ISRAEL WOULD LEAVE EGYPT AND RETURN TO CANAAN. WHEN HE DIED, HE TOLD THEM TO TAKE HIS BONES WITH THEM.

THE PEOPLE OF ISRAEL HAD COME INTO THEIR NEW HOME.

HIS BONES WERE FINALLY BURIED NEAR THE TOWN OF SHECHEM.

AND THERE, AT SHECHEM, JOSHUA CALLED A MEETING.

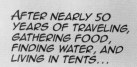

CHIRP...

CHIRP...

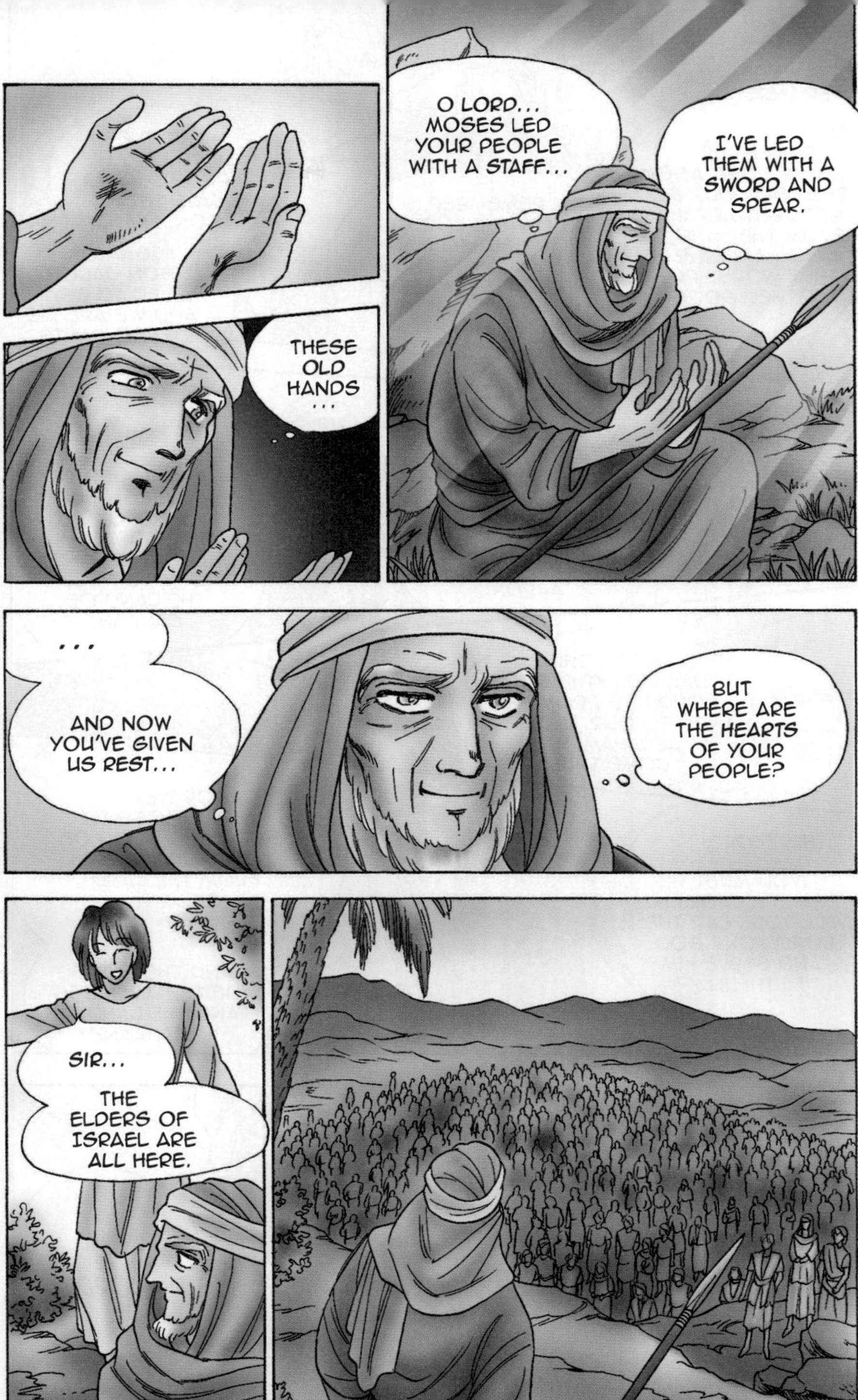
O LORD... MOSES LED YOUR PEOPLE WITH A STAFF...
I'VE LED THEM WITH A SWORD AND SPEAR.
THESE OLD HANDS ...
...
AND NOW YOU'VE GIVEN US REST...
BUT WHERE ARE THE HEARTS OF YOUR PEOPLE?
SIR...
THE ELDERS OF ISRAEL ARE ALL HERE.

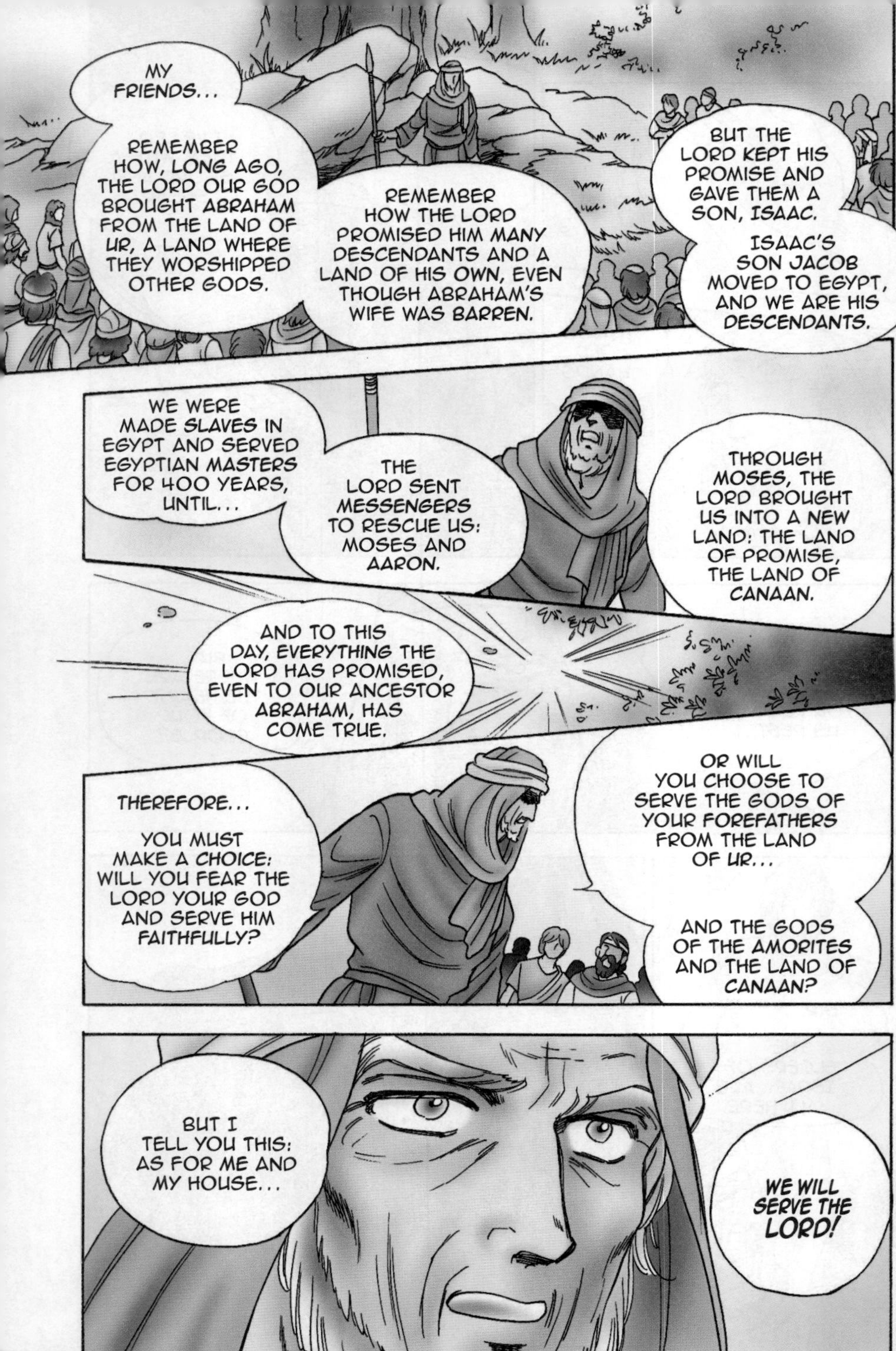
MY FRIENDS...
REMEMBER HOW, LONG AGO, THE LORD OUR GOD BROUGHT ABRAHAM FROM THE LAND OF UR, A LAND WHERE THEY WORSHIPPED OTHER GODS.
REMEMBER HOW THE LORD PROMISED HIM MANY DESCENDANTS AND A LAND OF HIS OWN, EVEN THOUGH ABRAHAM'S WIFE WAS BARREN.
BUT THE LORD KEPT HIS PROMISE AND GAVE THEM A SON, ISAAC.
ISAAC'S SON JACOB MOVED TO EGYPT, AND WE ARE HIS DESCENDANTS.
WE WERE MADE SLAVES IN EGYPT AND SERVED EGYPTIAN MASTERS FOR 400 YEARS, UNTIL...
THE LORD SENT MESSENGERS TO RESCUE US: MOSES AND AARON.
THROUGH MOSES, THE LORD BROUGHT US INTO A NEW LAND: THE LAND OF PROMISE, THE LAND OF CANAAN.
AND TO THIS DAY, EVERYTHING THE LORD HAS PROMISED, EVEN TO OUR ANCESTOR ABRAHAM, HAS COME TRUE.
THEREFORE...
YOU MUST MAKE A CHOICE: WILL YOU FEAR THE LORD YOUR GOD AND SERVE HIM FAITHFULLY?
OR WILL YOU CHOOSE TO SERVE THE GODS OF YOUR FOREFATHERS FROM THE LAND OF UR...
AND THE GODS OF THE AMORITES AND THE LAND OF CANAAN?
BUT I TELL YOU THIS: AS FOR ME AND MY HOUSE...
WE WILL SERVE THE LORD!

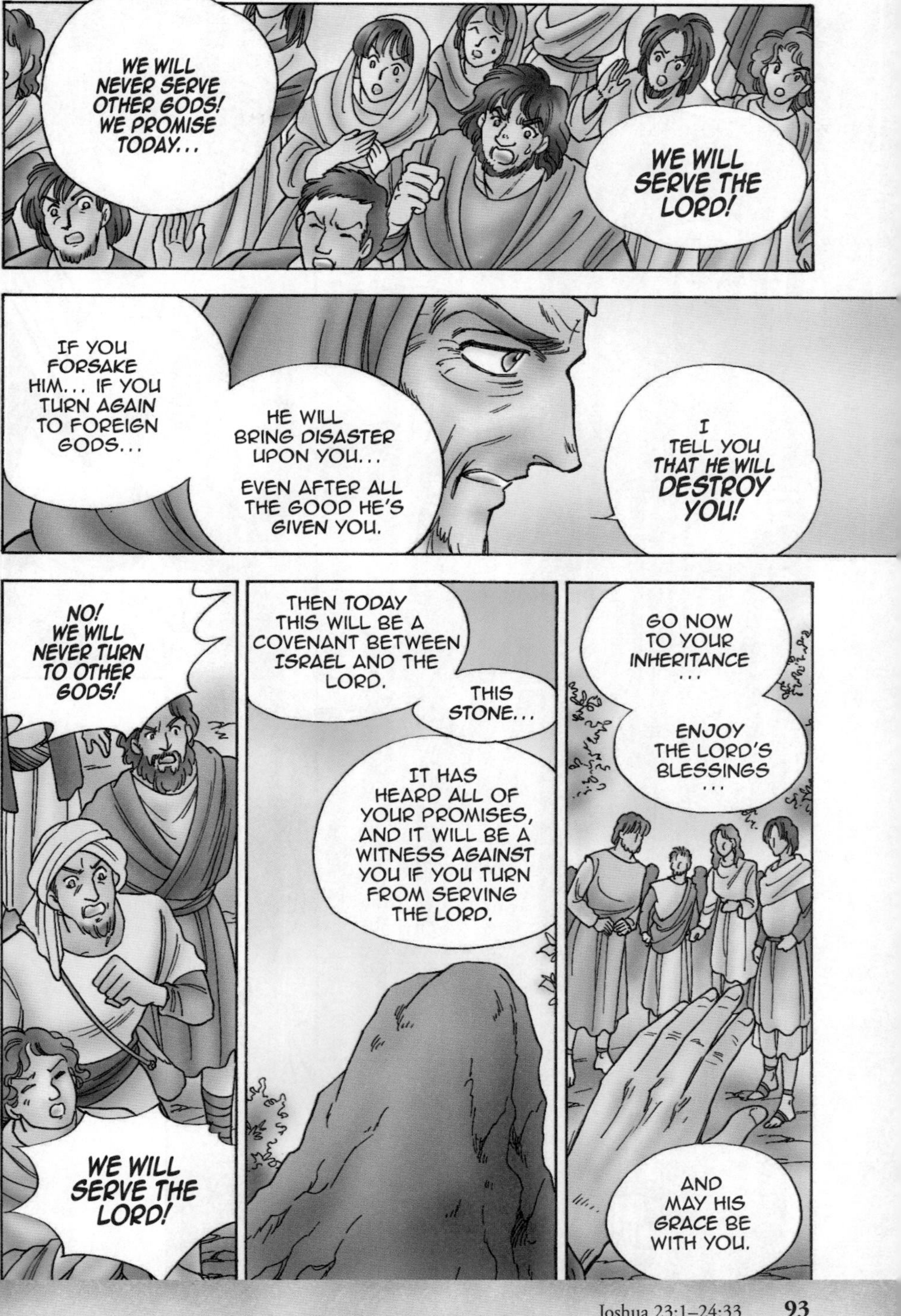
WE WILL NEVER SERVE OTHER GODS! WE PROMISE TODAY...
WE WILL SERVE THE LORD!
IF YOU FORSAKE HIM... IF YOU TURN AGAIN TO FOREIGN GODS...
HE WILL BRING DISASTER UPON YOU...
EVEN AFTER ALL THE GOOD HE'S GIVEN YOU.
I TELL YOU THAT HE WILL DESTROY YOU!
NO! WE WILL NEVER TURN TO OTHER GODS!
WE WILL SERVE THE LORD!
THEN TODAY THIS WILL BE A COVENANT BETWEEN ISRAEL AND THE LORD.
THIS STONE...
IT HAS HEARD ALL OF YOUR PROMISES, AND IT WILL BE A WITNESS AGAINST YOU IF YOU TURN FROM SERVING THE LORD.
GO NOW TO YOUR INHERITANCE...
ENJOY THE LORD'S BLESSINGS...
AND MAY HIS GRACE BE WITH YOU.

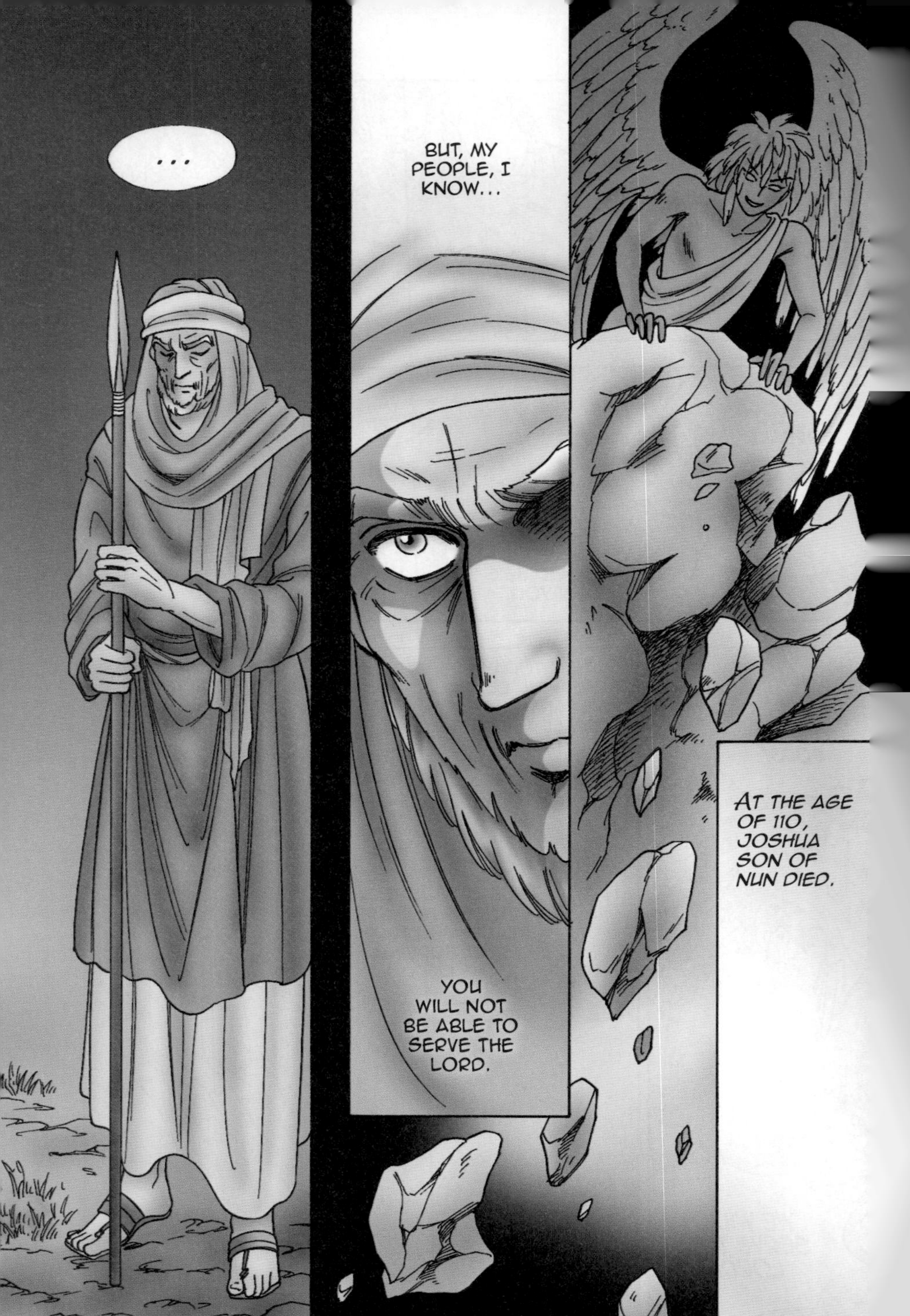
...
BUT, MY PEOPLE, I KNOW...
YOU WILL NOT BE ABLE TO SERVE THE LORD.
AT THE AGE OF 110, JOSHUA SON OF NUN DIED.

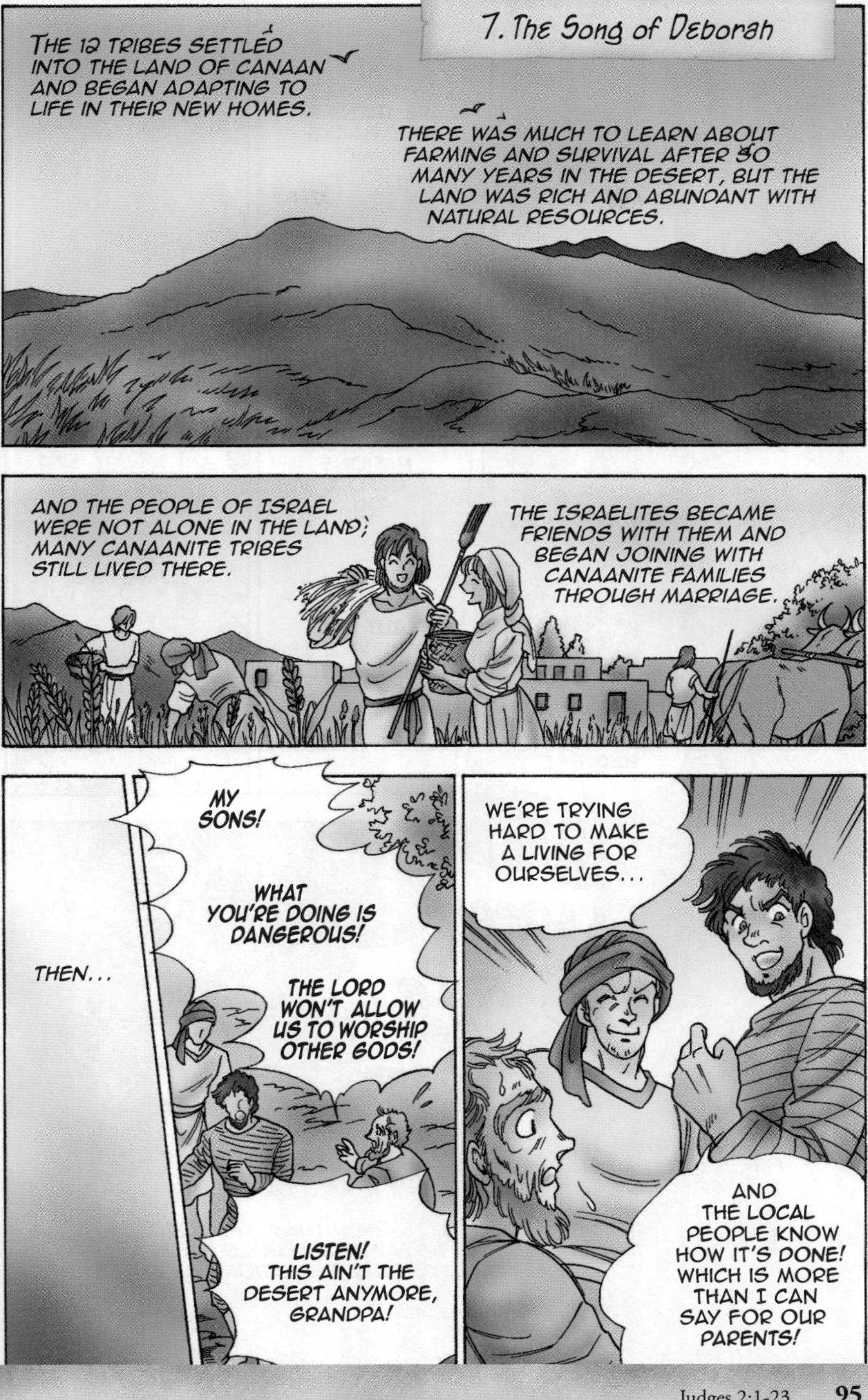
7. The Song of Deborah
THE 12 TRIBES SETTLED INTO THE LAND OF CANAAN AND BEGAN ADAPTING TO LIFE IN THEIR NEW HOMES.
THERE WAS MUCH TO LEARN ABOUT FARMING AND SURVIVAL AFTER SO MANY YEARS IN THE DESERT, BUT THE LAND WAS RICH AND ABUNDANT WITH NATURAL RESOURCES.
AND THE PEOPLE OF ISRAEL WERE NOT ALONE IN THE LAND; MANY CANAANITE TRIBES STILL LIVED THERE.
THE ISRAELITES BECAME FRIENDS WITH THEM AND BEGAN JOINING WITH CANAANITE FAMILIES THROUGH MARRIAGE.
THEN...
MY SONS!
WHAT YOU'RE DOING IS DANGEROUS!
THE LORD WON'T ALLOW US TO WORSHIP OTHER GODS!
LISTEN! THIS AIN'T THE DESERT ANYMORE, GRANDPA!
WE'RE TRYING HARD TO MAKE A LIVING FOR OURSELVES...
AND THE LOCAL PEOPLE KNOW HOW IT'S DONE! WHICH IS MORE THAN I CAN SAY FOR OUR PARENTS!

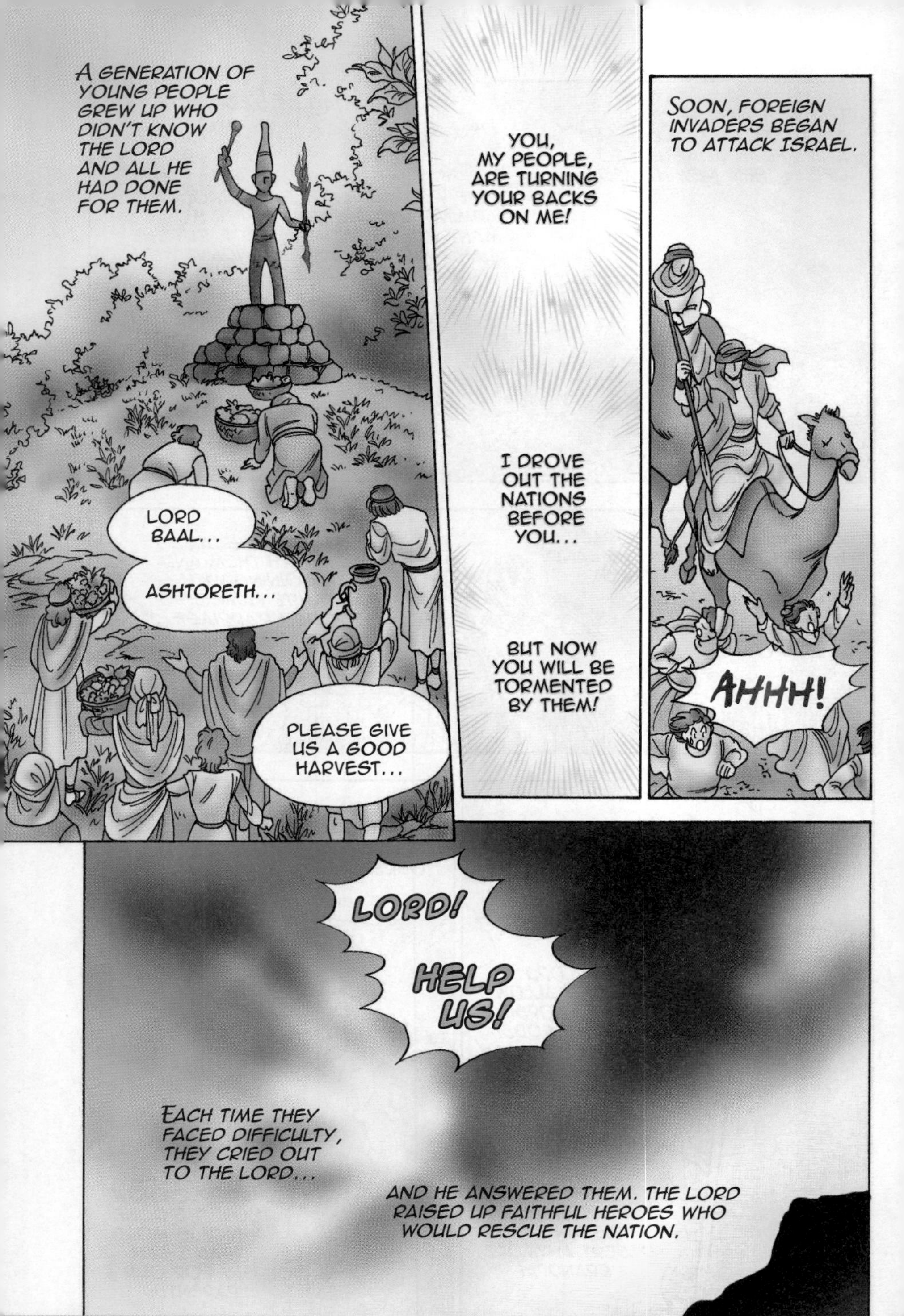
A GENERATION OF YOUNG PEOPLE GREW UP WHO DIDN'T KNOW THE LORD AND ALL HE HAD DONE FOR THEM.
LORD BAAL...
ASHTORETH...
PLEASE GIVE US A GOOD HARVEST...
YOU, MY PEOPLE, ARE TURNING YOUR BACKS ON ME!
I DROVE OUT THE NATIONS BEFORE YOU...
BUT NOW YOU WILL BE TORMENTED BY THEM!
SOON, FOREIGN INVADERS BEGAN TO ATTACK ISRAEL.
AHHH!
LORD!
HELP US!
EACH TIME THEY FACED DIFFICULTY, THEY CRIED OUT TO THE LORD...
AND HE ANSWERED THEM. THE LORD RAISED UP FAITHFUL HEROES WHO WOULD RESCUE THE NATION.

ONE OF THESE JUDGES WAS A PROPHET NAMED DEBORAH...

SHE HELD COURT UNDER A PALM TREE IN THE HILL COUNTRY OF EPHRAIM.

MADAM DEBORAH...

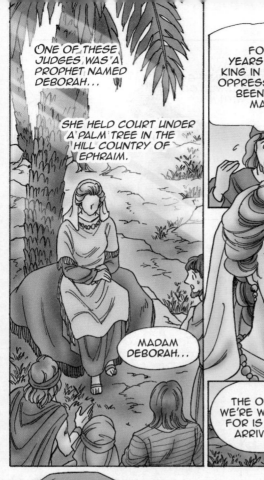

FOR 20 YEARS NOW THE KING IN HAZOR HAS OPPRESSED US! HE'S BEEN A BRUTAL MASTER...

ISN'T THERE ANY WAY YOU CAN HELP US?

YES, THE LORD HAS HEARD YOU...

AND HELP IS ON ITS WAY. IN FACT...

THE ONE WE'RE WAITING FOR IS JUST ARRIVING.

I AM BARAK.

I HAVE COME AT YOUR REQUEST.

DEBORAH?

BARAK...

LISTEN TO THE LORD'S COMMAND:

"CALL 10,000 MEN FROM NAPHTALI AND ZEBULUN TO MOUNT TABOR."

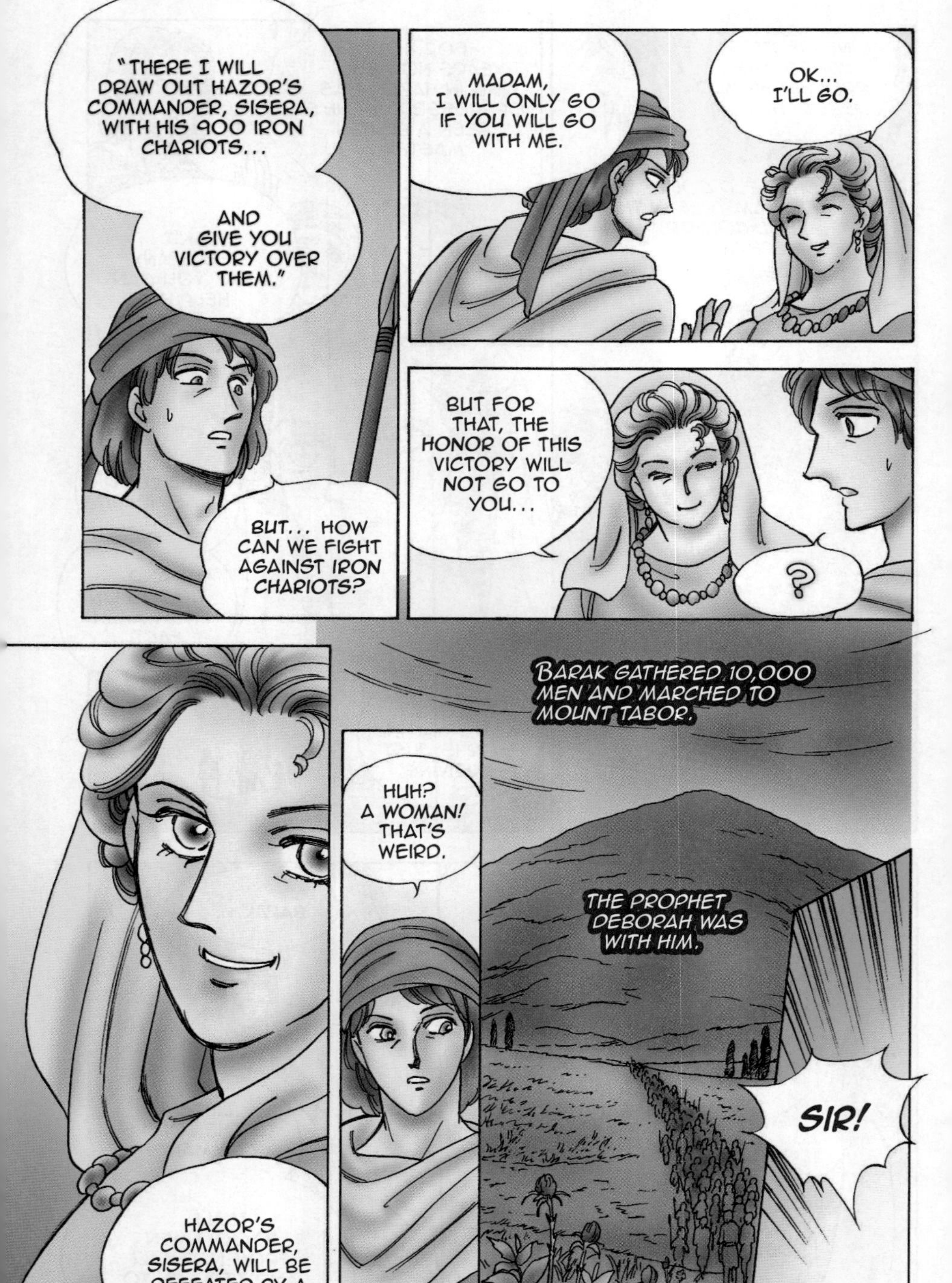

"THERE I WILL DRAW OUT HAZOR'S COMMANDER, SISERA, WITH HIS 900 IRON CHARIOTS...
AND GIVE YOU VICTORY OVER THEM."
BUT... HOW CAN WE FIGHT AGAINST IRON CHARIOTS?
MADAM, I WILL ONLY GO IF YOU WILL GO WITH ME.
OK... I'LL GO.
BUT FOR THAT, THE HONOR OF THIS VICTORY WILL NOT GO TO YOU...
?
HAZOR'S COMMANDER, SISERA, WILL BE DEFEATED BY A WOMAN.
HUH? A WOMAN! THAT'S WEIRD.
BARAK GATHERED 10,000 MEN AND MARCHED TO MOUNT TABOR.
THE PROPHET DEBORAH WAS WITH HIM.
SIR!

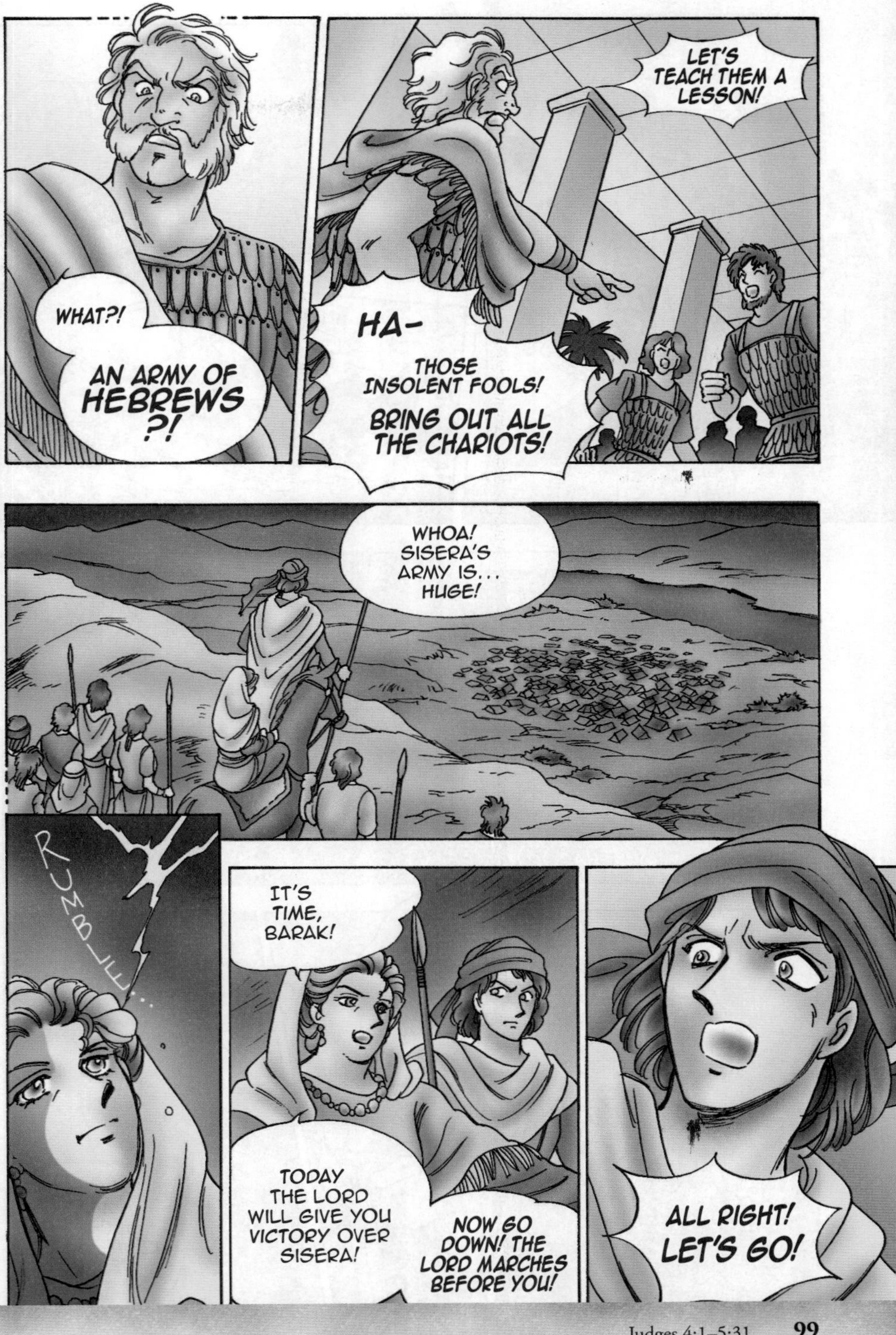
WHAT?!
AN ARMY OF HEBREWS ?!
LET'S TEACH THEM A LESSON!
HA-
THOSE INSOLENT FOOLS!
BRING OUT ALL THE CHARIOTS!
WHOA! SISERA'S ARMY IS... HUGE!
RUMBLE...
IT'S TIME, BARAK!
TODAY THE LORD WILL GIVE YOU VICTORY OVER SISERA!
NOW GO DOWN! THE LORD MARCHES BEFORE YOU!
ALL RIGHT! LET'S GO!

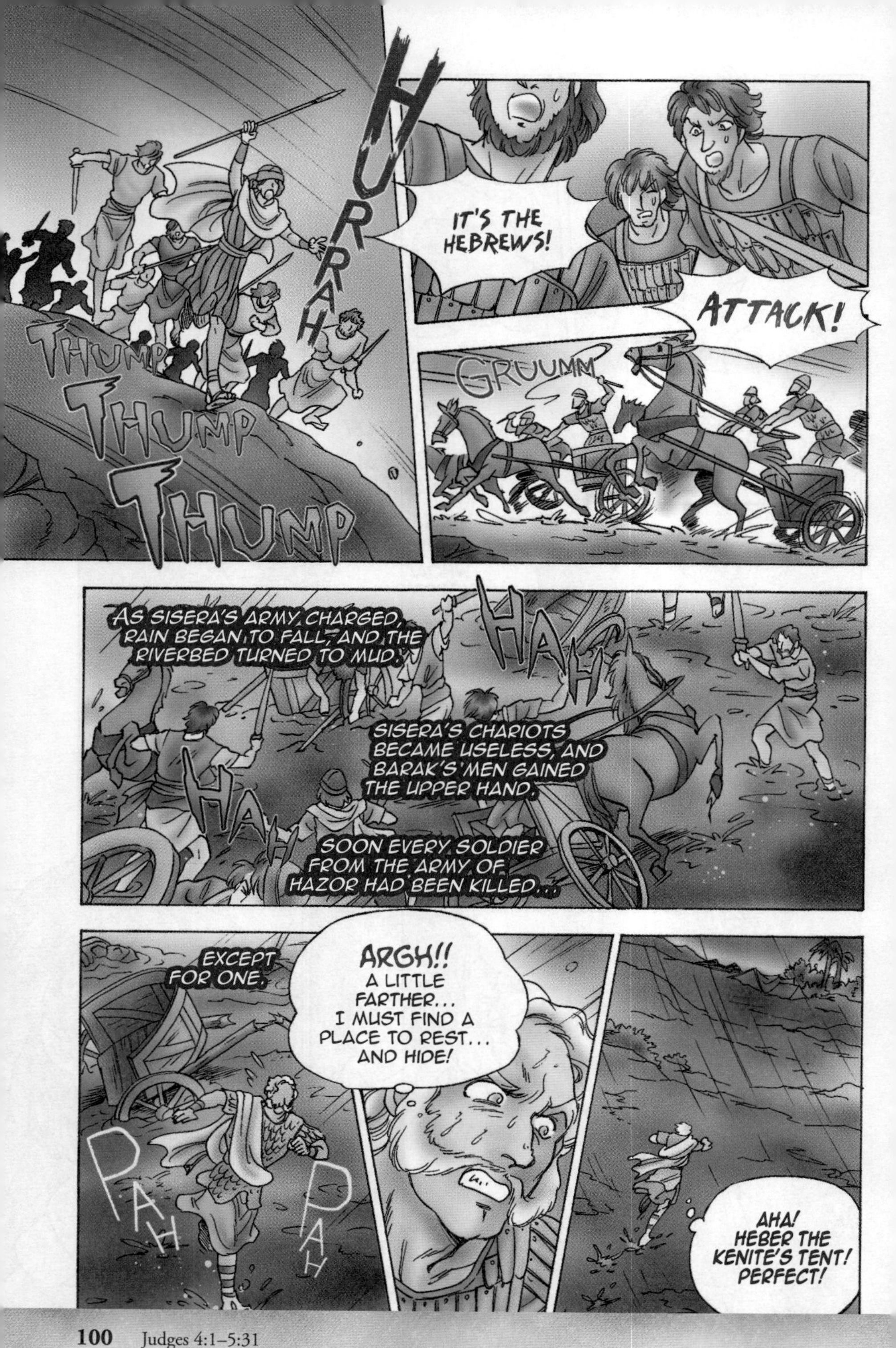
HURRAH
THUMP
THUMP
THUMP
IT'S THE HEBREWS!
ATTACK!
GRUUMM
AS SISERA'S ARMY CHARGED, RAIN BEGAN TO FALL, AND THE RIVERBED TURNED TO MUD.
HAH
SISERA'S CHARIOTS BECAME USELESS, AND BARAK'S MEN GAINED THE UPPER HAND.
HAH
SOON EVERY SOLDIER FROM THE ARMY OF HAZOR HAD BEEN KILLED...
EXCEPT FOR ONE.
ARGH!! A LITTLE FARTHER... I MUST FIND A PLACE TO REST... AND HIDE!
PAH
PAH
AHA! HEBER THE KENITE'S TENT! PERFECT!

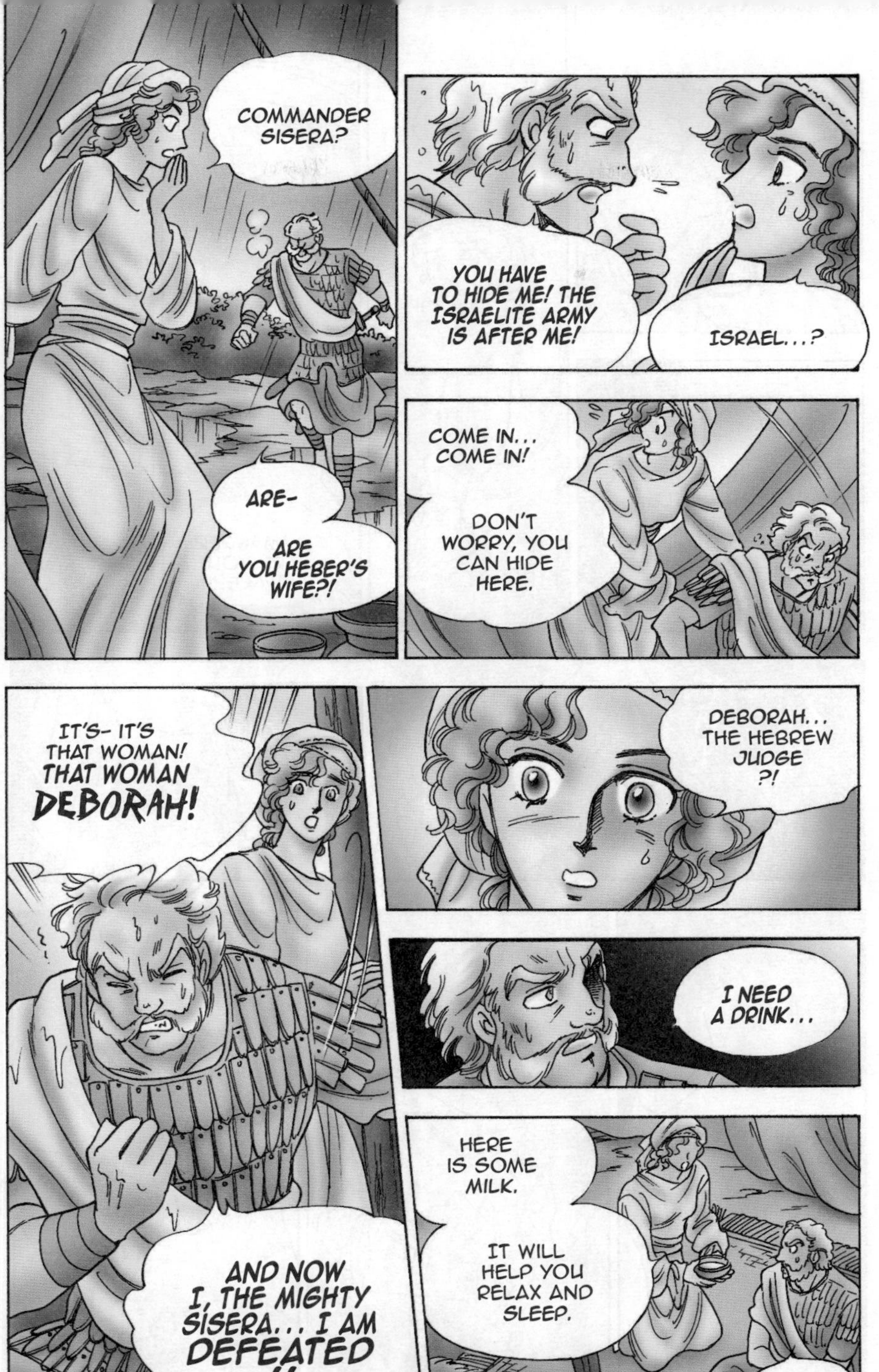

COMMANDER SISERA?
ARE-
ARE YOU HEBER'S WIFE?!
YOU HAVE TO HIDE ME! THE ISRAELITE ARMY IS AFTER ME!
ISRAEL...?
COME IN... COME IN!
DON'T WORRY, YOU CAN HIDE HERE.
IT'S- IT'S THAT WOMAN! THAT WOMAN DEBORAH!
AND NOW I, THE MIGHTY SISERA... I AM DEFEATED !!
DEBORAH... THE HEBREW JUDGE ?!
I NEED A DRINK...
HERE IS SOME MILK.
IT WILL HELP YOU RELAX AND SLEEP.
FINE.

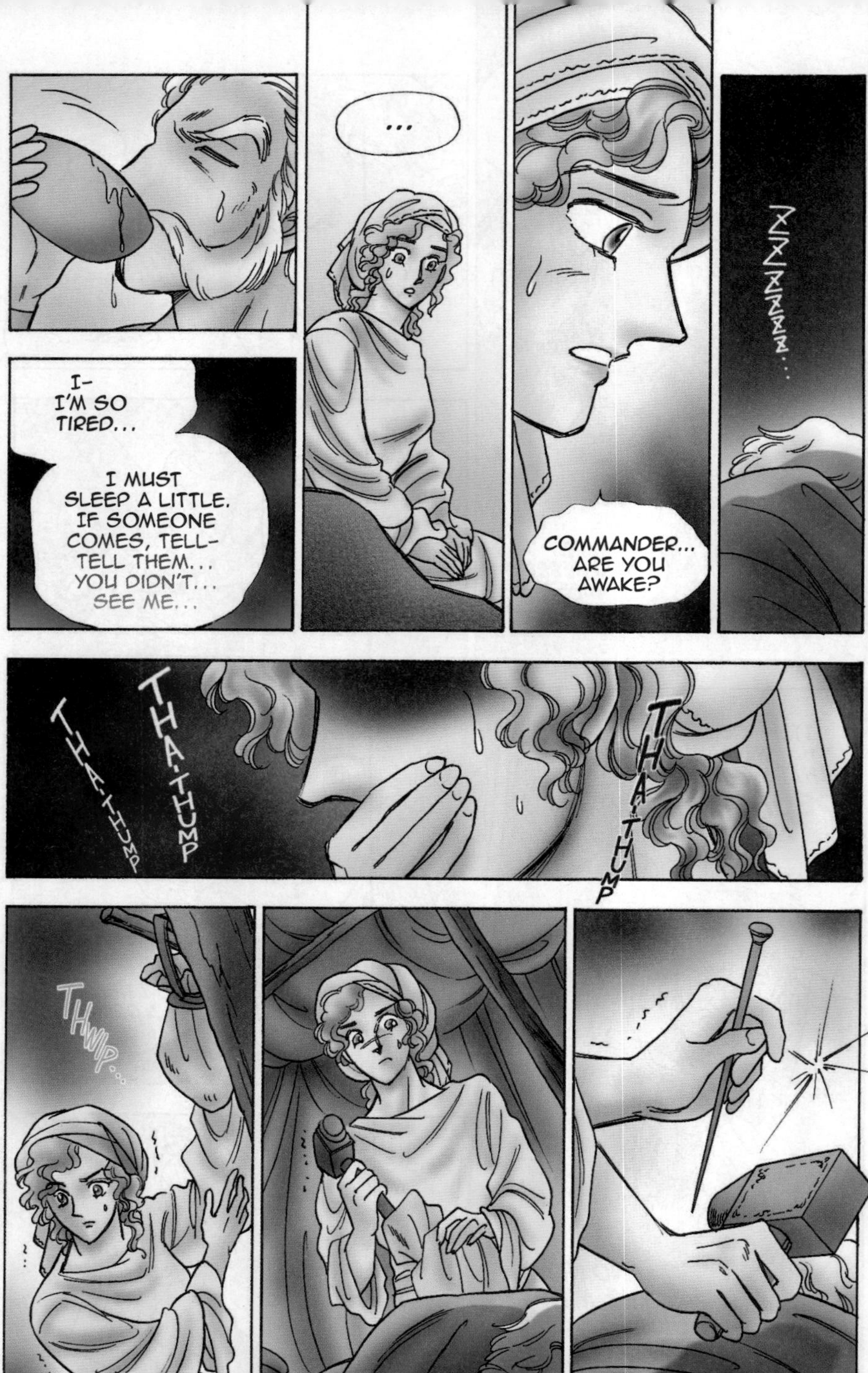
...
I-
I'M SO
TIRED...
I MUST
SLEEP A LITTLE.
IF SOMEONE
COMES, TELL-
TELL THEM...
YOU DIDN'T...
SEE ME...
COMMANDER...
ARE YOU
AWAKE?
ZZZZZZZ...
THA-THUMP
THA-THUMP
THA-THUMP
THWIP...

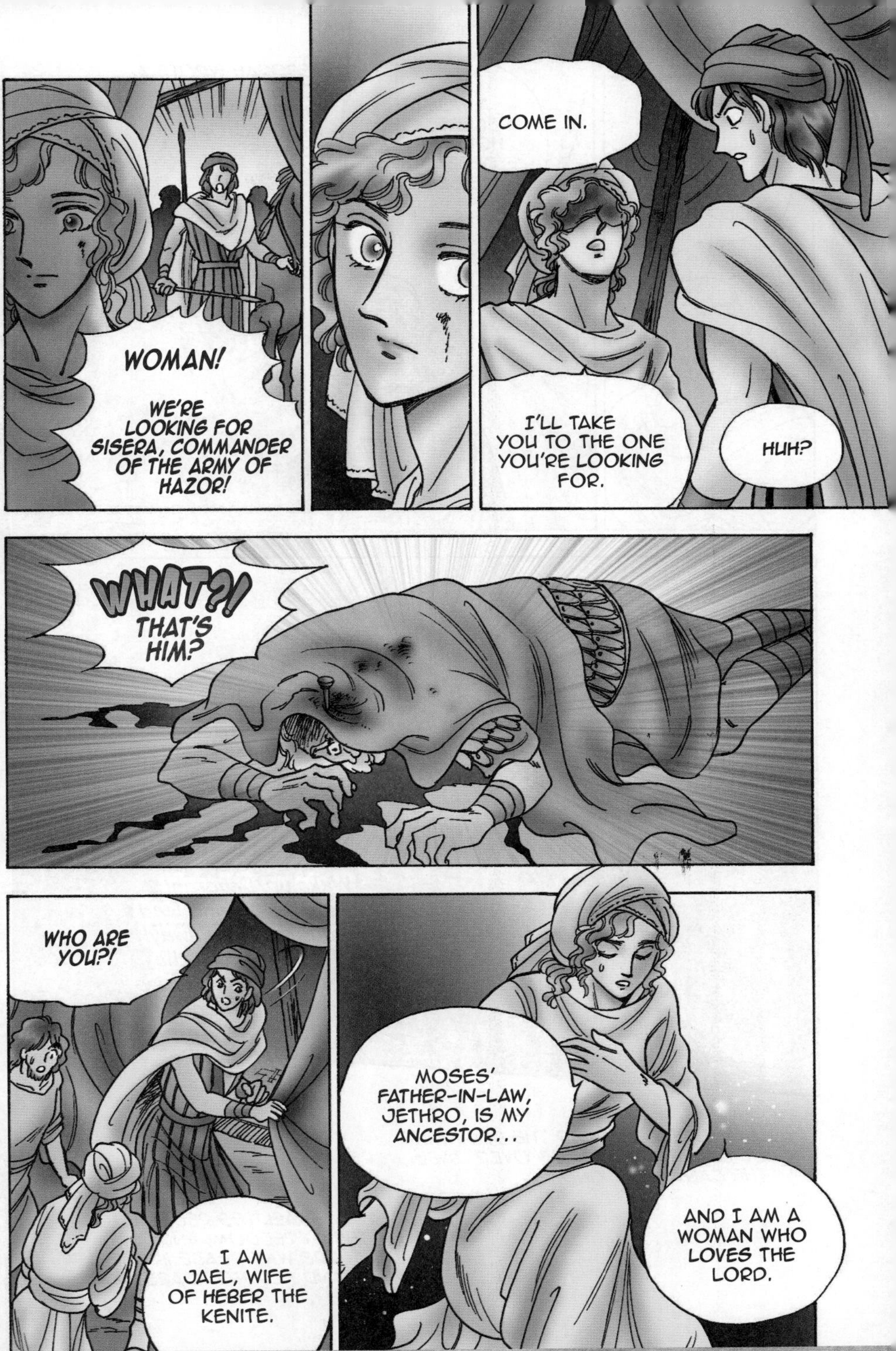
WOMAN!
WE'RE LOOKING FOR SISERA, COMMANDER OF THE ARMY OF HAZOR!
COME IN.
I'LL TAKE YOU TO THE ONE YOU'RE LOOKING FOR.
HUH?
WHAT?! THAT'S HIM?
WHO ARE YOU?!
I AM JAEL, WIFE OF HEBER THE KENITE.
MOSES' FATHER-IN-LAW, JETHRO, IS MY ANCESTOR...
AND I AM A WOMAN WHO LOVES THE LORD.

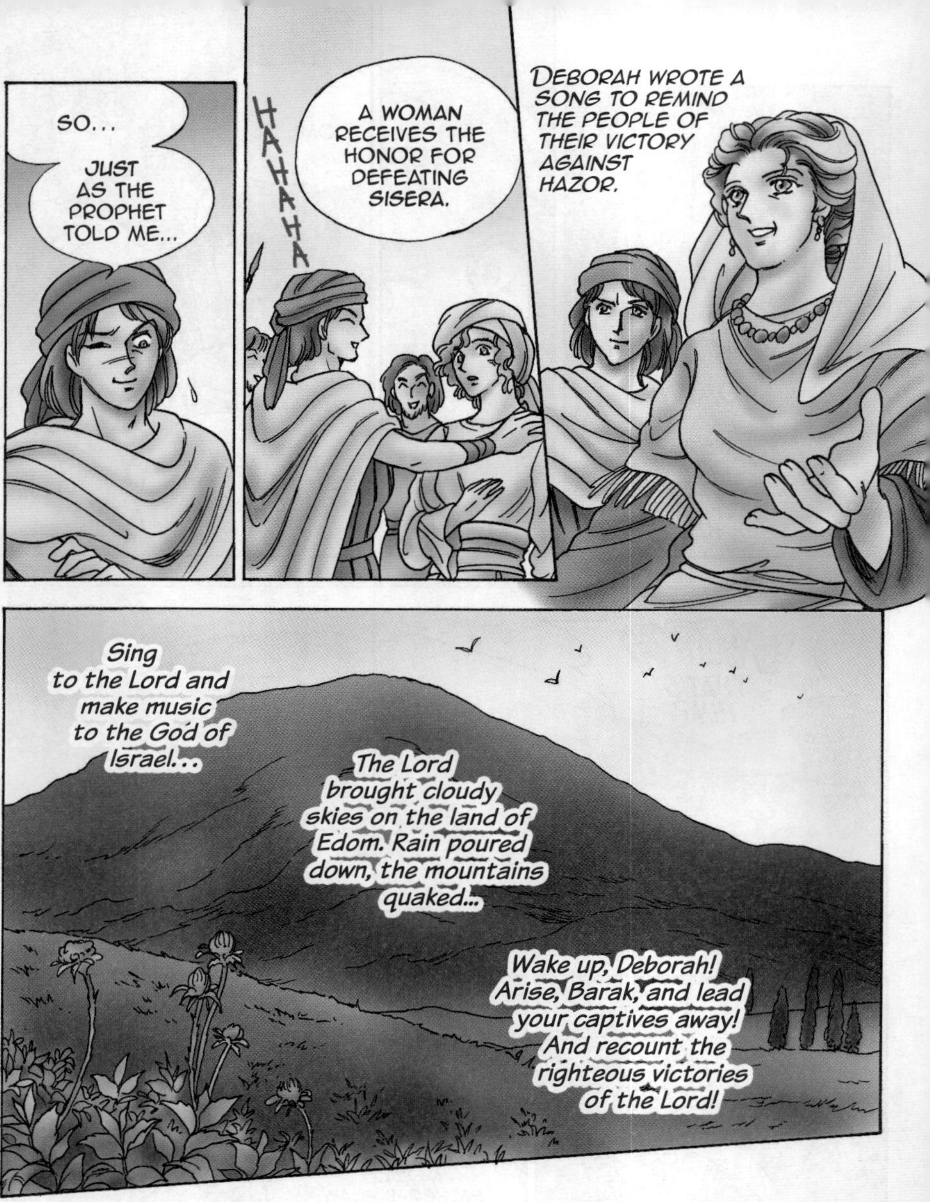
SO...
JUST AS THE PROPHET TOLD ME...
HAHAHAHA
A WOMAN RECEIVES THE HONOR FOR DEFEATING SISERA.
DEBORAH WROTE A SONG TO REMIND THE PEOPLE OF THEIR VICTORY AGAINST HAZOR.
Sing to the Lord and make music to the God of Israel...
The Lord brought cloudy skies on the land of Edom. Rain poured down, the mountains quaked...
Wake up, Deborah! Arise, Barak, and lead your captives away! And recount the righteous victories of the Lord!

THAT BATTLE MARKED THE BEGINNING OF SEVERAL VICTORIES OVER JABIN, THE CANAANITE KING.

THE ISRAELITES REGAINED THEIR FREEDOM, AND THERE WAS PEACE IN THE LAND FOR 40 YEARS.

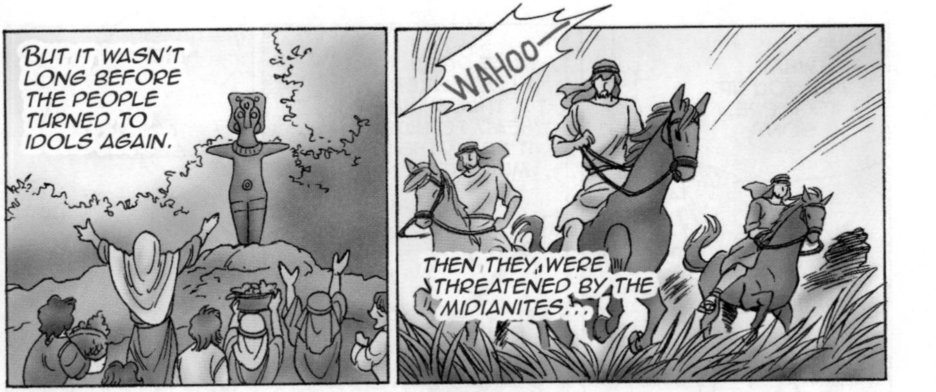
BUT IT WASN'T LONG BEFORE THE PEOPLE TURNED TO IDOLS AGAIN.
WAHOO—
THEN THEY WERE THREATENED BY THE MIDIANITES...

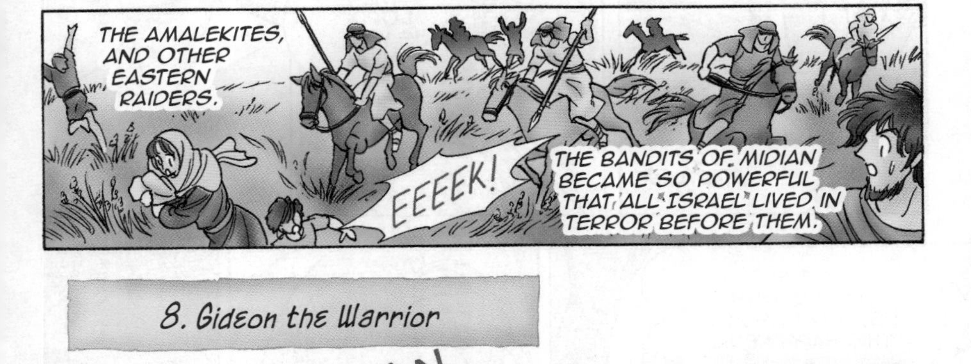
THE AMALEKITES, AND OTHER EASTERN RAIDERS.
EEEEK!
THE BANDITS OF MIDIAN BECAME SO POWERFUL THAT ALL ISRAEL LIVED IN TERROR BEFORE THEM.

8. Gideon the Warrior

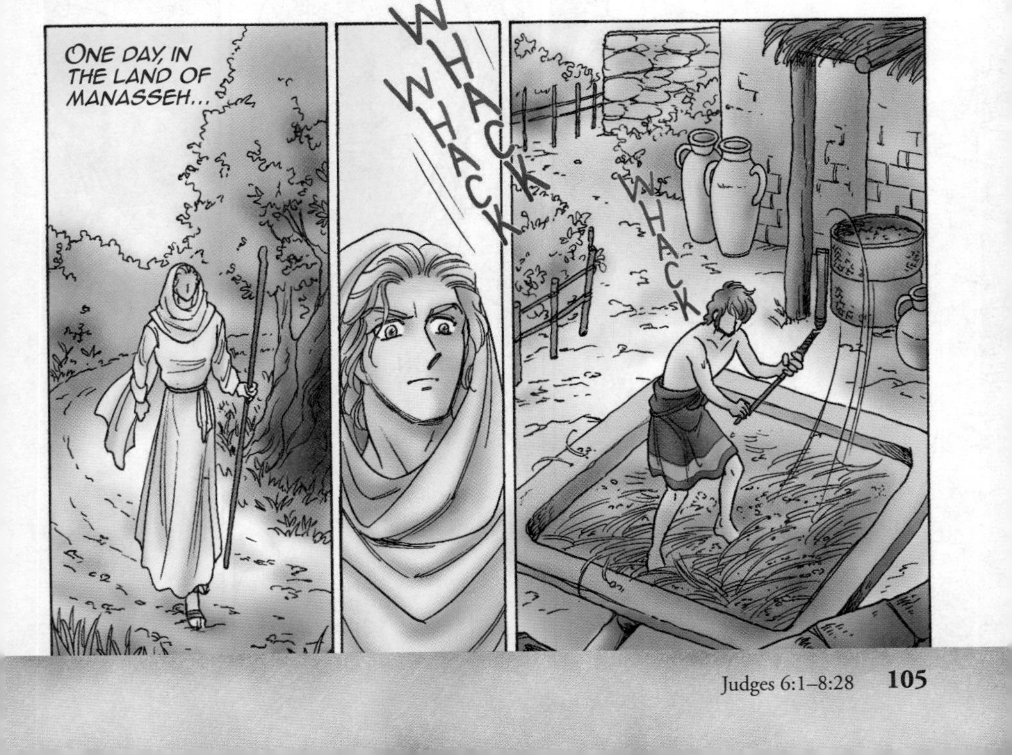
ONE DAY, IN THE LAND OF MANASSEH...
WHACK
WHACK
WHACK

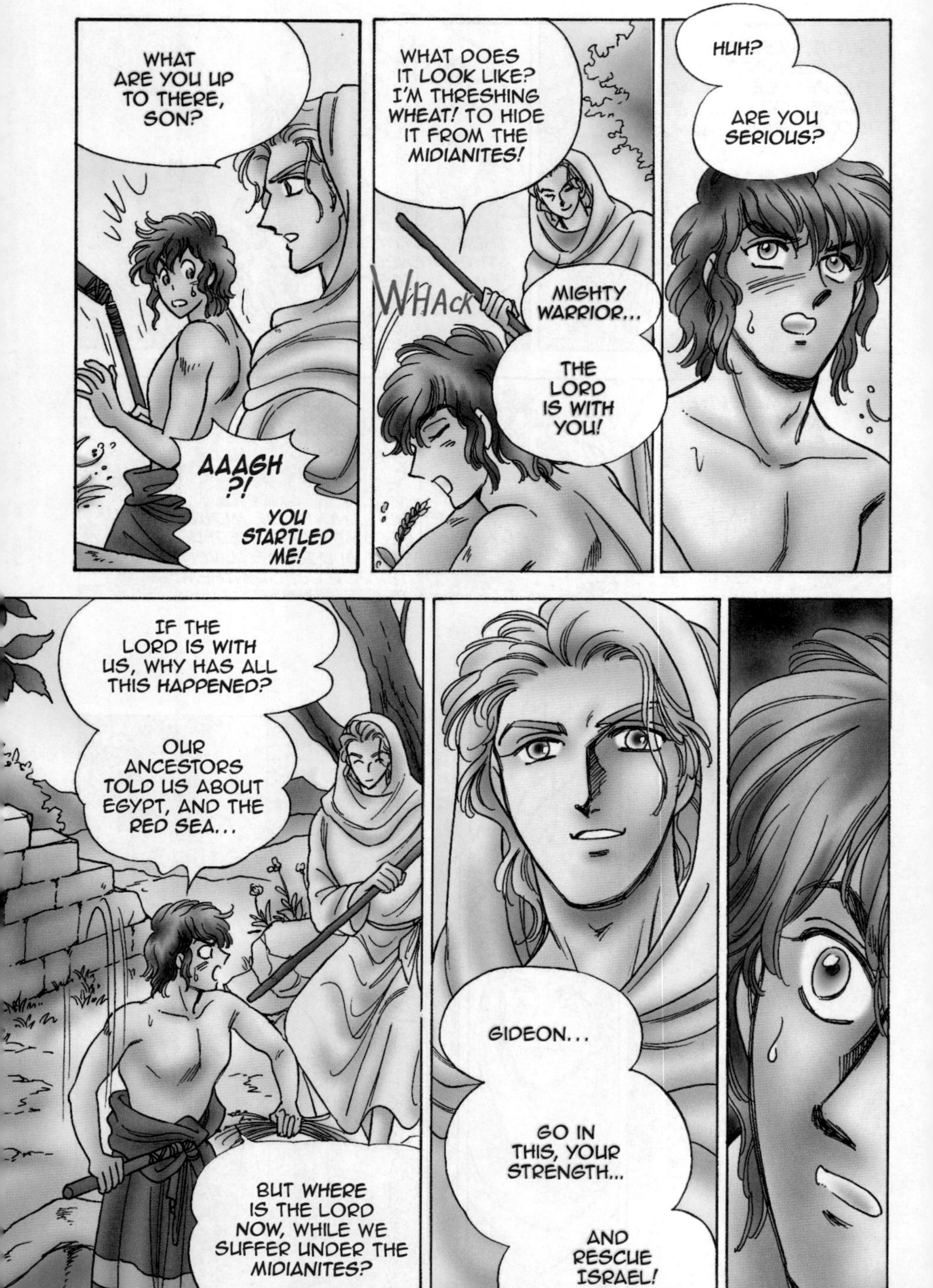
WHAT ARE YOU UP TO THERE, SON?
AAAGH ?!
YOU STARTLED ME!
WHAT DOES IT LOOK LIKE? I'M THRESHING WHEAT! TO HIDE IT FROM THE MIDIANITES!
WHACK
MIGHTY WARRIOR...
THE LORD IS WITH YOU!
HUH?
ARE YOU SERIOUS?
IF THE LORD IS WITH US, WHY HAS ALL THIS HAPPENED?
OUR ANCESTORS TOLD US ABOUT EGYPT, AND THE RED SEA...
BUT WHERE IS THE LORD NOW, WHILE WE SUFFER UNDER THE MIDIANITES?
GIDEON...
GO IN THIS, YOUR STRENGTH...
AND RESCUE ISRAEL!

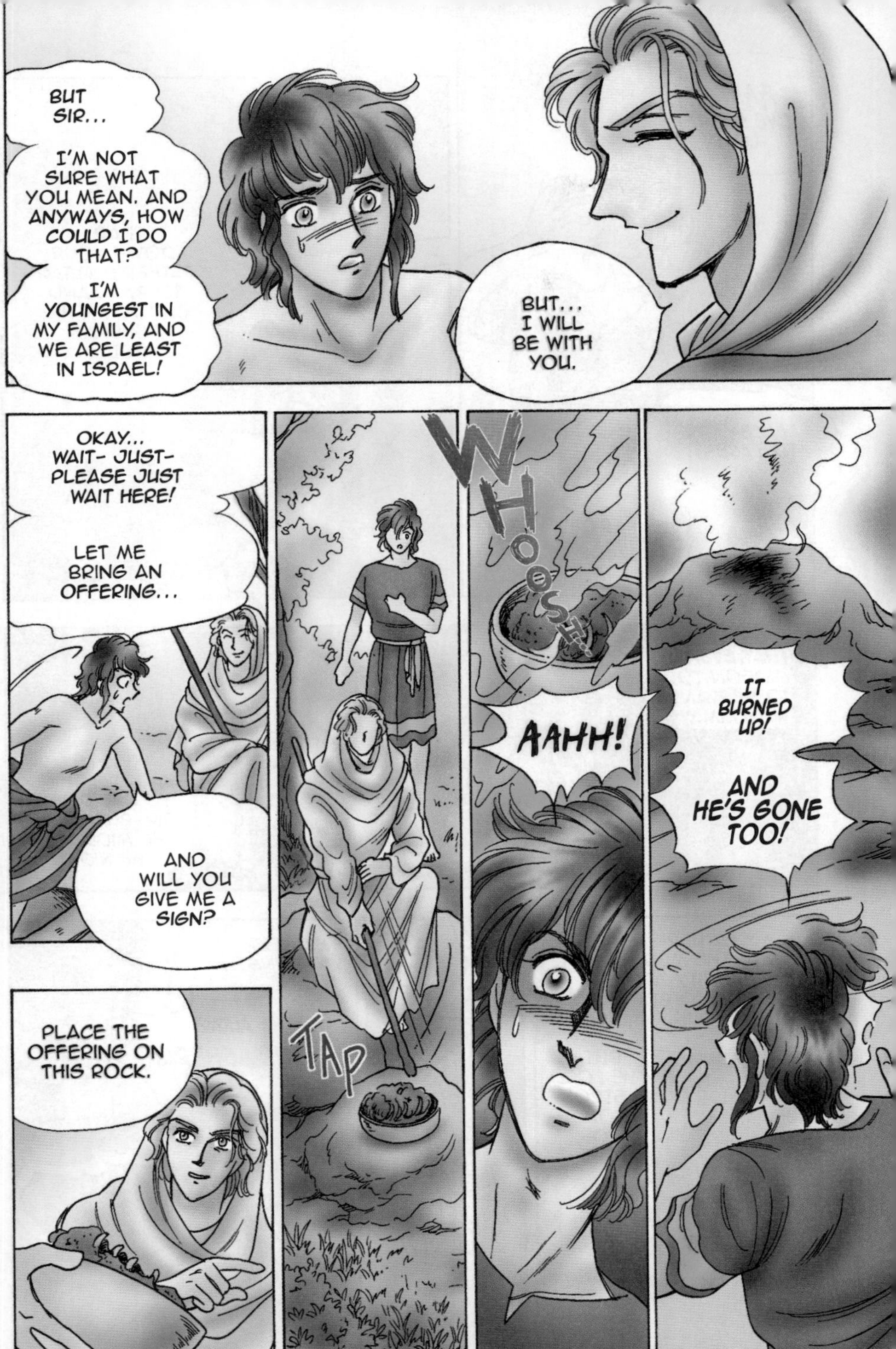
BUT SIR...
I'M NOT SURE WHAT YOU MEAN. AND ANYWAYS, HOW COULD I DO THAT?
I'M YOUNGEST IN MY FAMILY, AND WE ARE LEAST IN ISRAEL!
BUT... I WILL BE WITH YOU.
OKAY... WAIT- JUST- PLEASE JUST WAIT HERE!
LET ME BRING AN OFFERING...
AND WILL YOU GIVE ME A SIGN?
PLACE THE OFFERING ON THIS ROCK.
TAP
WHOOOSH...
AAHH!
IT BURNED UP!
AND HE'S GONE TOO!

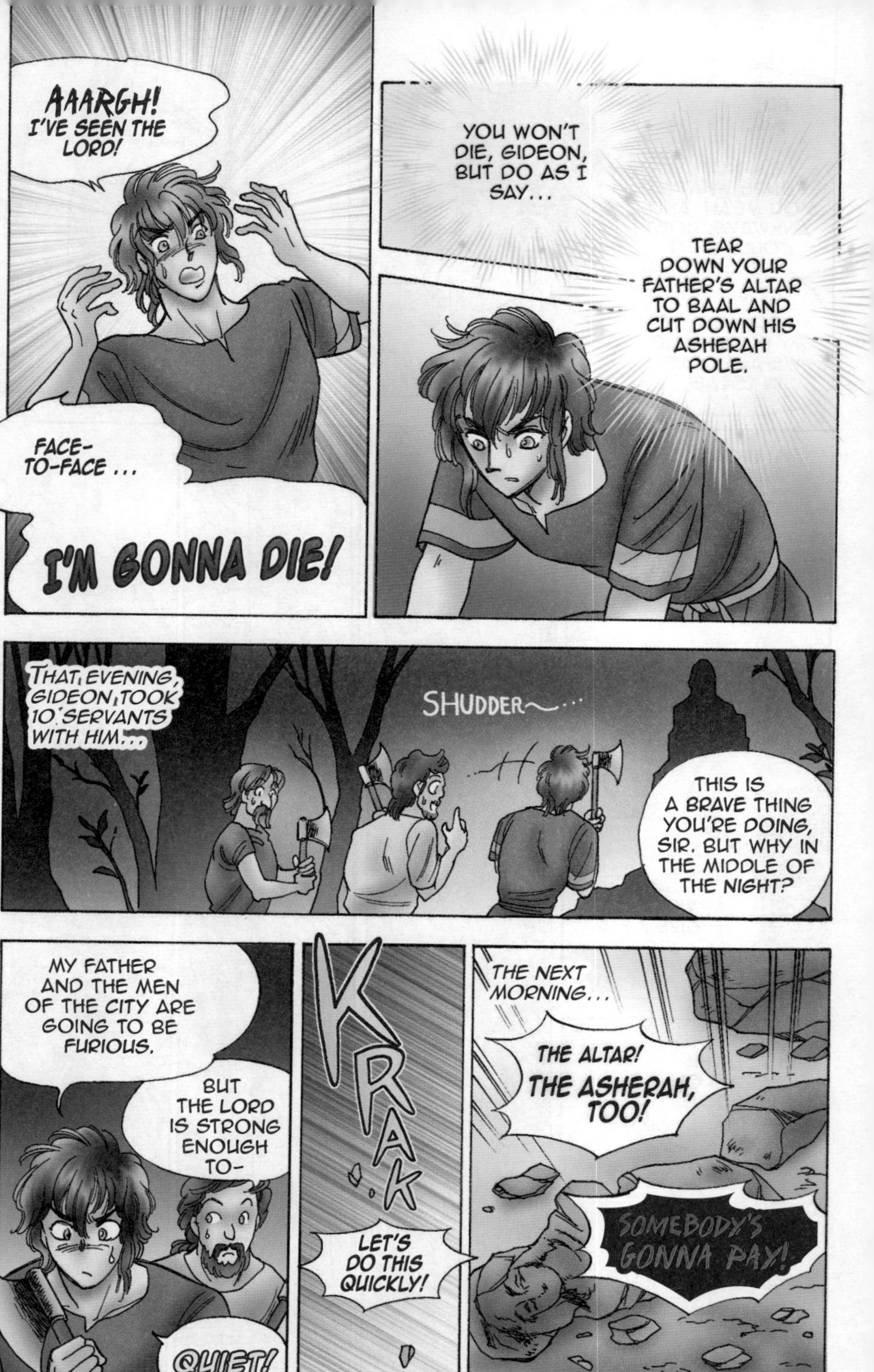
AAARGH! I'VE SEEN THE LORD!
FACE-TO-FACE ...
I'M GONNA DIE!
YOU WON'T DIE, GIDEON, BUT DO AS I SAY...
TEAR DOWN YOUR FATHER'S ALTAR TO BAAL AND CUT DOWN HIS ASHERAH POLE.
THAT EVENING, GIDEON TOOK 10 SERVANTS WITH HIM...
SHUDDER~...
THIS IS A BRAVE THING YOU'RE DOING, SIR. BUT WHY IN THE MIDDLE OF THE NIGHT?
MY FATHER AND THE MEN OF THE CITY ARE GOING TO BE FURIOUS.
BUT THE LORD IS STRONG ENOUGH TO-
QUIET!
KRAK
LET'S DO THIS QUICKLY!
THE NEXT MORNING...
THE ALTAR! THE ASHERAH, TOO!
SOMEBODY'S GONNA PAY!

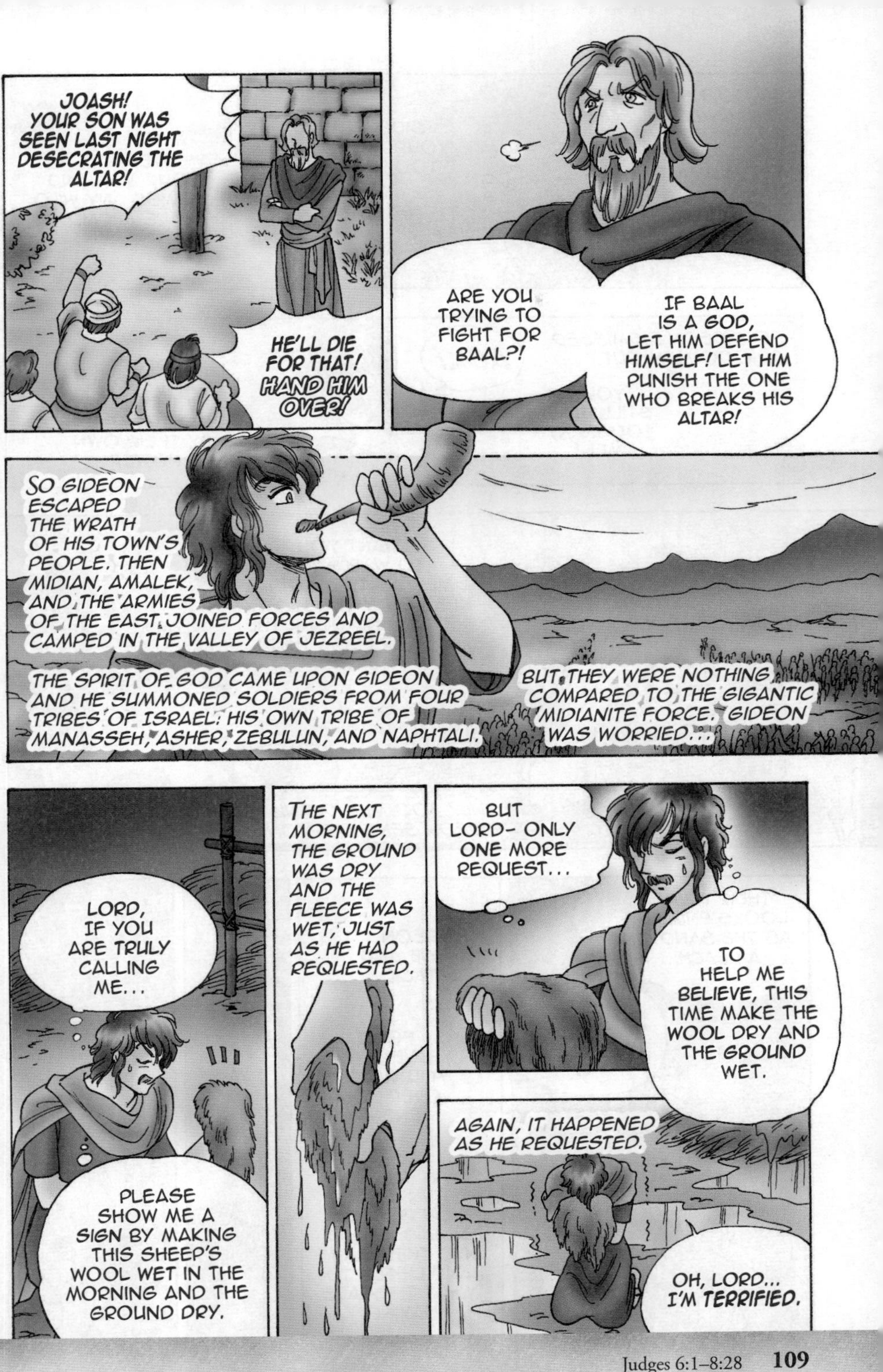
JOASH! YOUR SON WAS SEEN LAST NIGHT DESECRATING THE ALTAR!
HE'LL DIE FOR THAT! HAND HIM OVER!
ARE YOU TRYING TO FIGHT FOR BAAL?!
IF BAAL IS A GOD, LET HIM DEFEND HIMSELF! LET HIM PUNISH THE ONE WHO BREAKS HIS ALTAR!
SO GIDEON ESCAPED THE WRATH OF HIS TOWN'S PEOPLE. THEN MIDIAN, AMALEK, AND THE ARMIES OF THE EAST JOINED FORCES AND CAMPED IN THE VALLEY OF JEZREEL.
THE SPIRIT OF GOD CAME UPON GIDEON AND HE SUMMONED SOLDIERS FROM FOUR TRIBES OF ISRAEL: HIS OWN TRIBE OF MANASSEH, ASHER, ZEBULUN, AND NAPHTALI.
BUT THEY WERE NOTHING COMPARED TO THE GIGANTIC MIDIANITE FORCE. GIDEON WAS WORRIED...
LORD, IF YOU ARE TRULY CALLING ME...
PLEASE SHOW ME A SIGN BY MAKING THIS SHEEP'S WOOL WET IN THE MORNING AND THE GROUND DRY.
THE NEXT MORNING, THE GROUND WAS DRY AND THE FLEECE WAS WET, JUST AS HE HAD REQUESTED.
BUT LORD- ONLY ONE MORE REQUEST...
TO HELP ME BELIEVE, THIS TIME MAKE THE WOOL DRY AND THE GROUND WET.
AGAIN, IT HAPPENED AS HE REQUESTED.
OH, LORD... I'M TERRIFIED.

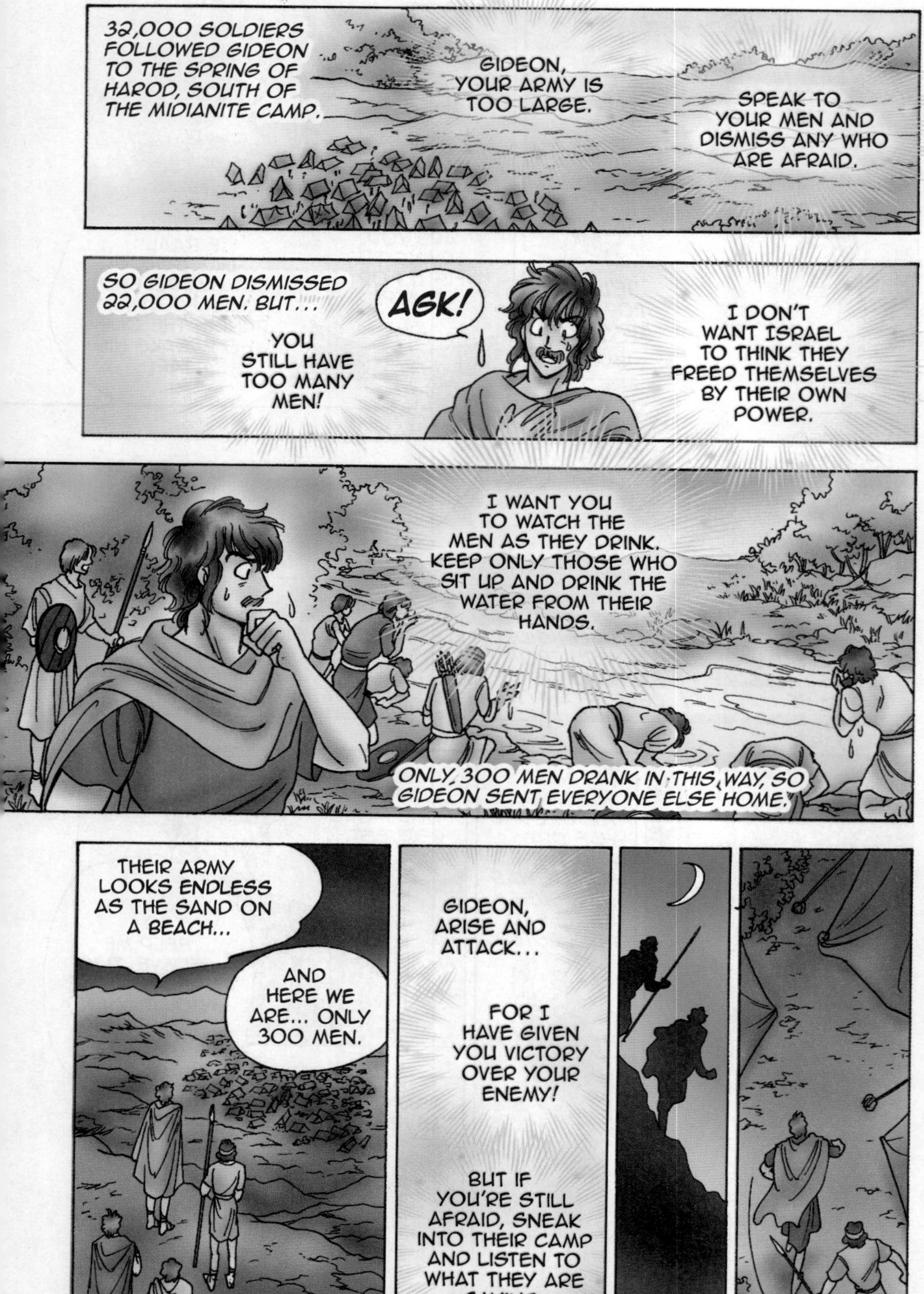
32,000 SOLDIERS FOLLOWED GIDEON TO THE SPRING OF HAROD, SOUTH OF THE MIDIANITE CAMP.
GIDEON, YOUR ARMY IS TOO LARGE.
SPEAK TO YOUR MEN AND DISMISS ANY WHO ARE AFRAID.
SO GIDEON DISMISSED 22,000 MEN. BUT...
YOU STILL HAVE TOO MANY MEN!
AGK!
I DON'T WANT ISRAEL TO THINK THEY FREED THEMSELVES BY THEIR OWN POWER.
I WANT YOU TO WATCH THE MEN AS THEY DRINK. KEEP ONLY THOSE WHO SIT UP AND DRINK THE WATER FROM THEIR HANDS.
ONLY 300 MEN DRANK IN THIS WAY, SO GIDEON SENT EVERYONE ELSE HOME.
THEIR ARMY LOOKS ENDLESS AS THE SAND ON A BEACH...
AND HERE WE ARE... ONLY 300 MEN.
GIDEON, ARISE AND ATTACK...
FOR I HAVE GIVEN YOU VICTORY OVER YOUR ENEMY!
BUT IF YOU'RE STILL AFRAID, SNEAK INTO THEIR CAMP AND LISTEN TO WHAT THEY ARE SAYING.

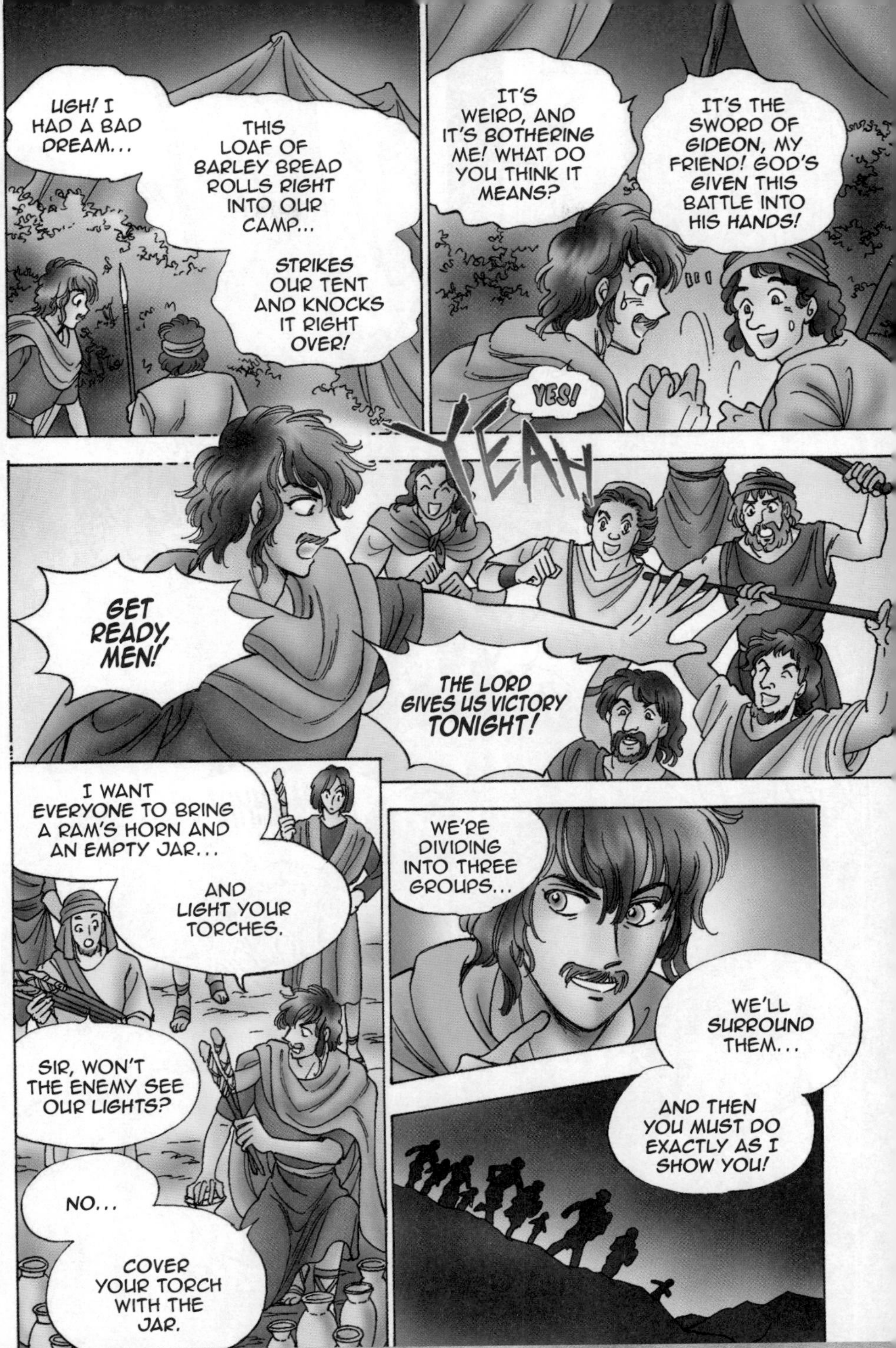
UGH! I HAD A BAD DREAM...
THIS LOAF OF BARLEY BREAD ROLLS RIGHT INTO OUR CAMP...
STRIKES OUR TENT AND KNOCKS IT RIGHT OVER!
IT'S WEIRD, AND IT'S BOTHERING ME! WHAT DO YOU THINK IT MEANS?
IT'S THE SWORD OF GIDEON, MY FRIEND! GOD'S GIVEN THIS BATTLE INTO HIS HANDS!
YES!
YEAH
GET READY, MEN!
THE LORD GIVES US VICTORY TONIGHT!
I WANT EVERYONE TO BRING A RAM'S HORN AND AN EMPTY JAR...
AND LIGHT YOUR TORCHES.
SIR, WON'T THE ENEMY SEE OUR LIGHTS?
NO...
COVER YOUR TORCH WITH THE JAR.
WE'RE DIVIDING INTO THREE GROUPS...
WE'LL SURROUND THEM...
AND THEN YOU MUST DO EXACTLY AS I SHOW YOU!

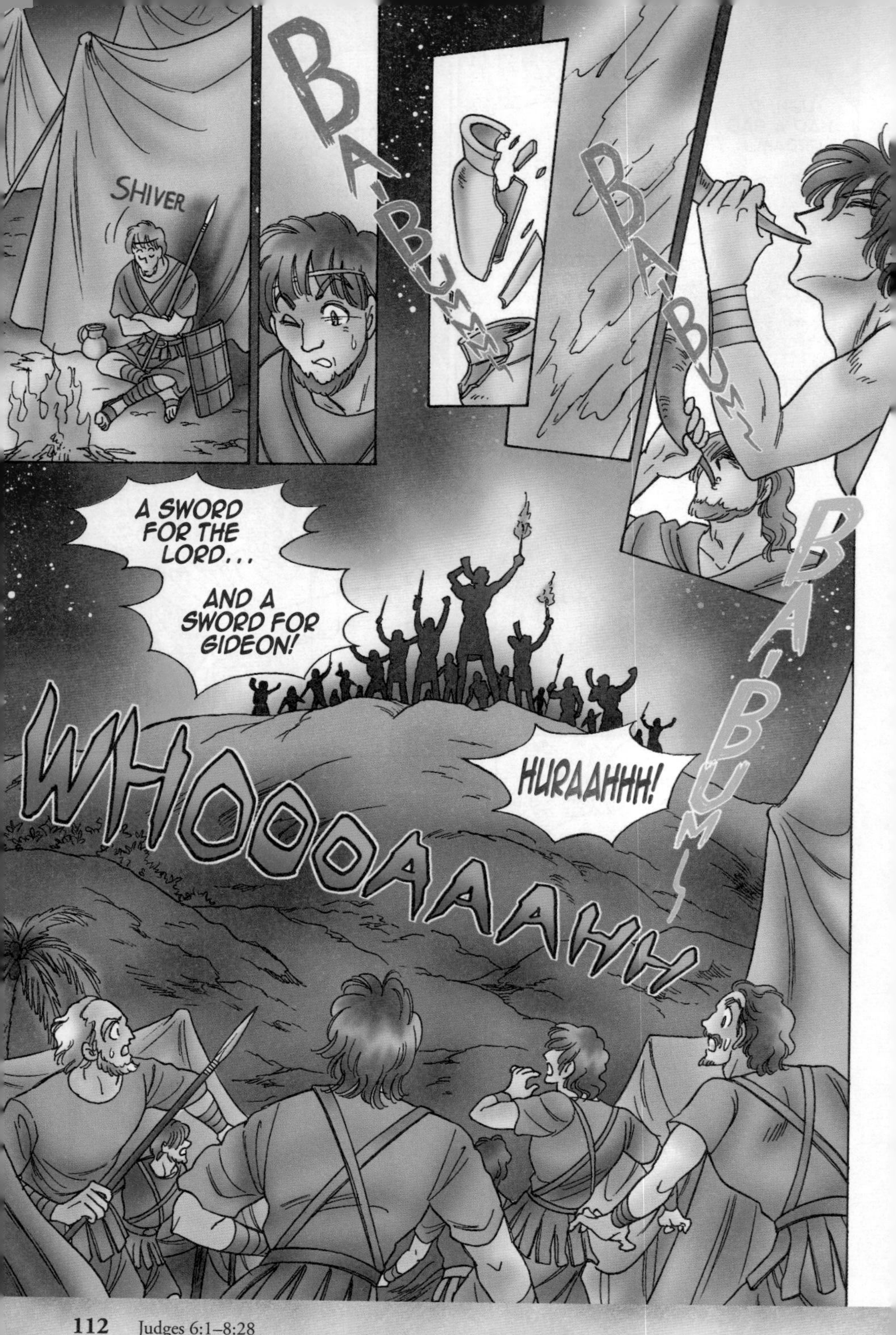

SHIVER
BA-BUMM!
BA-BUM
A SWORD FOR THE LORD...
AND A SWORD FOR GIDEON!
BA-BUM!
WHOOOAAAAHH
HURAAHHH!

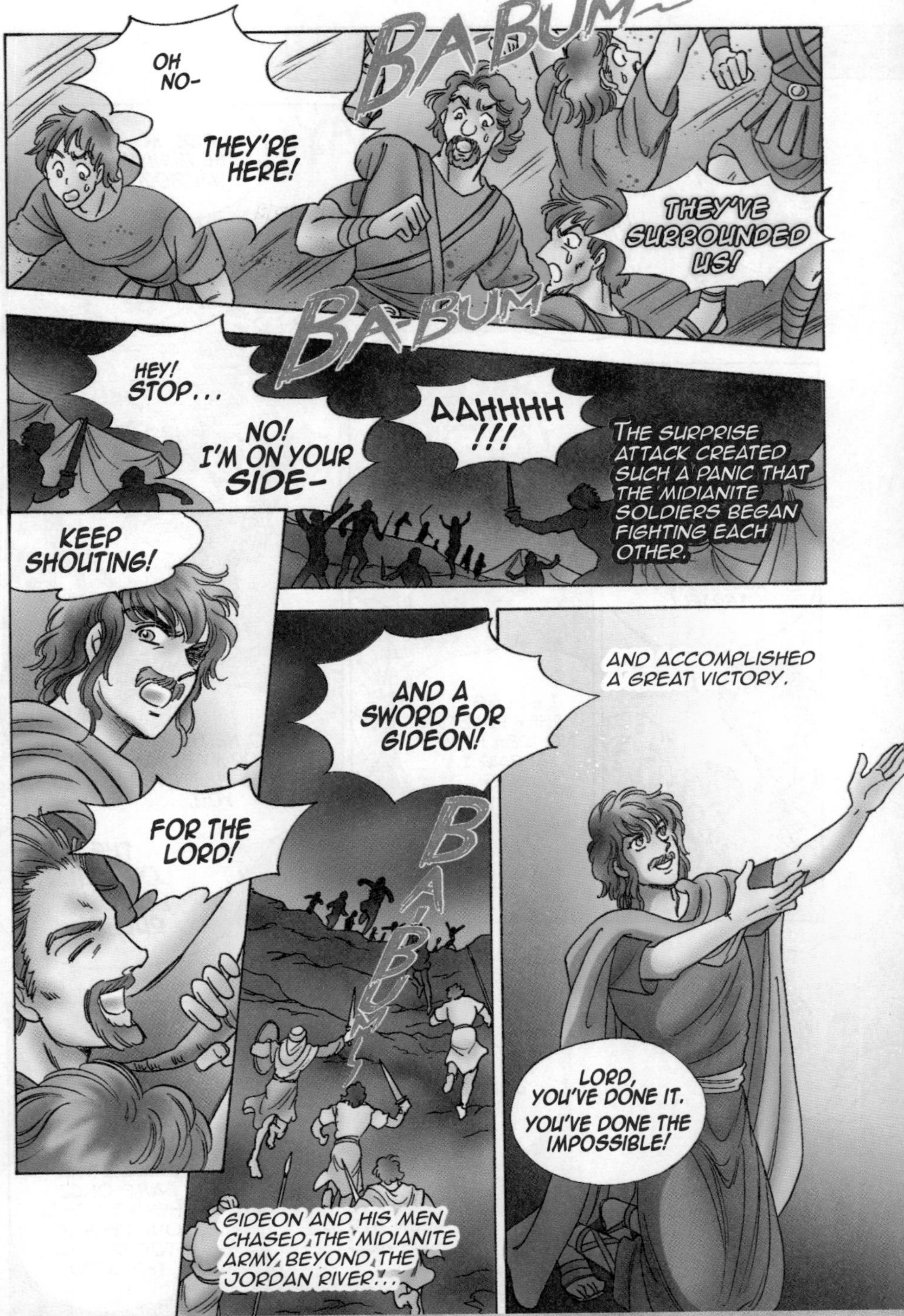

OH NO-
THEY'RE HERE!
BA-BUM
THEY'VE SURROUNDED US!
BA-BUM
HEY! STOP...
NO! I'M ON YOUR SIDE-
AAHHHH!!!
THE SURPRISE ATTACK CREATED SUCH A PANIC THAT THE MIDIANITE SOLDIERS BEGAN FIGHTING EACH OTHER.
KEEP SHOUTING!
FOR THE LORD!
AND A SWORD FOR GIDEON!
BA-BUM
GIDEON AND HIS MEN CHASED THE MIDIANITE ARMY BEYOND THE JORDAN RIVER...
AND ACCOMPLISHED A GREAT VICTORY.
LORD, YOU'VE DONE IT.
YOU'VE DONE THE IMPOSSIBLE!

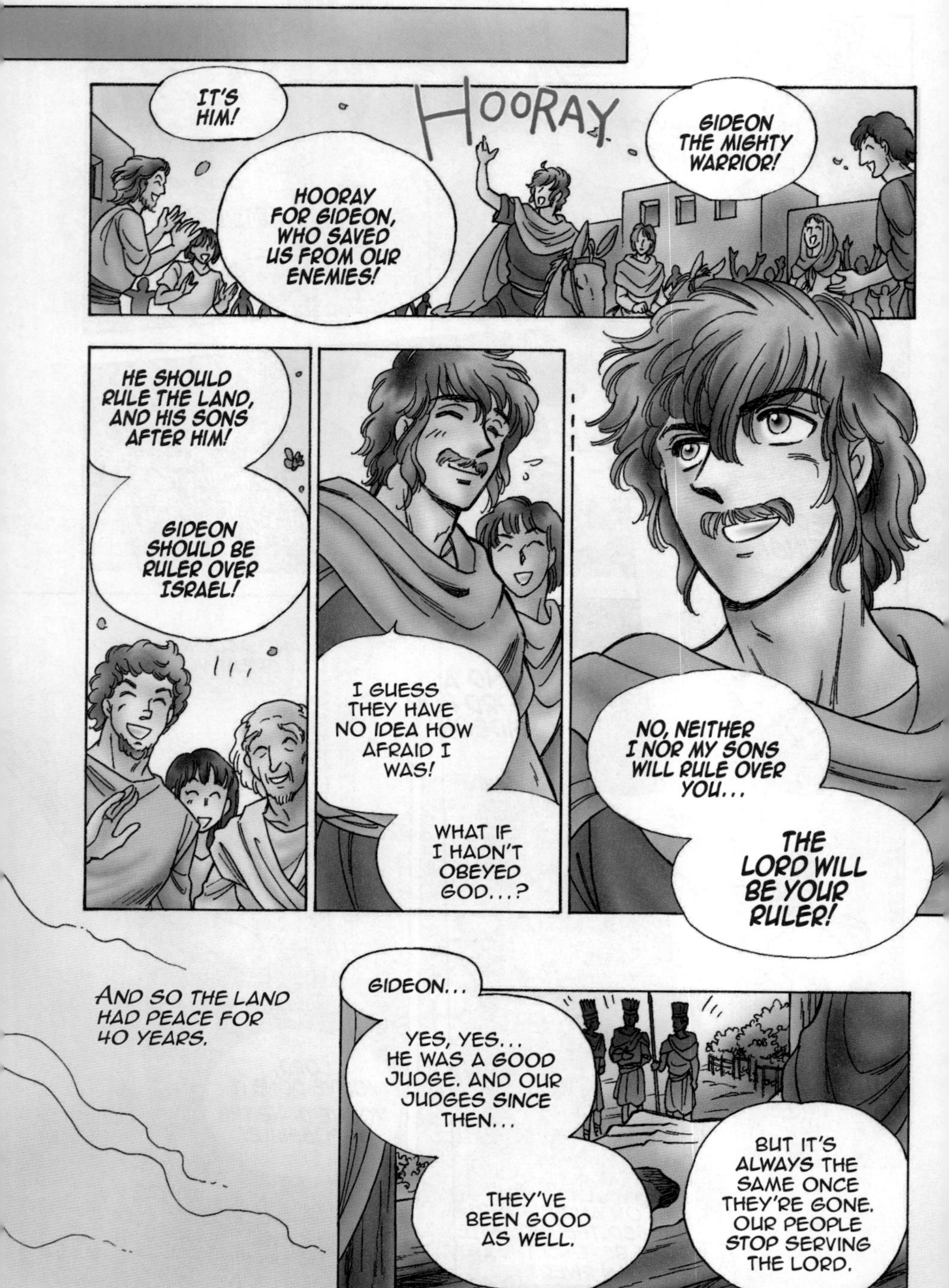
IT'S HIM!
HOORAY
HOORAY FOR GIDEON, WHO SAVED US FROM OUR ENEMIES!
GIDEON THE MIGHTY WARRIOR!
HE SHOULD RULE THE LAND, AND HIS SONS AFTER HIM!
GIDEON SHOULD BE RULER OVER ISRAEL!
I GUESS THEY HAVE NO IDEA HOW AFRAID I WAS!
WHAT IF I HADN'T OBEYED GOD...?
NO, NEITHER I NOR MY SONS WILL RULE OVER YOU...
THE LORD WILL BE YOUR RULER!
AND SO THE LAND HAD PEACE FOR 40 YEARS.
GIDEON...
YES, YES... HE WAS A GOOD JUDGE. AND OUR JUDGES SINCE THEN...
THEY'VE BEEN GOOD AS WELL.
BUT IT'S ALWAYS THE SAME ONCE THEY'RE GONE. OUR PEOPLE STOP SERVING THE LORD.

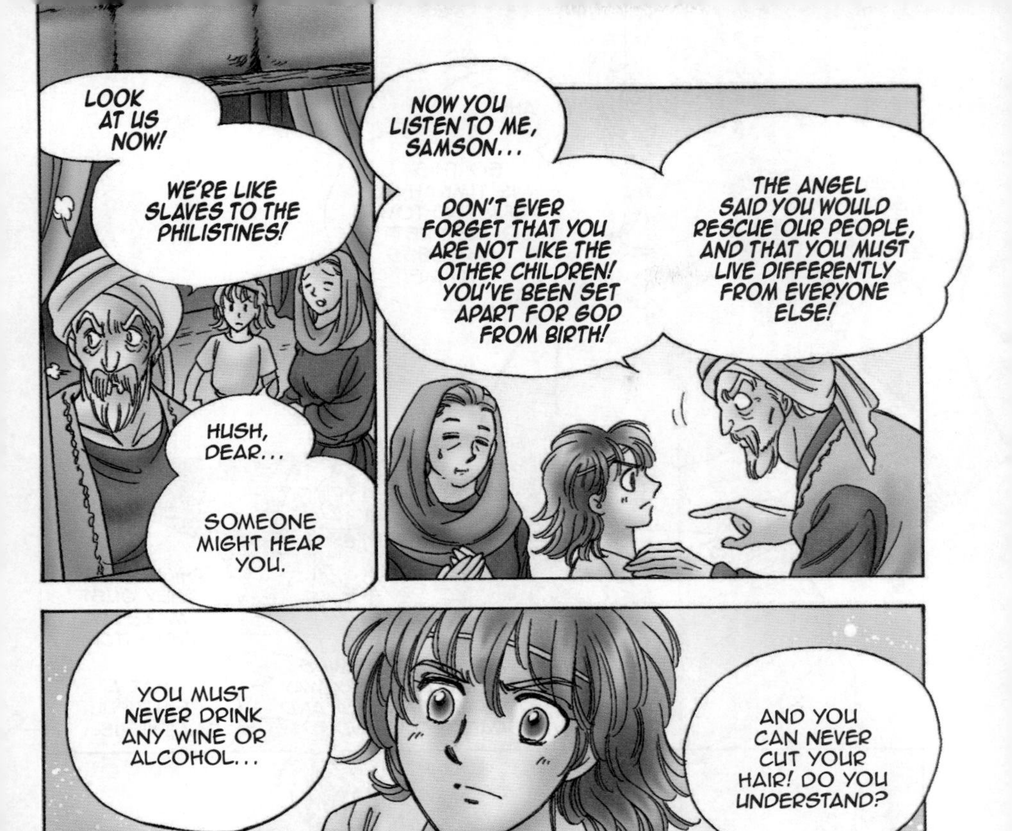
LOOK AT US NOW!
WE'RE LIKE SLAVES TO THE PHILISTINES!
HUSH, DEAR...
SOMEONE MIGHT HEAR YOU.
NOW YOU LISTEN TO ME, SAMSON...
DON'T EVER FORGET THAT YOU ARE NOT LIKE THE OTHER CHILDREN! YOU'VE BEEN SET APART FOR GOD FROM BIRTH!
THE ANGEL SAID YOU WOULD RESCUE OUR PEOPLE, AND THAT YOU MUST LIVE DIFFERENTLY FROM EVERYONE ELSE!
YOU MUST NEVER DRINK ANY WINE OR ALCOHOL...
AND YOU CAN NEVER CUT YOUR HAIR! DO YOU UNDERSTAND?
YES, DAD!
WHEN I GET OLDER...
I'M GONNA FIGHT THE PHILISTINES!

9. Mighty Samson

THE LORD BLESSED SAMSON, AND HE GREW INTO A POWERFUL YOUNG MAN.

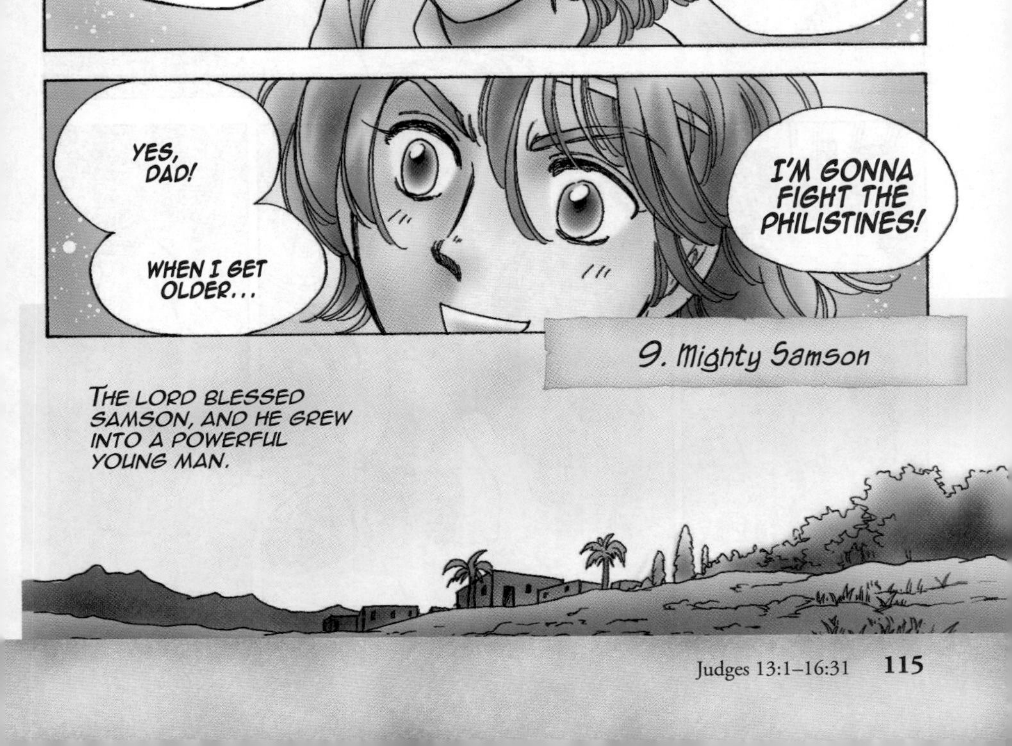

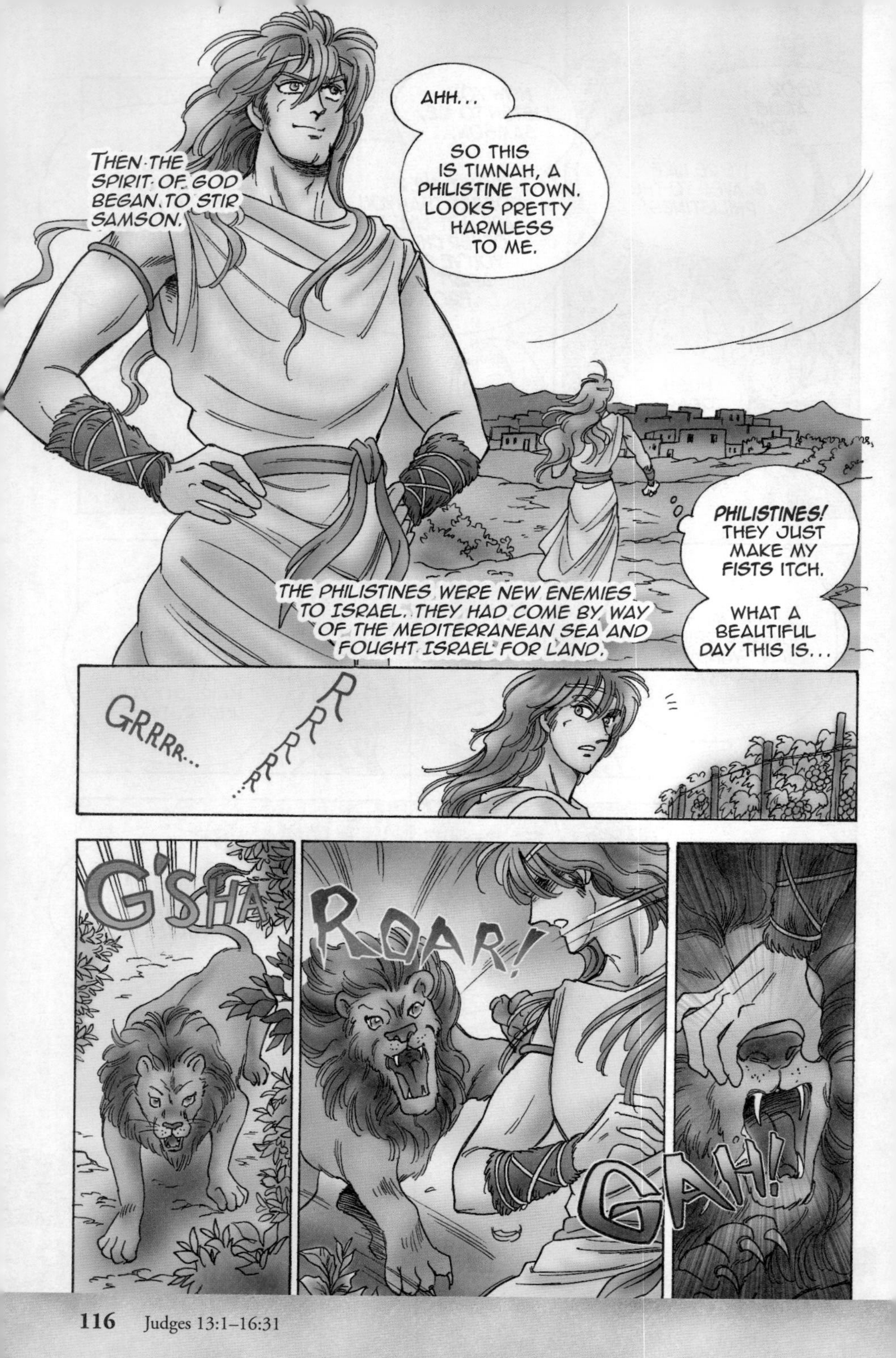
Then the spirit of God began to stir Samson.
Ahh...
So this is Timnah, a Philistine town. Looks pretty harmless to me.
Philistines! They just make my fists itch.
What a beautiful day this is...
The Philistines were new enemies to Israel. They had come by way of the Mediterranean Sea and fought Israel for land.
GRRRR...
...RRRRR
G'SHA
ROAR!
GAH!

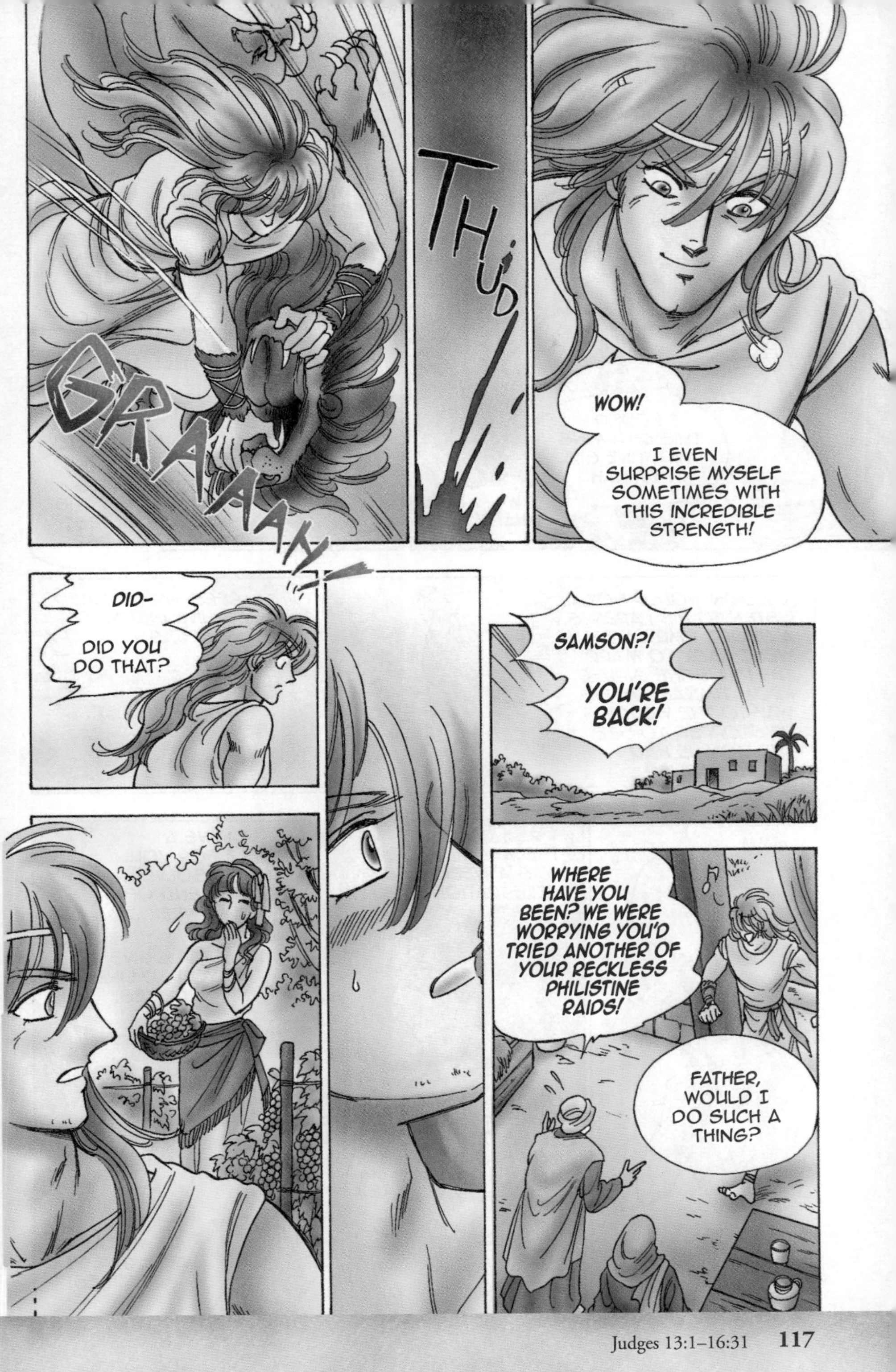
GRAAAAH!!
THUD
WOW!
I EVEN SURPRISE MYSELF SOMETIMES WITH THIS INCREDIBLE STRENGTH!
DID-
DID YOU DO THAT?
SAMSON?!
YOU'RE BACK!
WHERE HAVE YOU BEEN? WE WERE WORRYING YOU'D TRIED ANOTHER OF YOUR RECKLESS PHILISTINE RAIDS!
FATHER, WOULD I DO SUCH A THING?

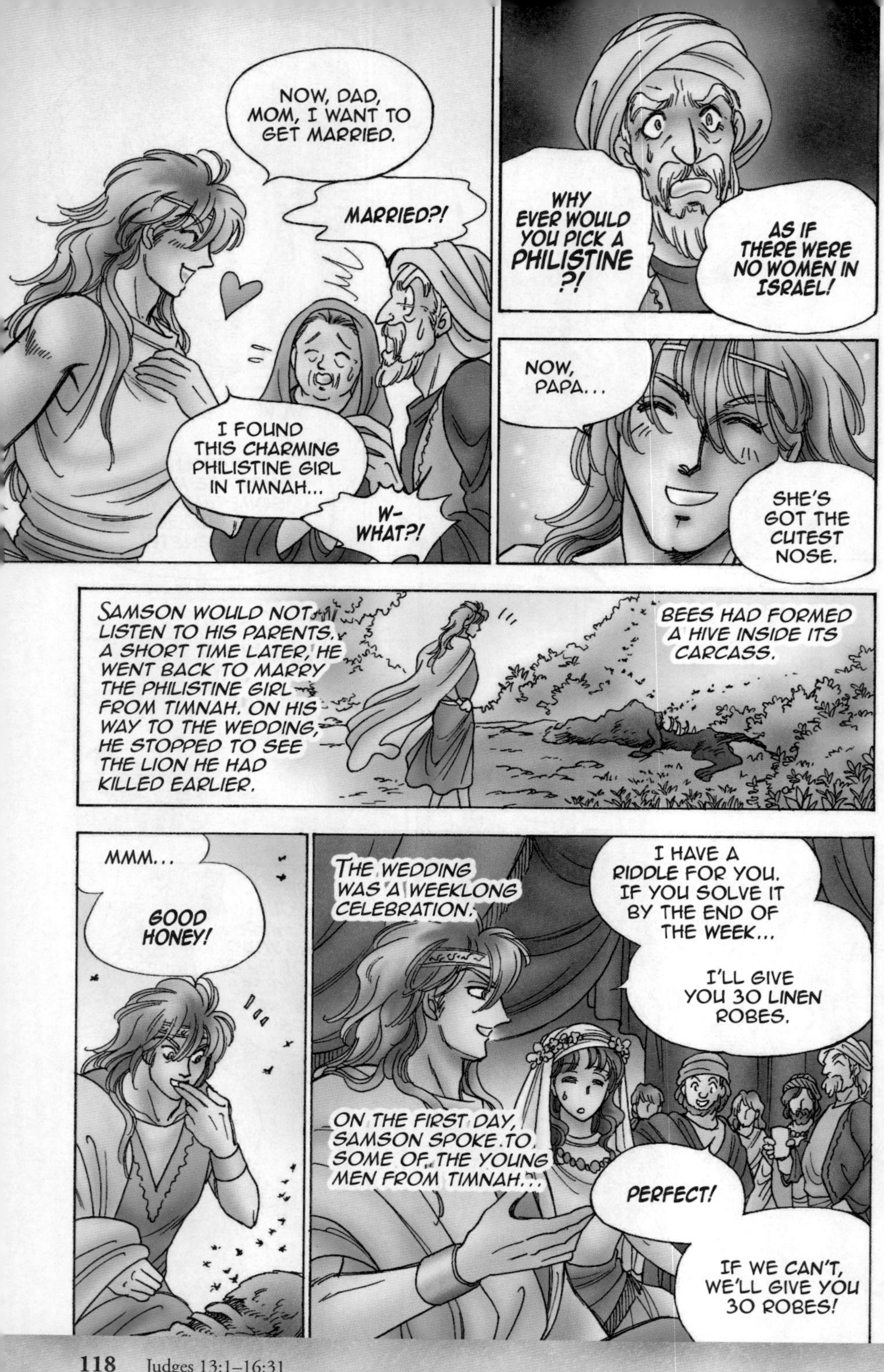
NOW, DAD, MOM, I WANT TO GET MARRIED.
MARRIED?!
I FOUND THIS CHARMING PHILISTINE GIRL IN TIMNAH...
W- WHAT?!
WHY EVER WOULD YOU PICK A PHILISTINE ?!
AS IF THERE WERE NO WOMEN IN ISRAEL!
NOW, PAPA...
SHE'S GOT THE CUTEST NOSE.
SAMSON WOULD NOT LISTEN TO HIS PARENTS. A SHORT TIME LATER, HE WENT BACK TO MARRY THE PHILISTINE GIRL FROM TIMNAH. ON HIS WAY TO THE WEDDING, HE STOPPED TO SEE THE LION HE HAD KILLED EARLIER.
BEES HAD FORMED A HIVE INSIDE ITS CARCASS.
MMM...
GOOD HONEY!
THE WEDDING WAS A WEEKLONG CELEBRATION.
I HAVE A RIDDLE FOR YOU. IF YOU SOLVE IT BY THE END OF THE WEEK...
I'LL GIVE YOU 30 LINEN ROBES.
ON THE FIRST DAY, SAMSON SPOKE TO SOME OF THE YOUNG MEN FROM TIMNAH...
PERFECT!
IF WE CAN'T, WE'LL GIVE YOU 30 ROBES!

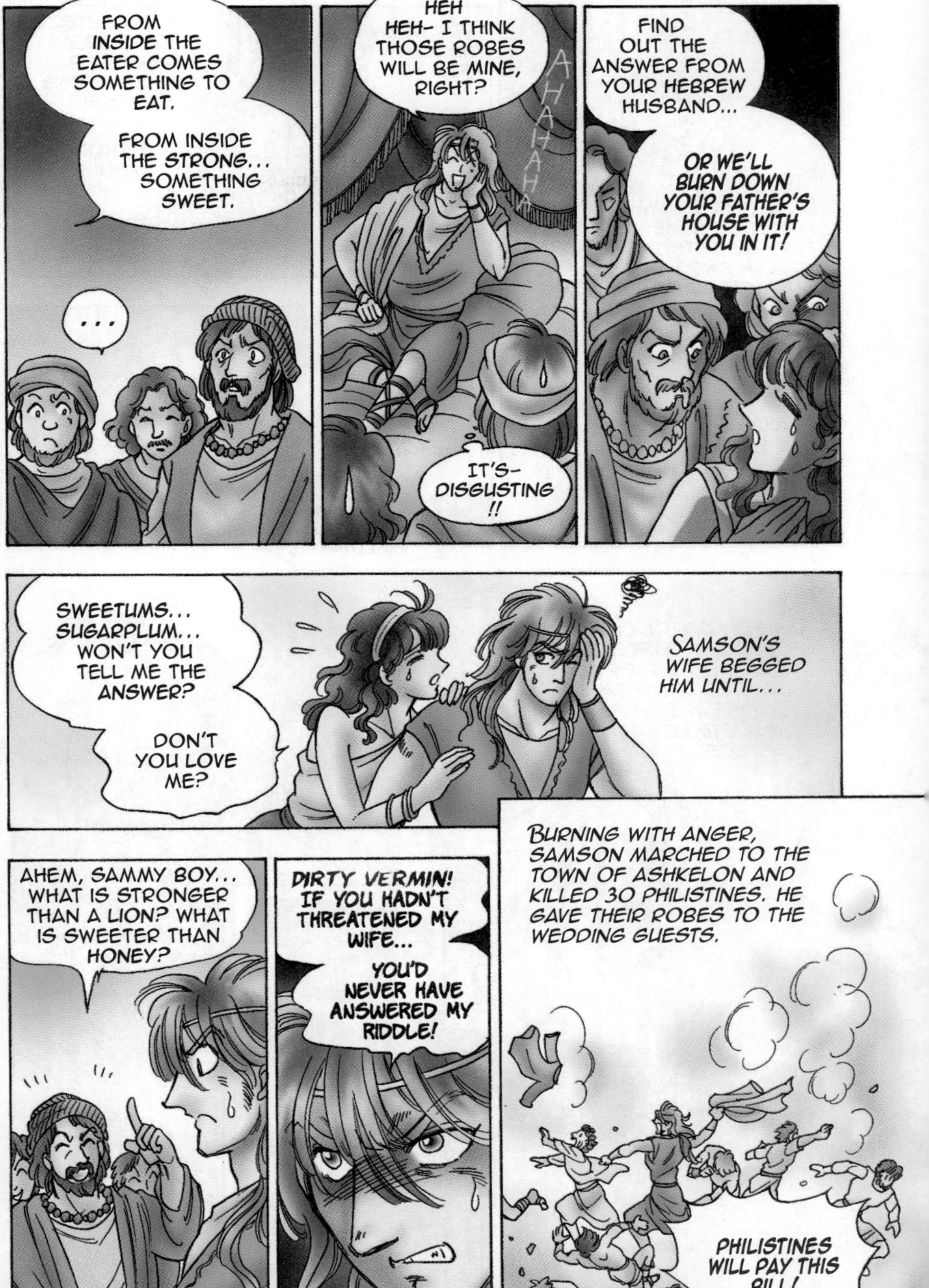

FROM INSIDE THE EATER COMES SOMETHING TO EAT.
FROM INSIDE THE STRONG... SOMETHING SWEET.
...
HEH HEH- I THINK THOSE ROBES WILL BE MINE, RIGHT?
AHAHAHA
IT'S- DISGUSTING !!
FIND OUT THE ANSWER FROM YOUR HEBREW HUSBAND...
OR WE'LL BURN DOWN YOUR FATHER'S HOUSE WITH YOU IN IT!
SWEETUMS... SUGARPLUM... WON'T YOU TELL ME THE ANSWER?
DON'T YOU LOVE ME?
SAMSON'S WIFE BEGGED HIM UNTIL...
AHEM, SAMMY BOY... WHAT IS STRONGER THAN A LION? WHAT IS SWEETER THAN HONEY?
DIRTY VERMIN! IF YOU HADN'T THREATENED MY WIFE...
YOU'D NEVER HAVE ANSWERED MY RIDDLE!
BURNING WITH ANGER, SAMSON MARCHED TO THE TOWN OF ASHKELON AND KILLED 30 PHILISTINES. HE GAVE THEIR ROBES TO THE WEDDING GUESTS.
PHILISTINES WILL PAY THIS BILL!

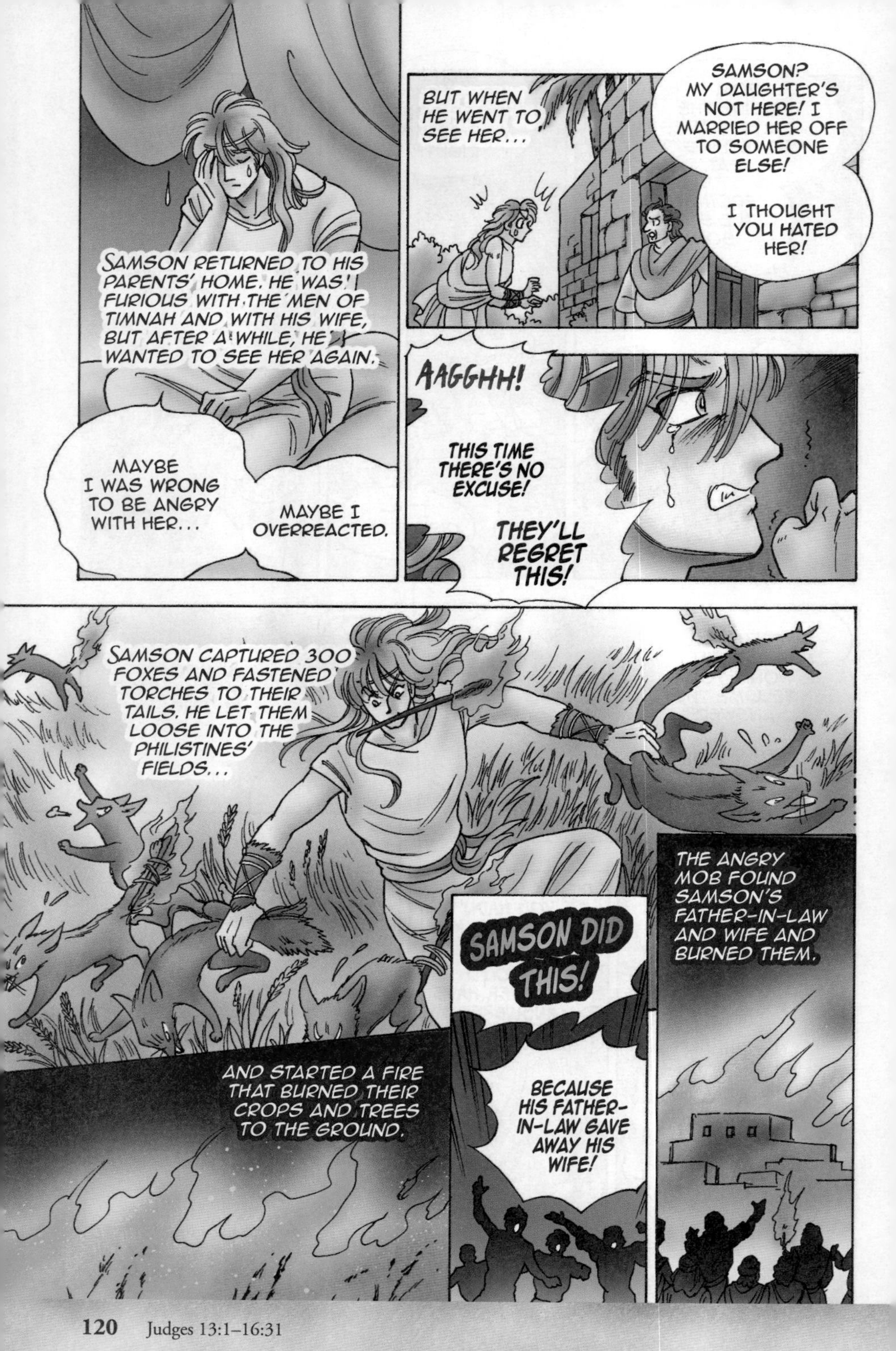
SAMSON RETURNED TO HIS PARENTS' HOME. HE WAS FURIOUS WITH THE MEN OF TIMNAH AND WITH HIS WIFE, BUT AFTER A WHILE, HE WANTED TO SEE HER AGAIN.
MAYBE I WAS WRONG TO BE ANGRY WITH HER...
MAYBE I OVERREACTED.
BUT WHEN HE WENT TO SEE HER...
SAMSON? MY DAUGHTER'S NOT HERE! I MARRIED HER OFF TO SOMEONE ELSE!
I THOUGHT YOU HATED HER!
AAGGHH!
THIS TIME THERE'S NO EXCUSE!
THEY'LL REGRET THIS!
SAMSON CAPTURED 300 FOXES AND FASTENED TORCHES TO THEIR TAILS. HE LET THEM LOOSE INTO THE PHILISTINES' FIELDS...
AND STARTED A FIRE THAT BURNED THEIR CROPS AND TREES TO THE GROUND.
SAMSON DID THIS!
BECAUSE HIS FATHER-IN-LAW GAVE AWAY HIS WIFE!
THE ANGRY MOB FOUND SAMSON'S FATHER-IN-LAW AND WIFE AND BURNED THEM.

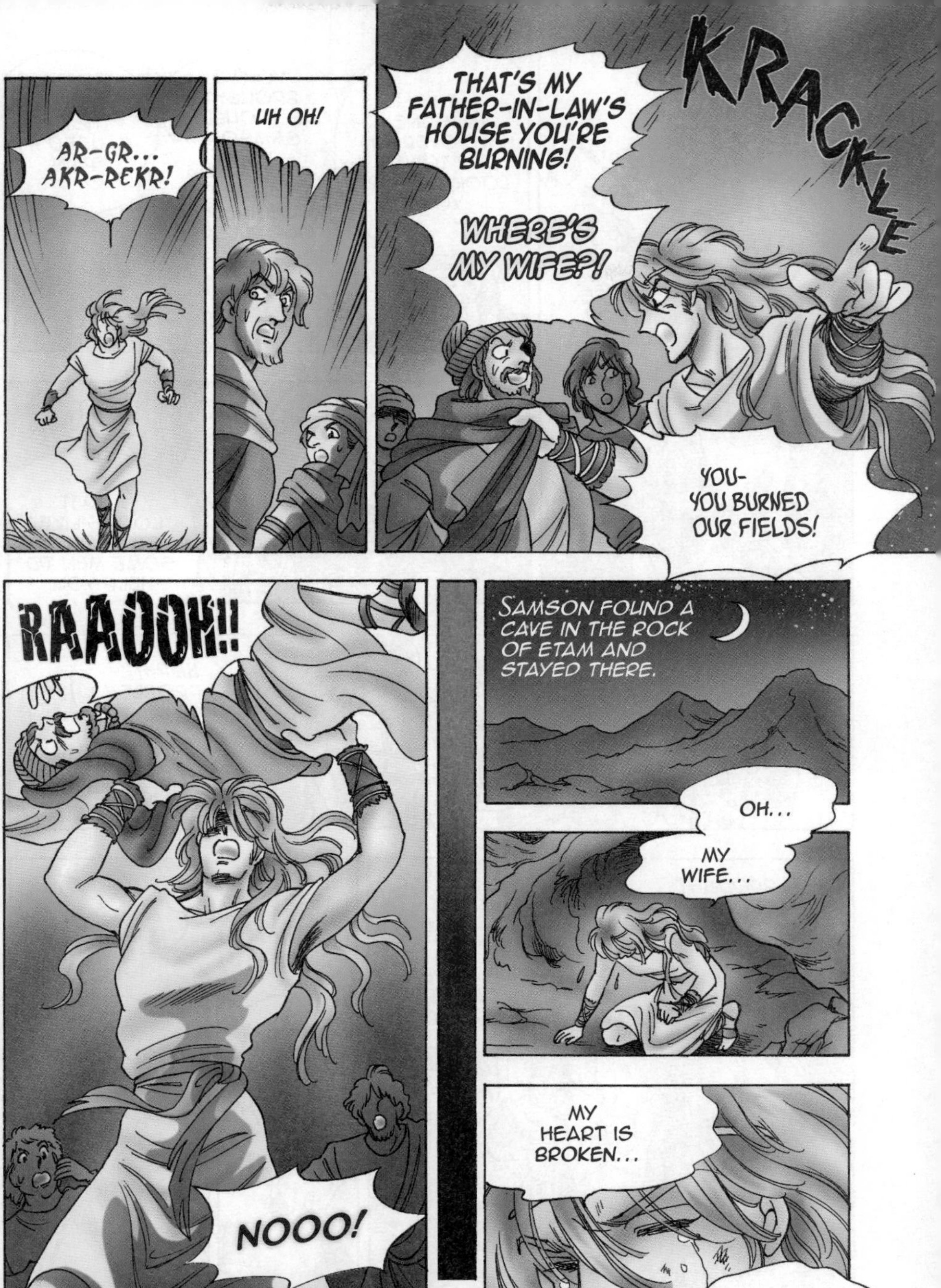
AR-GR... AKR-REKR!
UH OH!
THAT'S MY FATHER-IN-LAW'S HOUSE YOU'RE BURNING!
WHERE'S MY WIFE?!
KRACKLE
YOU- YOU BURNED OUR FIELDS!
RAAOOH!!
NOOO!
SAMSON FOUND A CAVE IN THE ROCK OF ETAM AND STAYED THERE.
OH...
MY WIFE...
MY HEART IS BROKEN...
I WILL NEVER LOVE AGAIN!

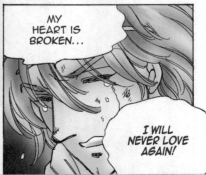

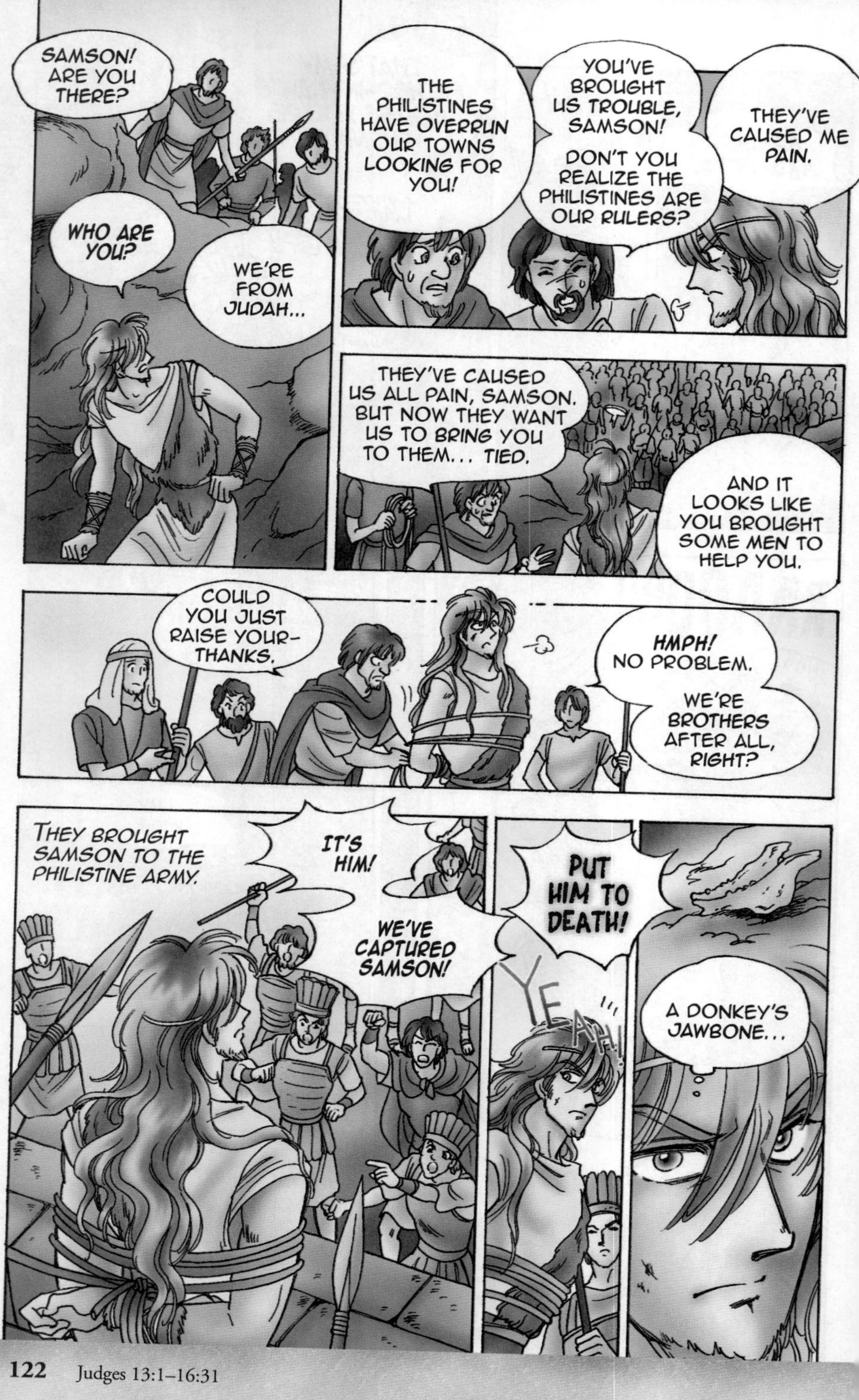
SAMSON! ARE YOU THERE?
WHO ARE YOU?
WE'RE FROM JUDAH...
THE PHILISTINES HAVE OVERRUN OUR TOWNS LOOKING FOR YOU!
YOU'VE BROUGHT US TROUBLE, SAMSON!
DON'T YOU REALIZE THE PHILISTINES ARE OUR RULERS?
THEY'VE CAUSED ME PAIN.
THEY'VE CAUSED US ALL PAIN, SAMSON. BUT NOW THEY WANT US TO BRING YOU TO THEM... TIED.
AND IT LOOKS LIKE YOU BROUGHT SOME MEN TO HELP YOU.
COULD YOU JUST RAISE YOUR- THANKS.
HMPH! NO PROBLEM.
WE'RE BROTHERS AFTER ALL, RIGHT?
THEY BROUGHT SAMSON TO THE PHILISTINE ARMY.
IT'S HIM!
WE'VE CAPTURED SAMSON!
PUT HIM TO DEATH!
YEAH!
A DONKEY'S JAWBONE...

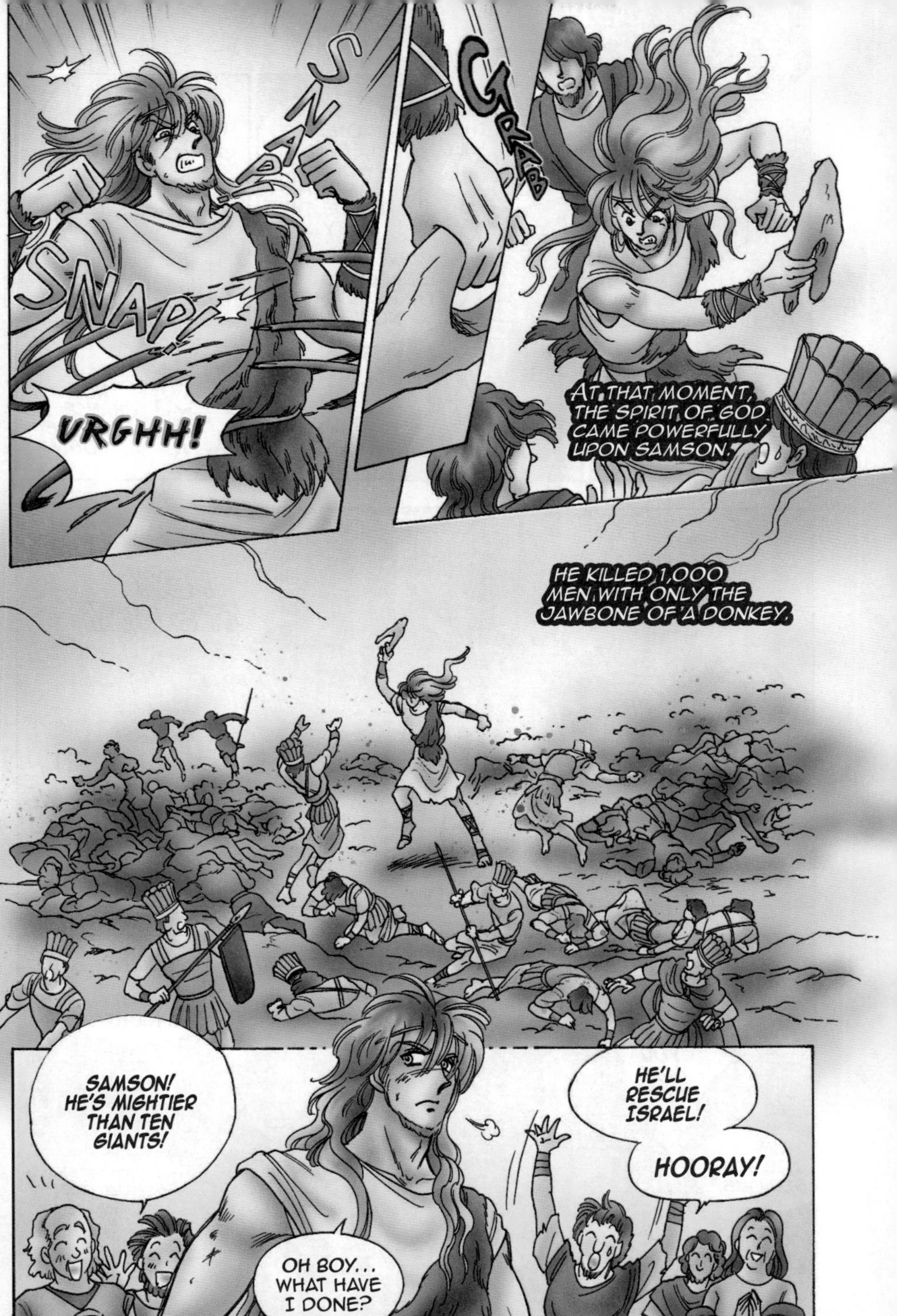
SNAP
SNAP!
URGHH!
GRABB
AT THAT MOMENT, THE SPIRIT OF GOD CAME POWERFULLY UPON SAMSON.
HE KILLED 1,000 MEN WITH ONLY THE JAWBONE OF A DONKEY.
SAMSON! HE'S MIGHTIER THAN TEN GIANTS!
HE'LL RESCUE ISRAEL!
HOORAY!
OH BOY... WHAT HAVE I DONE?

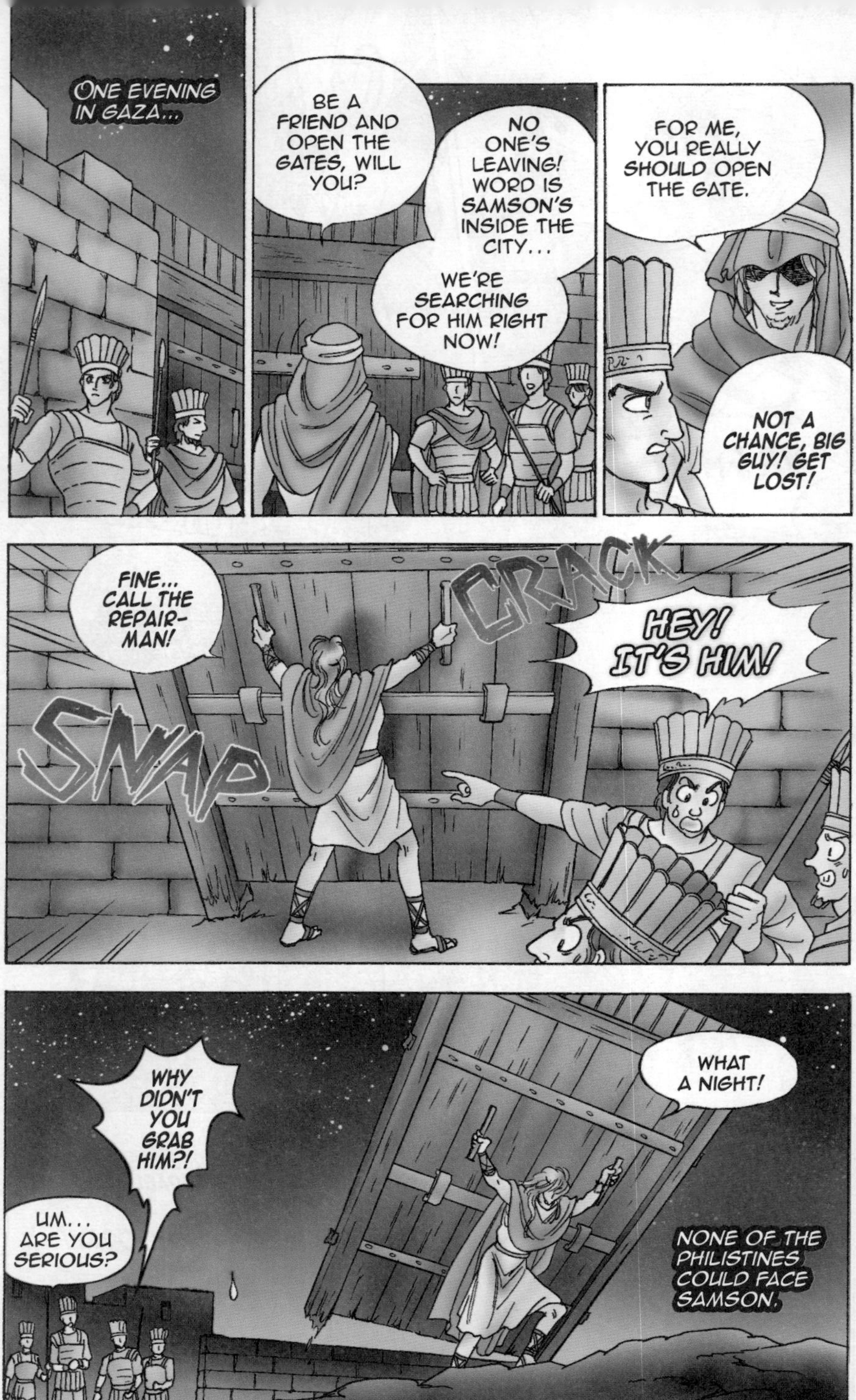

ONE EVENING IN GAZA...
BE A FRIEND AND OPEN THE GATES, WILL YOU?
NO ONE'S LEAVING! WORD IS SAMSON'S INSIDE THE CITY...
WE'RE SEARCHING FOR HIM RIGHT NOW!
FOR ME, YOU REALLY SHOULD OPEN THE GATE.
NOT A CHANCE, BIG GUY! GET LOST!
FINE... CALL THE REPAIR-MAN!
CRACK
HEY! IT'S HIM!
SNAP
WHY DIDN'T YOU GRAB HIM?!
UM... ARE YOU SERIOUS?
WHAT A NIGHT!
NONE OF THE PHILISTINES COULD FACE SAMSON.

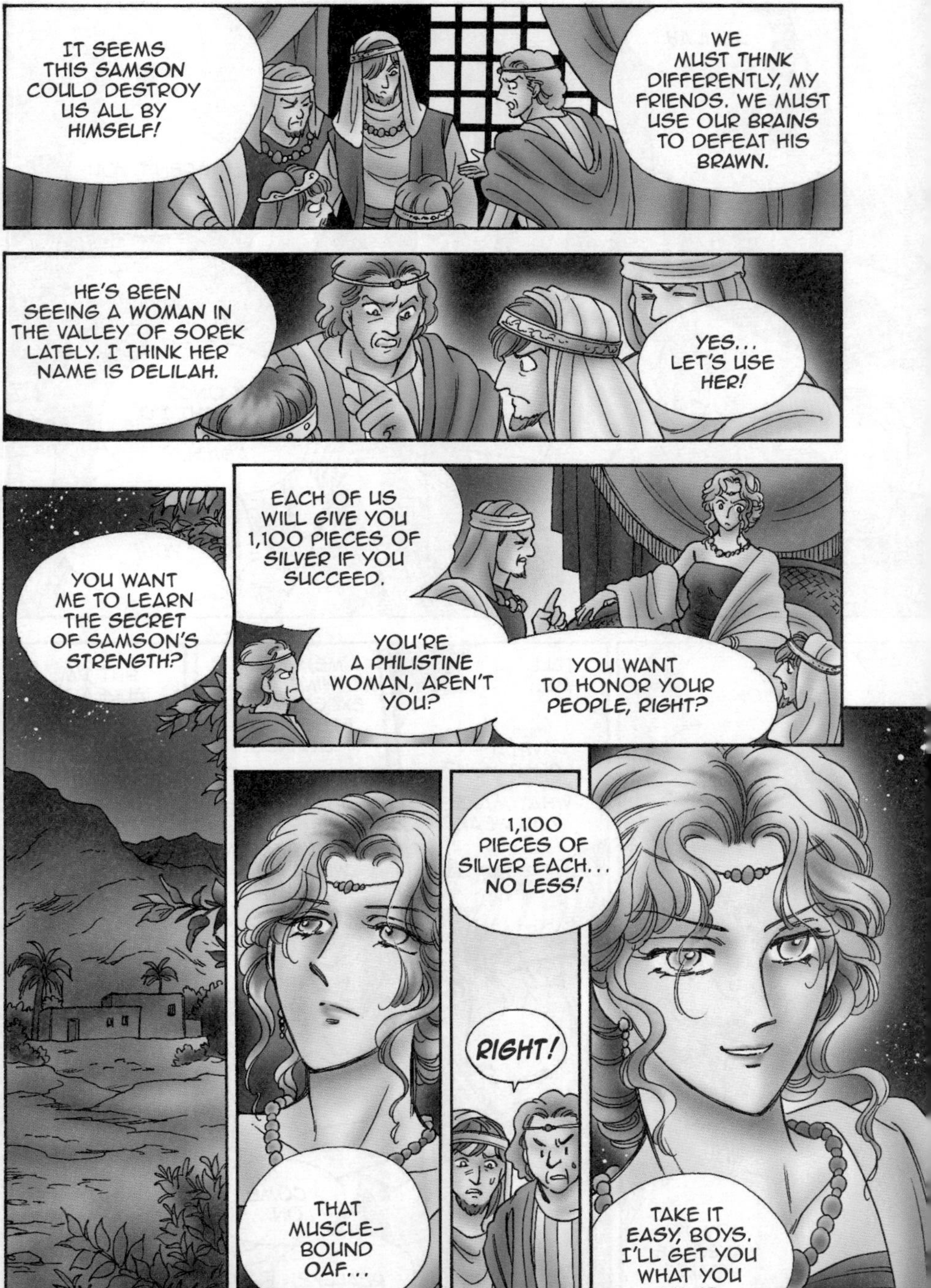
IT SEEMS THIS SAMSON COULD DESTROY US ALL BY HIMSELF!
WE MUST THINK DIFFERENTLY, MY FRIENDS. WE MUST USE OUR BRAINS TO DEFEAT HIS BRAWN.
HE'S BEEN SEEING A WOMAN IN THE VALLEY OF SOREK LATELY. I THINK HER NAME IS DELILAH.
YES... LET'S USE HER!
EACH OF US WILL GIVE YOU 1,100 PIECES OF SILVER IF YOU SUCCEED.
YOU WANT ME TO LEARN THE SECRET OF SAMSON'S STRENGTH?
YOU'RE A PHILISTINE WOMAN, AREN'T YOU?
YOU WANT TO HONOR YOUR PEOPLE, RIGHT?
1,100 PIECES OF SILVER EACH... NO LESS!
RIGHT!
THAT MUSCLE-BOUND OAF...
TAKE IT EASY, BOYS. I'LL GET YOU WHAT YOU WANT.

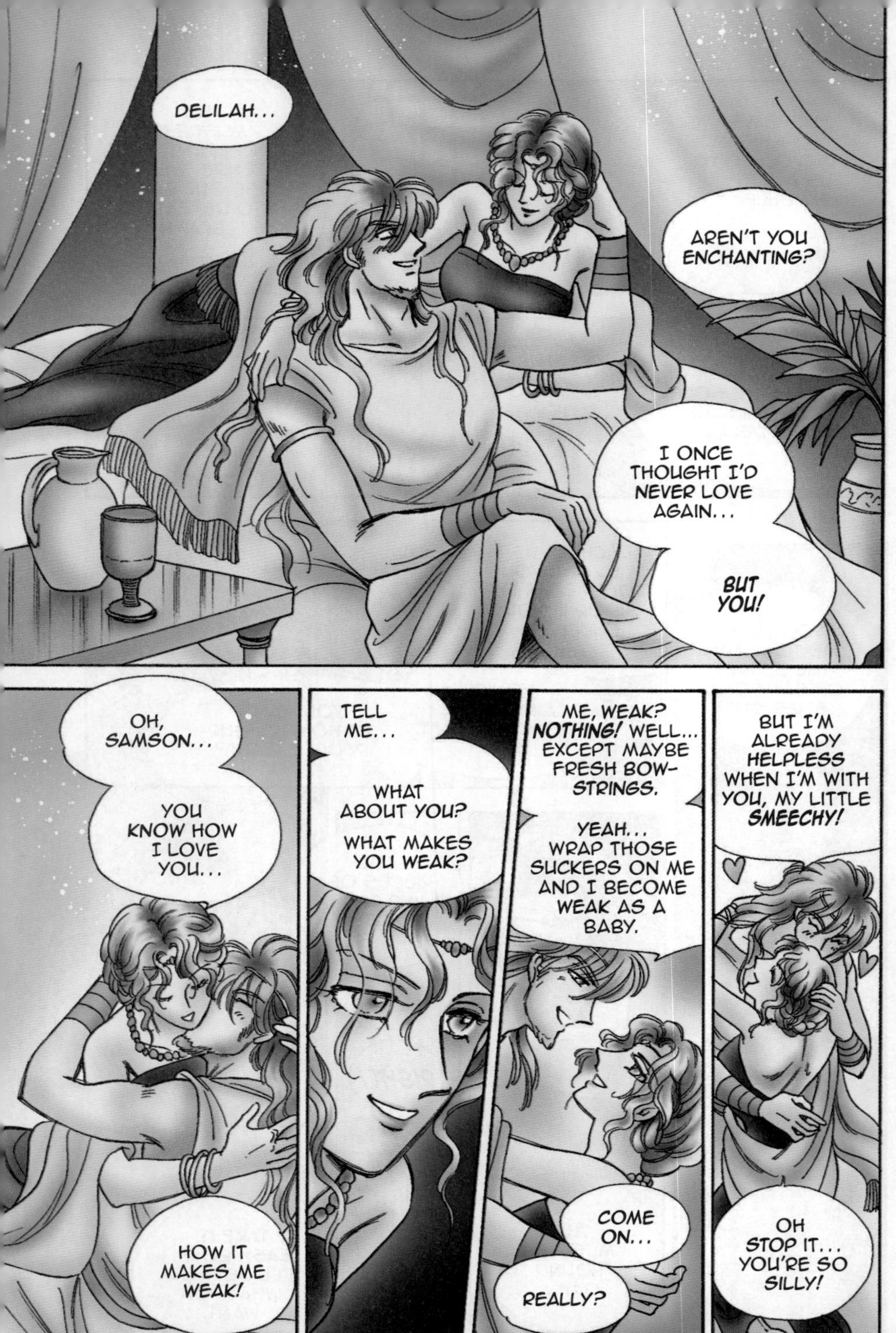
DELILAH...
AREN'T YOU ENCHANTING?
I ONCE THOUGHT I'D NEVER LOVE AGAIN...
BUT YOU!
OH, SAMSON...
YOU KNOW HOW I LOVE YOU...
HOW IT MAKES ME WEAK!
TELL ME...
WHAT ABOUT YOU?
WHAT MAKES YOU WEAK?
ME, WEAK? NOTHING! WELL... EXCEPT MAYBE FRESH BOW-STRINGS.
YEAH... WRAP THOSE SUCKERS ON ME AND I BECOME WEAK AS A BABY.
COME ON...
REALLY?
BUT I'M ALREADY HELPLESS WHEN I'M WITH YOU, MY LITTLE SMEECHY!
OH STOP IT... YOU'RE SO SILLY!

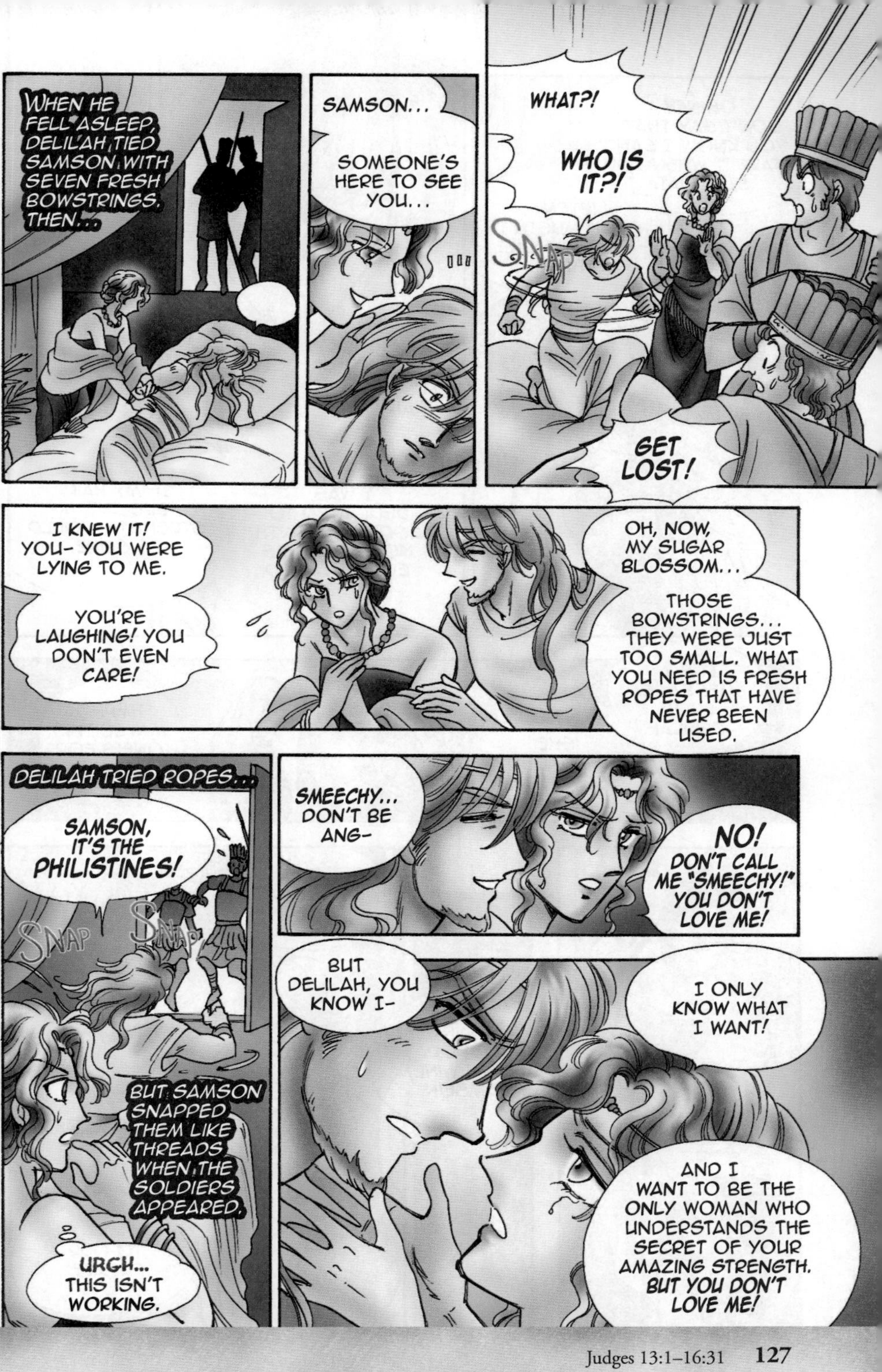
WHEN HE FELL ASLEEP, DELIL'AH TIED SAMSON WITH SEVEN FRESH BOWSTRINGS. THEN...
SAMSON...
SOMEONE'S HERE TO SEE YOU...
WHAT?!
WHO IS IT?!
SNAP
GET LOST!
I KNEW IT! YOU- YOU WERE LYING TO ME.
YOU'RE LAUGHING! YOU DON'T EVEN CARE!
OH, NOW, MY SUGAR BLOSSOM...
THOSE BOWSTRINGS... THEY WERE JUST TOO SMALL. WHAT YOU NEED IS FRESH ROPES THAT HAVE NEVER BEEN USED.
DELILAH TRIED ROPES...
SAMSON, IT'S THE PHILISTINES!
SNAP
SNAP
BUT SAMSON SNAPPED THEM LIKE THREADS WHEN THE SOLDIERS APPEARED.
URGH... THIS ISN'T WORKING.
SMEECHY... DON'T BE ANG-
NO! DON'T CALL ME "SMEECHY!" YOU DON'T LOVE ME!
BUT DELILAH, YOU KNOW I-
I ONLY KNOW WHAT I WANT!
AND I WANT TO BE THE ONLY WOMAN WHO UNDERSTANDS THE SECRET OF YOUR AMAZING STRENGTH. BUT YOU DON'T LOVE ME!

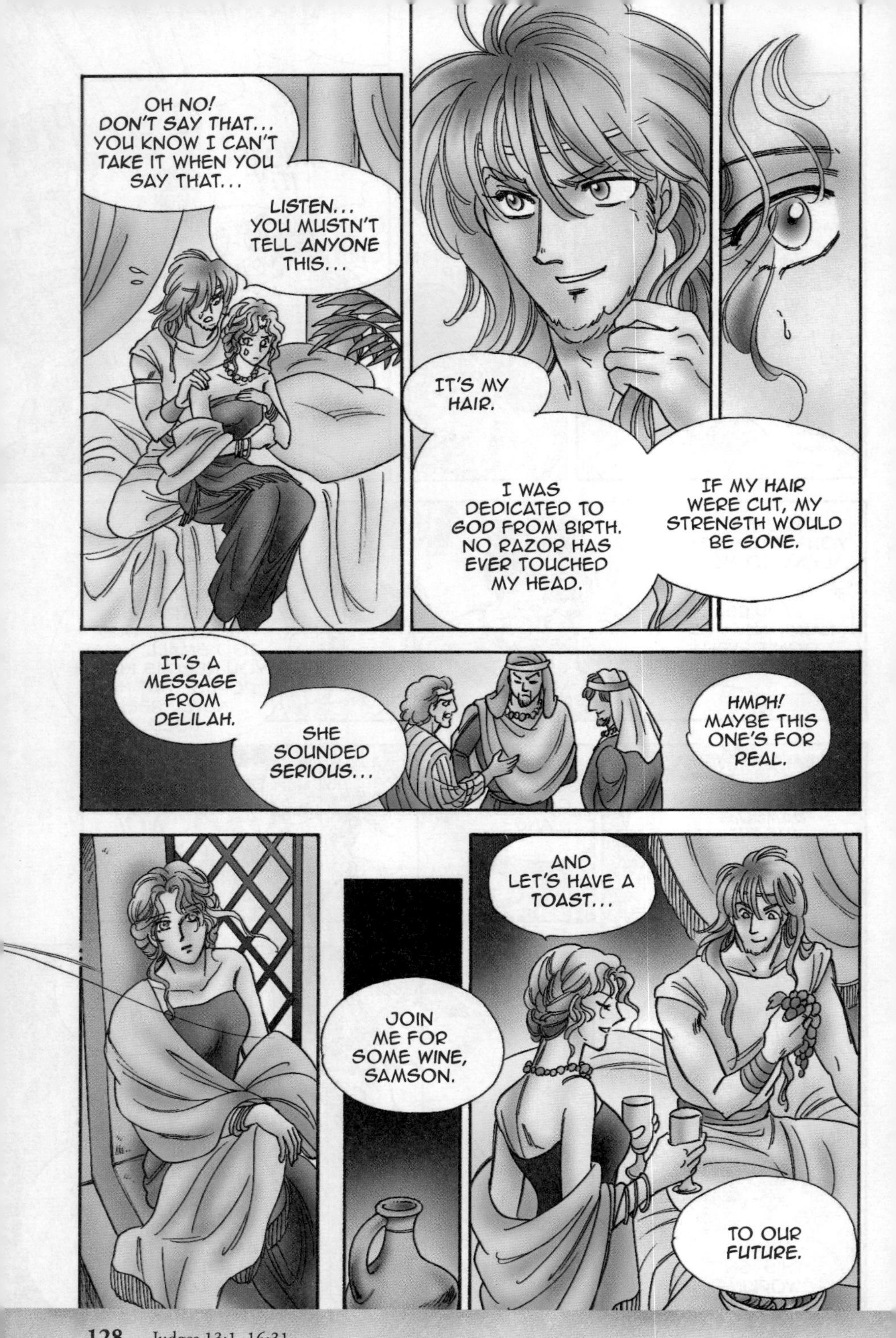
OH NO! DON'T SAY THAT... YOU KNOW I CAN'T TAKE IT WHEN YOU SAY THAT...
LISTEN... YOU MUSTN'T TELL ANYONE THIS...
IT'S MY HAIR.
I WAS DEDICATED TO GOD FROM BIRTH. NO RAZOR HAS EVER TOUCHED MY HEAD.
IF MY HAIR WERE CUT, MY STRENGTH WOULD BE GONE.
IT'S A MESSAGE FROM DELILAH.
SHE SOUNDED SERIOUS...
HMPH! MAYBE THIS ONE'S FOR REAL.
JOIN ME FOR SOME WINE, SAMSON.
AND LET'S HAVE A TOAST...
TO OUR FUTURE.

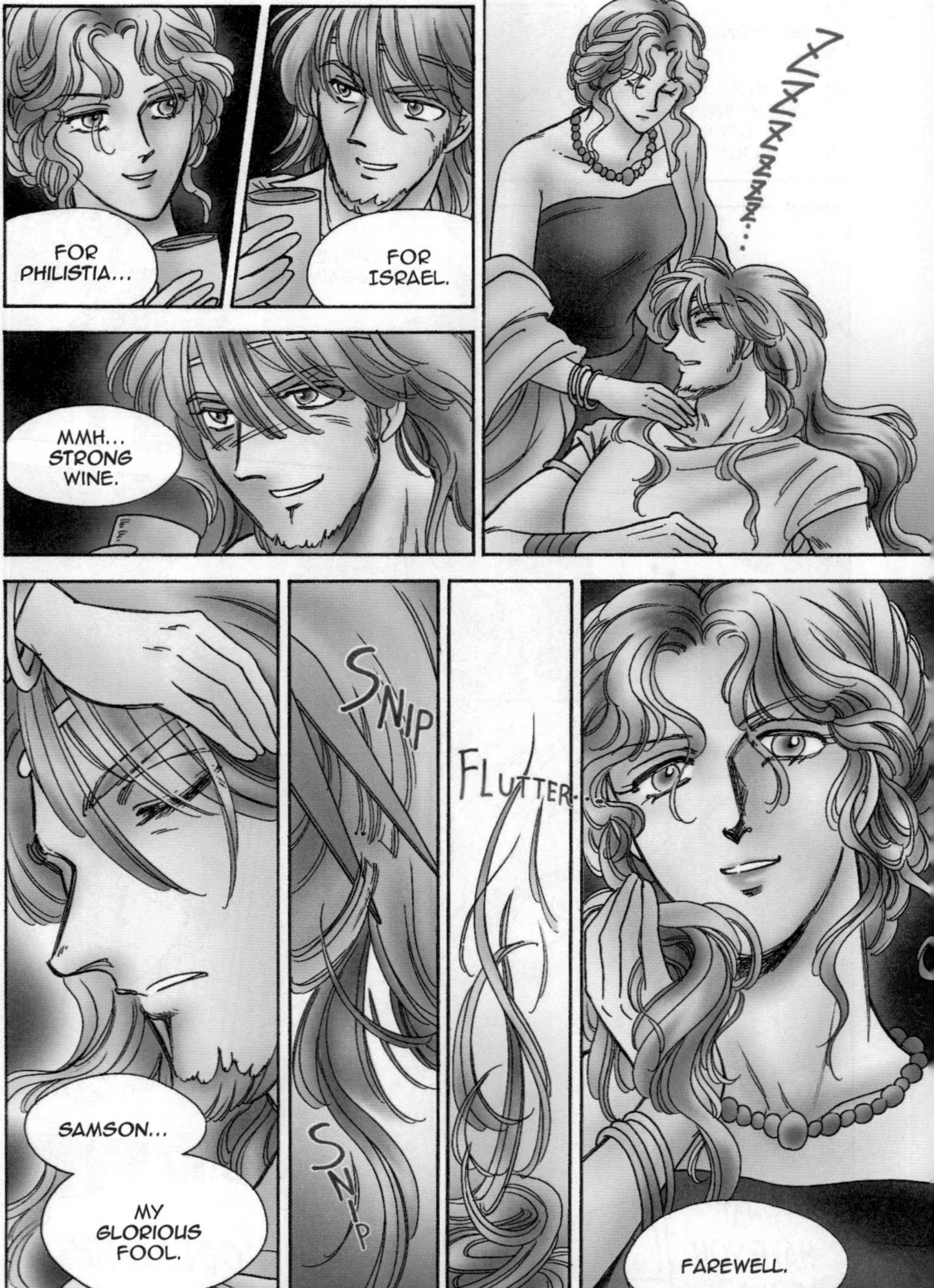
FOR PHILISTIA...
FOR ISRAEL.
MMH... STRONG WINE.
ZZZZZZZZ...
SAMSON...
MY GLORIOUS FOOL.
SNIP
SNIP
FLUTTER...
FAREWELL.

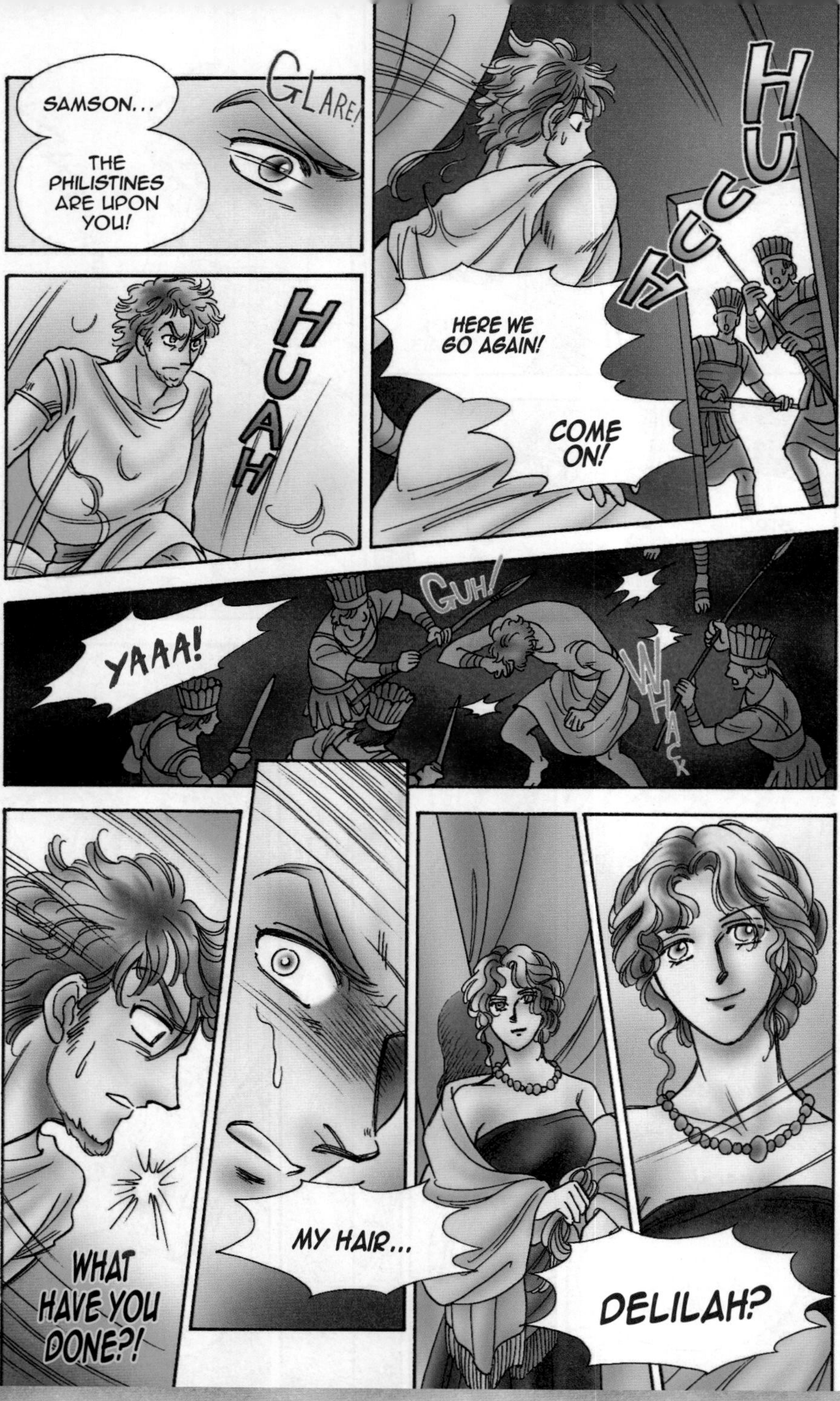
SAMSON...
THE PHILISTINES ARE UPON YOU!
GLARE!
HUUCUH
HUAH
HERE WE GO AGAIN!
COME ON!
GUH!
YAAA!
WHACK
WHAT HAVE YOU DONE?!
MY HAIR...
DELILAH?

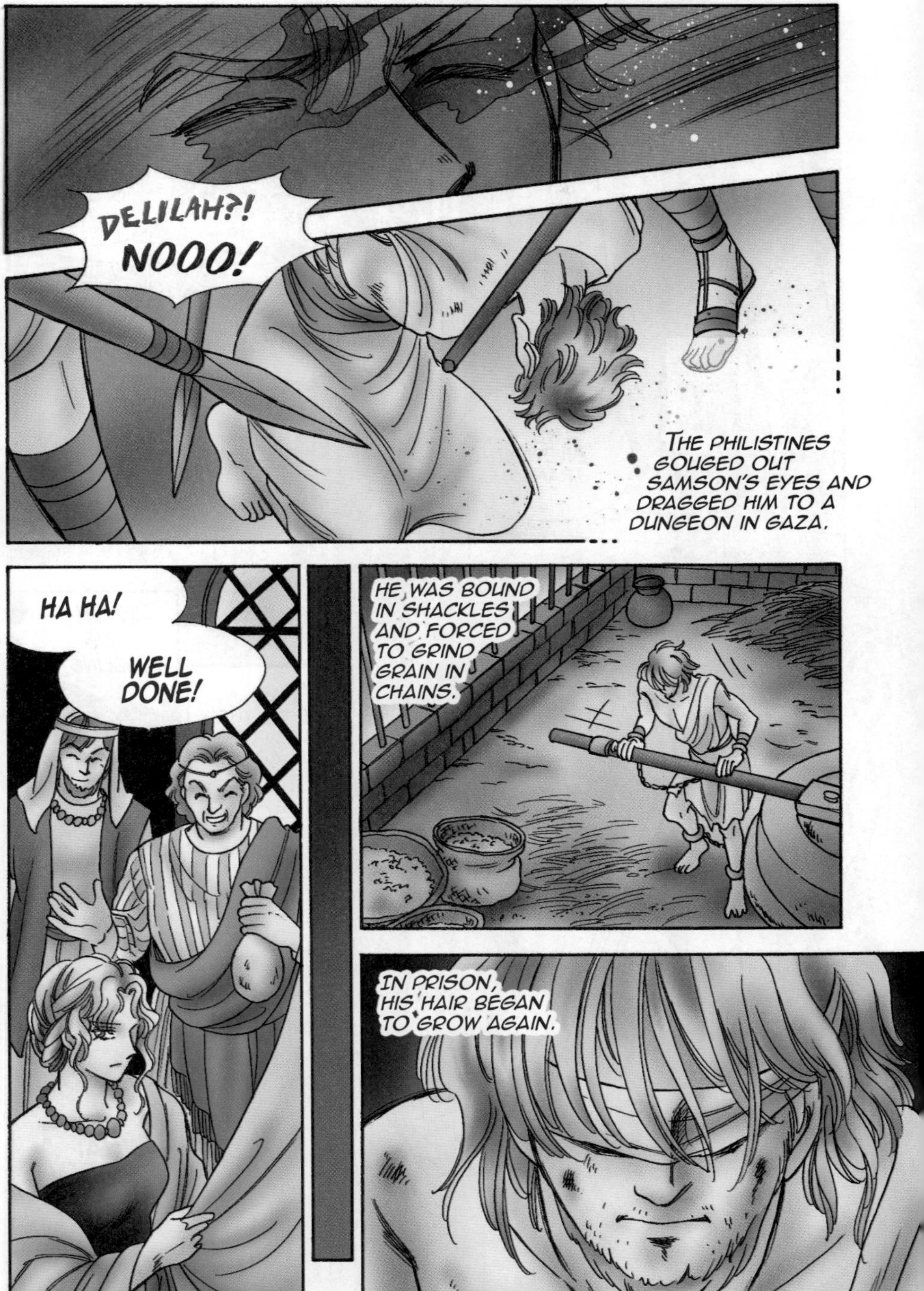
DELILAH?! NOOO!
THE PHILISTINES GOUGED OUT SAMSON'S EYES AND DRAGGED HIM TO A DUNGEON IN GAZA.
HA HA!
WELL DONE!
HE WAS BOUND IN SHACKLES AND FORCED TO GRIND GRAIN IN CHAINS.
IN PRISON, HIS HAIR BEGAN TO GROW AGAIN.

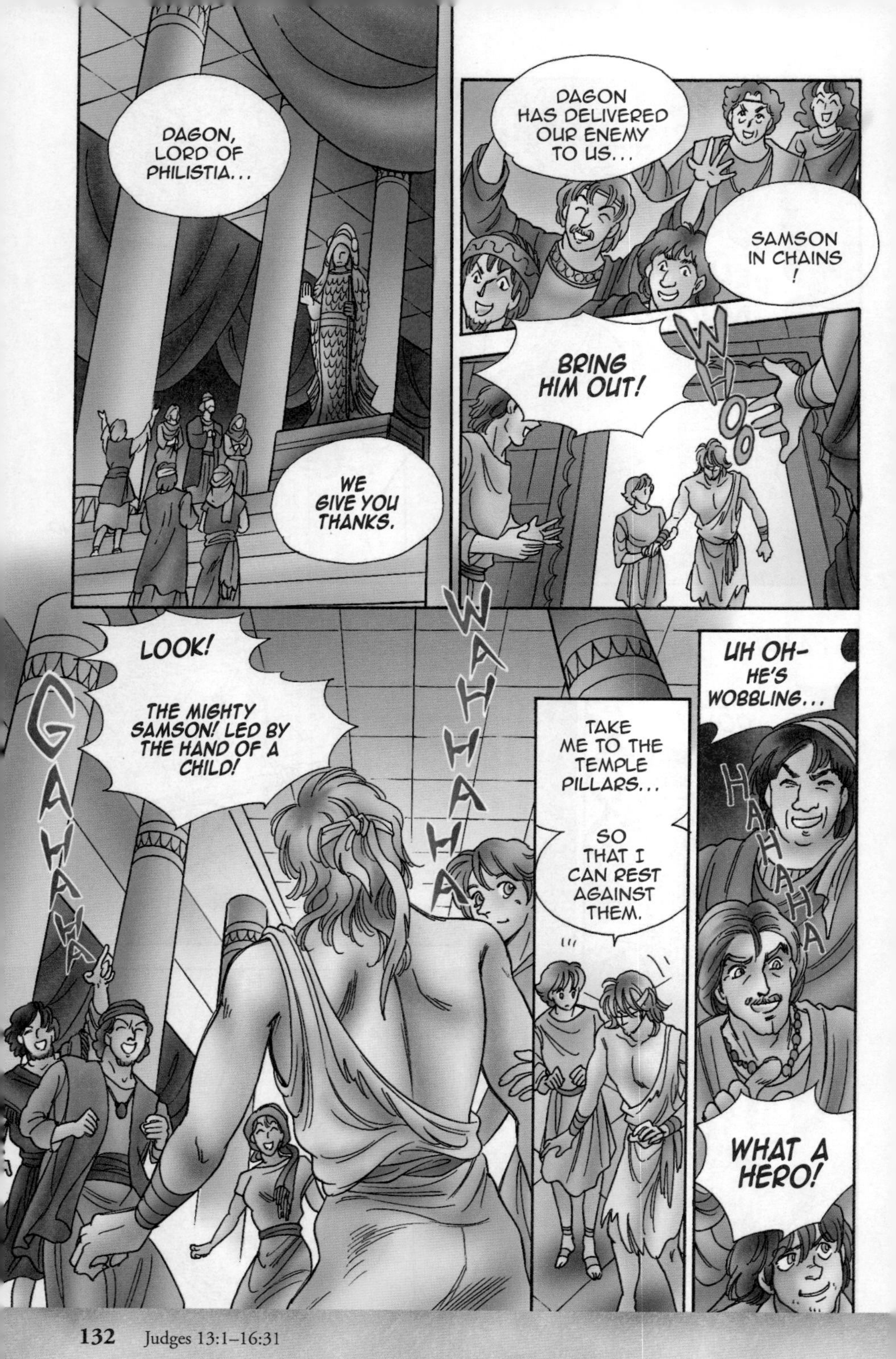
DAGON, LORD OF PHILISTIA...
WE GIVE YOU THANKS.
DAGON HAS DELIVERED OUR ENEMY TO US...
SAMSON IN CHAINS!
BRING HIM OUT!
WHOO
LOOK!
THE MIGHTY SAMSON! LED BY THE HAND OF A CHILD!
GAHAHAHA
WAHAHAHA
TAKE ME TO THE TEMPLE PILLARS...
SO THAT I CAN REST AGAINST THEM.
UH OH- HE'S WOBBLING...
HAHAHAHA
WHAT A HERO!

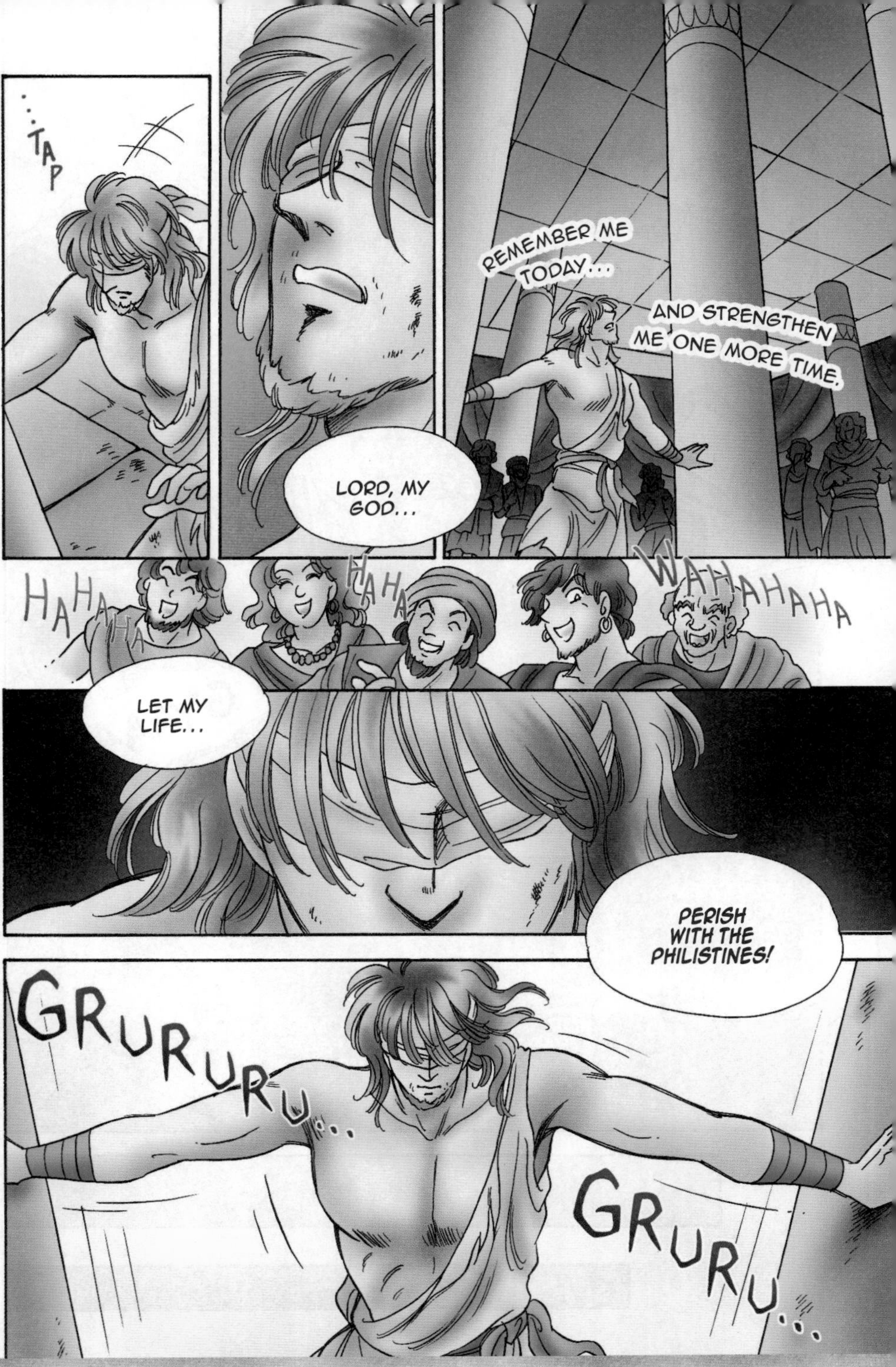
...TAP
LORD, MY GOD...
REMEMBER ME TODAY...
AND STRENGTHEN ME ONE MORE TIME.
HAHAHAHA
HAHA
WAHAHAHAHA
LET MY LIFE...
PERISH WITH THE PHILISTINES!
GRURURU...
GRURU...

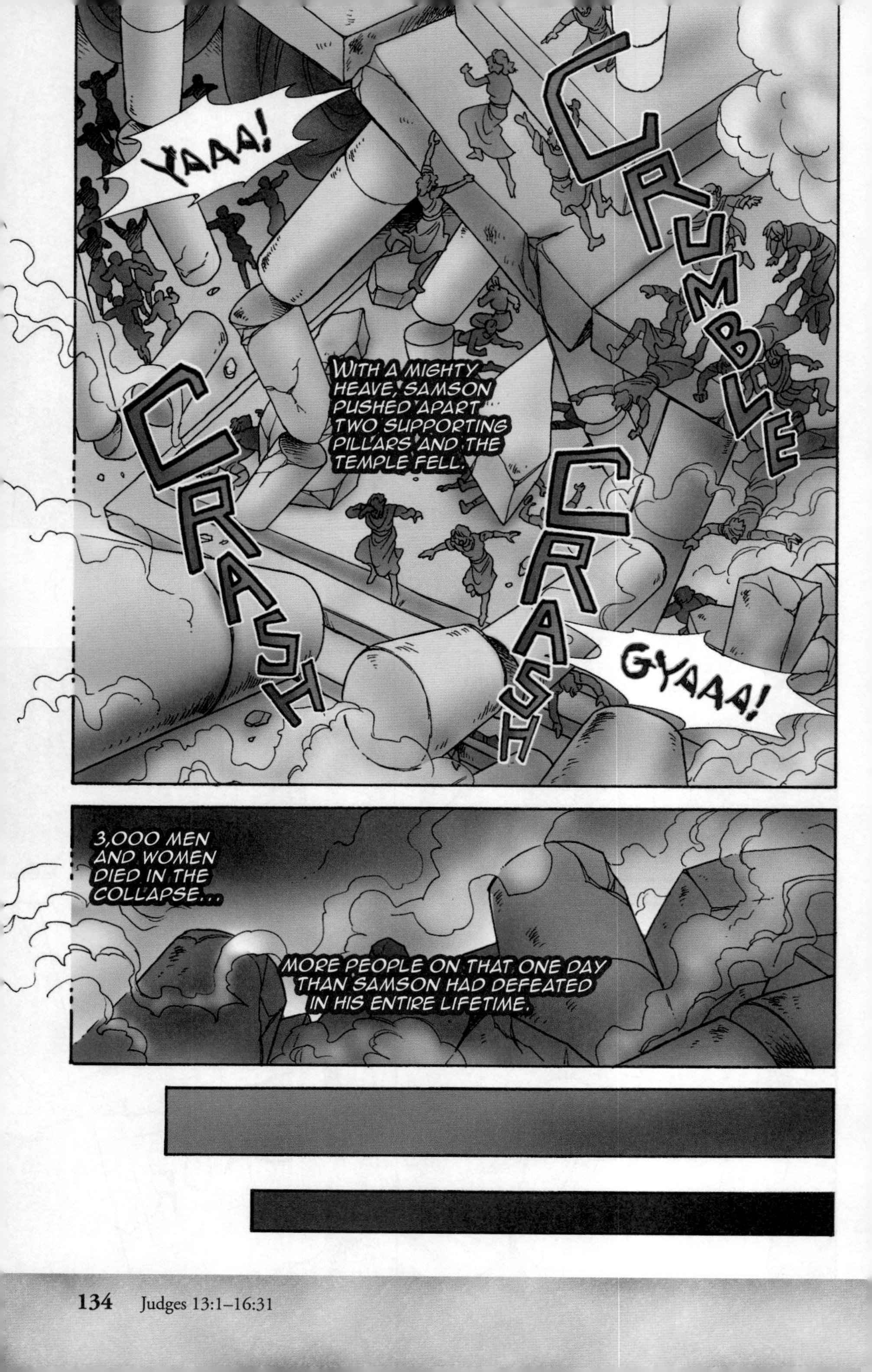
YAAA!
CRUMBLE
WITH A MIGHTY HEAVE, SAMSON PUSHED APART TWO SUPPORTING PILLARS AND THE TEMPLE FELL.
CRASH
CRASH
GYAAA!
3,000 MEN AND WOMEN DIED IN THE COLLAPSE...
MORE PEOPLE ON THAT ONE DAY THAN SAMSON HAD DEFEATED IN HIS ENTIRE LIFETIME.

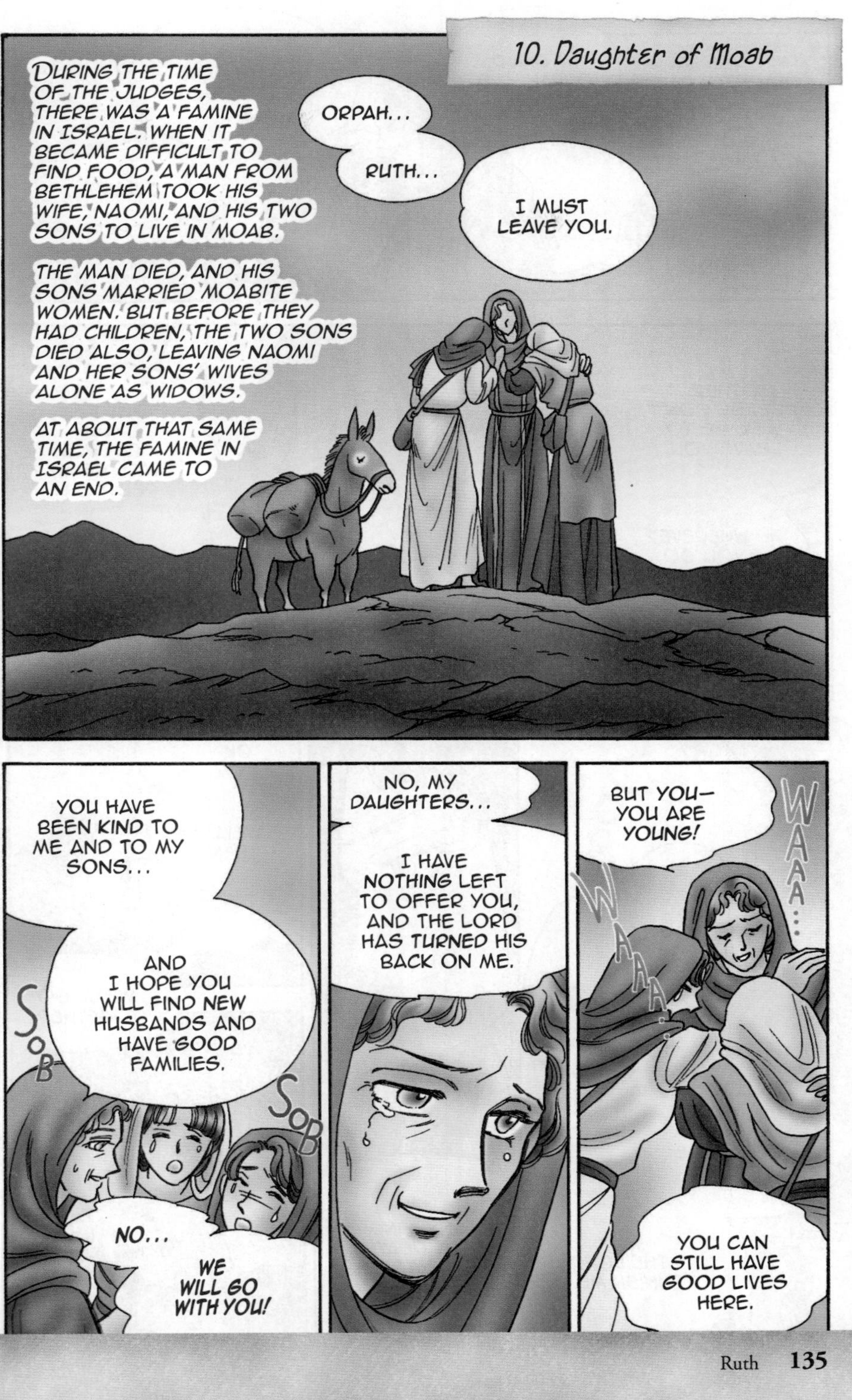
10. Daughter of Moab
DURING THE TIME OF THE JUDGES, THERE WAS A FAMINE IN ISRAEL. WHEN IT BECAME DIFFICULT TO FIND FOOD, A MAN FROM BETHLEHEM TOOK HIS WIFE, NAOMI, AND HIS TWO SONS TO LIVE IN MOAB.
THE MAN DIED, AND HIS SONS MARRIED MOABITE WOMEN. BUT BEFORE THEY HAD CHILDREN, THE TWO SONS DIED ALSO, LEAVING NAOMI AND HER SONS' WIVES ALONE AS WIDOWS.
AT ABOUT THAT SAME TIME, THE FAMINE IN ISRAEL CAME TO AN END.
ORPAH...
RUTH...
I MUST LEAVE YOU.
YOU HAVE BEEN KIND TO ME AND TO MY SONS...
AND I HOPE YOU WILL FIND NEW HUSBANDS AND HAVE GOOD FAMILIES.
SOB
SOB
NO...
WE WILL GO WITH YOU!
NO, MY DAUGHTERS...
I HAVE NOTHING LEFT TO OFFER YOU, AND THE LORD HAS TURNED HIS BACK ON ME.
BUT YOU— YOU ARE YOUNG!
WAAA...
WAAAA...
YOU CAN STILL HAVE GOOD LIVES HERE.

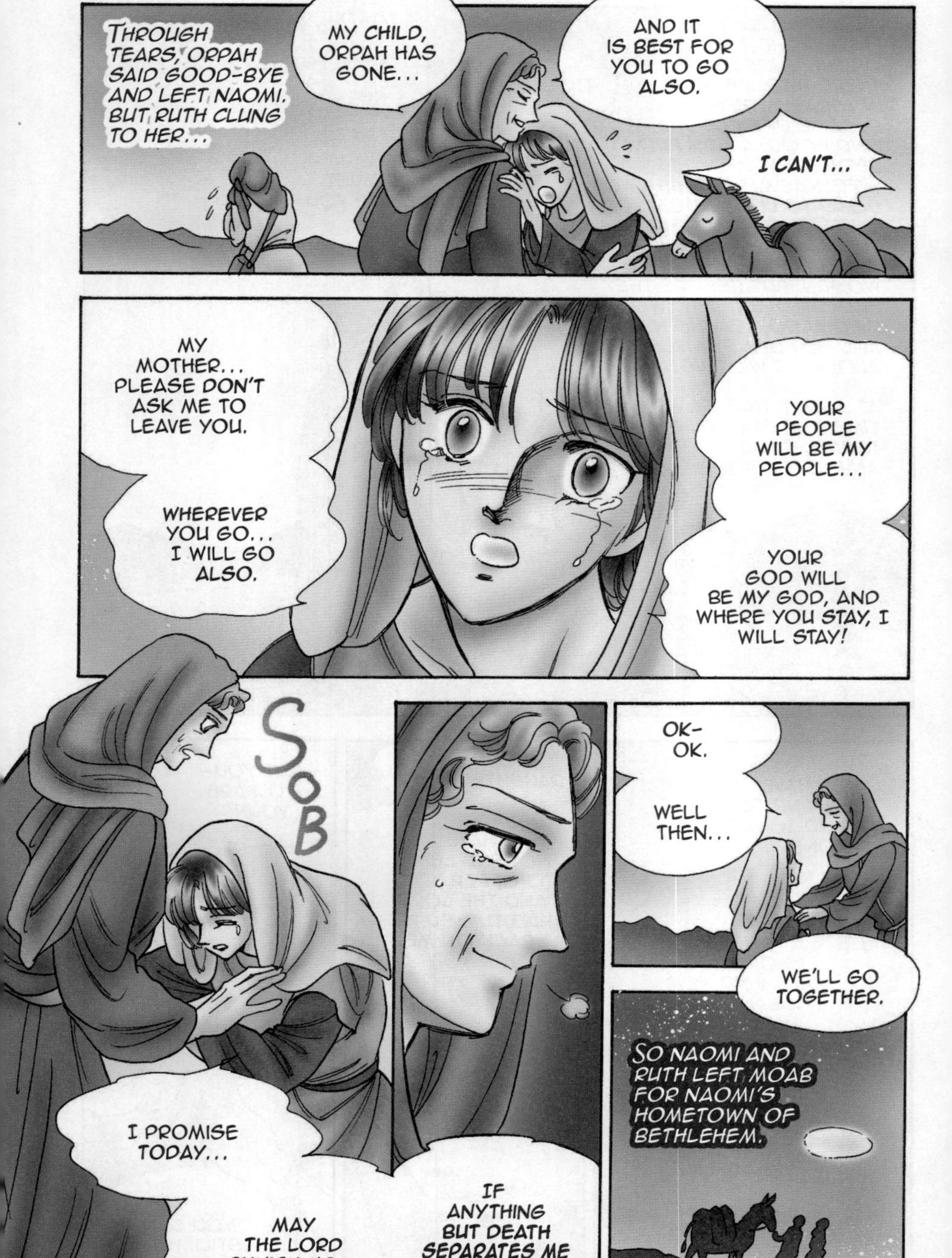
Through tears, Orpah said good-bye and left Naomi. But Ruth clung to her...
My child, Orpah has gone...
And it is best for you to go also.
I can't...
My mother... please don't ask me to leave you.
Wherever you go... I will go also.
Your people will be my people...
Your God will be my God, and where you stay, I will stay!
SOB
I promise today...
May the Lord punish me...
If anything but death separates me from you!
Ok-ok.
Well then...
We'll go together.
So Naomi and Ruth left Moab for Naomi's hometown of Bethlehem.

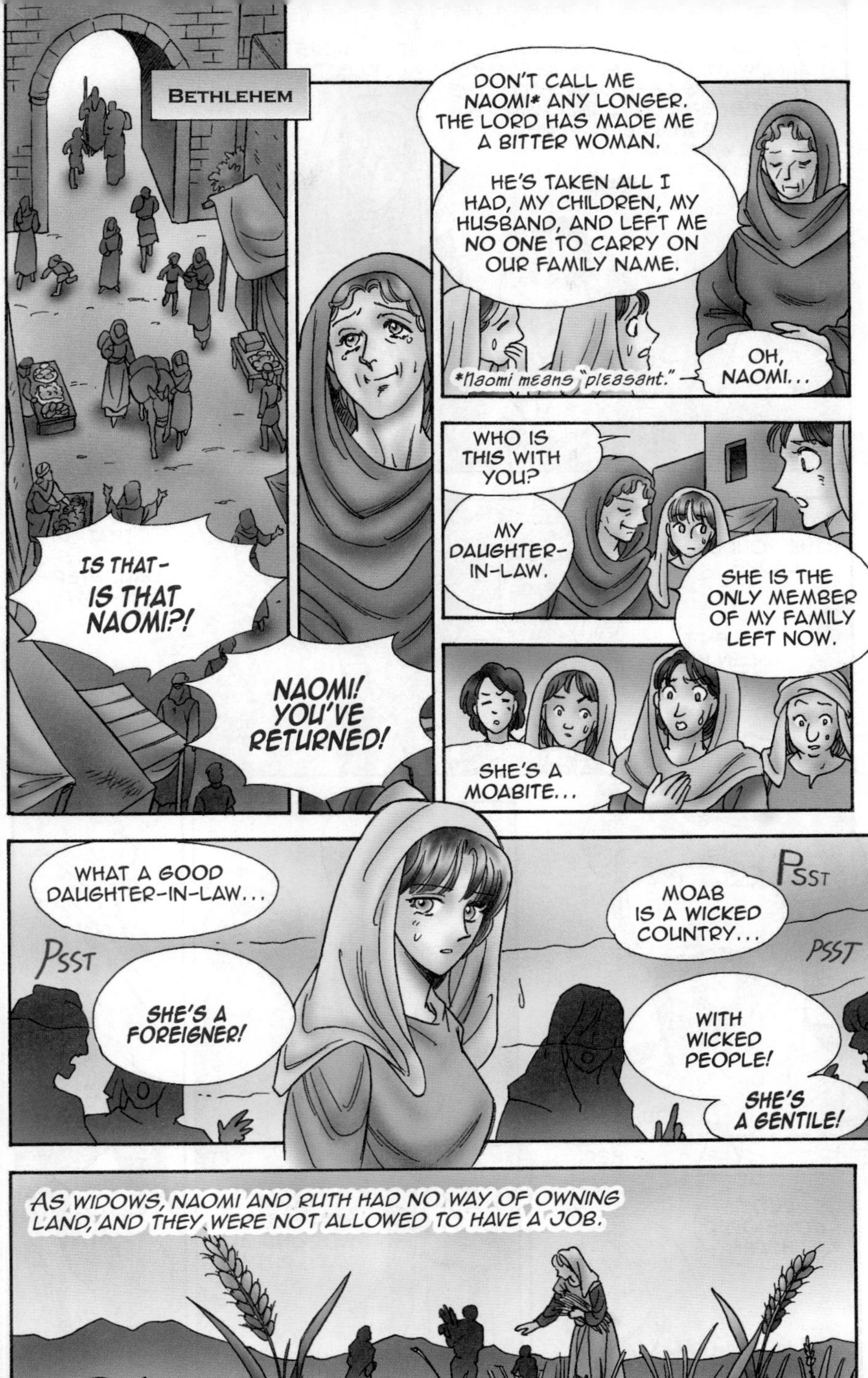
BETHLEHEM
IS THAT- IS THAT NAOMI?!
NAOMI! YOU'VE RETURNED!
DON'T CALL ME NAOMI* ANY LONGER. THE LORD HAS MADE ME A BITTER WOMAN.
HE'S TAKEN ALL I HAD, MY CHILDREN, MY HUSBAND, AND LEFT ME NO ONE TO CARRY ON OUR FAMILY NAME.
*Naomi means "pleasant."
OH, NAOMI...
WHO IS THIS WITH YOU?
MY DAUGHTER-IN-LAW.
SHE IS THE ONLY MEMBER OF MY FAMILY LEFT NOW.
SHE'S A MOABITE...
WHAT A GOOD DAUGHTER-IN-LAW...
PSST
SHE'S A FOREIGNER!
PSST
MOAB IS A WICKED COUNTRY...
PSST
WITH WICKED PEOPLE!
SHE'S A GENTILE!
AS WIDOWS, NAOMI AND RUTH HAD NO WAY OF OWNING LAND, AND THEY WERE NOT ALLOWED TO HAVE A JOB.

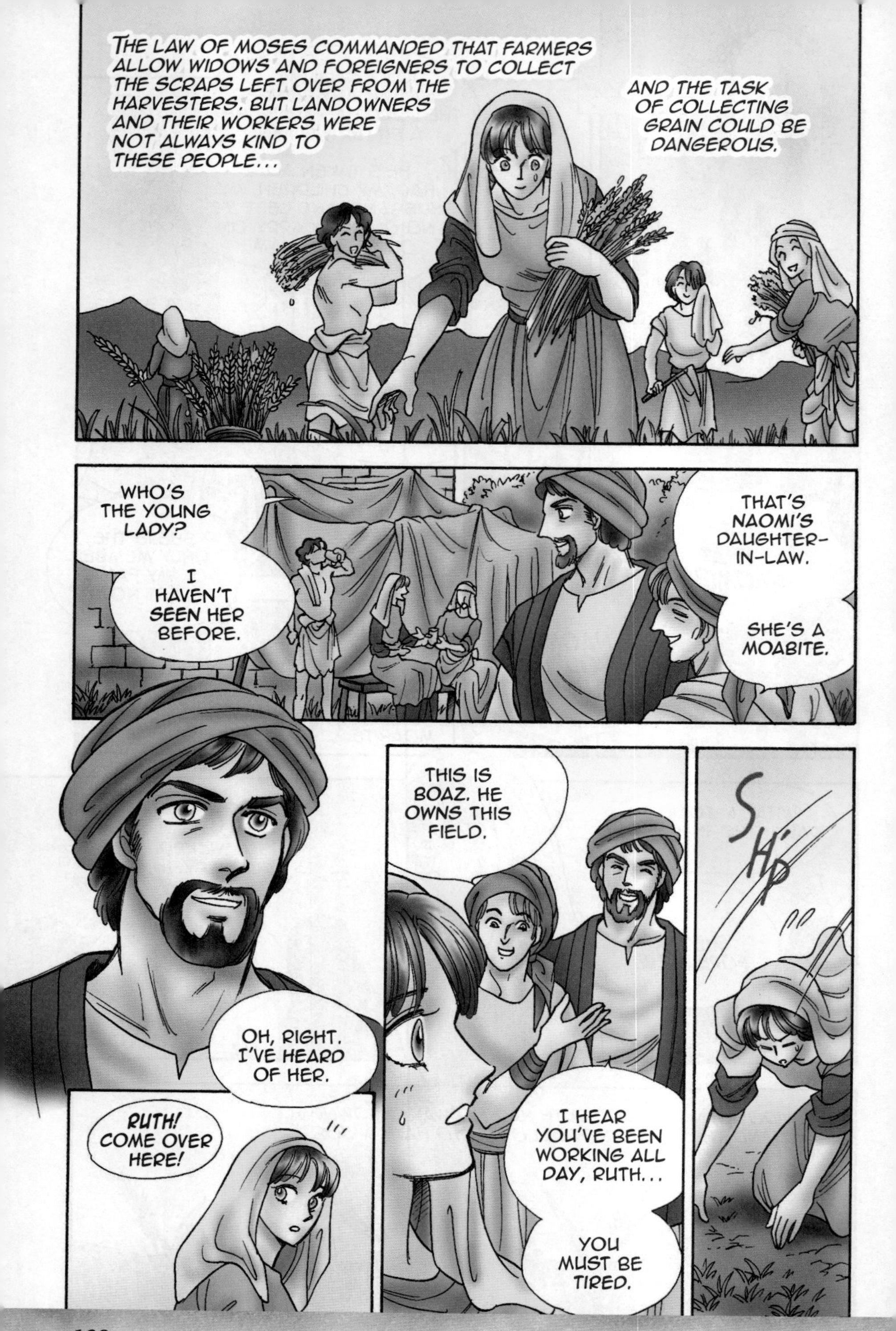
THE LAW OF MOSES COMMANDED THAT FARMERS ALLOW WIDOWS AND FOREIGNERS TO COLLECT THE SCRAPS LEFT OVER FROM THE HARVESTERS. BUT LANDOWNERS AND THEIR WORKERS WERE NOT ALWAYS KIND TO THESE PEOPLE...
AND THE TASK OF COLLECTING GRAIN COULD BE DANGEROUS.
WHO'S THE YOUNG LADY?
I HAVEN'T SEEN HER BEFORE.
THAT'S NAOMI'S DAUGHTER-IN-LAW.
SHE'S A MOABITE.
OH, RIGHT. I'VE HEARD OF HER.
RUTH! COME OVER HERE!
SHP
THIS IS BOAZ. HE OWNS THIS FIELD.
I HEAR YOU'VE BEEN WORKING ALL DAY, RUTH...
YOU MUST BE TIRED.

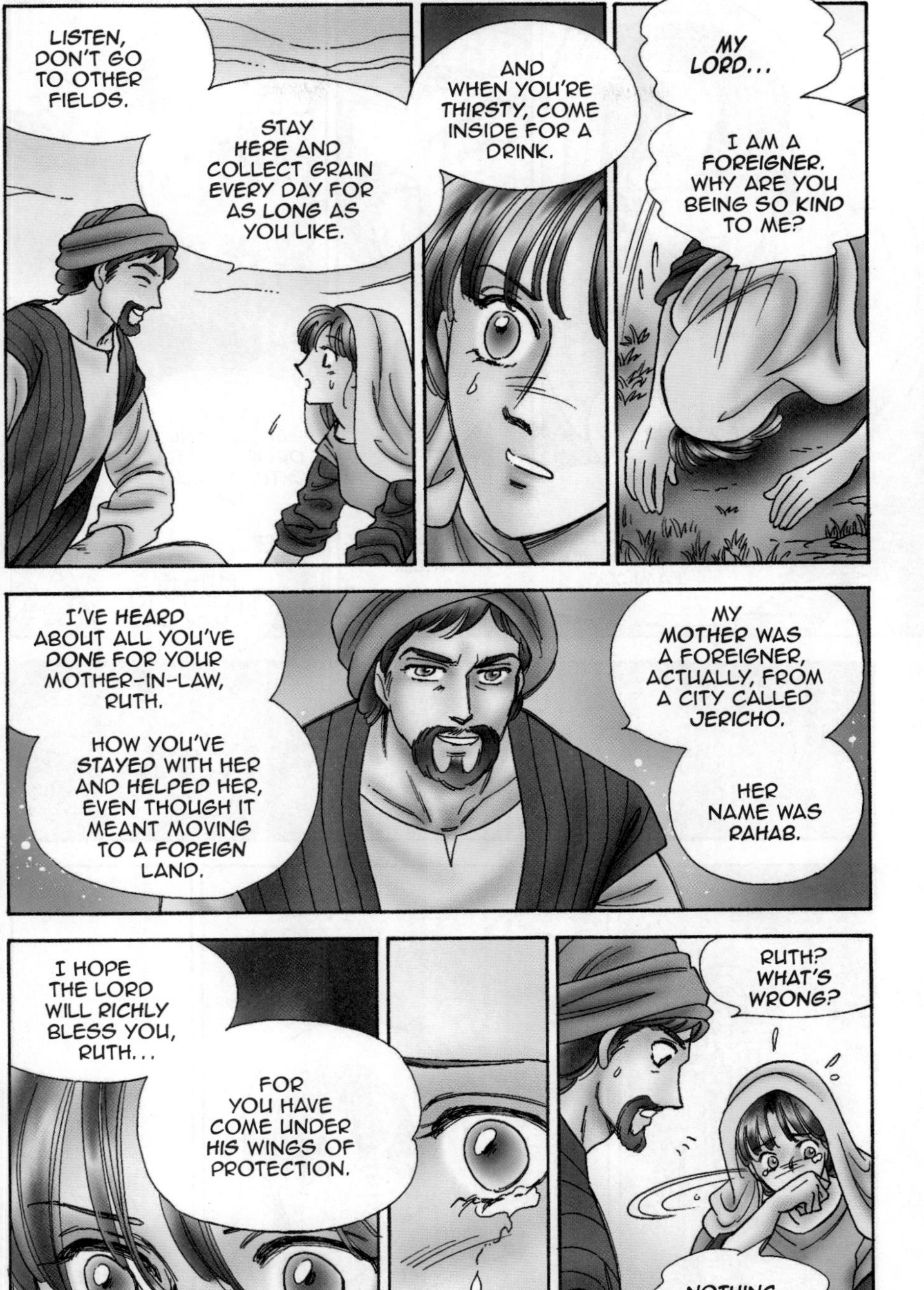
LISTEN, DON'T GO TO OTHER FIELDS.
STAY HERE AND COLLECT GRAIN EVERY DAY FOR AS LONG AS YOU LIKE.
AND WHEN YOU'RE THIRSTY, COME INSIDE FOR A DRINK.
MY LORD...
I AM A FOREIGNER. WHY ARE YOU BEING SO KIND TO ME?
I'VE HEARD ABOUT ALL YOU'VE DONE FOR YOUR MOTHER-IN-LAW, RUTH.
HOW YOU'VE STAYED WITH HER AND HELPED HER, EVEN THOUGH IT MEANT MOVING TO A FOREIGN LAND.
MY MOTHER WAS A FOREIGNER, ACTUALLY, FROM A CITY CALLED JERICHO.
HER NAME WAS RAHAB.
I HOPE THE LORD WILL RICHLY BLESS YOU, RUTH...
FOR YOU HAVE COME UNDER HIS WINGS OF PROTECTION.
RUTH? WHAT'S WRONG?
NOTHING-THANK YOU, SIR.

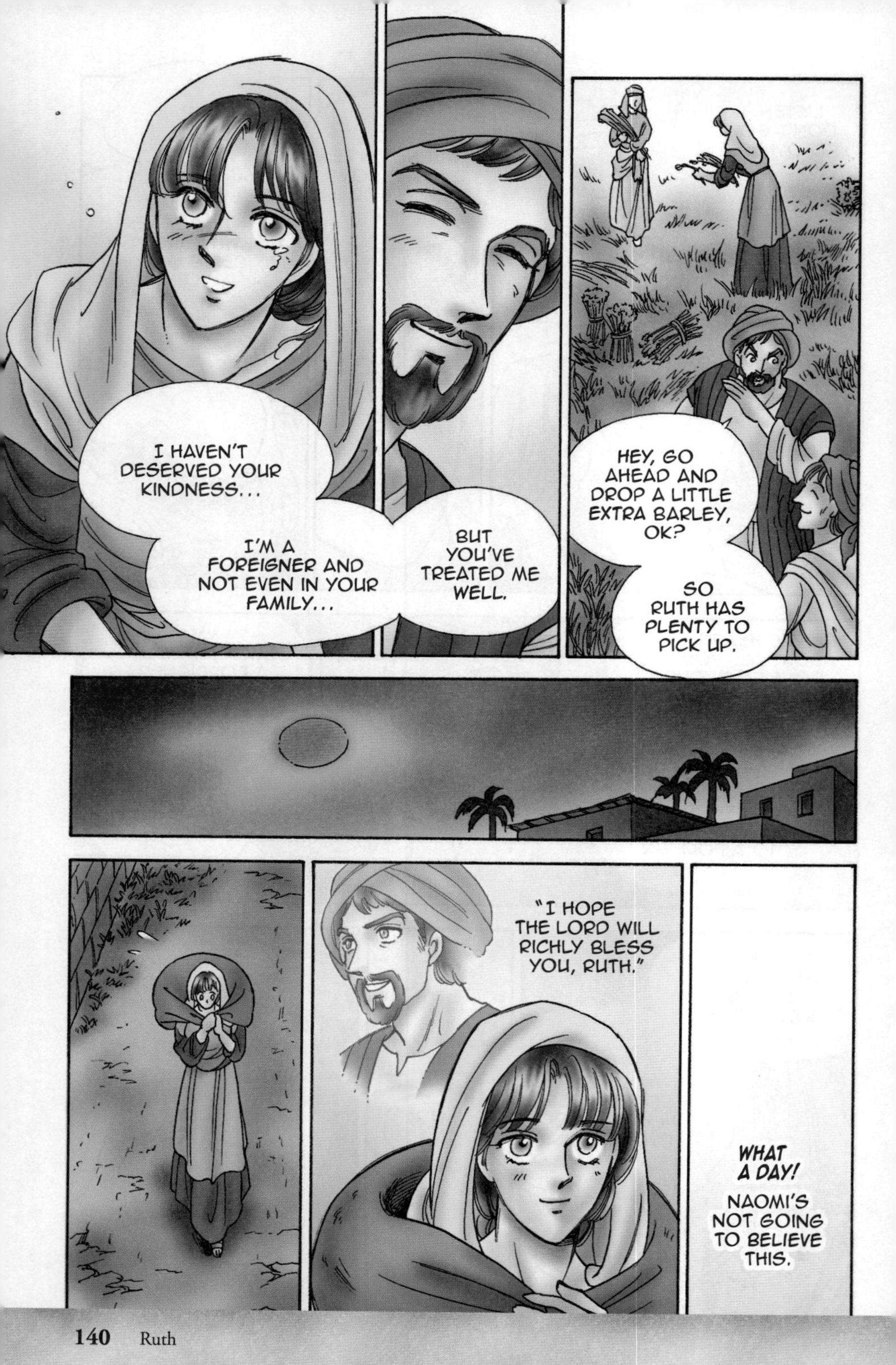
I HAVEN'T DESERVED YOUR KINDNESS...
I'M A FOREIGNER AND NOT EVEN IN YOUR FAMILY...
BUT YOU'VE TREATED ME WELL.
HEY, GO AHEAD AND DROP A LITTLE EXTRA BARLEY, OK?
SO RUTH HAS PLENTY TO PICK UP.
"I HOPE THE LORD WILL RICHLY BLESS YOU, RUTH."
WHAT A DAY!
NAOMI'S NOT GOING TO BELIEVE THIS.

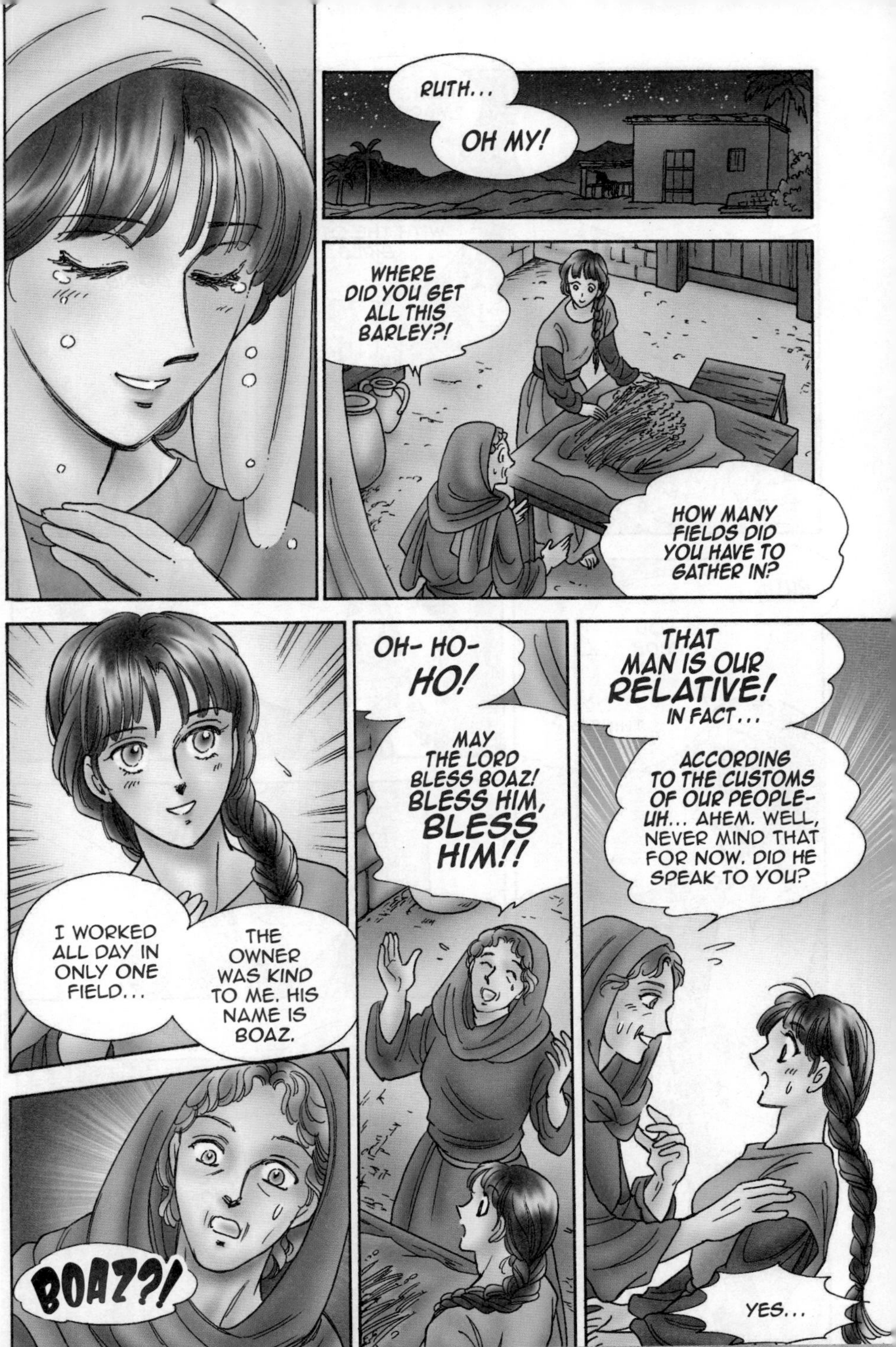
RUTH...
OH MY!
WHERE DID YOU GET ALL THIS BARLEY?!
HOW MANY FIELDS DID YOU HAVE TO GATHER IN?
I WORKED ALL DAY IN ONLY ONE FIELD...
THE OWNER WAS KIND TO ME. HIS NAME IS BOAZ.
BOAZ?!
OH- HO- HO!
MAY THE LORD BLESS BOAZ! BLESS HIM, BLESS HIM!!
THAT MAN IS OUR RELATIVE! IN FACT...
ACCORDING TO THE CUSTOMS OF OUR PEOPLE- UH... AHEM. WELL, NEVER MIND THAT FOR NOW. DID HE SPEAK TO YOU?
YES...

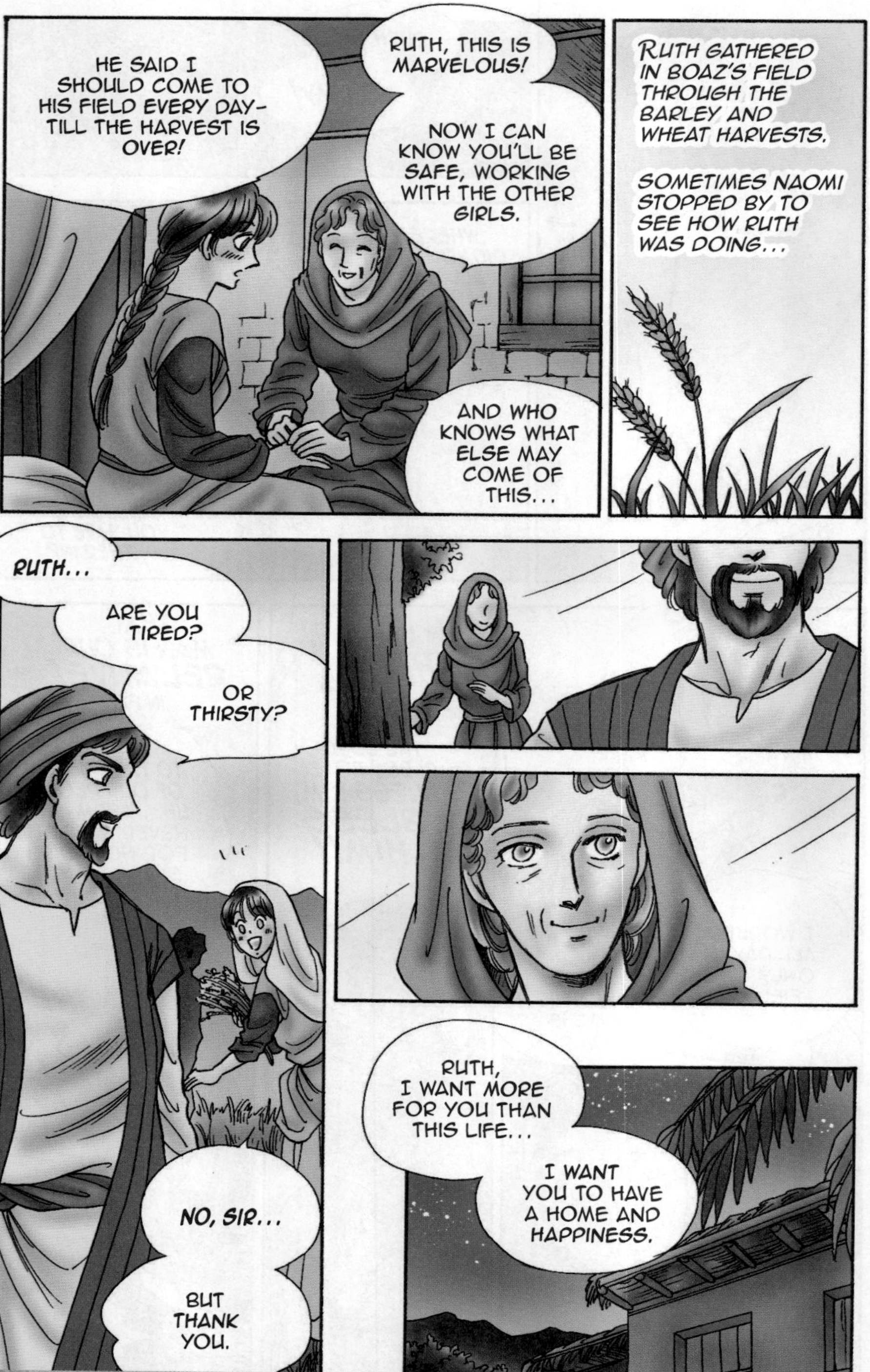
HE SAID I SHOULD COME TO HIS FIELD EVERY DAY-TILL THE HARVEST IS OVER!
RUTH, THIS IS MARVELOUS!
NOW I CAN KNOW YOU'LL BE SAFE, WORKING WITH THE OTHER GIRLS.
AND WHO KNOWS WHAT ELSE MAY COME OF THIS...
RUTH GATHERED IN BOAZ'S FIELD THROUGH THE BARLEY AND WHEAT HARVESTS.
SOMETIMES NAOMI STOPPED BY TO SEE HOW RUTH WAS DOING...
RUTH...
ARE YOU TIRED?
OR THIRSTY?
...
NO, SIR...
BUT THANK YOU.
RUTH, I WANT MORE FOR YOU THAN THIS LIFE...
I WANT YOU TO HAVE A HOME AND HAPPINESS.

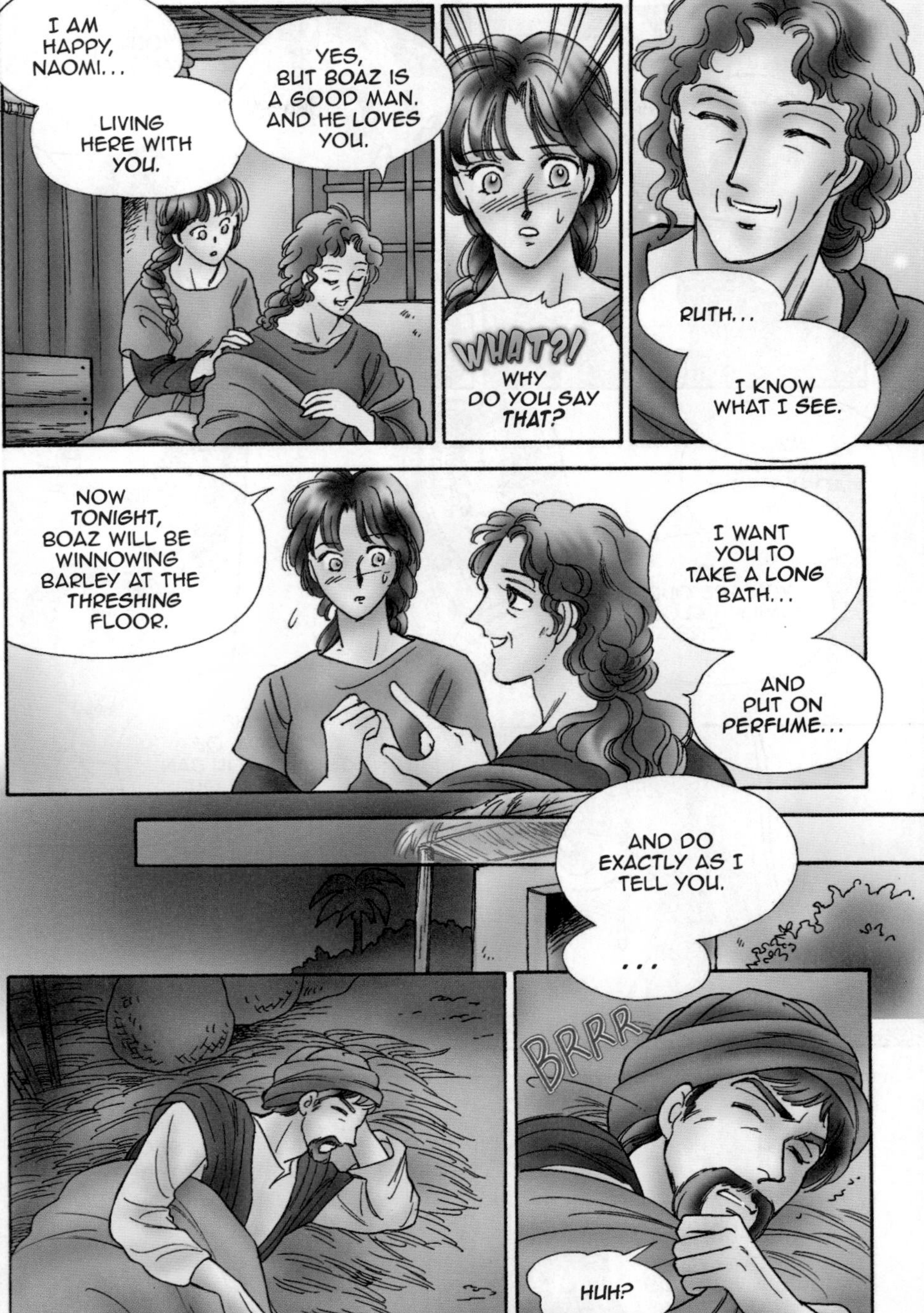
I AM HAPPY, NAOMI...
LIVING HERE WITH YOU.
YES, BUT BOAZ IS A GOOD MAN. AND HE LOVES YOU.
WHAT?!
WHY DO YOU SAY THAT?
RUTH...
I KNOW WHAT I SEE.
NOW TONIGHT, BOAZ WILL BE WINNOWING BARLEY AT THE THRESHING FLOOR.
I WANT YOU TO TAKE A LONG BATH...
AND PUT ON PERFUME...
AND DO EXACTLY AS I TELL YOU.
...
BRRR
HUH?

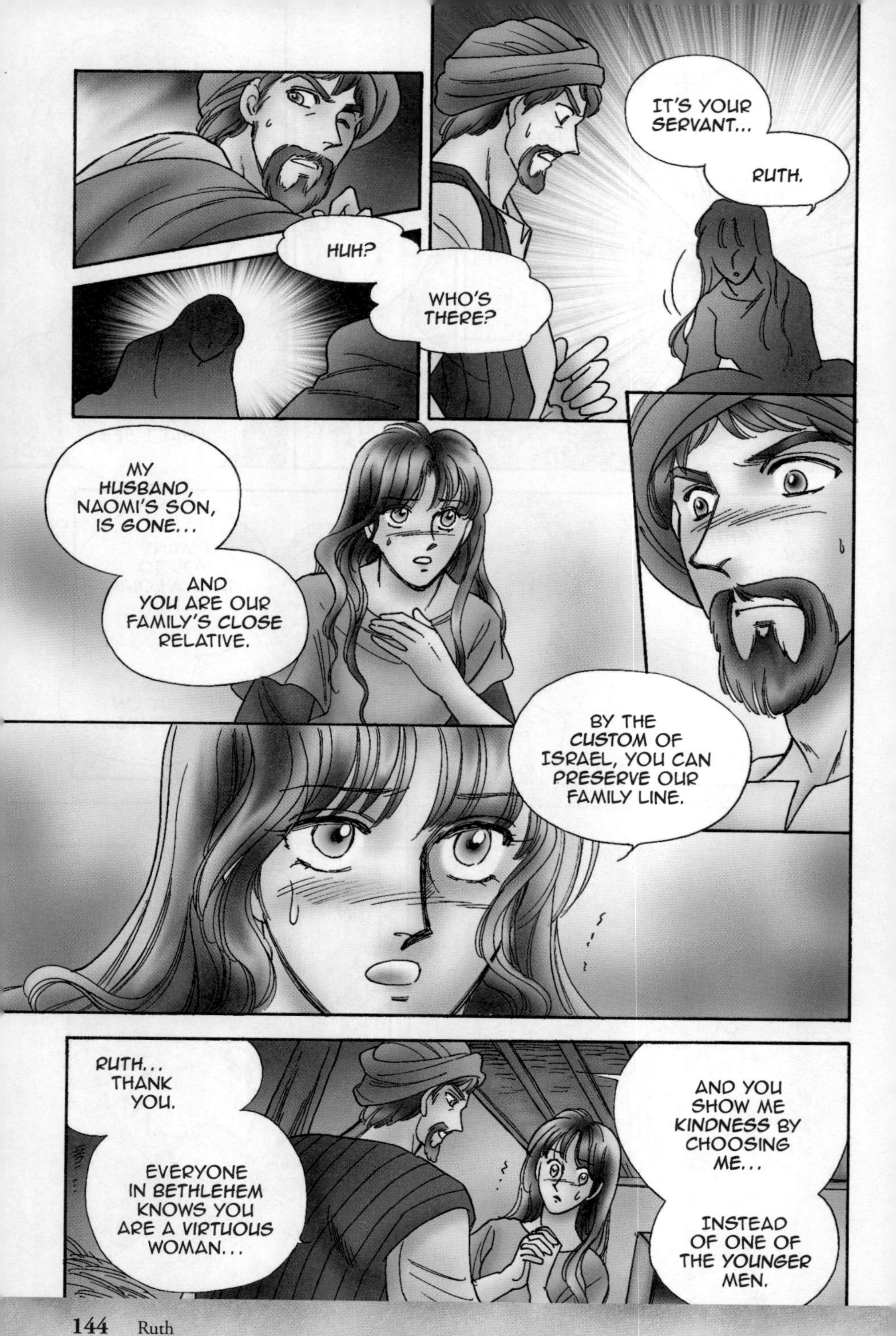
HUH?
WHO'S THERE?
IT'S YOUR SERVANT...
RUTH.
MY HUSBAND, NAOMI'S SON, IS GONE...
AND YOU ARE OUR FAMILY'S CLOSE RELATIVE.
BY THE CUSTOM OF ISRAEL, YOU CAN PRESERVE OUR FAMILY LINE.
RUTH... THANK YOU.
EVERYONE IN BETHLEHEM KNOWS YOU ARE A VIRTUOUS WOMAN...
AND YOU SHOW ME KINDNESS BY CHOOSING ME...
INSTEAD OF ONE OF THE YOUNGER MEN.

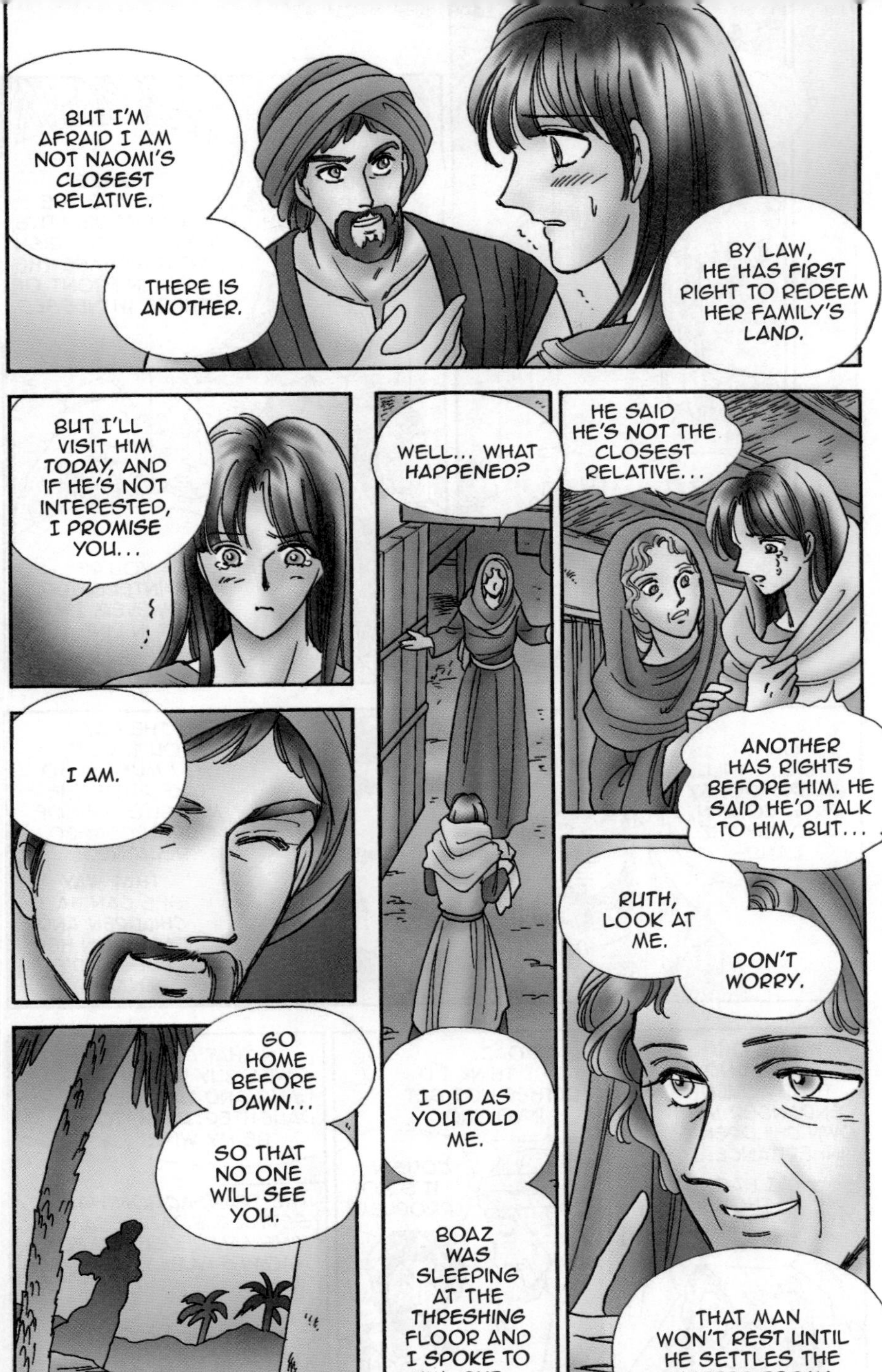
BUT I'M AFRAID I AM NOT NAOMI'S CLOSEST RELATIVE.
THERE IS ANOTHER.
BY LAW, HE HAS FIRST RIGHT TO REDEEM HER FAMILY'S LAND.
BUT I'LL VISIT HIM TODAY, AND IF HE'S NOT INTERESTED, I PROMISE YOU...
I AM.
GO HOME BEFORE DAWN...
SO THAT NO ONE WILL SEE YOU.
WELL... WHAT HAPPENED?
I DID AS YOU TOLD ME.
BOAZ WAS SLEEPING AT THE THRESHING FLOOR AND I SPOKE TO HIM. BUT...
HE SAID HE'S NOT THE CLOSEST RELATIVE...
ANOTHER HAS RIGHTS BEFORE HIM. HE SAID HE'D TALK TO HIM, BUT...
RUTH, LOOK AT ME.
DON'T WORRY.
THAT MAN WON'T REST UNTIL HE SETTLES THE MATTER TODAY.

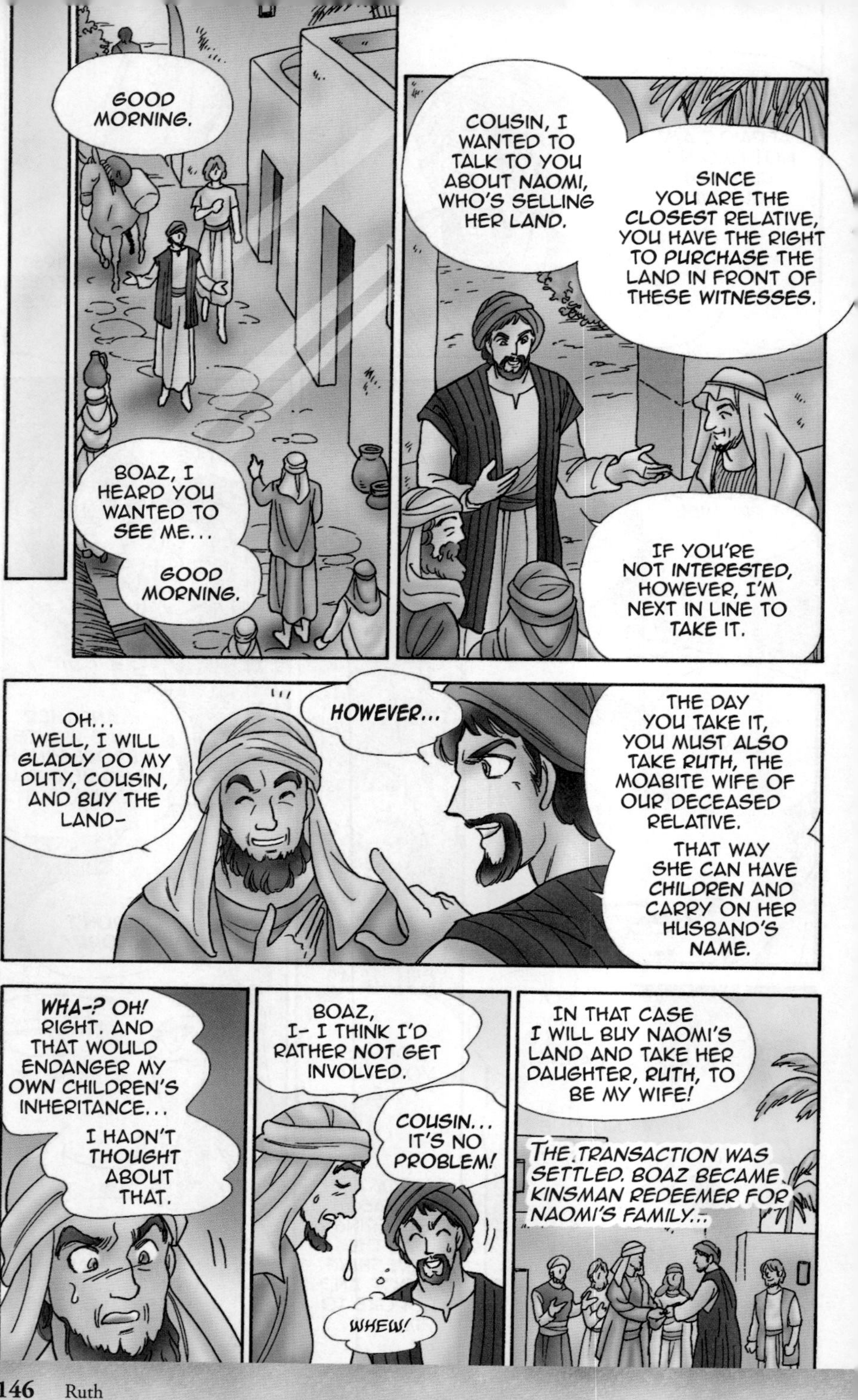
GOOD MORNING.
BOAZ, I HEARD YOU WANTED TO SEE ME...
GOOD MORNING.
COUSIN, I WANTED TO TALK TO YOU ABOUT NAOMI, WHO'S SELLING HER LAND.
SINCE YOU ARE THE CLOSEST RELATIVE, YOU HAVE THE RIGHT TO PURCHASE THE LAND IN FRONT OF THESE WITNESSES.
IF YOU'RE NOT INTERESTED, HOWEVER, I'M NEXT IN LINE TO TAKE IT.
OH... WELL, I WILL GLADLY DO MY DUTY, COUSIN, AND BUY THE LAND-
HOWEVER...
THE DAY YOU TAKE IT, YOU MUST ALSO TAKE RUTH, THE MOABITE WIFE OF OUR DECEASED RELATIVE.
THAT WAY SHE CAN HAVE CHILDREN AND CARRY ON HER HUSBAND'S NAME.
WHA-? OH! RIGHT. AND THAT WOULD ENDANGER MY OWN CHILDREN'S INHERITANCE...
I HADN'T THOUGHT ABOUT THAT.
BOAZ, I- I THINK I'D RATHER NOT GET INVOLVED.
COUSIN... IT'S NO PROBLEM!
WHEW!
IN THAT CASE I WILL BUY NAOMI'S LAND AND TAKE HER DAUGHTER, RUTH, TO BE MY WIFE!
THE TRANSACTION WAS SETTLED. BOAZ BECAME KINSMAN REDEEMER FOR NAOMI'S FAMILY...

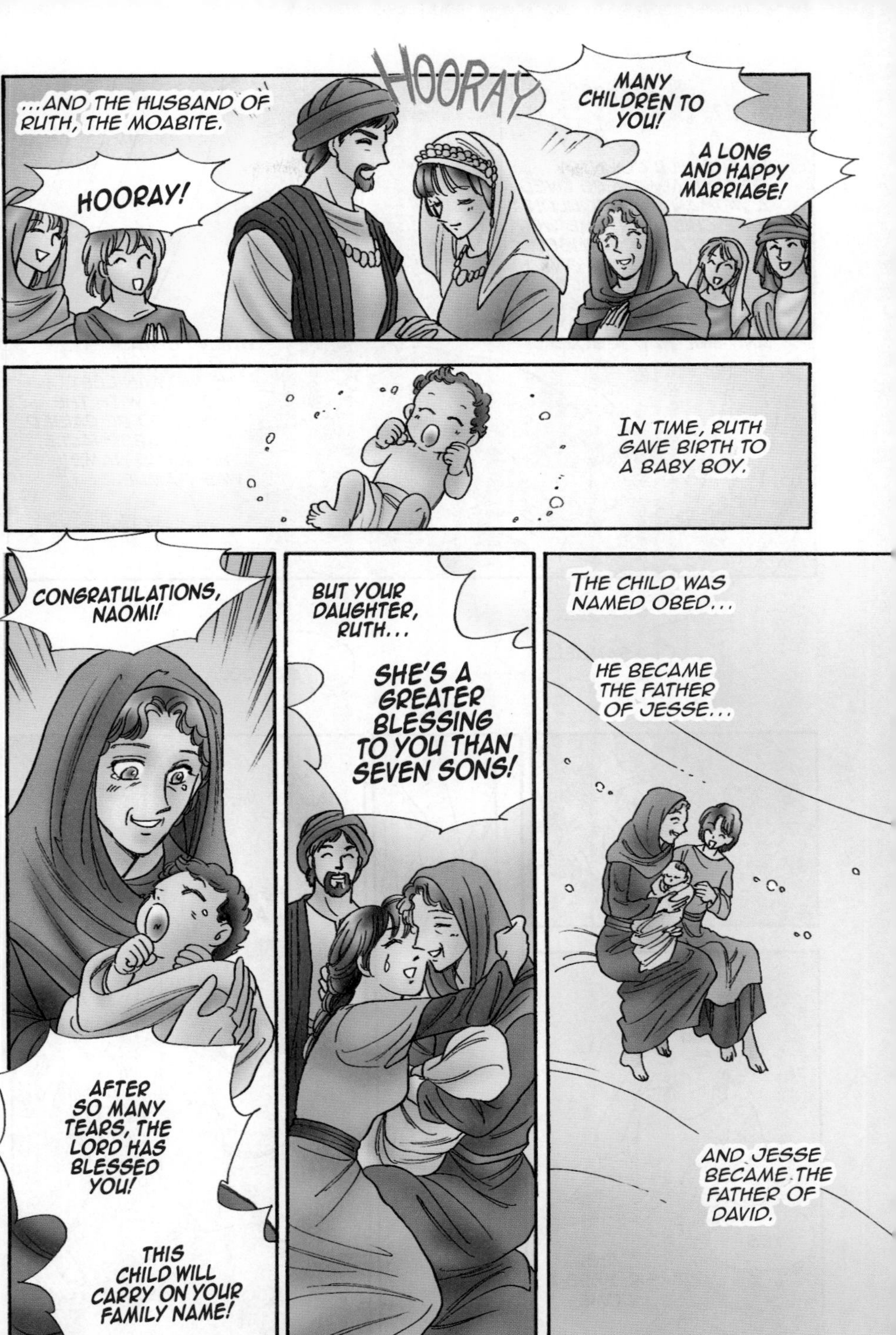

...AND THE HUSBAND OF RUTH, THE MOABITE.
HOORAY
MANY CHILDREN TO YOU!
HOORAY!
A LONG AND HAPPY MARRIAGE!
IN TIME, RUTH GAVE BIRTH TO A BABY BOY.
CONGRATULATIONS, NAOMI!
AFTER SO MANY TEARS, THE LORD HAS BLESSED YOU!
THIS CHILD WILL CARRY ON YOUR FAMILY NAME!
BUT YOUR DAUGHTER, RUTH...
SHE'S A GREATER BLESSING TO YOU THAN SEVEN SONS!
THE CHILD WAS NAMED OBED...
HE BECAME THE FATHER OF JESSE...
AND JESSE BECAME THE FATHER OF DAVID.

11. Samuel

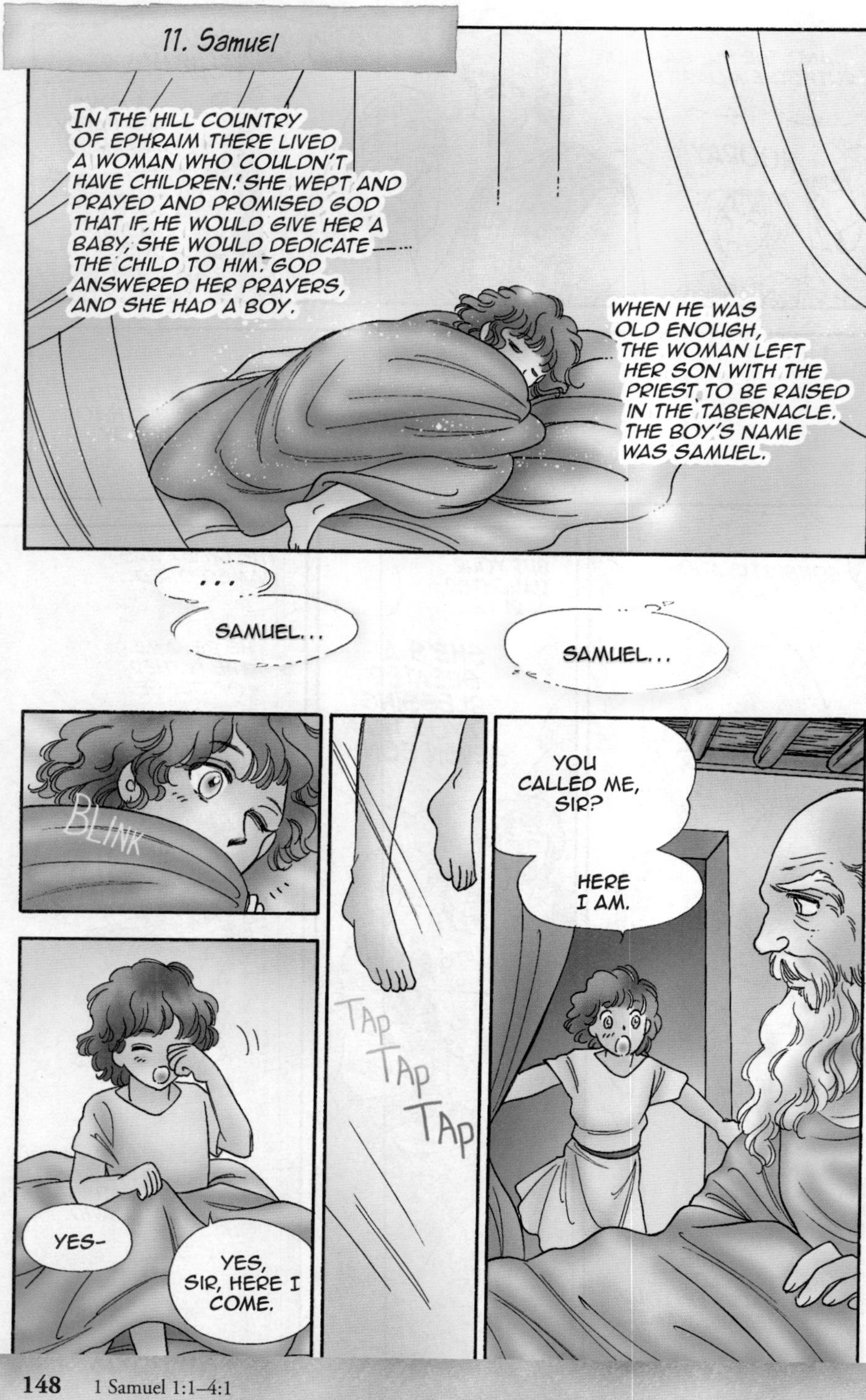

In the hill country of Ephraim there lived a woman who couldn't have children. She wept and prayed and promised God that if he would give her a baby, she would dedicate the child to him. God answered her prayers, and she had a boy.
When he was old enough, the woman left her son with the priest to be raised in the tabernacle. The boy's name was Samuel.
...
Samuel...
Samuel...
BLINK
...
TAP TAP TAP
Yes-
Yes, sir, here I come.
You called me, sir?
Here I am.

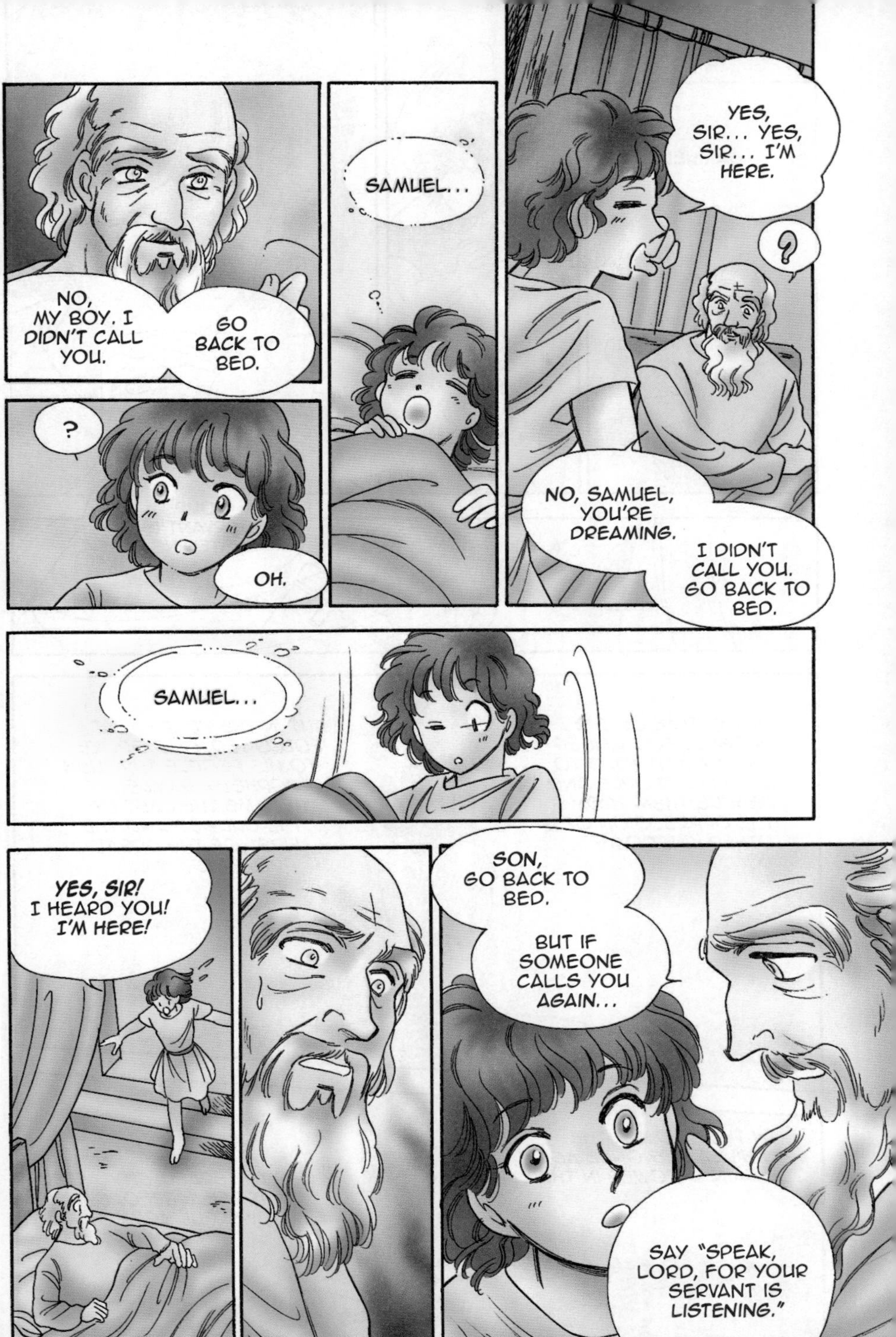
NO, MY BOY. I DIDN'T CALL YOU.
GO BACK TO BED.
?
OH.
SAMUEL...
YES, SIR... YES, SIR... I'M HERE.
?
NO, SAMUEL, YOU'RE DREAMING.
I DIDN'T CALL YOU. GO BACK TO BED.
SAMUEL...
YES, SIR! I HEARD YOU! I'M HERE!
SON, GO BACK TO BED.
BUT IF SOMEONE CALLS YOU AGAIN...
SAY "SPEAK, LORD, FOR YOUR SERVANT IS LISTENING."

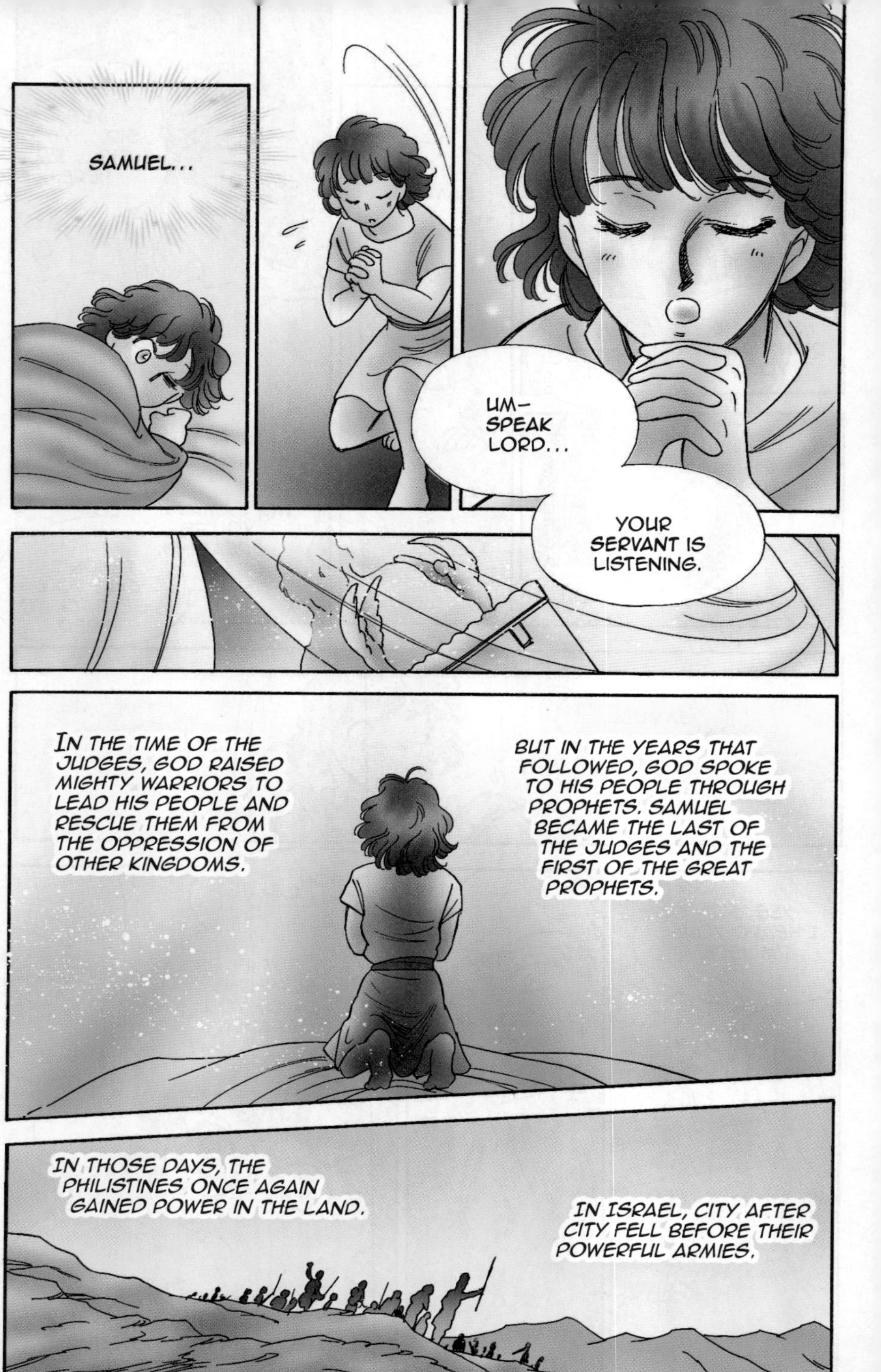
SAMUEL...
UM–
SPEAK
LORD...
YOUR
SERVANT IS
LISTENING.
IN THE TIME OF THE JUDGES, GOD RAISED MIGHTY WARRIORS TO LEAD HIS PEOPLE AND RESCUE THEM FROM THE OPPRESSION OF OTHER KINGDOMS.
BUT IN THE YEARS THAT FOLLOWED, GOD SPOKE TO HIS PEOPLE THROUGH PROPHETS. SAMUEL BECAME THE LAST OF THE JUDGES AND THE FIRST OF THE GREAT PROPHETS.
IN THOSE DAYS, THE PHILISTINES ONCE AGAIN GAINED POWER IN THE LAND.
IN ISRAEL, CITY AFTER CITY FELL BEFORE THEIR POWERFUL ARMIES.

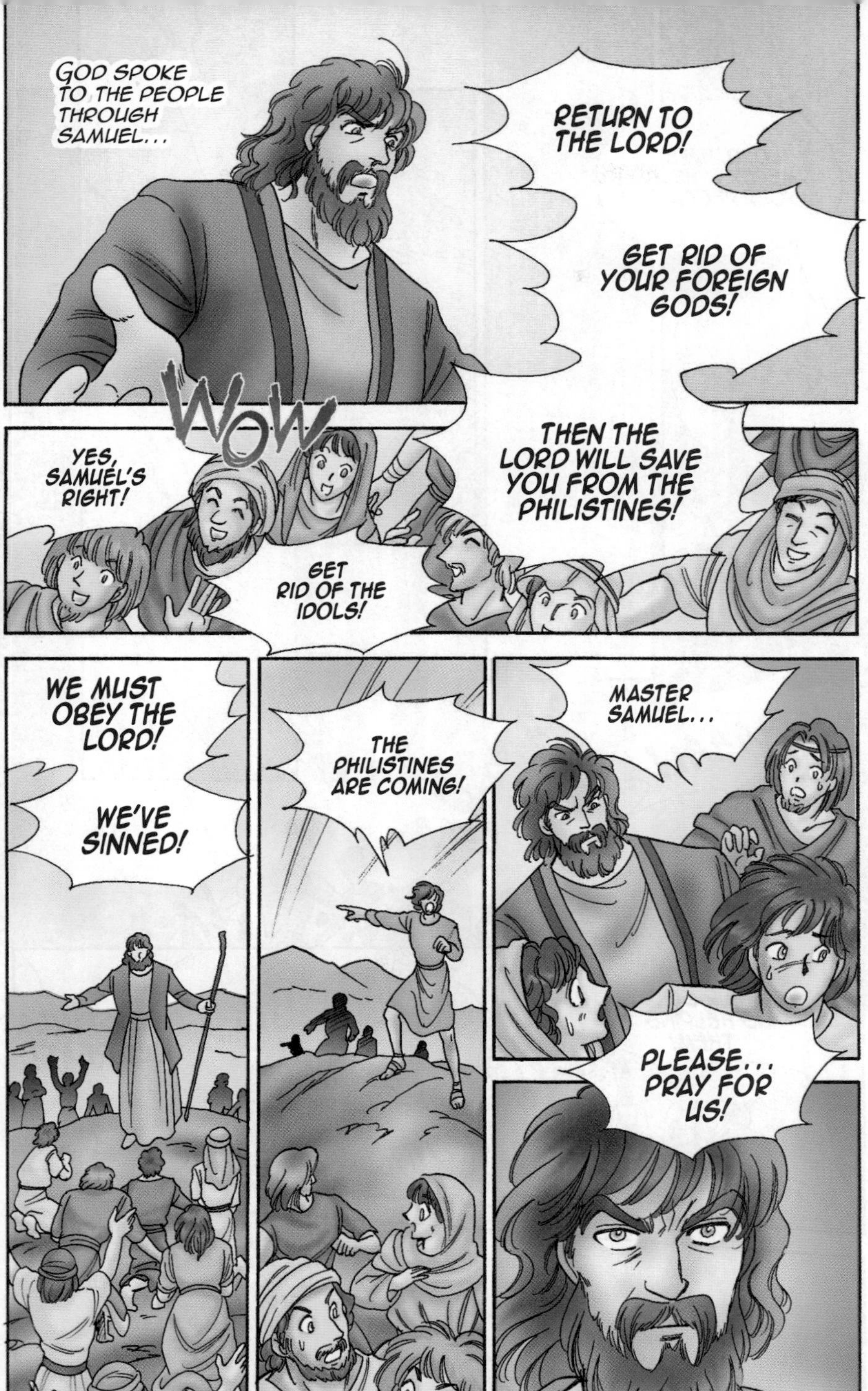

GOD SPOKE TO THE PEOPLE THROUGH SAMUEL...
RETURN TO THE LORD!
GET RID OF YOUR FOREIGN GODS!
WOW
YES, SAMUEL'S RIGHT!
THEN THE LORD WILL SAVE YOU FROM THE PHILISTINES!
GET RID OF THE IDOLS!
WE MUST OBEY THE LORD!
WE'VE SINNED!
THE PHILISTINES ARE COMING!
MASTER SAMUEL...
PLEASE... PRAY FOR US!

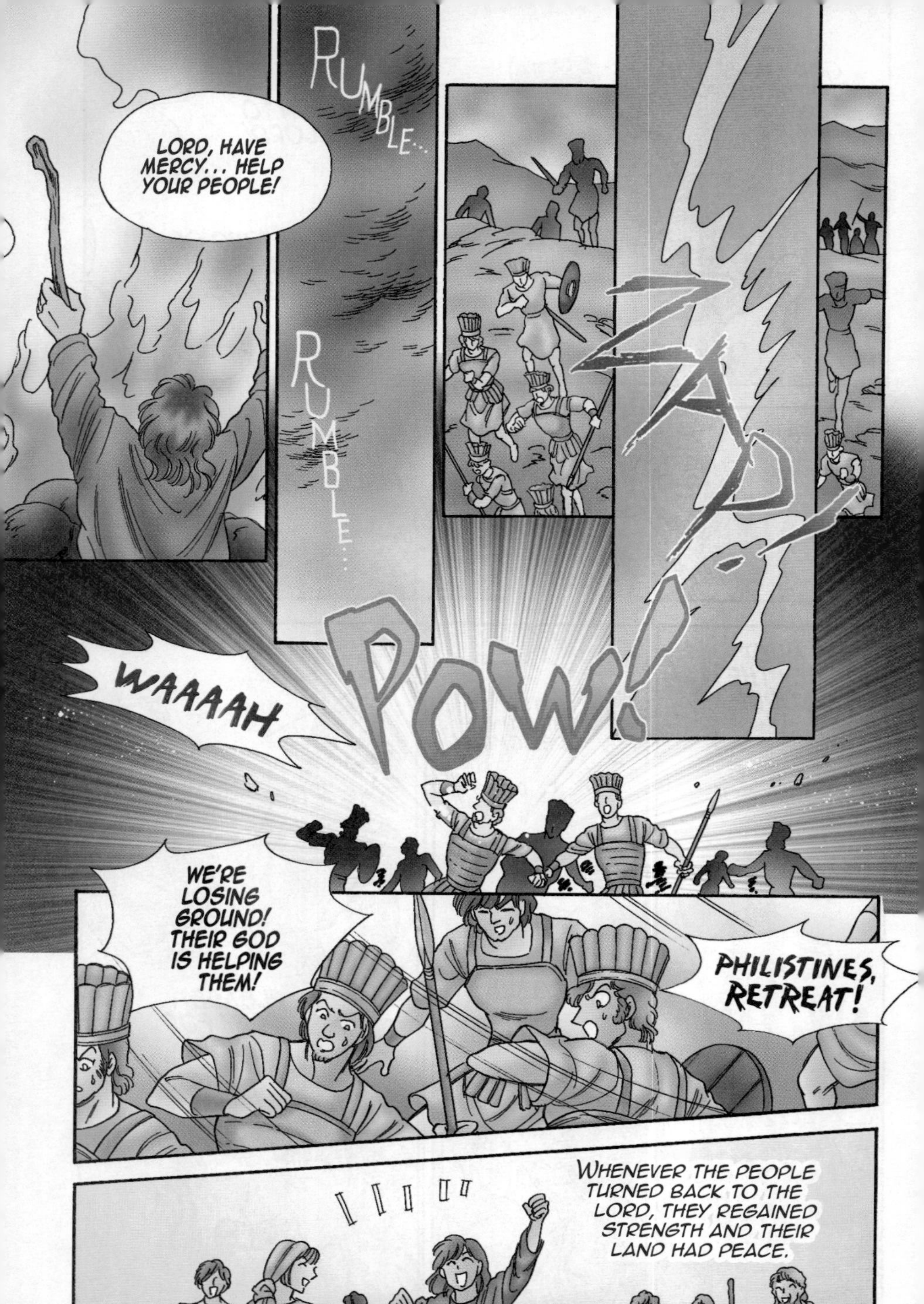
LORD, HAVE MERCY... HELP YOUR PEOPLE!
RUMBLE...
RUMBLE...
ZAP!
POW!
WAAAAH
WE'RE LOSING GROUND! THEIR GOD IS HELPING THEM!
PHILISTINES, RETREAT!
WHENEVER THE PEOPLE TURNED BACK TO THE LORD, THEY REGAINED STRENGTH AND THEIR LAND HAD PEACE.

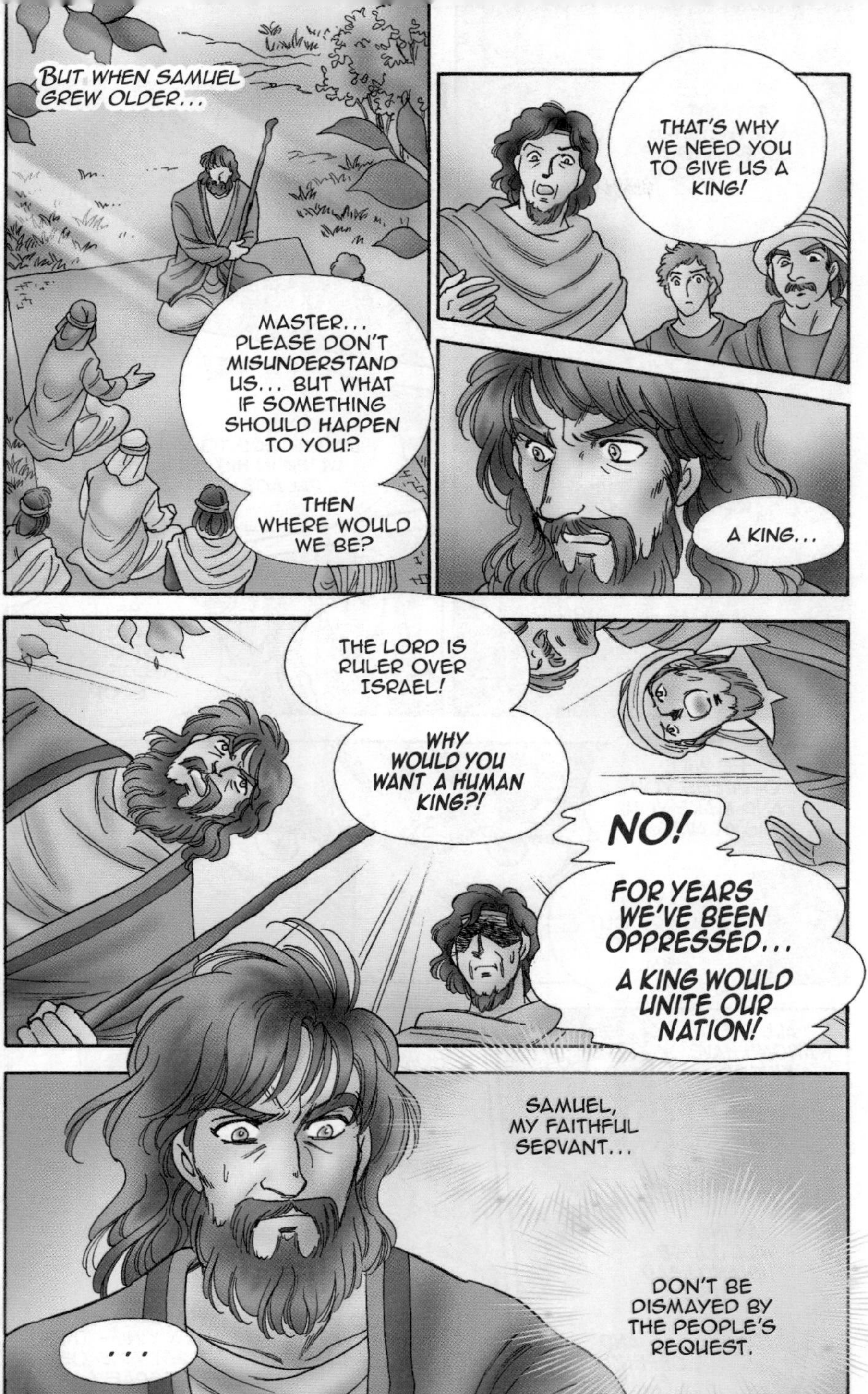

BUT WHEN SAMUEL GREW OLDER...
MASTER... PLEASE DON'T MISUNDERSTAND US... BUT WHAT IF SOMETHING SHOULD HAPPEN TO YOU?
THEN WHERE WOULD WE BE?
THAT'S WHY WE NEED YOU TO GIVE US A KING!
A KING...
THE LORD IS RULER OVER ISRAEL!
WHY WOULD YOU WANT A HUMAN KING?!
NO!
FOR YEARS WE'VE BEEN OPPRESSED...
A KING WOULD UNITE OUR NATION!
SAMUEL, MY FAITHFUL SERVANT...
DON'T BE DISMAYED BY THE PEOPLE'S REQUEST.
...

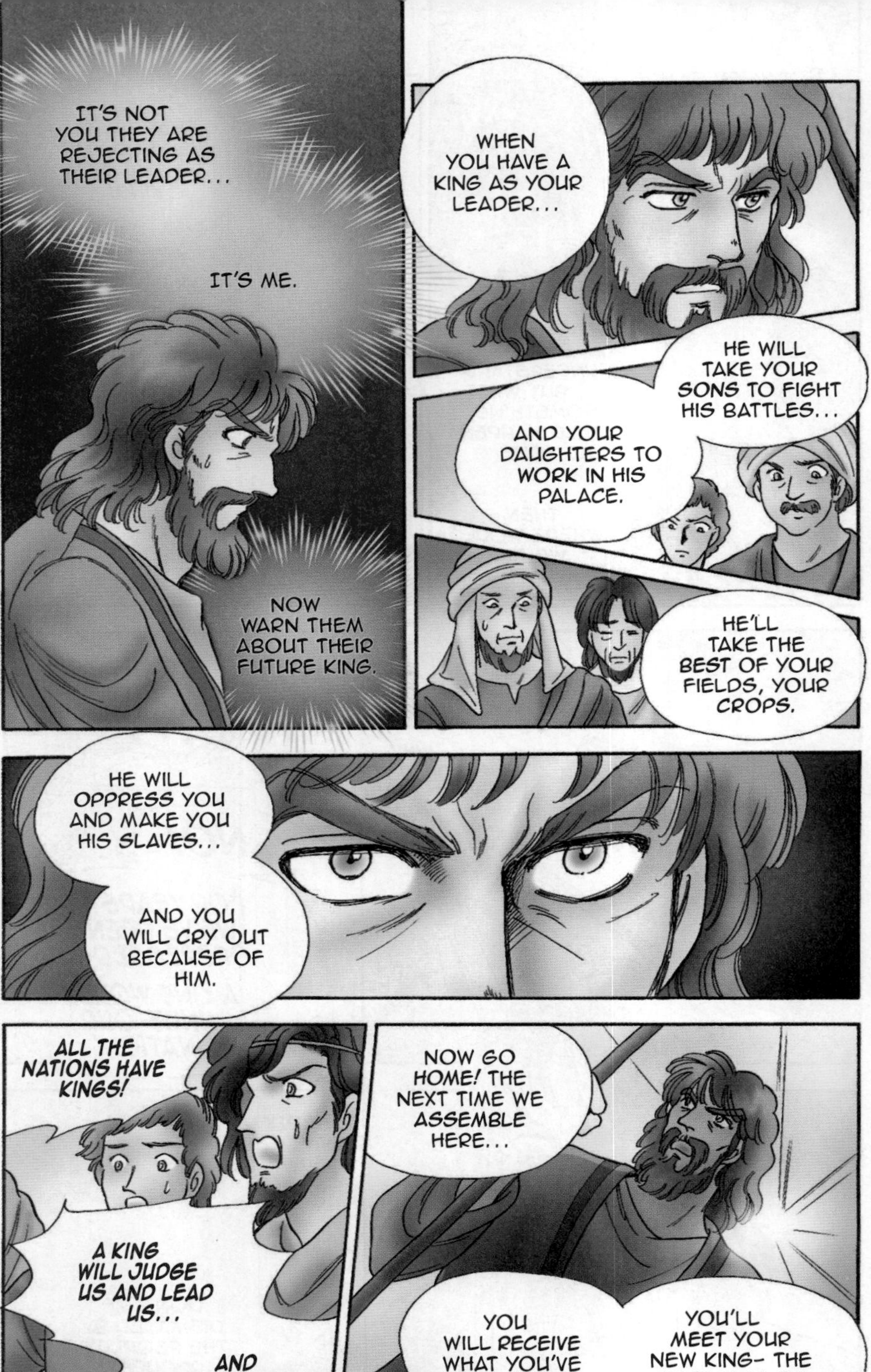
IT'S NOT YOU THEY ARE REJECTING AS THEIR LEADER...
IT'S ME.
NOW WARN THEM ABOUT THEIR FUTURE KING.
WHEN YOU HAVE A KING AS YOUR LEADER...
HE WILL TAKE YOUR SONS TO FIGHT HIS BATTLES...
AND YOUR DAUGHTERS TO WORK IN HIS PALACE.
HE'LL TAKE THE BEST OF YOUR FIELDS, YOUR CROPS.
HE WILL OPPRESS YOU AND MAKE YOU HIS SLAVES...
AND YOU WILL CRY OUT BECAUSE OF HIM.
ALL THE NATIONS HAVE KINGS!
A KING WILL JUDGE US AND LEAD US...
AND DEFEND OUR FAMILIES!
NOW GO HOME! THE NEXT TIME WE ASSEMBLE HERE...
YOU WILL RECEIVE WHAT YOU'VE ASKED FOR!
YOU'LL MEET YOUR NEW KING- THE FIRST KING OF ISRAEL!

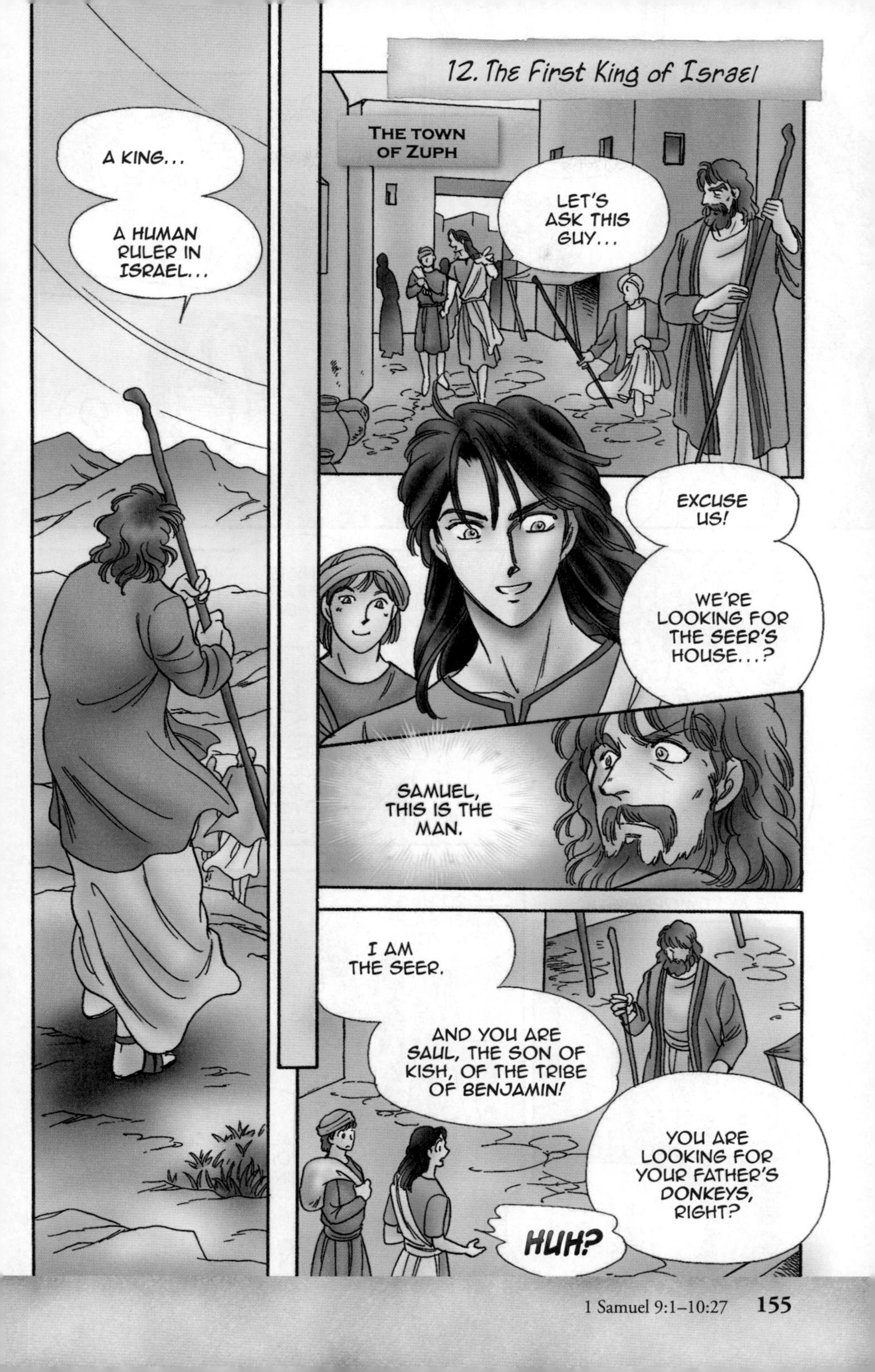
12. The First King of Israel
A KING...
A HUMAN RULER IN ISRAEL...
THE TOWN OF ZUPH
LET'S ASK THIS GUY...
EXCUSE US!
WE'RE LOOKING FOR THE SEER'S HOUSE...?
SAMUEL, THIS IS THE MAN.
I AM THE SEER.
AND YOU ARE SAUL, THE SON OF KISH, OF THE TRIBE OF BENJAMIN!
YOU ARE LOOKING FOR YOUR FATHER'S DONKEYS, RIGHT?
HUH?

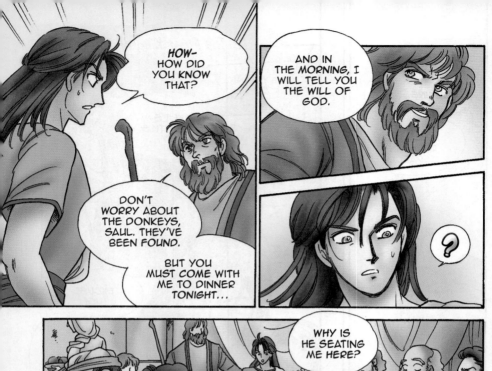

HOW— HOW DID YOU KNOW THAT?

AND IN THE MORNING, I WILL TELL YOU THE WILL OF GOD.

DON'T WORRY ABOUT THE DONKEYS, SAUL. THEY'VE BEEN FOUND.

BUT YOU MUST COME WITH ME TO DINNER TONIGHT...

?

WHY IS HE SEATING ME HERE?

WHO'S THIS YOUNG GUY?

... ?

SAMUEL HAD INVITED THE TOWN LEADERS TO A MEAL, AND HE PUT SAUL IN THE SEAT OF HONOR.

THE NEXT MORNING...

THE LORD HAS A MESSAGE FOR YOU.

ALL ISRAEL HOPES FOR A KING TO LEAD THEM...

AND THE LORD HAS CHOSEN YOU.

LISTEN TO ME, SON OF KISH...

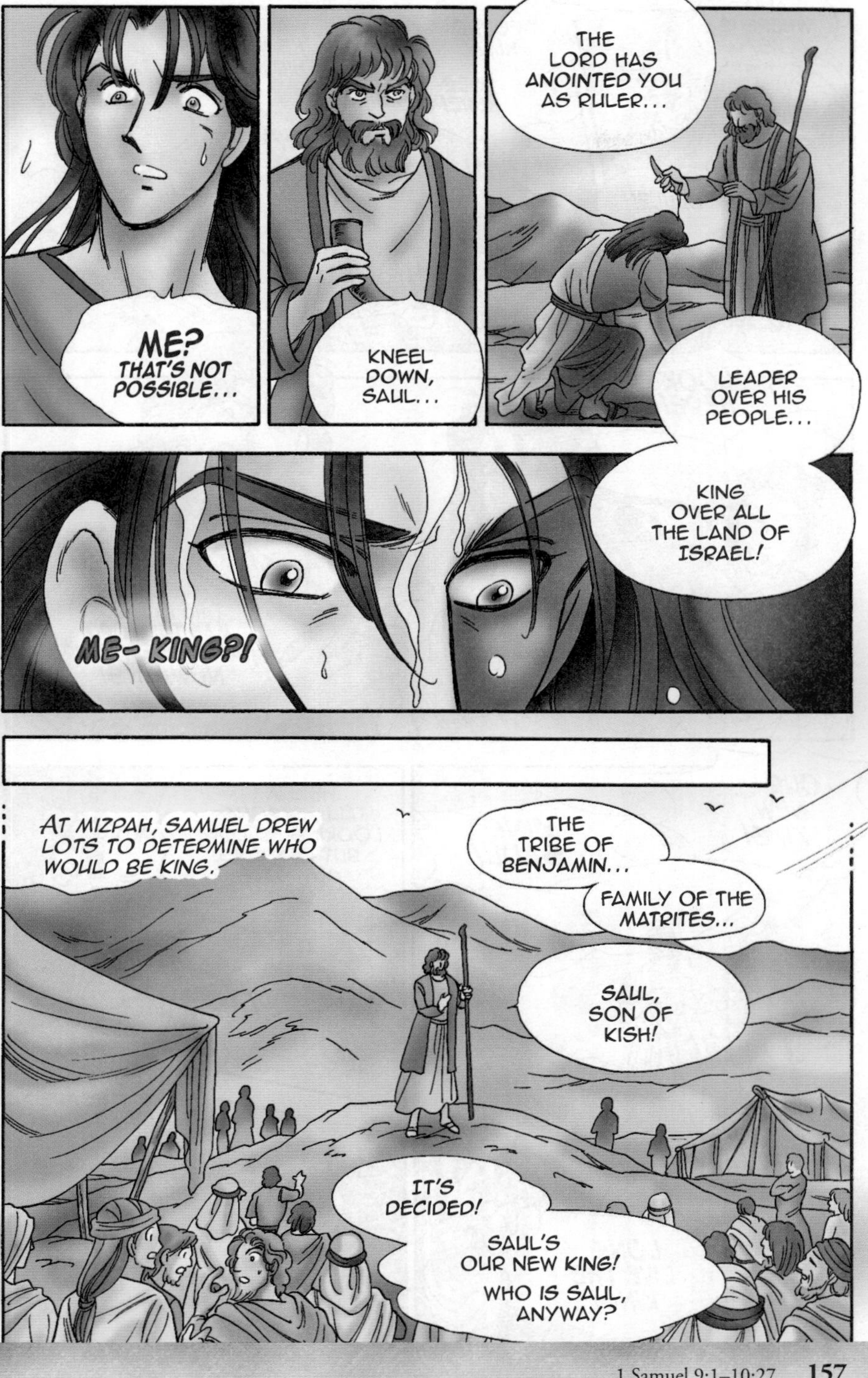
ME? THAT'S NOT POSSIBLE...
KNEEL DOWN, SAUL...
THE LORD HAS ANOINTED YOU AS RULER...
LEADER OVER HIS PEOPLE...
KING OVER ALL THE LAND OF ISRAEL!
ME- KING?!
AT MIZPAH, SAMUEL DREW LOTS TO DETERMINE WHO WOULD BE KING.
THE TRIBE OF BENJAMIN...
FAMILY OF THE MATRITES...
SAUL, SON OF KISH!
IT'S DECIDED!
SAUL'S OUR NEW KING!
WHO IS SAUL, ANYWAY?

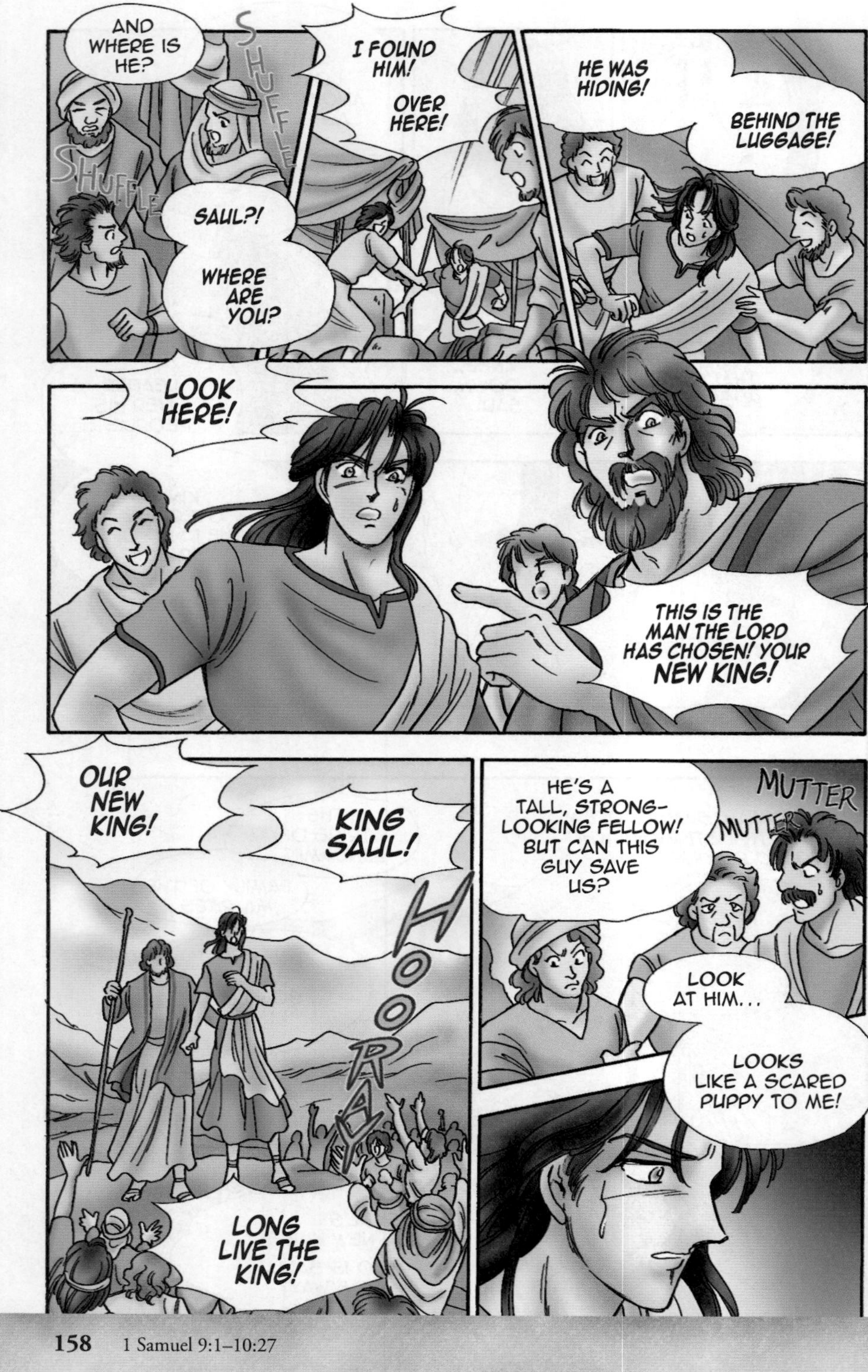
AND WHERE IS HE?
SHUFFLE
SHUFFLE
SAUL?!
WHERE ARE YOU?
I FOUND HIM!
OVER HERE!
HE WAS HIDING!
BEHIND THE LUGGAGE!
LOOK HERE!
THIS IS THE MAN THE LORD HAS CHOSEN! YOUR NEW KING!
OUR NEW KING!
KING SAUL!
HOORAY
LONG LIVE THE KING!
MUTTER
MUTTER
HE'S A TALL, STRONG-LOOKING FELLOW! BUT CAN THIS GUY SAVE US?
LOOK AT HIM...
LOOKS LIKE A SCARED PUPPY TO ME!

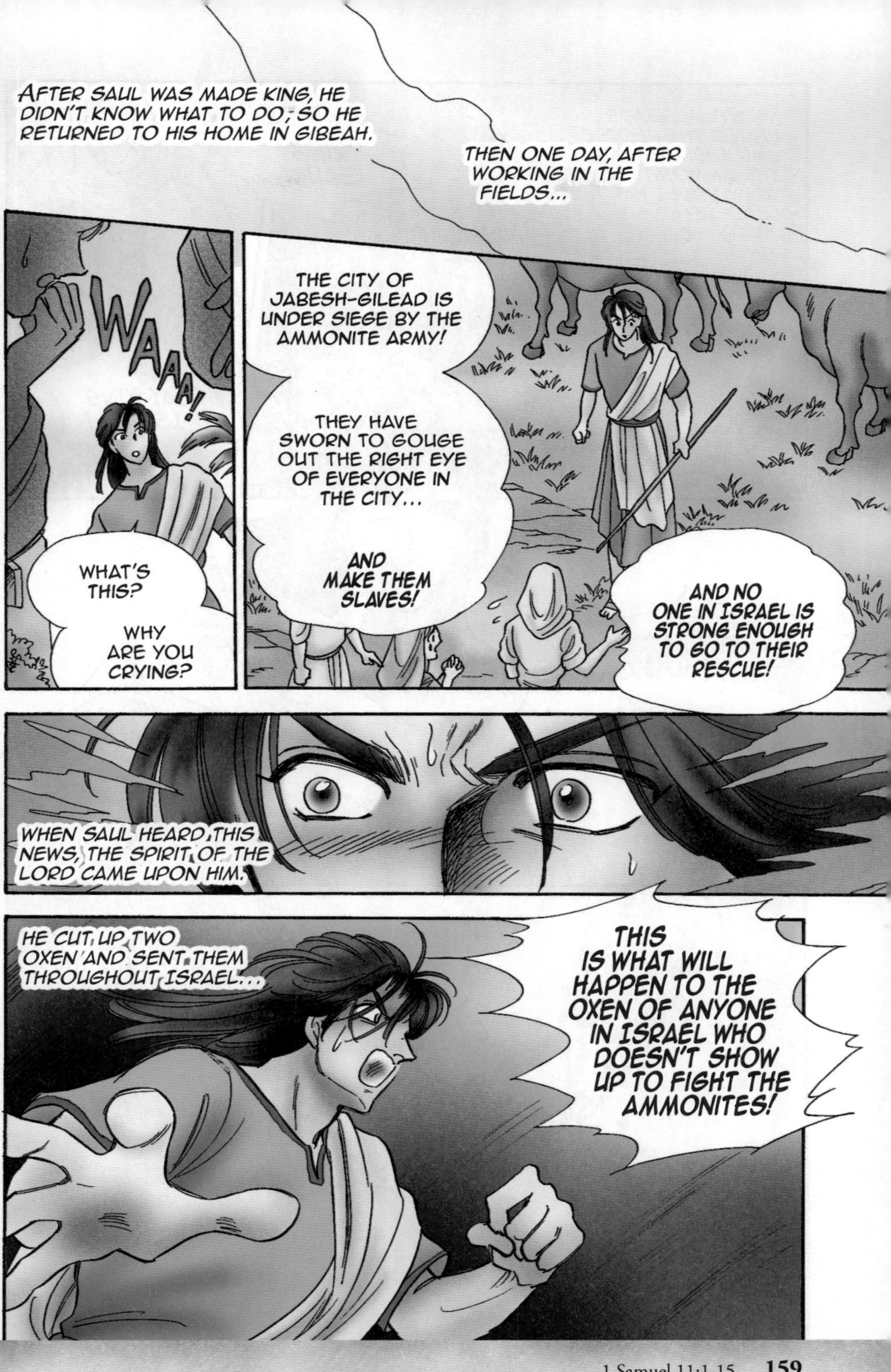
AFTER SAUL WAS MADE KING, HE DIDN'T KNOW WHAT TO DO, SO HE RETURNED TO HIS HOME IN GIBEAH.
THEN ONE DAY, AFTER WORKING IN THE FIELDS...
WAAAA!
WHAT'S THIS?
WHY ARE YOU CRYING?
THE CITY OF JABESH-GILEAD IS UNDER SIEGE BY THE AMMONITE ARMY!
THEY HAVE SWORN TO GOUGE OUT THE RIGHT EYE OF EVERYONE IN THE CITY...
AND MAKE THEM SLAVES!
AND NO ONE IN ISRAEL IS STRONG ENOUGH TO GO TO THEIR RESCUE!
WHEN SAUL HEARD THIS NEWS, THE SPIRIT OF THE LORD CAME UPON HIM.
HE CUT UP TWO OXEN AND SENT THEM THROUGHOUT ISRAEL...
THIS IS WHAT WILL HAPPEN TO THE OXEN OF ANYONE IN ISRAEL WHO DOESN'T SHOW UP TO FIGHT THE AMMONITES!

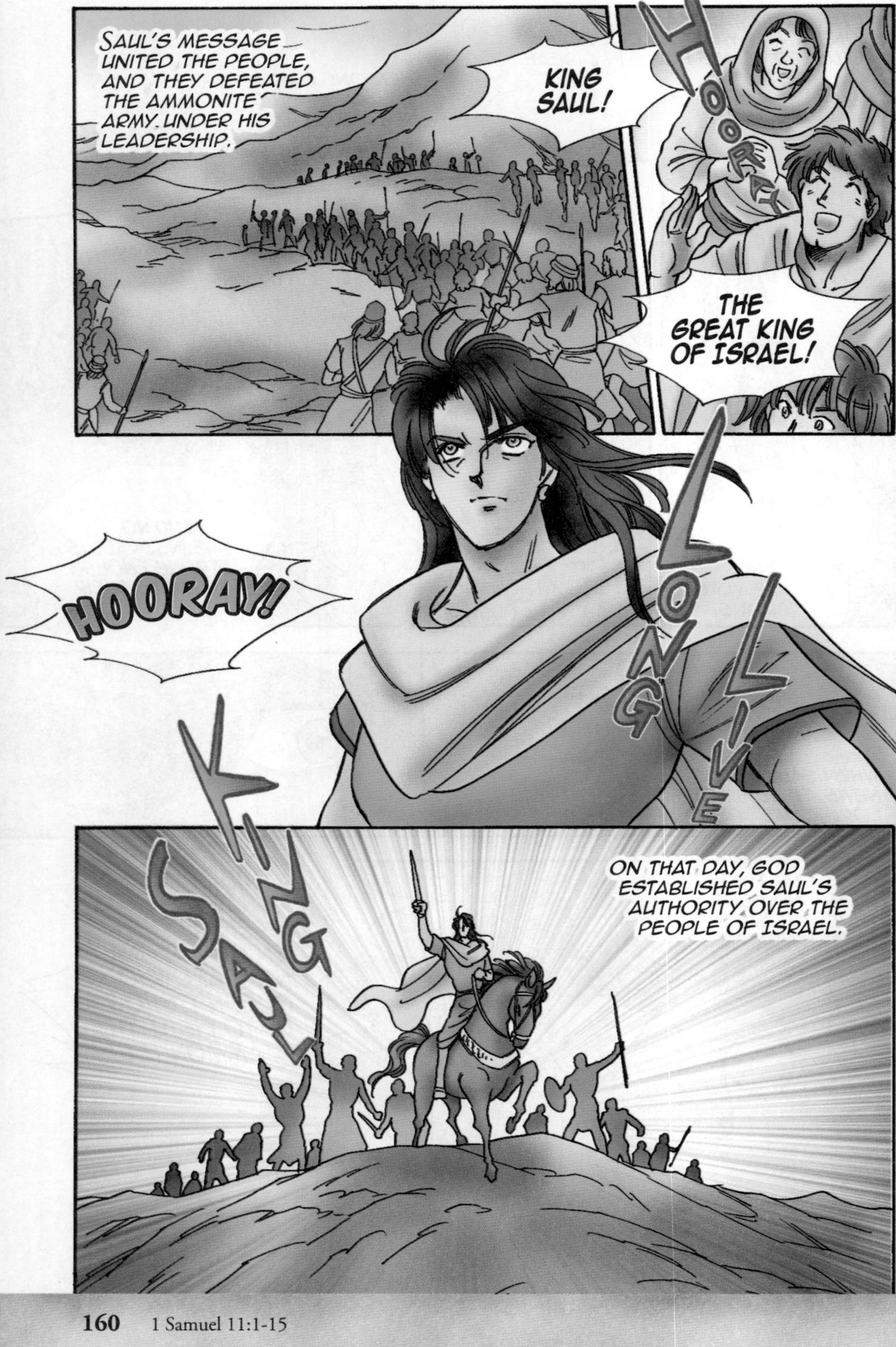
SAUL'S MESSAGE UNITED THE PEOPLE, AND THEY DEFEATED THE AMMONITE ARMY UNDER HIS LEADERSHIP.
KING SAUL!
HOORAY
THE GREAT KING OF ISRAEL!
HOORAY!
LONG LIVE
KING SAUL
ON THAT DAY, GOD ESTABLISHED SAUL'S AUTHORITY OVER THE PEOPLE OF ISRAEL.

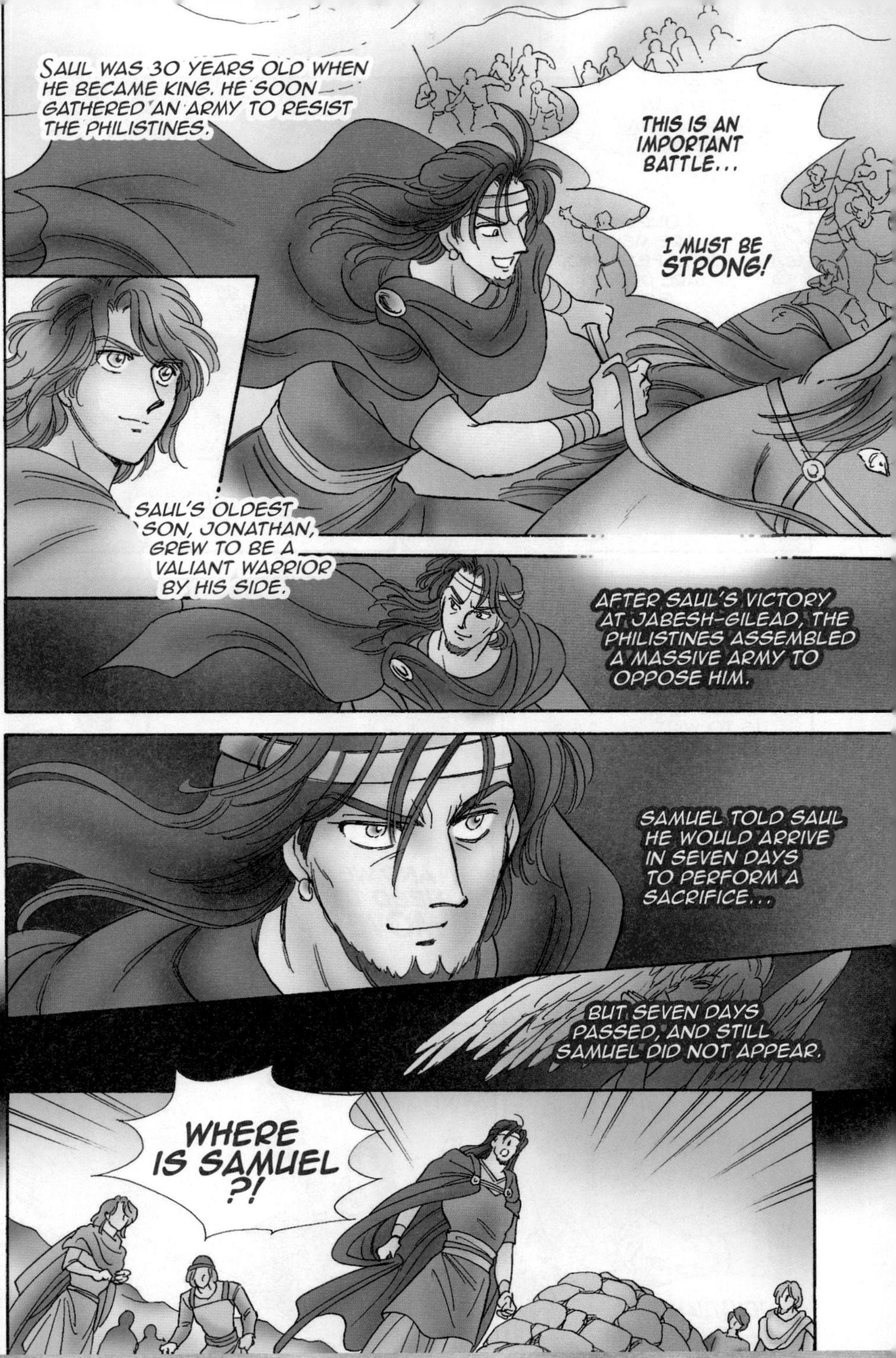
SAUL WAS 30 YEARS OLD WHEN HE BECAME KING. HE SOON GATHERED AN ARMY TO RESIST THE PHILISTINES.
THIS IS AN IMPORTANT BATTLE...
I MUST BE STRONG!
SAUL'S OLDEST SON, JONATHAN, GREW TO BE A VALIANT WARRIOR BY HIS SIDE.
AFTER SAUL'S VICTORY AT JABESH-GILEAD, THE PHILISTINES ASSEMBLED A MASSIVE ARMY TO OPPOSE HIM.
SAMUEL TOLD SAUL HE WOULD ARRIVE IN SEVEN DAYS TO PERFORM A SACRIFICE...
BUT SEVEN DAYS PASSED, AND STILL SAMUEL DID NOT APPEAR.
WHERE IS SAMUEL ?!

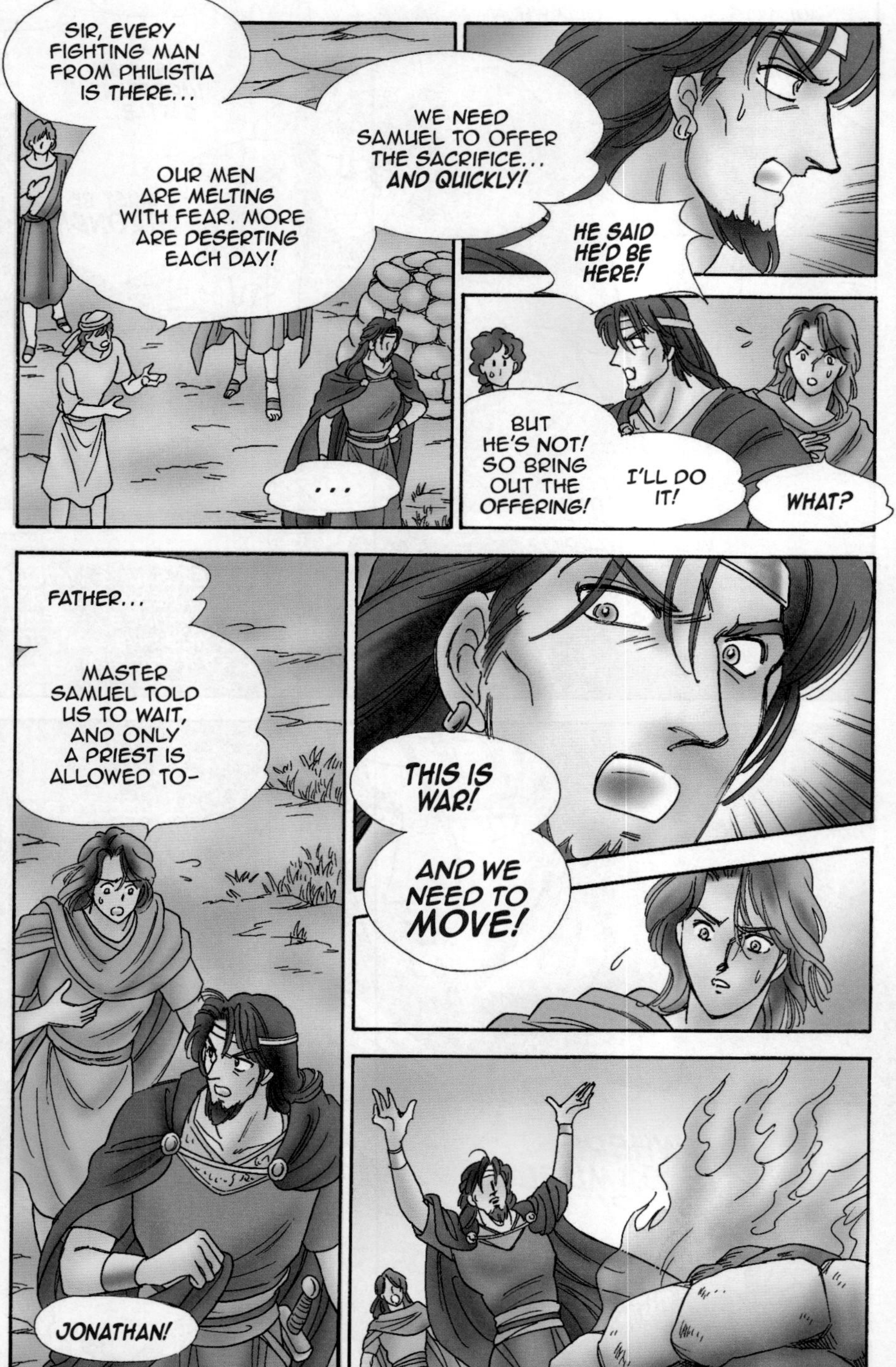
SIR, EVERY FIGHTING MAN FROM PHILISTIA IS THERE...
OUR MEN ARE MELTING WITH FEAR. MORE ARE DESERTING EACH DAY!
...
WE NEED SAMUEL TO OFFER THE SACRIFICE... AND QUICKLY!
HE SAID HE'D BE HERE!
BUT HE'S NOT! SO BRING OUT THE OFFERING!
I'LL DO IT!
WHAT?
FATHER...
MASTER SAMUEL TOLD US TO WAIT, AND ONLY A PRIEST IS ALLOWED TO-
JONATHAN!
THIS IS WAR!
AND WE NEED TO MOVE!

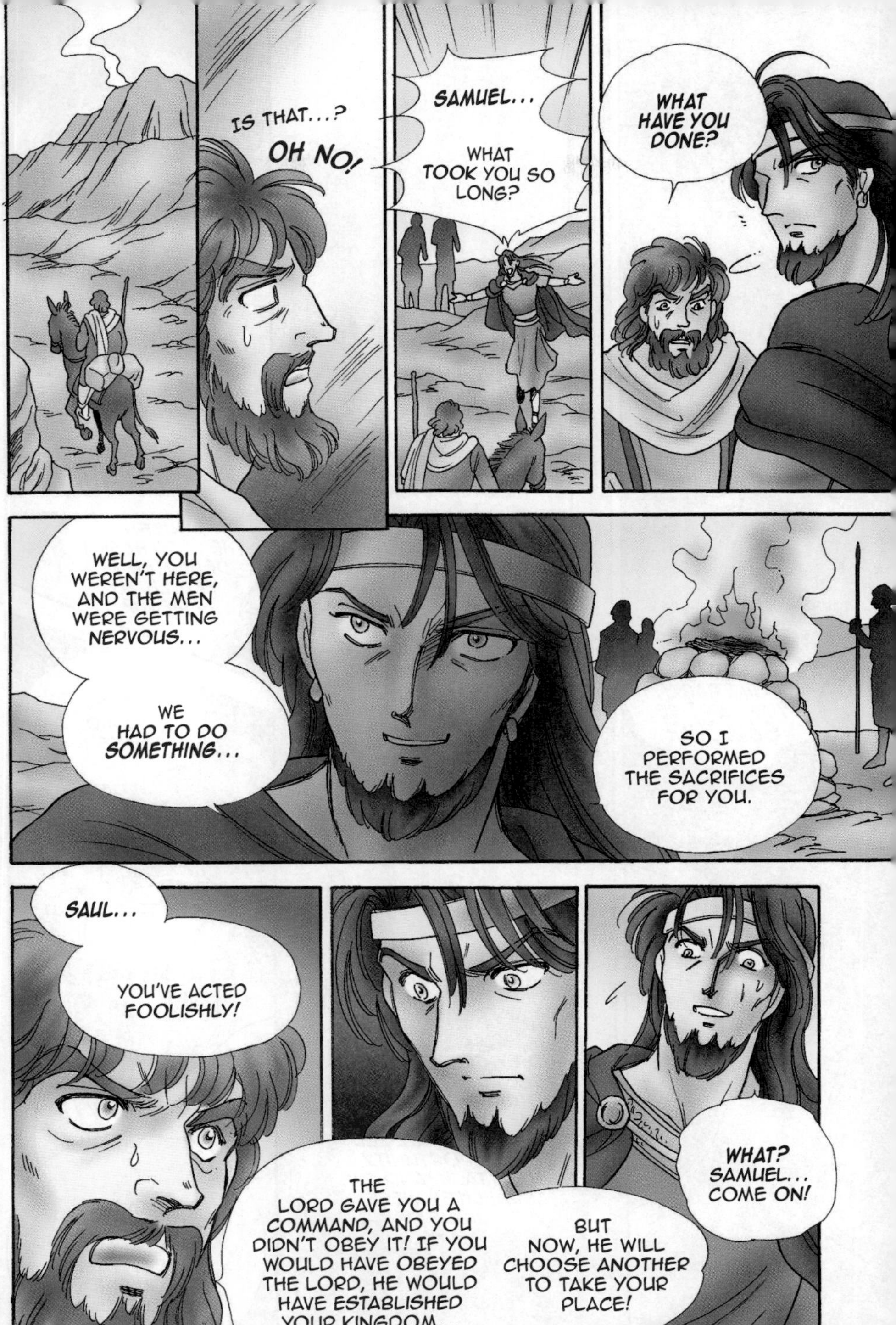
IS THAT...?
OH NO!
SAMUEL...
WHAT TOOK YOU SO LONG?
WHAT HAVE YOU DONE?
WELL, YOU WEREN'T HERE, AND THE MEN WERE GETTING NERVOUS...
WE HAD TO DO SOMETHING...
SO I PERFORMED THE SACRIFICES FOR YOU.
SAUL...
YOU'VE ACTED FOOLISHLY!
WHAT? SAMUEL... COME ON!
THE LORD GAVE YOU A COMMAND, AND YOU DIDN'T OBEY IT! IF YOU WOULD HAVE OBEYED THE LORD, HE WOULD HAVE ESTABLISHED YOUR KINGDOM...
BUT NOW, HE WILL CHOOSE ANOTHER TO TAKE YOUR PLACE!

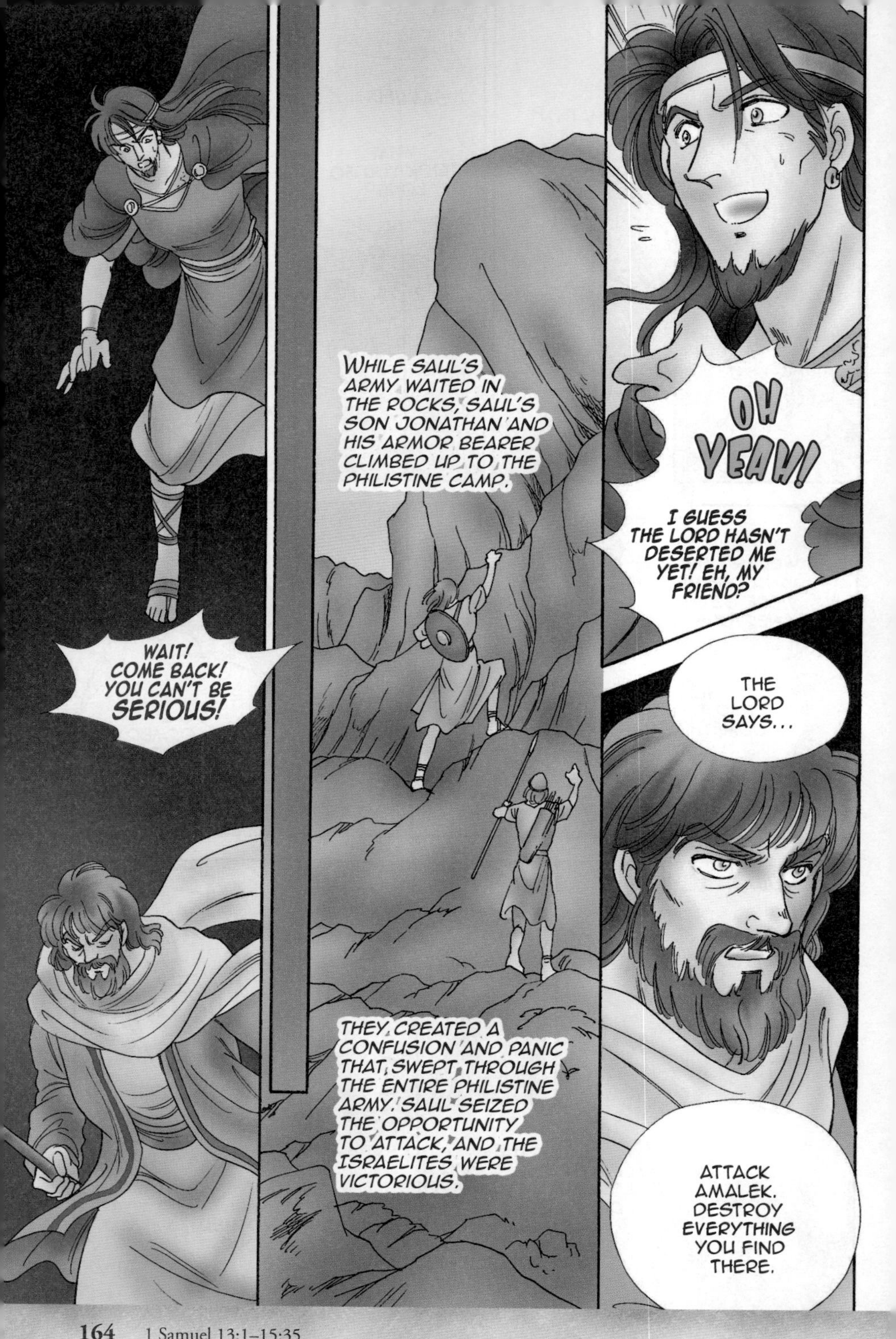
WAIT! COME BACK! YOU CAN'T BE SERIOUS!
WHILE SAUL'S ARMY WAITED IN THE ROCKS, SAUL'S SON JONATHAN AND HIS ARMOR BEARER CLIMBED UP TO THE PHILISTINE CAMP.
THEY CREATED A CONFUSION AND PANIC THAT SWEPT THROUGH THE ENTIRE PHILISTINE ARMY. SAUL SEIZED THE OPPORTUNITY TO ATTACK, AND THE ISRAELITES WERE VICTORIOUS.
OH YEAH!
I GUESS THE LORD HASN'T DESERTED ME YET! EH, MY FRIEND?
THE LORD SAYS...
ATTACK AMALEK. DESTROY EVERYTHING YOU FIND THERE.

THIS TIME, SAUL MUSTERED 200,000 SOLDIERS TO ATTACK THE AMALEKITES. HOWEVER...

SAMUEL... I REGRET THAT I HAVE MADE SAUL KING.

HE HAS NOT BEEN FAITHFUL TO ME OR OBEYED MY COMMANDS.

SAMUEL, HELLO, OLD FRIEND!

I HAVE DESTROYED EVERYTHING, JUST AS THE LORD COMMANDED!

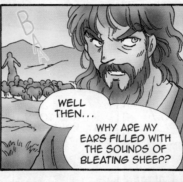

WELL THEN...

WHY ARE MY EARS FILLED WITH THE SOUNDS OF BLEATING SHEEP?

OH, THAT...

AHEM— WELL NOW, YOU JUST WOULDN'T BELIEVE THE HERDS WE FOUND!

"SACRIFICES," I THOUGHT. "THESE ARE PERFECT FOR SACRIFICES..."

BE SILENT!

THE LORD SPOKE TO ME ABOUT YOU LAST NIGHT!

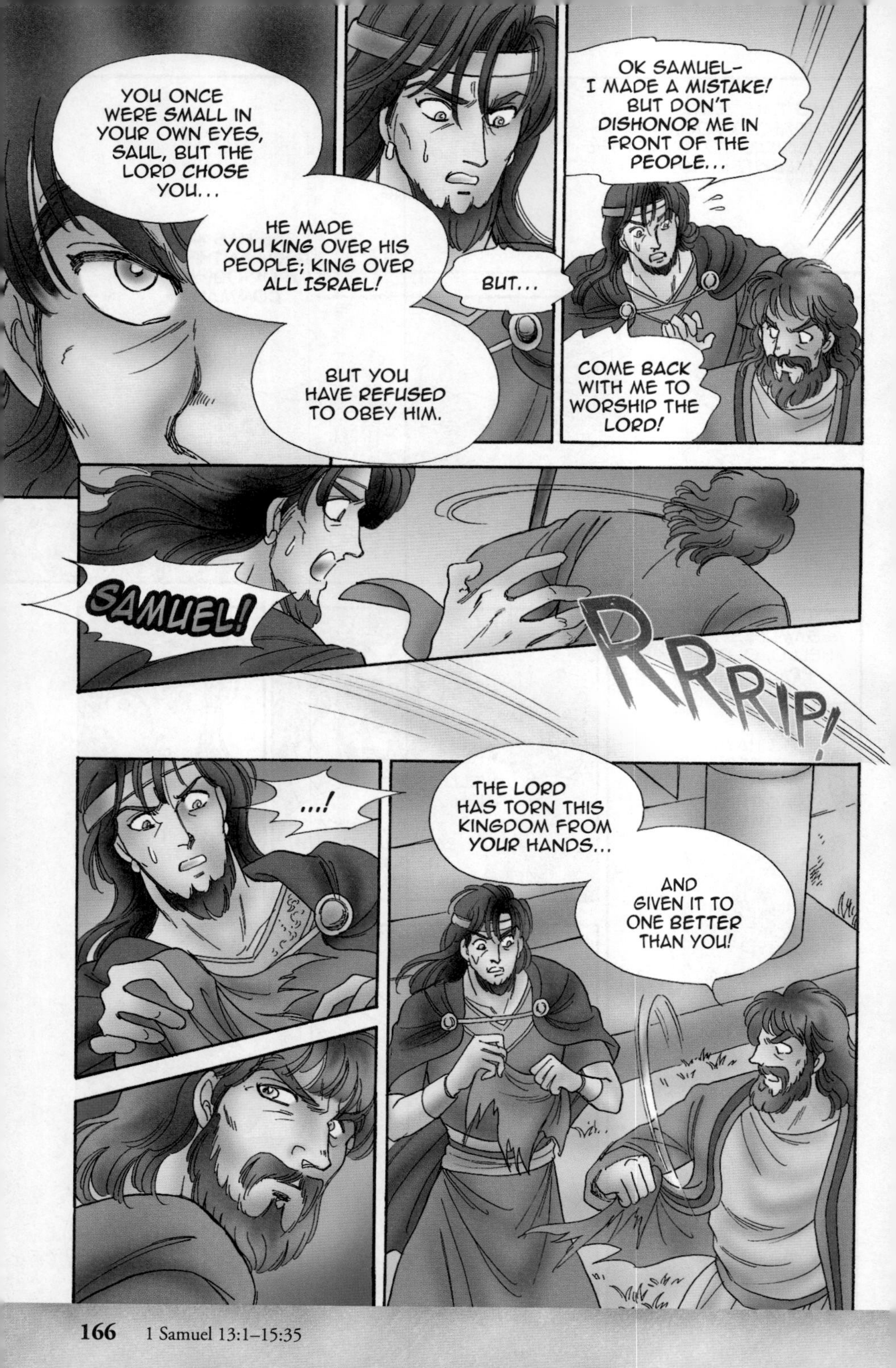
YOU ONCE WERE SMALL IN YOUR OWN EYES, SAUL, BUT THE LORD CHOSE YOU...
HE MADE YOU KING OVER HIS PEOPLE; KING OVER ALL ISRAEL!
BUT...
BUT YOU HAVE REFUSED TO OBEY HIM.
OK SAMUEL- I MADE A MISTAKE! BUT DON'T DISHONOR ME IN FRONT OF THE PEOPLE...
COME BACK WITH ME TO WORSHIP THE LORD!
SAMUEL!
RRRIP!
...!
THE LORD HAS TORN THIS KINGDOM FROM YOUR HANDS...
AND GIVEN IT TO ONE BETTER THAN YOU!

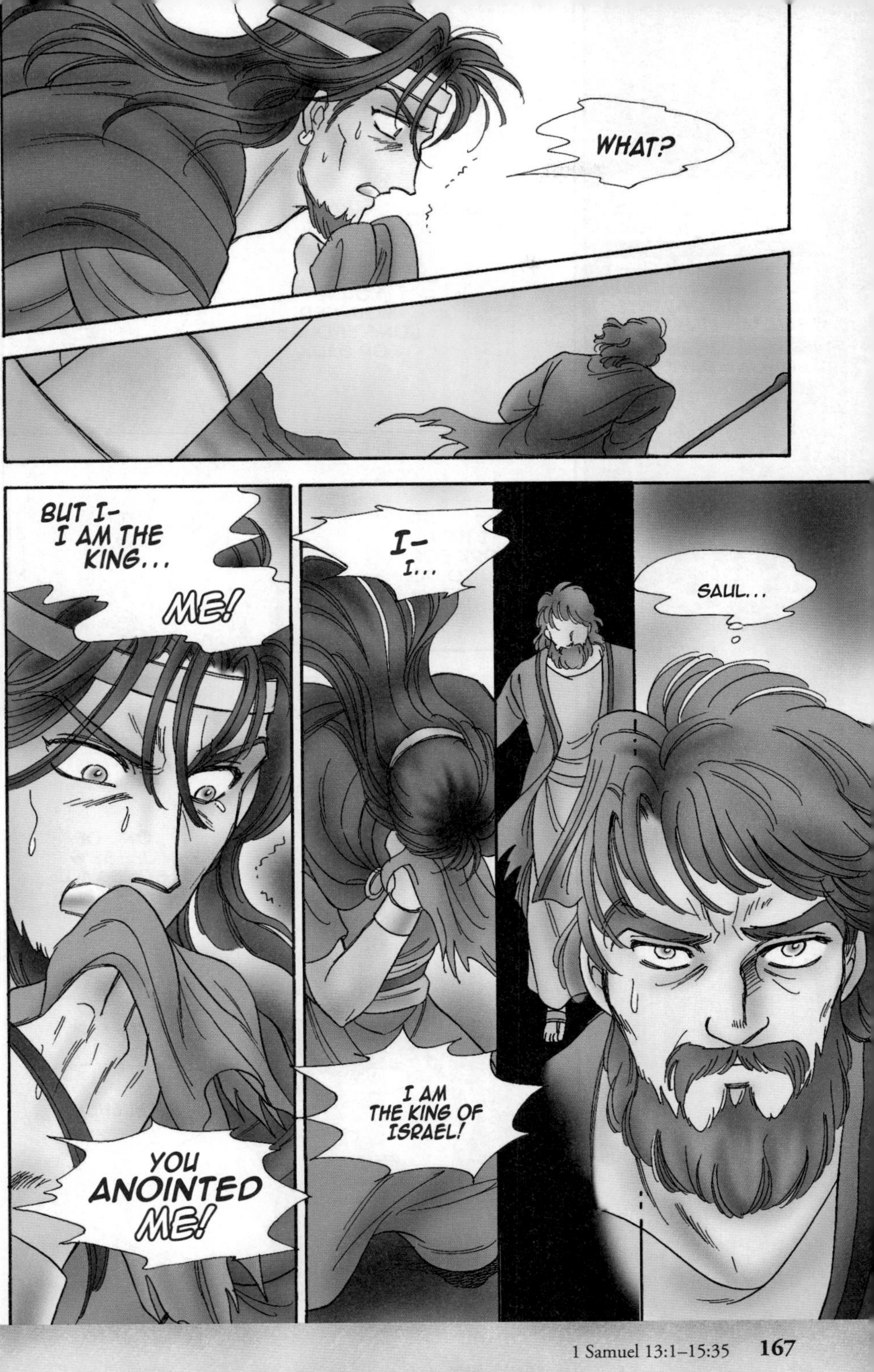

WHAT?
BUT I-
I AM THE
KING...
ME!
YOU
ANOINTED
ME!
I-
I...
I AM
THE KING OF
ISRAEL!
SAUL...

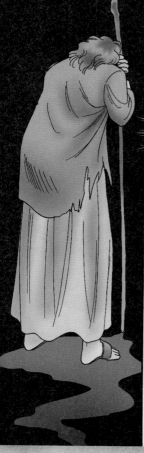

THAT WAS THE LAST TIME SAMUEL MET SAUL FACE-TO-FACE.

HE GRIEVED A LONG TIME BECAUSE THE LORD HAD REJECTED SAUL AS KING.

BUT ONE DAY...

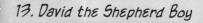

SAMUEL...

YOU'VE MOURNED LONG ENOUGH FOR SAUL.

I HAVE WORK FOR YOU TO DO.

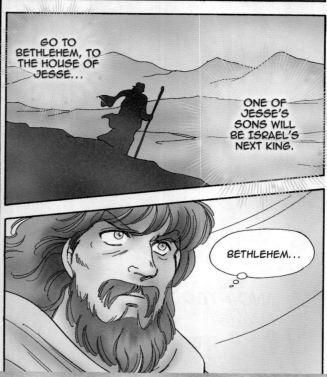

GO TO BETHLEHEM, TO THE HOUSE OF JESSE...

ONE OF JESSE'S SONS WILL BE ISRAEL'S NEXT KING.

BETHLEHEM...

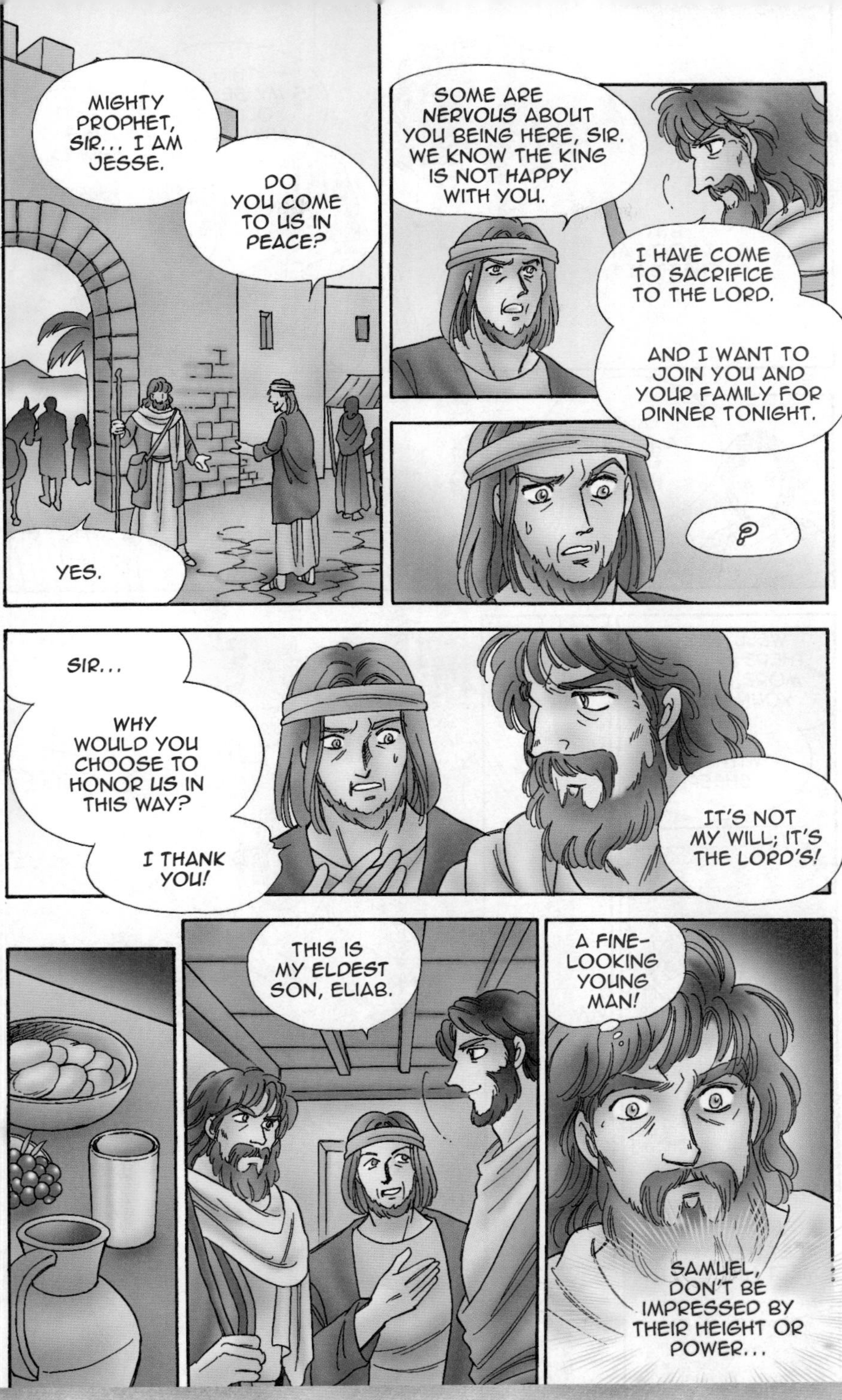
MIGHTY PROPHET, SIR... I AM JESSE.
DO YOU COME TO US IN PEACE?
YES.
SOME ARE NERVOUS ABOUT YOU BEING HERE, SIR. WE KNOW THE KING IS NOT HAPPY WITH YOU.
I HAVE COME TO SACRIFICE TO THE LORD.
AND I WANT TO JOIN YOU AND YOUR FAMILY FOR DINNER TONIGHT.
?
SIR...
WHY WOULD YOU CHOOSE TO HONOR US IN THIS WAY?
I THANK YOU!
IT'S NOT MY WILL; IT'S THE LORD'S!
THIS IS MY ELDEST SON, ELIAB.
A FINE-LOOKING YOUNG MAN!
SAMUEL, DON'T BE IMPRESSED BY THEIR HEIGHT OR POWER...

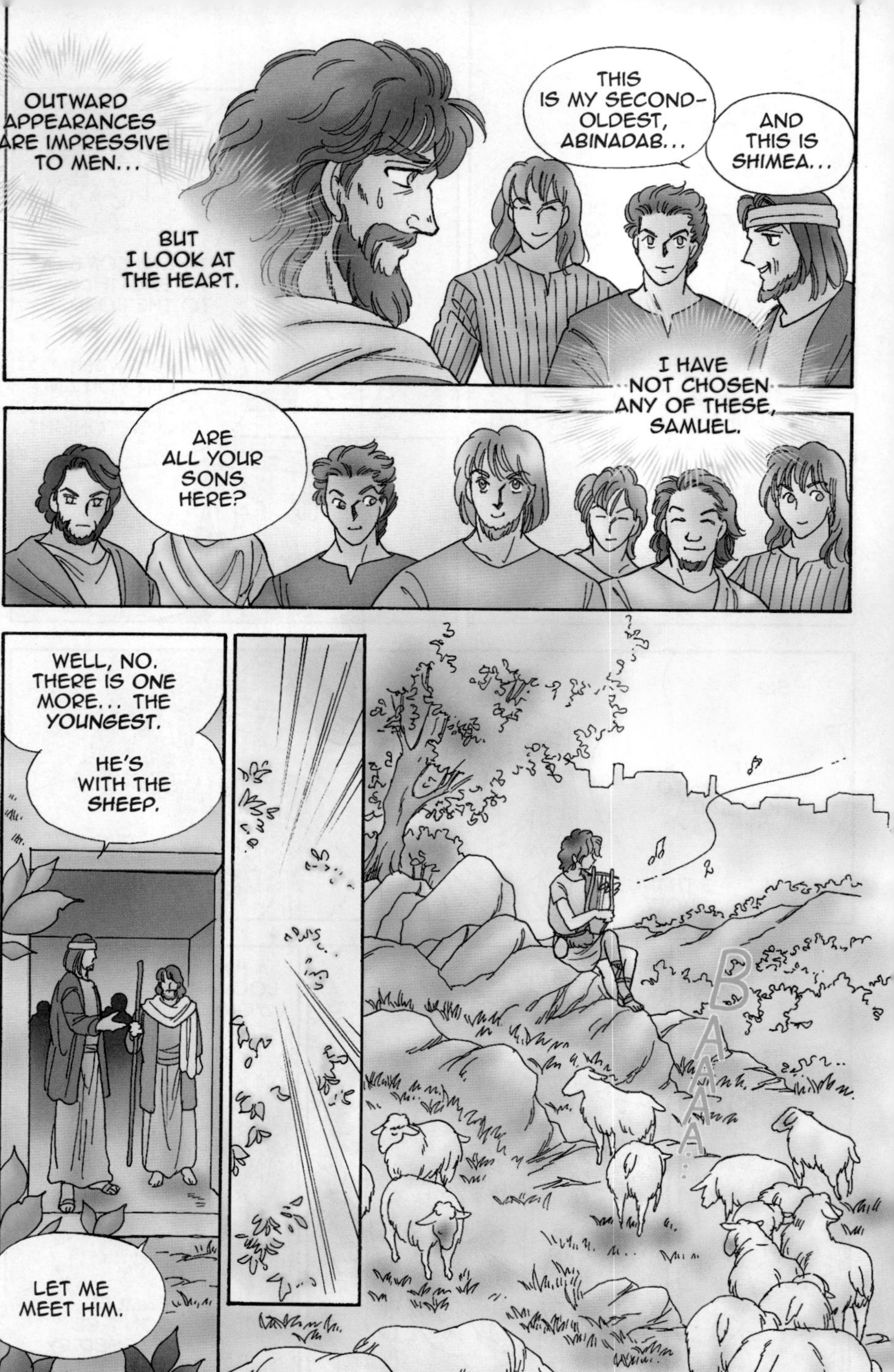
OUTWARD APPEARANCES ARE IMPRESSIVE TO MEN...
BUT I LOOK AT THE HEART.
THIS IS MY SECOND-OLDEST, ABINADAB...
AND THIS IS SHIMEA...
I HAVE NOT CHOSEN ANY OF THESE, SAMUEL.
ARE ALL YOUR SONS HERE?
WELL, NO. THERE IS ONE MORE... THE YOUNGEST.
HE'S WITH THE SHEEP.
LET ME MEET HIM.
BAAAA...

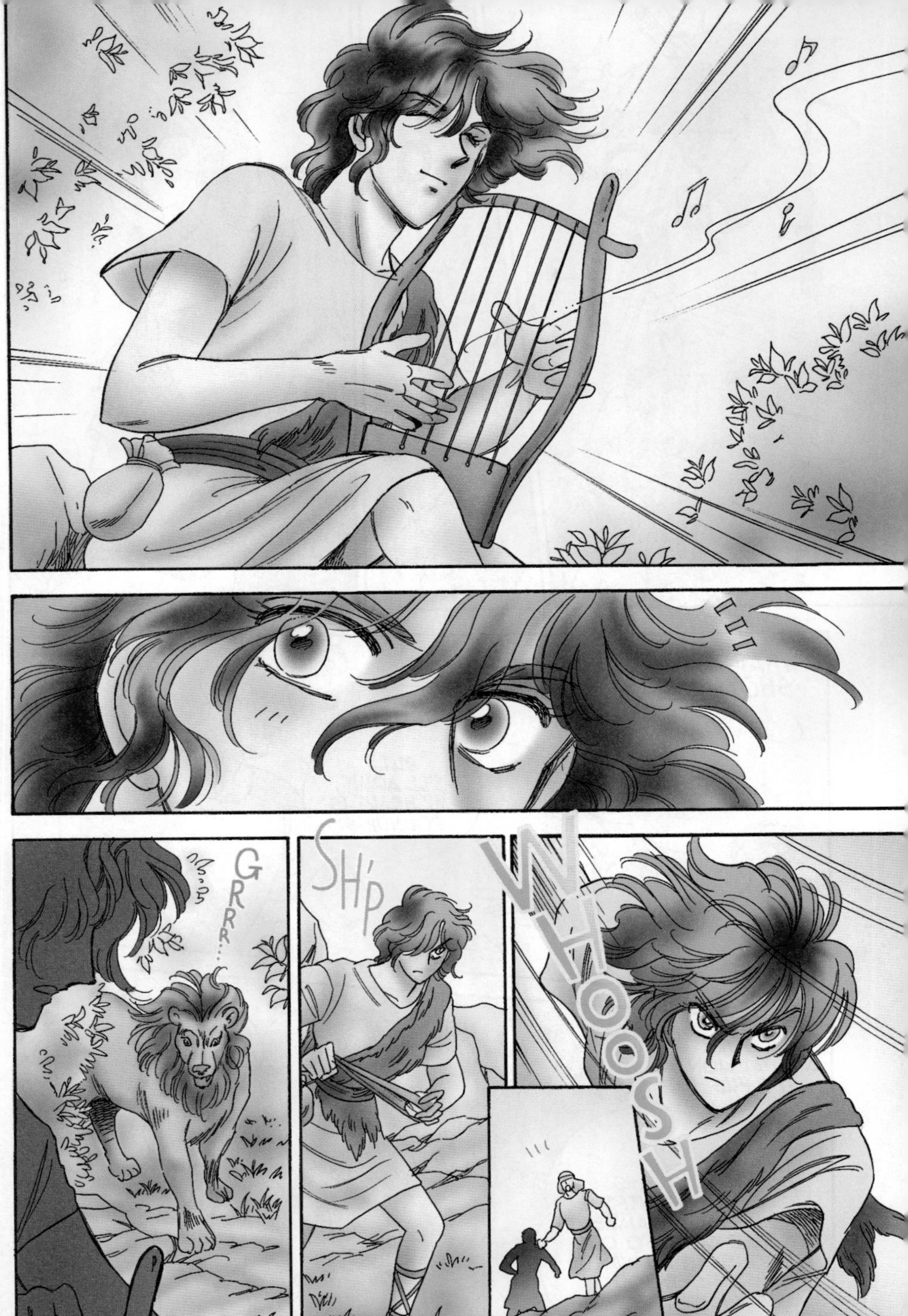
GRRR...
SH'P
WHOOSH

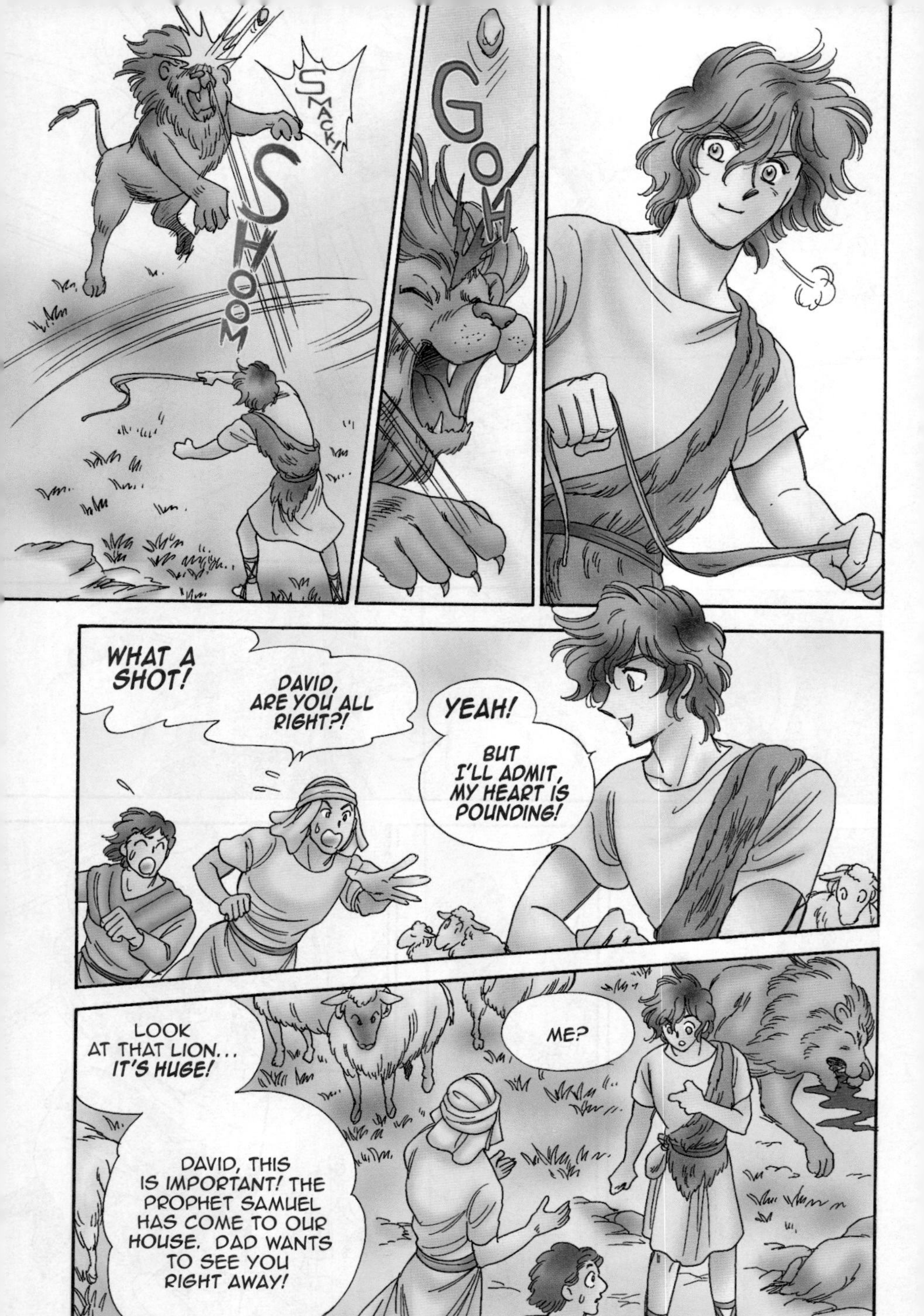
SMACK!
SHOOM
GOH
WHAT A SHOT!
DAVID, ARE YOU ALL RIGHT?!
YEAH!
BUT I'LL ADMIT, MY HEART IS POUNDING!
LOOK AT THAT LION... IT'S HUGE!
ME?
DAVID, THIS IS IMPORTANT! THE PROPHET SAMUEL HAS COME TO OUR HOUSE. DAD WANTS TO SEE YOU RIGHT AWAY!

DAD!

I'M HERE!

THIS IS MY YOUNGEST SON, DAVID.

THIS IS THE ONE. ANOINT HIM.

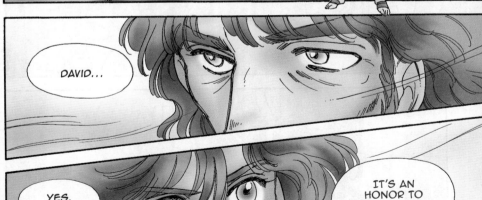

DAVID...

YES, SIR.

IT'S AN HONOR TO MEET YOU, SIR.

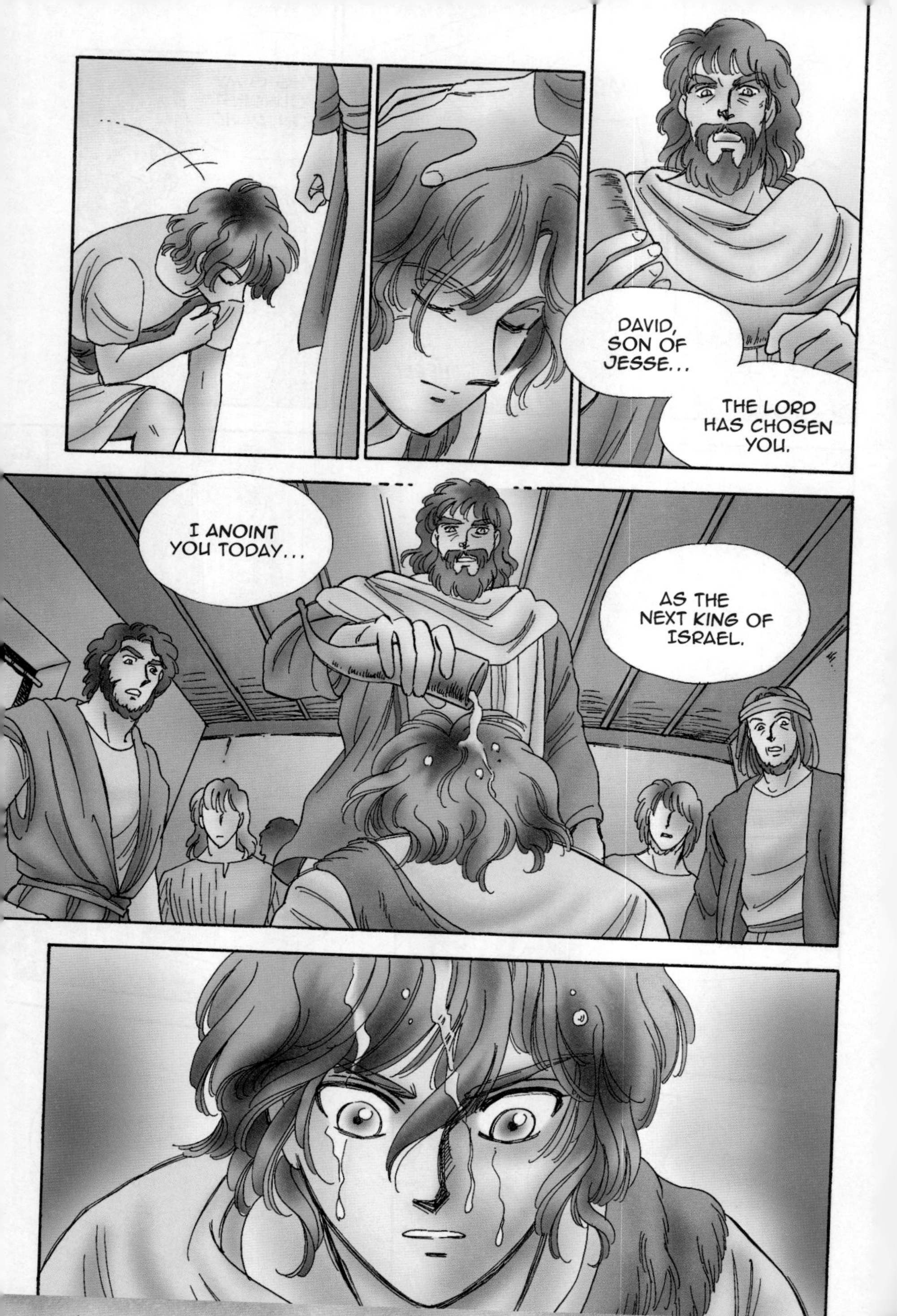
DAVID, SON OF JESSE...
THE LORD HAS CHOSEN YOU.
I ANOINT YOU TODAY...
AS THE NEXT KING OF ISRAEL.

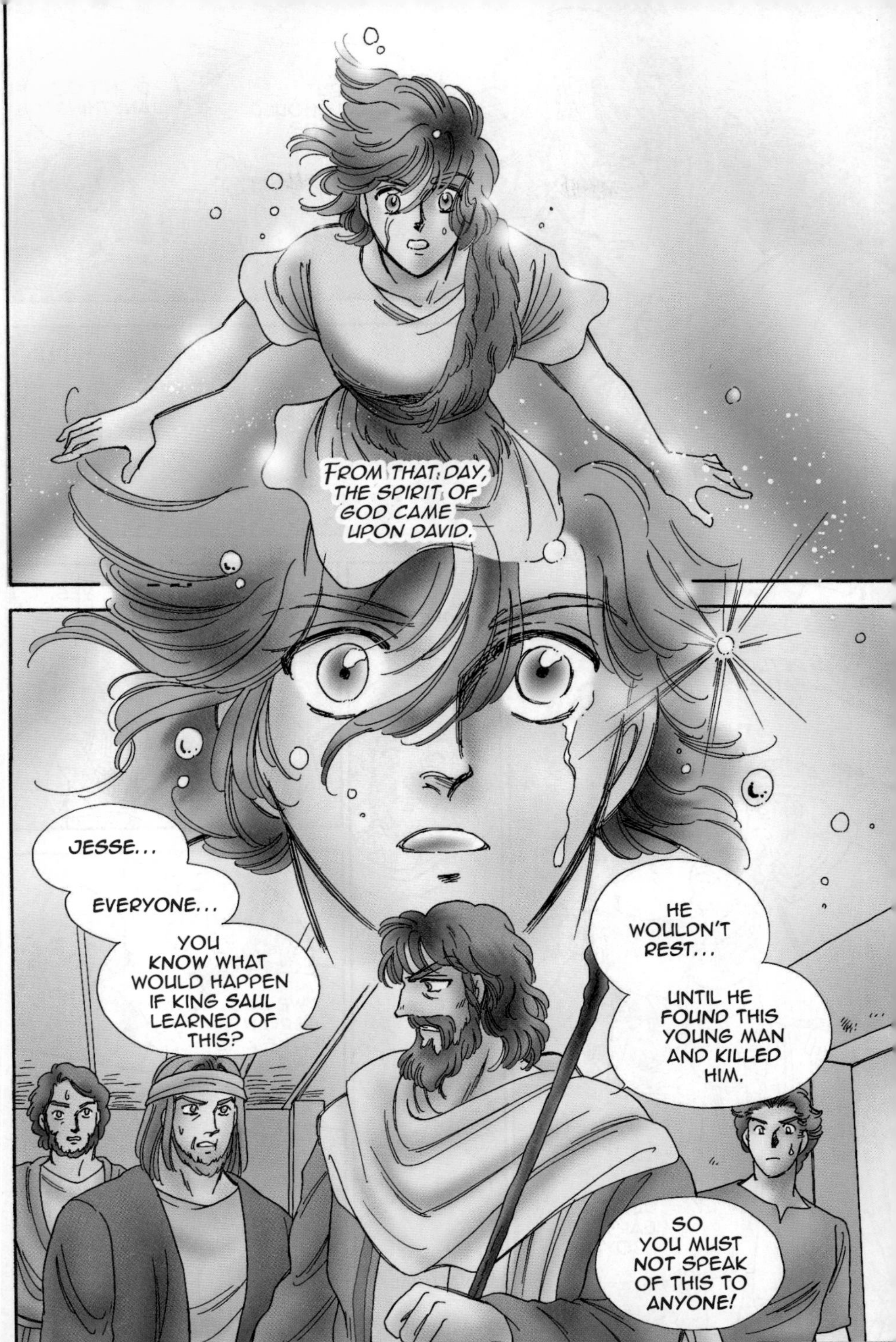
FROM THAT DAY, THE SPIRIT OF GOD CAME UPON DAVID.
JESSE...
EVERYONE...
YOU KNOW WHAT WOULD HAPPEN IF KING SAUL LEARNED OF THIS?
HE WOULDN'T REST...
UNTIL HE FOUND THIS YOUNG MAN AND KILLED HIM.
SO YOU MUST NOT SPEAK OF THIS TO ANYONE!

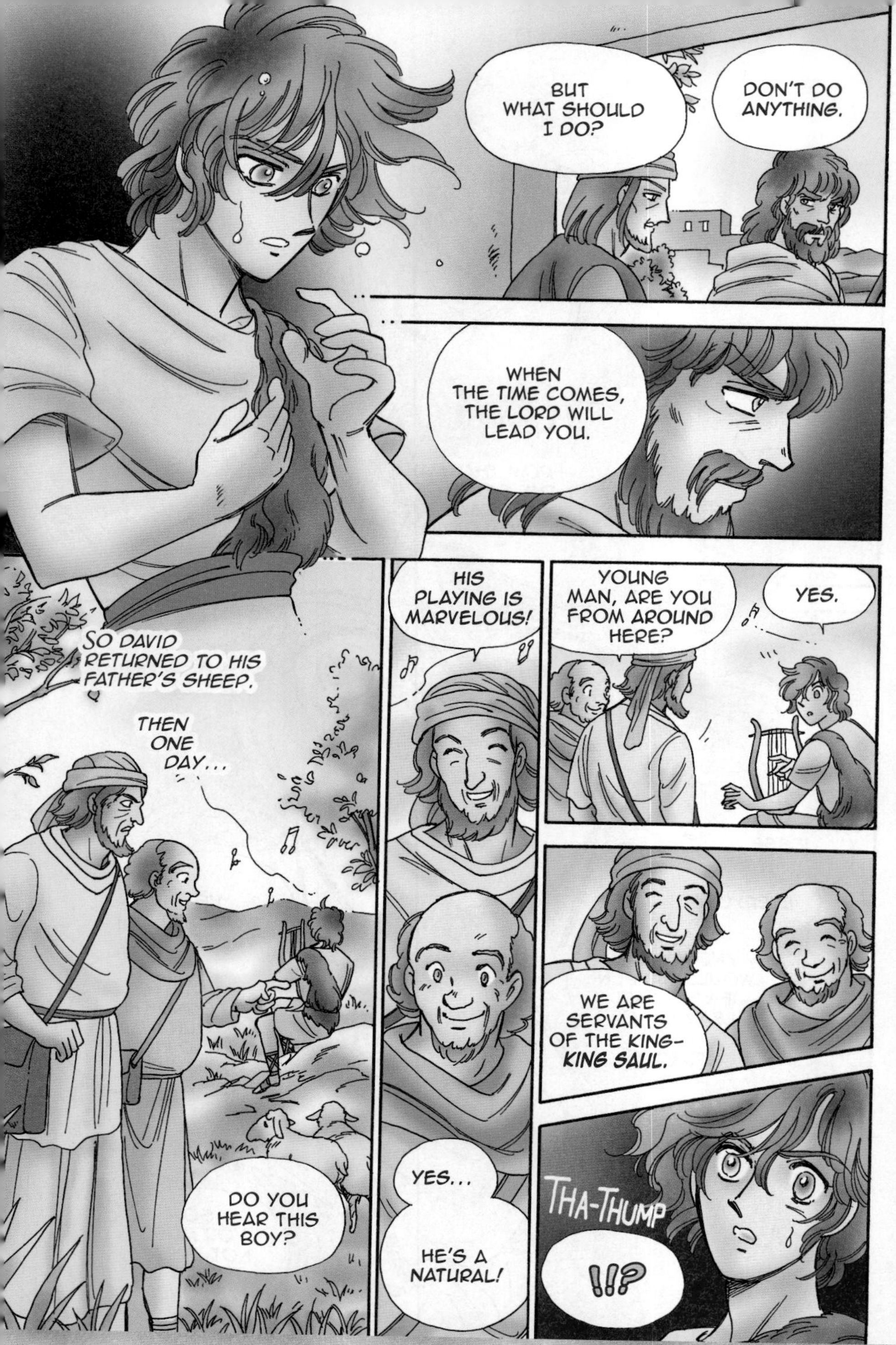
BUT WHAT SHOULD I DO?
DON'T DO ANYTHING.
WHEN THE TIME COMES, THE LORD WILL LEAD YOU.
SO DAVID RETURNED TO HIS FATHER'S SHEEP.
THEN ONE DAY...
DO YOU HEAR THIS BOY?
HIS PLAYING IS MARVELOUS!
YES...
HE'S A NATURAL!
YOUNG MAN, ARE YOU FROM AROUND HERE?
YES.
WE ARE SERVANTS OF THE KING- KING SAUL.
THA-THUMP
!!?

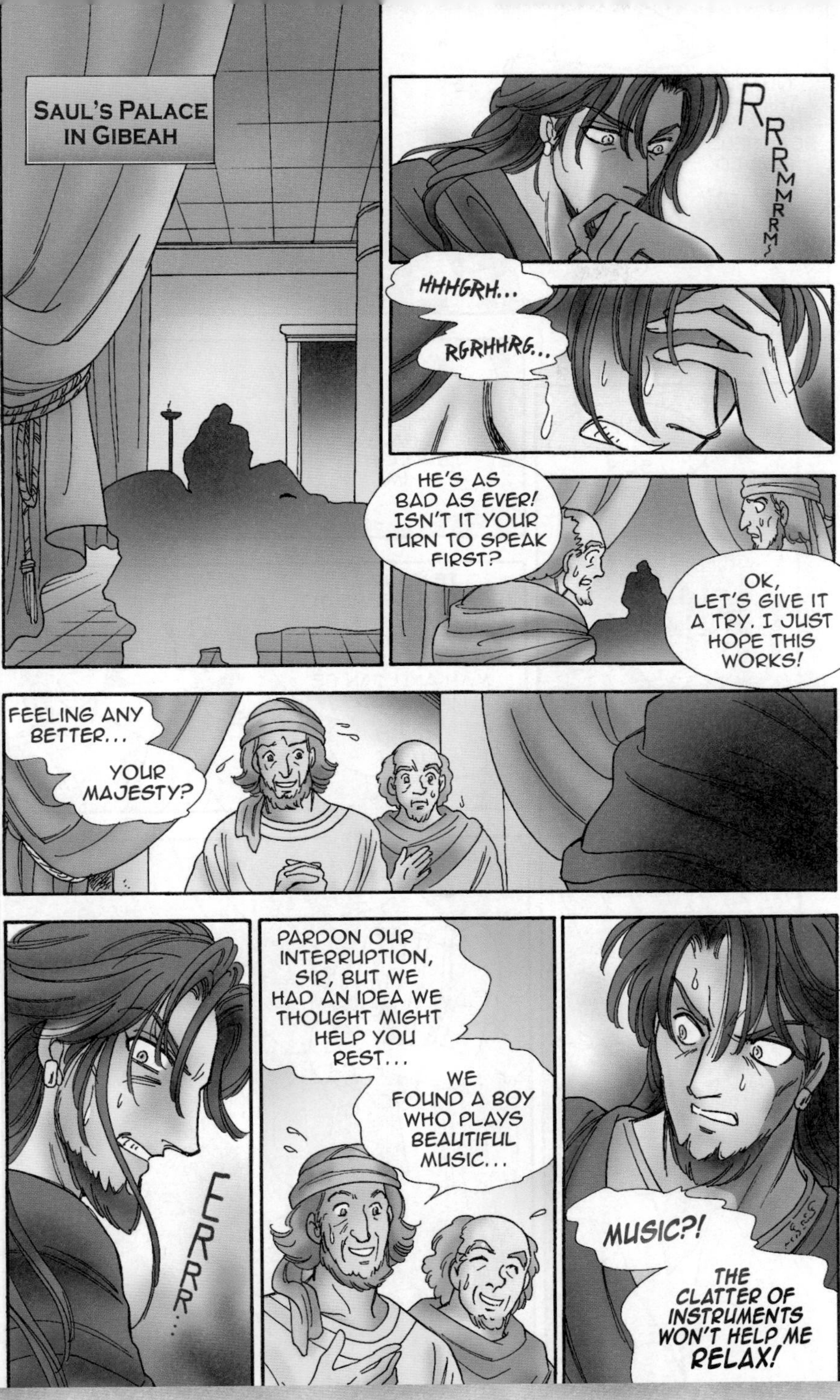
SAUL'S PALACE IN GIBEAH
RRRMMRRM~
HHHGRH...
RGRHHRG...
HE'S AS BAD AS EVER! ISN'T IT YOUR TURN TO SPEAK FIRST?
OK, LET'S GIVE IT A TRY. I JUST HOPE THIS WORKS!
FEELING ANY BETTER...
YOUR MAJESTY?
ERRRR...
PARDON OUR INTERRUPTION, SIR, BUT WE HAD AN IDEA WE THOUGHT MIGHT HELP YOU REST...
WE FOUND A BOY WHO PLAYS BEAUTIFUL MUSIC...
MUSIC?!
THE CLATTER OF INSTRUMENTS WON'T HELP ME RELAX!

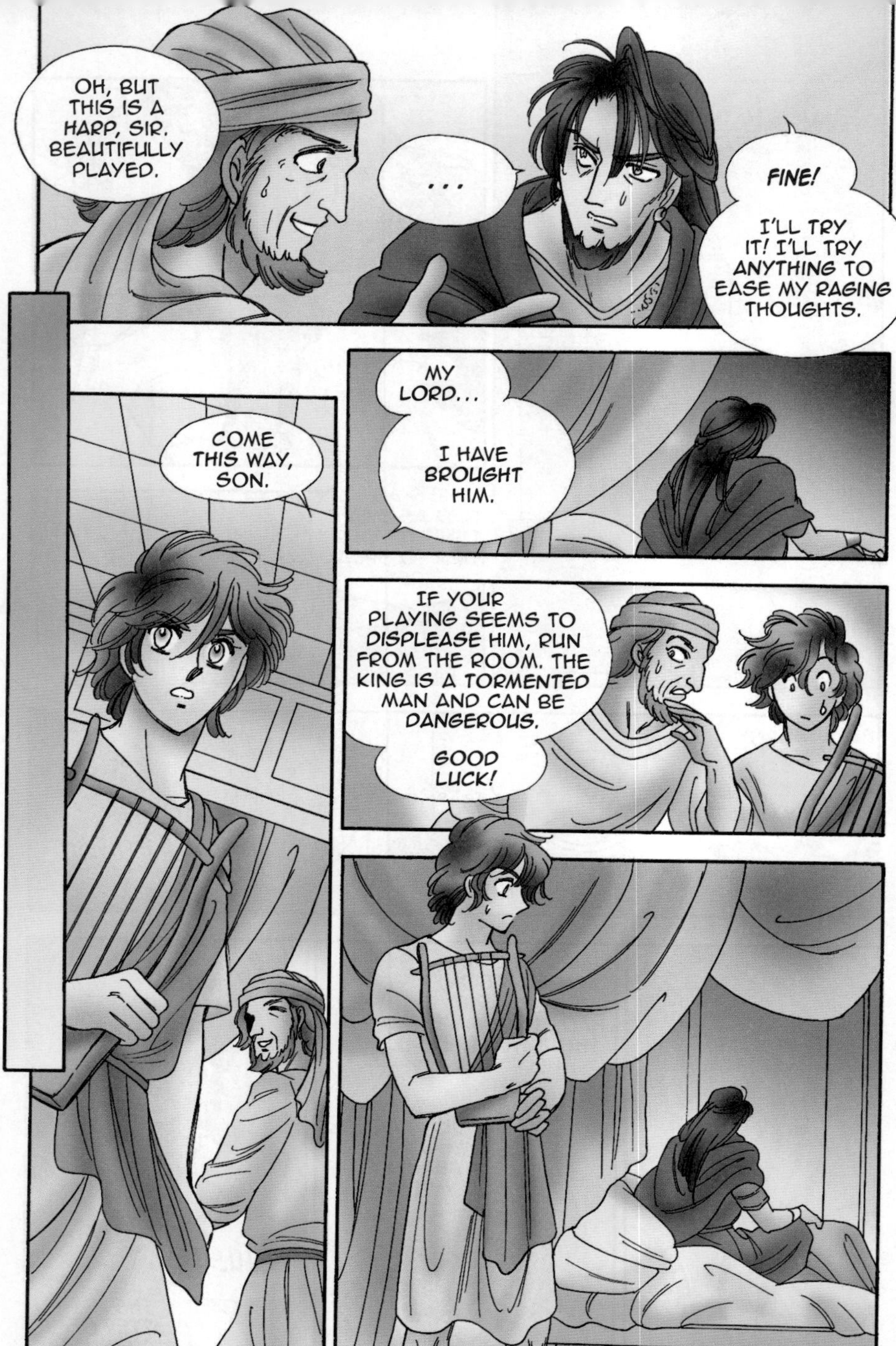
OH, BUT THIS IS A HARP, SIR. BEAUTIFULLY PLAYED.
...
FINE!
I'LL TRY IT! I'LL TRY ANYTHING TO EASE MY RAGING THOUGHTS.
COME THIS WAY, SON.
MY LORD...
I HAVE BROUGHT HIM.
IF YOUR PLAYING SEEMS TO DISPLEASE HIM, RUN FROM THE ROOM. THE KING IS A TORMENTED MAN AND CAN BE DANGEROUS.
GOOD LUCK!

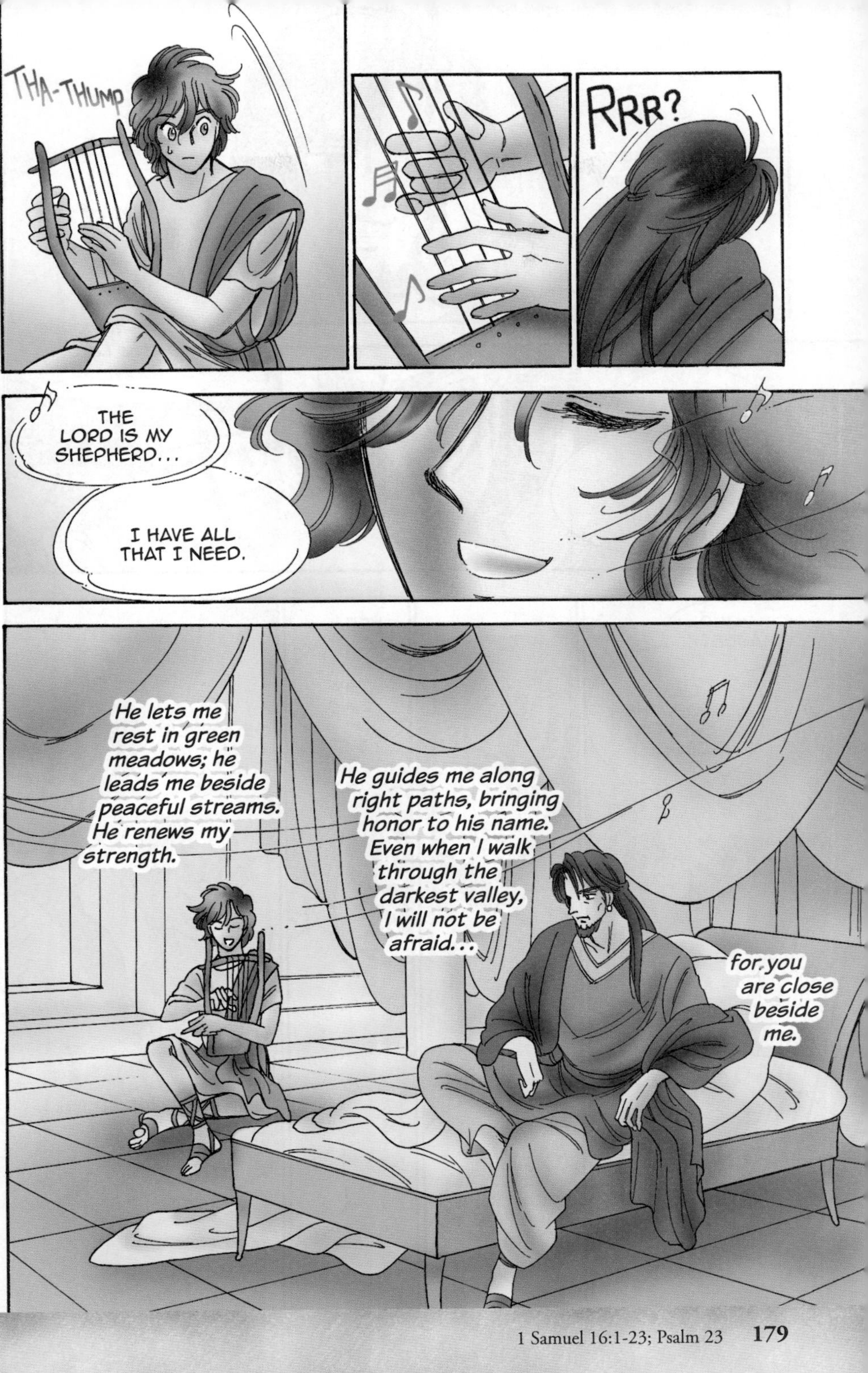
THA-THUMP
RRR?
THE LORD IS MY SHEPHERD...
I HAVE ALL THAT I NEED.
He lets me rest in green meadows; he leads me beside peaceful streams. He renews my strength.
He guides me along right paths, bringing honor to his name. Even when I walk through the darkest valley, I will not be afraid...
for you are close beside me.

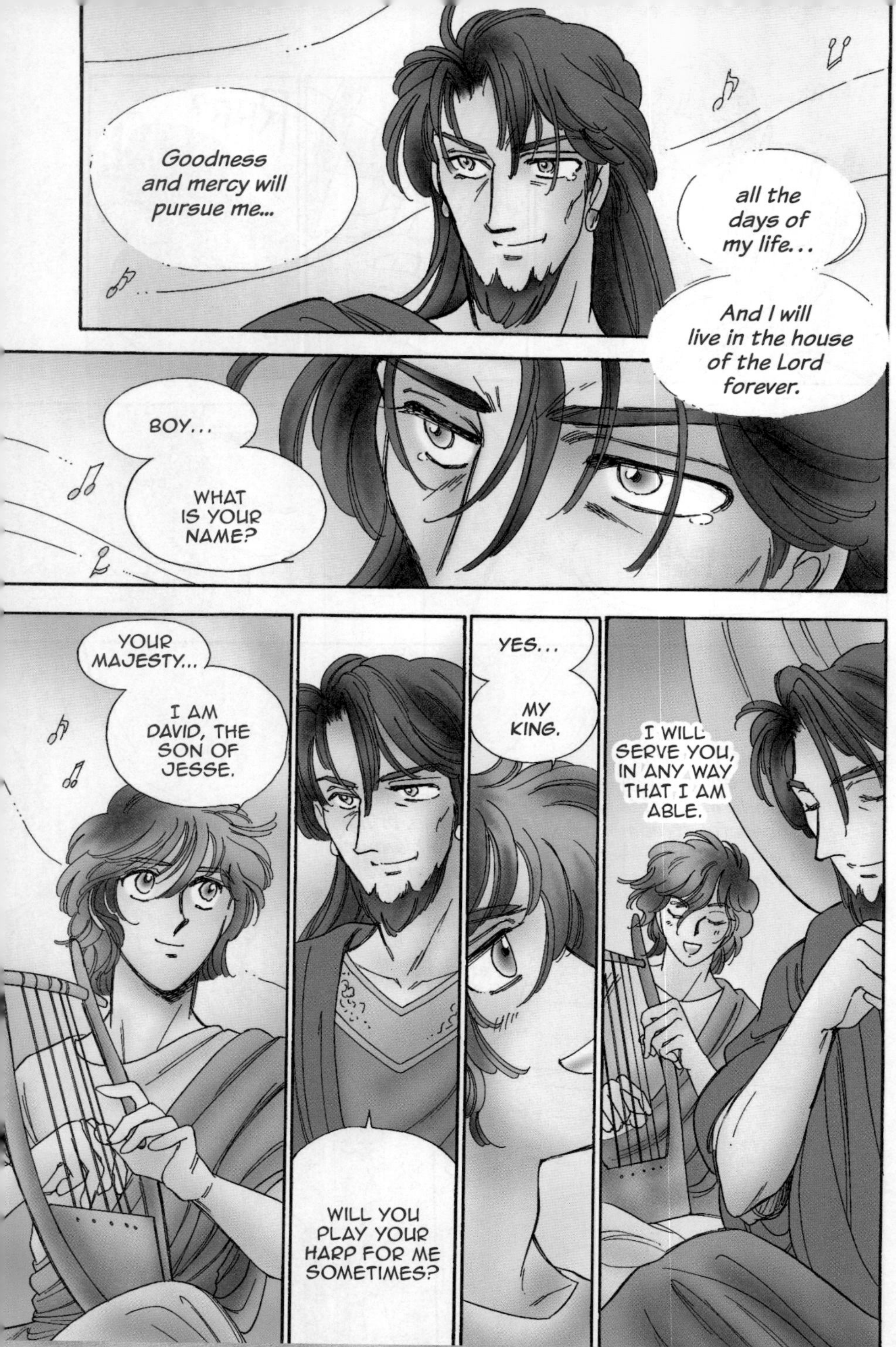
Goodness and mercy will pursue me...
all the days of my life. . .
And I will live in the house of the Lord forever.
BOY. . .
WHAT IS YOUR NAME?
YOUR MAJESTY...
I AM DAVID, THE SON OF JESSE.
YES. . .
MY KING.
WILL YOU PLAY YOUR HARP FOR ME SOMETIMES?
I WILL SERVE YOU, IN ANY WAY THAT I AM ABLE.

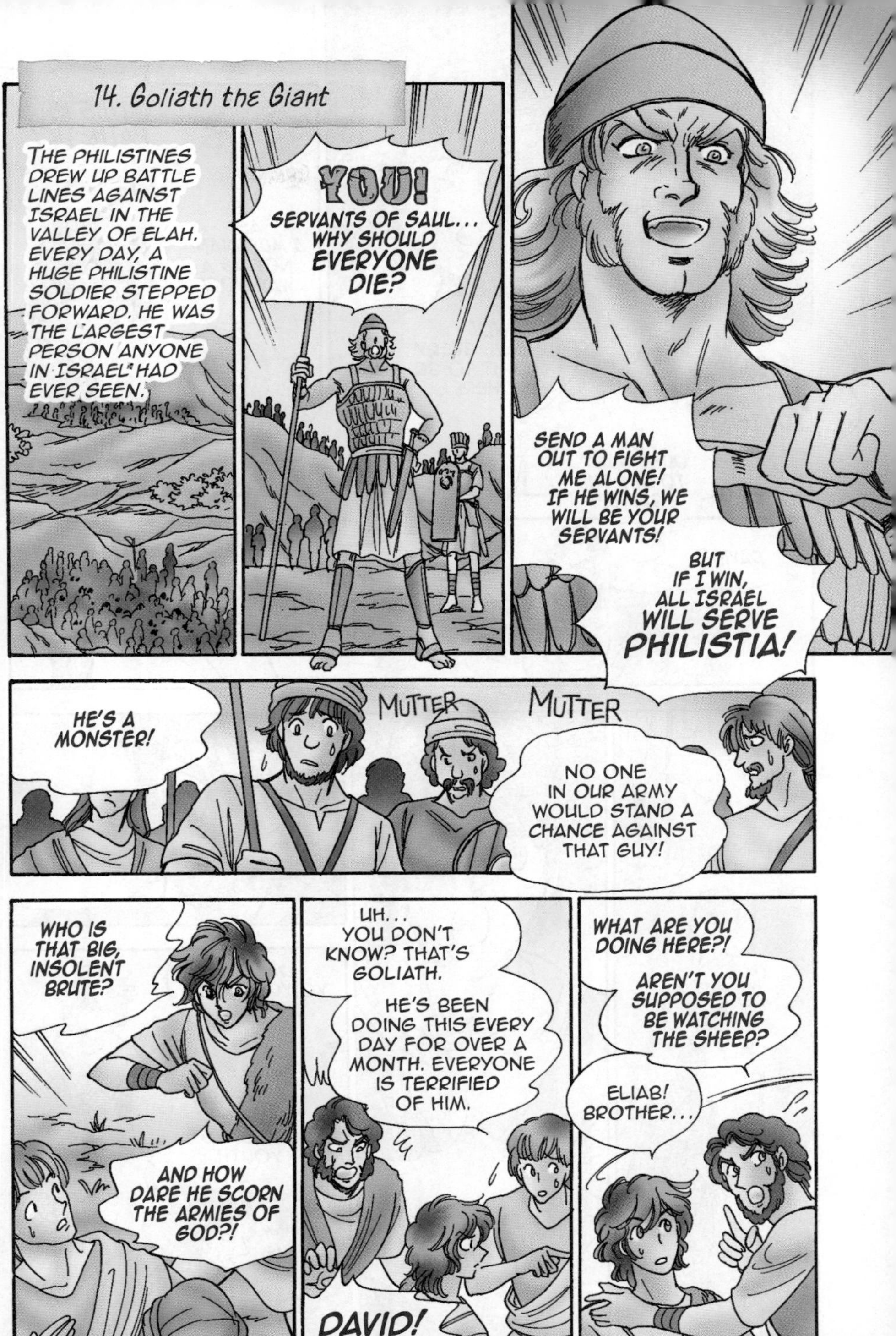
14. Goliath the Giant
THE PHILISTINES DREW UP BATTLE LINES AGAINST ISRAEL IN THE VALLEY OF ELAH. EVERY DAY, A HUGE PHILISTINE SOLDIER STEPPED FORWARD. HE WAS THE LARGEST PERSON ANYONE IN ISRAEL HAD EVER SEEN.
YOU! SERVANTS OF SAUL... WHY SHOULD EVERYONE DIE?
SEND A MAN OUT TO FIGHT ME ALONE! IF HE WINS, WE WILL BE YOUR SERVANTS!
BUT IF I WIN, ALL ISRAEL WILL SERVE PHILISTIA!
HE'S A MONSTER!
MUTTER
MUTTER
NO ONE IN OUR ARMY WOULD STAND A CHANCE AGAINST THAT GUY!
WHO IS THAT BIG, INSOLENT BRUTE?
AND HOW DARE HE SCORN THE ARMIES OF GOD?!
UH... YOU DON'T KNOW? THAT'S GOLIATH.
HE'S BEEN DOING THIS EVERY DAY FOR OVER A MONTH. EVERYONE IS TERRIFIED OF HIM.
DAVID!
WHAT ARE YOU DOING HERE?!
AREN'T YOU SUPPOSED TO BE WATCHING THE SHEEP?
ELIAB! BROTHER...

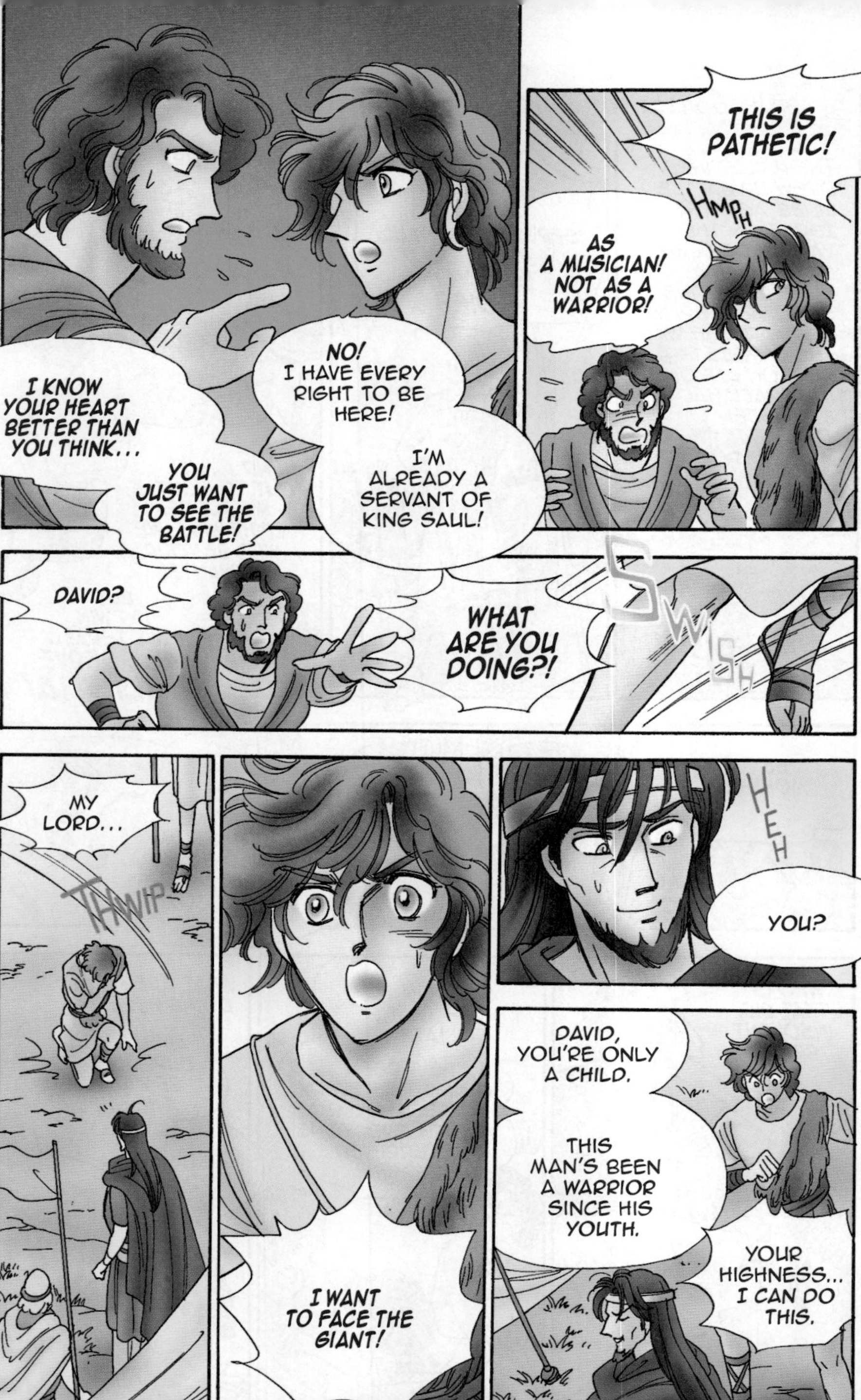
I KNOW YOUR HEART BETTER THAN YOU THINK...
YOU JUST WANT TO SEE THE BATTLE!
NO! I HAVE EVERY RIGHT TO BE HERE!
I'M ALREADY A SERVANT OF KING SAUL!
THIS IS PATHETIC!
HMPH
AS A MUSICIAN! NOT AS A WARRIOR!
DAVID?
WHAT ARE YOU DOING?!
SWISH
MY LORD...
THWIP
I WANT TO FACE THE GIANT!
HEH
YOU?
DAVID, YOU'RE ONLY A CHILD.
THIS MAN'S BEEN A WARRIOR SINCE HIS YOUTH.
YOUR HIGHNESS... I CAN DO THIS.

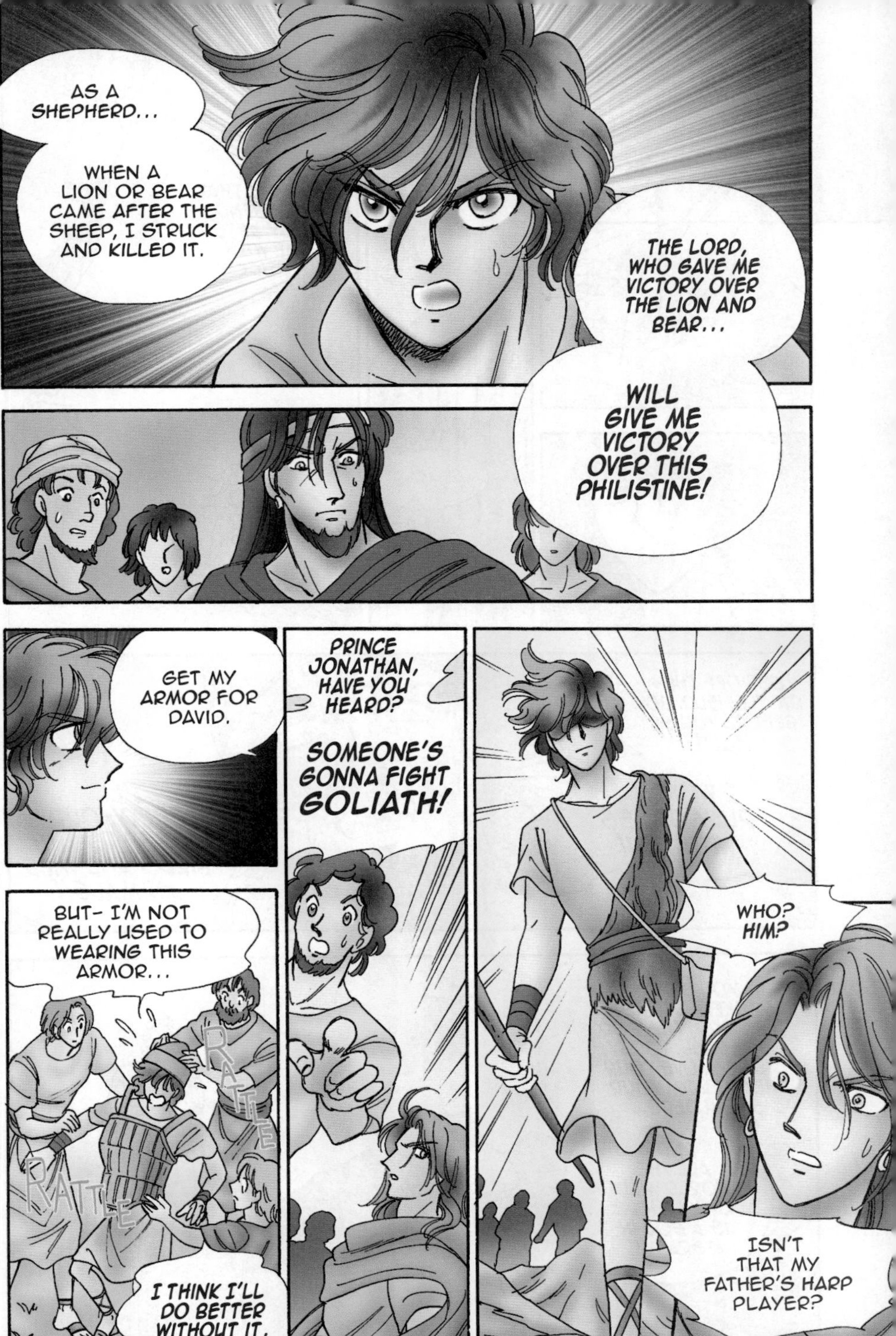
AS A SHEPHERD...
WHEN A LION OR BEAR CAME AFTER THE SHEEP, I STRUCK AND KILLED IT.
THE LORD, WHO GAVE ME VICTORY OVER THE LION AND BEAR...
WILL GIVE ME VICTORY OVER THIS PHILISTINE!
GET MY ARMOR FOR DAVID.
BUT- I'M NOT REALLY USED TO WEARING THIS ARMOR...
RATTLE
RATTLE
I THINK I'LL DO BETTER WITHOUT IT.
PRINCE JONATHAN, HAVE YOU HEARD?
SOMEONE'S GONNA FIGHT GOLIATH!
WHO? HIM?
ISN'T THAT MY FATHER'S HARP PLAYER?

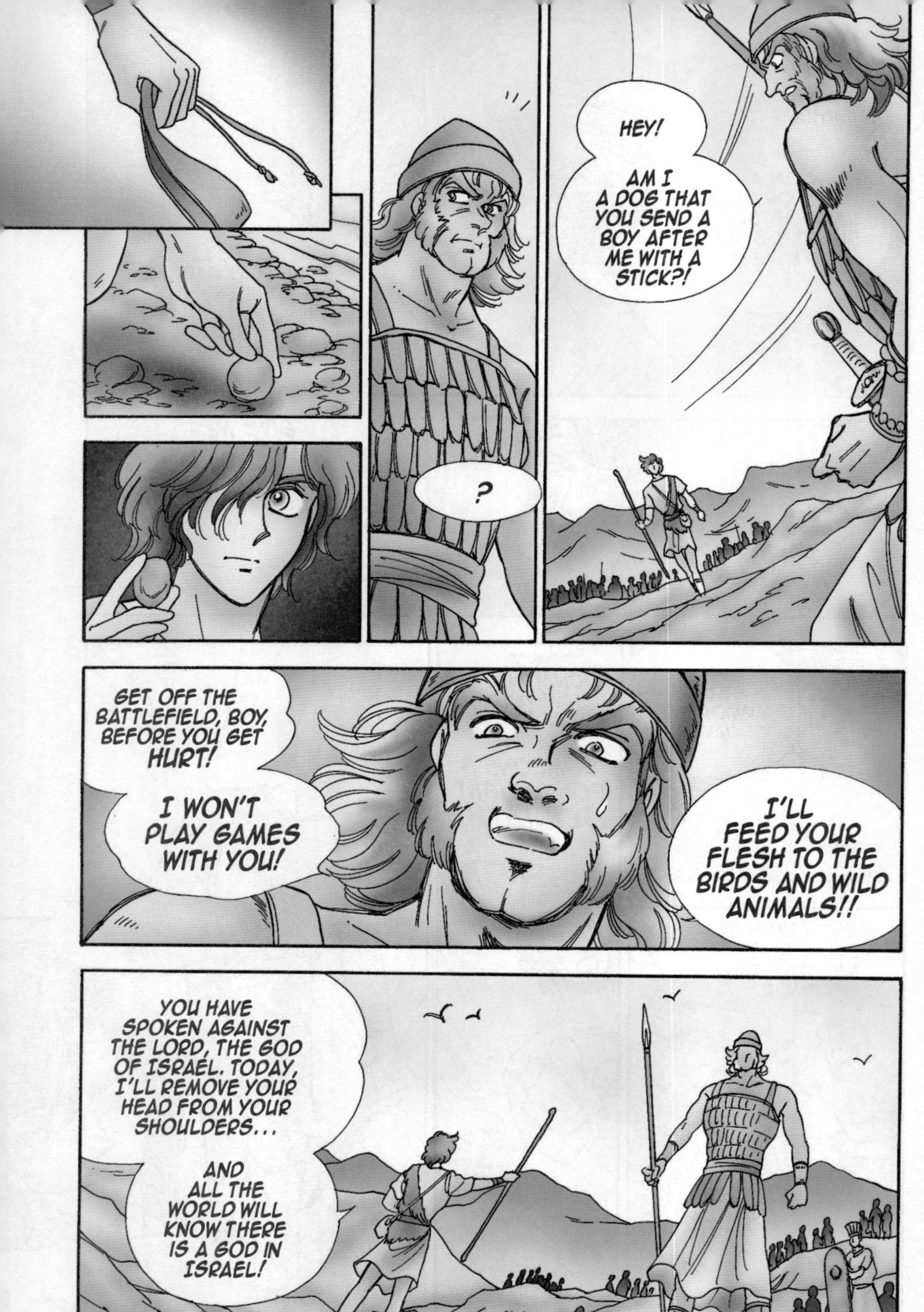
?
HEY!
AM I A DOG THAT YOU SEND A BOY AFTER ME WITH A STICK?!
GET OFF THE BATTLEFIELD, BOY, BEFORE YOU GET HURT!
I WON'T PLAY GAMES WITH YOU!
I'LL FEED YOUR FLESH TO THE BIRDS AND WILD ANIMALS!!
YOU HAVE SPOKEN AGAINST THE LORD, THE GOD OF ISRAEL. TODAY, I'LL REMOVE YOUR HEAD FROM YOUR SHOULDERS...
AND ALL THE WORLD WILL KNOW THERE IS A GOD IN ISRAEL!

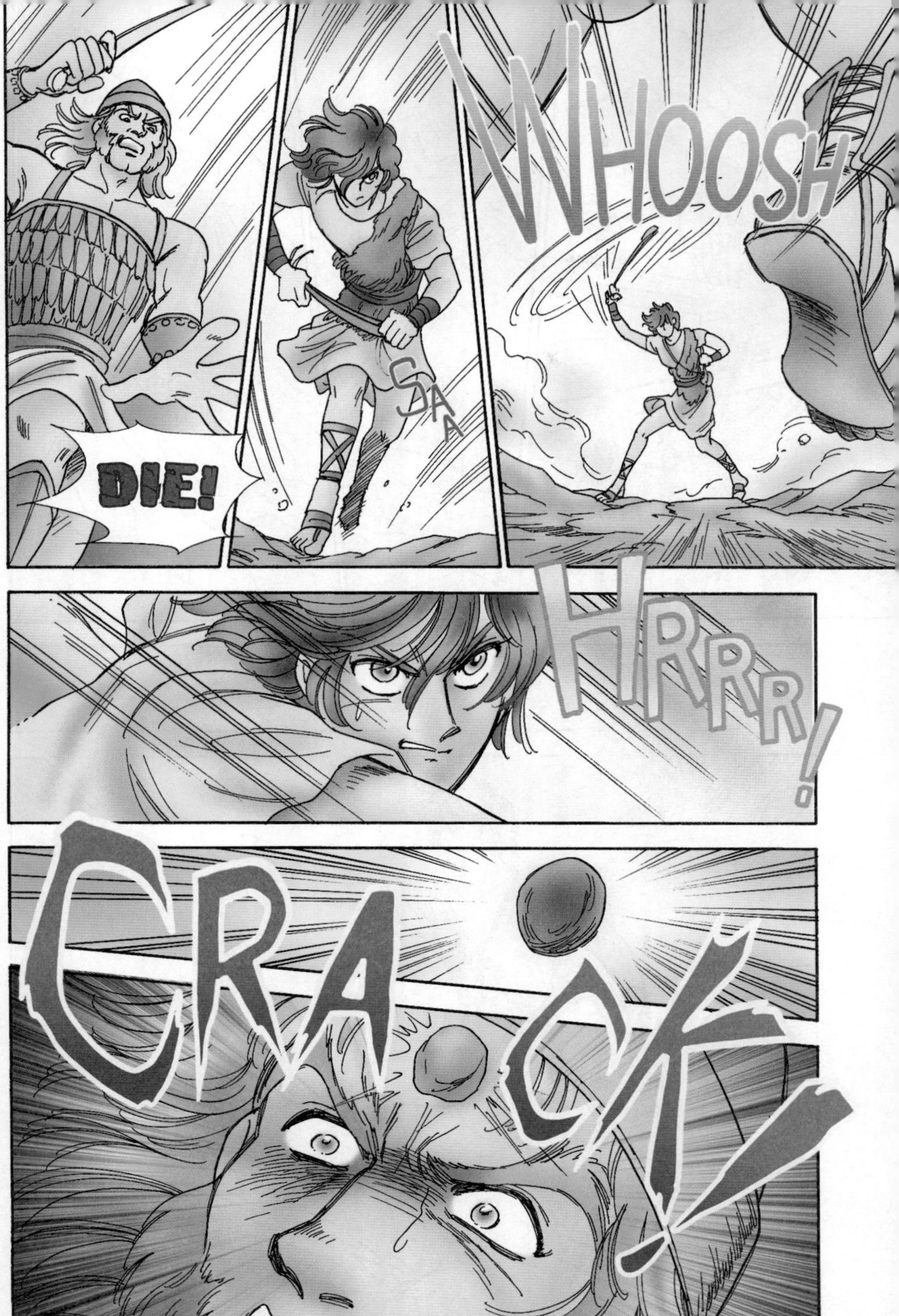
DIE!
SAA
WHOOSH
HRRR!
CRACK!

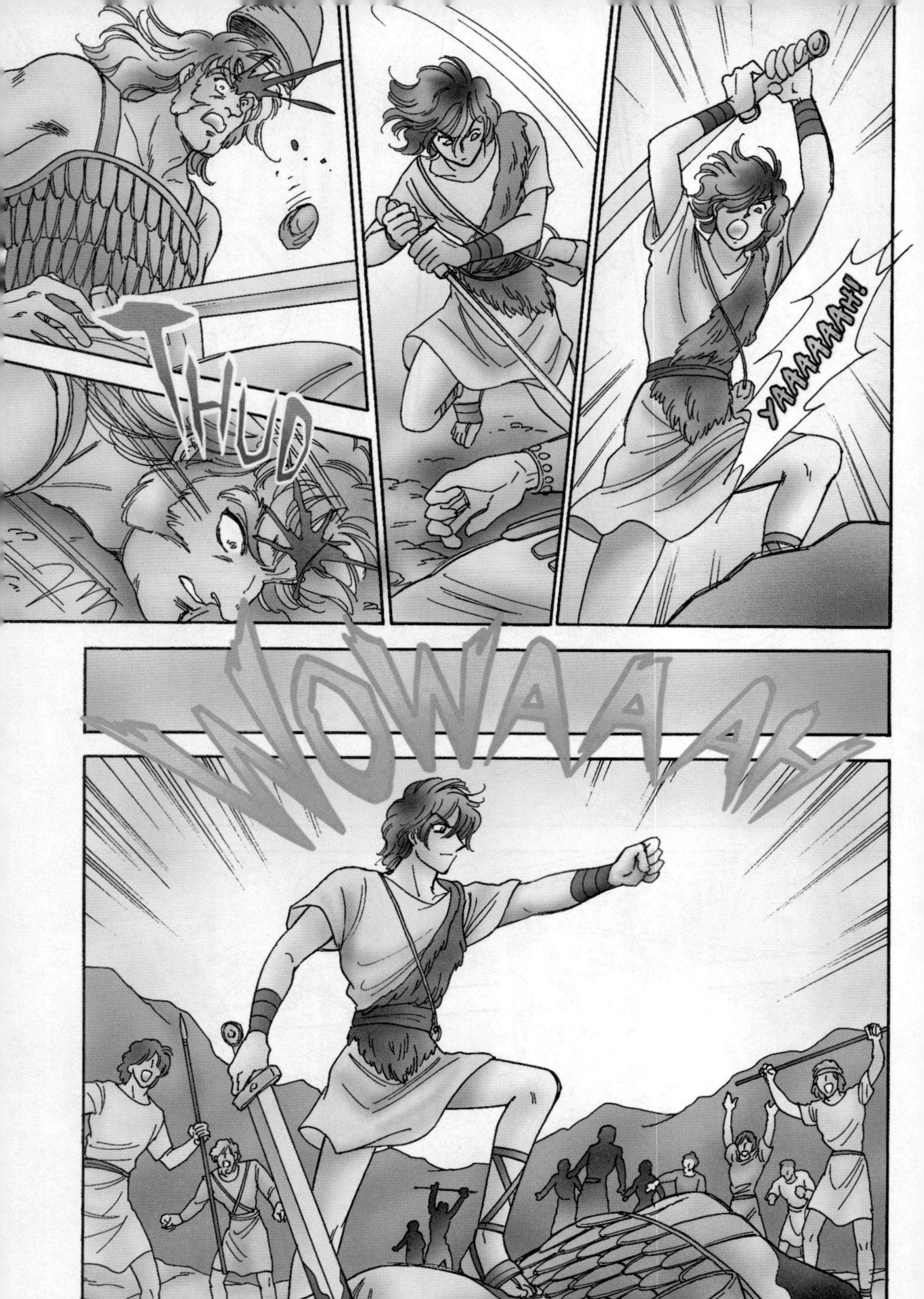
THUD
YAAAAAAH!
WOWAAAH

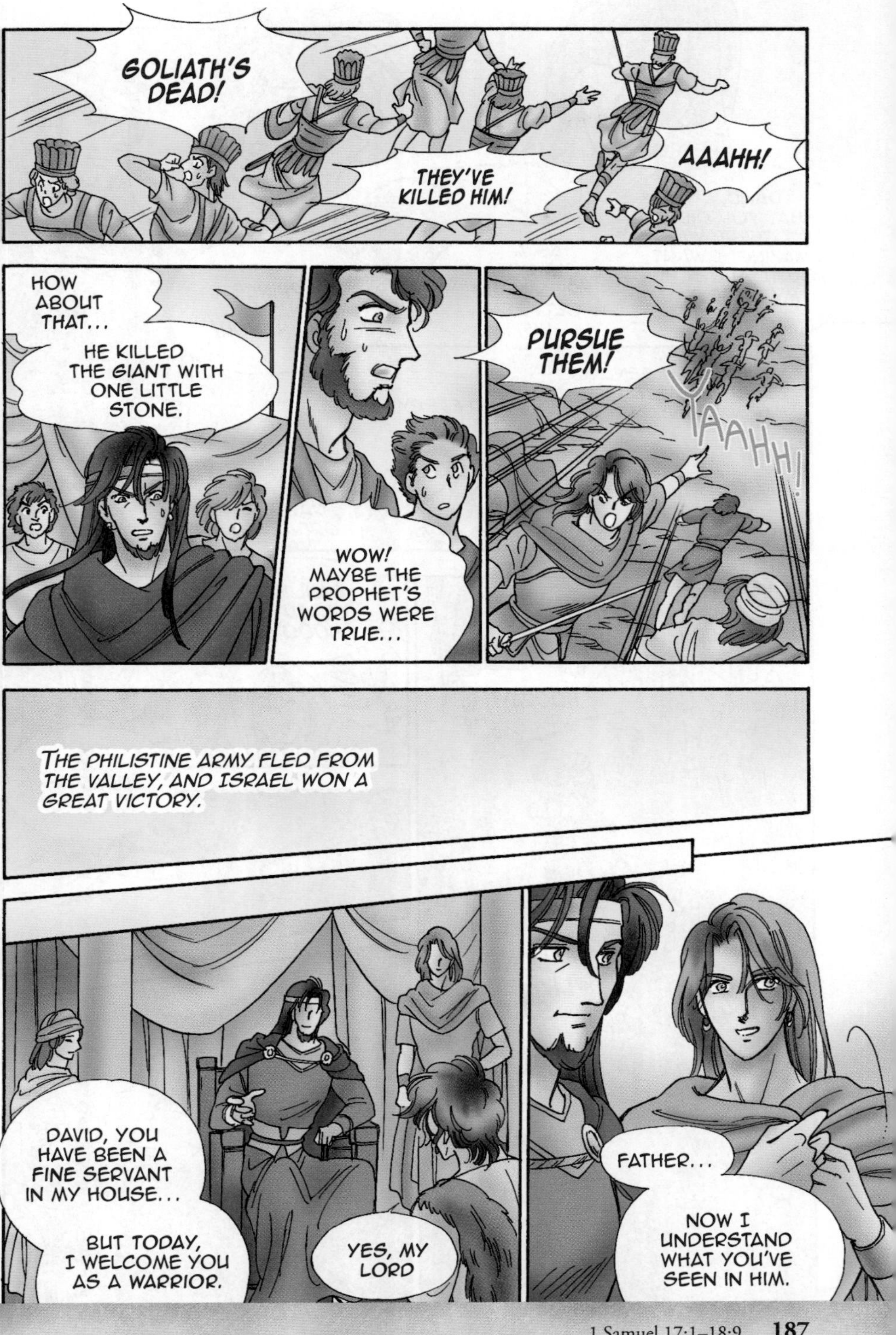
GOLIATH'S DEAD!
THEY'VE KILLED HIM!
AAAHH!
HOW ABOUT THAT...
HE KILLED THE GIANT WITH ONE LITTLE STONE.
WOW! MAYBE THE PROPHET'S WORDS WERE TRUE...
PURSUE THEM!
YAAHH!
THE PHILISTINE ARMY FLED FROM THE VALLEY, AND ISRAEL WON A GREAT VICTORY.
DAVID, YOU HAVE BEEN A FINE SERVANT IN MY HOUSE...
BUT TODAY, I WELCOME YOU AS A WARRIOR.
YES, MY LORD
FATHER...
NOW I UNDERSTAND WHAT YOU'VE SEEN IN HIM.

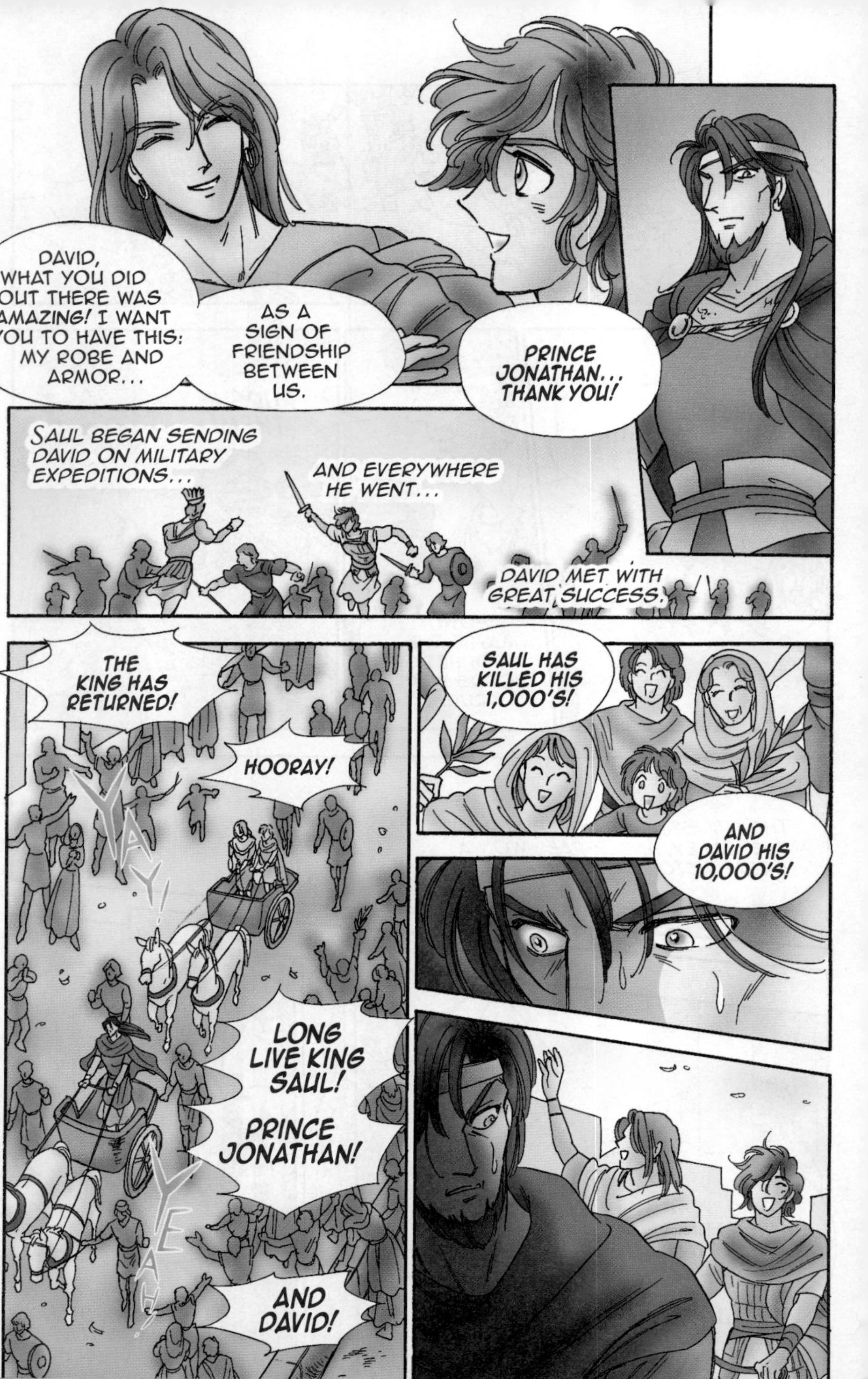
DAVID, WHAT YOU DID OUT THERE WAS AMAZING! I WANT YOU TO HAVE THIS: MY ROBE AND ARMOR...
AS A SIGN OF FRIENDSHIP BETWEEN US.
PRINCE JONATHAN... THANK YOU!
SAUL BEGAN SENDING DAVID ON MILITARY EXPEDITIONS...
AND EVERYWHERE HE WENT...
DAVID MET WITH GREAT SUCCESS.
THE KING HAS RETURNED!
HOORAY!
YAAY!
LONG LIVE KING SAUL!
PRINCE JONATHAN!
YEEAAH!
AND DAVID!
SAUL HAS KILLED HIS 1,000'S!
AND DAVID HIS 10,000'S!

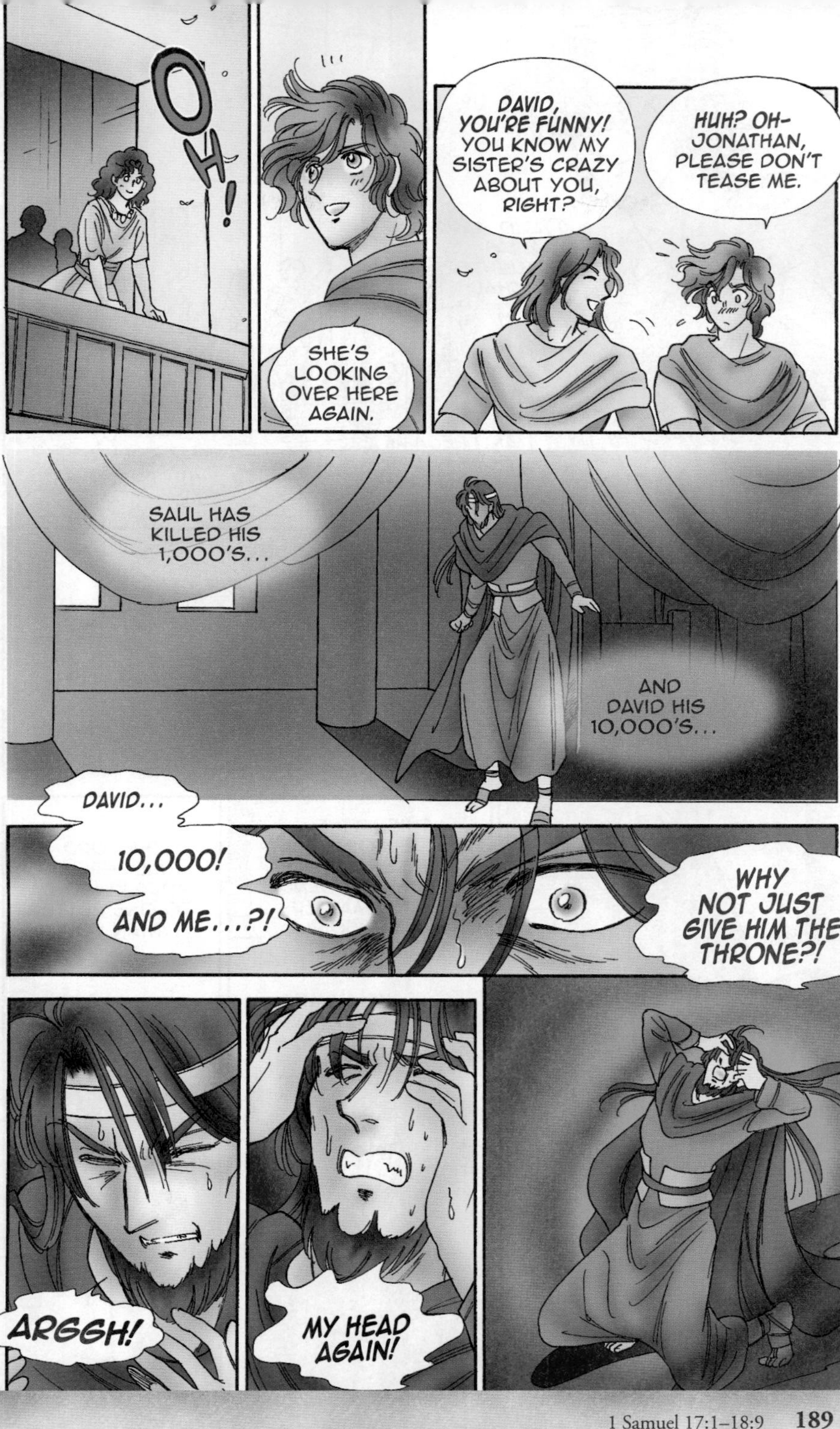
OH!
SHE'S LOOKING OVER HERE AGAIN.
DAVID, YOU'RE FUNNY! YOU KNOW MY SISTER'S CRAZY ABOUT YOU, RIGHT?
HUH? OH- JONATHAN, PLEASE DON'T TEASE ME.
SAUL HAS KILLED HIS 1,000'S...
AND DAVID HIS 10,000'S...
DAVID...
10,000!
AND ME...?!
WHY NOT JUST GIVE HIM THE THRONE?!
ARGGH!
MY HEAD AGAIN!

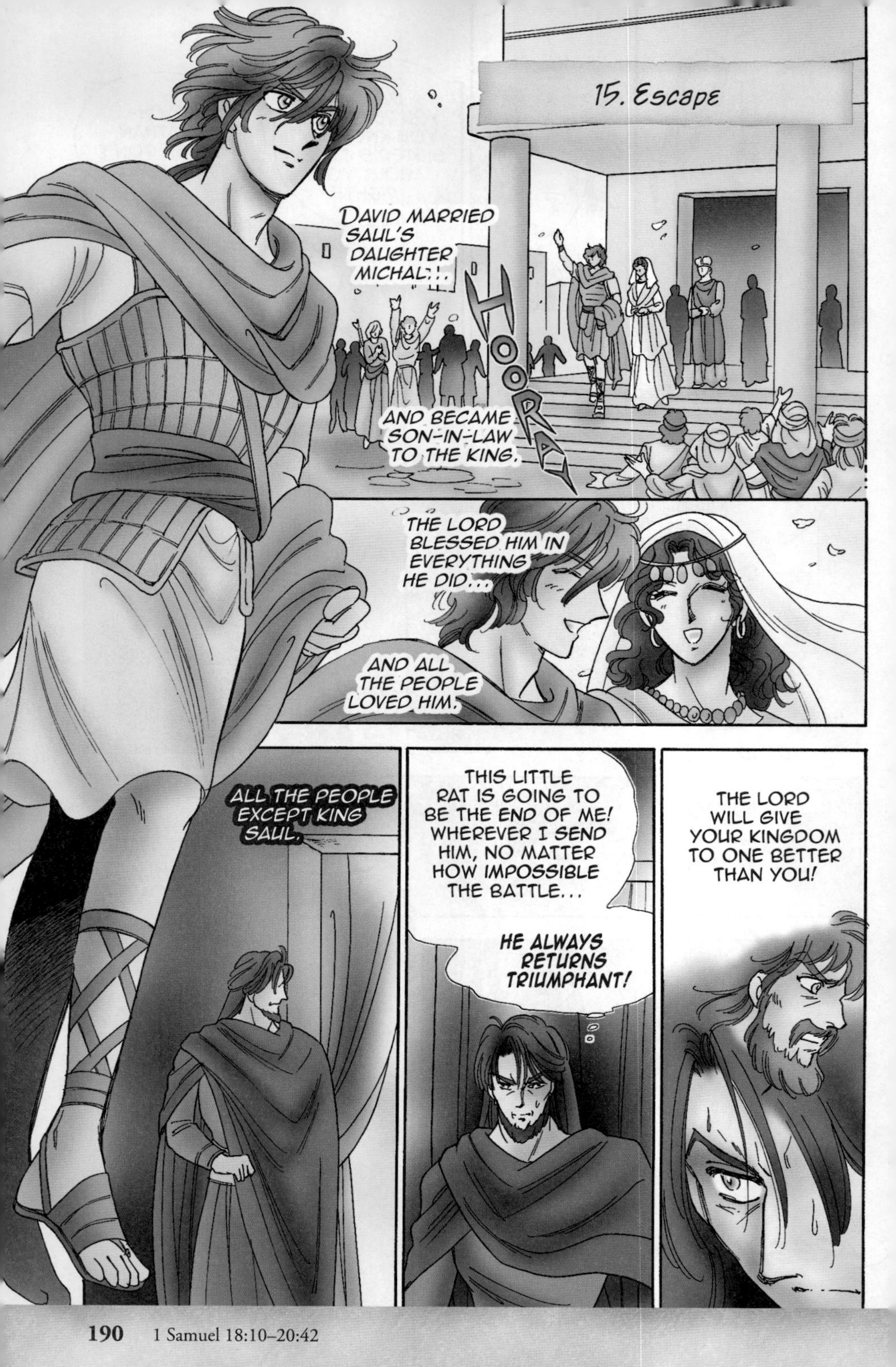
15. Escape
DAVID MARRIED SAUL'S DAUGHTER MICHAL...
HOORAY
AND BECAME SON-IN-LAW TO THE KING.
THE LORD BLESSED HIM IN EVERYTHING HE DID...
AND ALL THE PEOPLE LOVED HIM.
ALL THE PEOPLE EXCEPT KING SAUL.
THIS LITTLE RAT IS GOING TO BE THE END OF ME! WHEREVER I SEND HIM, NO MATTER HOW IMPOSSIBLE THE BATTLE...
HE ALWAYS RETURNS TRIUMPHANT!
THE LORD WILL GIVE YOUR KINGDOM TO ONE BETTER THAN YOU!

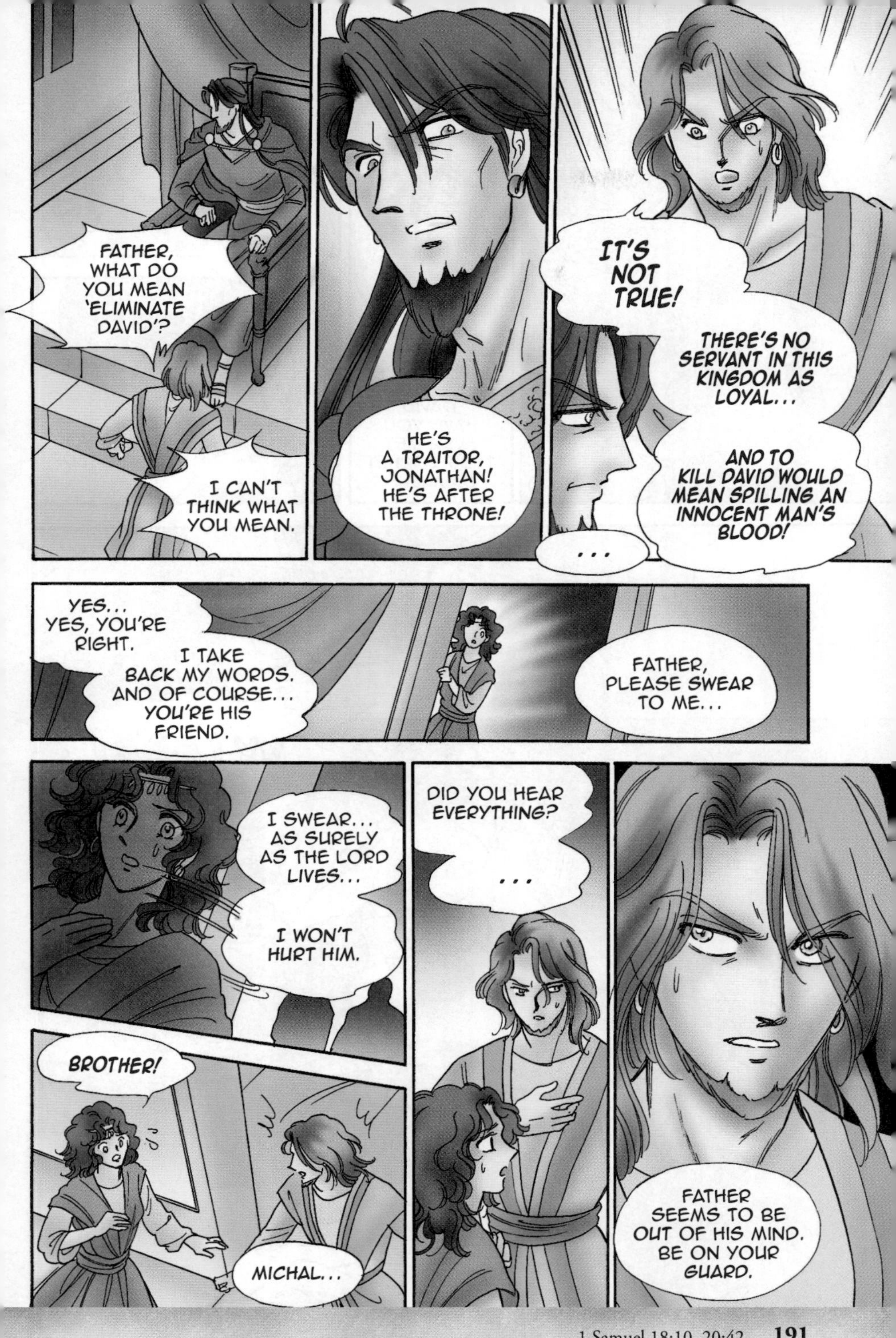
FATHER, WHAT DO YOU MEAN 'ELIMINATE DAVID'?
I CAN'T THINK WHAT YOU MEAN.
HE'S A TRAITOR, JONATHAN! HE'S AFTER THE THRONE!
IT'S NOT TRUE!
THERE'S NO SERVANT IN THIS KINGDOM AS LOYAL...
AND TO KILL DAVID WOULD MEAN SPILLING AN INNOCENT MAN'S BLOOD!
...
YES... YES, YOU'RE RIGHT.
I TAKE BACK MY WORDS. AND OF COURSE... YOU'RE HIS FRIEND.
FATHER, PLEASE SWEAR TO ME...
I SWEAR... AS SURELY AS THE LORD LIVES...
I WON'T HURT HIM.
BROTHER!
MICHAL...
DID YOU HEAR EVERYTHING?
...
FATHER SEEMS TO BE OUT OF HIS MIND. BE ON YOUR GUARD.

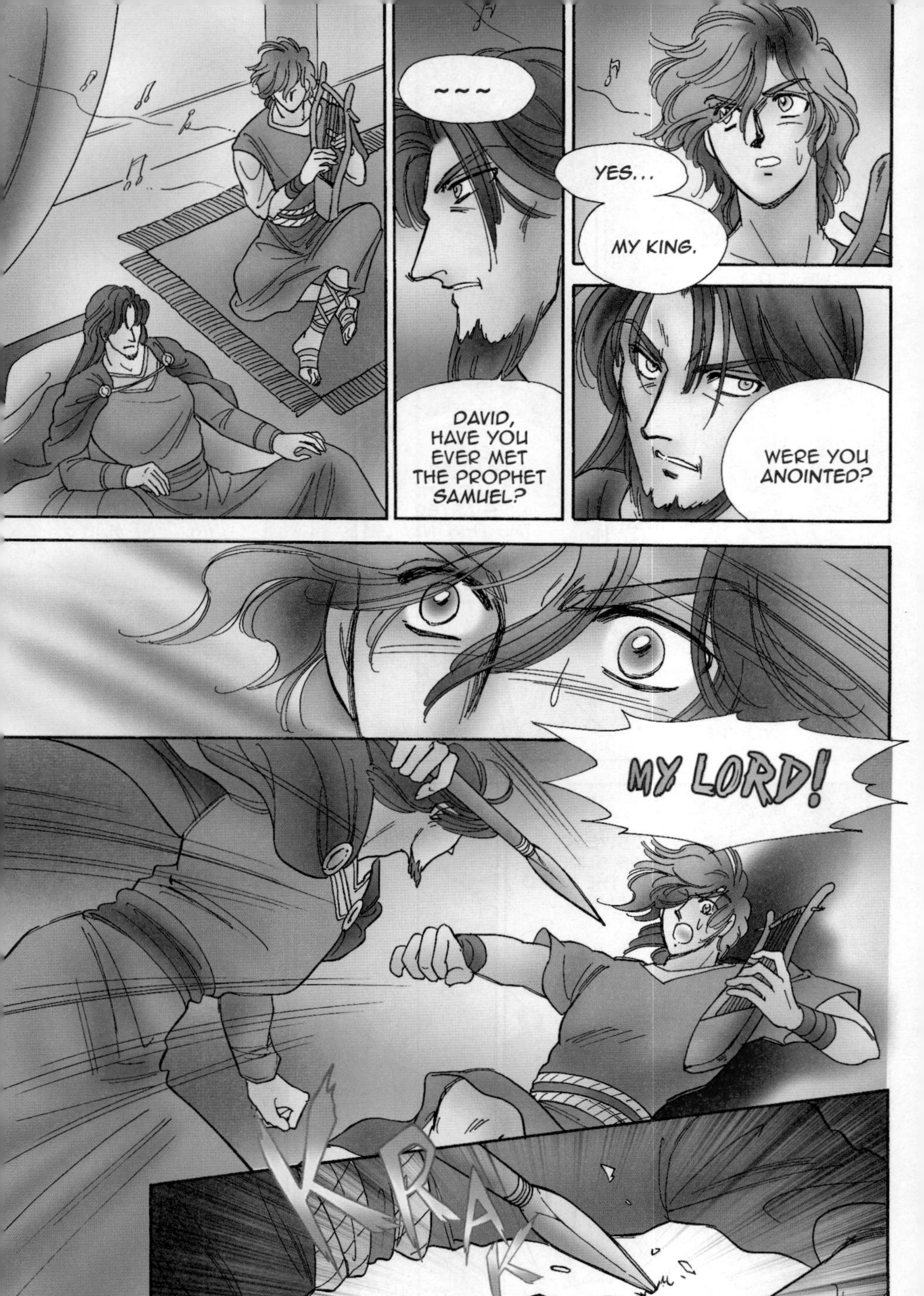

YES...
MY KING.
DAVID, HAVE YOU EVER MET THE PROPHET SAMUEL?
WERE YOU ANOINTED?
MY LORD!
KRAK

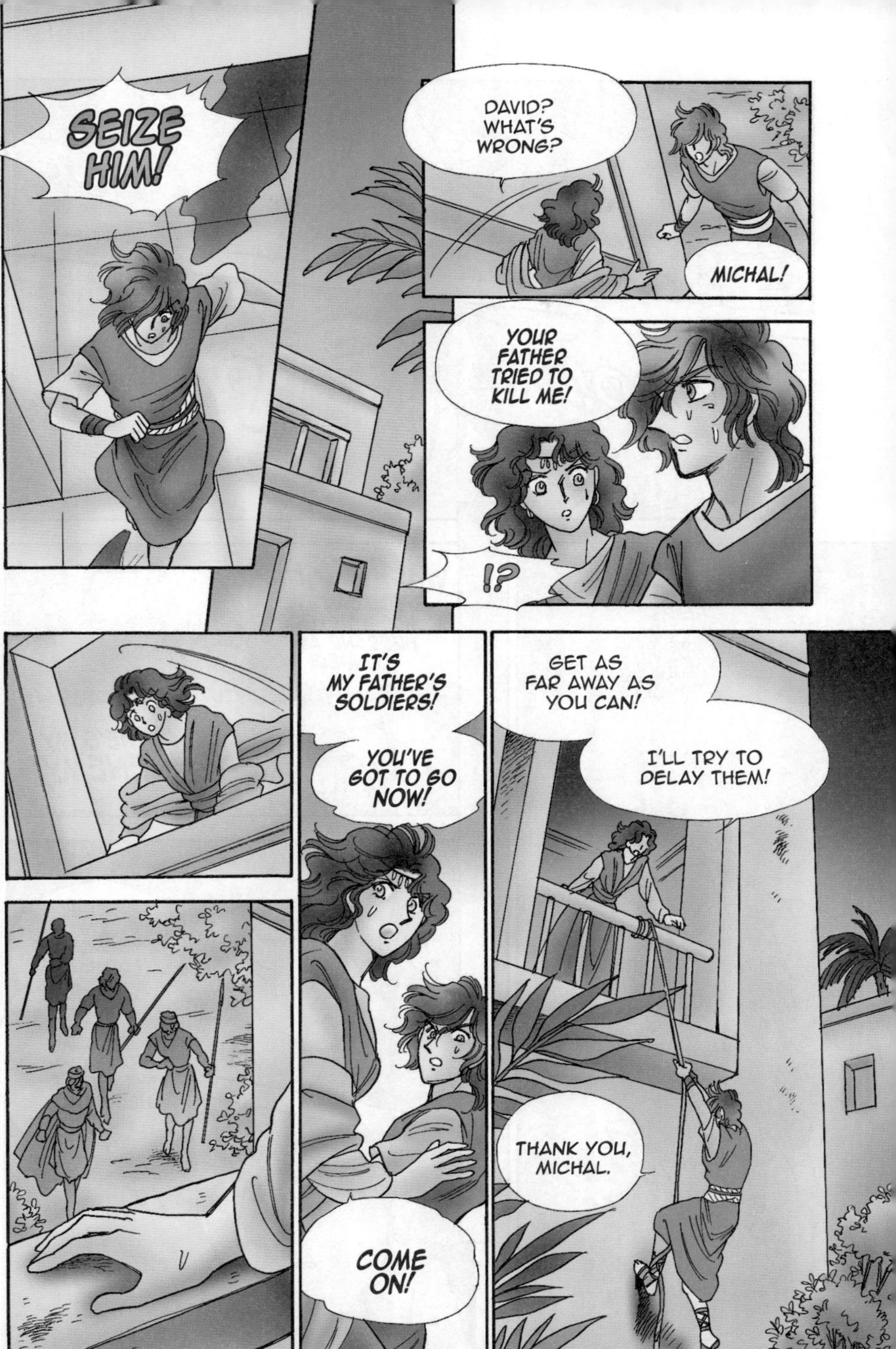
SEIZE HIM!
DAVID? WHAT'S WRONG?
MICHAL!
YOUR FATHER TRIED TO KILL ME!
!?
IT'S MY FATHER'S SOLDIERS!
YOU'VE GOT TO GO NOW!
GET AS FAR AWAY AS YOU CAN!
I'LL TRY TO DELAY THEM!
THANK YOU, MICHAL.
COME ON!

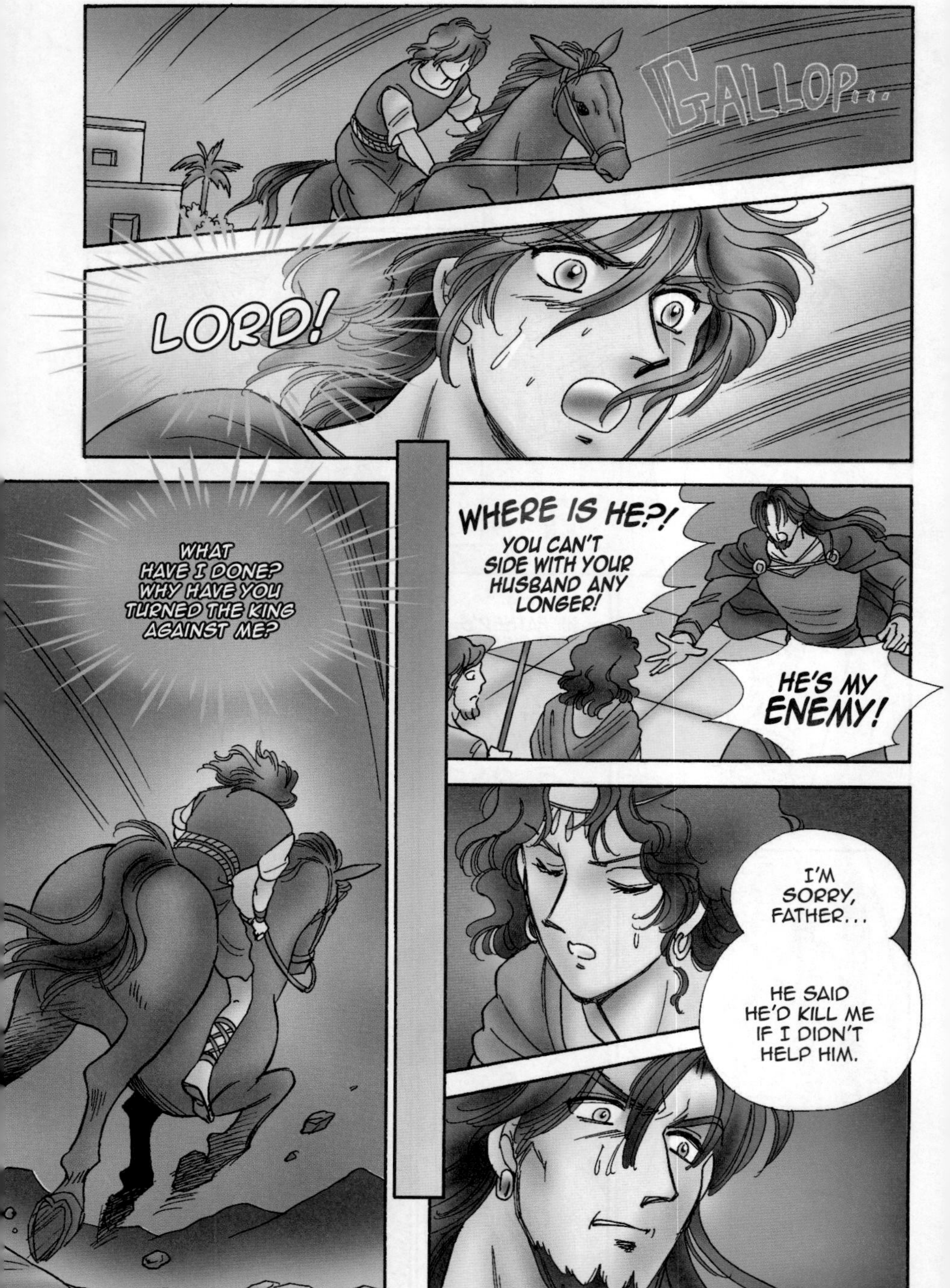
GALLOP...
LORD!
WHAT HAVE I DONE? WHY HAVE YOU TURNED THE KING AGAINST ME?
WHERE IS HE?!
YOU CAN'T SIDE WITH YOUR HUSBAND ANY LONGER!
HE'S MY ENEMY!
I'M SORRY, FATHER...
HE SAID HE'D KILL ME IF I DIDN'T HELP HIM.

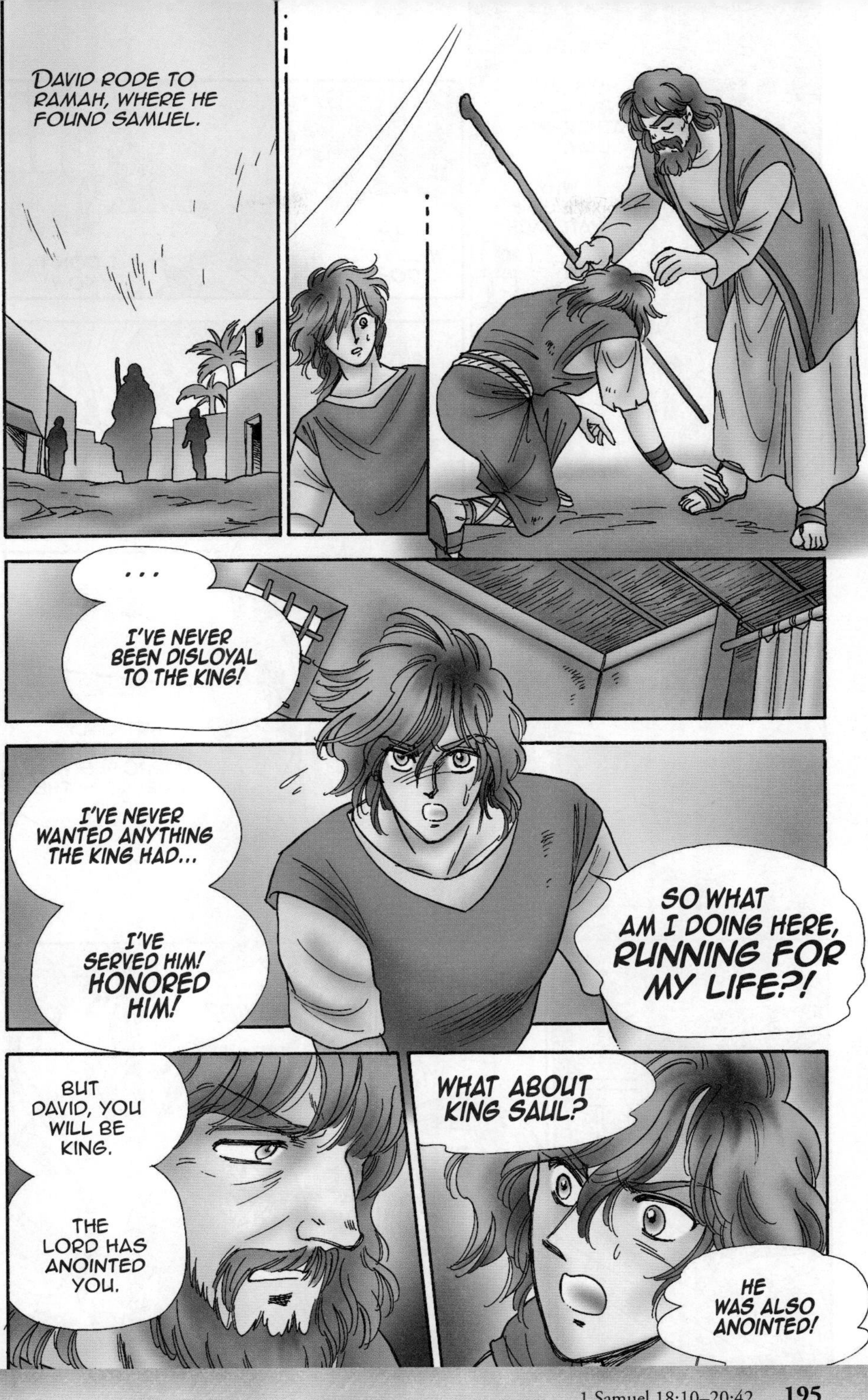
DAVID RODE TO RAMAH, WHERE HE FOUND SAMUEL.
. . .
I'VE NEVER BEEN DISLOYAL TO THE KING!
I'VE NEVER WANTED ANYTHING THE KING HAD...
I'VE SERVED HIM! HONORED HIM!
SO WHAT AM I DOING HERE, RUNNING FOR MY LIFE?!
BUT DAVID, YOU WILL BE KING.
THE LORD HAS ANOINTED YOU.
WHAT ABOUT KING SAUL?
HE WAS ALSO ANOINTED!

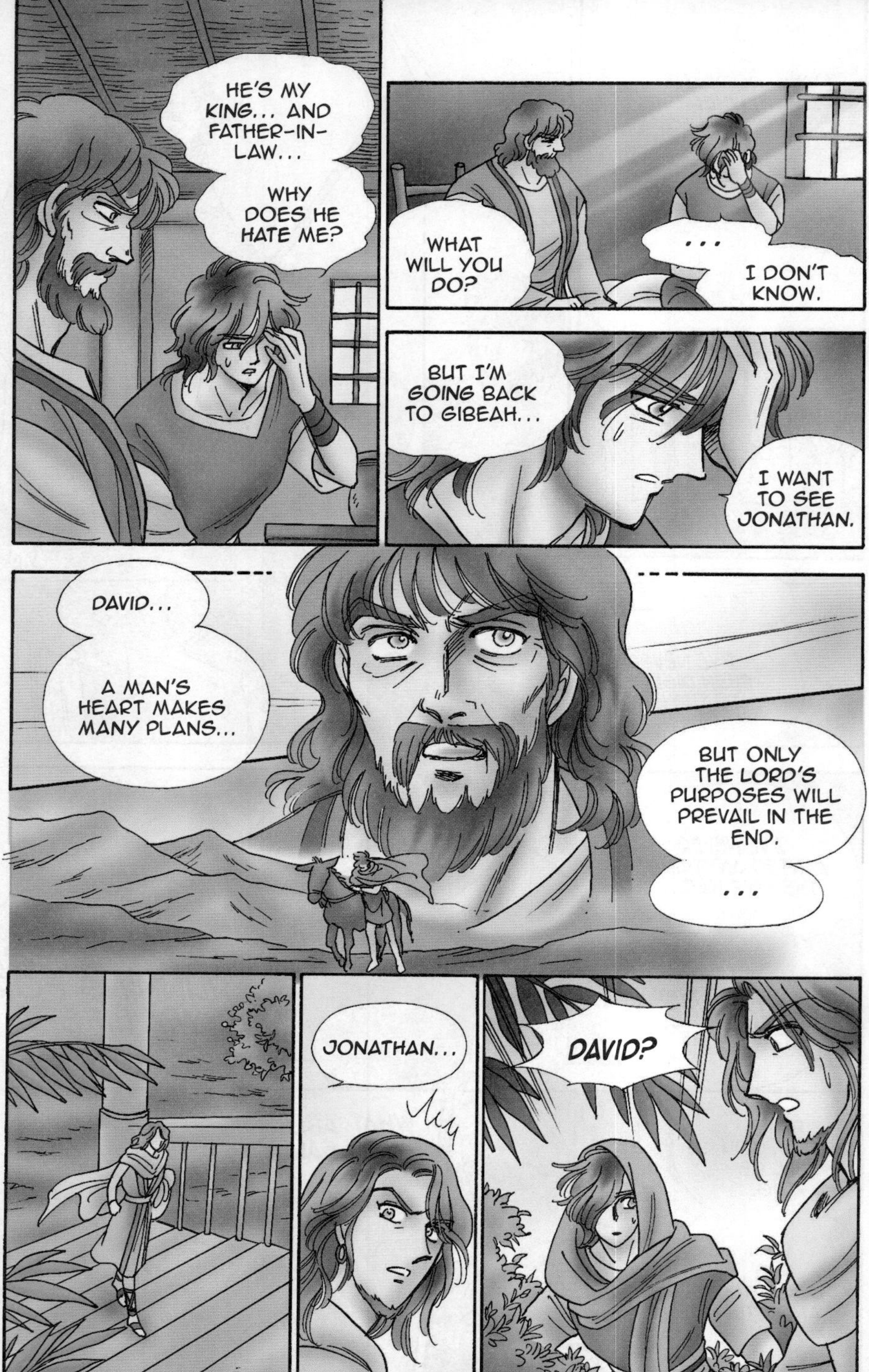
HE'S MY KING... AND FATHER-IN-LAW...
WHY DOES HE HATE ME?
WHAT WILL YOU DO?
...
I DON'T KNOW.
BUT I'M GOING BACK TO GIBEAH...
I WANT TO SEE JONATHAN.
DAVID...
A MAN'S HEART MAKES MANY PLANS...
BUT ONLY THE LORD'S PURPOSES WILL PREVAIL IN THE END.
...
JONATHAN...
DAVID?

DAVID, YOU'RE SAFE!

JONATHAN!

IS MICHAL SAFE?

YES!

I WAS WORRIED WHEN I LEFT...

SHE'S FINE.

WHAT IS IT, JONATHAN...?

WHAT HAVE I DONE TO MAKE HIM HATE ME LIKE THIS?

I'M ALONE...

AND I FEEL LIKE AN ENEMY OF THE ENTIRE KINGDOM.

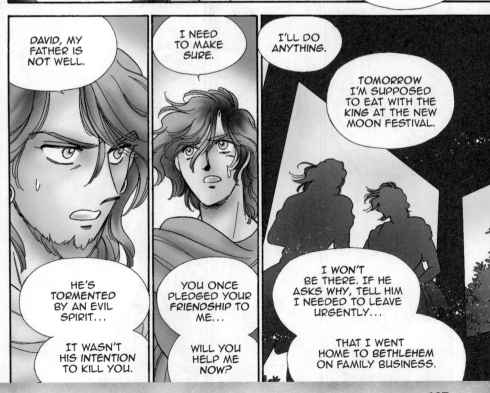

DAVID, MY FATHER IS NOT WELL.

HE'S TORMENTED BY AN EVIL SPIRIT...

IT WASN'T HIS INTENTION TO KILL YOU.

I NEED TO MAKE SURE.

YOU ONCE PLEDGED YOUR FRIENDSHIP TO ME...

WILL YOU HELP ME NOW?

I'LL DO ANYTHING.

TOMORROW I'M SUPPOSED TO EAT WITH THE KING AT THE NEW MOON FESTIVAL.

I WON'T BE THERE. IF HE ASKS WHY, TELL HIM I NEEDED TO LEAVE URGENTLY...

THAT I WENT HOME TO BETHLEHEM ON FAMILY BUSINESS.

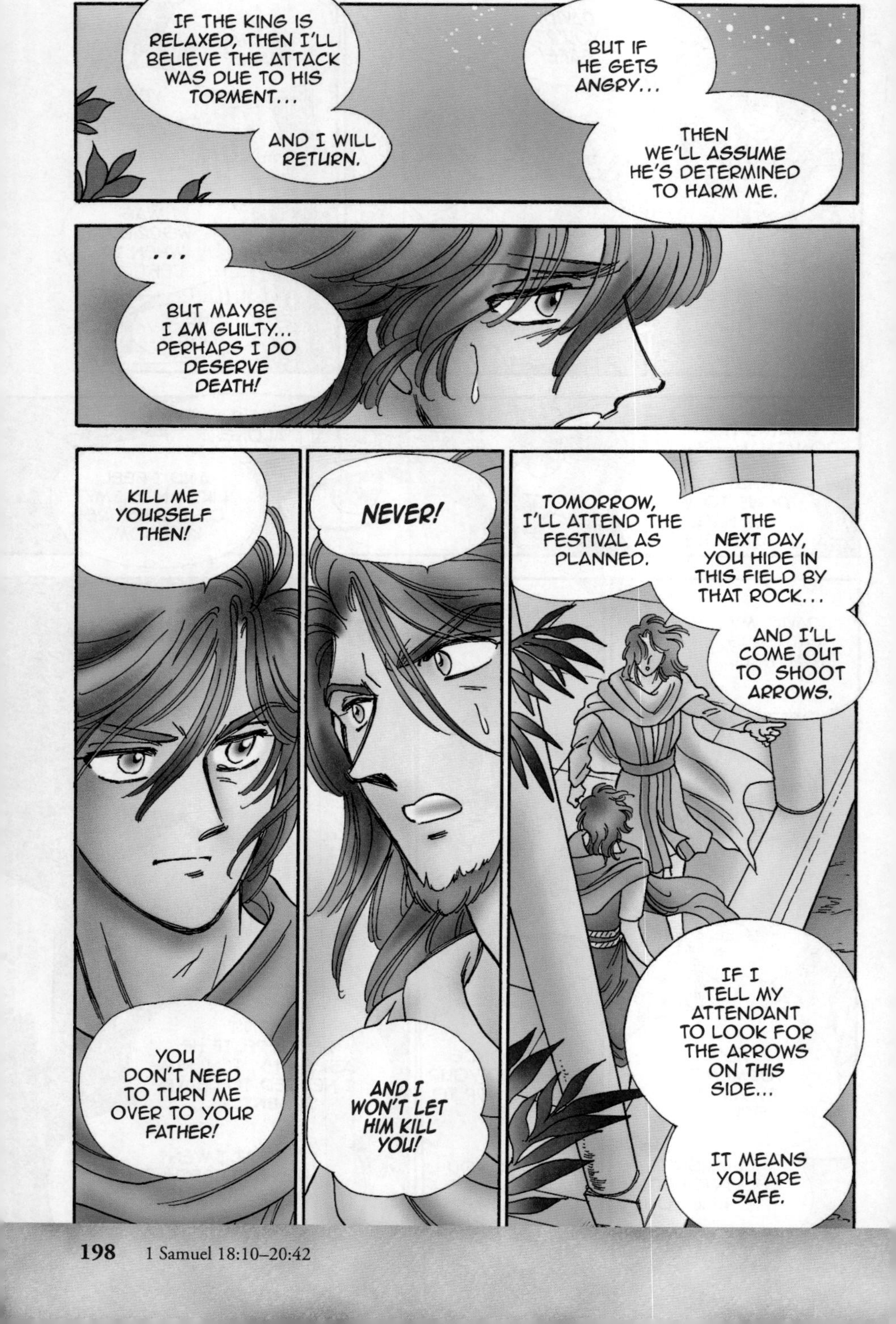
IF THE KING IS RELAXED, THEN I'LL BELIEVE THE ATTACK WAS DUE TO HIS TORMENT...
AND I WILL RETURN.
BUT IF HE GETS ANGRY...
THEN WE'LL ASSUME HE'S DETERMINED TO HARM ME.
...
BUT MAYBE I AM GUILTY... PERHAPS I DO DESERVE DEATH!
KILL ME YOURSELF THEN!
YOU DON'T NEED TO TURN ME OVER TO YOUR FATHER!
NEVER!
AND I WON'T LET HIM KILL YOU!
TOMORROW, I'LL ATTEND THE FESTIVAL AS PLANNED.
THE NEXT DAY, YOU HIDE IN THIS FIELD BY THAT ROCK...
AND I'LL COME OUT TO SHOOT ARROWS.
IF I TELL MY ATTENDANT TO LOOK FOR THE ARROWS ON THIS SIDE...
IT MEANS YOU ARE SAFE.

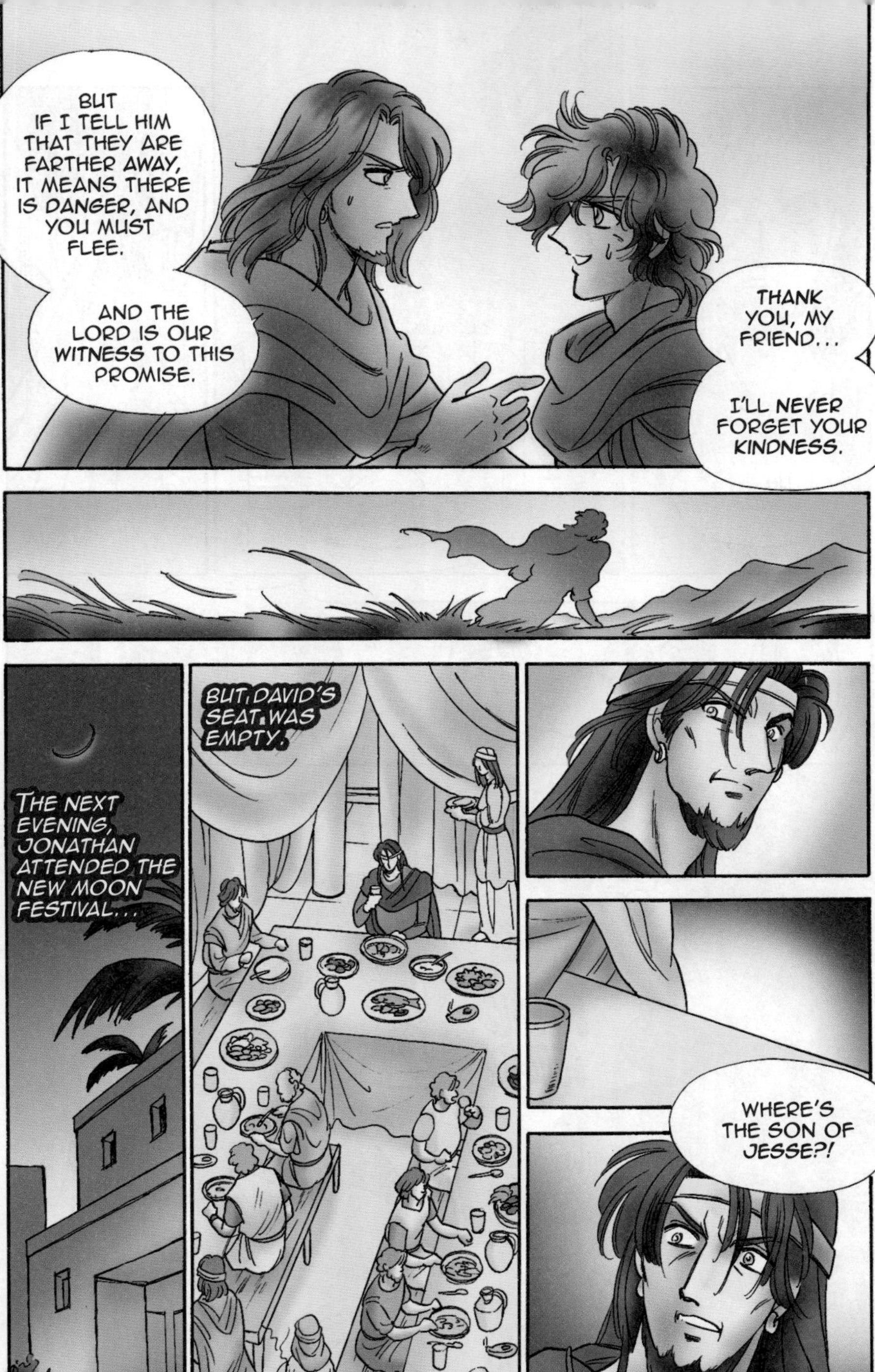
BUT IF I TELL HIM THAT THEY ARE FARTHER AWAY, IT MEANS THERE IS DANGER, AND YOU MUST FLEE.
AND THE LORD IS OUR WITNESS TO THIS PROMISE.
THANK YOU, MY FRIEND...
I'LL NEVER FORGET YOUR KINDNESS.
THE NEXT EVENING, JONATHAN ATTENDED THE NEW MOON FESTIVAL...
BUT DAVID'S SEAT WAS EMPTY.
WHERE'S THE SON OF JESSE?!

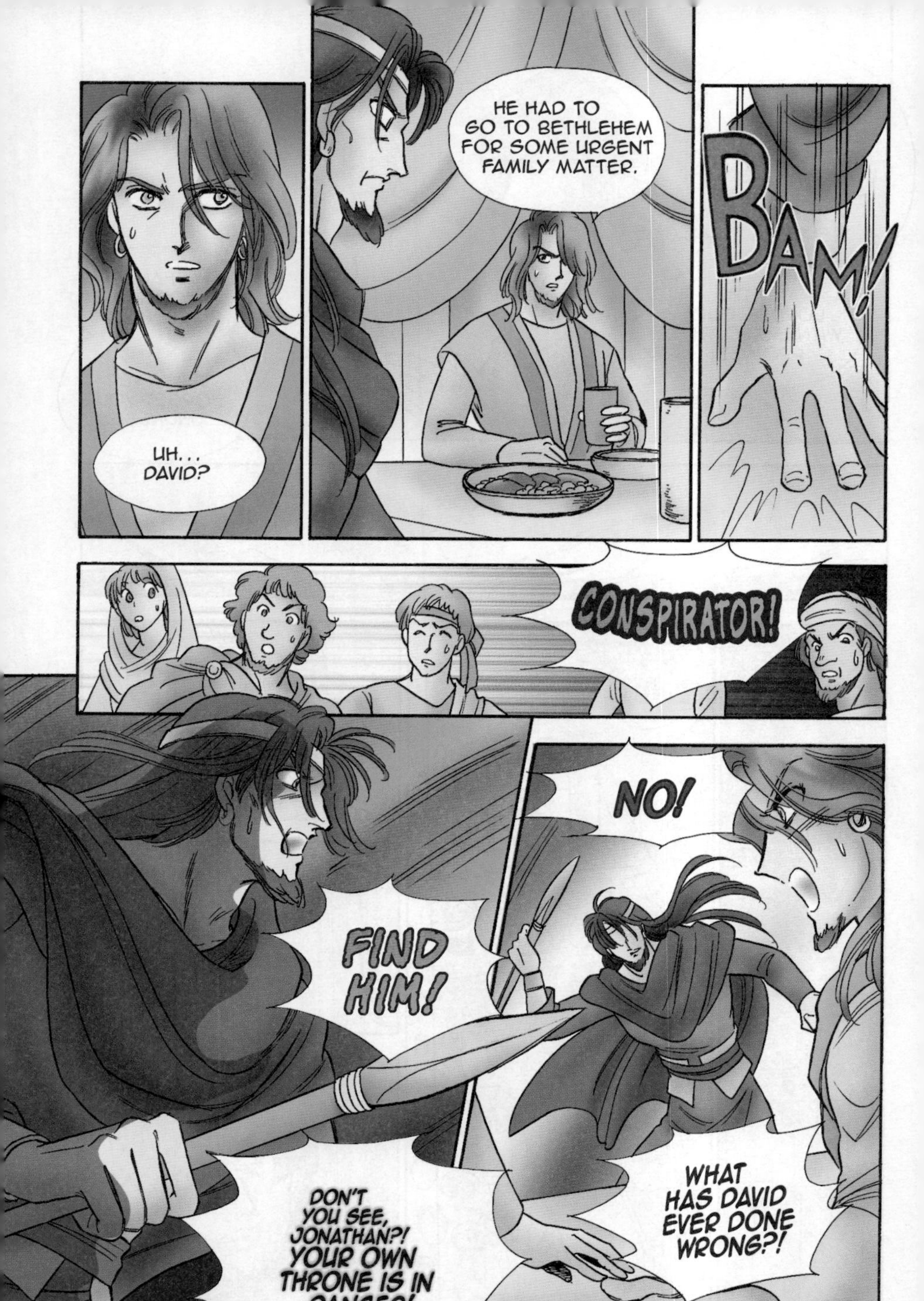
UH. . . DAVID?
HE HAD TO GO TO BETHLEHEM FOR SOME URGENT FAMILY MATTER.
BAM!
CONSPIRATOR!
FIND HIM!
DON'T YOU SEE, JONATHAN?! YOUR OWN THRONE IS IN DANGER!
NO!
WHAT HAS DAVID EVER DONE WRONG?!

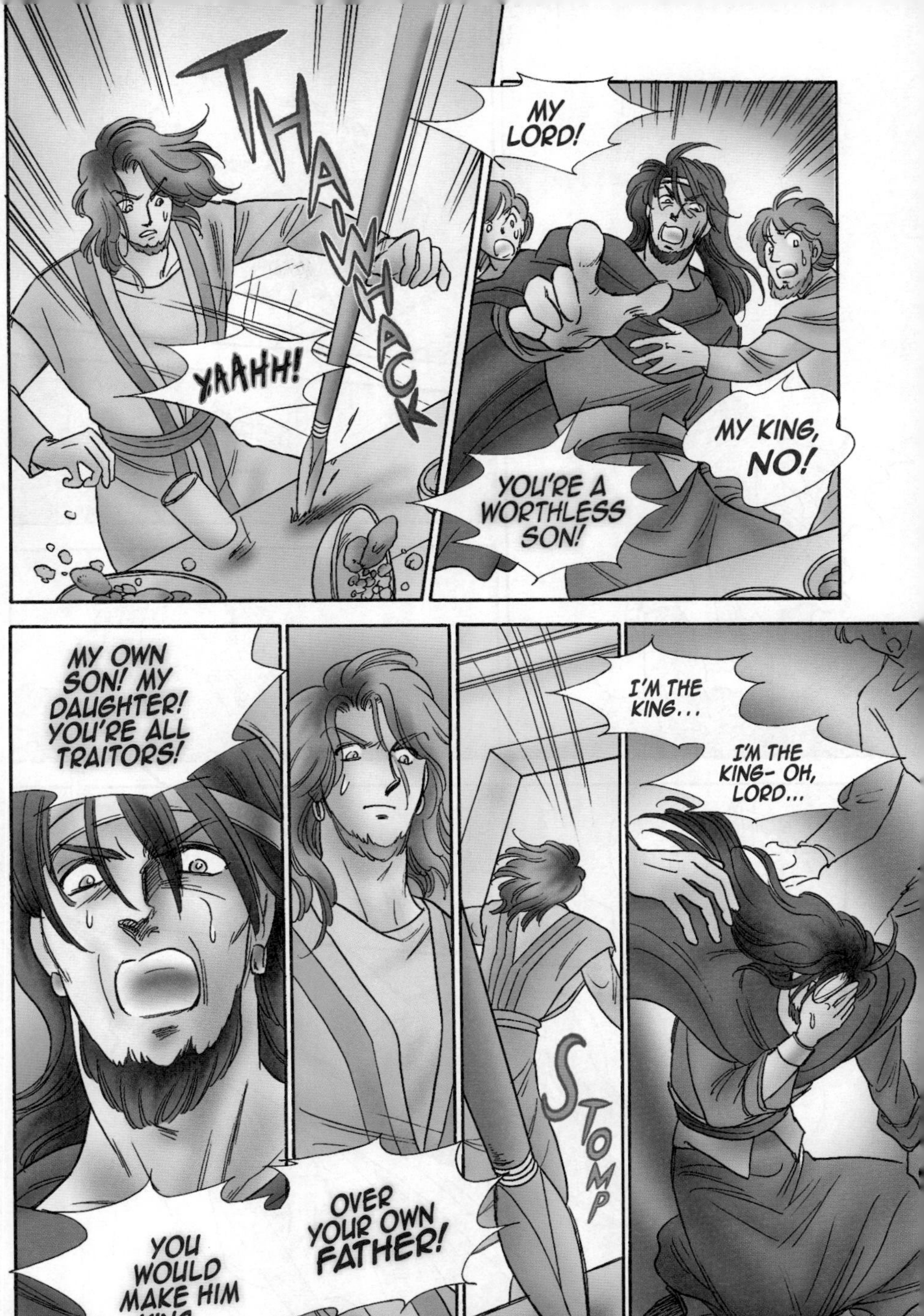
THAWHACK
YAAHH!
MY LORD!
MY KING, NO!
YOU'RE A WORTHLESS SON!
MY OWN SON! MY DAUGHTER! YOU'RE ALL TRAITORS!
YOU WOULD MAKE HIM KING...
OVER YOUR OWN FATHER!
STOMP
I'M THE KING...
I'M THE KING- OH, LORD...

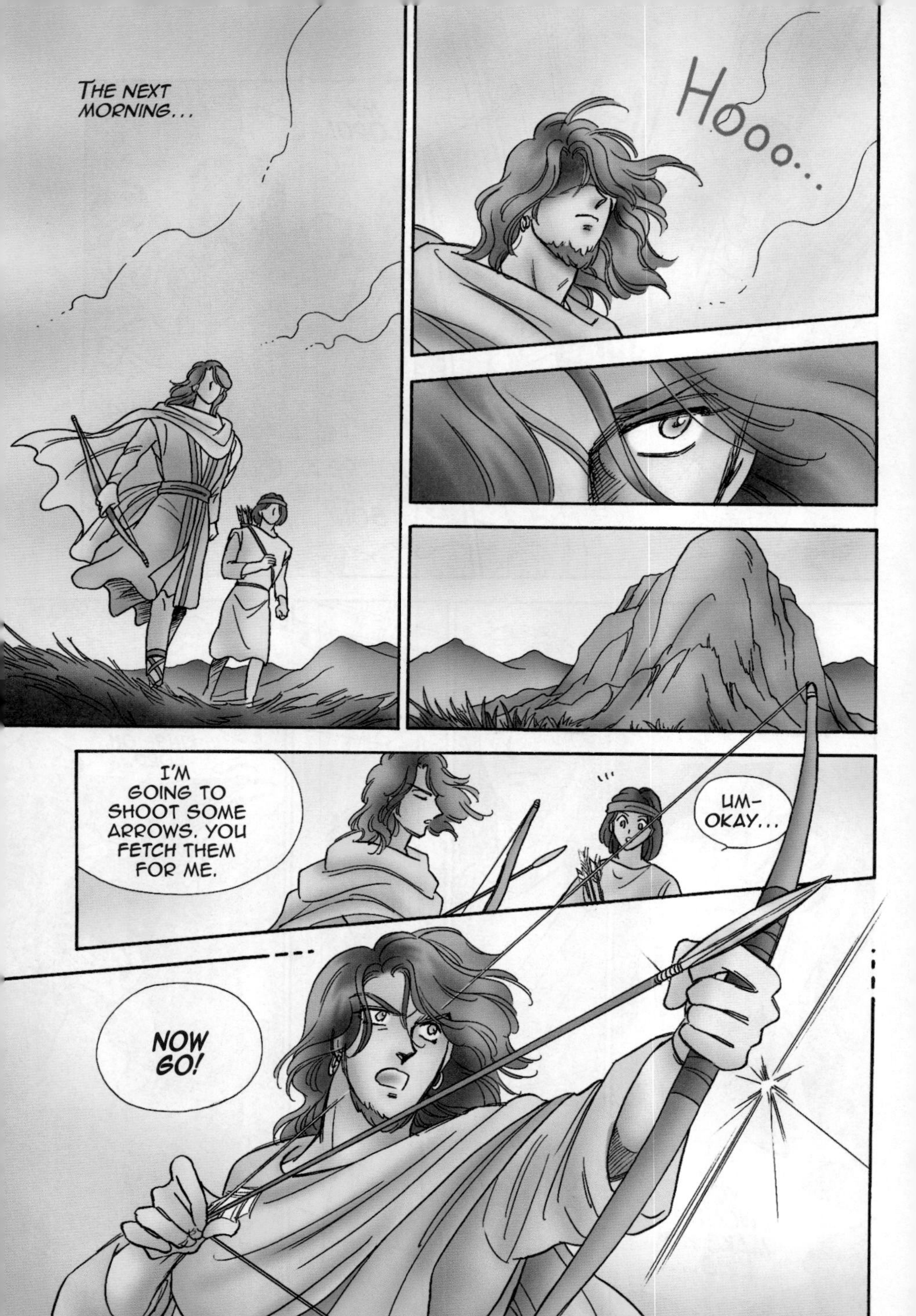
THE NEXT MORNING...
Hooo...
I'M GOING TO SHOOT SOME ARROWS. YOU FETCH THEM FOR ME.
UM-OKAY...
NOW GO!

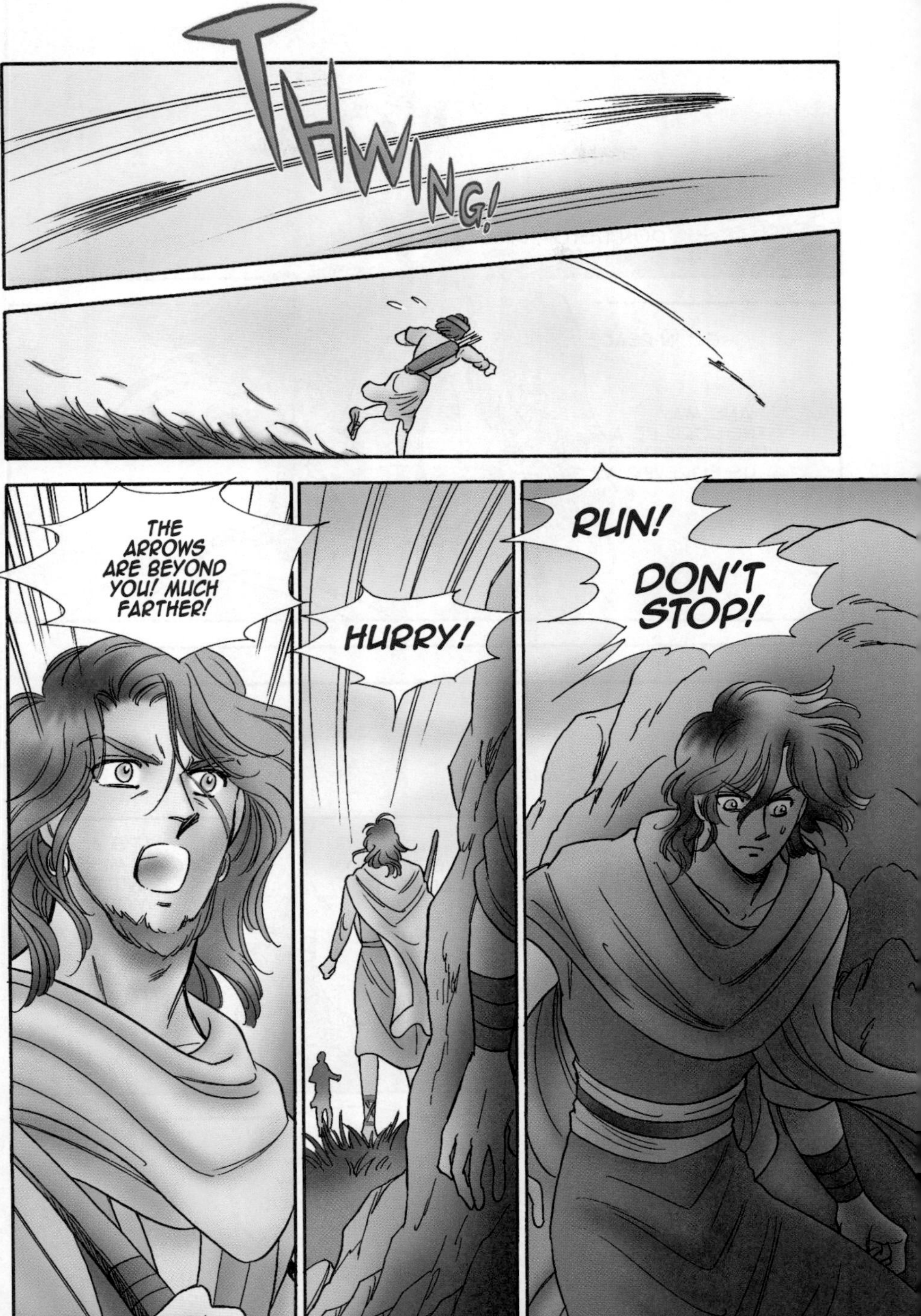
THWING!
THE ARROWS ARE BEYOND YOU! MUCH FARTHER!
HURRY!
RUN!
DON'T STOP!

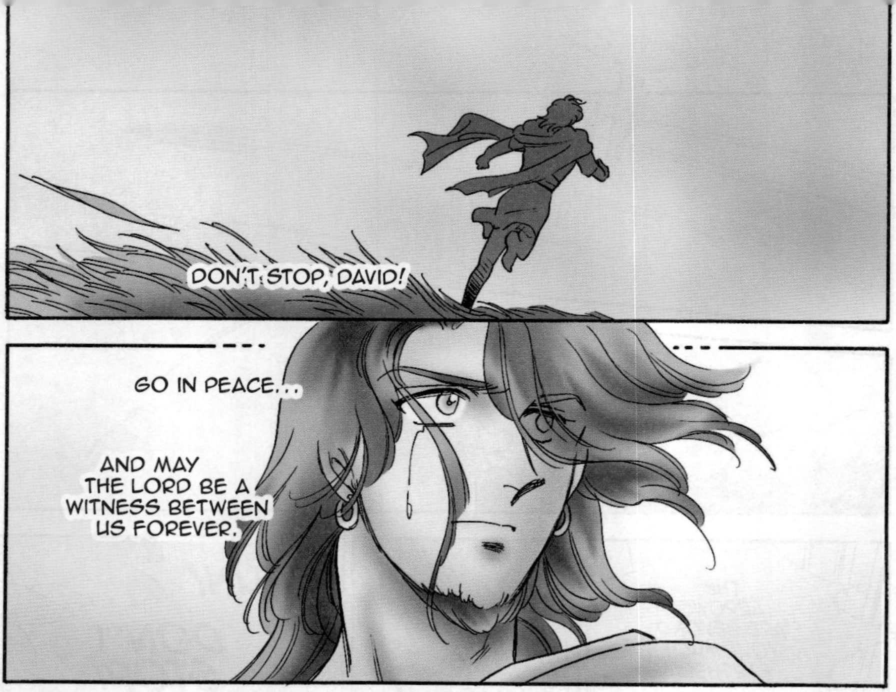
DON'T STOP, DAVID!
GO IN PEACE...
AND MAY THE LORD BE A WITNESS BETWEEN US FOREVER.

16. On the Run

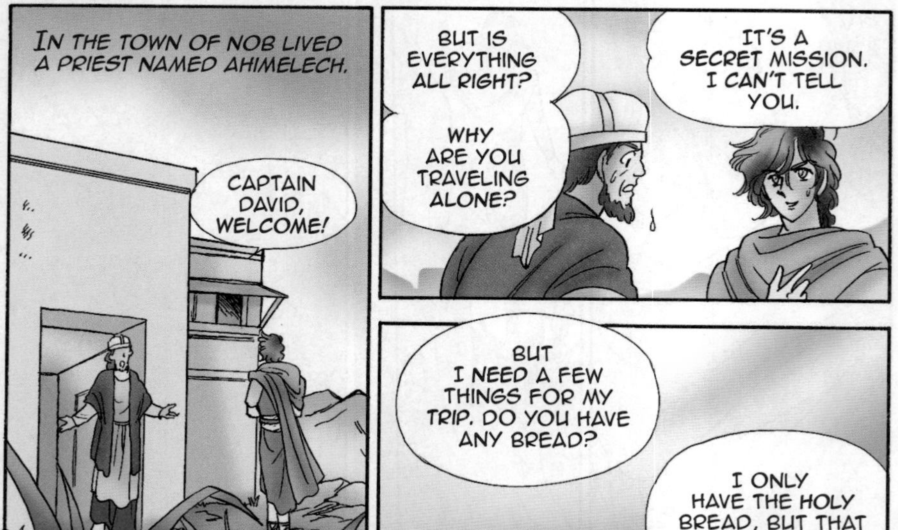
IN THE TOWN OF NOB LIVED A PRIEST NAMED AHIMELECH.
CAPTAIN DAVID, WELCOME!
BUT IS EVERYTHING ALL RIGHT?
WHY ARE YOU TRAVELING ALONE?
IT'S A SECRET MISSION. I CAN'T TELL YOU.
BUT I NEED A FEW THINGS FOR MY TRIP. DO YOU HAVE ANY BREAD?
I ONLY HAVE THE HOLY BREAD, BUT THAT SHOULD BE OK FOR YOU.

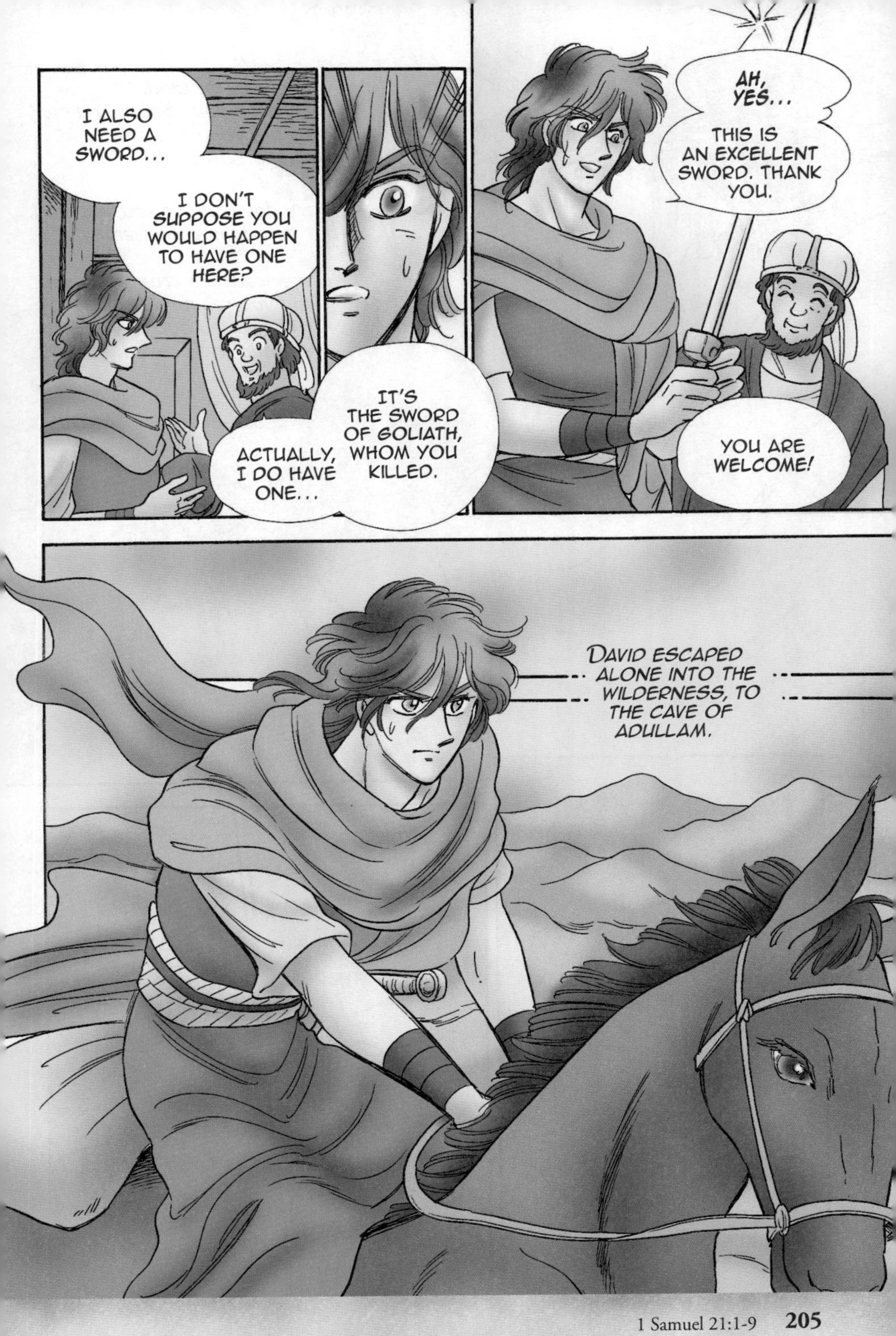

I ALSO NEED A SWORD...
I DON'T SUPPOSE YOU WOULD HAPPEN TO HAVE ONE HERE?
ACTUALLY, I DO HAVE ONE...
IT'S THE SWORD OF GOLIATH, WHOM YOU KILLED.
AH, YES...
THIS IS AN EXCELLENT SWORD. THANK YOU.
YOU ARE WELCOME!
DAVID ESCAPED ALONE INTO THE WILDERNESS, TO THE CAVE OF ADULLAM.

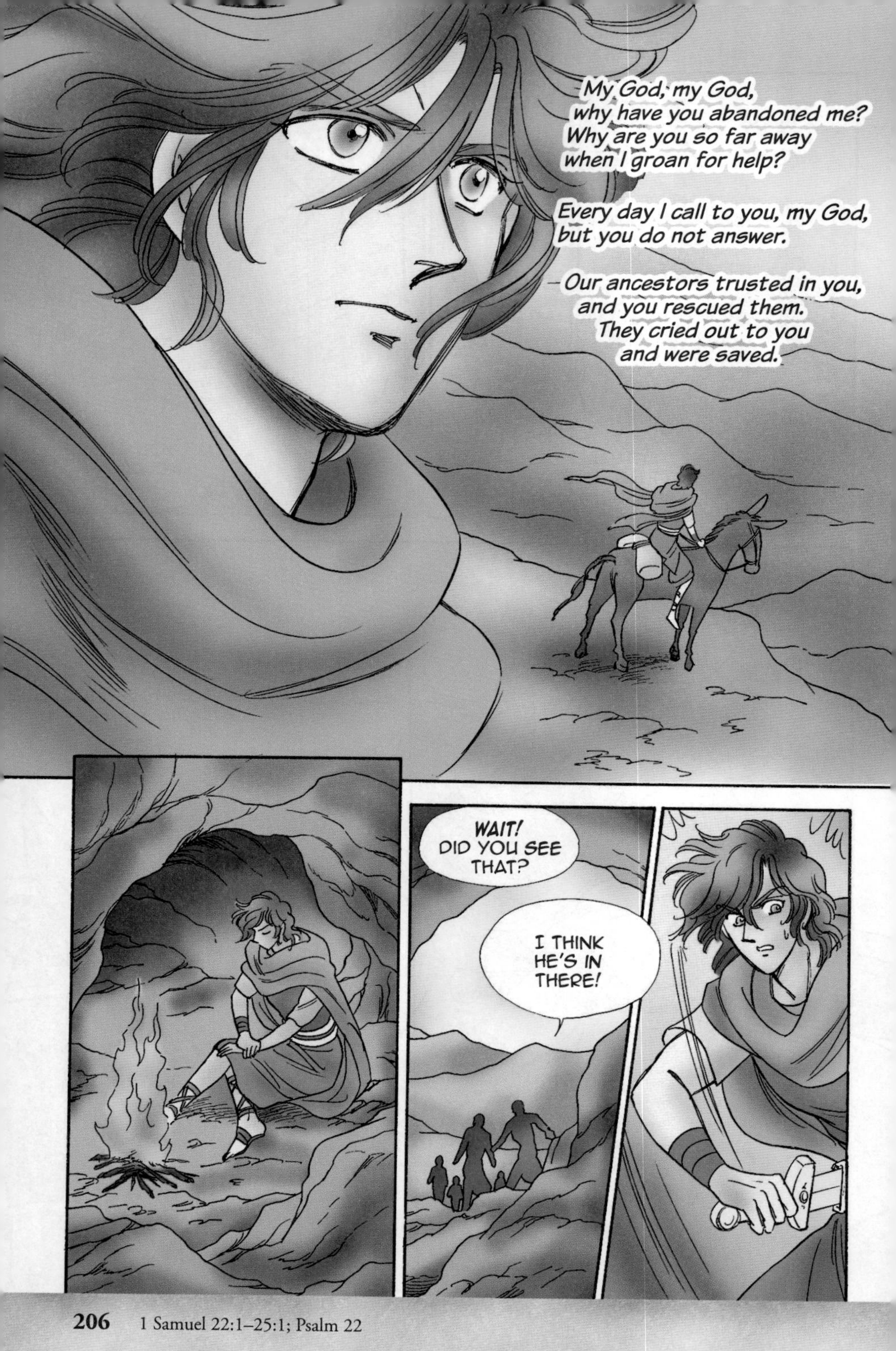

My God, my God,
why have you abandoned me?
Why are you so far away
when I groan for help?
Every day I call to you, my God,
but you do not answer.
Our ancestors trusted in you,
and you rescued them.
They cried out to you
and were saved.
WAIT! DID YOU SEE THAT?
I THINK HE'S IN THERE!

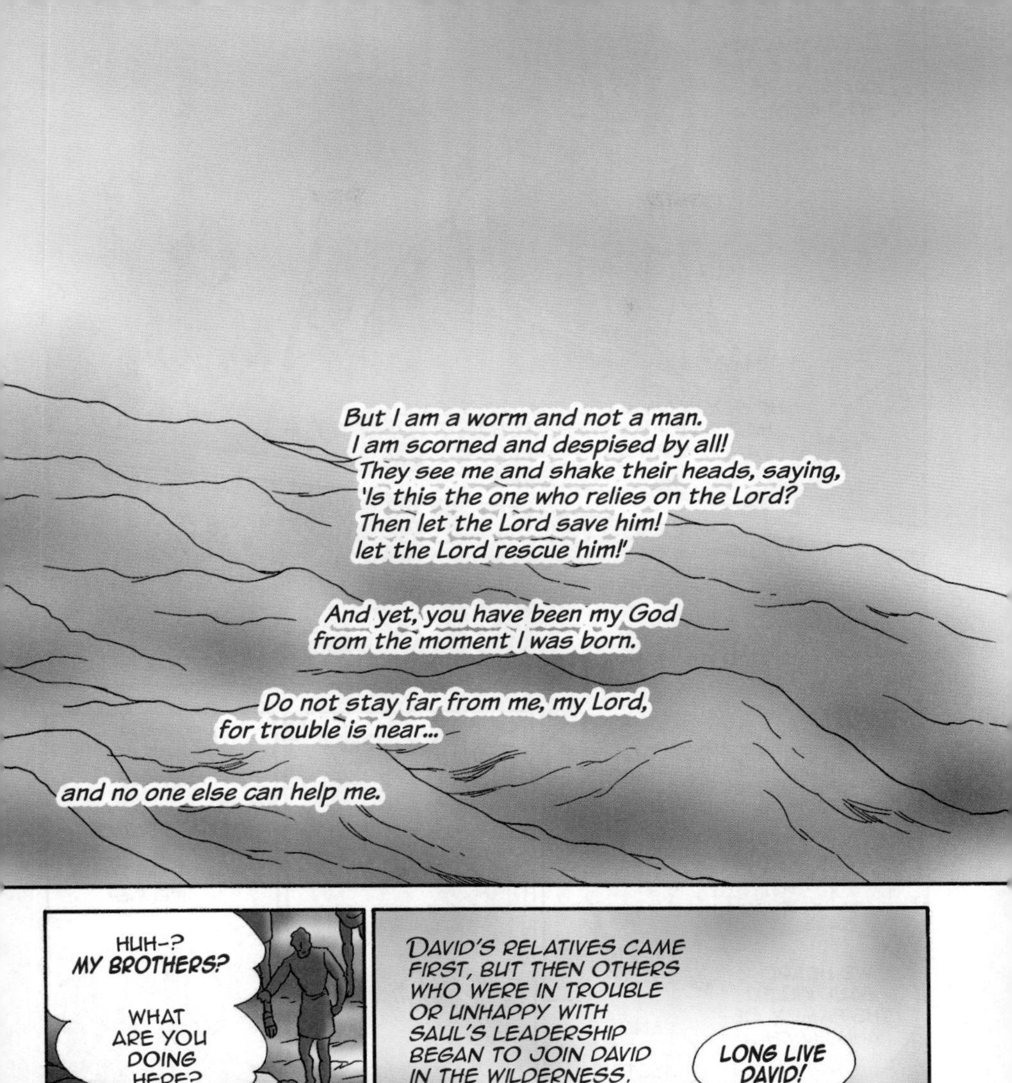
But I am a worm and not a man.
I am scorned and despised by all!
They see me and shake their heads, saying,
'Is this the one who relies on the Lord?
Then let the Lord save him!
let the Lord rescue him!'
And yet, you have been my God
from the moment I was born.
Do not stay far from me, my Lord,
for trouble is near...
and no one else can help me.

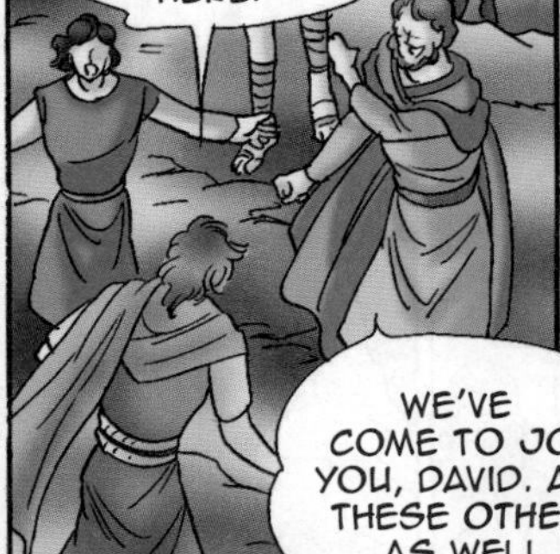
HUH-? MY BROTHERS?
WHAT ARE YOU DOING HERE?
WE'VE COME TO JOIN YOU, DAVID. AND THESE OTHERS AS WELL.

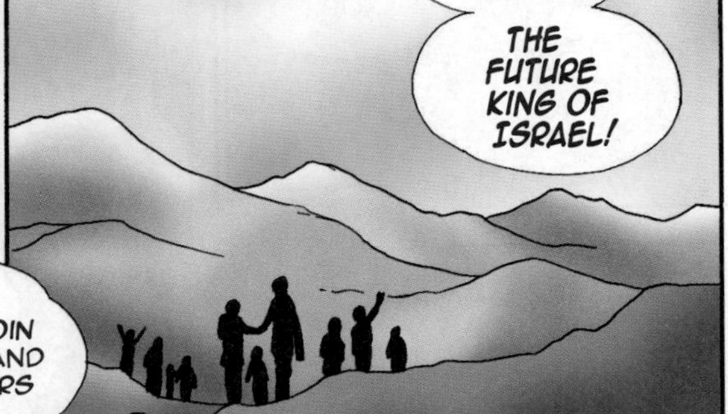
DAVID'S RELATIVES CAME FIRST, BUT THEN OTHERS WHO WERE IN TROUBLE OR UNHAPPY WITH SAUL'S LEADERSHIP BEGAN TO JOIN DAVID IN THE WILDERNESS.
LONG LIVE DAVID!
THE FUTURE KING OF ISRAEL!

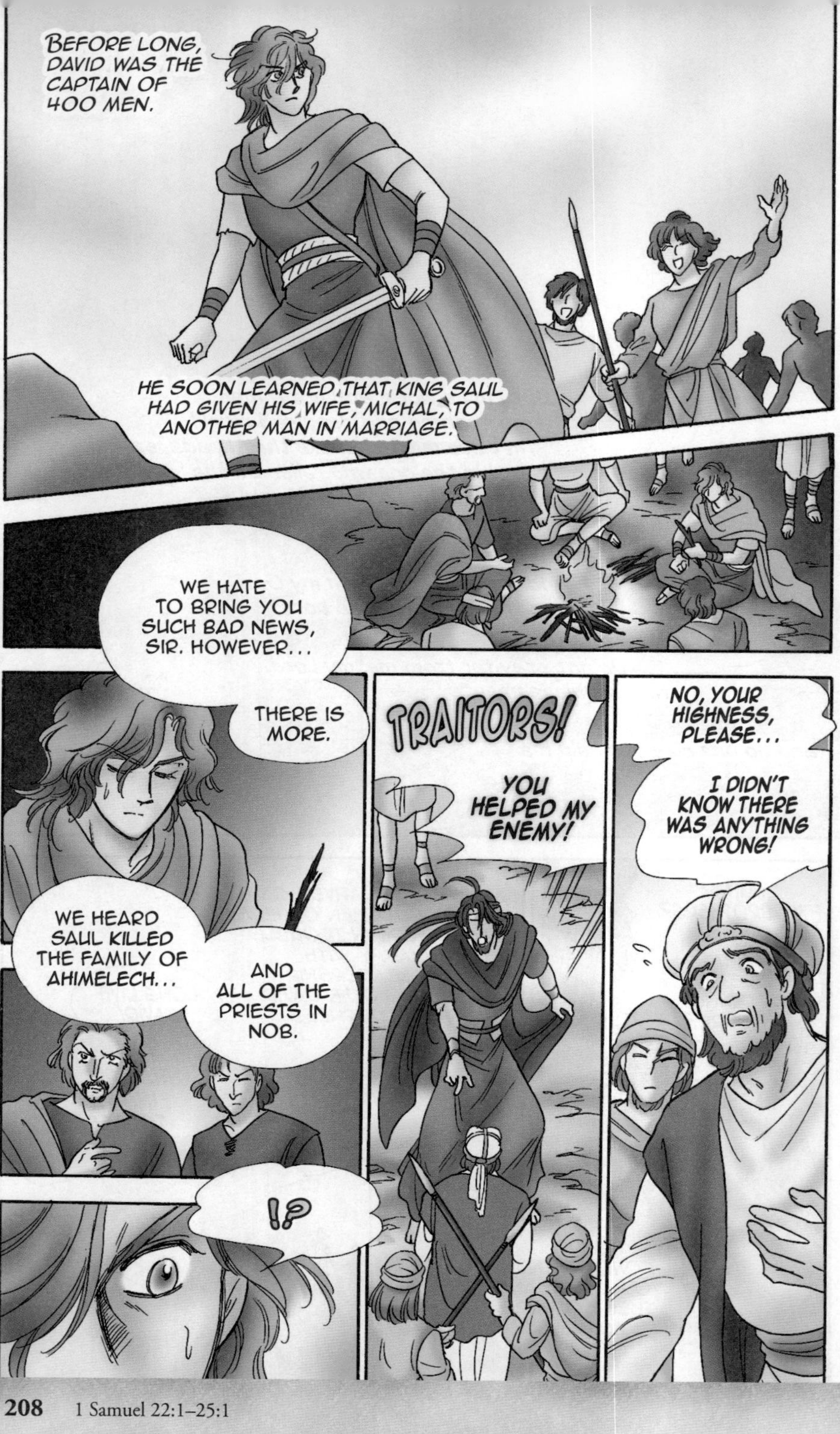
BEFORE LONG, DAVID WAS THE CAPTAIN OF 400 MEN.
HE SOON LEARNED THAT KING SAUL HAD GIVEN HIS WIFE, MICHAL, TO ANOTHER MAN IN MARRIAGE.
WE HATE TO BRING YOU SUCH BAD NEWS, SIR. HOWEVER...
THERE IS MORE.
WE HEARD SAUL KILLED THE FAMILY OF AHIMELECH...
AND ALL OF THE PRIESTS IN NOB.
!?
TRAITORS!
YOU HELPED MY ENEMY!
NO, YOUR HIGHNESS, PLEASE...
I DIDN'T KNOW THERE WAS ANYTHING WRONG!

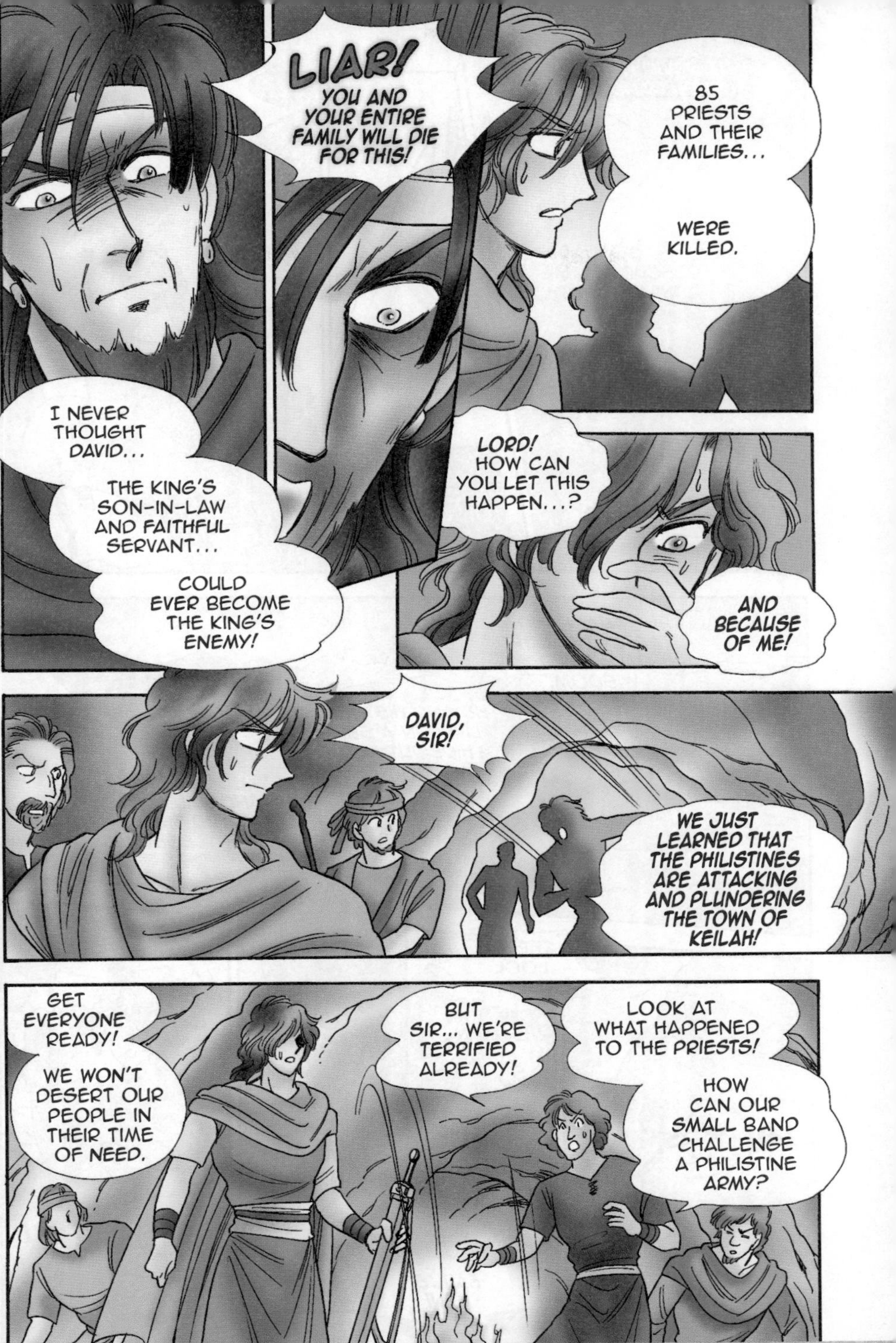

LIAR!
YOU AND YOUR ENTIRE FAMILY WILL DIE FOR THIS!
85 PRIESTS AND THEIR FAMILIES...
WERE KILLED.
I NEVER THOUGHT DAVID...
THE KING'S SON-IN-LAW AND FAITHFUL SERVANT...
COULD EVER BECOME THE KING'S ENEMY!
LORD! HOW CAN YOU LET THIS HAPPEN...?
AND BECAUSE OF ME!
DAVID, SIR!
WE JUST LEARNED THAT THE PHILISTINES ARE ATTACKING AND PLUNDERING THE TOWN OF KEILAH!
GET EVERYONE READY!
WE WON'T DESERT OUR PEOPLE IN THEIR TIME OF NEED.
BUT SIR... WE'RE TERRIFIED ALREADY!
LOOK AT WHAT HAPPENED TO THE PRIESTS!
HOW CAN OUR SMALL BAND CHALLENGE A PHILISTINE ARMY?

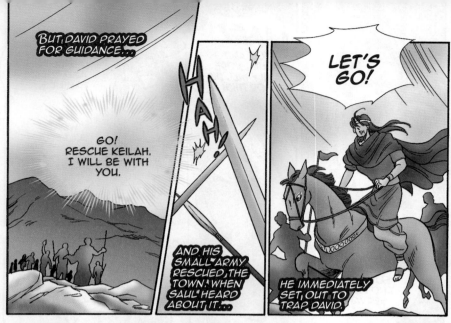

BUT, DAVID PRAYED FOR GUIDANCE...

GO! RESCUE KEILAH. I WILL BE WITH YOU.

HA!

LET'S GO!

AND HIS SMALL ARMY RESCUED THE TOWN. WHEN SAUL HEARD ABOUT IT...

HE IMMEDIATELY SET OUT TO TRAP DAVID.

BUT, AGAIN AND AGAIN THE LORD GAVE DAVID WISDOM.

HE AND HIS MEN LIVED IN A SECRET HIDEOUT IN THE WILDERNESS...

AND SAUL HUNTED THEM RELENTLESSLY.

THEY LOOK LIKE...

SOMEONE'S COMING!

SAUL'S MEN!

SIR, COME QUICKLY!

JONATHAN!

DAVID!

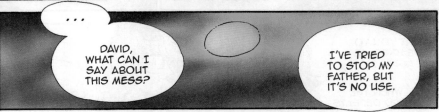

. . .

DAVID, WHAT CAN I SAY ABOUT THIS MESS?

I'VE TRIED TO STOP MY FATHER, BUT IT'S NO USE.

NOW HE KNOWS ABOUT THIS PLACE.

HE'S PROBABLY ALREADY ON HIS WAY TO FIND YOU.

WE'LL PREPARE TO LEAVE AT ONCE.

. . .

OF COURSE, DAVID...

HE CAN'T DO ANYTHING TO YOU.

BUT I CAME HERE...

BECAUSE I WANTED TO MAKE ONE THING CLEAR.

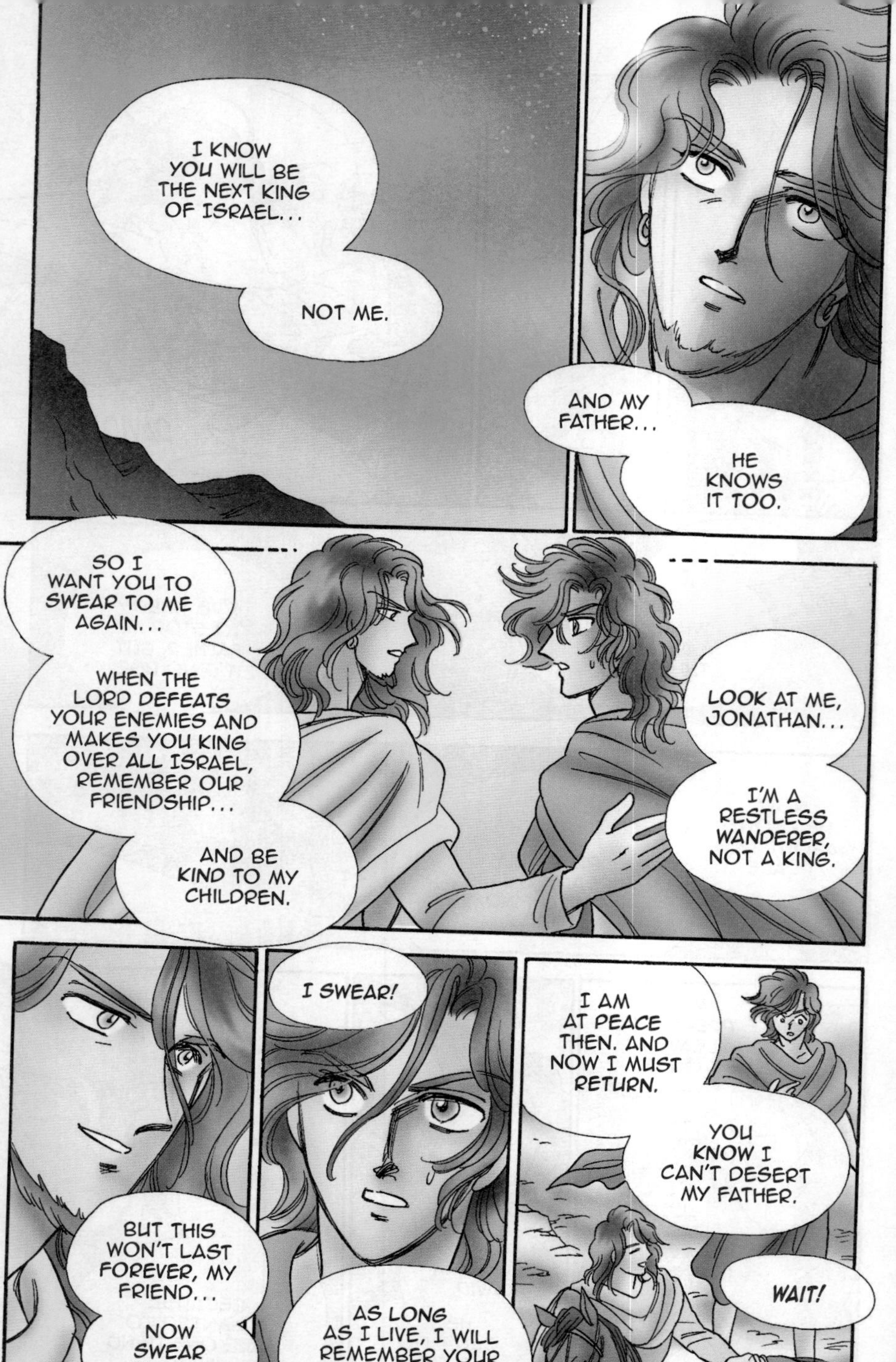

I KNOW YOU WILL BE THE NEXT KING OF ISRAEL...
NOT ME.
AND MY FATHER...
HE KNOWS IT TOO.
SO I WANT YOU TO SWEAR TO ME AGAIN...
WHEN THE LORD DEFEATS YOUR ENEMIES AND MAKES YOU KING OVER ALL ISRAEL, REMEMBER OUR FRIENDSHIP...
AND BE KIND TO MY CHILDREN.
LOOK AT ME, JONATHAN...
I'M A RESTLESS WANDERER, NOT A KING.
BUT THIS WON'T LAST FOREVER, MY FRIEND...
NOW SWEAR TO ME!
I SWEAR!
AS LONG AS I LIVE, I WILL REMEMBER YOUR DESCENDANTS.
I AM AT PEACE THEN. AND NOW I MUST RETURN.
YOU KNOW I CAN'T DESERT MY FATHER.
WAIT!

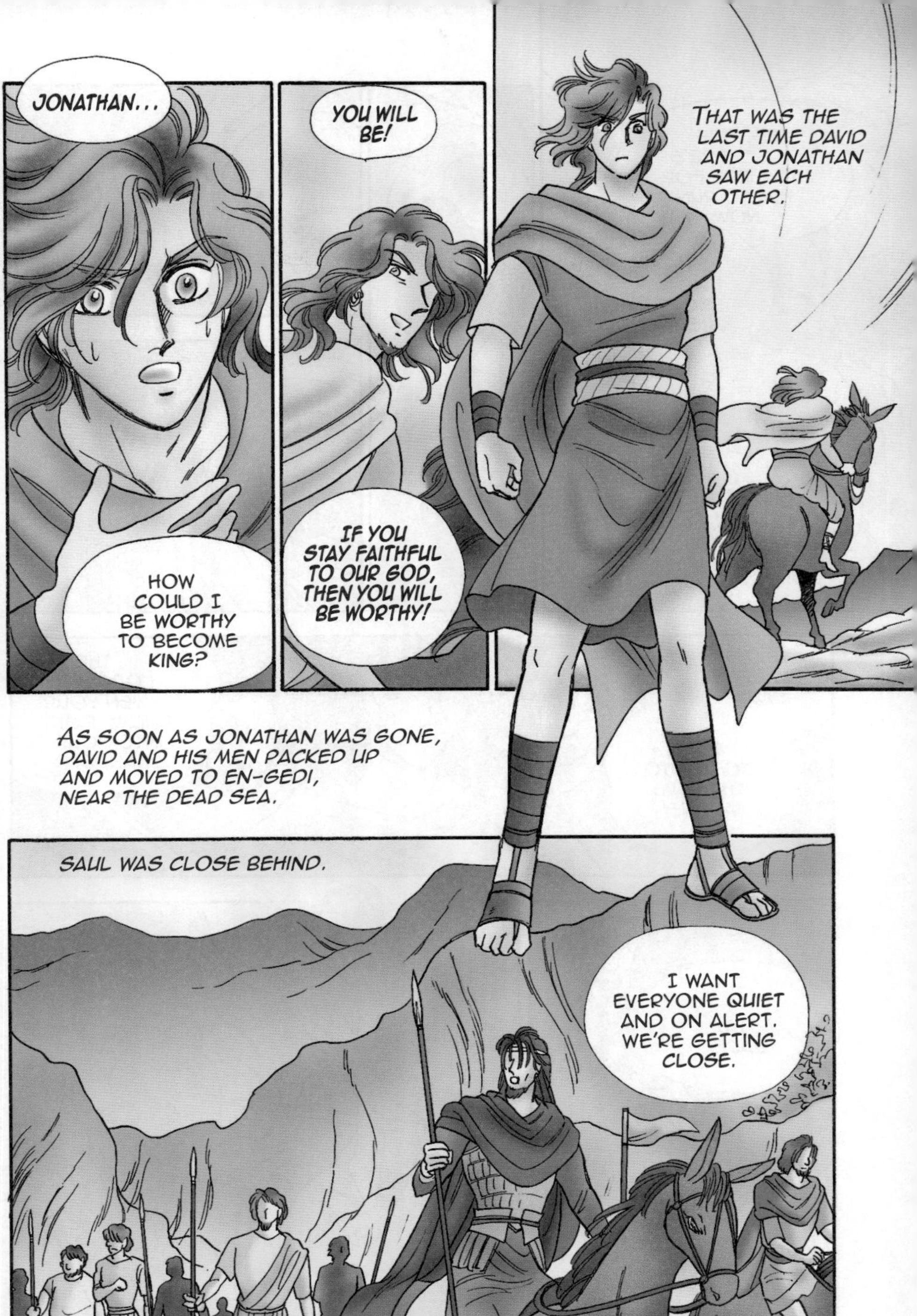
JONATHAN...
HOW COULD I BE WORTHY TO BECOME KING?
YOU WILL BE!
IF YOU STAY FAITHFUL TO OUR GOD, THEN YOU WILL BE WORTHY!
THAT WAS THE LAST TIME DAVID AND JONATHAN SAW EACH OTHER.
AS SOON AS JONATHAN WAS GONE, DAVID AND HIS MEN PACKED UP AND MOVED TO EN-GEDI, NEAR THE DEAD SEA.
SAUL WAS CLOSE BEHIND.
I WANT EVERYONE QUIET AND ON ALERT. WE'RE GETTING CLOSE.

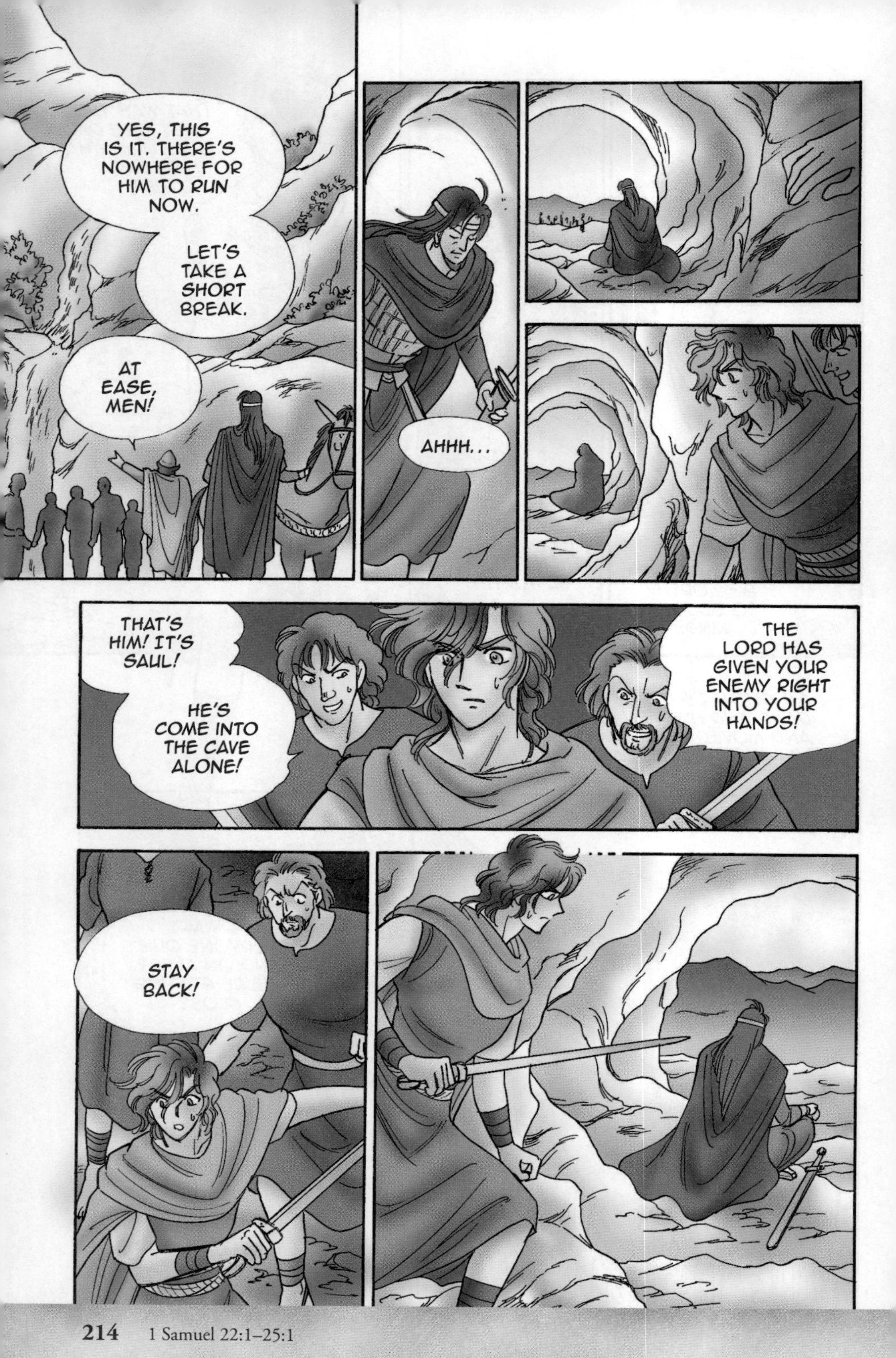
YES, THIS IS IT. THERE'S NOWHERE FOR HIM TO RUN NOW.
LET'S TAKE A SHORT BREAK.
AT EASE, MEN!
AHHH...
THAT'S HIM! IT'S SAUL!
HE'S COME INTO THE CAVE ALONE!
THE LORD HAS GIVEN YOUR ENEMY RIGHT INTO YOUR HANDS!
STAY BACK!

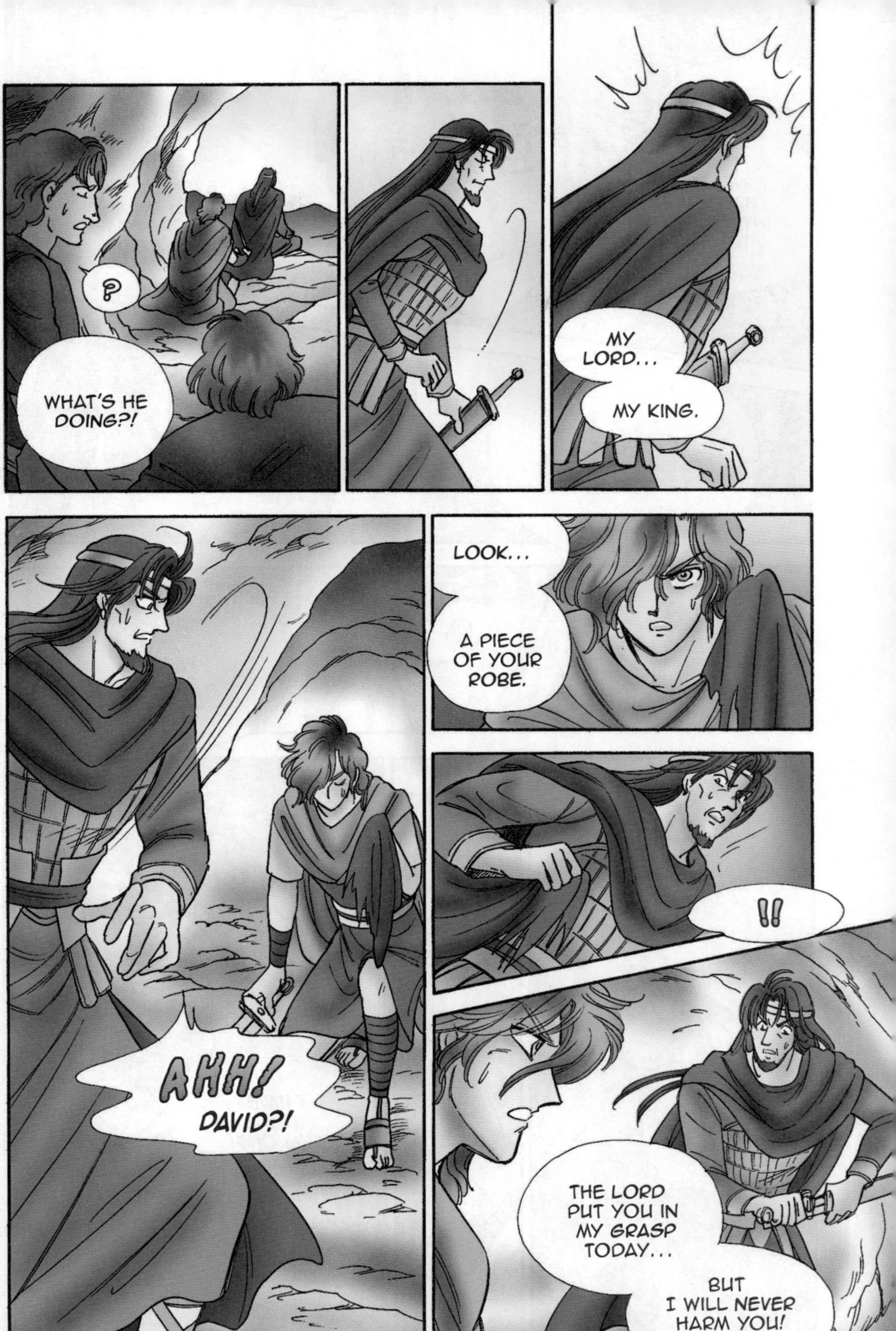
?
WHAT'S HE DOING?!
MY LORD...
MY KING.
AHH!
DAVID?!
LOOK...
A PIECE OF YOUR ROBE.
!!
THE LORD PUT YOU IN MY GRASP TODAY...
BUT I WILL NEVER HARM YOU!

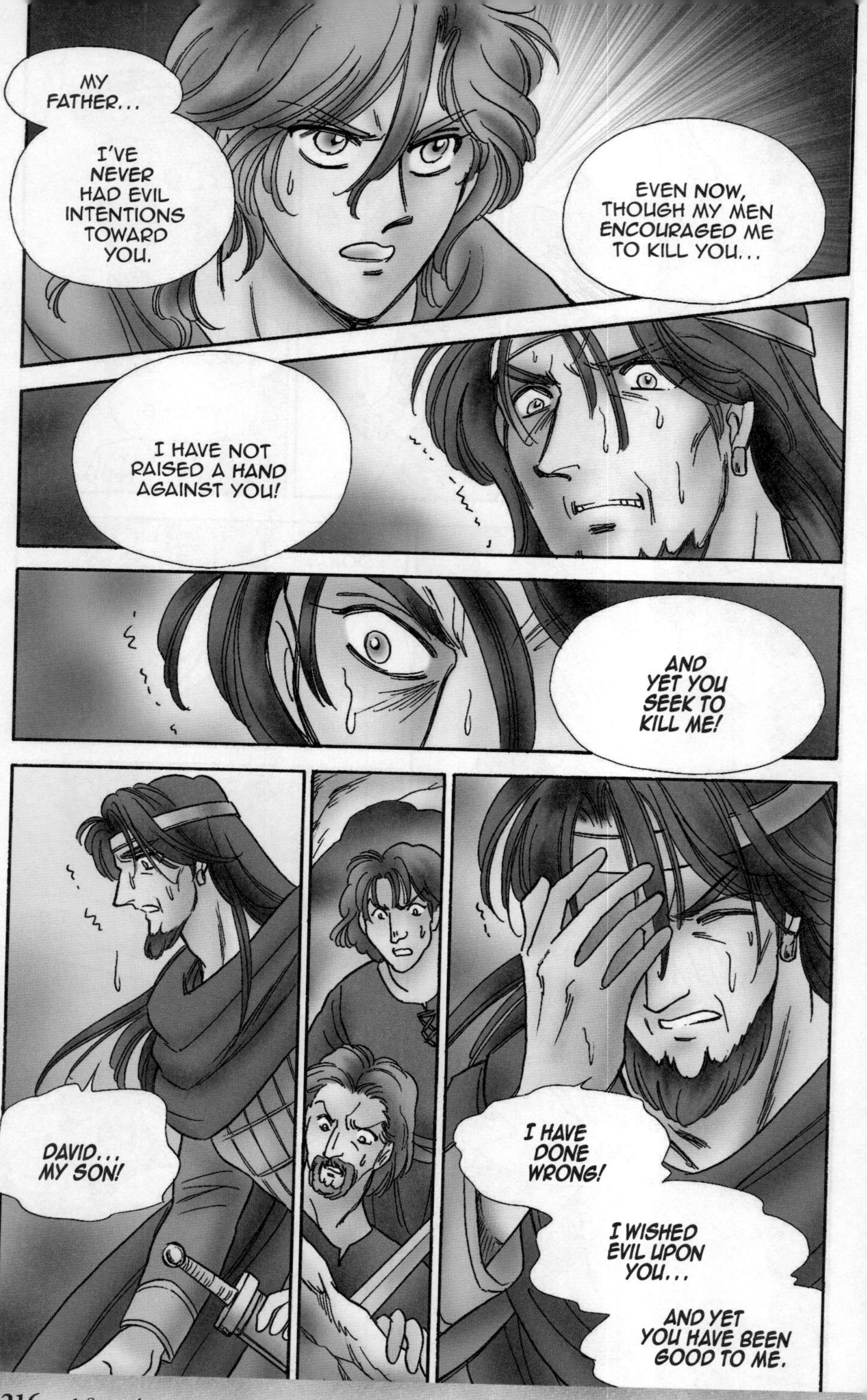
MY FATHER...
I'VE NEVER HAD EVIL INTENTIONS TOWARD YOU.
EVEN NOW, THOUGH MY MEN ENCOURAGED ME TO KILL YOU...
I HAVE NOT RAISED A HAND AGAINST YOU!
AND YET YOU SEEK TO KILL ME!
DAVID... MY SON!
I HAVE DONE WRONG!
I WISHED EVIL UPON YOU...
AND YET YOU HAVE BEEN GOOD TO ME.

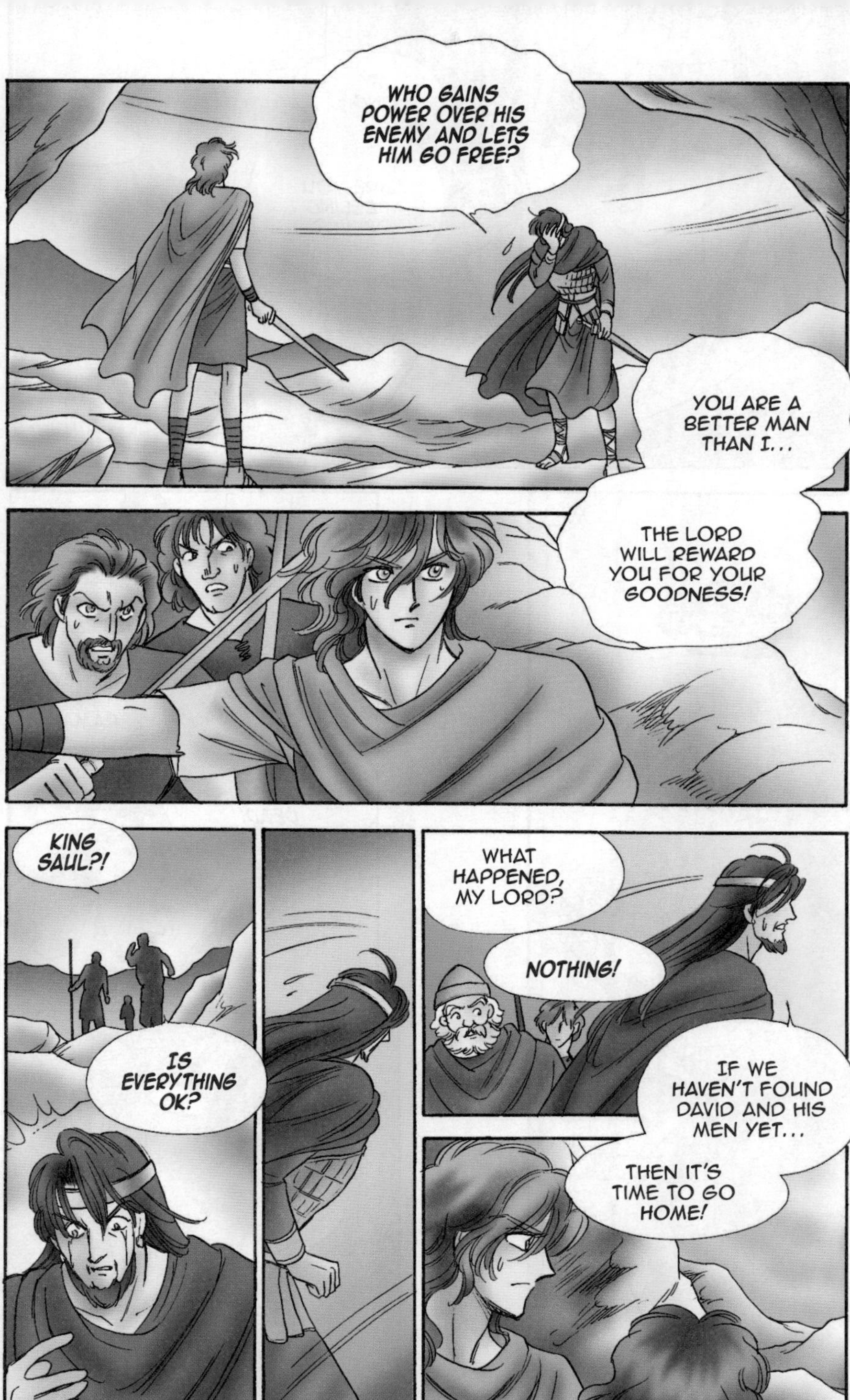
WHO GAINS POWER OVER HIS ENEMY AND LETS HIM GO FREE?
YOU ARE A BETTER MAN THAN I...
THE LORD WILL REWARD YOU FOR YOUR GOODNESS!
KING SAUL?!
IS EVERYTHING OK?
WHAT HAPPENED, MY LORD?
NOTHING!
IF WE HAVEN'T FOUND DAVID AND HIS MEN YET...
THEN IT'S TIME TO GO HOME!

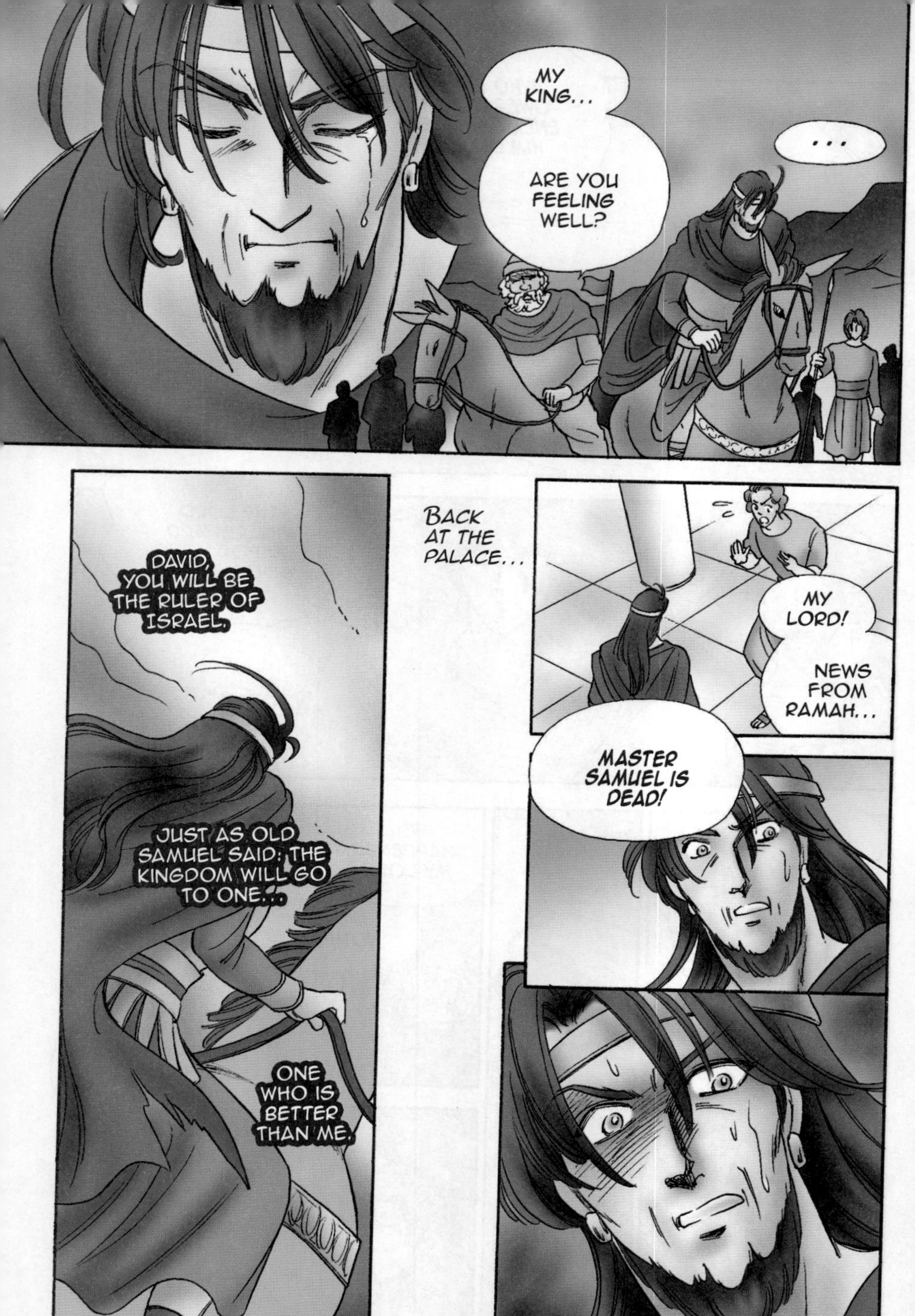
MY KING...
ARE YOU FEELING WELL?
...
DAVID, YOU WILL BE THE RULER OF ISRAEL.
JUST AS OLD SAMUEL SAID: THE KINGDOM WILL GO TO ONE...
ONE WHO IS BETTER THAN ME.
BACK AT THE PALACE...
MY LORD!
NEWS FROM RAMAH...
MASTER SAMUEL IS DEAD!

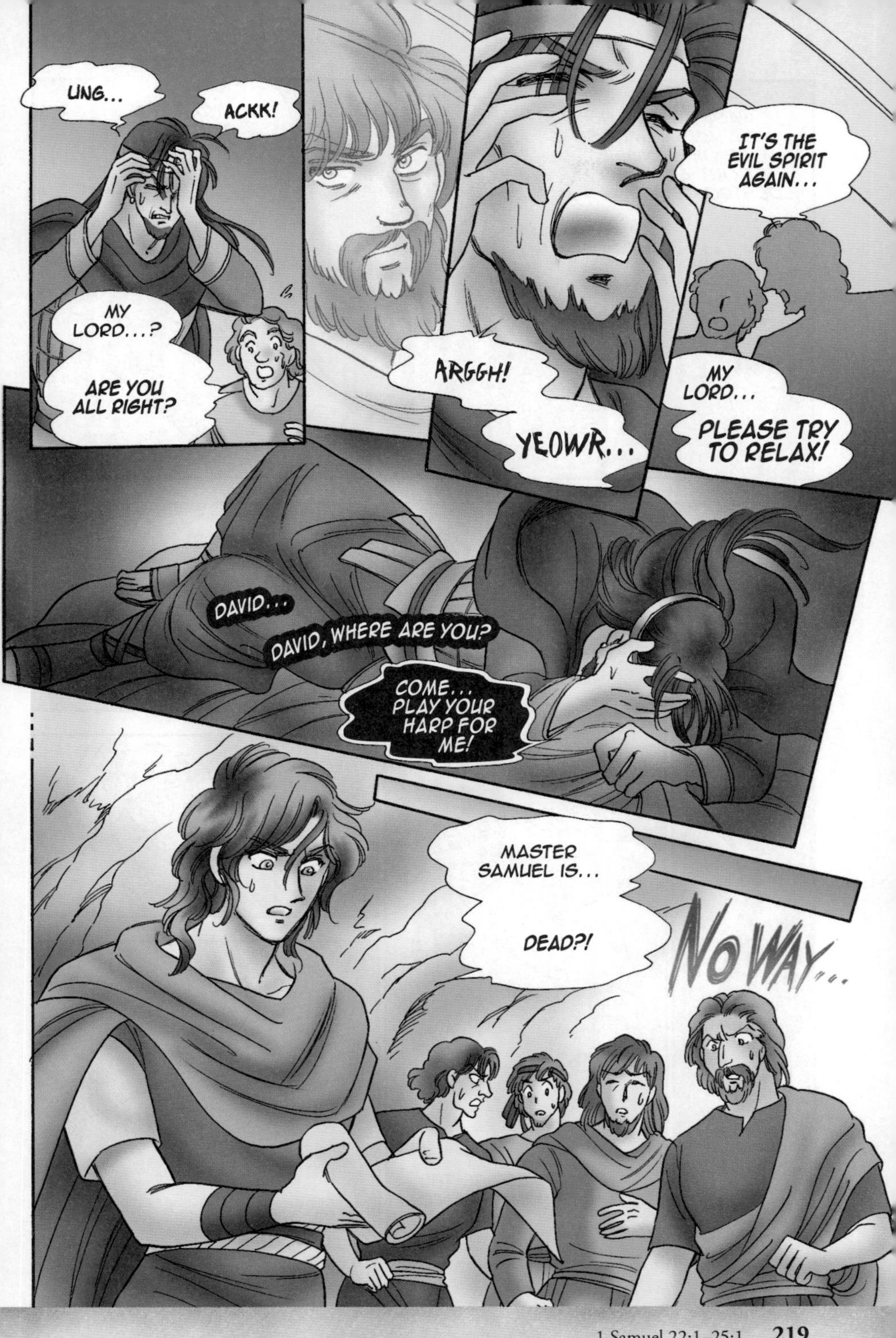
UNG...
ACKK!
MY LORD...?
ARE YOU ALL RIGHT?
IT'S THE EVIL SPIRIT AGAIN...
ARGGH!
YEOWR...
MY LORD...
PLEASE TRY TO RELAX!
DAVID...
DAVID, WHERE ARE YOU?
COME... PLAY YOUR HARP FOR ME!
MASTER SAMUEL IS...
DEAD?!
NO WAY...

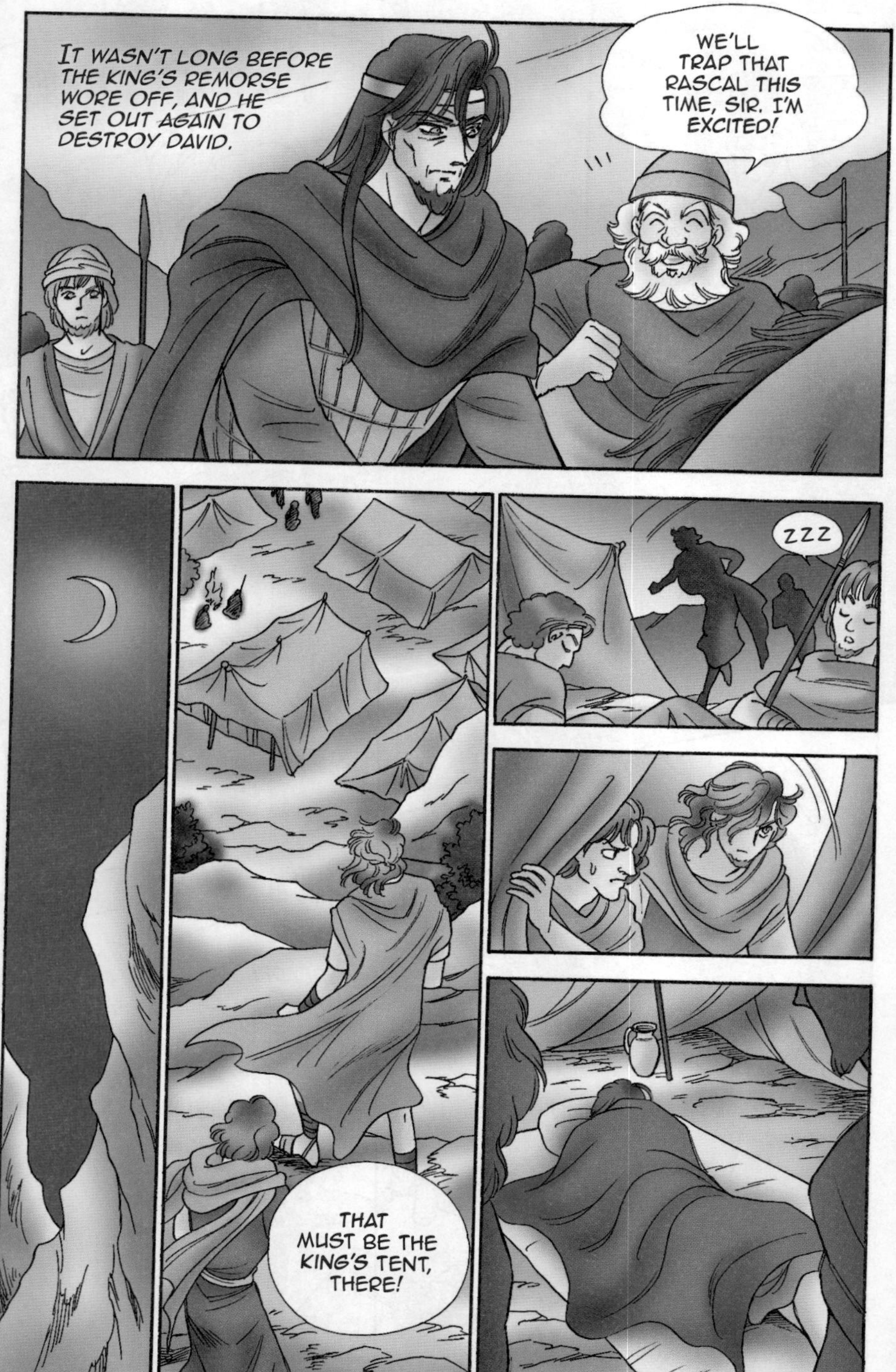
IT WASN'T LONG BEFORE THE KING'S REMORSE WORE OFF, AND HE SET OUT AGAIN TO DESTROY DAVID.
WE'LL TRAP THAT RASCAL THIS TIME, SIR. I'M EXCITED!
ZZZ
THAT MUST BE THE KING'S TENT, THERE!

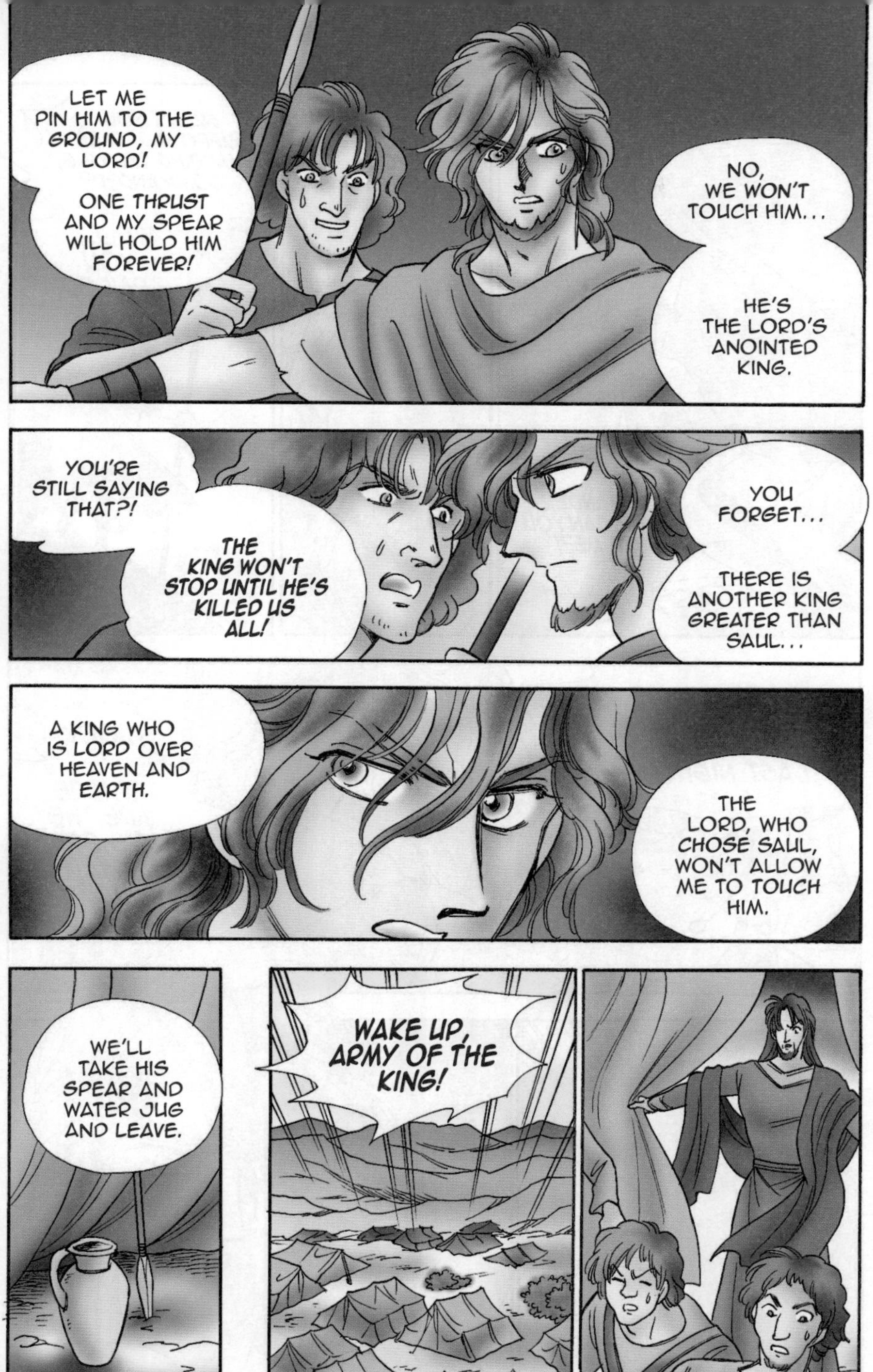
LET ME PIN HIM TO THE GROUND, MY LORD!
ONE THRUST AND MY SPEAR WILL HOLD HIM FOREVER!
NO, WE WON'T TOUCH HIM...
HE'S THE LORD'S ANOINTED KING.
YOU'RE STILL SAYING THAT?!
THE KING WON'T STOP UNTIL HE'S KILLED US ALL!
YOU FORGET...
THERE IS ANOTHER KING GREATER THAN SAUL...
A KING WHO IS LORD OVER HEAVEN AND EARTH.
THE LORD, WHO CHOSE SAUL, WON'T ALLOW ME TO TOUCH HIM.
WE'LL TAKE HIS SPEAR AND WATER JUG AND LEAVE.
WAKE UP, ARMY OF THE KING!

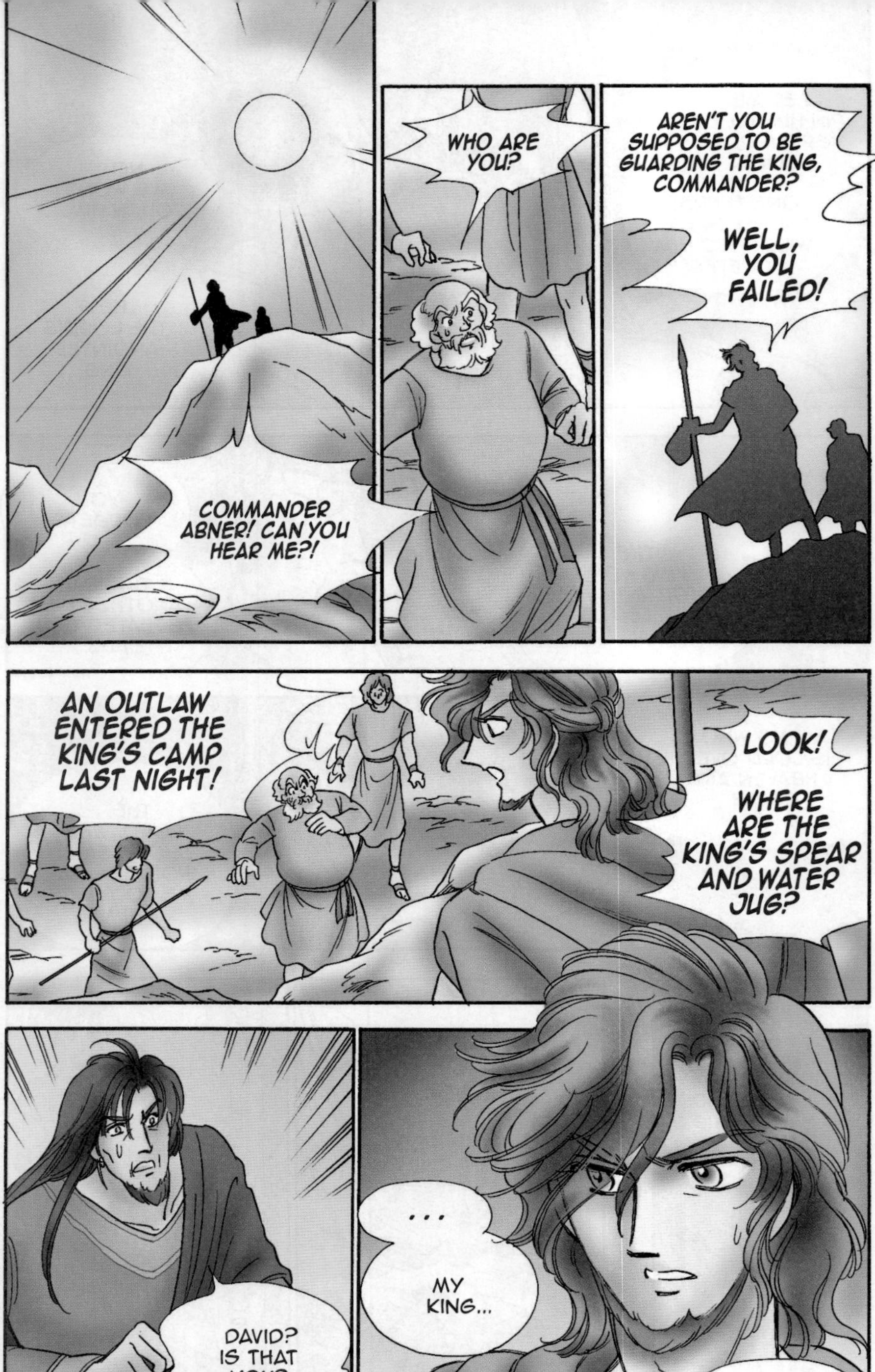
COMMANDER ABNER! CAN YOU HEAR ME?!
WHO ARE YOU?
AREN'T YOU SUPPOSED TO BE GUARDING THE KING, COMMANDER?
WELL, YOU FAILED!
AN OUTLAW ENTERED THE KING'S CAMP LAST NIGHT!
LOOK!
WHERE ARE THE KING'S SPEAR AND WATER JUG?
DAVID? IS THAT YOU?
...
MY KING...
IT'S ME.

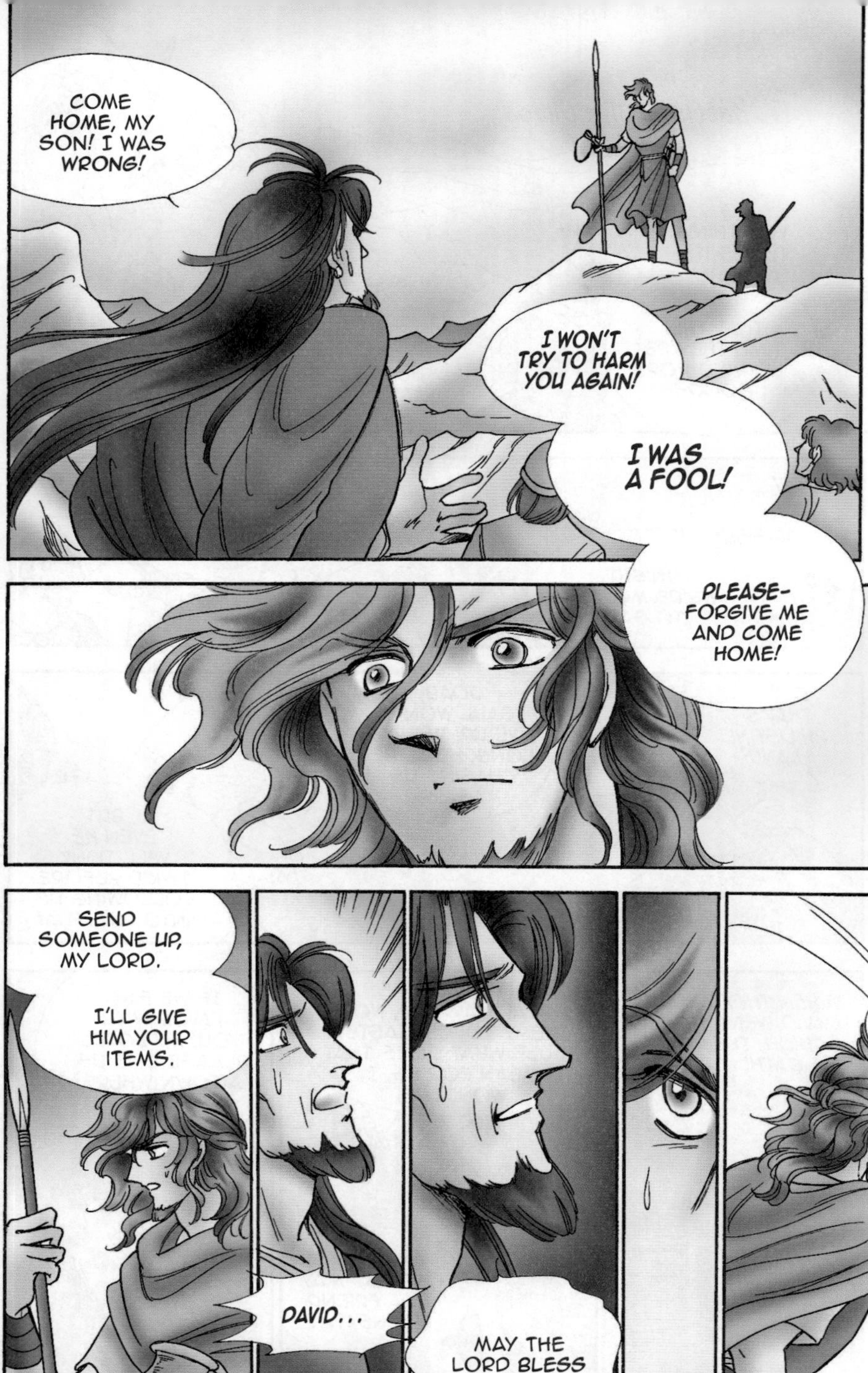
COME HOME, MY SON! I WAS WRONG!
I WON'T TRY TO HARM YOU AGAIN!
I WAS A FOOL!
PLEASE- FORGIVE ME AND COME HOME!
SEND SOMEONE UP, MY LORD.
I'LL GIVE HIM YOUR ITEMS.
DAVID...
MAY THE LORD BLESS YOU.

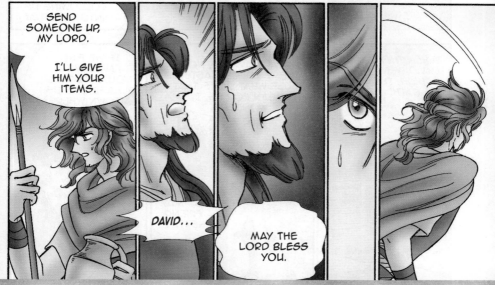

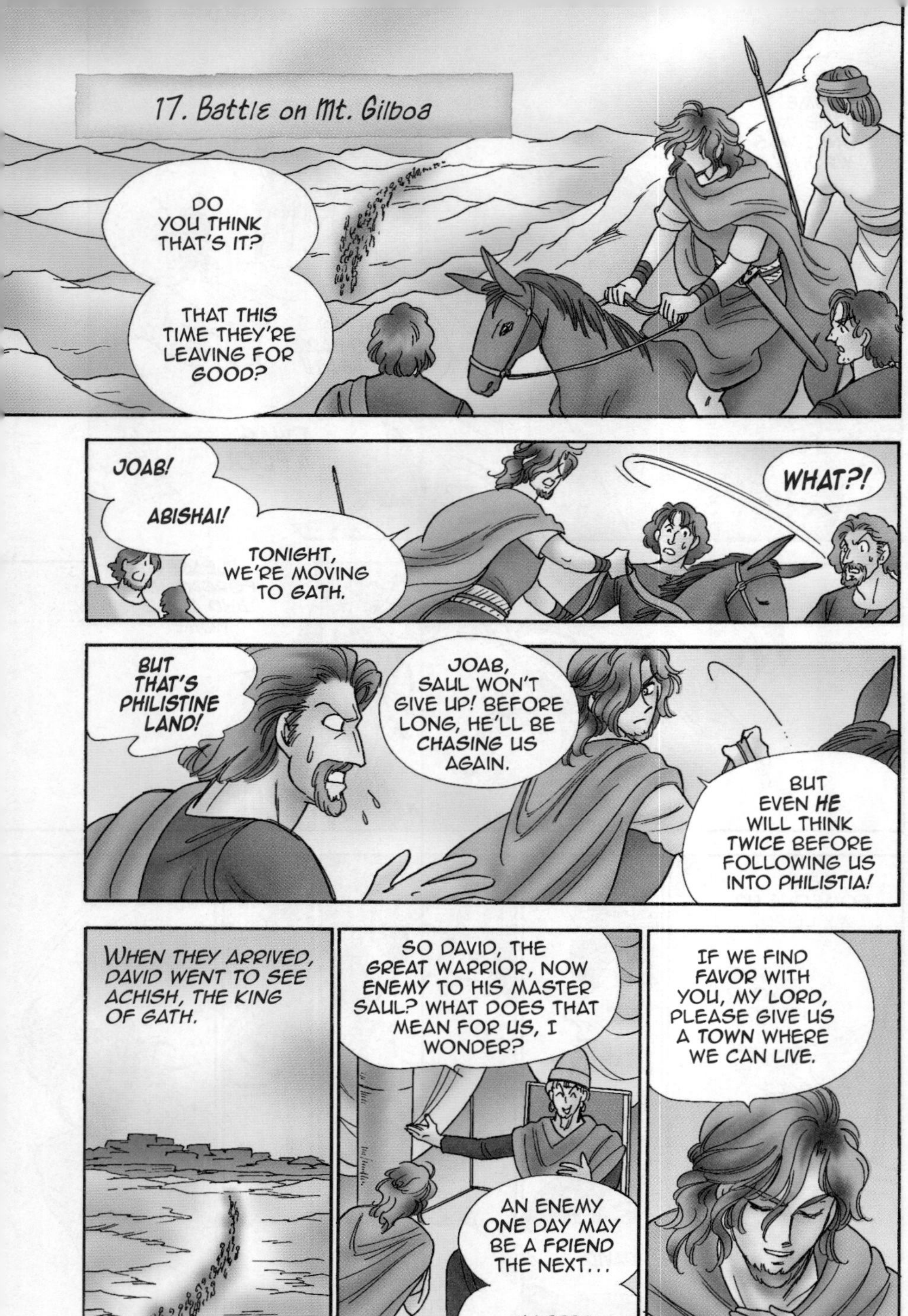
17. Battle on Mt. Gilboa
DO YOU THINK THAT'S IT?
THAT THIS TIME THEY'RE LEAVING FOR GOOD?
JOAB!
ABISHAI!
TONIGHT, WE'RE MOVING TO GATH.
WHAT?!
BUT THAT'S PHILISTINE LAND!
JOAB, SAUL WON'T GIVE UP! BEFORE LONG, HE'LL BE CHASING US AGAIN.
BUT EVEN HE WILL THINK TWICE BEFORE FOLLOWING US INTO PHILISTIA!
WHEN THEY ARRIVED, DAVID WENT TO SEE ACHISH, THE KING OF GATH.
SO DAVID, THE GREAT WARRIOR, NOW ENEMY TO HIS MASTER SAUL? WHAT DOES THAT MEAN FOR US, I WONDER?
AN ENEMY ONE DAY MAY BE A FRIEND THE NEXT...
MASTER ACHISH.
IF WE FIND FAVOR WITH YOU, MY LORD, PLEASE GIVE US A TOWN WHERE WE CAN LIVE.

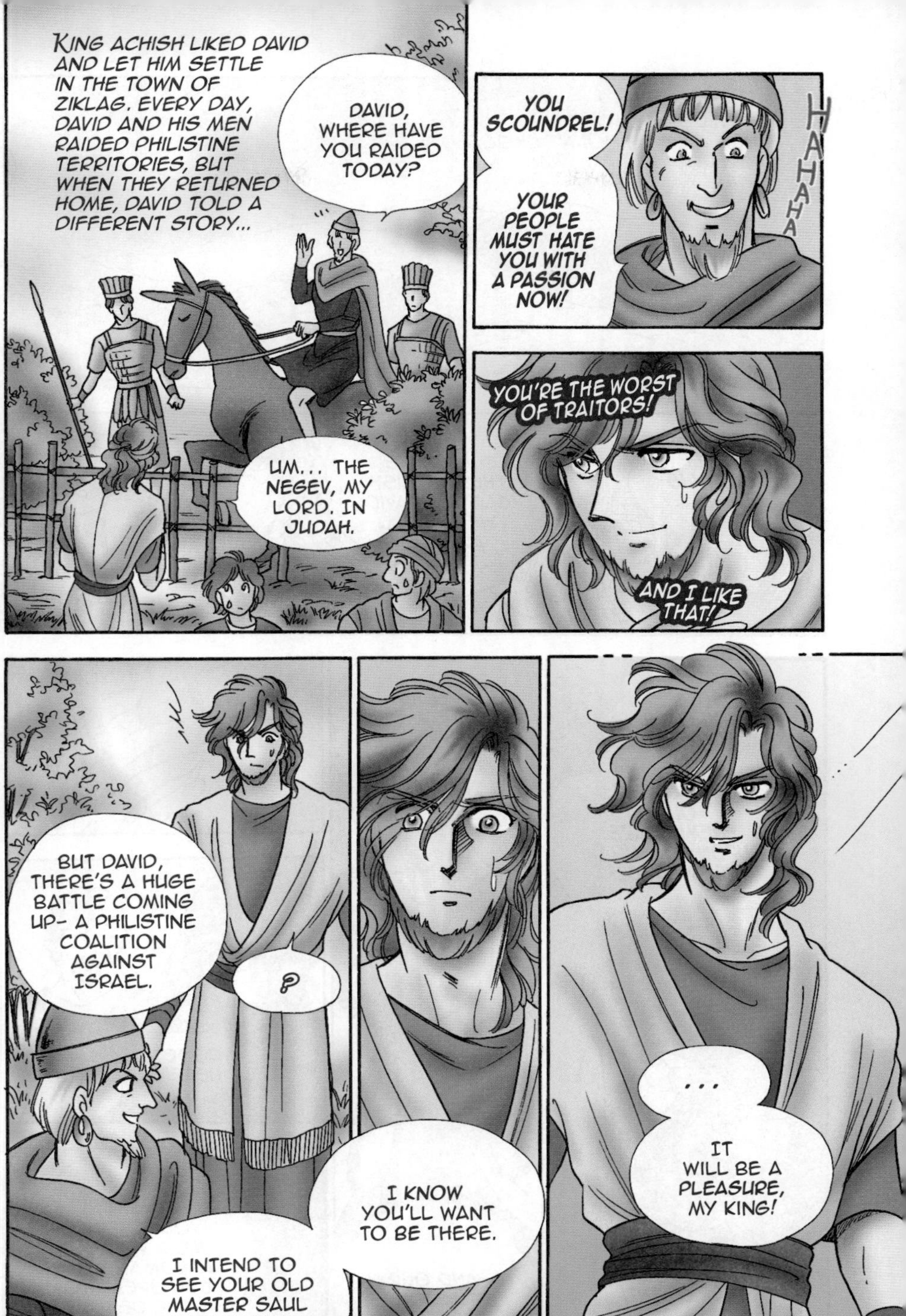
KING ACHISH LIKED DAVID AND LET HIM SETTLE IN THE TOWN OF ZIKLAG. EVERY DAY, DAVID AND HIS MEN RAIDED PHILISTINE TERRITORIES, BUT WHEN THEY RETURNED HOME, DAVID TOLD A DIFFERENT STORY...
DAVID, WHERE HAVE YOU RAIDED TODAY?
UM... THE NEGEV, MY LORD. IN JUDAH.
YOU SCOUNDREL!
YOUR PEOPLE MUST HATE YOU WITH A PASSION NOW!
HAHAHAHA
YOU'RE THE WORST OF TRAITORS!
AND I LIKE THAT!
BUT DAVID, THERE'S A HUGE BATTLE COMING UP- A PHILISTINE COALITION AGAINST ISRAEL.
?
I INTEND TO SEE YOUR OLD MASTER SAUL FINALLY TAKEN DOWN!
I KNOW YOU'LL WANT TO BE THERE.
...
IT WILL BE A PLEASURE, MY KING!

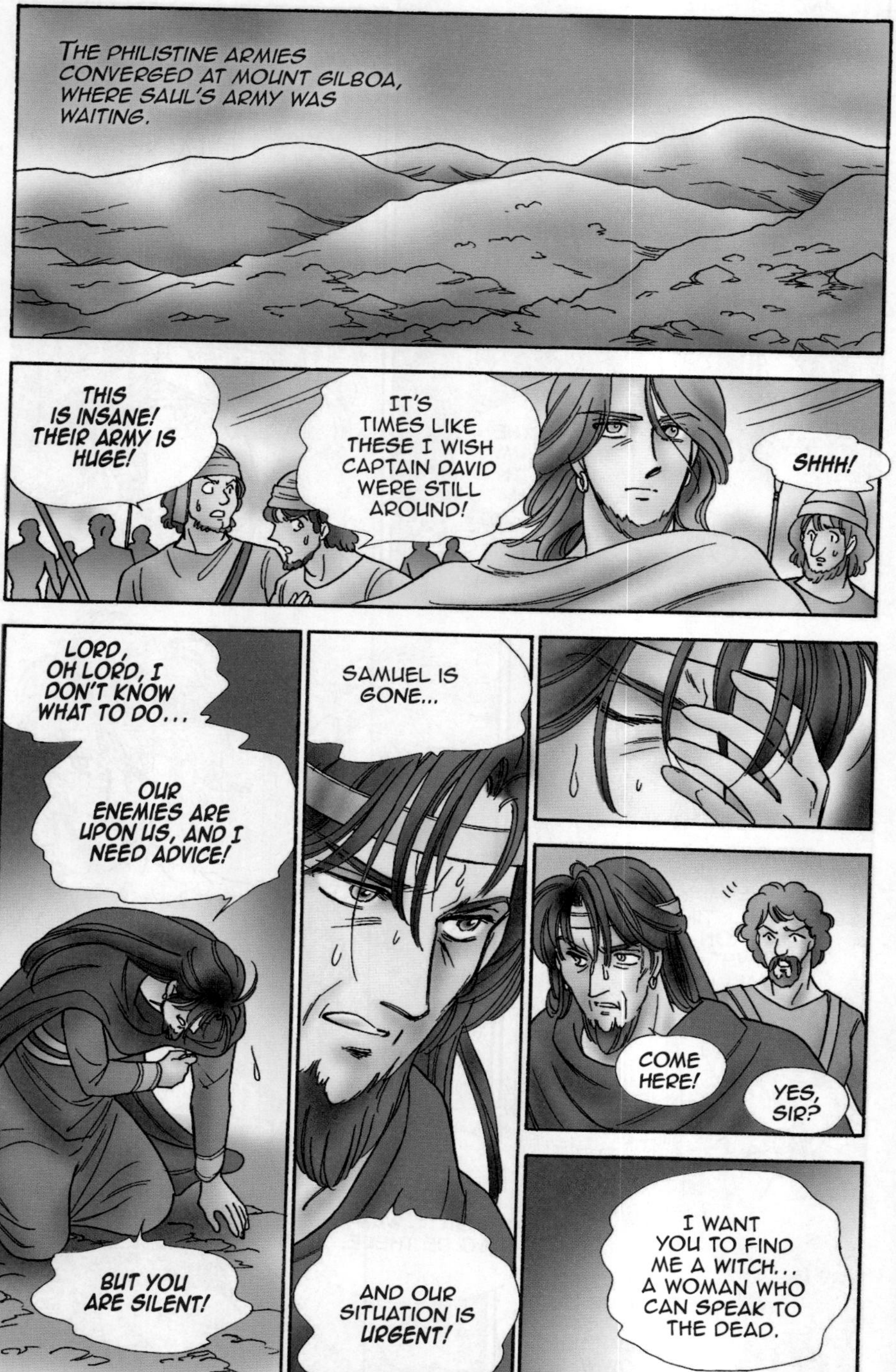
THE PHILISTINE ARMIES CONVERGED AT MOUNT GILBOA, WHERE SAUL'S ARMY WAS WAITING.
THIS IS INSANE! THEIR ARMY IS HUGE!
IT'S TIMES LIKE THESE I WISH CAPTAIN DAVID WERE STILL AROUND!
SHHH!
LORD, OH LORD, I DON'T KNOW WHAT TO DO...
OUR ENEMIES ARE UPON US, AND I NEED ADVICE!
BUT YOU ARE SILENT!
SAMUEL IS GONE...
AND OUR SITUATION IS URGENT!
COME HERE!
YES, SIR?
I WANT YOU TO FIND ME A WITCH... A WOMAN WHO CAN SPEAK TO THE DEAD.

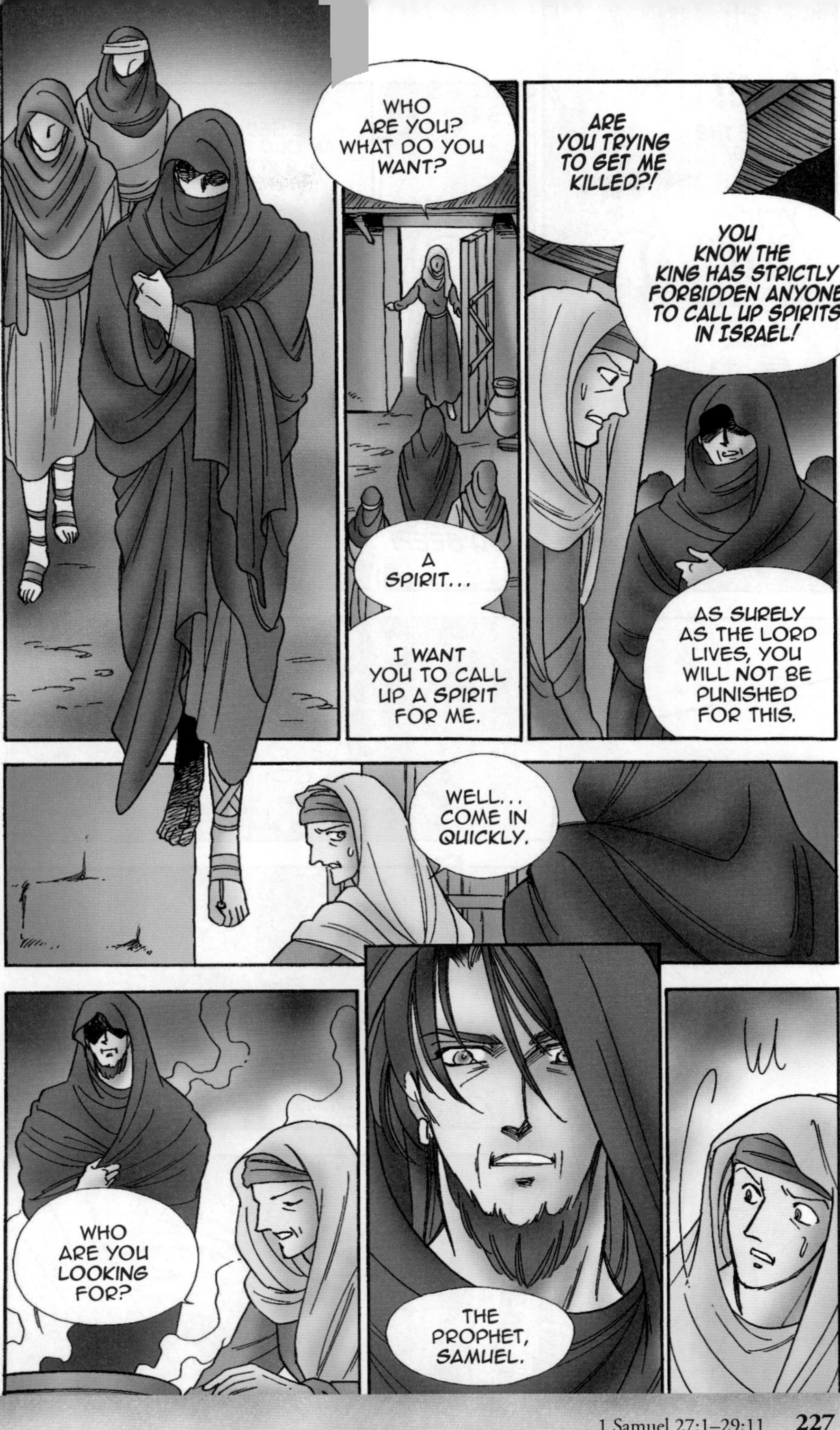
WHO ARE YOU? WHAT DO YOU WANT?
A SPIRIT...
I WANT YOU TO CALL UP A SPIRIT FOR ME.
ARE YOU TRYING TO GET ME KILLED?!
YOU KNOW THE KING HAS STRICTLY FORBIDDEN ANYONE TO CALL UP SPIRITS IN ISRAEL!
AS SURELY AS THE LORD LIVES, YOU WILL NOT BE PUNISHED FOR THIS.
WELL... COME IN QUICKLY.
WHO ARE YOU LOOKING FOR?
THE PROPHET, SAMUEL.

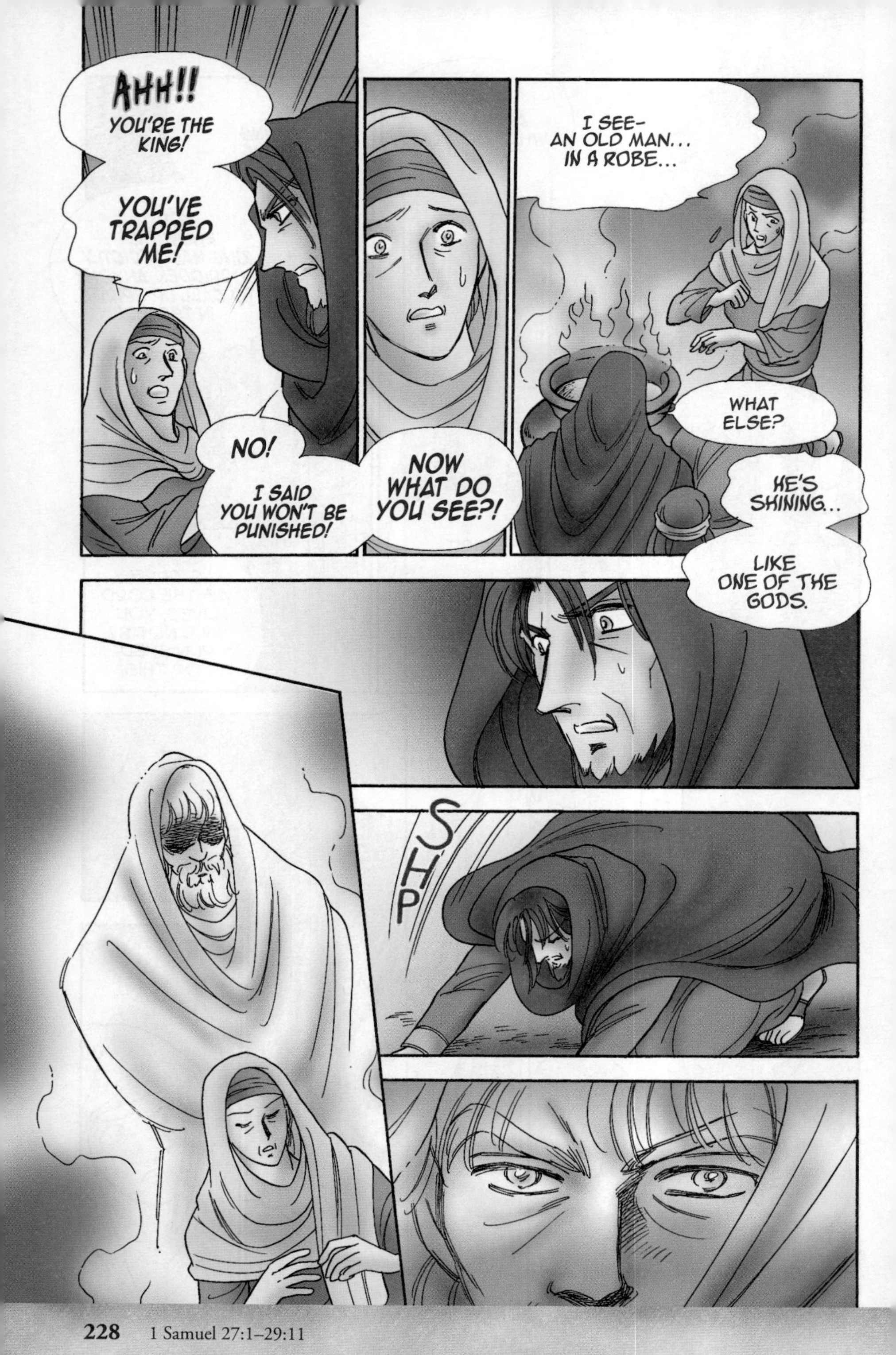
AHH!! YOU'RE THE KING!
YOU'VE TRAPPED ME!
NO!
I SAID YOU WON'T BE PUNISHED!
NOW WHAT DO YOU SEE?!
I SEE- AN OLD MAN... IN A ROBE...
WHAT ELSE?
HE'S SHINING...
LIKE ONE OF THE GODS.
SHP

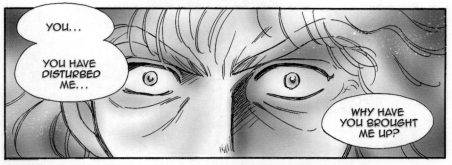

YOU...

YOU HAVE DISTURBED ME...

WHY HAVE YOU BROUGHT ME UP?

MAS-MASTER SAMUEL...

I'VE ASKED THE LORD...

BUT HE DOESN'T GIVE ME ANY DREAMS OR PROPHETS TO HELP ME!

WHY DO YOU CONSULT ME...

NOW THAT THE LORD IS YOUR ENEMY?!

HE HAS TORN THIS KINGDOM FROM YOUR HAND, AS HE SAID HE WOULD...

AND GIVEN IT TO ANOTHER! HE IS GIVING IT TO DAVID!

I'M IN TROUBLE!

THE PHILISTINES ARE UPON US AND I- I DON'T KNOW WHAT TO DO!

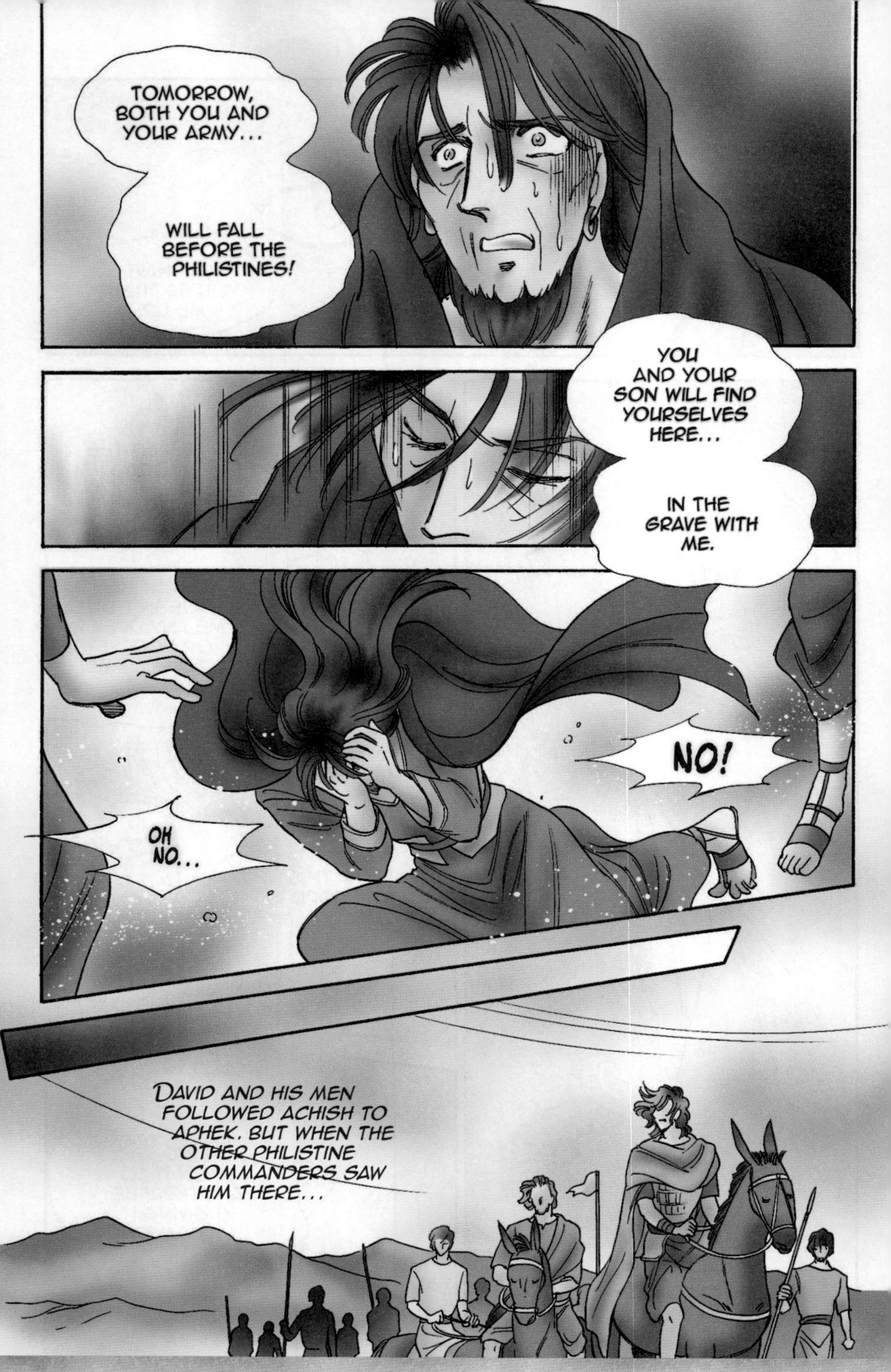
TOMORROW, BOTH YOU AND YOUR ARMY...
WILL FALL BEFORE THE PHILISTINES!
YOU AND YOUR SON WILL FIND YOURSELVES HERE...
IN THE GRAVE WITH ME.
NO!
OH NO...
DAVID AND HIS MEN FOLLOWED ACHISH TO APHEK. BUT WHEN THE OTHER PHILISTINE COMMANDERS SAW HIM THERE...

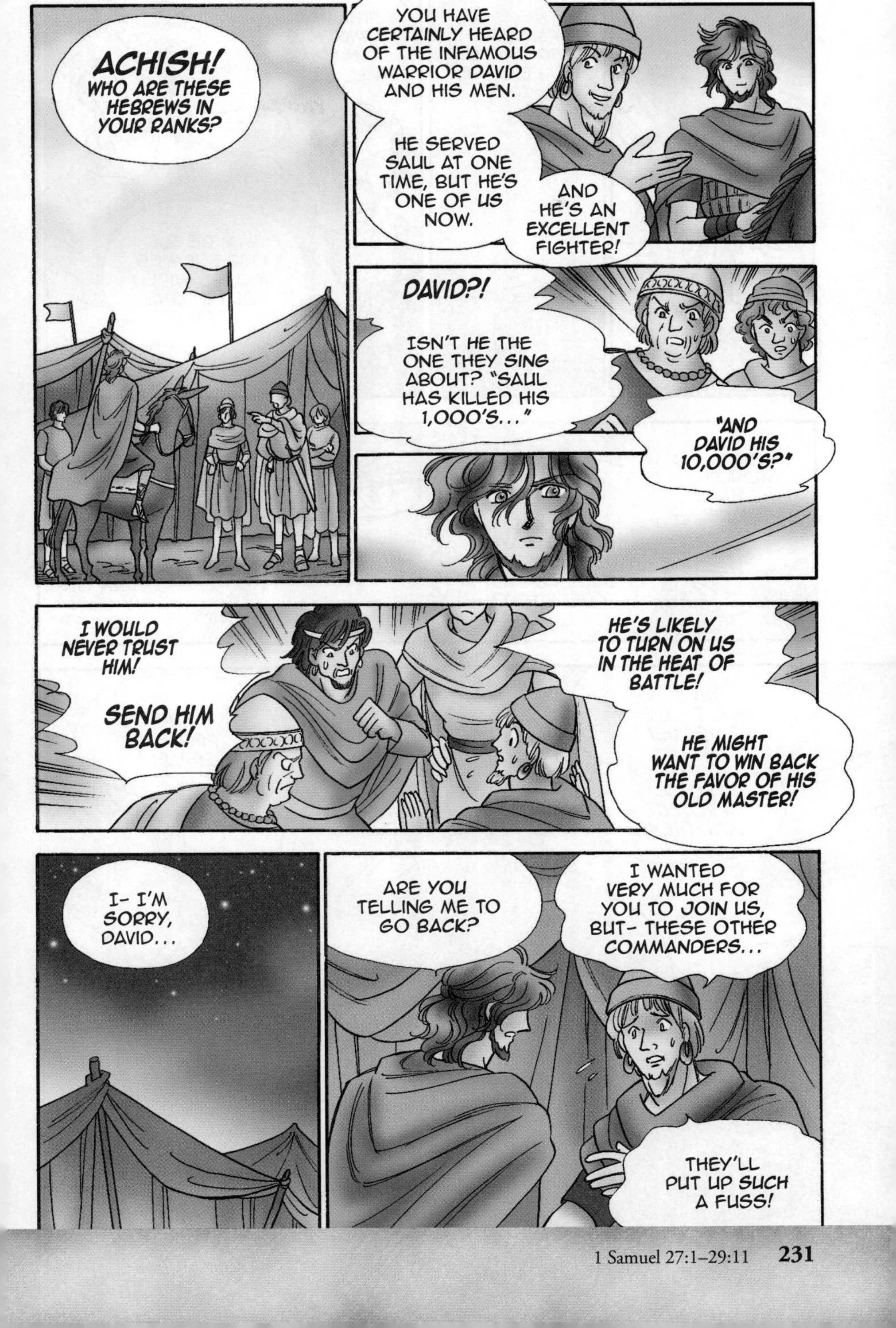
ACHISH! WHO ARE THESE HEBREWS IN YOUR RANKS?
YOU HAVE CERTAINLY HEARD OF THE INFAMOUS WARRIOR DAVID AND HIS MEN.
HE SERVED SAUL AT ONE TIME, BUT HE'S ONE OF US NOW.
AND HE'S AN EXCELLENT FIGHTER!
DAVID?!
ISN'T HE THE ONE THEY SING ABOUT? "SAUL HAS KILLED HIS 1,000'S..."
"AND DAVID HIS 10,000'S?"
I WOULD NEVER TRUST HIM!
SEND HIM BACK!
HE'S LIKELY TO TURN ON US IN THE HEAT OF BATTLE!
HE MIGHT WANT TO WIN BACK THE FAVOR OF HIS OLD MASTER!
I- I'M SORRY, DAVID...
ARE YOU TELLING ME TO GO BACK?
I WANTED VERY MUCH FOR YOU TO JOIN US, BUT- THESE OTHER COMMANDERS...
THEY'LL PUT UP SUCH A FUSS!

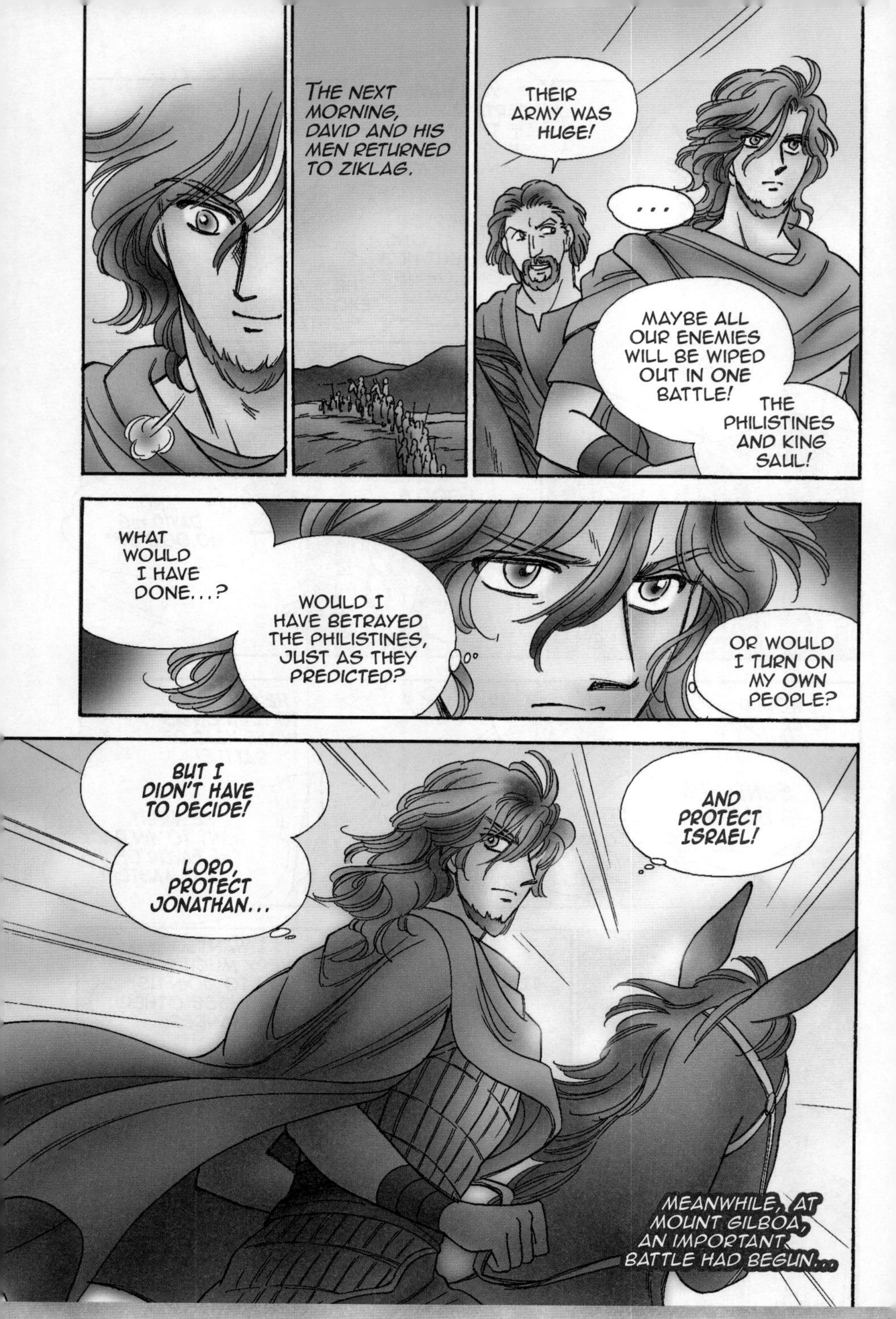
THE NEXT MORNING, DAVID AND HIS MEN RETURNED TO ZIKLAG.
THEIR ARMY WAS HUGE!
. . .
MAYBE ALL OUR ENEMIES WILL BE WIPED OUT IN ONE BATTLE!
THE PHILISTINES AND KING SAUL!
WHAT WOULD I HAVE DONE. . .?
WOULD I HAVE BETRAYED THE PHILISTINES, JUST AS THEY PREDICTED?
OR WOULD I TURN ON MY OWN PEOPLE?
BUT I DIDN'T HAVE TO DECIDE!
LORD, PROTECT JONATHAN. . .
AND PROTECT ISRAEL!
MEANWHILE, AT MOUNT GILBOA, AN IMPORTANT BATTLE HAD BEGUN. . .

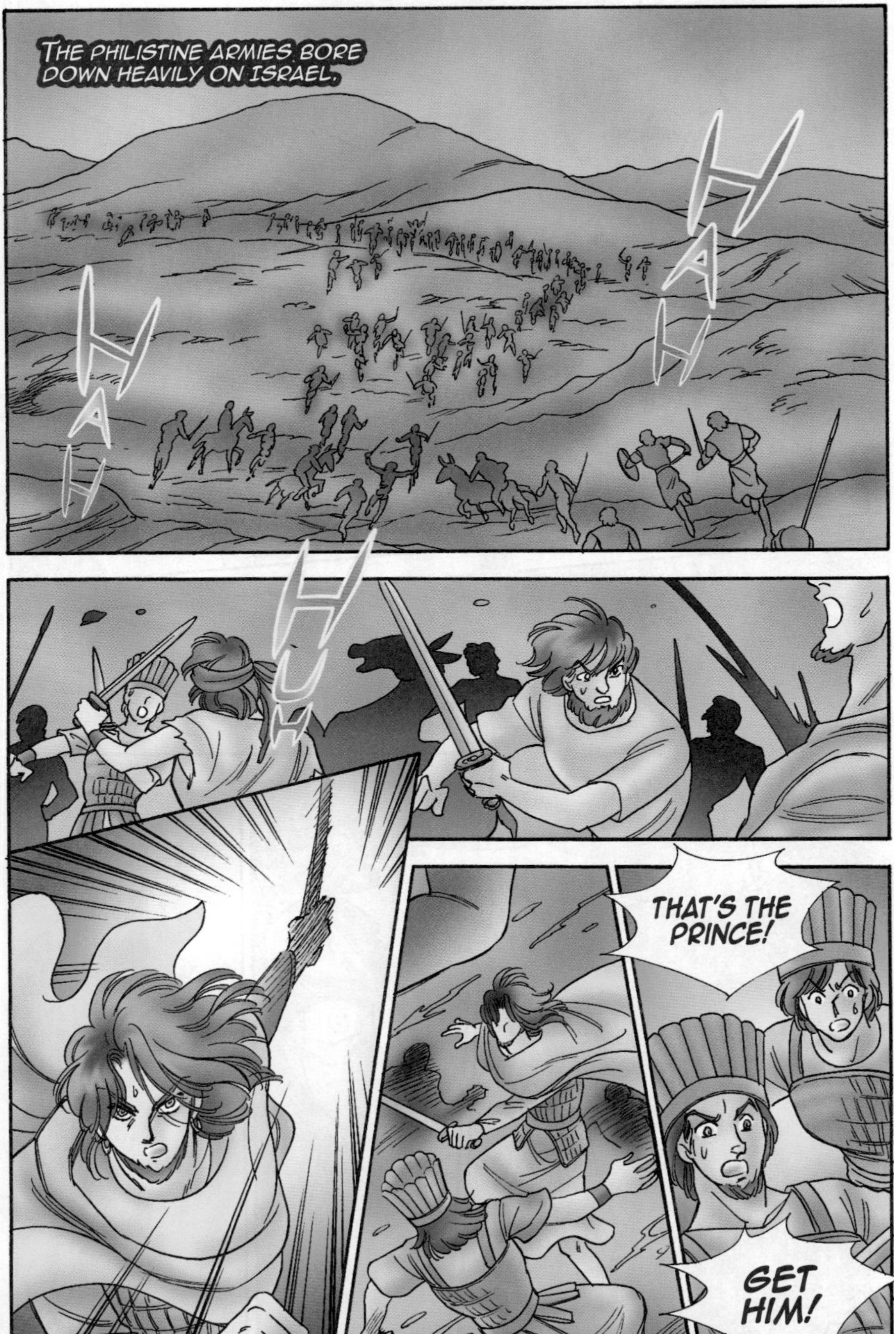
THE PHILISTINE ARMIES BORE DOWN HEAVILY ON ISRAEL.
HAH
HAH
HUH
THAT'S THE PRINCE!
GET HIM!

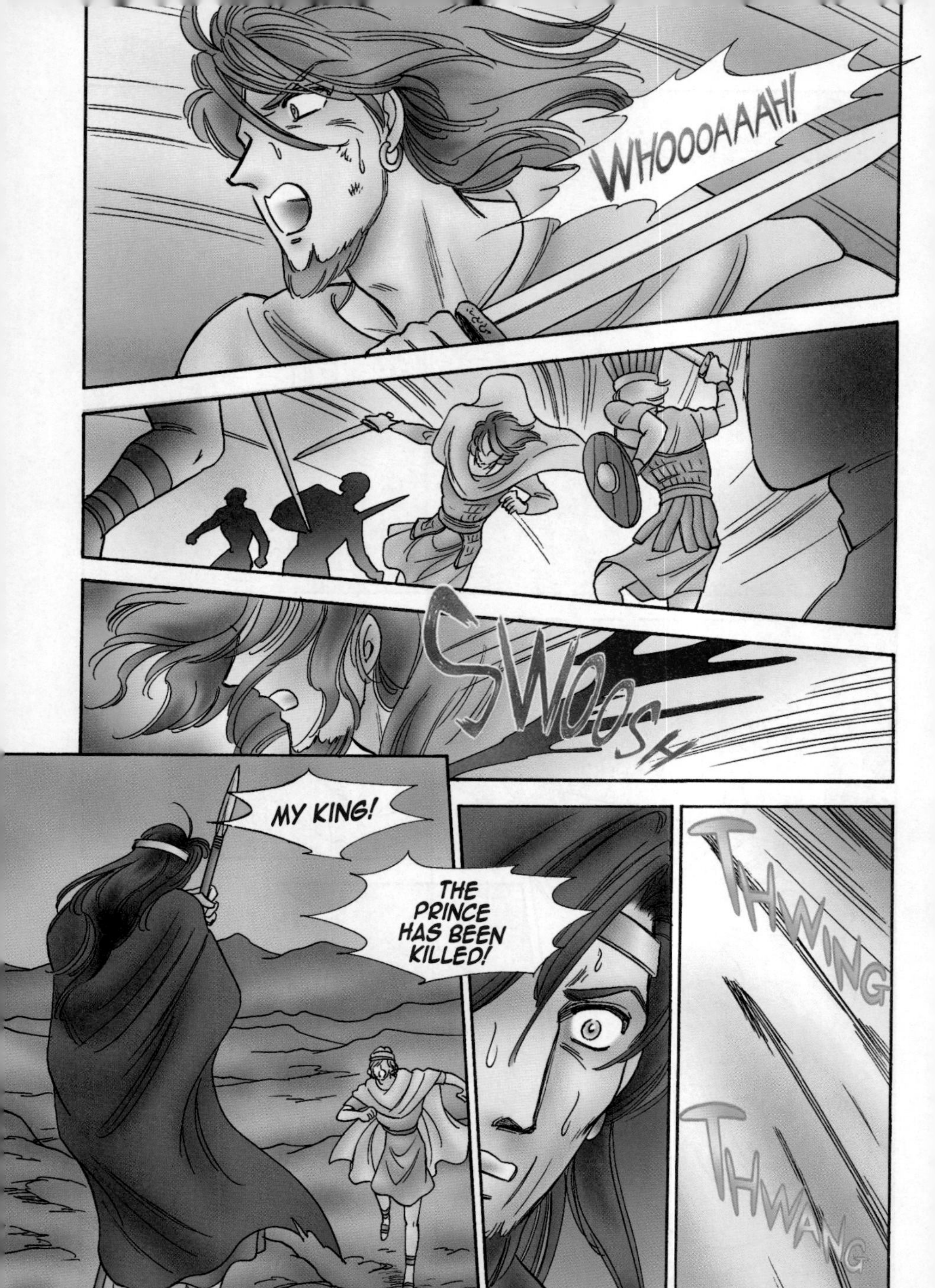
WHOOOAAAH!
SWOOSH
MY KING!
THE PRINCE HAS BEEN KILLED!
THWING
THWANG

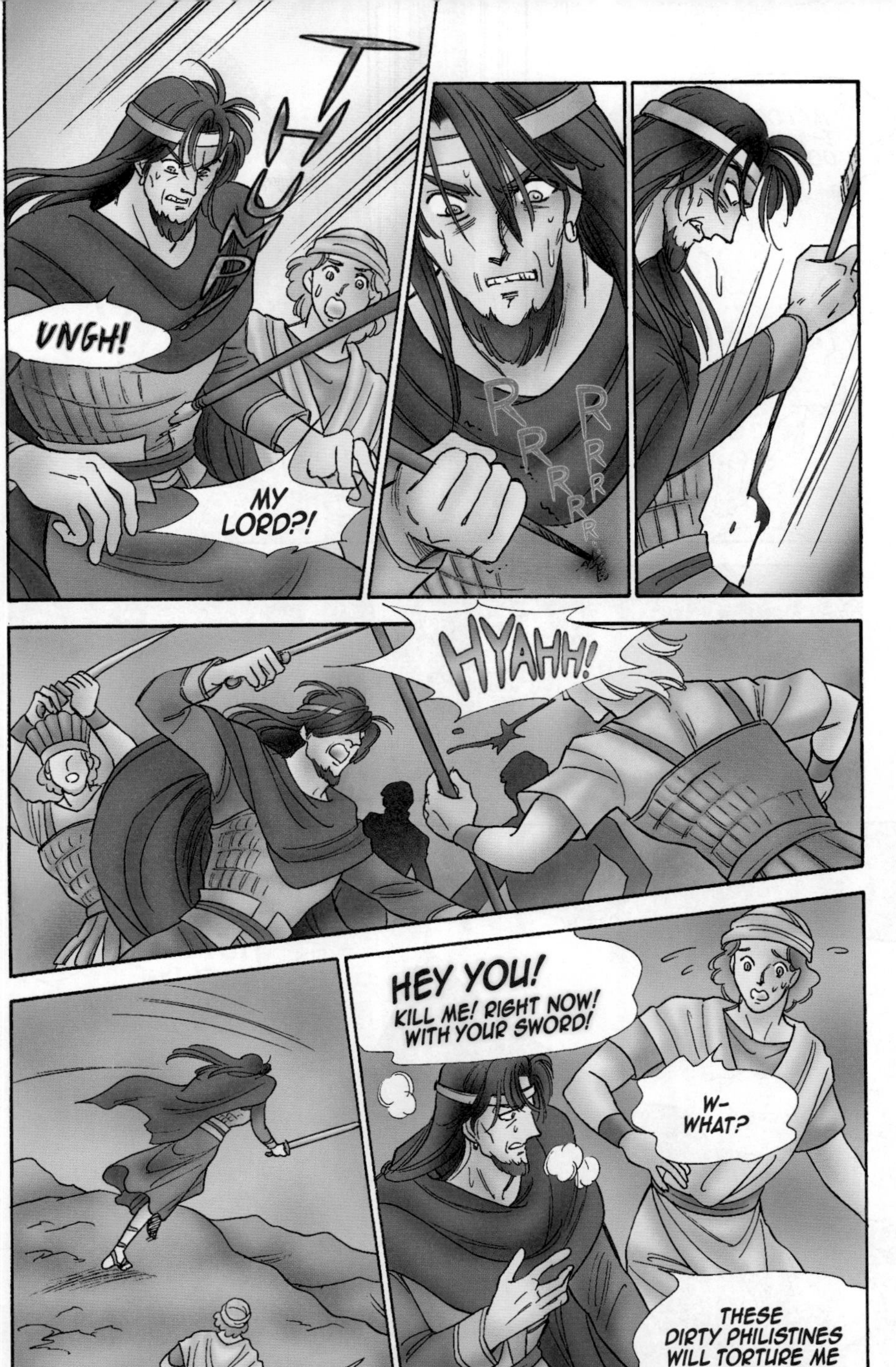
THUMP
UNGH!
MY LORD?!
RRRRRR
RRRRR
HYAHH!
HEY YOU!
KILL ME! RIGHT NOW! WITH YOUR SWORD!
W- WHAT?
THESE DIRTY PHILISTINES WILL TORTURE ME IF THEY CAPTURE ME ALIVE!

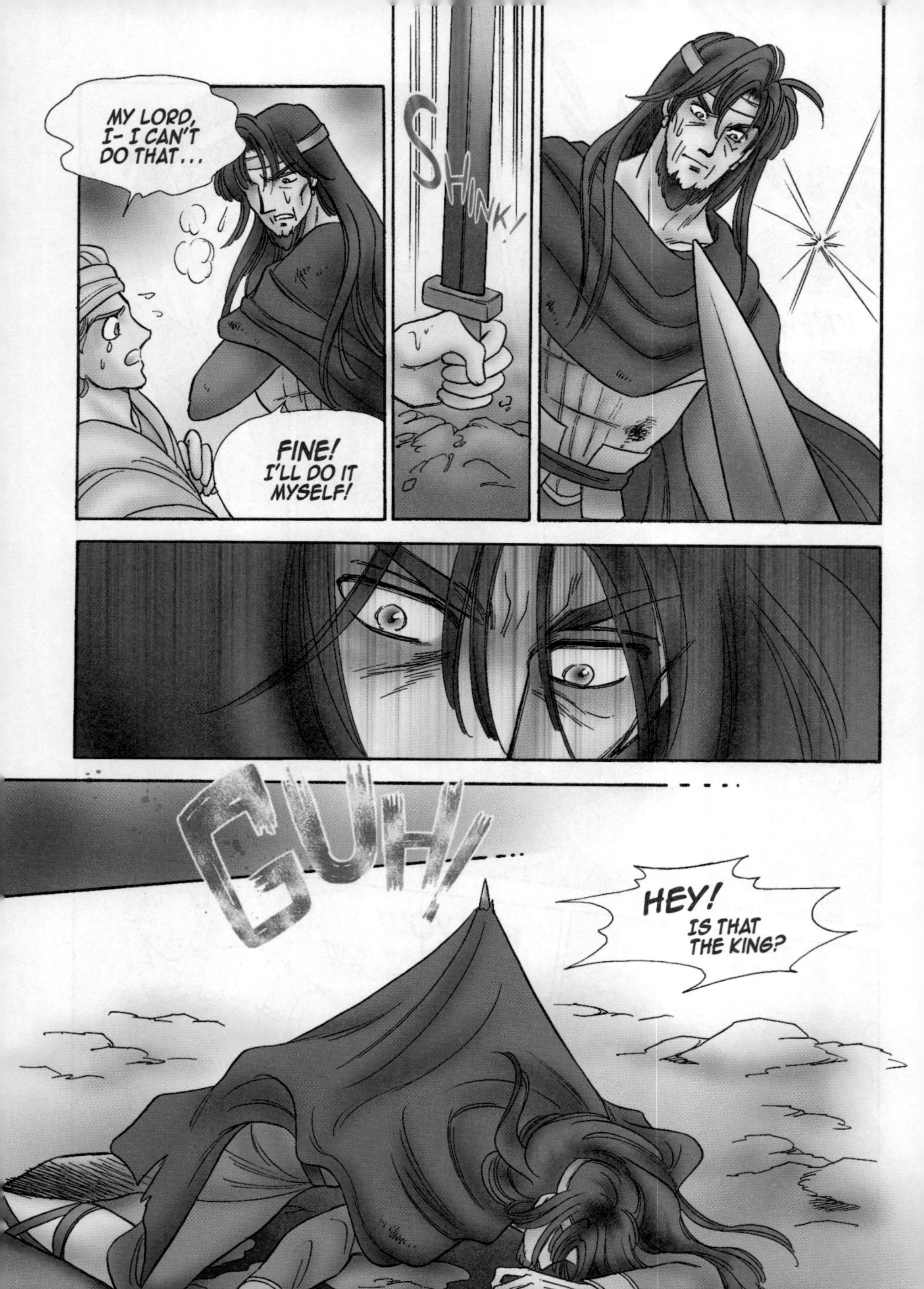
MY LORD, I- I CAN'T DO THAT . . .
FINE! I'LL DO IT MYSELF!
SHINK!
GUH!
HEY! IS THAT THE KING?

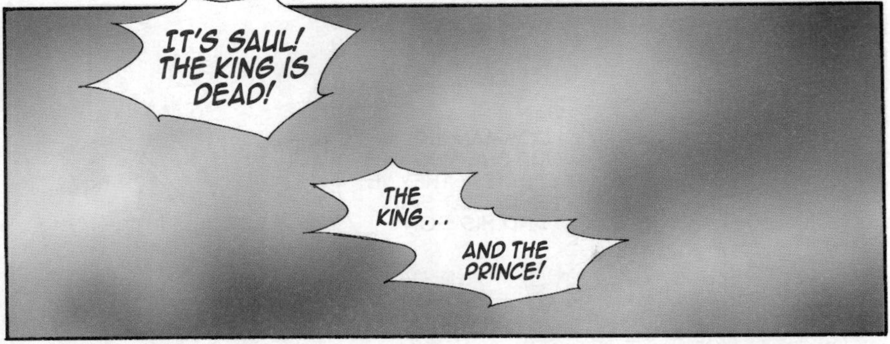
IT'S SAUL! THE KING IS DEAD!
THE KING...
AND THE PRINCE!

SAUL'S SURVIVING SOLDIERS FLED FROM THE BATTLEFIELD...

AND ISRAEL WAS DEFEATED.

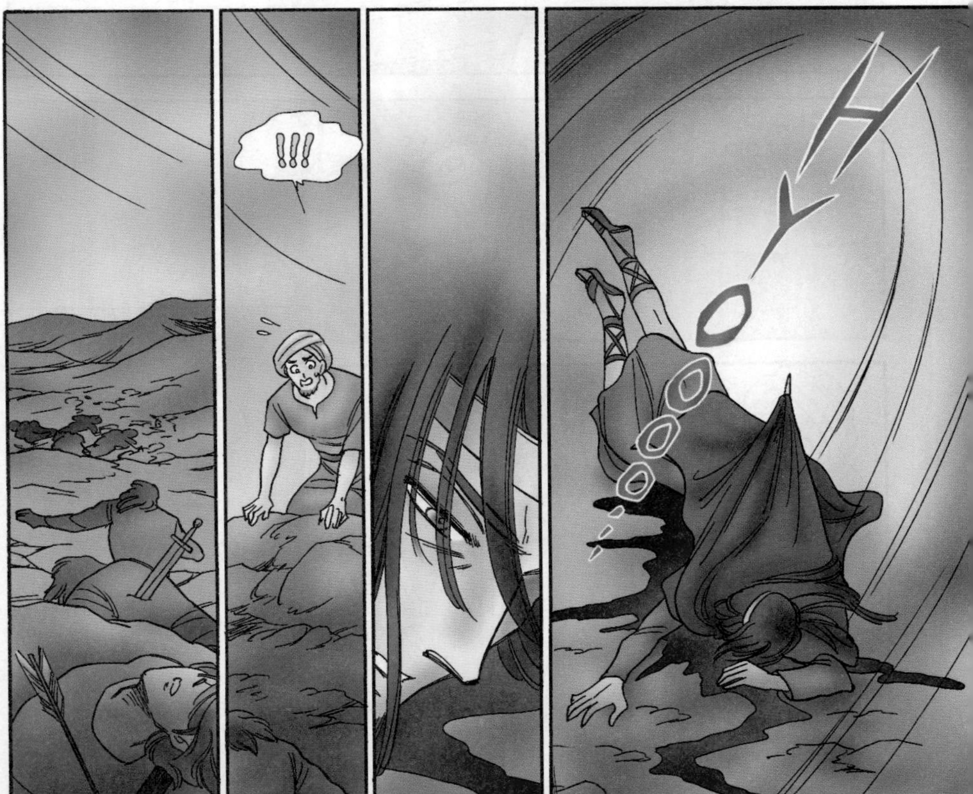
!!!
HYOOOO

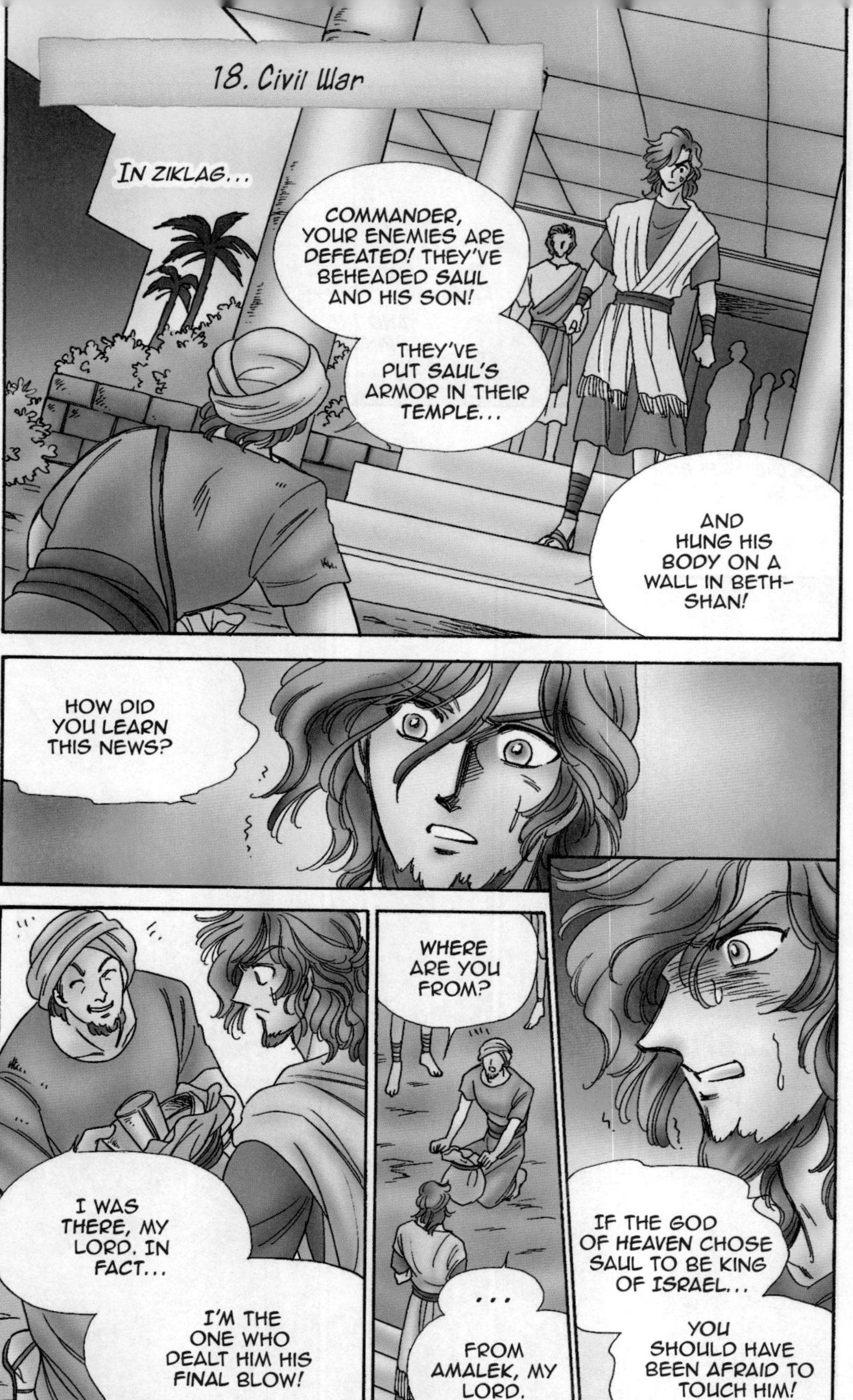
18. Civil War
In Ziklag...
COMMANDER, YOUR ENEMIES ARE DEFEATED! THEY'VE BEHEADED SAUL AND HIS SON!
THEY'VE PUT SAUL'S ARMOR IN THEIR TEMPLE...
AND HUNG HIS BODY ON A WALL IN BETH-SHAN!
HOW DID YOU LEARN THIS NEWS?
I WAS THERE, MY LORD. IN FACT...
I'M THE ONE WHO DEALT HIM HIS FINAL BLOW!
WHERE ARE YOU FROM?
...
FROM AMALEK, MY LORD.
IF THE GOD OF HEAVEN CHOSE SAUL TO BE KING OF ISRAEL...
YOU SHOULD HAVE BEEN AFRAID TO TOUCH HIM!

KILL HIM!

JONATHAN!

....!

Oh, how the mighty heroes have fallen!

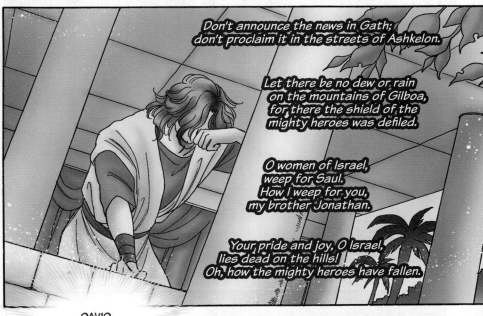

Don't announce the news in Gath; don't proclaim it in the streets of Ashkelon.

Let there be no dew or rain on the mountains of Gilboa, for there the shield of the mighty heroes was defiled.

O women of Israel, weep for Saul. How I weep for you, my brother Jonathan.

Your pride and joy, O Israel, lies dead on the hills! Oh, how the mighty heroes have fallen.

DAVID, GO UP TO HEBRON.

ON HEARING FROM THE LORD, DAVID AND HIS MEN LEFT ZIKLAG.

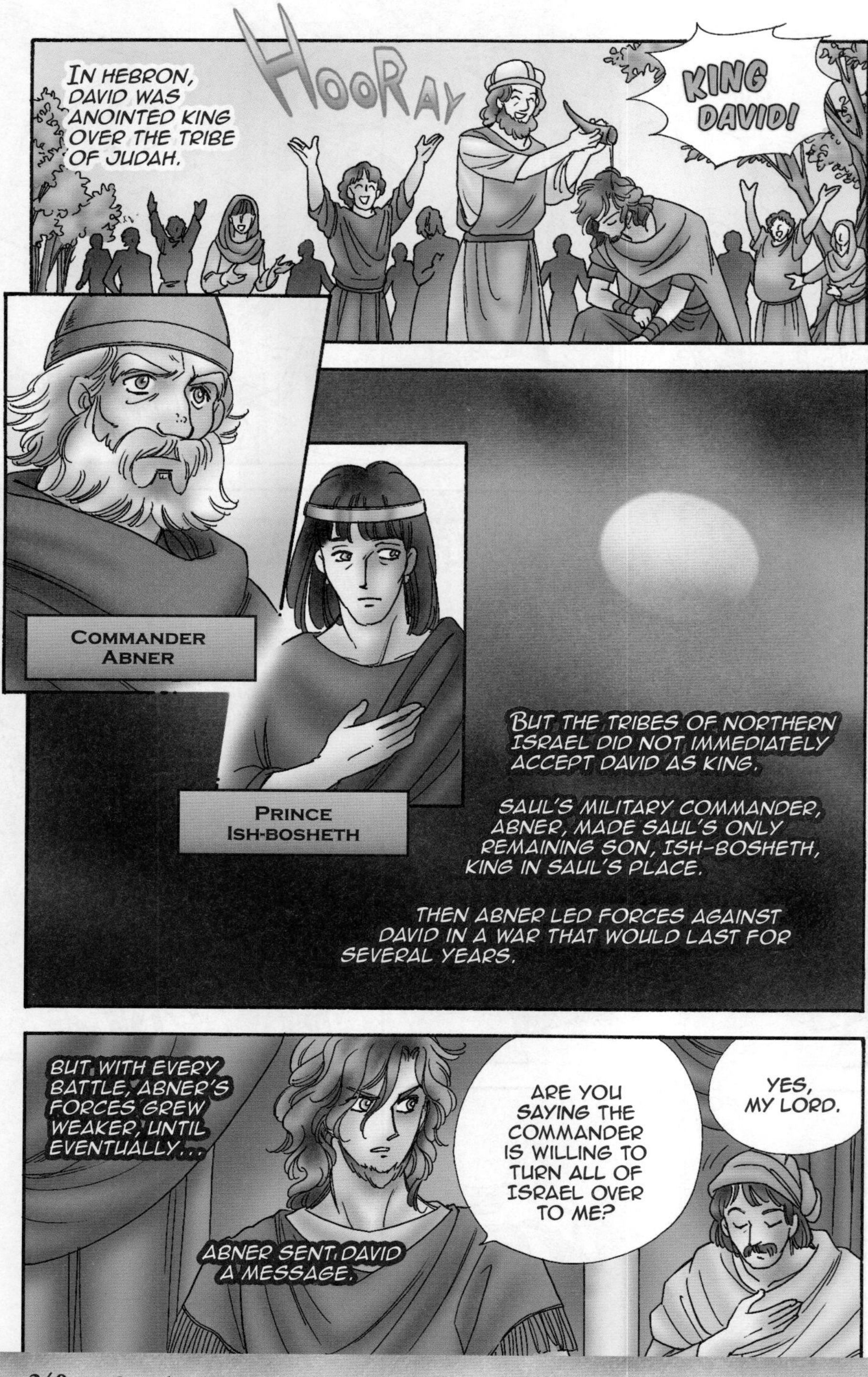
IN HEBRON, DAVID WAS ANOINTED KING OVER THE TRIBE OF JUDAH.
HOORAY
KING DAVID!
COMMANDER ABNER
PRINCE ISH-BOSHETH
BUT THE TRIBES OF NORTHERN ISRAEL DID NOT IMMEDIATELY ACCEPT DAVID AS KING.
SAUL'S MILITARY COMMANDER, ABNER, MADE SAUL'S ONLY REMAINING SON, ISH-BOSHETH, KING IN SAUL'S PLACE.
THEN ABNER LED FORCES AGAINST DAVID IN A WAR THAT WOULD LAST FOR SEVERAL YEARS.
BUT WITH EVERY BATTLE, ABNER'S FORCES GREW WEAKER, UNTIL EVENTUALLY...
ABNER SENT DAVID A MESSAGE.
ARE YOU SAYING THE COMMANDER IS WILLING TO TURN ALL OF ISRAEL OVER TO ME?
YES, MY LORD.

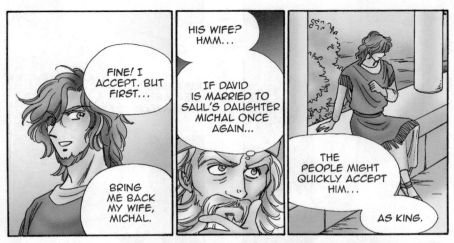

FINE! I ACCEPT. BUT FIRST...

BRING ME BACK MY WIFE, MICHAL.

HIS WIFE? HMM...

IF DAVID IS MARRIED TO SAUL'S DAUGHTER MICHAL ONCE AGAIN...

THE PEOPLE MIGHT QUICKLY ACCEPT HIM...

AS KING.

IT'S BEEN A LONG WAR, AND I JUST DON'T WANT ANY MORE FIGHTING AMONG THE PEOPLE OF ISRAEL...

I WILL MAKE SURE YOU RECEIVE THE ENTIRE KINGDOM.

MICHAL... YOU'RE HERE!

DAVID, WAIT. IT'S BEEN A LONG TIME SINCE I WAS YOUR WIFE.

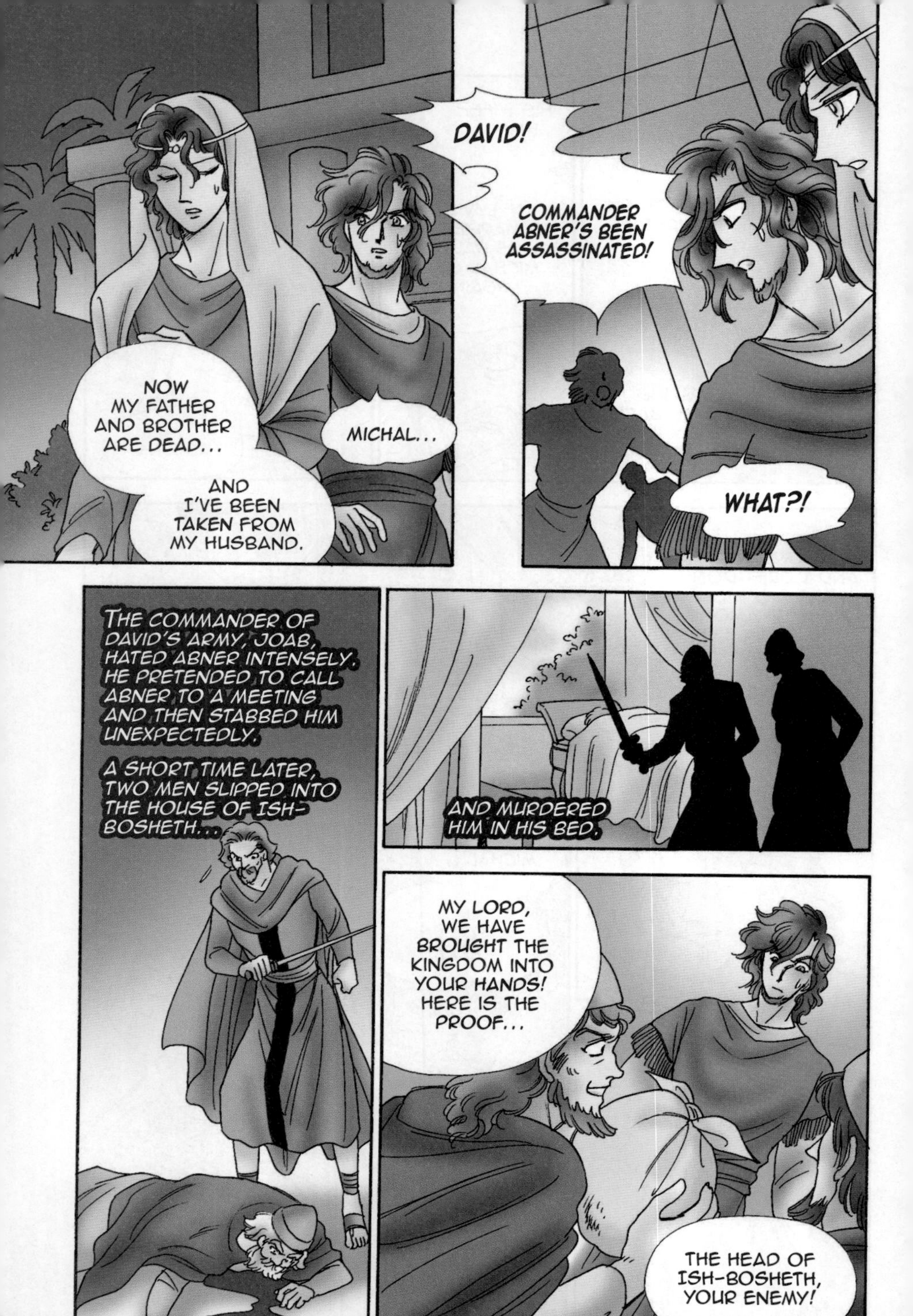
NOW MY FATHER AND BROTHER ARE DEAD...
AND I'VE BEEN TAKEN FROM MY HUSBAND.
MICHAL...
DAVID!
COMMANDER ABNER'S BEEN ASSASSINATED!
WHAT?!
THE COMMANDER OF DAVID'S ARMY, JOAB, HATED ABNER INTENSELY. HE PRETENDED TO CALL ABNER TO A MEETING AND THEN STABBED HIM UNEXPECTEDLY.
A SHORT TIME LATER, TWO MEN SLIPPED INTO THE HOUSE OF ISH-BOSHETH...
AND MURDERED HIM IN HIS BED.
MY LORD, WE HAVE BROUGHT THE KINGDOM INTO YOUR HANDS! HERE IS THE PROOF...
THE HEAD OF ISH-BOSHETH, YOUR ENEMY!

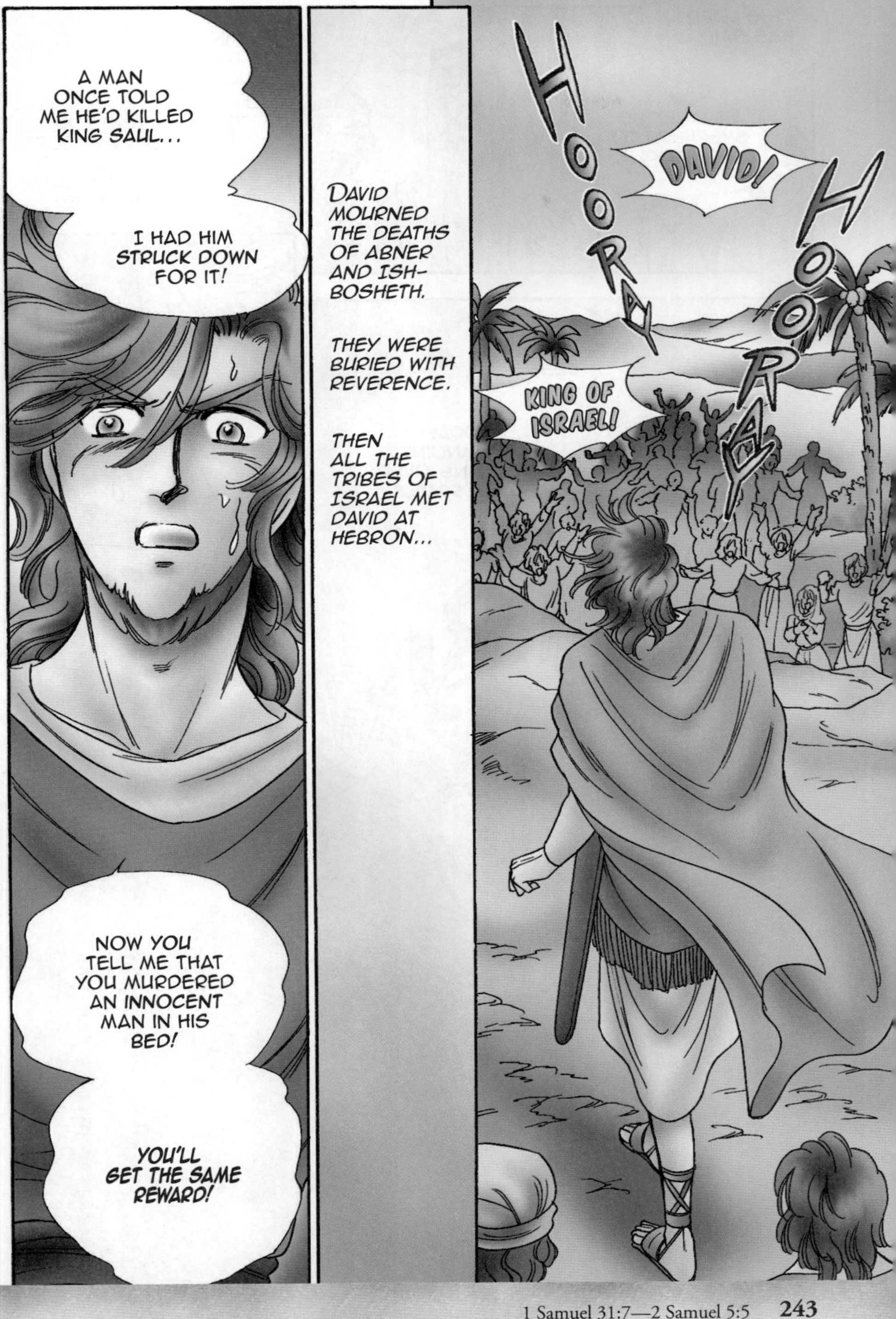
A MAN ONCE TOLD ME HE'D KILLED KING SAUL...
I HAD HIM STRUCK DOWN FOR IT!
NOW YOU TELL ME THAT YOU MURDERED AN INNOCENT MAN IN HIS BED!
YOU'LL GET THE SAME REWARD!
DAVID MOURNED THE DEATHS OF ABNER AND ISH-BOSHETH.
THEY WERE BURIED WITH REVERENCE.
THEN ALL THE TRIBES OF ISRAEL MET DAVID AT HEBRON...
HOORAY
DAVID!
HOORAY
KING OF ISRAEL!

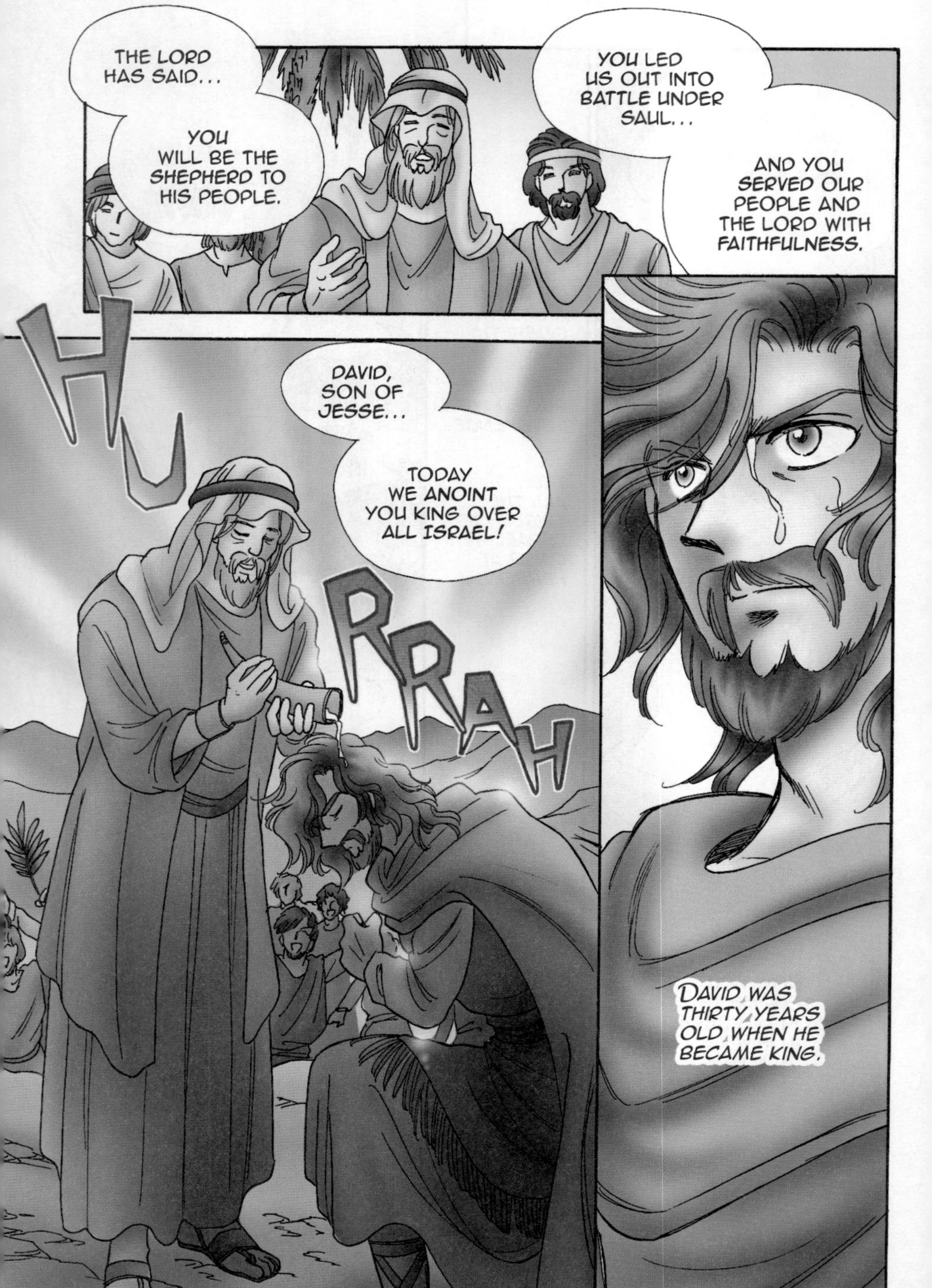
THE LORD HAS SAID...
YOU WILL BE THE SHEPHERD TO HIS PEOPLE.
YOU LED US OUT INTO BATTLE UNDER SAUL...
AND YOU SERVED OUR PEOPLE AND THE LORD WITH FAITHFULNESS.
HU
DAVID, SON OF JESSE...
TODAY WE ANOINT YOU KING OVER ALL ISRAEL!
RRRAH
DAVID WAS THIRTY YEARS OLD WHEN HE BECAME KING.

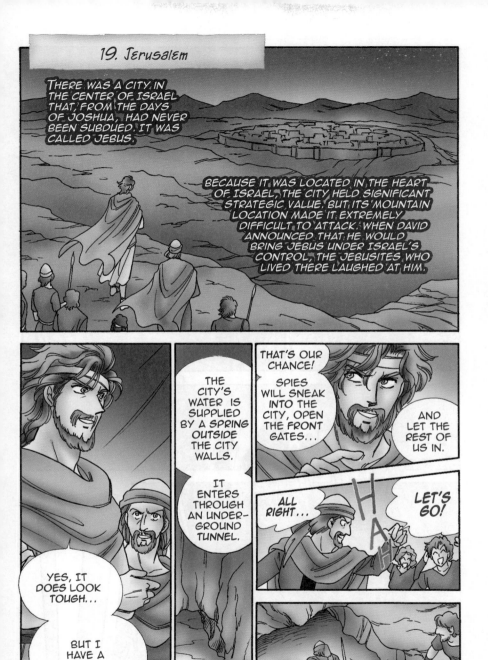

19. Jerusalem

THERE WAS A CITY IN THE CENTER OF ISRAEL THAT, FROM THE DAYS OF JOSHUA, HAD NEVER BEEN SUBDUED. IT WAS CALLED JEBUS.

BECAUSE IT WAS LOCATED IN THE HEART OF ISRAEL, THE CITY HELD SIGNIFICANT STRATEGIC VALUE, BUT ITS MOUNTAIN LOCATION MADE IT EXTREMELY DIFFICULT TO ATTACK. WHEN DAVID ANNOUNCED THAT HE WOULD BRING JEBUS UNDER ISRAEL'S CONTROL, THE JEBUSITES WHO LIVED THERE LAUGHED AT HIM.

THE CITY'S WATER IS SUPPLIED BY A SPRING OUTSIDE THE CITY WALLS.

IT ENTERS THROUGH AN UNDERGROUND TUNNEL.

THAT'S OUR CHANCE! SPIES WILL SNEAK INTO THE CITY, OPEN THE FRONT GATES...

AND LET THE REST OF US IN.

ALL RIGHT...

HAH

LET'S GO!

YES, IT DOES LOOK TOUGH...

BUT I HAVE A PLAN.

TELL US, SIR.

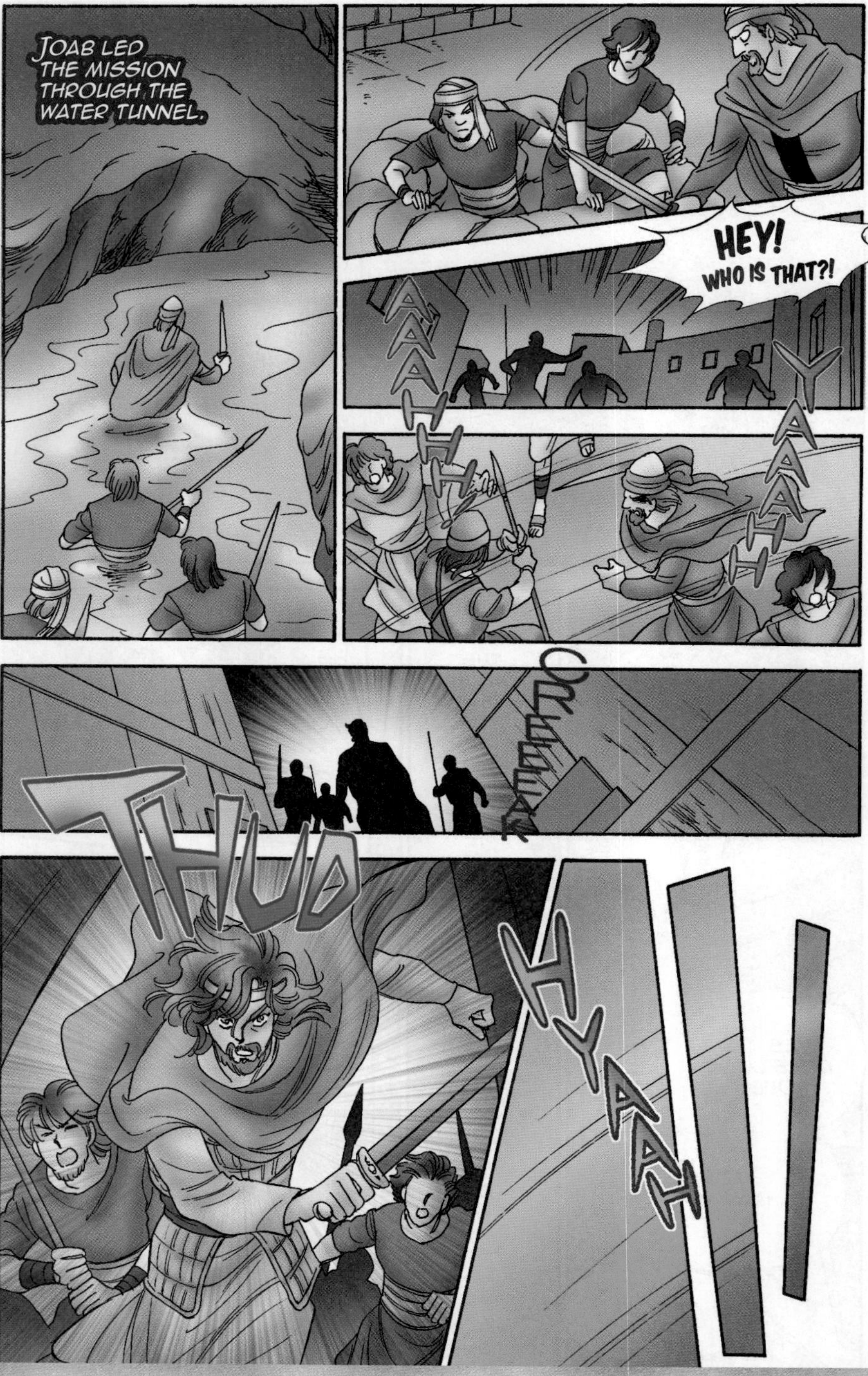

JOAB LED THE MISSION THROUGH THE WATER TUNNEL.
HEY! WHO IS THAT?!
AAAAHHH
YAAAAHH
CREEEEAK
THUD
HYAAAH

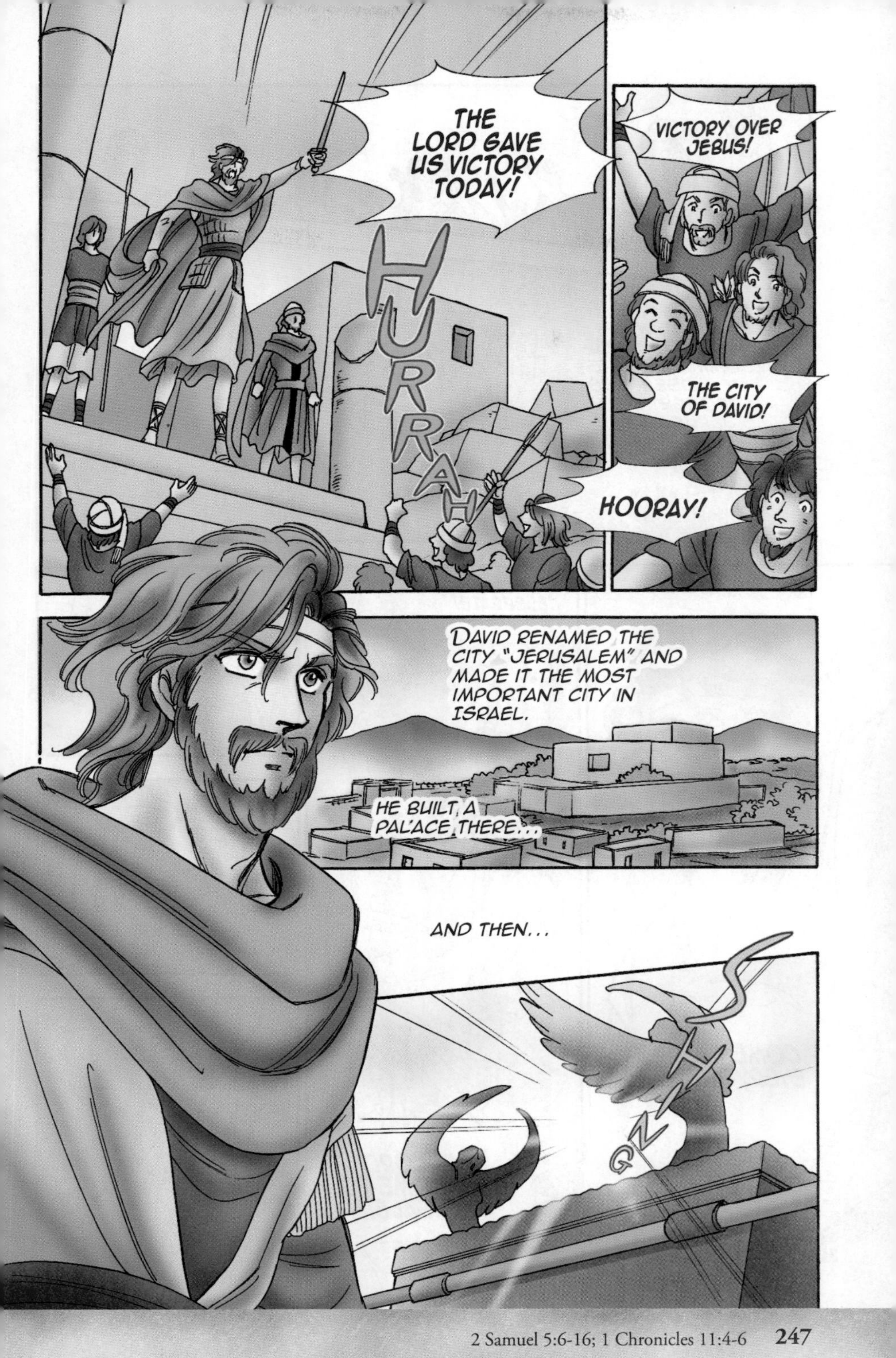
THE LORD GAVE US VICTORY TODAY!
HURRAH
VICTORY OVER JEBUS!
THE CITY OF DAVID!
HOORAY!
DAVID RENAMED THE CITY "JERUSALEM" AND MADE IT THE MOST IMPORTANT CITY IN ISRAEL.
HE BUILT A PAL'ACE THERE...
AND THEN...
SHING

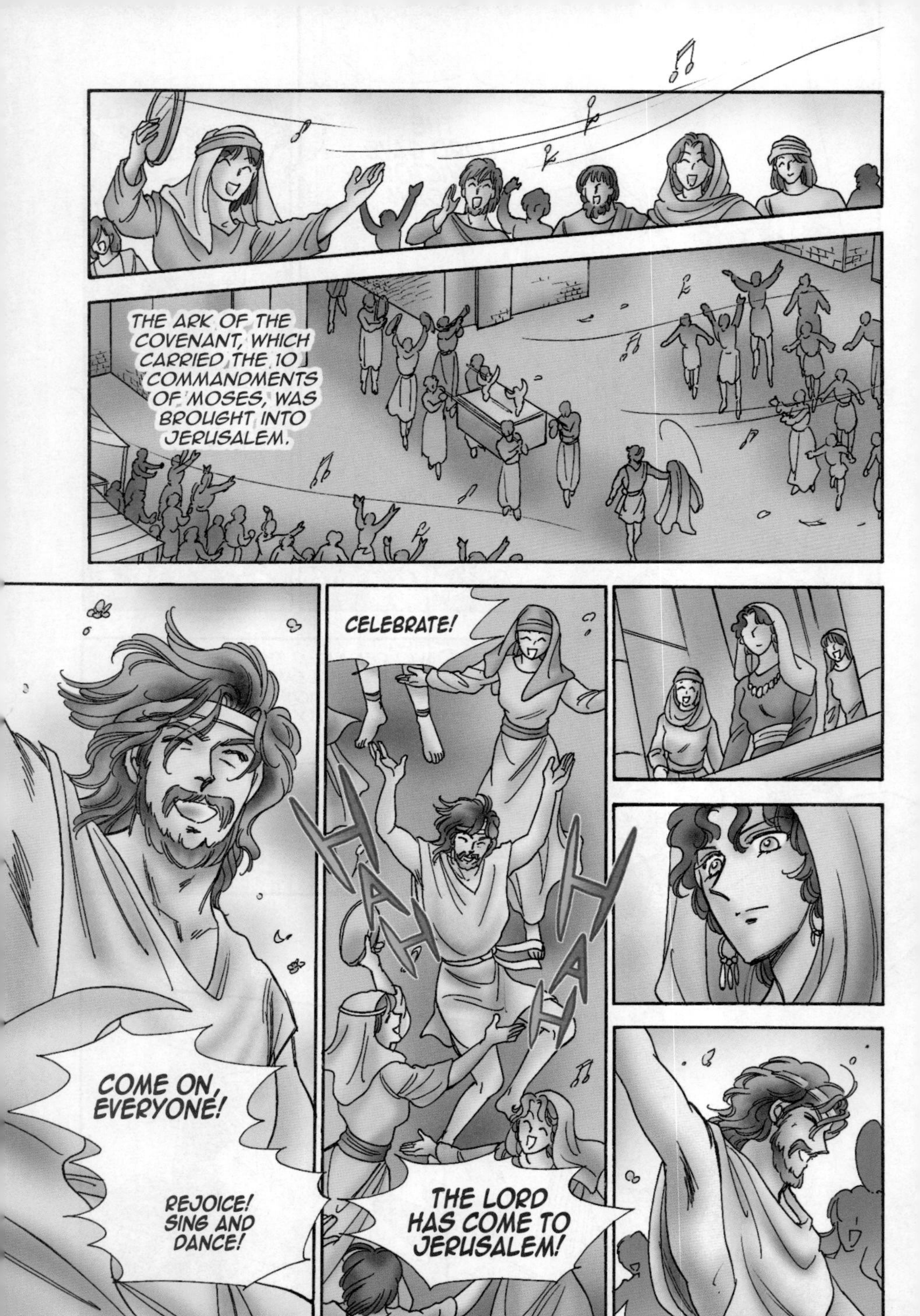
THE ARK OF THE COVENANT, WHICH CARRIED THE 10 COMMANDMENTS OF MOSES, WAS BROUGHT INTO JERUSALEM.
COME ON, EVERYONE!
REJOICE! SING AND DANCE!
CELEBRATE!
HAHA
HAHAH
THE LORD HAS COME TO JERUSALEM!

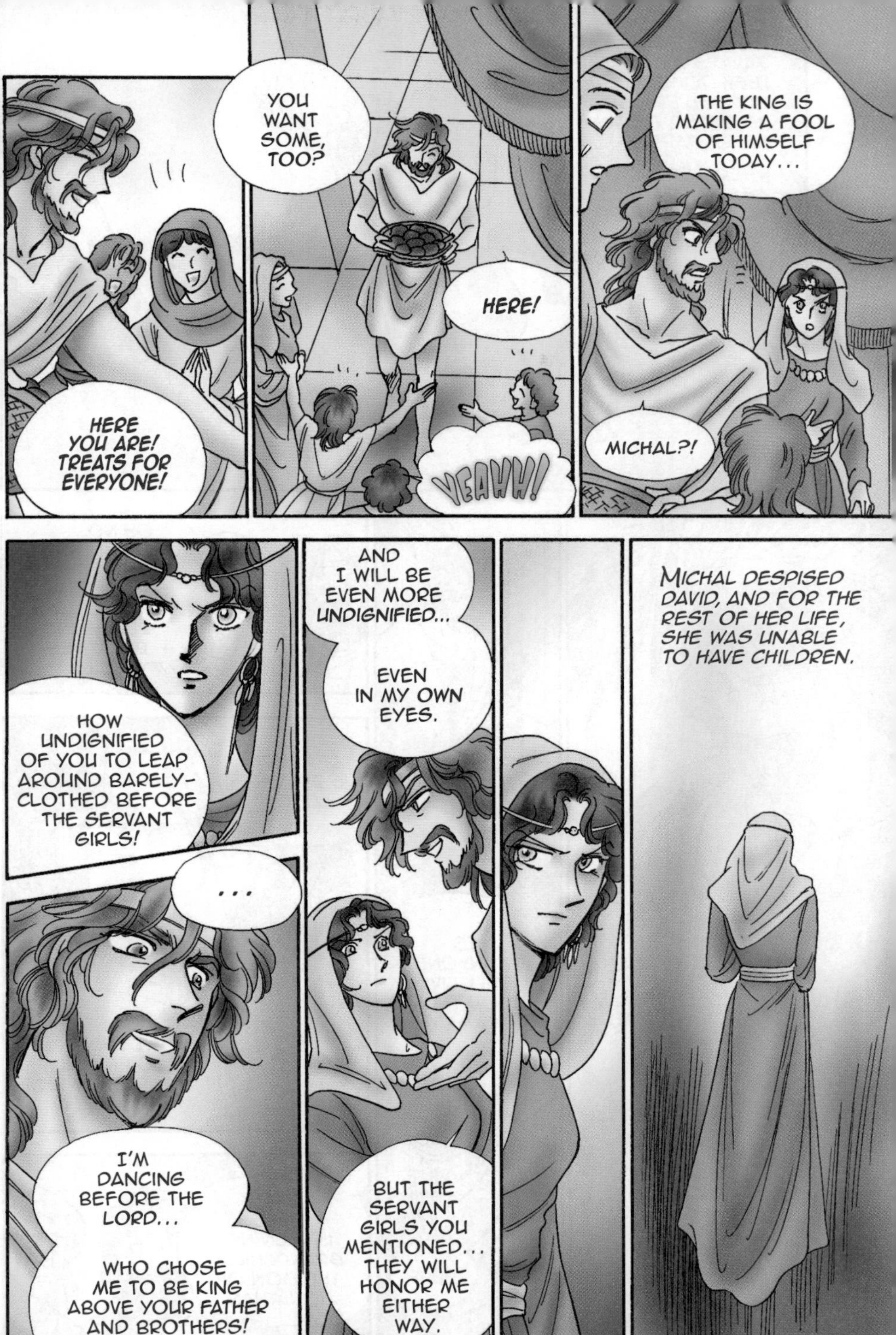
HERE YOU ARE! TREATS FOR EVERYONE!
YOU WANT SOME, TOO?
HERE!
YEAHH!
THE KING IS MAKING A FOOL OF HIMSELF TODAY...
MICHAL?!
HOW UNDIGNIFIED OF YOU TO LEAP AROUND BARELY-CLOTHED BEFORE THE SERVANT GIRLS!
...
I'M DANCING BEFORE THE LORD...
WHO CHOSE ME TO BE KING ABOVE YOUR FATHER AND BROTHERS!
AND I WILL BE EVEN MORE UNDIGNIFIED...
EVEN IN MY OWN EYES.
BUT THE SERVANT GIRLS YOU MENTIONED... THEY WILL HONOR ME EITHER WAY.
MICHAL DESPISED DAVID, AND FOR THE REST OF HER LIFE, SHE WAS UNABLE TO HAVE CHILDREN.

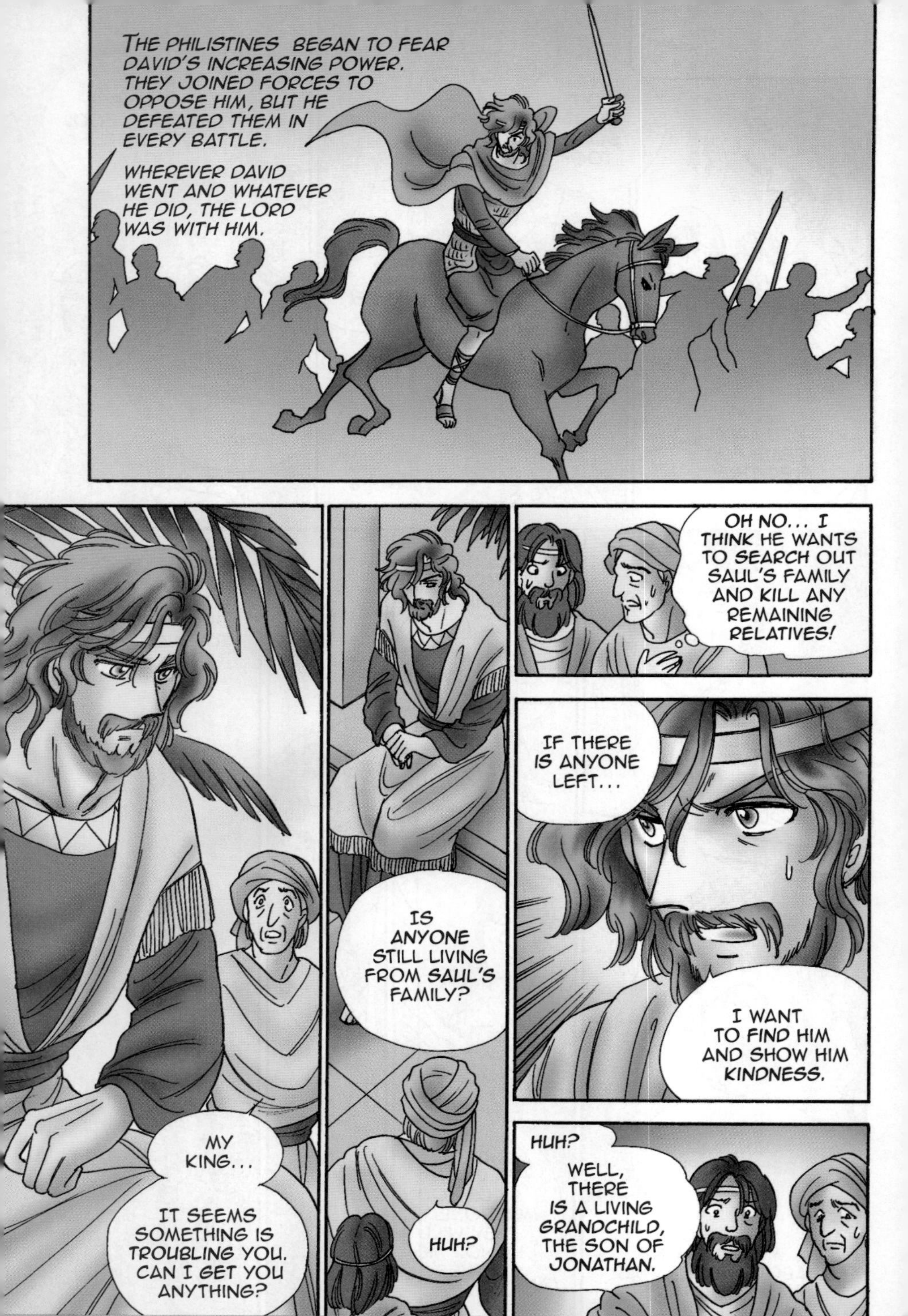

THE PHILISTINES BEGAN TO FEAR DAVID'S INCREASING POWER. THEY JOINED FORCES TO OPPOSE HIM, BUT HE DEFEATED THEM IN EVERY BATTLE.
WHEREVER DAVID WENT AND WHATEVER HE DID, THE LORD WAS WITH HIM.
MY KING...
IT SEEMS SOMETHING IS TROUBLING YOU. CAN I GET YOU ANYTHING?
IS ANYONE STILL LIVING FROM SAUL'S FAMILY?
HUH?
OH NO... I THINK HE WANTS TO SEARCH OUT SAUL'S FAMILY AND KILL ANY REMAINING RELATIVES!
IF THERE IS ANYONE LEFT...
I WANT TO FIND HIM AND SHOW HIM KINDNESS.
HUH?
WELL, THERE IS A LIVING GRANDCHILD, THE SON OF JONATHAN.

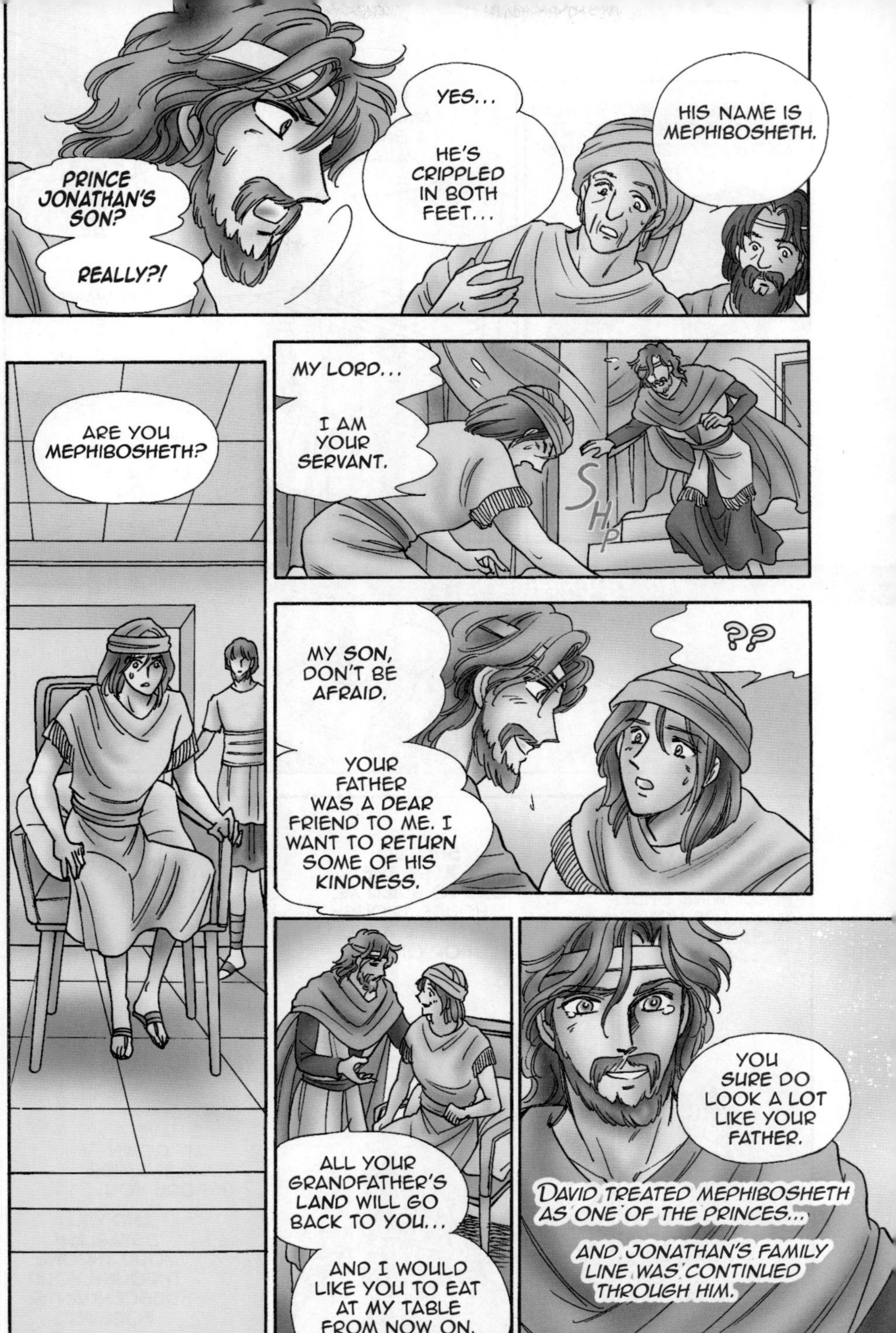
PRINCE JONATHAN'S SON?
REALLY?!
YES...
HE'S CRIPPLED IN BOTH FEET...
HIS NAME IS MEPHIBOSHETH.
ARE YOU MEPHIBOSHETH?
MY LORD...
I AM YOUR SERVANT.
SHP
MY SON, DON'T BE AFRAID.
YOUR FATHER WAS A DEAR FRIEND TO ME. I WANT TO RETURN SOME OF HIS KINDNESS.
??
ALL YOUR GRANDFATHER'S LAND WILL GO BACK TO YOU...
AND I WOULD LIKE YOU TO EAT AT MY TABLE FROM NOW ON.
YOU SURE DO LOOK A LOT LIKE YOUR FATHER.
DAVID TREATED MEPHIBOSHETH AS ONE OF THE PRINCES...
AND JONATHAN'S FAMILY LINE WAS CONTINUED THROUGH HIM.

WITH SAMUEL GONE, GOD RAISED UP THE PROPHET NATHAN TO BRING GOD'S WORD TO THE PEOPLE.

NATHAN...

YES, DAVID?

HERE I AM, LIVING IN A SPLENDID PALACE...

WHILE THE ARK OF THE LORD IS STILL IN A TENT.

I WANT TO BUILD A TEMPLE FOR THE ARK.

DO AS YOU WISH. THE LORD IS WITH YOU.

BUT THAT NIGHT...

NATHAN, GO AND TELL MY SERVANT DAVID...

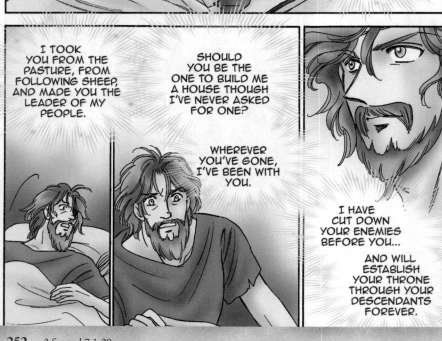

I TOOK YOU FROM THE PASTURE, FROM FOLLOWING SHEEP, AND MADE YOU THE LEADER OF MY PEOPLE.

SHOULD YOU BE THE ONE TO BUILD ME A HOUSE THOUGH I'VE NEVER ASKED FOR ONE?

WHEREVER YOU'VE GONE, I'VE BEEN WITH YOU.

I HAVE CUT DOWN YOUR ENEMIES BEFORE YOU...

AND WILL ESTABLISH YOUR THRONE THROUGH YOUR DESCENDANTS FOREVER.

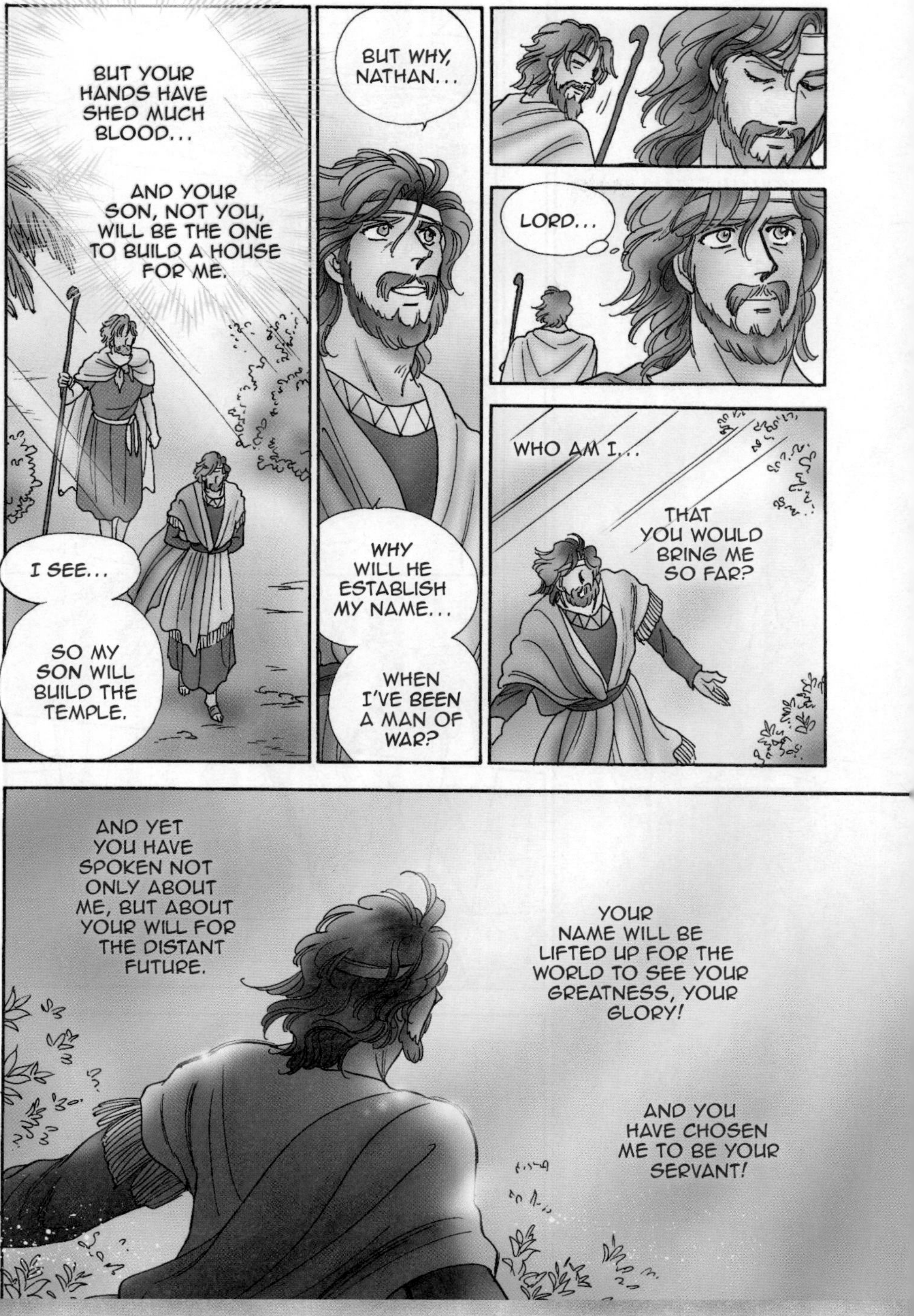
BUT YOUR HANDS HAVE SHED MUCH BLOOD...
AND YOUR SON, NOT YOU, WILL BE THE ONE TO BUILD A HOUSE FOR ME.
I SEE...
SO MY SON WILL BUILD THE TEMPLE.
BUT WHY, NATHAN...
WHY WILL HE ESTABLISH MY NAME...
WHEN I'VE BEEN A MAN OF WAR?
LORD...
WHO AM I...
THAT YOU WOULD BRING ME SO FAR?
AND YET YOU HAVE SPOKEN NOT ONLY ABOUT ME, BUT ABOUT YOUR WILL FOR THE DISTANT FUTURE.
YOUR NAME WILL BE LIFTED UP FOR THE WORLD TO SEE YOUR GREATNESS, YOUR GLORY!
AND YOU HAVE CHOSEN ME TO BE YOUR SERVANT!

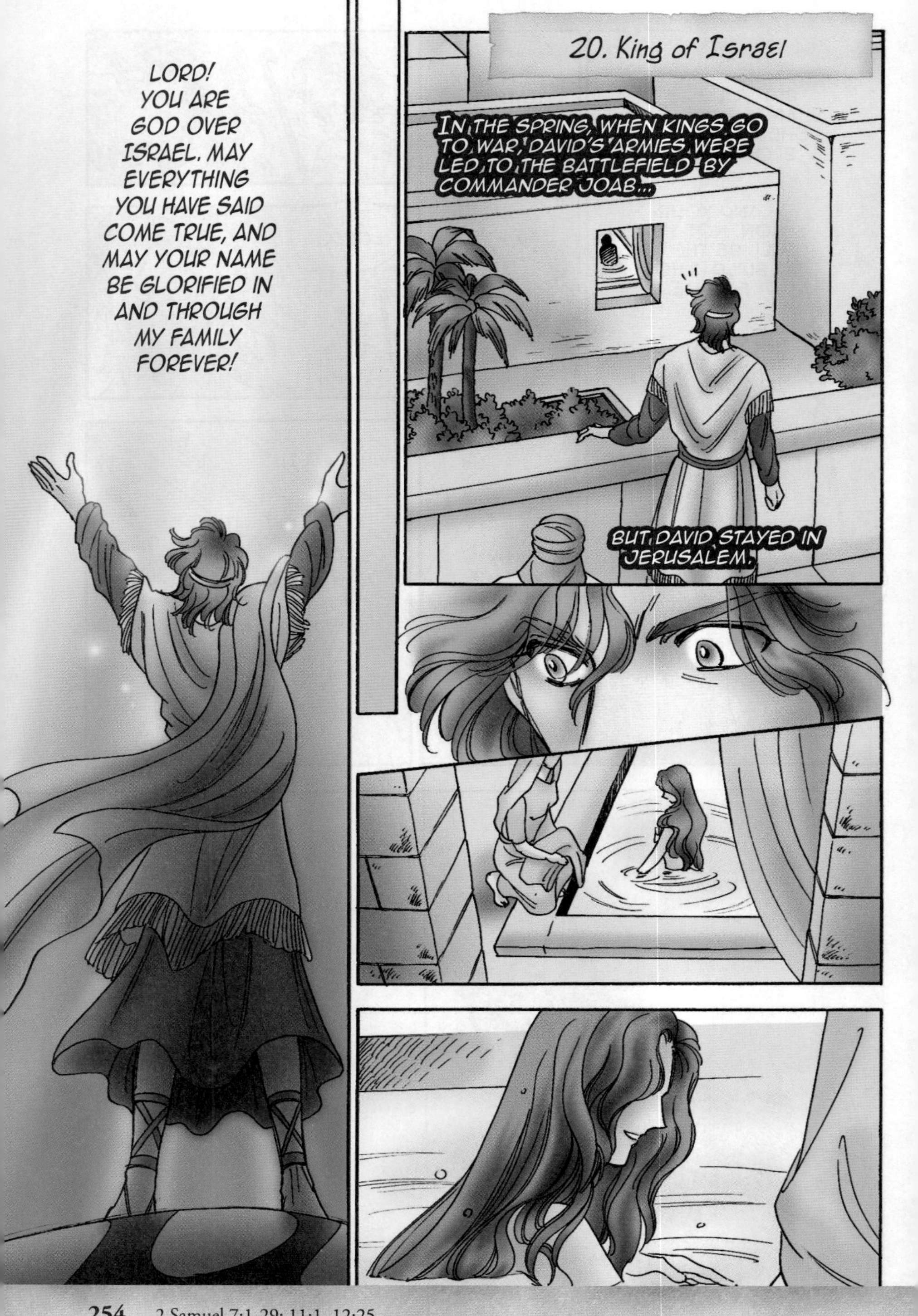
LORD! YOU ARE GOD OVER ISRAEL. MAY EVERYTHING YOU HAVE SAID COME TRUE, AND MAY YOUR NAME BE GLORIFIED IN AND THROUGH MY FAMILY FOREVER!
20. King of Israel
IN THE SPRING, WHEN KINGS GO TO WAR, DAVID'S ARMIES WERE LED TO THE BATTLEFIELD BY COMMANDER JOAB...
BUT DAVID STAYED IN JERUSALEM.

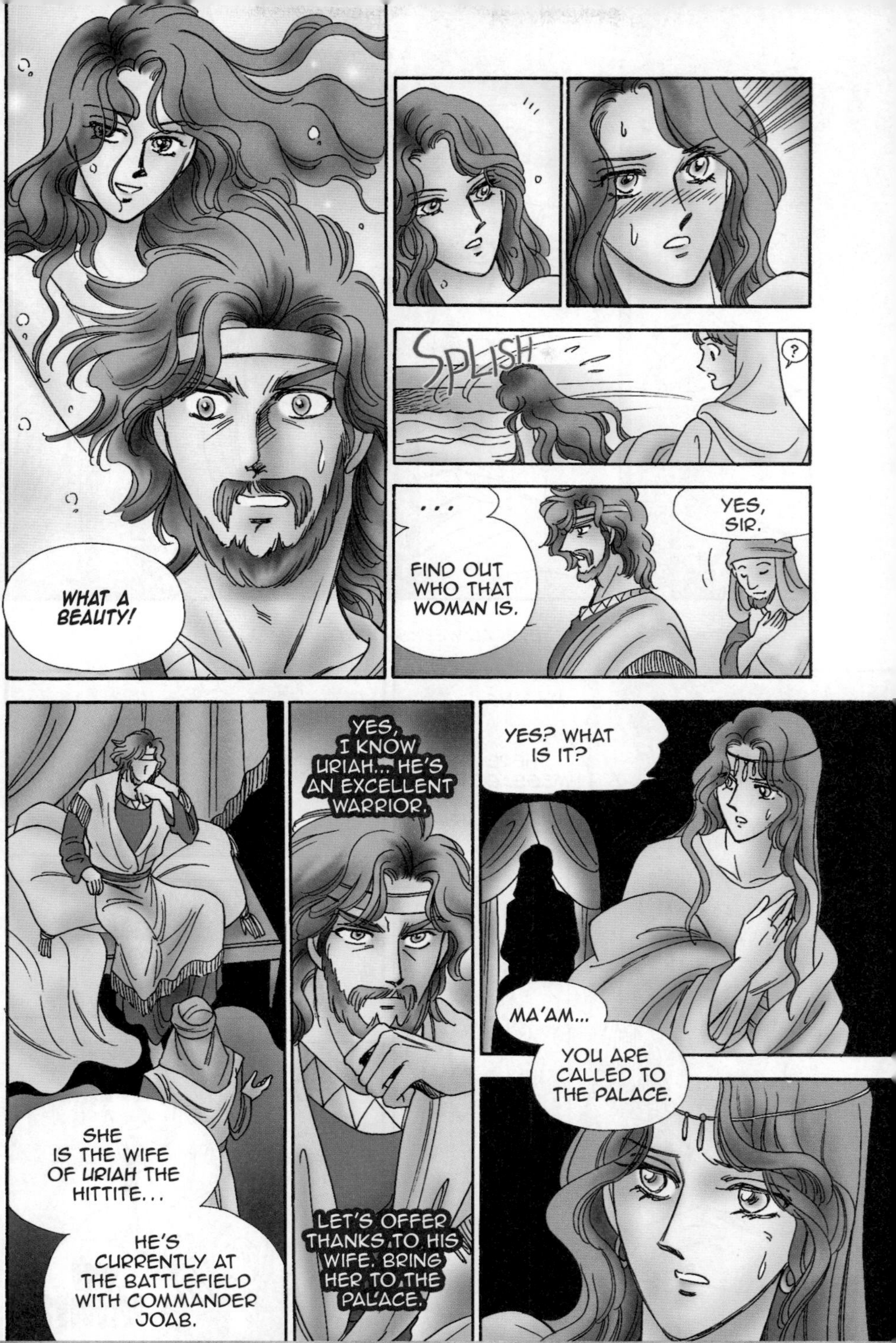

SPLISH
?
WHAT A BEAUTY!
...
FIND OUT WHO THAT WOMAN IS.
YES, SIR.
SHE IS THE WIFE OF URIAH THE HITTITE...
HE'S CURRENTLY AT THE BATTLEFIELD WITH COMMANDER JOAB.
YES, I KNOW URIAH... HE'S AN EXCELLENT WARRIOR.
LET'S OFFER THANKS TO HIS WIFE. BRING HER TO THE PALACE.
YES? WHAT IS IT?
MA'AM...
YOU ARE CALLED TO THE PALACE.

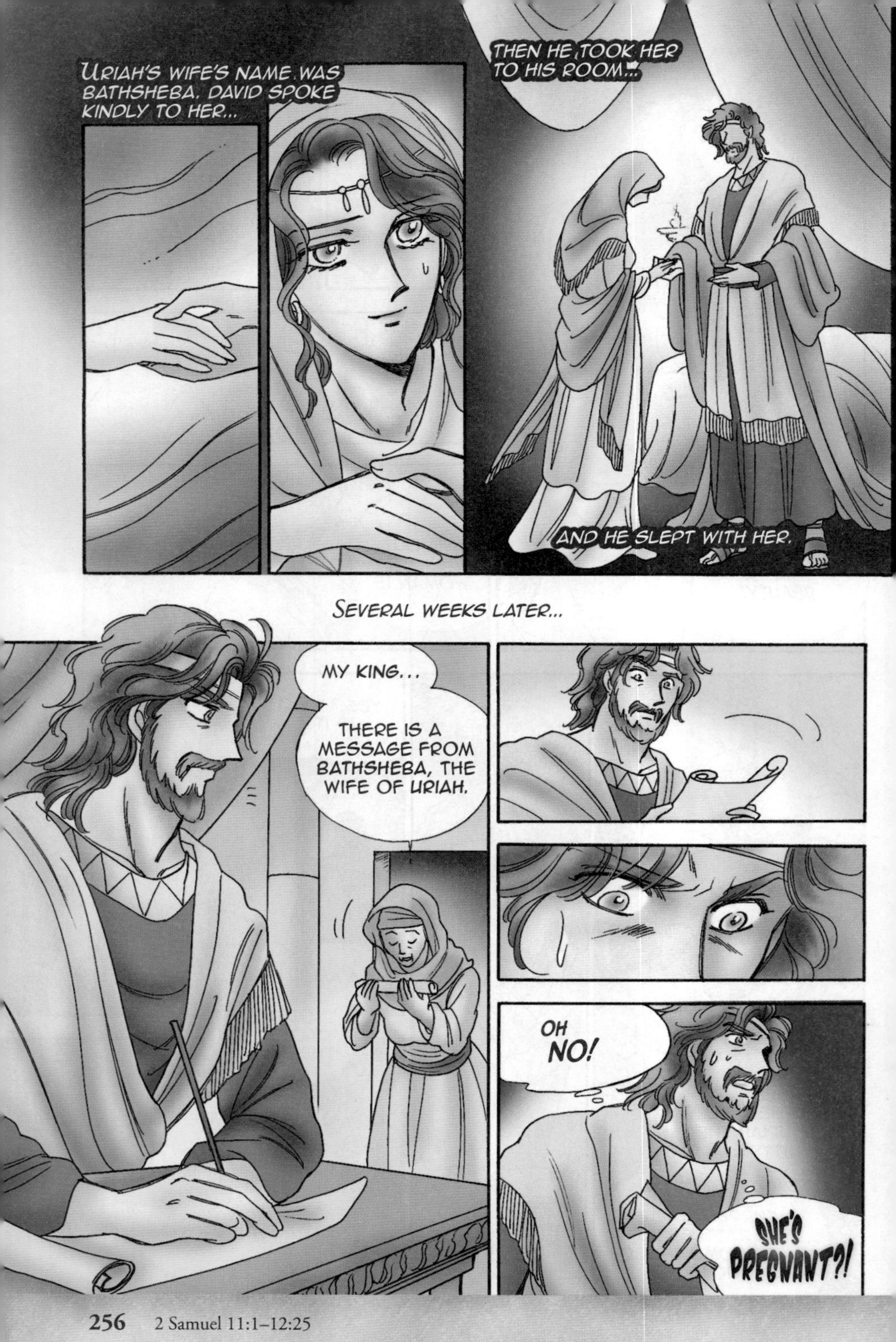
URIAH'S WIFE'S NAME WAS BATHSHEBA. DAVID SPOKE KINDLY TO HER...
THEN HE TOOK HER TO HIS ROOM...
AND HE SLEPT WITH HER.
SEVERAL WEEKS LATER...
MY KING...
THERE IS A MESSAGE FROM BATHSHEBA, THE WIFE OF URIAH.
OH NO!
SHE'S PREGNANT?!

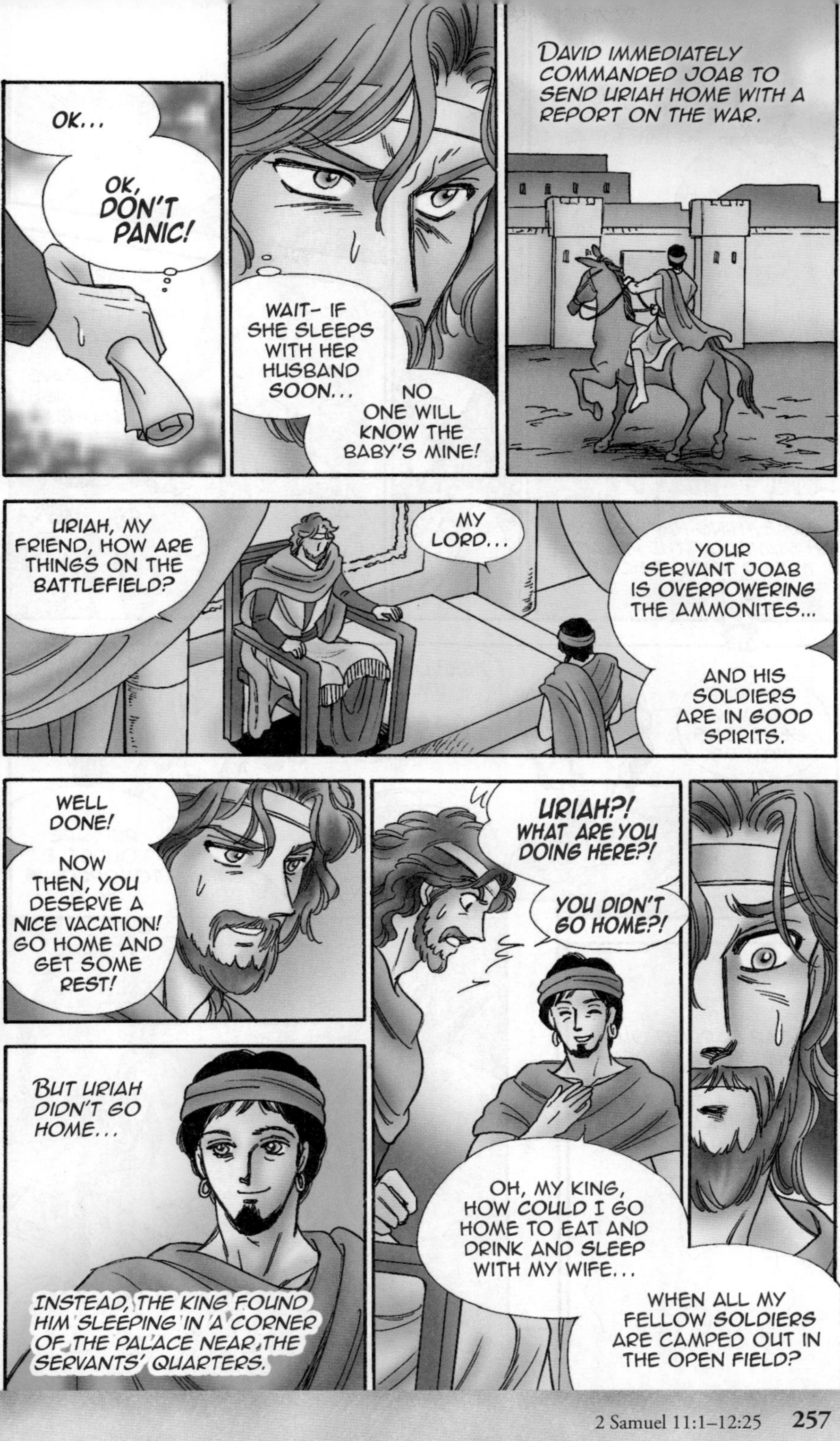
OK...
OK, DON'T PANIC!
WAIT- IF SHE SLEEPS WITH HER HUSBAND SOON...
NO ONE WILL KNOW THE BABY'S MINE!
DAVID IMMEDIATELY COMMANDED JOAB TO SEND URIAH HOME WITH A REPORT ON THE WAR.
URIAH, MY FRIEND, HOW ARE THINGS ON THE BATTLEFIELD?
MY LORD...
YOUR SERVANT JOAB IS OVERPOWERING THE AMMONITES...
AND HIS SOLDIERS ARE IN GOOD SPIRITS.
WELL DONE!
NOW THEN, YOU DESERVE A NICE VACATION! GO HOME AND GET SOME REST!
BUT URIAH DIDN'T GO HOME...
INSTEAD, THE KING FOUND HIM SLEEPING IN A CORNER OF THE PALACE NEAR THE SERVANTS' QUARTERS.
URIAH?! WHAT ARE YOU DOING HERE?!
YOU DIDN'T GO HOME?!
OH, MY KING, HOW COULD I GO HOME TO EAT AND DRINK AND SLEEP WITH MY WIFE...
WHEN ALL MY FELLOW SOLDIERS ARE CAMPED OUT IN THE OPEN FIELD?

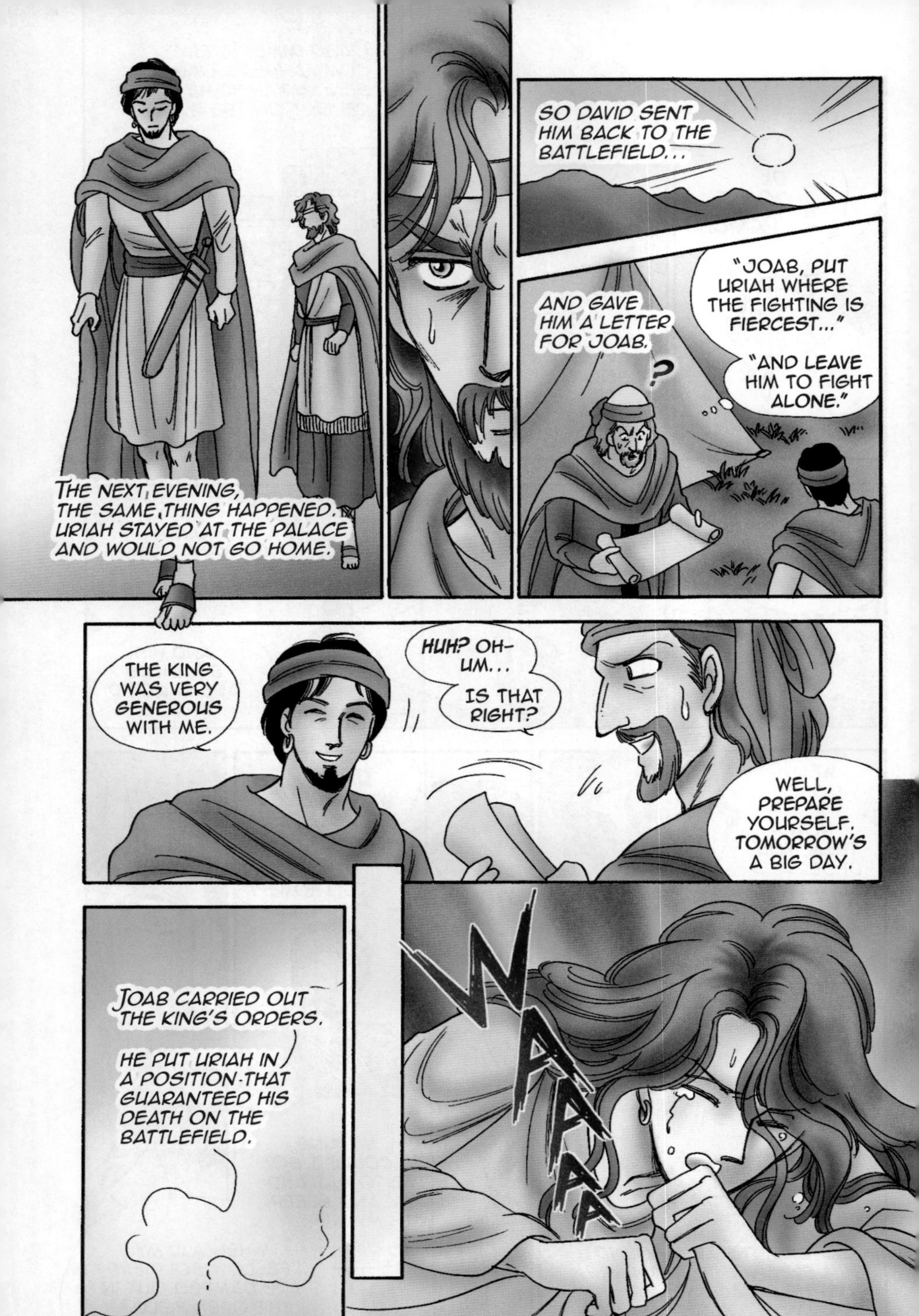
THE NEXT EVENING, THE SAME THING HAPPENED. URIAH STAYED AT THE PALACE AND WOULD NOT GO HOME.
SO DAVID SENT HIM BACK TO THE BATTLEFIELD...
AND GAVE HIM A LETTER FOR JOAB.
"JOAB, PUT URIAH WHERE THE FIGHTING IS FIERCEST..."
"AND LEAVE HIM TO FIGHT ALONE."
?
THE KING WAS VERY GENEROUS WITH ME.
HUH? OH-UM...
IS THAT RIGHT?
WELL, PREPARE YOURSELF. TOMORROW'S A BIG DAY.
JOAB CARRIED OUT THE KING'S ORDERS.
HE PUT URIAH IN A POSITION THAT GUARANTEED HIS DEATH ON THE BATTLEFIELD.
WAAAAA

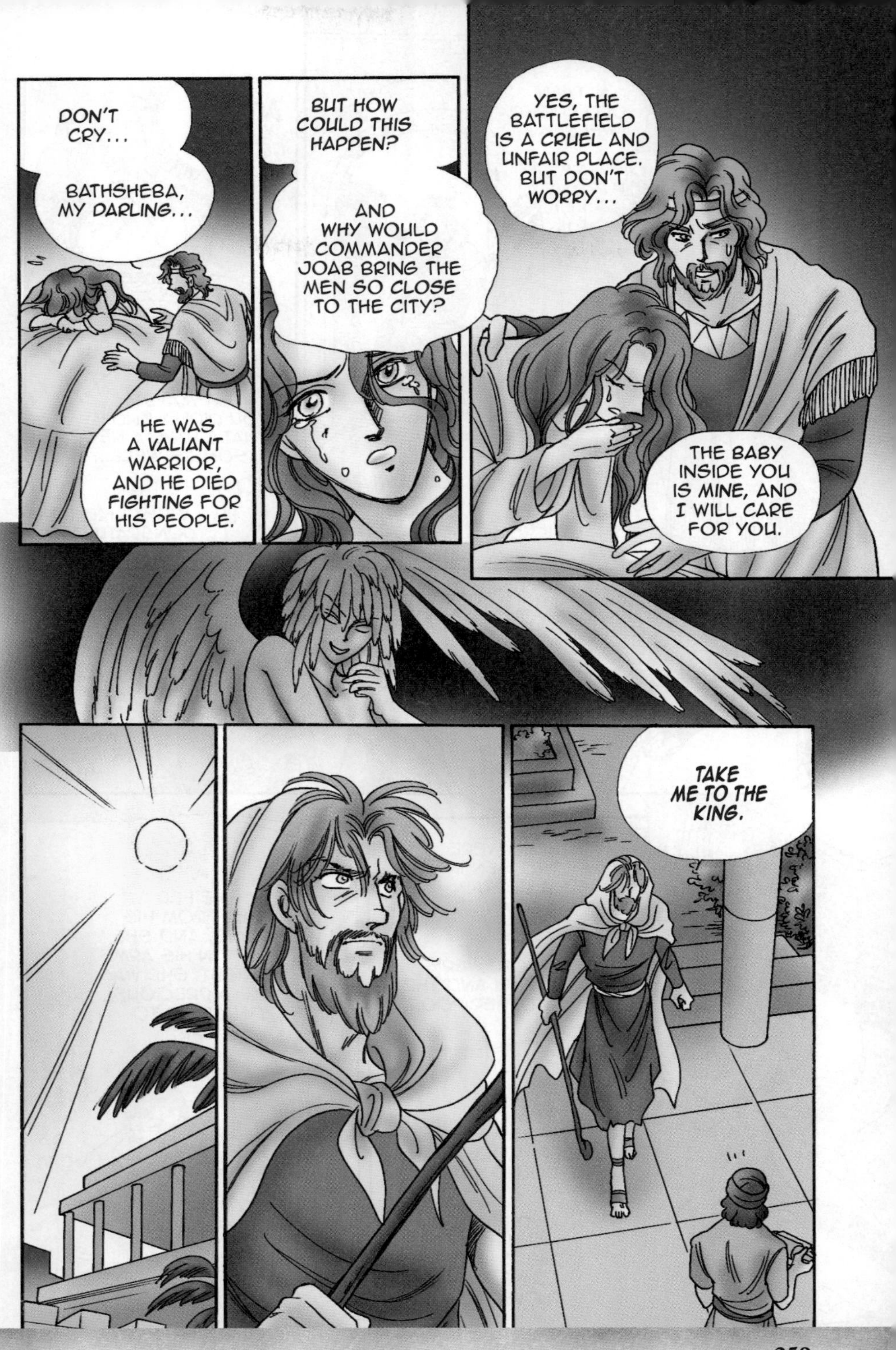
DON'T CRY...
BATHSHEBA, MY DARLING...
HE WAS A VALIANT WARRIOR, AND HE DIED FIGHTING FOR HIS PEOPLE.
BUT HOW COULD THIS HAPPEN?
AND WHY WOULD COMMANDER JOAB BRING THE MEN SO CLOSE TO THE CITY?
YES, THE BATTLEFIELD IS A CRUEL AND UNFAIR PLACE. BUT DON'T WORRY...
THE BABY INSIDE YOU IS MINE, AND I WILL CARE FOR YOU.
TAKE ME TO THE KING.

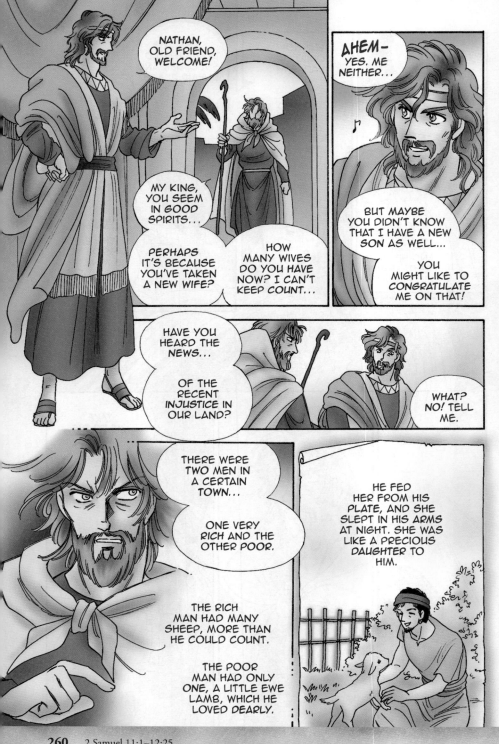

NATHAN, OLD FRIEND, WELCOME!

MY KING, YOU SEEM IN GOOD SPIRITS...

PERHAPS IT'S BECAUSE YOU'VE TAKEN A NEW WIFE?

HOW MANY WIVES DO YOU HAVE NOW? I CAN'T KEEP COUNT...

AHEM— YES. ME NEITHER...

BUT MAYBE YOU DIDN'T KNOW THAT I HAVE A NEW SON AS WELL...

YOU MIGHT LIKE TO CONGRATULATE ME ON THAT!

HAVE YOU HEARD THE NEWS...

OF THE RECENT INJUSTICE IN OUR LAND?

WHAT? NO! TELL ME.

THERE WERE TWO MEN IN A CERTAIN TOWN...

ONE VERY RICH AND THE OTHER POOR.

THE RICH MAN HAD MANY SHEEP, MORE THAN HE COULD COUNT.

THE POOR MAN HAD ONLY ONE, A LITTLE EWE LAMB, WHICH HE LOVED DEARLY.

HE FED HER FROM HIS PLATE, AND SHE SLEPT IN HIS ARMS AT NIGHT. SHE WAS LIKE A PRECIOUS DAUGHTER TO HIM.

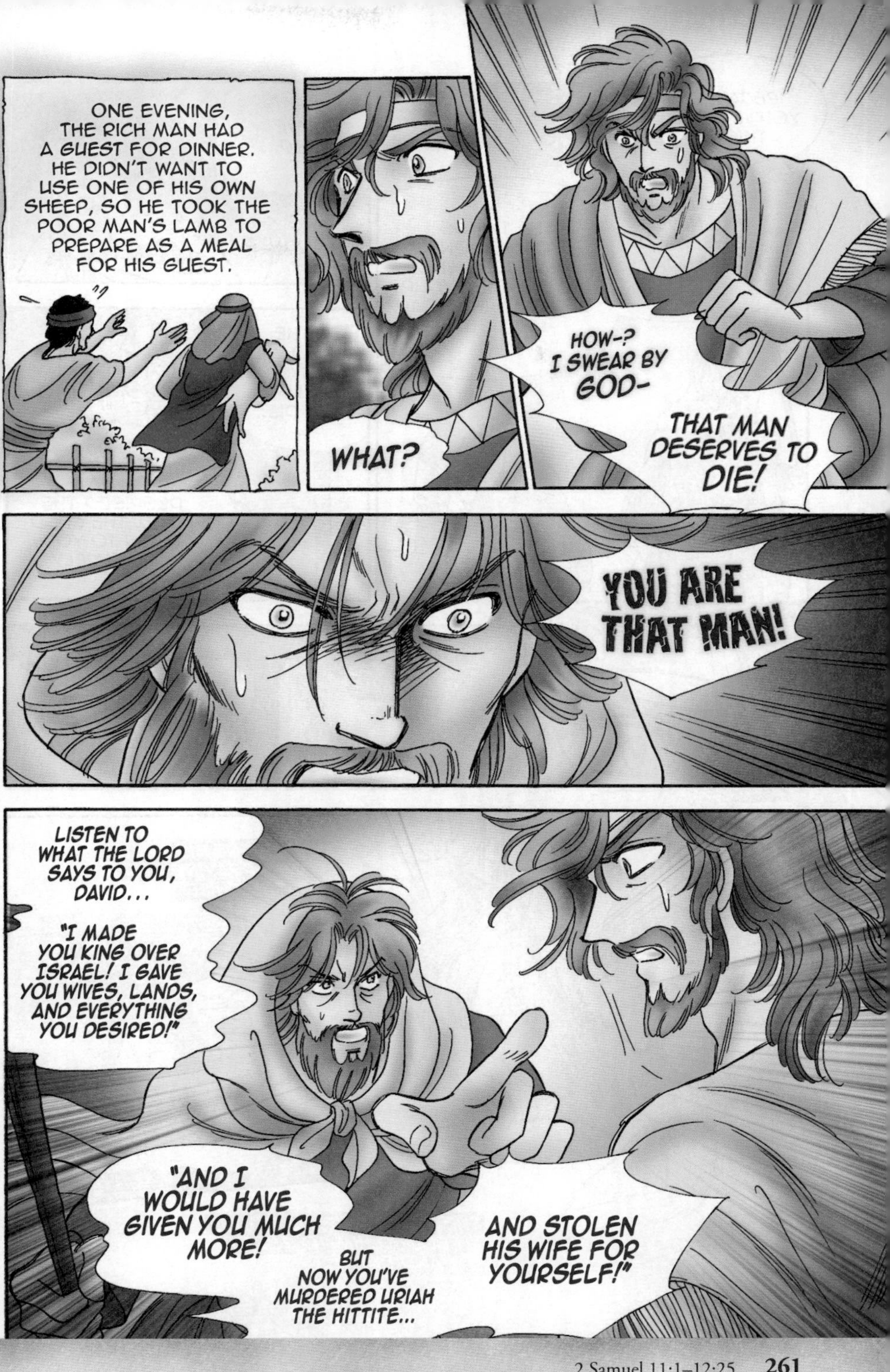
ONE EVENING, THE RICH MAN HAD A GUEST FOR DINNER. HE DIDN'T WANT TO USE ONE OF HIS OWN SHEEP, SO HE TOOK THE POOR MAN'S LAMB TO PREPARE AS A MEAL FOR HIS GUEST.
WHAT?
HOW-? I SWEAR BY GOD-
THAT MAN DESERVES TO DIE!
YOU ARE THAT MAN!
LISTEN TO WHAT THE LORD SAYS TO YOU, DAVID...
"I MADE YOU KING OVER ISRAEL! I GAVE YOU WIVES, LANDS, AND EVERYTHING YOU DESIRED!"
"AND I WOULD HAVE GIVEN YOU MUCH MORE!
BUT NOW YOU'VE MURDERED URIAH THE HITTITE...
AND STOLEN HIS WIFE FOR YOURSELF!"

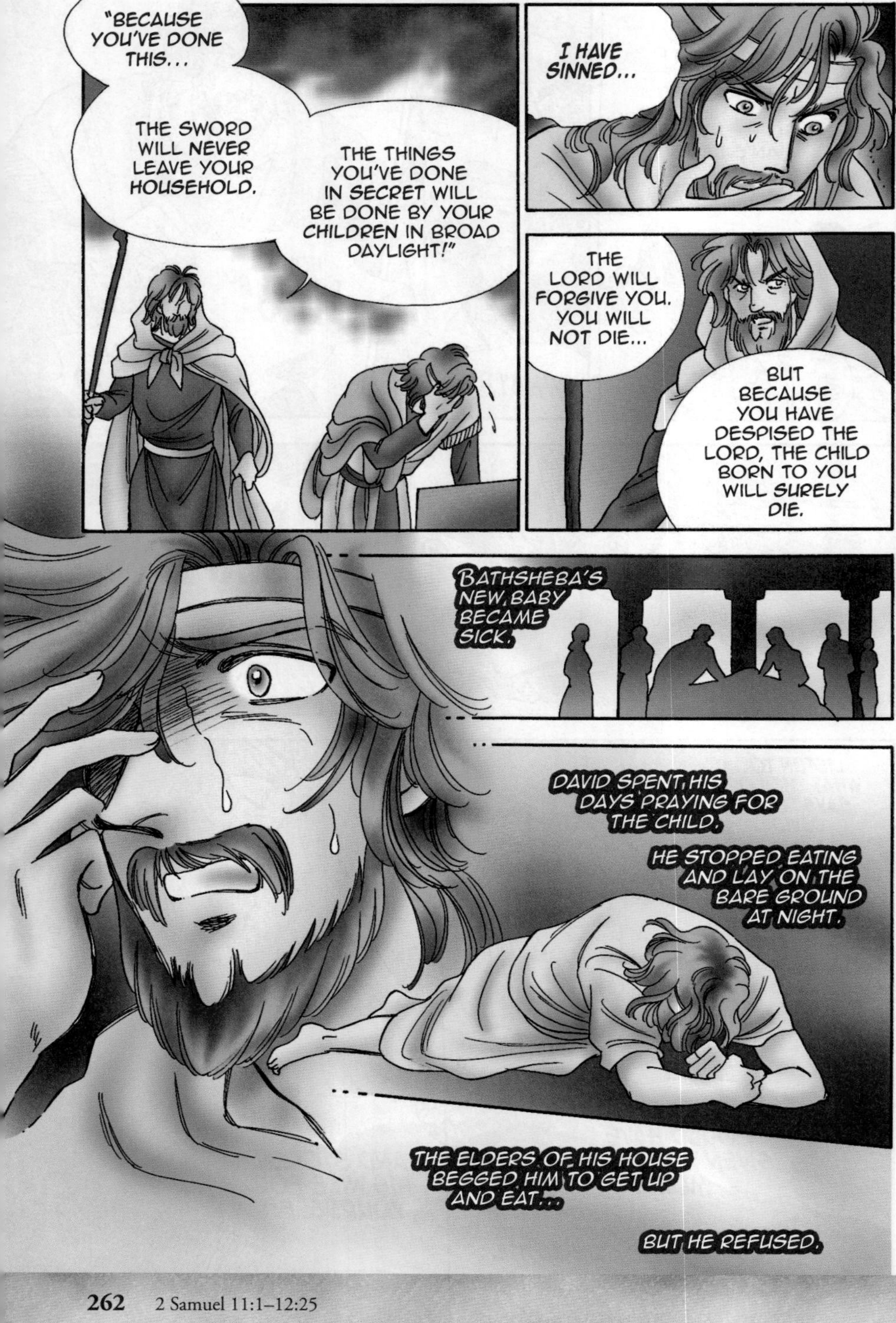
"BECAUSE YOU'VE DONE THIS...
THE SWORD WILL NEVER LEAVE YOUR HOUSEHOLD.
THE THINGS YOU'VE DONE IN SECRET WILL BE DONE BY YOUR CHILDREN IN BROAD DAYLIGHT!"
I HAVE SINNED...
THE LORD WILL FORGIVE YOU. YOU WILL NOT DIE...
BUT BECAUSE YOU HAVE DESPISED THE LORD, THE CHILD BORN TO YOU WILL SURELY DIE.
BATHSHEBA'S NEW BABY BECAME SICK.
DAVID SPENT HIS DAYS PRAYING FOR THE CHILD.
HE STOPPED EATING AND LAY ON THE BARE GROUND AT NIGHT.
THE ELDERS OF HIS HOUSE BEGGED HIM TO GET UP AND EAT...
BUT HE REFUSED.

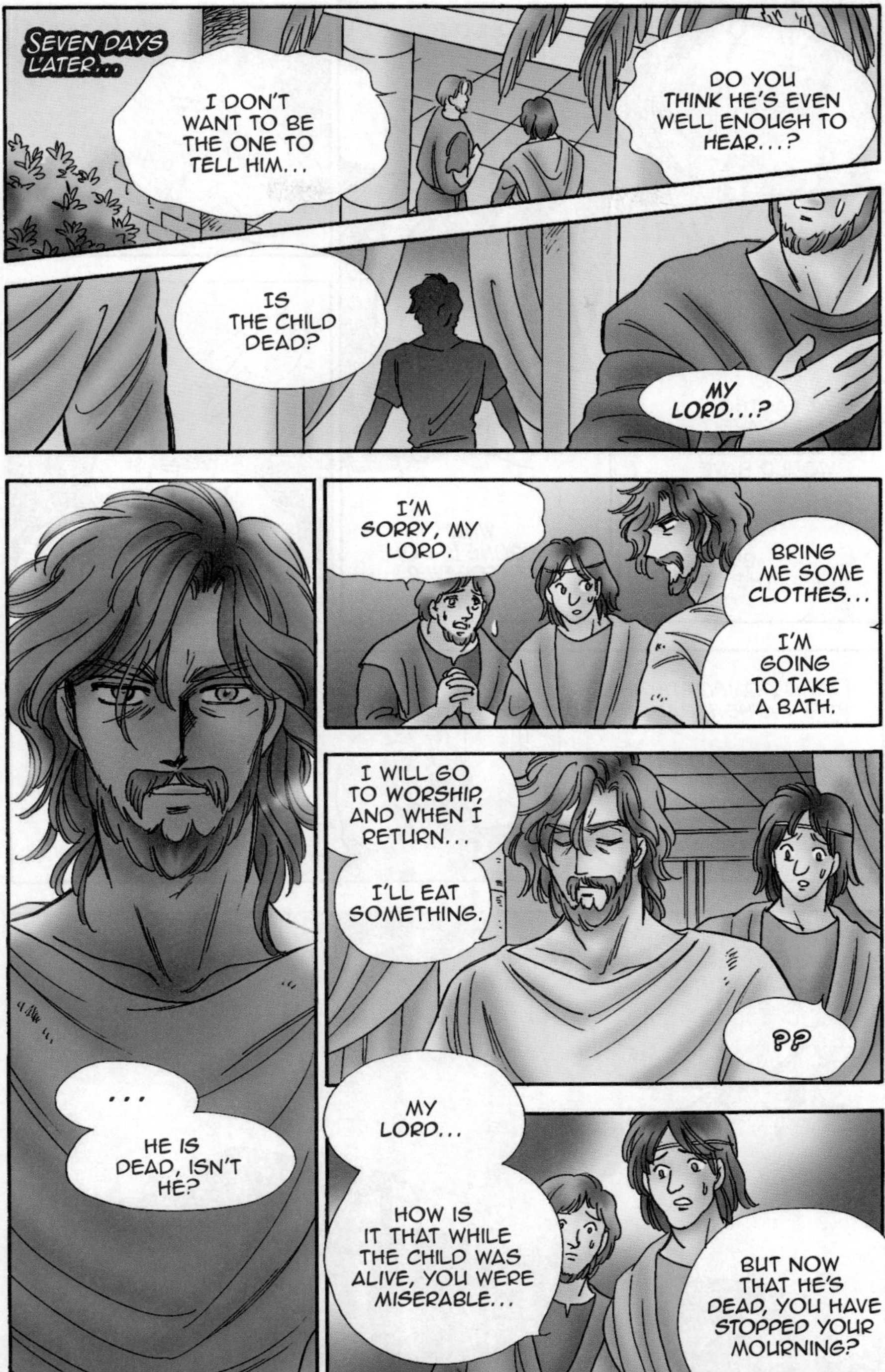
SEVEN DAYS LATER...
I DON'T WANT TO BE THE ONE TO TELL HIM...
DO YOU THINK HE'S EVEN WELL ENOUGH TO HEAR...?
MY LORD...?
IS THE CHILD DEAD?
...
HE IS DEAD, ISN'T HE?
I'M SORRY, MY LORD.
BRING ME SOME CLOTHES...
I'M GOING TO TAKE A BATH.
I WILL GO TO WORSHIP, AND WHEN I RETURN...
I'LL EAT SOMETHING.
??
MY LORD...
HOW IS IT THAT WHILE THE CHILD WAS ALIVE, YOU WERE MISERABLE...
BUT NOW THAT HE'S DEAD, YOU HAVE STOPPED YOUR MOURNING?

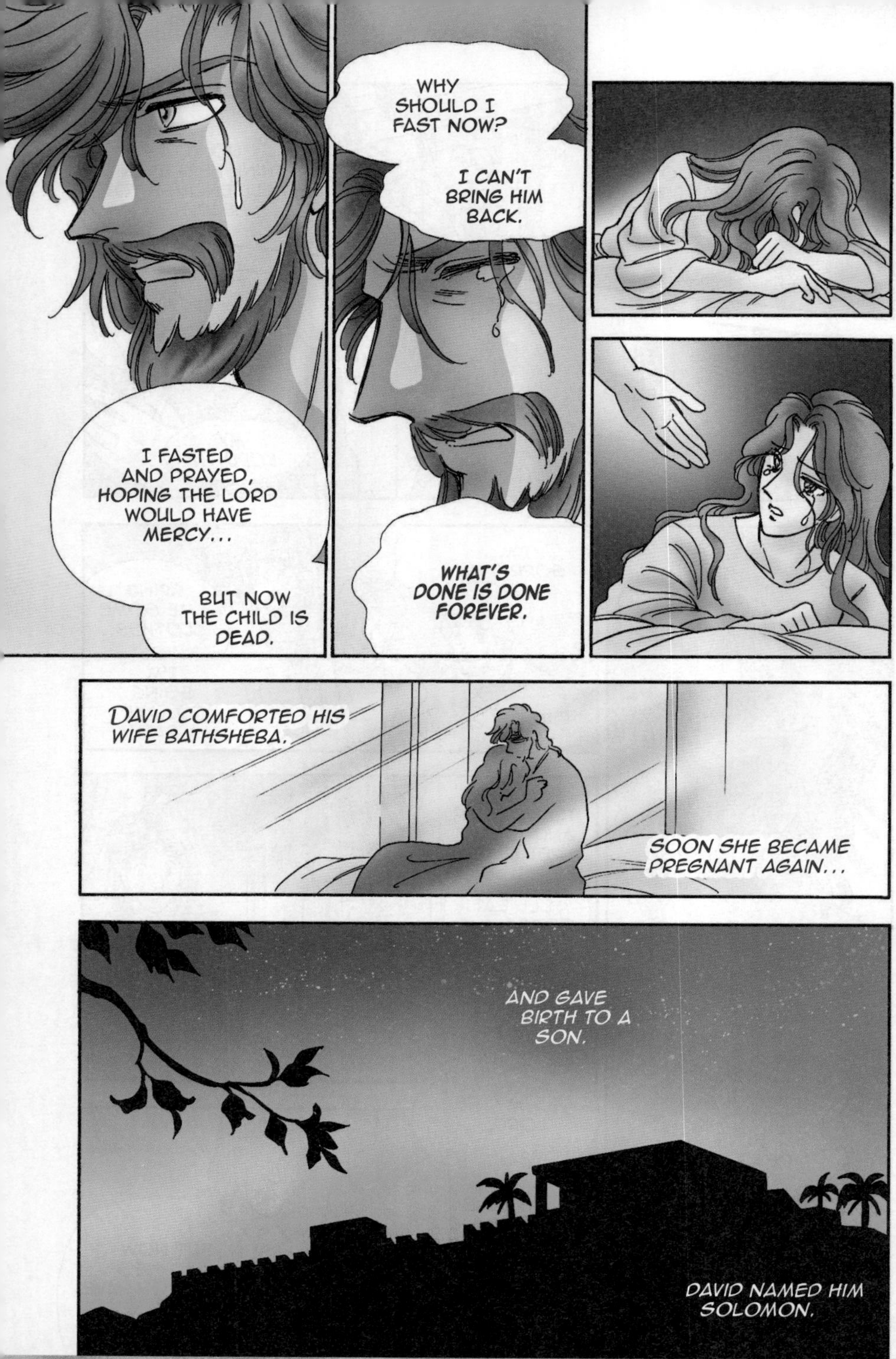
I FASTED AND PRAYED, HOPING THE LORD WOULD HAVE MERCY...
BUT NOW THE CHILD IS DEAD.
WHY SHOULD I FAST NOW?
I CAN'T BRING HIM BACK.
WHAT'S DONE IS DONE FOREVER.
DAVID COMFORTED HIS WIFE BATHSHEBA.
SOON SHE BECAME PREGNANT AGAIN...
AND GAVE BIRTH TO A SON.
DAVID NAMED HIM SOLOMON.

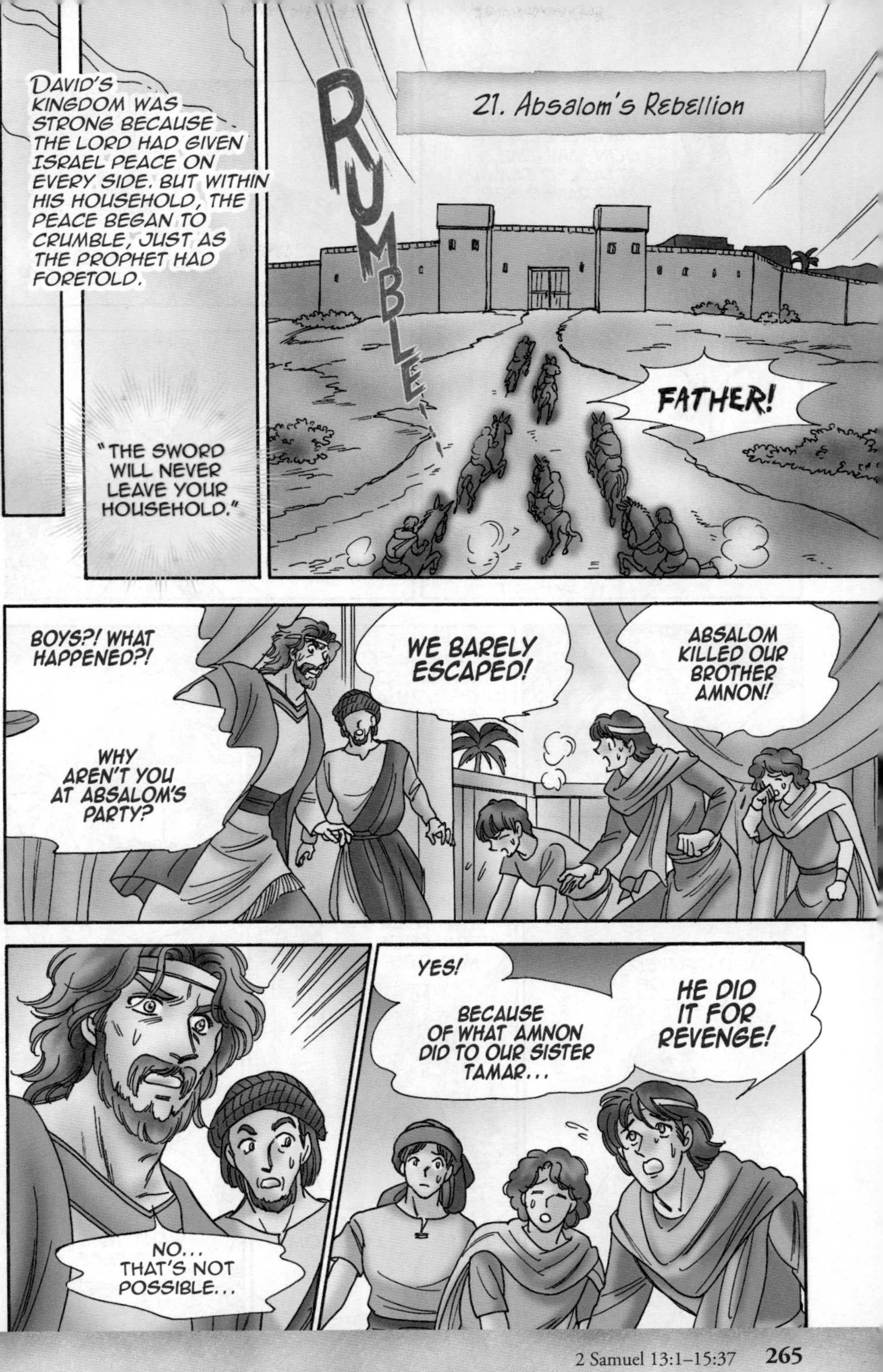
21. Absalom's Rebellion
David's kingdom was strong because the Lord had given Israel peace on every side. But within his household, the peace began to crumble, just as the prophet had foretold.
"The sword will never leave your household."
RUMBLE...
FATHER!
BOYS?! WHAT HAPPENED?!
WHY AREN'T YOU AT ABSALOM'S PARTY?
WE BARELY ESCAPED!
ABSALOM KILLED OUR BROTHER AMNON!
NO... THAT'S NOT POSSIBLE...
YES!
BECAUSE OF WHAT AMNON DID TO OUR SISTER TAMAR...
HE DID IT FOR REVENGE!

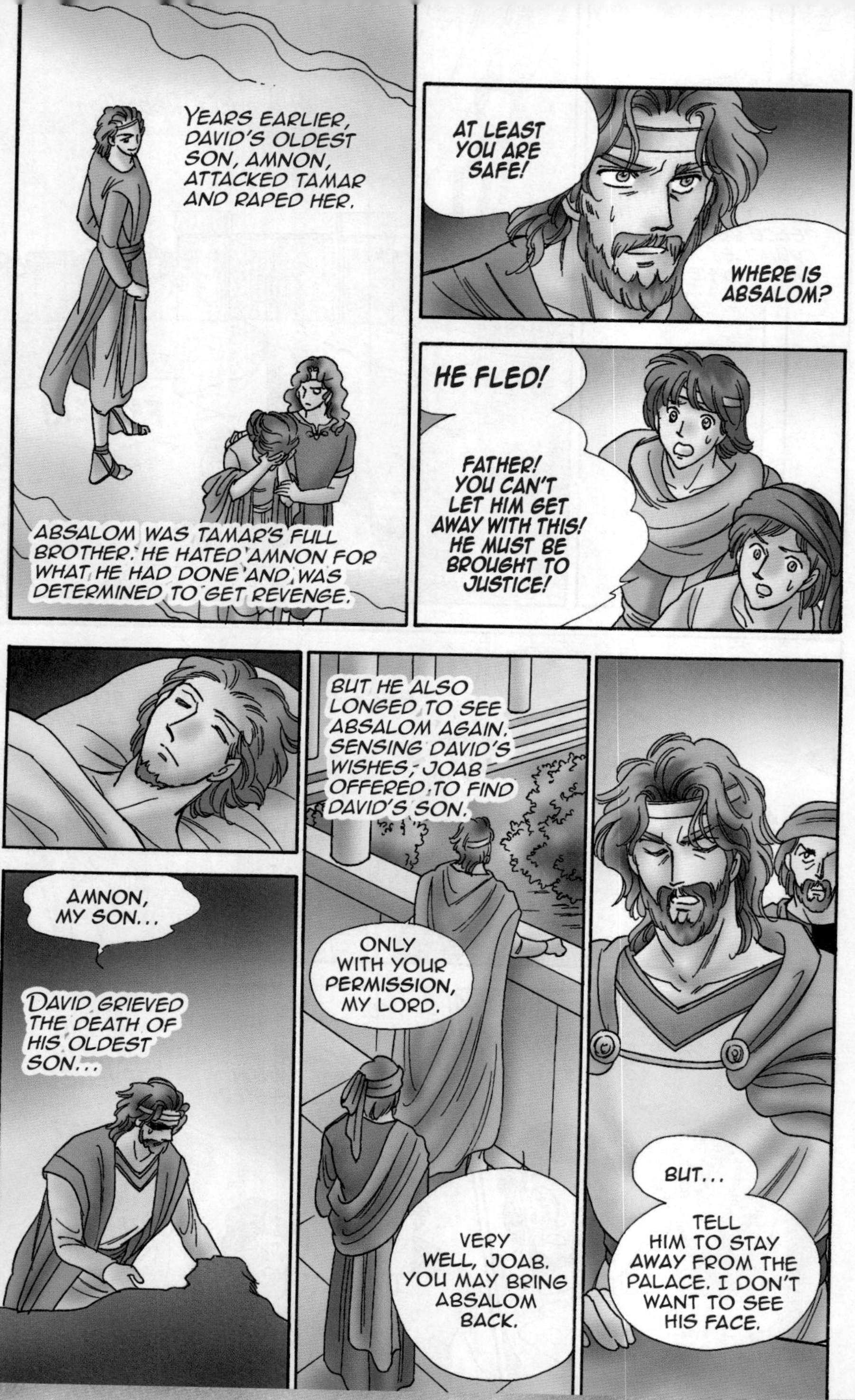
YEARS EARLIER, DAVID'S OLDEST SON, AMNON, ATTACKED TAMAR AND RAPED HER.
ABSALOM WAS TAMAR'S FULL BROTHER. HE HATED AMNON FOR WHAT HE HAD DONE AND WAS DETERMINED TO GET REVENGE.
AT LEAST YOU ARE SAFE!
WHERE IS ABSALOM?
HE FLED!
FATHER! YOU CAN'T LET HIM GET AWAY WITH THIS! HE MUST BE BROUGHT TO JUSTICE!
AMNON, MY SON...
DAVID GRIEVED THE DEATH OF HIS OLDEST SON...
BUT HE ALSO LONGED TO SEE ABSALOM AGAIN. SENSING DAVID'S WISHES, JOAB OFFERED TO FIND DAVID'S SON.
ONLY WITH YOUR PERMISSION, MY LORD.
VERY WELL, JOAB. YOU MAY BRING ABSALOM BACK.
BUT...
TELL HIM TO STAY AWAY FROM THE PALACE. I DON'T WANT TO SEE HIS FACE.

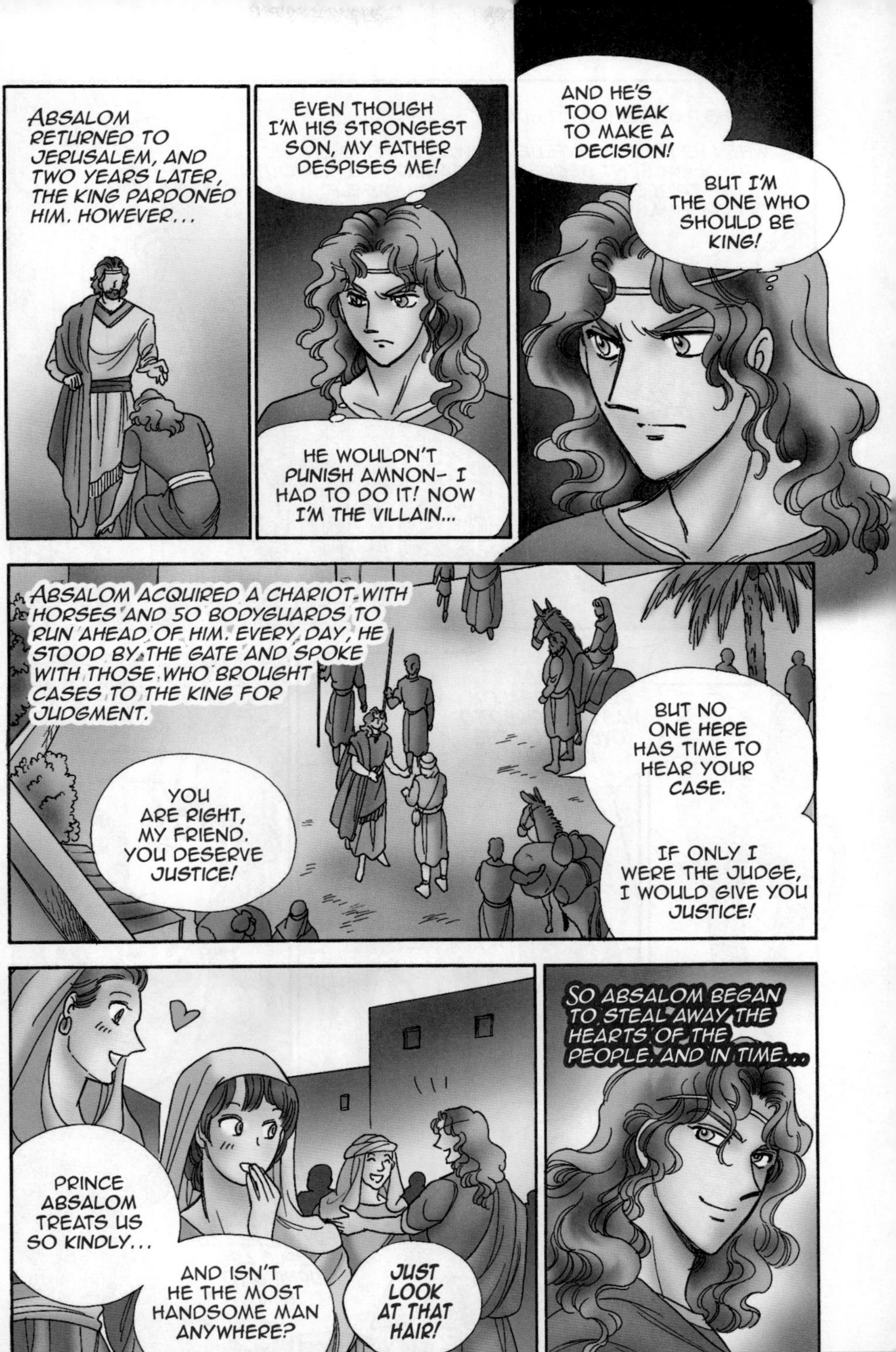
ABSALOM RETURNED TO JERUSALEM, AND TWO YEARS LATER, THE KING PARDONED HIM. HOWEVER...
EVEN THOUGH I'M HIS STRONGEST SON, MY FATHER DESPISES ME!
HE WOULDN'T PUNISH AMNON– I HAD TO DO IT! NOW I'M THE VILLAIN...
AND HE'S TOO WEAK TO MAKE A DECISION!
BUT I'M THE ONE WHO SHOULD BE KING!
ABSALOM ACQUIRED A CHARIOT WITH HORSES AND 50 BODYGUARDS TO RUN AHEAD OF HIM. EVERY DAY, HE STOOD BY THE GATE AND SPOKE WITH THOSE WHO BROUGHT CASES TO THE KING FOR JUDGMENT.
YOU ARE RIGHT, MY FRIEND. YOU DESERVE JUSTICE!
BUT NO ONE HERE HAS TIME TO HEAR YOUR CASE.
IF ONLY I WERE THE JUDGE, I WOULD GIVE YOU JUSTICE!
PRINCE ABSALOM TREATS US SO KINDLY...
AND ISN'T HE THE MOST HANDSOME MAN ANYWHERE?
JUST LOOK AT THAT HAIR!
SO ABSALOM BEGAN TO STEAL AWAY THE HEARTS OF THE PEOPLE. AND IN TIME...

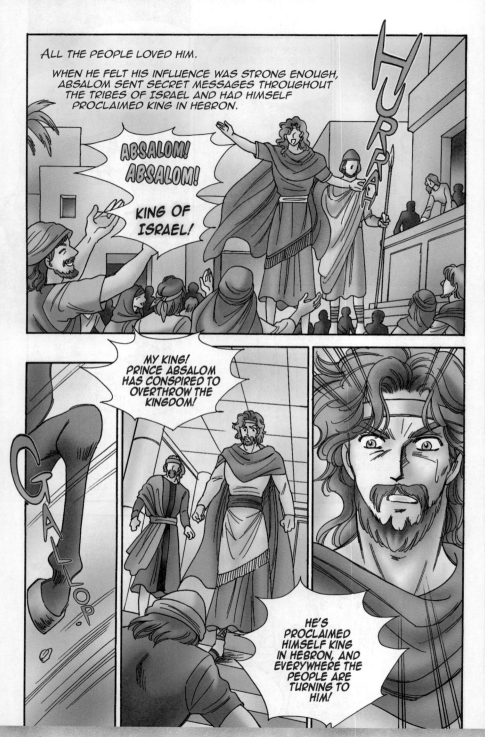

ALL THE PEOPLE LOVED HIM.

WHEN HE FELT HIS INFLUENCE WAS STRONG ENOUGH, ABSALOM SENT SECRET MESSAGES THROUGHOUT THE TRIBES OF ISRAEL AND HAD HIMSELF PROCLAIMED KING IN HEBRON.

ABSALOM! ABSALOM!

KING OF ISRAEL!

MY KING! PRINCE ABSALOM HAS CONSPIRED TO OVERTHROW THE KINGDOM!

HE'S PROCLAIMED HIMSELF KING IN HEBRON, AND EVERYWHERE THE PEOPLE ARE TURNING TO HIM!

THEN WE MUST FLEE AT ONCE!

FATHER?

THEY'LL COME STRAIGHT HERE AND NONE OF US WILL ESCAPE!

I WON'T DRAG ISRAEL INTO ANOTHER CIVIL WAR.

MY LORD!

MY KING...

WE ARE WITH YOU!

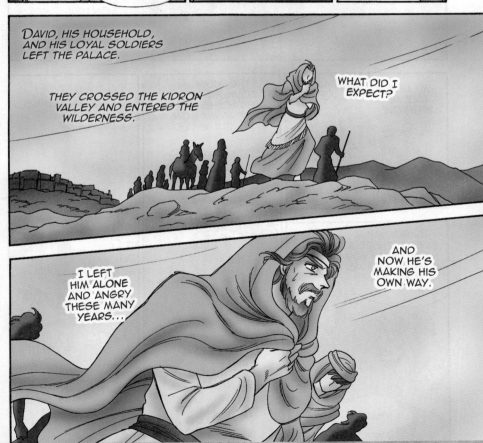

DAVID, HIS HOUSEHOLD, AND HIS LOYAL SOLDIERS LEFT THE PALACE.

THEY CROSSED THE KIDRON VALLEY AND ENTERED THE WILDERNESS.

WHAT DID I EXPECT?

I LEFT HIM ALONE AND ANGRY THESE MANY YEARS...

AND NOW HE'S MAKING HIS OWN WAY.

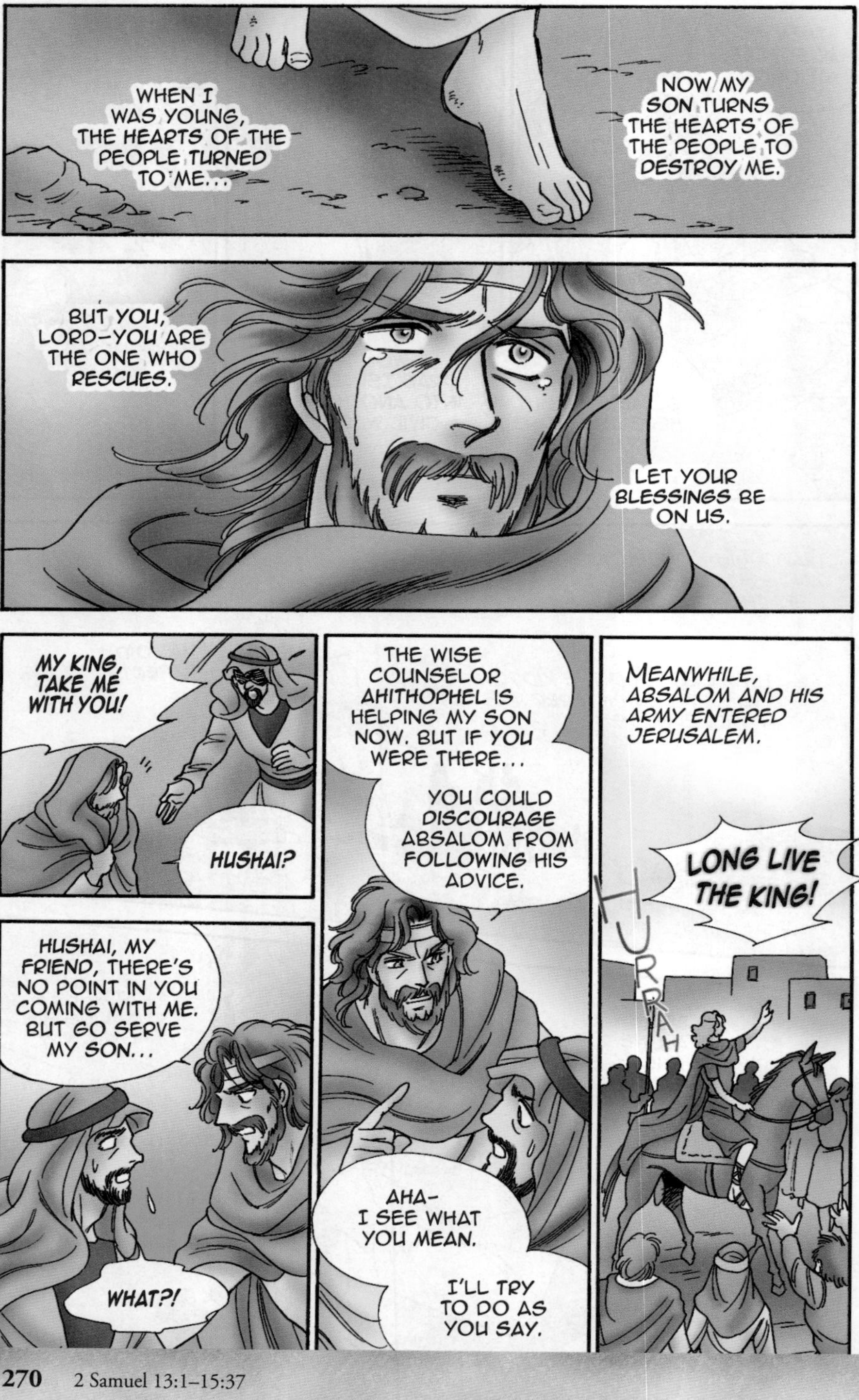
WHEN I WAS YOUNG, THE HEARTS OF THE PEOPLE TURNED TO ME...
NOW MY SON TURNS THE HEARTS OF THE PEOPLE TO DESTROY ME.
BUT YOU, LORD—YOU ARE THE ONE WHO RESCUES.
LET YOUR BLESSINGS BE ON US.
MY KING, TAKE ME WITH YOU!
HUSHAI?
HUSHAI, MY FRIEND, THERE'S NO POINT IN YOU COMING WITH ME. BUT GO SERVE MY SON...
WHAT?!
THE WISE COUNSELOR AHITHOPHEL IS HELPING MY SON NOW. BUT IF YOU WERE THERE...
YOU COULD DISCOURAGE ABSALOM FROM FOLLOWING HIS ADVICE.
AHA- I SEE WHAT YOU MEAN.
I'LL TRY TO DO AS YOU SAY.
MEANWHILE, ABSALOM AND HIS ARMY ENTERED JERUSALEM.
LONG LIVE THE KING!
HURRAH

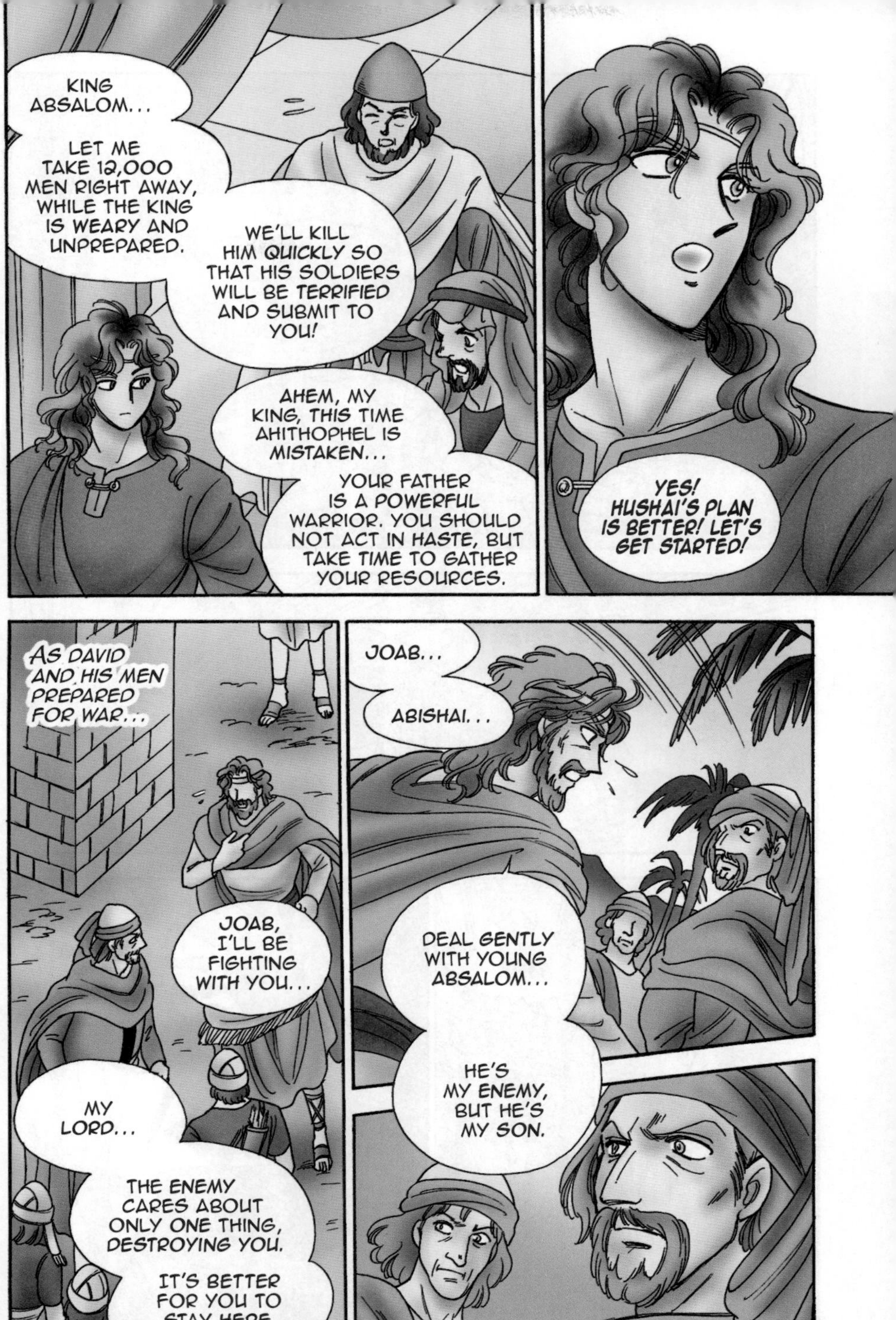
KING ABSALOM...
LET ME TAKE 12,000 MEN RIGHT AWAY, WHILE THE KING IS WEARY AND UNPREPARED.
WE'LL KILL HIM QUICKLY SO THAT HIS SOLDIERS WILL BE TERRIFIED AND SUBMIT TO YOU!
AHEM, MY KING, THIS TIME AHITHOPHEL IS MISTAKEN...
YOUR FATHER IS A POWERFUL WARRIOR. YOU SHOULD NOT ACT IN HASTE, BUT TAKE TIME TO GATHER YOUR RESOURCES.
YES! HUSHAI'S PLAN IS BETTER! LET'S GET STARTED!
AS DAVID AND HIS MEN PREPARED FOR WAR...
JOAB, I'LL BE FIGHTING WITH YOU...
MY LORD...
THE ENEMY CARES ABOUT ONLY ONE THING, DESTROYING YOU.
IT'S BETTER FOR YOU TO STAY HERE.
JOAB...
ABISHAI...
DEAL GENTLY WITH YOUNG ABSALOM...
HE'S MY ENEMY, BUT HE'S MY SON.

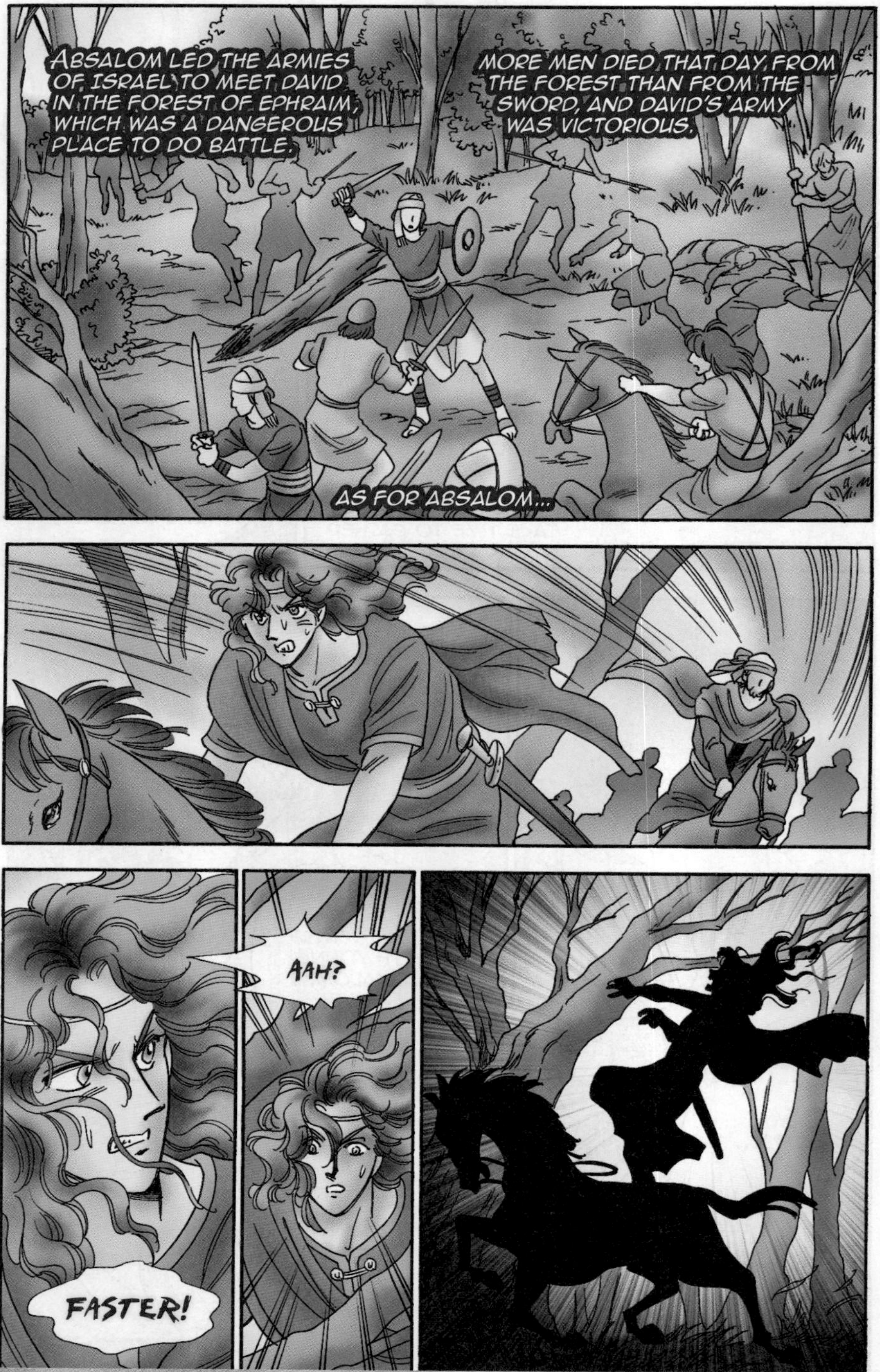
Absalom led the armies of Israel to meet David in the forest of Ephraim, which was a dangerous place to do battle.
More men died that day from the forest than from the sword, and David's army was victorious.
As for Absalom...
Aah?
Faster!

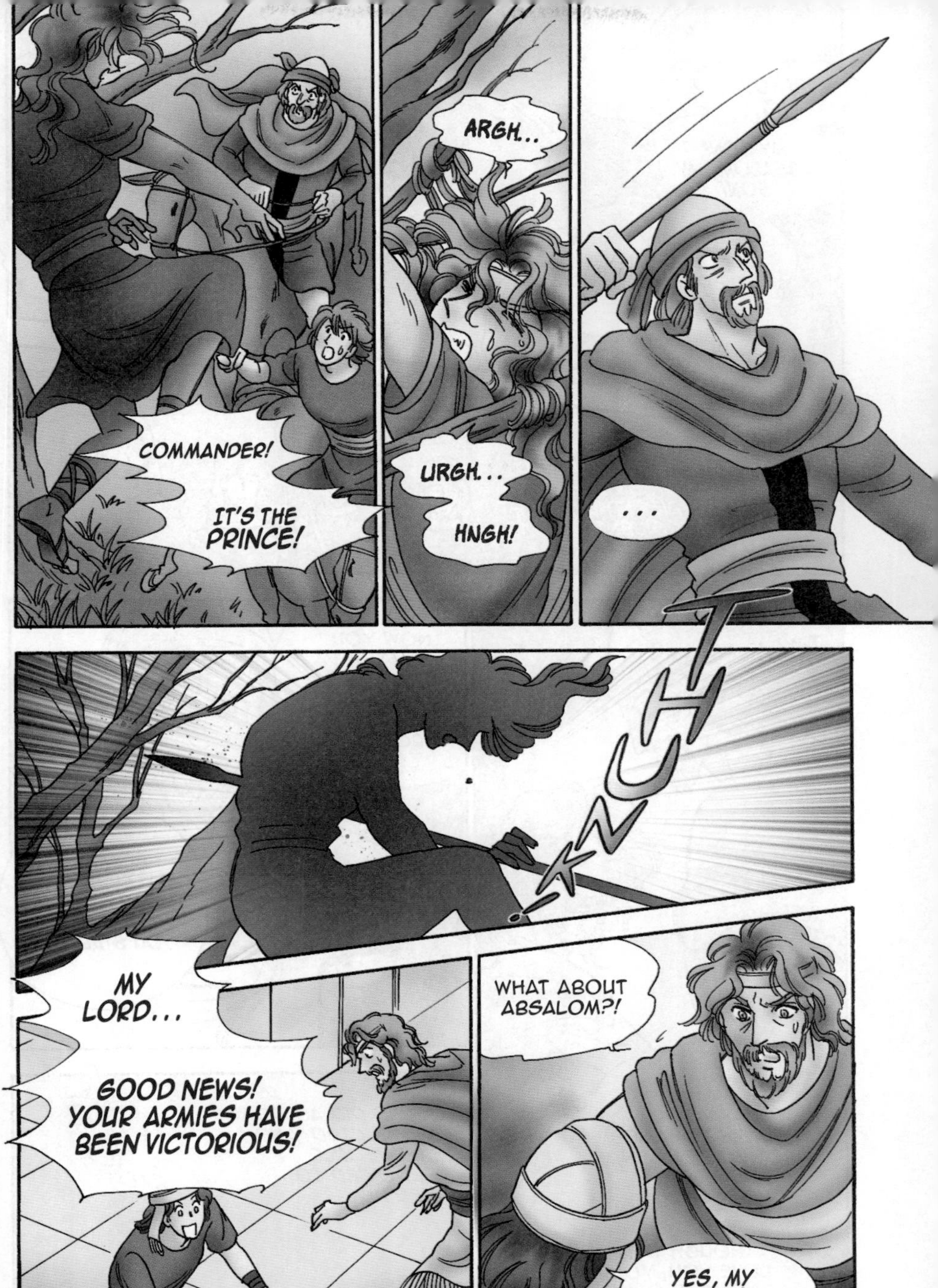
COMMANDER!
IT'S THE PRINCE!
ARGH...
URGH...
HNGH!
...
THUNK!
MY LORD...
GOOD NEWS! YOUR ARMIES HAVE BEEN VICTORIOUS!
WHAT ABOUT ABSALOM?!
YES, MY LORD!
THE TRAITOR WAS KILLED!

OH NO, NO...

MY SON! ABSALOM, MY SON!

IF ONLY I COULD HAVE DIED INSTEAD OF YOU!

NOW IT'S TOO LATE!

WHY, LORD? WHY?!

THE SOLDIERS' JOY TURNED TO SADNESS, WHEN THEY SAW THE KING'S GRIEF. THEY CREPT INTO THE CITY, SILENTLY, AS IF THEY HAD LOST THE BATTLE.

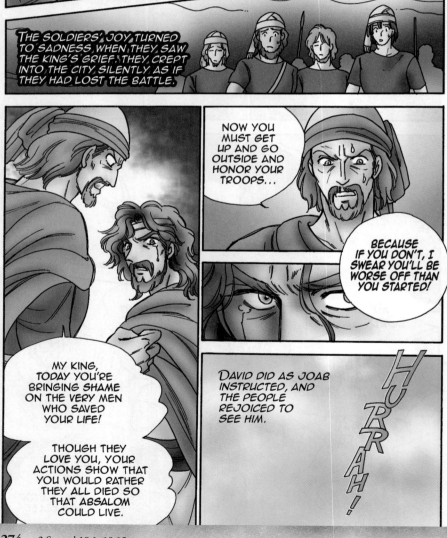

NOW YOU MUST GET UP AND GO OUTSIDE AND HONOR YOUR TROOPS...

BECAUSE IF YOU DON'T, I SWEAR YOU'LL BE WORSE OFF THAN YOU STARTED!

MY KING, TODAY YOU'RE BRINGING SHAME ON THE VERY MEN WHO SAVED YOUR LIFE!

THOUGH THEY LOVE YOU, YOUR ACTIONS SHOW THAT YOU WOULD RATHER THEY ALL DIED SO THAT ABSALOM COULD LIVE.

DAVID DID AS JOAB INSTRUCTED, AND THE PEOPLE REJOICED TO SEE HIM.

HURRAH!

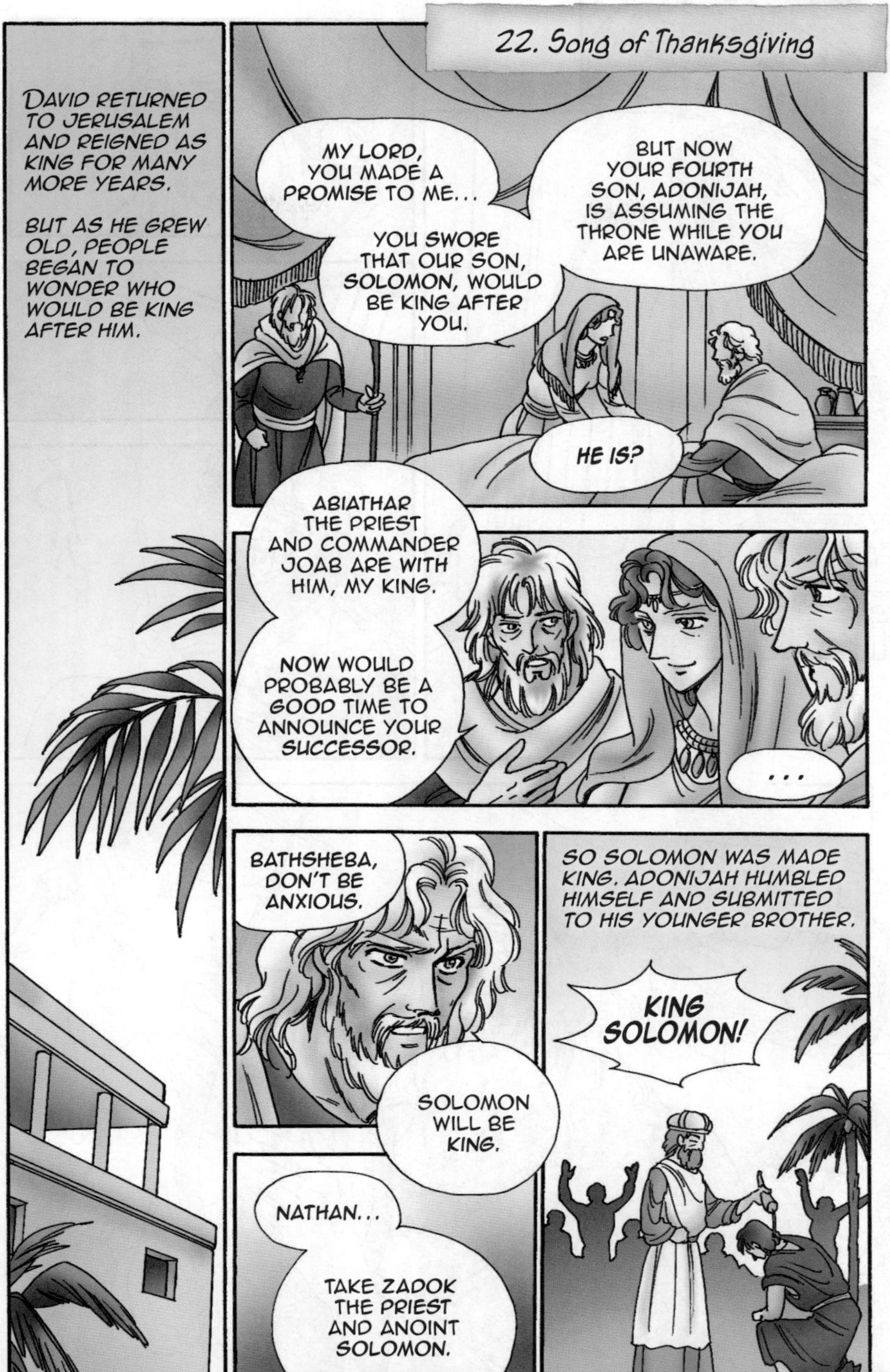
22. Song of Thanksgiving
DAVID RETURNED TO JERUSALEM AND REIGNED AS KING FOR MANY MORE YEARS.
BUT AS HE GREW OLD, PEOPLE BEGAN TO WONDER WHO WOULD BE KING AFTER HIM.
MY LORD, YOU MADE A PROMISE TO ME...
YOU SWORE THAT OUR SON, SOLOMON, WOULD BE KING AFTER YOU.
BUT NOW YOUR FOURTH SON, ADONIJAH, IS ASSUMING THE THRONE WHILE YOU ARE UNAWARE.
HE IS?
ABIATHAR THE PRIEST AND COMMANDER JOAB ARE WITH HIM, MY KING.
NOW WOULD PROBABLY BE A GOOD TIME TO ANNOUNCE YOUR SUCCESSOR.
...
BATHSHEBA, DON'T BE ANXIOUS.
SOLOMON WILL BE KING.
NATHAN...
TAKE ZADOK THE PRIEST AND ANOINT SOLOMON.
SO SOLOMON WAS MADE KING. ADONIJAH HUMBLED HIMSELF AND SUBMITTED TO HIS YOUNGER BROTHER.
KING SOLOMON!

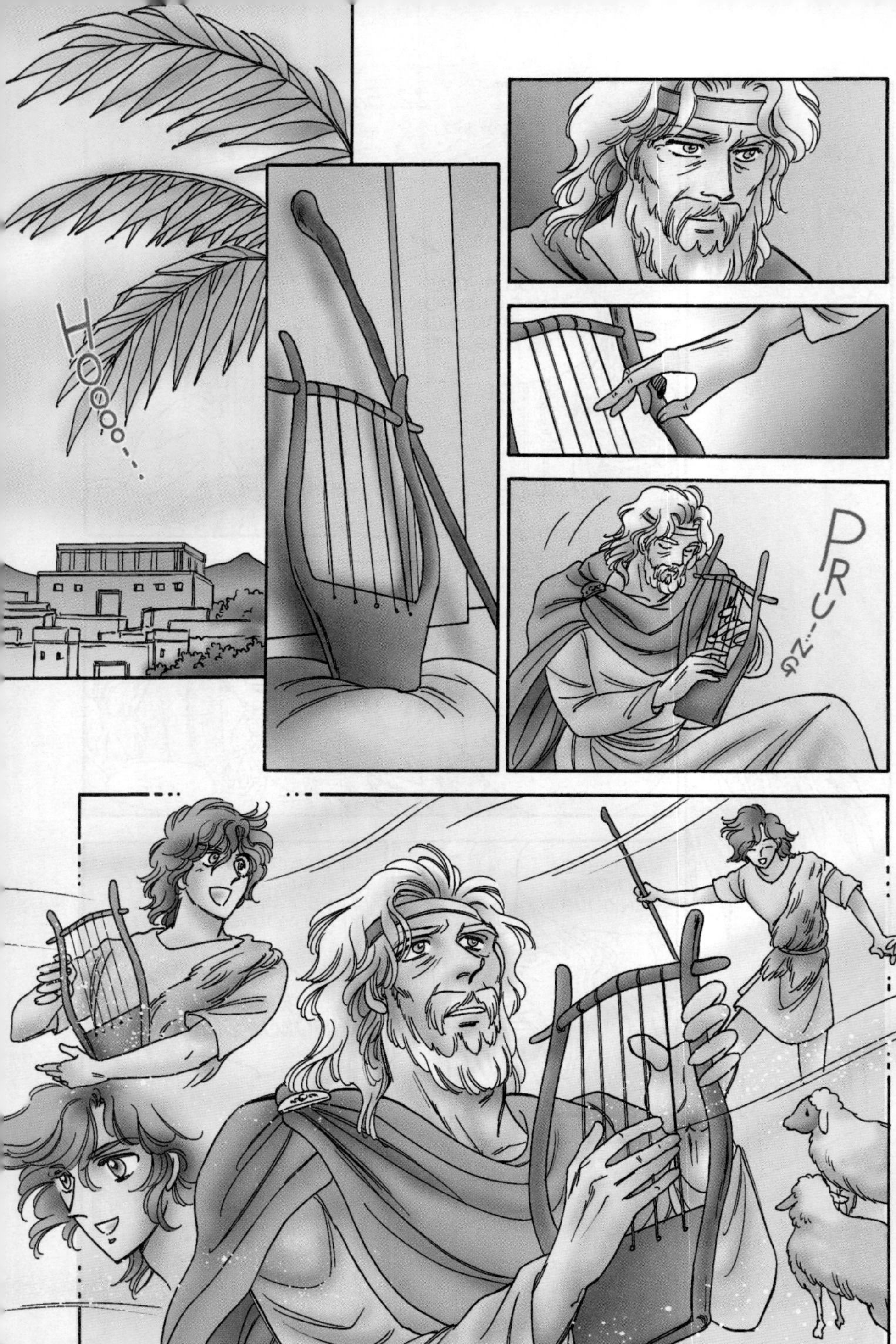

HOOOO...
PRU-N-G

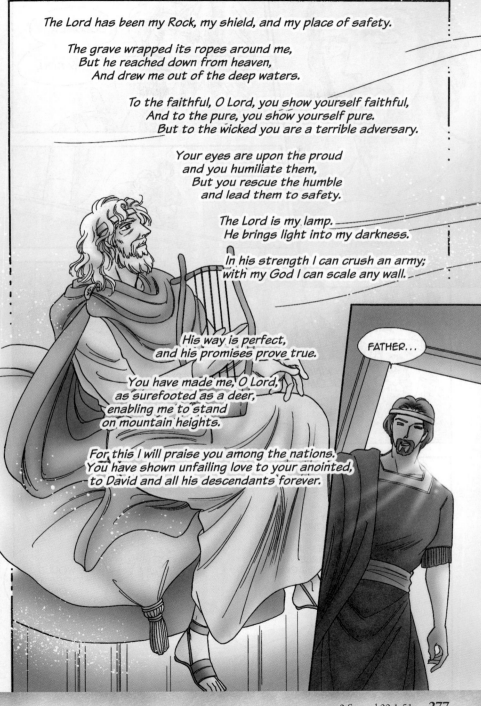

The Lord has been my Rock, my shield, and my place of safety.

The grave wrapped its ropes around me,
But he reached down from heaven,
And drew me out of the deep waters.

To the faithful, O Lord, you show yourself faithful,
And to the pure, you show yourself pure.
But to the wicked you are a terrible adversary.

Your eyes are upon the proud
and you humiliate them,
But you rescue the humble
and lead them to safety.

The Lord is my lamp.
He brings light into my darkness.

In his strength I can crush an army;
with my God I can scale any wall.

His way is perfect,
and his promises prove true.

You have made me, O Lord,
as surefooted as a deer,
enabling me to stand
on mountain heights.

For this I will praise you among the nations.
You have shown unfailing love to your anointed,
to David and all his descendants forever.

FATHER...

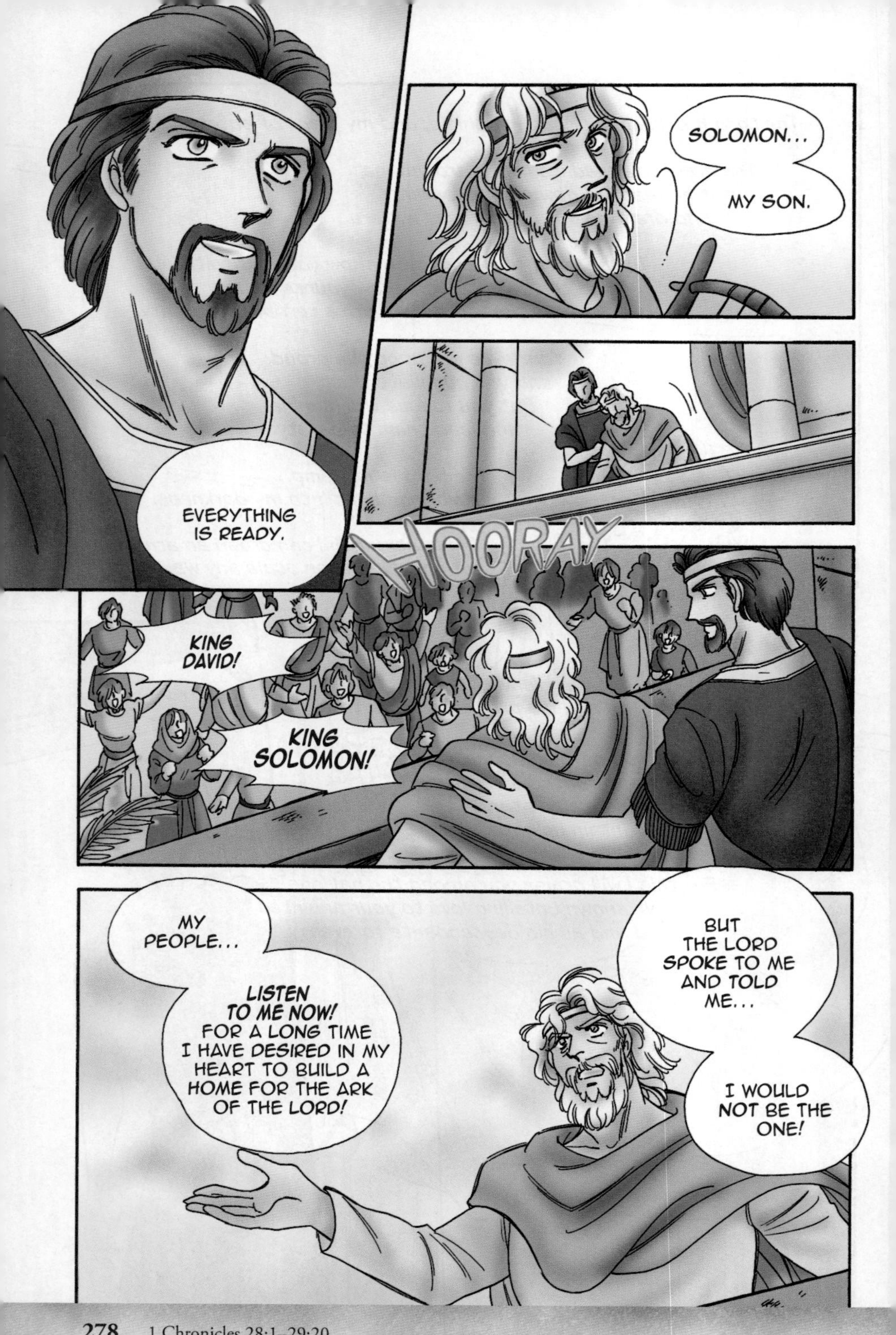
EVERYTHING IS READY.
SOLOMON...
MY SON.
HOORAY
KING DAVID!
KING SOLOMON!
MY PEOPLE...
LISTEN TO ME NOW! FOR A LONG TIME I HAVE DESIRED IN MY HEART TO BUILD A HOME FOR THE ARK OF THE LORD!
BUT THE LORD SPOKE TO ME AND TOLD ME...
I WOULD NOT BE THE ONE!

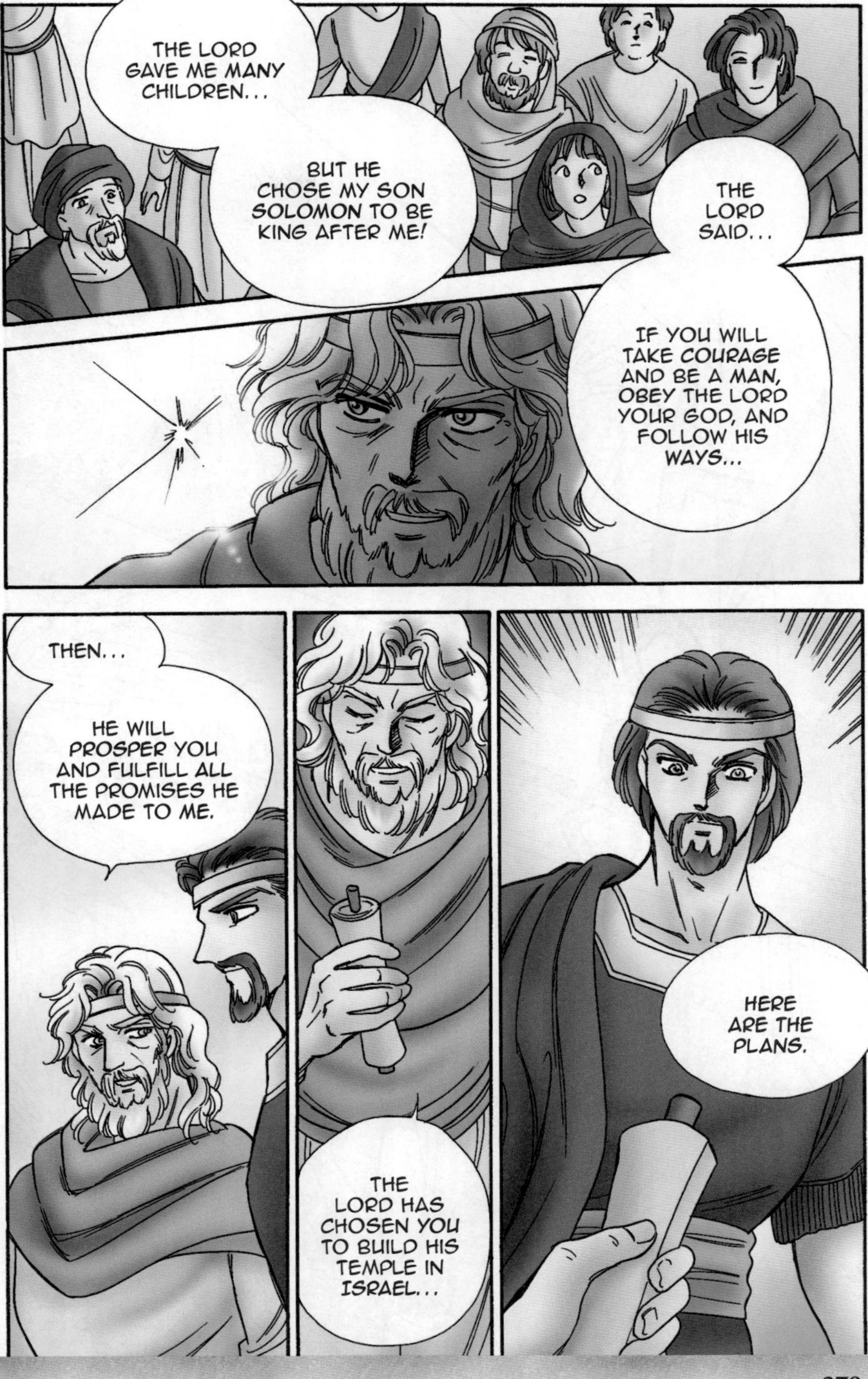
THE LORD GAVE ME MANY CHILDREN...
BUT HE CHOSE MY SON SOLOMON TO BE KING AFTER ME!
THE LORD SAID...
IF YOU WILL TAKE COURAGE AND BE A MAN, OBEY THE LORD YOUR GOD, AND FOLLOW HIS WAYS...
THEN...
HE WILL PROSPER YOU AND FULFILL ALL THE PROMISES HE MADE TO ME.
THE LORD HAS CHOSEN YOU TO BUILD HIS TEMPLE IN ISRAEL...
HERE ARE THE PLANS.

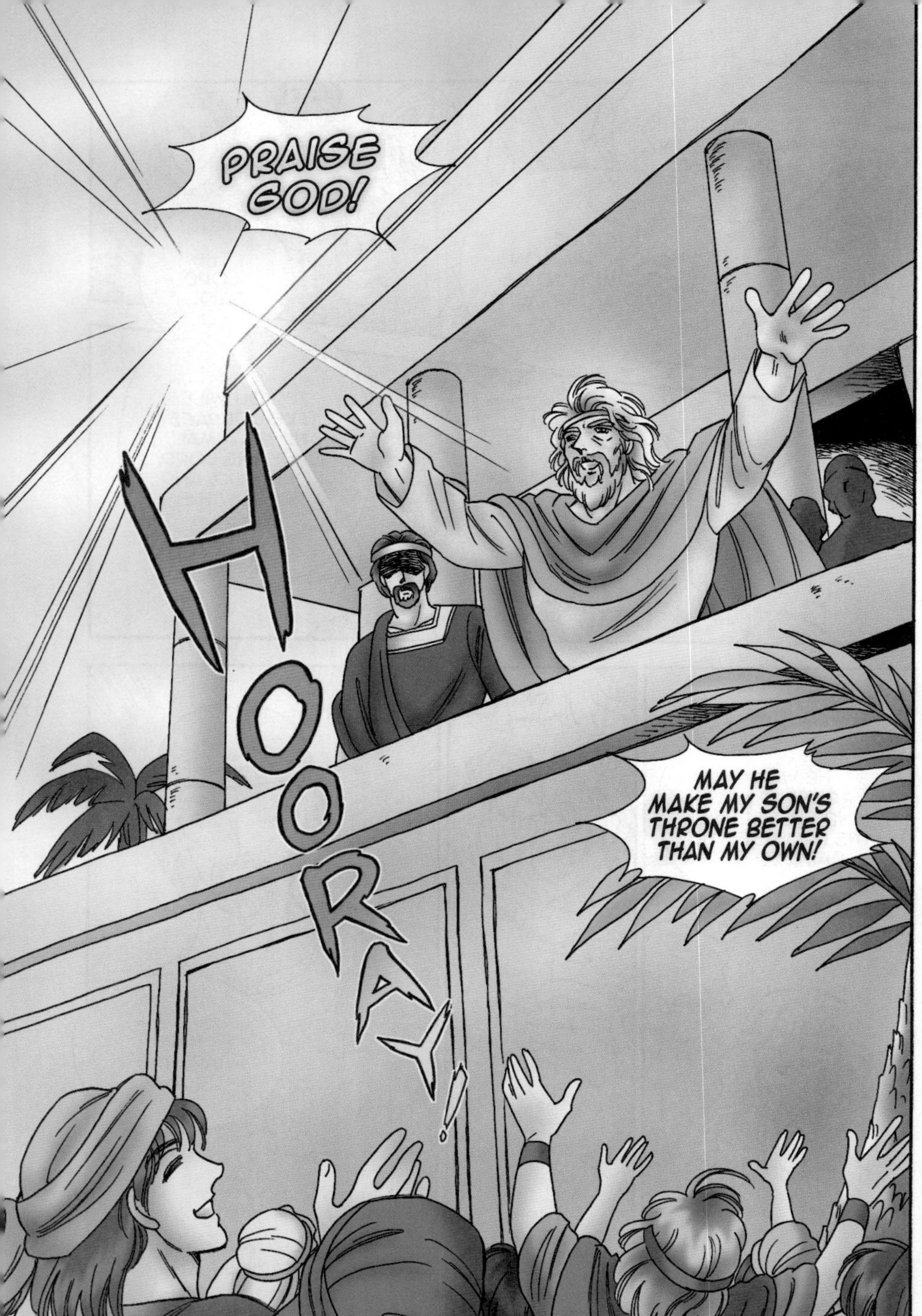
PRAISE GOD!
HOORAY!
MAY HE MAKE MY SON'S THRONE BETTER THAN MY OWN!

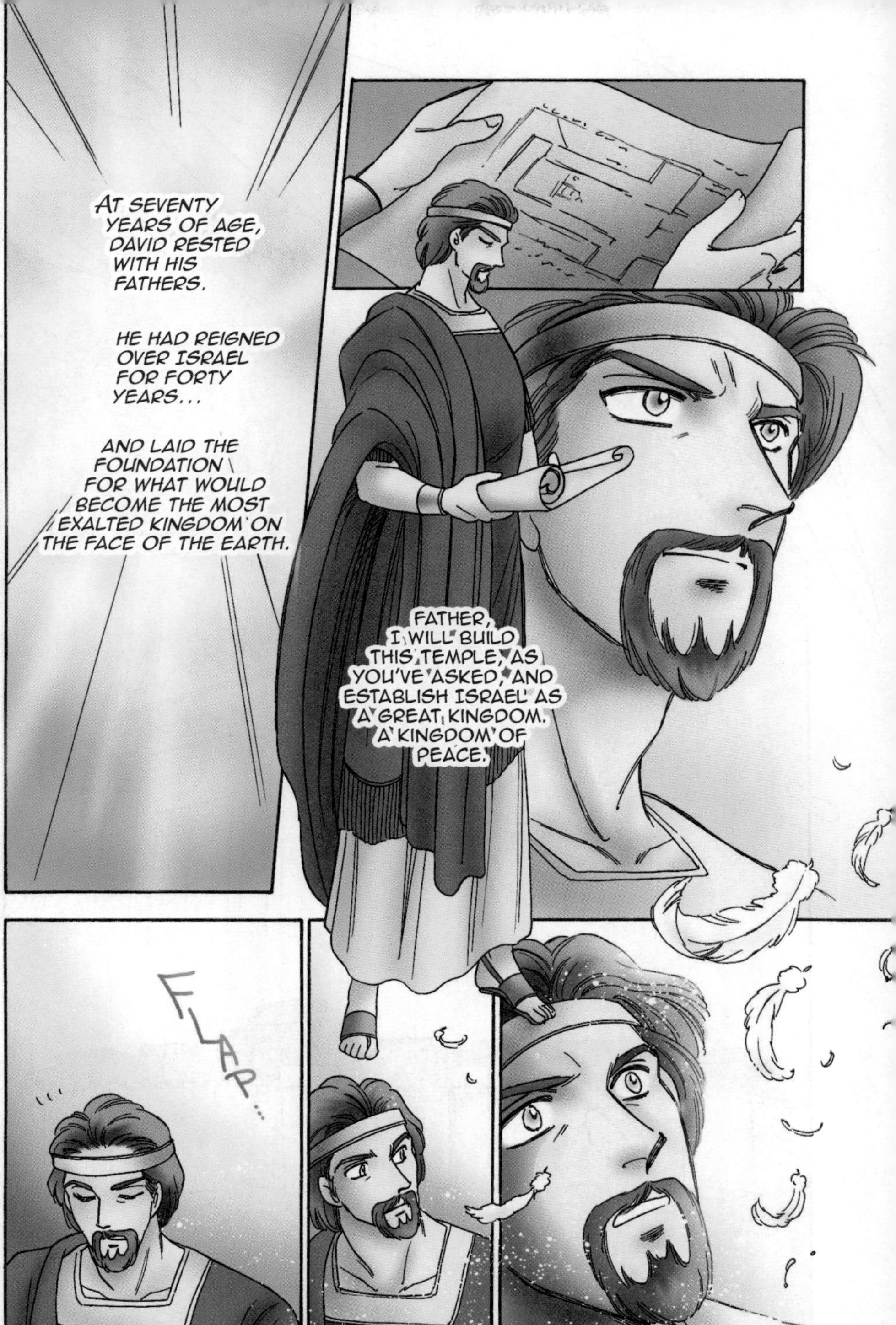
AT SEVENTY YEARS OF AGE, DAVID RESTED WITH HIS FATHERS.
HE HAD REIGNED OVER ISRAEL FOR FORTY YEARS...
AND LAID THE FOUNDATION FOR WHAT WOULD BECOME THE MOST EXALTED KINGDOM ON THE FACE OF THE EARTH.
FATHER, I WILL BUILD THIS TEMPLE, AS YOU'VE ASKED, AND ESTABLISH ISRAEL AS A GREAT KINGDOM. A KINGDOM OF PEACE.
FLAP...

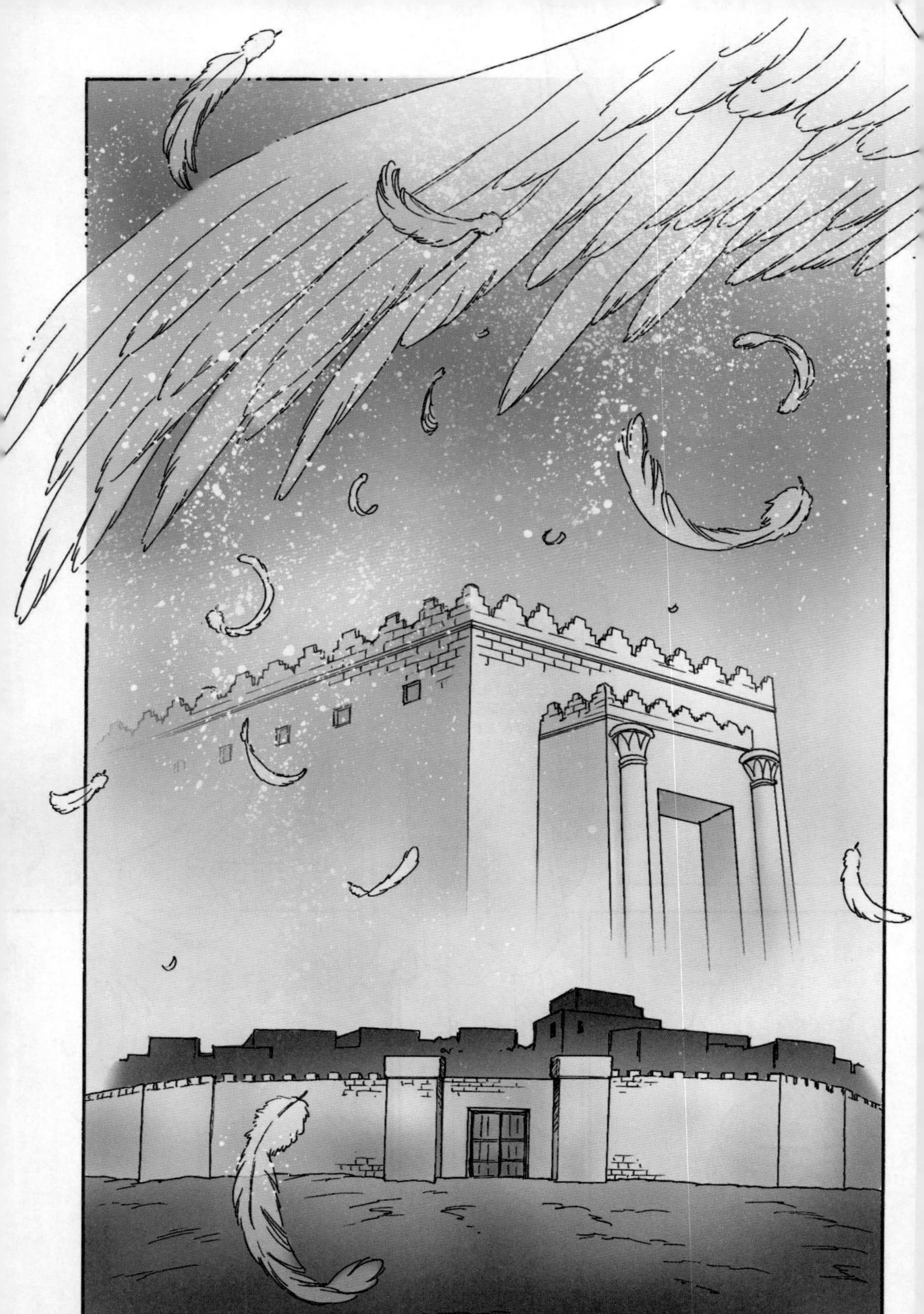

JOURNEY TO THE PROMISED LAND
THROUGH THE WILDERNESS TO CANAAN

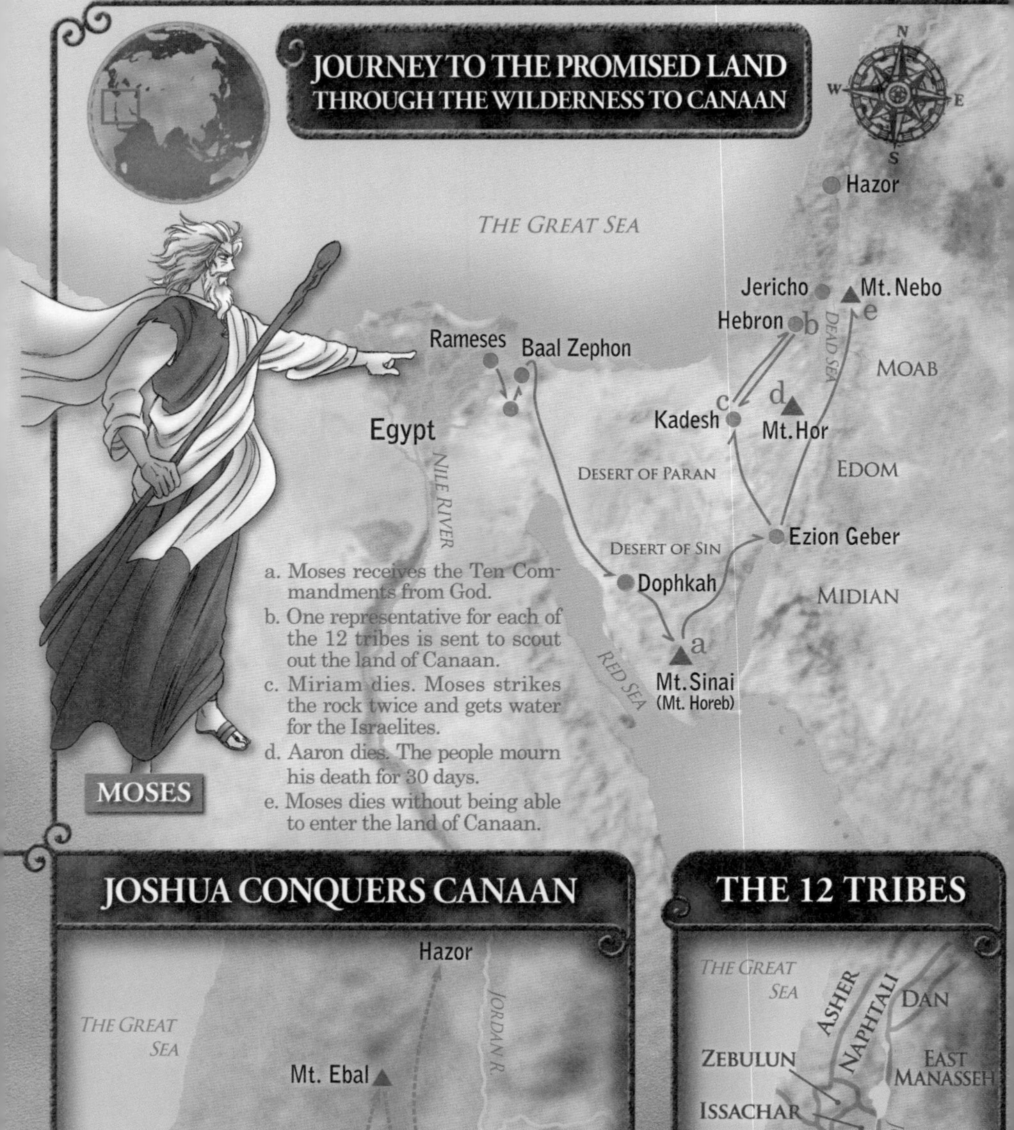

N
W
E
S
Hazor
THE GREAT SEA
Jericho
Mt. Nebo
Hebron
b
e
DEAD SEA
Rameses
Baal Zephon
MOAB
c
d
Kadesh
Mt. Hor
Egypt
NILE RIVER
DESERT OF PARAN
EDOM
Ezion Geber
DESERT OF SIN
Dophkah
MIDIAN
a
RED SEA
Mt. Sinai
(Mt. Horeb)
MOSES

a. Moses receives the Ten Commandments from God.

b. One representative for each of the 12 tribes is sent to scout out the land of Canaan.

c. Miriam dies. Moses strikes the rock twice and gets water for the Israelites.

d. Aaron dies. The people mourn his death for 30 days.

e. Moses dies without being able to enter the land of Canaan.

JOSHUA CONQUERS CANAAN

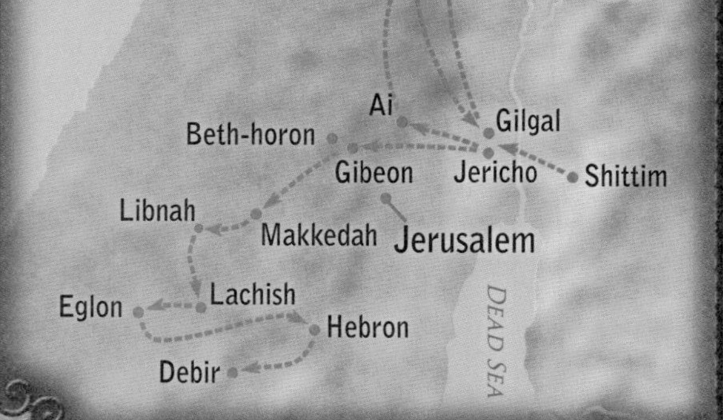

Hazor
THE GREAT SEA
JORDAN R.
Mt. Ebal
Ai
Gilgal
Beth-horon
Gibeon
Jericho
Shittim
Libnah
Makkedah
Jerusalem
Lachish
Eglon
Hebron
Debir
DEAD SEA

THE 12 TRIBES

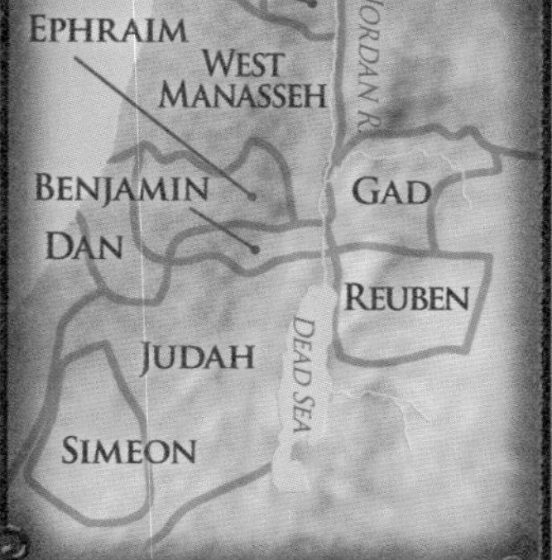

THE GREAT SEA
ASHER
NAPHTALI
DAN
ZEBULUN
EAST MANASSEH
ISSACHAR
EPHRAIM
JORDAN R.
WEST MANASSEH
BENJAMIN
GAD
DAN
REUBEN
JUDAH
DEAD SEA
SIMEON

THE FOOTPRINTS OF SAUL AND DAVID

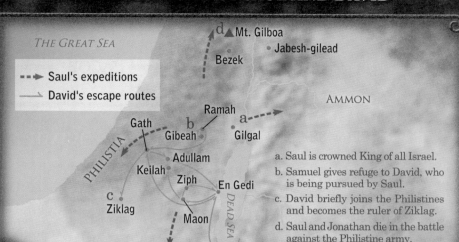

THE GREAT SEA

- ➤ Saul's expeditions
- ➤ David's escape routes

d ▲ Mt. Gilboa
• Jabesh-gilead
Bezek

AMMON

Ramah
Gath
b
a
Gibeah
Gilgal
PHILISTIA
Adullam
Keilah
Ziph
c
En Gedi
Ziklag
DEAD SEA
Maon

AMALEK

a. Saul is crowned King of all Israel.
b. Samuel gives refuge to David, who is being pursued by Saul.
c. David briefly joins the Philistines and becomes the ruler of Ziklag.
d. Saul and Jonathan die in the battle against the Philistine army.

BATTLES DAVID FOUGHT

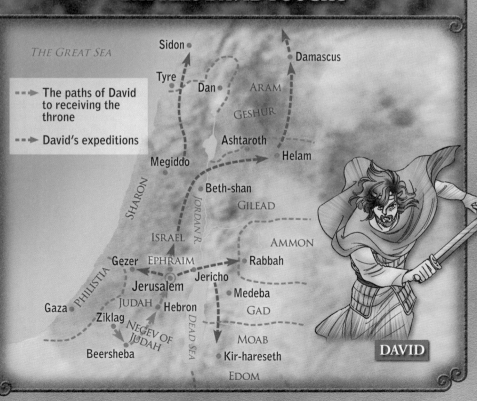

THE GREAT SEA

- ➤ The paths of David to receiving the throne
- ➤ David's expeditions

Sidon •
• Damascus
Tyre •
Dan •
ARAM
GESHUR
Ashtaroth
Megiddo
• Helam
Beth-shan
GILEAD
ISRAEL
AMMON
Gezer
EPHRAIM
• Rabbah
Jerusalem
Jericho
Gaza •
JUDAH
• Medeba
Ziklag
Hebron
GAD
NEGEV OF JUDAH
MOAB
Beersheba
• Kir-hareseth
EDOM

SHARON
JORDAN R.
PHILISTIA
DEAD SEA

DAVID

CHARACTER INTRODUCTIONS & FAMILY TREE

LEAH — JACOB

REUBEN SIMEON THE TRIBE OF LEVI THE TRIBE OF JUDAH

MIRIAM

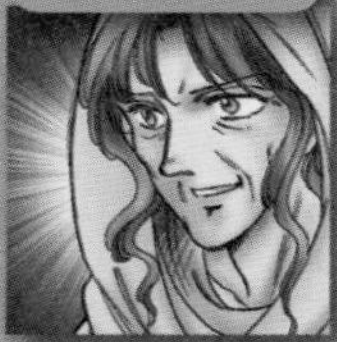

Moses' sister. She helps Moses' work along with Aaron. There was a time she forgot her duty as a prophet and criticized Moses. As a result, she was temporarily struck with a skin disease.

AARON

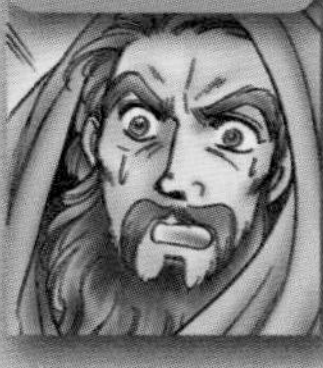

Moses' brother. He helps in Moses' work and helps lead the Israelites. The people cry out for a tangible deity, and Aaron compromises by allowing them to worship a false god. This act becomes the first breaking of the Ten Commandments, right after Moses received them from God.

MOSES

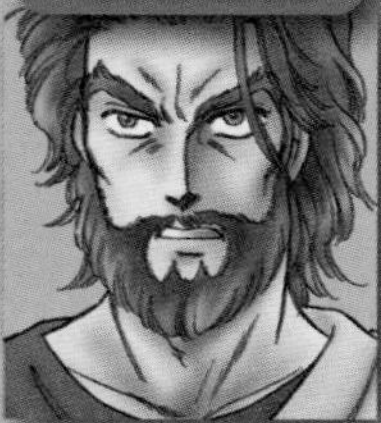

He leads the Israelites out of Egypt and receives the Ten Commandments from God at Mount Sinai. Although Moses performs various miracles in the wilderness for the people of Israel, he himself is not able to enter into the Promised Land. He does, however, fulfill his duties till the very end.

CALEB

SALMON

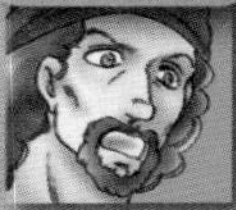

Caleb and Joshua together scout out the land of Canaan and are later able to enter the Promised Land. When the land is apportioned, Caleb inherits the town of Hebron.

RUTH

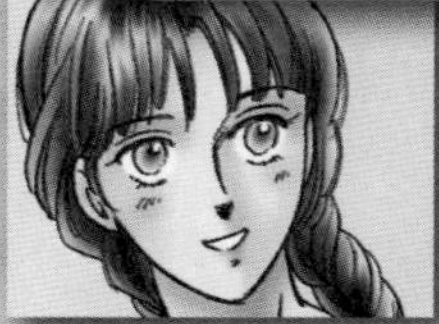

After the death of her husband, the Gentile Ruth accompanies her mother-in-law, Naomi, and worships Naomi's God as her own. Ruth meets Boaz as she is gleaning in his grain fields.

ELEAZAR ITHAMAR

ZERUIAH

JOAB

SAMUEL

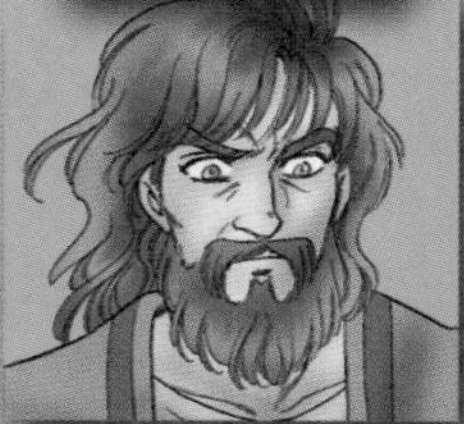

A prophet from the town of Ramah. He becomes a servant of God through the prayers of his faithful mother, Hannah. He leads Israel in its time of transition.

ELI

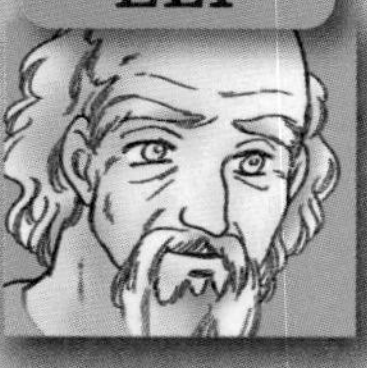

A high priest who serves God in the Holy Place. The boy Samuel serves under Eli.

RACHEL →

ISSACHAR ZEBULUN DINAH GAD ASHER

RAHAB

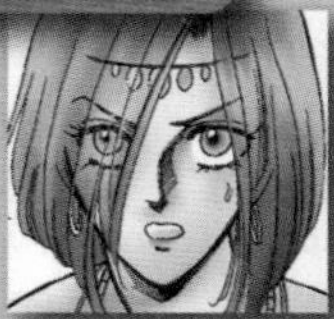

A prostitute who comes to the aid of two spies sent by Joshua to scout out the land of Jericho. Due to this, God protects her entire family when Jericho falls to the Israelites.

DEBORAH

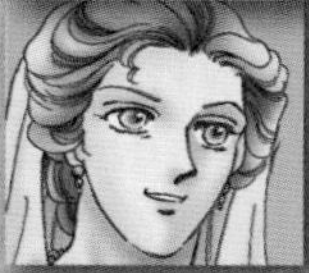

Lappidoth's wife and also a prophet, who becomes a judge at the time of Israel's rule over Canaan. She sides with Barak and gives him God's prophecies. Barak leads his warriors to victory over King Jabin of Canaan.

BOAZ

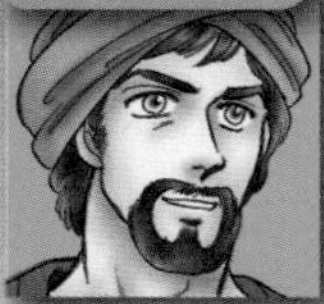

A relative of Naomi's husband, Elimelech. He is the owner of the grain fields where Ruth is working – a very wise and kindhearted person. He purchases Elimelech's land and marries Ruth.

OBED

JESSE

DAVID

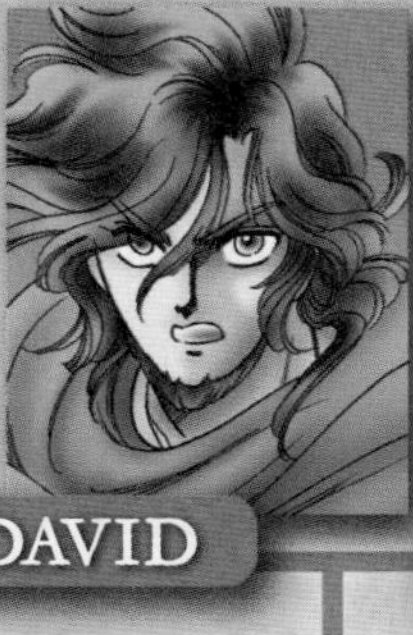

The second king of Israel. As a boy, he was a shepherd. He captures King Saul's attention by downing Goliath with a stone to the head, and is invited to serve at the king's palace. Soon, he is sought after by jealous Saul, who threatens his life. Although a faithful man of God, David sins by committing adultery with Bathsheba. Overall, however, he becomes the greatest king who unites and develops Israel into one solid kingdom.

MAACAH

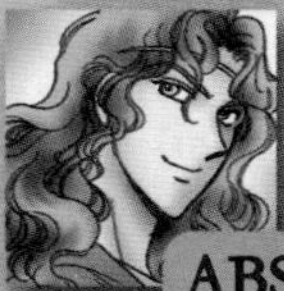

ABSALOM

A son of David. Harboring a grudge for what happened to his sister Tamar, he kills his half-brother Amnon. Absalom then rebels against his father, David, although David dearly loves him.

BATHSHEBA

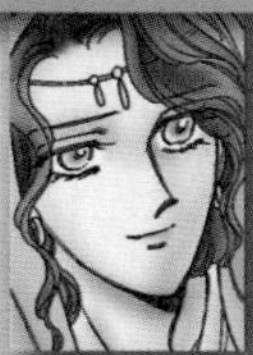

The wife of Uriah the Hittite. She catches David's eye and is invited to his palace. In order to conceal their sin of adultery and marry Bathsheba, David sends her husband into the front lines and has him killed. David and Bathsheba's first child dies, but they receive a second child, Solomon.

SOLOMON

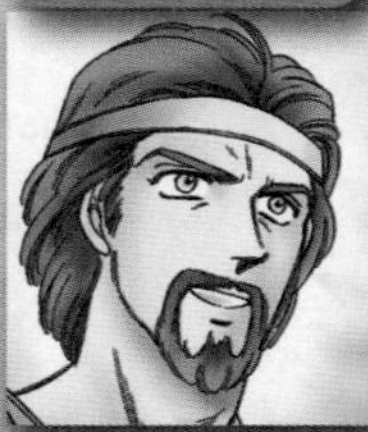

King David chooses his son Solomon to succeed him on the throne. He becomes king and constructs the Temple. By the great wisdom given by God, Solomon causes Israel to prosper and become a widely renowned nation.

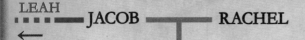

LEAH
◄┄┄┄┄ **JACOB** ━━━━━ **RACHEL**

JOSEPH　　THE TRIBE OF **BENJAMIN**　　THE TRIBE OF **DAN**　　THE TRIBE OF **NAPHTALI**

With Deborah's prophecies and encouragement, Barak leads the Israelites to victory in the battle with King Jabin of Canaan.

BARAK

THE TRIBE OF **MANASSEH**　　THE TRIBE OF **EPHRAIM**

GIDEON

NUN

SAMSON

A hero appointed by God even before his birth. His long hair is the source of his strength, but he is deceived by his beloved Delilah and falls into the hands of the Philistines. At the end of his life he kills nearly 3,000 Philistines.

JOSHUA

Gideon experiences a miracle through an angel of God. He destroys the altars of Baal and is appointed by God to cut down the Asherah pole. Gideon rescues the people of Israel from the Midianites.

SAUL

The first king of Israel. He tries to rule the kingdom without obedience to God. At first Saul is fond of David, yet soon thereafter his heart turns jealous and he attempts to kill him. Saul dies a tragic death.

The next leader chosen for the nation of Israel after Moses. Under Moses, he and Caleb scout out the land of Canaan for 40 days and bring back encouraging news for Israel. Under Joshua's leadership, Canaan is conquered and the land of Israel is divided among the 12 tribes.

JONATHAN

The firstborn of Saul. Jonathan is deeply bonded to David in true friendship, and he pledges loyalty to him. After Jonathan's death, David is deeply grieved, but he keeps his promise and takes care of Jonathan's offspring.